S0-EIB-945

DIPLOMACY AND TRADE IN THE CHINESE WORLD 589-1276

HANDBOOK OF ORIENTAL STUDIES
HANDBUCH DER ORIENTALISTIK

SECTION FOUR

CHINA

edited by

S.F. TEISER · M. KERN

VOLUME EIGHTEEN

DIPLOMACY AND TRADE IN THE CHINESE WORLD 589-1276

DIPLOMACY AND TRADE IN THE CHINESE WORLD 589-1276

BY

HANS BIELENSTEIN

BRILL
LEIDEN · BOSTON
2005

This book is printed on acid-free paper.

Library of Congress Cataloging-in-Publication Data

Bielenstein, Hans.
Diplomacy and trade in the Chinese world, 589-1276 / Hans Bielenstein.
p. cm. — (Handbuch der Orientalistik, ISSN 0169-9520 = Handbook of Oriental studies, Section 4, China)
Includes bibliographical references and index.
ISBN 90-04-14416-1 (alk. paper)
1. China—Commerce—History. 2. China—Foreign relations—To 1644. 3. China—History—Sui dynasty, 581-618. 4. China—History—Tang dynasty, 618-907. 5. China—History—Song dynasty, 960-1279. I. Title. II. Handbuch der Orientalistik. Vierte Abteilung, China.

HF3835.B54 2005
327.51'009'021—dc22

2005042011

ISSN 0169-9520
ISBN 90 04 14416 1

PRINTED IN THE NETHERLANDS

CONTENTS

LIST OF MAPS

THE SOURCES

The chief sources for the current work are the dynastic histories. They were for this time compiled by committees, each presided over by a well-known scholar, the *Sui shu* by Wei Cheng (580-643), the *Pei shih* by Li Yen-shou (fl.629), the *Chiu T'ang-shu* by Liu Hsü (887-946), the *Hsin T'ang shu* by Ou-yang Hsiu (1007-1072),[1] the *Chiu Wu-tai shih* by Hsüeh Chü-cheng (912-981), the *Wu-tai shih-chi* by Ou-yang Hsiu,[2] the *Sung shih*, *Liao shih*, and *Chin shih* by T'o-t'o (1313-1355), and the *Yüan shih* by Wang Yi (1321-1372). These histories give information about foreign states and tribes, their rulers, and their relations to China and each other. The imperial annals have brief, well-dated accounts. Later chapters devoted to foreign countries or peoples are poorer in dates but richer in information. Important tribes are given chapters of their own, lesser ones are lumped together. For instance, *Chiu T'ang shu* has individual chapters for the Turks, Uighurs, and Tibetans, followed by chapters on the Southern Barbarians, Western Barbarians, Eastern Barbarians, and Northern Barbarians.

In addition to the dynastic histories, valuable material is available elsewhere. There are, first of all, the texts called *Collected Matters of Importance* (*Hui-yao*). The *T'ang hui-yao* and *Wu-tai hui-yao* were both completed by Wang P'u (922-982) in 961. The *Sung hui-yao* was reconstituted as the *Sung hui-yao kao* from the *Yung-lo ta-tien* by Hsü Sung (1781-1848).

Then there are the encyclopaedias. The *T'ung-tien* was compiled by Tu Yu (735-812). It is an important source but has no relevant information beyond the reign of Hsüan-tsung (712-756). The *Ts'e-fu-yüan-kuei* by Wang Ch'in-jo, Yang Yi and others was completed in 1013. It covers the period from Sui through the Five Dynasties, and its chapters on "Tribute Missions" have numerous well-dated entries. The *Wen-hsien*

[1] It is a peculiarity of the *Hsin T'ang shu* that the Imperial Annals never refer to foreign missions directly. The entries will say that the Tibetans or Turks requested peace or sought a marriage, which naturally had to be done by way of missions, but mention no envoys. This must have been an editorial decision by Ou-yang Hsiu himself.

[2] Compiled by Ou-yang Hsiu alone. It was later referred to as the *Hsin Wu-tai shih*, and I quote it under that name.

t'ung-k'ao by Ma Tuan-lin (fl. 1273) builds on the *T'ung-tien* and has entries down to 1224. It is especially informative on the Sung.

Finally, the *Tzu-chih t'ung-chien* by Ssu-ma Kuang (1019-1086) becomes increasingly important. It ends with the Five Dynasties, and the closer we get to Ssu-ma Kuang's own time the more new information is offered, all presented with the author's usual admirable clarity. Li T'ao (1115-1184) wrote a continuation of Ssu-ma Kuang's work, called the *Hsü Tzu-chih t'ung-chien ch'ang-pien*. It covers the period 960-1100 and has useful information not found elsewhere.

There are, of course, sources available in languages other than Chinese, such as Arabic, Korean, Japanese, and perhaps Tibetan, but the Chinese are by far the richest. I had to restrict my work to a maneagable proportion, and therefore base it on the Chinese corpus of information.

In Han times, foreign missions to China had been relatively rare and the dynastic historians had every reason to record them with pride. During the Six Dynasties, missions increased in number. But these dynasties were brief, and their archival records consequently limited. The dynastic historians had trouble filling their works, which can be seen from the fact that they padded them with lengthy and unnecessary quotations from e.g. memorials. They had no need to save space. Under the T'ang, and Sung, the situation changed. Archival materials became so abundant that the compilers had to be careful to keep their dynastic histories within manageable bounds. This must be their reason for ignoring some of the missions. Fortunately, the other works mentioned above, especially the *Ts'e-fu yüan-kuei* and *Hsü Tzu-chih t'ung-chien ch'ang-pien*, showed a special interest in them. It will be seen that by a pooling of all information, statistical analysis is, in fact, possible.

The sources mention, at times, missions from obscure and otherwise unknown states and tribes. These are disregarded by me. I only discuss in this work foreign countries and peoples which have sections under their own headings in the dynastic histories and encyclopaedias.

Among Western general histories, the *Cambridge History of China* and Otto Franke's *Geschichte des Chinesischen Reiches* are the most comprehensive. The latter can be uncritical and has to be used with caution.[3] For the Liao, in spite of its sociological jargon, Karl Wittfogel's history

---

[3] See my *Six Dynasties*, vol.I, p.8.

is an impressive achievement. *China among Equals* is a splendid work, edited by Morris Rossabi. Special respect is due to the works of Herbert Franke, and Michael Rogers, and Edward Schafer's charming *The Golden Peaches of Samarkand*.

I follow my usual habit of working from the sources up and not from my imagination down. This means that I rarely find it necessary to quote secondary literature. I prefer not to engage in needless polemics. Let my interpretation of the sources speak for itself. If others agree with me, so much the better. Should we differ, let future generations of scholars decide the rights and wrongs. I see no need to refer to all available literature just because it is there, including the host of works in Chinese and Japanese. I restrict myself therefore intentionally to giving a list of quoted literature. Those, who are interested in comprehensive bibliographies, are refered to the *Cambridge History of China* and the above-mentioned work of Rossaby.

INTRODUCTION

This work is a sequel to the chapter on EMBASSIES in my *The Six Dynasties*, vol.II (*Bulletin of the Museum of Far Eastern* Antiquities, vol. 69, 1996). It is chiefly a study of the exchange of missions and the goods they brought. Government trade is therefore a major theme of this work. Military conflicts are mentioned only in passing, whenever they help to elucidate diplomatic reactions.

I am not concerned with the theory of foreign policy, with Chinese diplomacy in a broad, international context, or how the imperial courts perceived foreign ethnic groups. High-level debates and decisions at the court on how to cope with powerful foreign peoples, and the strategies of diplomatic specialists such as a P'ei Chü (d. ca.630) are beyond the scope of this work. So are diplomatic correspondences, or the reminiscences of envoys. An exhaustive study of such matters would require several books in their own right. Neither do I discuss private, foreign travellers such as Buddhist monks. They did not represent their countries. I deal with the actual technique of foreign relations, i.e. chiefly with the exchange of missions and the goods they brought.

Obviously, China and its immediate neighbours had other relations than mere trade. Borders had to be delineated, peace had to be concluded, technology and books were exchanged, and so on. Where the sources dwell on these matters, I have given them full attention. For countries which were situated more distantly from China, trade became the exclusive purpose of the missions. The states in Afghanistan, the Middle East, India, and on the islands to the south did not have to reckon with China as a great power, and they did not have to pay homage to the Son of Heaven. All they wanted was Chinese goods. If their envoys went through motions which signified submission, this was no more than smart business practice.

The Chinese saw it differently and liked to believe that the emperor or Son of Heaven was destined to govern the world. This concept of a universal ruler was hard to maintain in times of internal division or strong foreign neighbours, when emperors had to accomodate themselves to the existance of other emperors, and rival courts had to devise means of coexistance. It was nevertheless shared by all, whether Chinese or aliens. It meant that foreign kings and chiefs were considered potential subjects who held their offices as only "acting" or "probationary" rulers until they were recognized by an emperor and their territories thereby theoretically accepted as subordinate units. It happened that the Chinese at such ocassions gave new names to the foreign countries, although these were no more than bookkeeping terms. The process of recognition was repeated with each new emperor. The foreign rulers were usually willing to receive titles and sometimes even coveted them, but did not, of course, thereby become vassals. In fact, they had no problem in accepting titles from more than one emperor simultaneously.

A further consequence of this concept was that missions from foreign countries were considered "tribute missions", their gifts or merchandise "tribute", and letters from their rulers "memorials". In actual fact, most letters were at the Chinese court translated, rephrased, or even invented in accordance with Chinese imperial terminology, so that alien kings and chiefs are made to refer to themselves as the emperor's "subjects" or "slaves" and as "kowtowing" to him. For instance, a "memorial" of 977 supposedly said: "I, the king of Po-ni, Hsiang-ta, kotow" (*Sung shih* 489:19b; *Wen-hsien t'ung-k'ao* 332:18b). Even more outrageously, the king of Koguryŏ, Kao Yüan (Yŏng-yang Wang), is supposed in 598 to have presented a "memorial" in which he "apologized" and referred to himself as a "shit" (*Pei shih* 94:9b).[1]

Conversely, letters from Chinese emperors to foreign rulers were called "edicts", and these were not sent but "bestowed".

Western, Chinese, and Japanese scholars have frequently fallen into the trap of accepting the terminology of the Chinese dynastic historians as authentic, and hence submission and tribute of foreign countries to China have to them been historical truths. In actual fact, excepting Chiao-chih/Annam, real tribute was never paid to China, only by China to the Eastern Turks, Uighurs, Hsia, Liao, and Chin. I will therefore avoid Chinese dynastic phraseology and say "letter" for "memorial", "gifts" for "tribute", and "to recognize" for "to enfeoff" or "invest", and I will avoid such words as "edict" in Chinese communications to foreigners, and "apology" for the offer of a foreign ruler to restore normality.

Foreign envoys were commonly granted Chinese titles and, if they

---

[1] Ma Tuan-lin says of the "memorial" of the king of Chu-lien of 1015 that there can be no doubt that it was a Chinese composition and that it does not show any evidence whatever of foreign origin. See Hirth and Rockhill, *Chao Ju-kua* p.99, note 3 and my *Six Dynasties*, vol.II, pp.80-81.

came more than once, even "promoted". It pleased the court to believe that it thereby expanded its bureaucacy beyond the borders, although in reality the titles were purely nominal.

Missions went naturally in two directions, to and from China, but the sources are richer on the former. The larger countries sent missions of their own. Smaller ones sometimes attached their envoys to missions of larger states. All brought presents. These were not always accepted. Those which were, were catalogued, evaluated for recompensation, employed for conspicuous consumption, put to practical use, or placed in the Imperial Storehouse for Offerings.[2]

The missions could be large and apart from the chief envoy and his deputy included physicians, clerks, attendants, cooks, grooms, and military escorts. These received travel money and food allowances from their home countries in accordance with their ranks. Once they had crossed the border, the host country took care of all further travel expenses, housing, food, and drink. In China, foreign envoys fell under the jurisdiction of the Herald who was one of the ministers of the central government. It was therefore in the interest of the Chinese government to limit the size of foreign missions, and orders were issued to that effect. If missions came unannounced, Chinese border or port officials had to report their arrival to the capital before they were allowed to proceed. It happened that permission was not granted.

The purpose of the missions to and from China and between its neighbours embraced the entire range of diplomatic relations: to offer good-will, to discuss protocol, to form alliances for war, to make peace, to delineate borders, to spy, to negotiate joint markets, to request or arrange marriages, to ask for books and medicines, to congratulate on a New Year's Day or birthday, to inquire about health, to announce an enthronement or death, to condole and sacrifice, to contribute to funeral expenses, to attend a burial, to confer posthumous titles, and to convey testamentary gifts. The Chinese also had an insatiable appetite for knowledge of the customs of foreign peoples, their geographical settings, the names of their rulers, and curent events. But all missions and their personnel engaged in trade, and some exclusively so. Not only did foreign countries expect payments for their gifts, but there are cases on record where they stated what they expected in return. This

---

[2] On Feb.16, 1264, the Southern Sung sold pearls, aromatics, elephant tusks, rhinoceros horns and other goods from the Imperial Storehouse for Offerings in a last effort to raise money for the defense against the Mongols (*Sung shih* 45:17a).

may have been a common practice.[3] The Chinese received many goods of great value to them, either for purposes of luxury or utility.

All foreign countries were ranked in relation to each other. This listing decided their precedence at the Chinese court and sometimes led to quarrels among the ambassadors. Envoys were not always received by the emperor. He might be absent from the capital or the country might be considered too unimportant to merit an audience or banquet.

The envoys were not diplomats in the modern sense, with special training for foreign relations and knowledge of foreign languages. Some Chinese envoys showed egregious tactlessness and sino-centric arrogance. Few were sent on more than one mission. Their employment was not without inconvenience or danger and could lead to punishment for improper behaviour, and death through illness, accident, hardship or even execution. Foreign climate, food and drink could be distressing.[4] But the commissions were lucrative. Envoys brought goods of their own for profitable trade, and even if this is mentioned only sporadically in the sources, it must have been a general practice. The members of the missions also received valuable gifts from heir hosts in accordance with their ranks. It was not unusual for certain countries to employ Buddhist priests as envoys, and it is not always easy to decide when monks were arriving in an official capacity or for purposes of their monasteries or their own. It is equally difficult to determine whether Arab shipmasters represented the caliphate or were private entrepeneurs. Some countries along the maritime routes south of Asia employed Arabs as their envoys, because these were experienced travellers with good connections. During T'ang, envoys from states in frequent contact with China were issued bronze fishes, divided into halves, for purpose of identification. One half was kept in the capital, the other was carried in a brocade "fish wallet" by the envoy. By melding the two parts, an envoy proved his authenticity. Fish wallets were common imperial presents to the envoys. In Sung times, the fish wallets were still used but tallies were not.

---

[3] In addition to this government-level trade, there flourished, of course, a much larger volume of private commerce conducted via port towns, border toll stations, and joint markets, and controlled by special commissioners. This commerce had no part in foreign relations and will be referred to only occasionally.

[4] One Sung envoy in 1176 gave advice on how to prevent ones ears from falling off in the bitter cold of the north. See H.Franke in Rossabi ed., *China among Equals*, p.135.

CONTINENTAL SOUTH ASIA AND THE ISLANDS

During the Six Dynasties, trade connections between continental South Asia and the islands had been lively.[1] After the reunification of China in 589 by the Sui, foreign missions continued to arrive. But the Sui also made active attempts of its own to establish relations. In 607, the Master of Affairs of Military Garrisons, Ch'ang Chün, and the Master of Affairs of the Bureau of Forestry and Crafts, Wang Chün-cheng, volunteered to go as envoys to the state of Ch'ih-t'u. Emperor Yang was greatly pleased and bestowed on them 100 bolts of silk each. In the 10th month (Oct./Nov.), they embarked in Nan-hai commandery, presumably Canton, After having sailed for twenty days, they encountered favourable winds, passed the Chiao-shih Mountain and reached the Ling-chia-po-pa-to Island. They then reached the Shih-tzu Rocks, from whereon there was a chain of islands. After another two or three days, they saw from a distance the mountains of the Lang-ya-hsü State.[2] Thereafter, they reached the Chi-lung Island on the border of Ch'ih-t'u. On their return, they encountered shoals of green flying fish. After more than ten days, they reached Lin-yi (in central and southern Vietnam). To the southeast, there were mountains. The sea water turned yellow and smelled rank. They were stuck in the slime for one day. It was said to be the excrements of big fish. They then reached Chiao-chih, i.e. the Hanoi area (*Sui shu* 82:4a-5a; *Wen-hsien t'ung-k'ao* 331:13a).

This account is obviously based on the report of the envoys after their return, and it is interesting for two reasons. It brings out the eagerness of Emperor Yang for foreign relations and trade. It also is an example of sailing directions prepared by Chinese travellers from their own experiences or based on information provided by foreigners. As will be seen, the ancient historians availed themselves of such records in attempting to describe the locations of foreign countries in relation to China and to each other. The trouble is that the accounts are contradictory. Modern attempts to identify the various states in continental South Asia and the islands during the time under discus-

[1] See my *Six Dynasties*, vol.II, pp.80 ff.
[2] *Wen-hsien t'ung-k'ao* has Lang-ya-hsiu.

sion, based on ancient sailing directions as well as modern linguistics, have therefore often been inconclusive. The most ambitious effort is that of Hirth and Rockhill in their annotated translation of Chao Ju-kua's *Chu-fan chih.*[3]

Chao Ju-kua was a Maritime Trade Commissioner in the great port of Ch'üan-chou on the Fu-chien coast, who wrote his account in the middle of the 13th century. His sources are earlier works and informants among the seafarers. He lists under their own headings 54 countries and cities.[4] 14 of these had a "tributary" relationships with China and are therefore of special interest to us. Others had direct or indirect trade connections with China, while the rest was only known by hearsay.

Hirth and Rockhill, with great ingenuity, have attempted to identifiy the ancient names with modern places. In a number of cases they obviously are right. In others, they have been too bold.

Let us now list the foreign countries in continental South Asia and on the islands which had official relations with China between 589 and 1276, and see what can be known about their locations.[5]

Chiao-chih, Chiao chou or An-nan: Situated in present northern Vietnam. In the West, usually called Annam.

Lin-yi or Huan-wang: Situated in present central and southern Vietnam except its southermost part.

Chan-ch'eng: This was Champa, the successor state of Lin-yi.

To-mien: According to *Ts'e-fu yü*an-*kuei* p.5025, it was situated south of Lin-yi, bordering on the sea. It must have been a small country in present southernmost Vietnam.

Wu-hsün: According to *Wen-hsien t'ung-k'ao* 332:17b, it was situated at the sea near Champa. It therefore must have been another small country in present southernmost Vietnam.

P'u-p'o:[6] According to *Wen-hsien t'ung-k'ao* 332:17b, it was situated at the sea near Champa. It therefore must have been another small country in present southernmost Vietnam.

---

[3] Friedrich Hirth and W.W.Rockhill, *Chau Ju-kua on the Chinese and Arab Trade in the Twelfth and Thirteenth Centuries.* For a brief account of the mission in 607, see ibid. p.8 and note 2.

[4] Including Silla, Japan, and the Chinese island of Hai-nan.

[5] See maps 1 and 2. I am here concerned only with the locations of countries which have entries in their own rights in the dynastic histories and encyclopaedias. For the historical times when these states existed or had relations with China see below.

[6] By *Wen-hsien t'ung-k'ao* called P'u-p'o-chung.

San-ma-lan: According to *Wen-hsien t'ung-k'ao* 332:17b, it was situated at the sea near Champa. It therefore must have been still another small country in present southernmost Vietnam.

Fu-nan: Situated in present southern Cambodia and southernmost Vietnam.

Chen-la: This was the Khmer Kingdom in present Cambodia.

Seng-kao: *Ts'e-fu yüan-kuei* p.5024 calls it a small country in the southern wilderness. According to *Wen-hsien t'ung-k'ao* 131:12b, it was situated northwest of Chen-la and was annexed by it after 650-656.

Wu-ling: *Ts'e-fu yüan-kuei* p.5024 calls it a small country in the southern wilderness. According to *Wen-hsien t'ung-k'ao* 131:12b, it was annexed by Chen-la after 650-656.

Chia-cha: *Ts'e-fu yüan-kuei* p.5024 calls it a small country in the southern wilderness. According to *Wen-hsien t'ung-k'ao* 131:12b, it was annexed by Chen-la after 650-656.

Chiu-mi: *Ts'e-fu yüan-kuei*, p.5024, calls it a small country in the southern wilderness. According to *Wen-hsien t'ung-k'ao* 131:12b, it was annexed by Chen-la after 650-656.

Chan-po or Chan-p'o: Schafer[7] places this country in Cambodia but then calls it "a country unknown to us".

Lo-hu: According to *Sung shih* 31:6b, and Chao Ju-kua[8] it was a dependency of Chen-la. Following Gerini and Pelliot, Hirth and Rockhill[9] identify it with Lopburi on the lower Menam.

Chen-li-fu: According to *Wen-hsien t'ung-k'ao* 332:14a and Chao Ju-kua,[10] it was a dependency of Chen-la. Following Gerini, Hirth and Rockhill[11] identify it with Chanthabun on the east coast of the Gulf of Siam, i.e. they place it in southeastern Thailand adjoining Cambodia.

Ch'ih-t'u: The "Red Earth" country. This was the state reached by the Sui mission of 607. According to *Sui shu* 82:3a and *Wen-hsien t'ung-k'ao* 331:12b, the people were a separate tribe of Fu-nan, their country was situated in the southern ocean, more than 100 days of sea travel distant [from China], and it had received its name because

---

[7] Schafer, *Golden Peaches*, pp.81, 83.

[8] Hirth and Rockhill, *Chao Ju-kua*, p.53.

[9] Op.cit., p.56, note 10.

[10] Op.cit., p.53.

[11] Op.cit., p.56, note 10.

the colour of the earth there was often red. Hirth and Rockhill[12] identify it as Siam (Thailand). But this does not agree with the *Sui shu* statement 82:3a that Ch'ih-t'u in the north bordered on the great ocean and that it apparently was an island. The location of Ch'ih-t'u is therefore uncertain.

To-ho-lo: According to *Chiu T'ang shu* 197:3a, it bordered on P'an-p'an in the south, on Chen-la in the east, and on the great ocean in the west. Schafer[13] identifies it as Dvāravati in southern Thailand. This is contradicted by *Hsin T'ang shu* 222C:4a and *Wen-hsien t'ung-k'ao* 332:16a according to which To-ho-lo was reached from Canton in 5 months. That would mean a much greater distance than that from Canton to Thailand.[14]

T'ou-ho: According to *Hsin T'ang shu* 222C:4b and *Wen-hsien t'ung-k'ao* 332:14a, it was situated on a great island in the southern ocean, south of Chen-la and southwest of Canton, and reached by sea from Canton in 100 days.

Chou-mei-liu: According to *Sung shih* 489:24a, travelling eastward from this country one reached Champa after a journey of 50 days, southeastward She-p'o after a journey of 45 days, and northeastward Canton after a journey of 135 days.

P'o-li: According to *Sui shu* 82:7b, one reached this state after having passed Ch'ih-t'u. According to *Chiu T'ang shu* 197:2a, it was situated on an island southeast of Lin-yi. According to *T'ang hui-yao* 99:11b, it was a country in the southern wilderness, situated southeast of Lin-yi, about 10,000 *li* distant by sea. According to Hirth and Rockhill,[15] it was probably situated on the Malay Peninsula. Schafer says that P'o-li was Bali.[16] In short, there is a complete lack of agreement.

Lo-ch'a: According to *Wen-hsien t'ung-k'ao* 332:12b, it was situated east of the P'o-li state. Since the location of P'o-li is uncertain, the same is true for Lo-ch'a.[17]

San-fo-ch'i or Shi-li-fo-shih: According to *Sung shih* 489:12a, it was a neighbour of Champa, situated between Chen-la and She-p'o and separated from all three of them by the sea. According to Chao Ju-

[12] Op.cit., p.8.

[13] *Golden Peaches*, p.237.

[14] See also below sub T'o-huan and Ko-lo-she.

[15] *Chau Ju-kua* p.280.

[16] *Golden Peaches*, p.26.

[17] Needham, *Science and Civilisation*, vol.4:1, p.115 note e, identifies it with Pahang on the east coast of Malaya.

kua, it was reached by sea from China in a little over one month.[18] All authorities agree that this was the Buddhist state of Śrivijaya in eastern Sumatra.

To-p'o-teng: According to *Chiu T'ang shu* 197:3a, it was situated 2 months' sea voyage south of Lin-yi. It bordered on K'o-ling in the east and on the great ocean in the north. Schafer[19] surmises that this might be Sumatra.

K'o-ling: According to *Chiu T'ang shu* 197:3a, it was situated on an island in the south. According to *Hsin T'ang shu* 222C:3b and *Wen-hsien t'ung-k'ao* 332:16a, it was situated in the southern ocean facing P'o-li in the east and [To-]p'o-teng in the west. Both texts equate K'o-ling with She-p'o. Hirth and Rockhill[20] conclude the K'o-ling[21] was western Java and propose[22] that the name is a transscription of Kalinga in India, from where the Hindu settlers of Java had for the most part come. They observe, however that Gerini places the country on the Malay Peninsula. Schafer calls the state Kalinga.[23] It may well be that K'o-ling was on Java, in which case it was a predecessor of She-p'o. Their dates overlap, however. K'o-ling appears in the Chinese sources from 640 to 860-874, She-p'o from 820.

She-p'o: According to *Sung shih* 489:15b and *Wen-hsien t'ung-k'ao* 332:14b, it was situated in the southern ocean. According to *Sung shih* 489:17b and *Wen-hsien t'ung-k'ao* 332:15a, it had an old enmity with San-fo-ch'i. According to Chao Ju-kua, it was reached from Ch'üan-chou after a sea voyage of about a month.[24] All authorities agree that this was Java. In that case, She-p'o stands for the Hindu kingdom of Mataram and its sucessors, which indeed were hostile to the Buddhist San-fo-ch'i.

Po-ni: According to *Sung shih* 489:18a-18b and *Wen-hsien t'ung-k'ao* 332:18b, it was situated southwest[25] [of China] in the great ocean, 45 days' journey from She-p'o, 40 days from San-fo-ch'i, and 30 days from Champa. Hirth and Rockhill[26] conclude that Po-ni was

[18] Hirth and Rockhill, *Chao Ju-kua*, p.60.
[19] *Golden Peaches*, p.136.
[20] *Chau Ju-kua*, p.273.
[21] They call it Ho-ling.
[22] *Chao Ju-kua*, p.78-79, note 1.
[23] *Golden Peaches*, pp.83, 101, 103, 245.
[24] Hirth and Rockhill, *Chao Ju-kua*, p.75.
[25] Chao Ju-kua says southeast. See Hirth and Rockhill p.155.
[26] *Chao Ju-kua*, p.158, note 1, and p.280.

Borneo but note that Gerini places it on the east coast of Sumatra. If Po-ni was situated in northern Borneo, the sailing distances would be about right.

T'o-huan: According to *Chiu T'ang shu* 197:2b, it was situated in the great ocean southwest of Lin-yi, more than 3 months' voyage distant from Chiao-chih, bordering in the southeast on To-ho-lo.[27] According to Schafer,[28] it probably was one of the Moluccas.

Mo-yi: *Sung shih* and *Wen-hsien t'ung-k'ao* say nothing about the location of this country. According to Hirth and Rockhill,[29] Chao Ju-kua used this name[30] as applying to Mindoro and Luzon, if not all the Philippine Islands.

Ko-lo-she: According to *T'ung-tien* 18:71b, *Ts'e-fu yüan-kuei* p.5025, and *Wen-hsien t'ung-k'ao* 332:16b, it was situated south of the southern ocean and bordered in the east on To-ho-lo.[31]

Kan-t'ang: According to *Hsin T'ang shu* 222C:2a and *Wen-hsien t'ung-k'ao* 331:12b, it was situated south of the ocean.

Chu-na or Shu-na: According to *Hsin T'ang shu* 222C:2a, it was reached by sea from Chiao-chih in 3 months. According to *Wen-hsien t'ung-k'ao* 331:12b, it was situated 2 months' voyage south of Fu-nan.

To-mo-ch'ang: According to *Hsin T'ang shu* 222C:5a and *Wen-hsien t'ung-k'ao* 332:16b, it was situated on an island and northward faced K'o-ling.

P'an-p'an:[32] According to *Chiu T'ang shu* 197:2a, it was situated at the sea, 40 days distant by ship from Chiao chou (Chiao-chih). According to *T'ung-tien* 188:70b, it was a big island in the southern ocean. Herrmann[33] shows it on the northern part of the Malay Peninsula. According to Schafer,[34] P'an-p'an was once powerful on the Malay Peninsula.

Tan-tan:[35] According to *Hsin T'ang shu* 222C:5b, it was situated

[27] If this is true, To-ho-lo cannot have been Dvāravati in present Thailand.

[28] *Golden Peaches*, pp.101-102.

[29] *Chao Ju-kua*, p.160, note 1, and 277.

[30] He wrote it Ma-yi.

[31] This is still another argument against To-ho-lo being Dvāravati.

[32] *Sui shu*, *Chiu T'ang shu*, *Hsin T'ang shu*, and *Ts'e-fu yüan-kuei* write the name with radical 108, *T'ung-tien* and *Wen-hsien t'ung-k'ao* with radical 75.

[33] *Atlas*, p. 39.

[34] *Golden Peaches*, p.81.

[35] *Sui shu* and *Wen-hsien t'ung-k'ao* transliterate the name with the character for "cinnabar", *Hsin T'ang shu* and *Ts'e-fu yüan-kuei* with the homophone for "odd".

southeast of Chen chou, i.e. of modern Hai-nan.[36]

P'iao: It was situated near Nan-chao, apparently in eastern Burma. In 802, P'iao attached envoys to a mission sent by Nan-chao to the T'ang court. Nan-chao was situated in western Yün-nan.

P'u-tuan or P'u-kan: Hirth and Rockhill[37] speculate that P'u-tuan and P'u-kan might be the same country. That is, in fact, the case. Chao Ju-kua records that P'u-kan sent a mission to Sung in 1004. *Sung shih* 7:3, 7b; 490:19b lists the same mission as coming from P'u-tuan. The two names were therefore interchangable. According to the *Ling-wai tai-ta*,[38] P'u-kan was 5 days' journey distant from Ta-li, i.e. Nan-chao.[39] That distance is clearly the same as the one later covered by the Burma Road. There is general agreement that P'u-tuan/P'u-kan was Pagan in central Burma.

Shih-tzu: According to *Liang shu* 54:24a, Shih-tzu was situated next to India. According to *Hsin T'ang-shu* 222C:9a, it was situated in the southern ocean. According to *T'ang hui-yao* 100:12a, it was situated in the southwestwern ocean. Hirth and Rockhill[40] identify Shih-tzu as Ceylon and state that Fa-hsien was the first to use this name. According to Legge,[41] the founding of the kingdom was ascribed to an Indian merchant adventurer, whose father's name was Singha "the Lion" . From this, the name of the state was derived: Singhala, the Singha Kingdom or Kingdom of the Lion. Schafer[42] notes that Ceylon was called the "Lion Country". *T'ang hui-yao* 100:16a records that in ancient times the Buddha went to this country. This refers, of course, to the legend that he visited Ceylon. But misled by the name, the same text 100:12a claims that Shih-tzu got its name because the people there were able to tame and rear lions. There are not and have never been any lions on Ceylon. It is nevertheless certain that Shih-tzu stands for Ceylon.

T'ien-chu: This is India.

Chu-lien: According to *Sung shih* 489:20a and *Wen-hsien t'ung-k'ao* 332:19a, it was situated 411,400 *li* distant from Canton. Hirth and

---

[36] Needham, *Science and Civilsation*, vol.4:1, p.115 note e, follows Gerini in identifying Tan-tan with Kelantan in Malaya.
[37] *Chao Ju-kua*, p.59 note 1.
[38] By Chou Ch'ü-fei, written in 1178. See Hirth and Rockhill p. 22 note 2.
[39] See Hirth and Rockhill, *Chao Ju-kua*, p.59 note 1.
[40] *Chao Ju-kua*, p.12 note 4, and p. 281.
[41] *Record of Buddhist Kingdoms*, pp.100-101 note 5.
[42] *Golden Peaches*, p.12.

Rockhill[43] observe that all figures connected with Chu-lien in Chinese accounts are inexclicably exaggerated. They propose that Chu-lien stands for the Chola Dominion or Coromandel Coast.[44]

Wu-ch'a or Wu-ch'ang or Wu-tu: According to *T'ung-tien* 188:72a, it was situated in central India. According to *T'ang hui-yao* 99:23b and *Wen-hsien t'ung-k'ao* 332:16a; 338:51b, it was situated in southern India. According to *Tzu-chih t'ung-chien* p.6740, it was situated west of the Arabs.

Na-chieh: According to *Wen-hsien t'ung-k'ao* 338:51b, it was a depend ency of central India.

Ni-p'o-lo: This is Nepal.

Ts'eng-t'an: According to *Sung shih* 490:21b, it was situated in the southern ocean. According to *Sung shih* 490:21b and *Wen-hsien t'ung-k'ao* 332:20a, the envoys of 1071 had travelled to Canton via San-fo-ch'i for 160 days. Hirth and Rockhill[45] surmise that this might be Zanzibar in Africa and that it is practically the same country as Chao Ju-kua's Ts'eng-pa.

Of these 44 countries, I conclude that only about half can be identified with any degree of confidence (maps 1 and 2). As might be expected, most of these were situated on the continent, in Vietnam, Cambodia, Thailand, Burma, and India. The Chinese historians knew less about the islands. While the sea captains understood how to navigate the oceans to and from their destinations, the written records are vague or contradictory. We can only be certain about the states on eastern Sumatra, Java, Ceylon, and perhaps Borneo, i.e. those on the largest islands.

Let us now see what can be learned from China's relations with the foreign countries in continental South Asia and on the islands.

CHIAO-CHIH

This territory in northern Vietnam, rich in agriculture and before the Sung an important transit point for overseas trade, had been a colonial part of the Chinese empire since 214 B.C. Its name derived from that of a Chinese commandery, situated in Chiao Province (Chiao chou).

[43] *Chao Ju-kua*, p.99 note 2.

[44] Op.cit., pp.93 and 272.

[45] Op.cit., p.127 note 4, and p.283.

Chiao-chih finally gained independence during the Five Dynasties.

After the rule of a number of local strongmen, Ting Lien became the king of Chiao-chih. On Aug.19, 973, his envoys to the Sung court offered regional objects.[46] T'ai-tsu appointed him Acting Grand Master, Military Commissioner of the non-existant Army Which Quiets the Sea, and Protector General of Annam. The envoys were appointed to Chinese nominal offices[47] (*Sung shih* 3:3b; 488:2a; *Wen-hsien t'ung-k'ao* 330:4b).

On July 4, 975, Ting Lien's envoys offered rhinoceros horns,[48] elephant tusks, and aromatic drugs. That autumn, T'ai-tsu appointed him Commander Unequalled in Honours,[49] reconfirmed him as Acting Grand Master, and recognized him as king of Chiao-chih commandery[50] (*Sung shih* 3:8a; 488:2a; *Wen-hsien t'ung-k'ao* 330:4b).

After T'ai-tsung had ascended the Sung throne on Nov.14, 976, envoys from Ting Lien congratulated and offered regional objects in the 12th month (Jan./Feb., 978) of the Chinese year 977 (*Sung shih* 488:2b; *Sung hui-yao kao* 10122:2a; *Wen-hsien t'ung-k'ao* 330:4b).

Ting Lien was in 979 succeeded by his younger brother Hsüan.[51] A Sung mission arrived after Lien's death. In the winter of 980, envoys from Hsüan offered regional objects. Soon thereafter, he was overthrown and placed under house arrest by the high dignitary Li

---

[46] *Sung hui-yao kao* 10122:1b dates this mission in the 4th month (May/June). When the sources state that foreign countries sent missions, the dates refer to the times when they were received, not to the times when they departed from their home countries.

[47] The nominal offices conferred on envoys mentioned in this chapter were Supreme Pillar of State, Grand Commandant, Grandee for Court Service, Grandee for Closing Court, Imperial Household Grandee of the Golden Seal and Purple Ribbon, Imperial Household Grandee of the Silver Seal and Blue Ribbon, Grandee Secretary, Palace Inspector Examining the Halls, Supernumerary Gentleman of the Ministry of Personnel, General-in-chief of the Guards of the Golden Mace of the Right, General-in-chief Who Maintains Obedience and Longs for Civilization, General of the Gentlemen, General of the Gentlemen Who Maintain Obedience, General Who Brings Repose to the Distance, General Who Cherishes the Distance, General Who Cherishes Civilization, General Who Scouts and Attacks, and Chief Commandant of the Courageous Garrison. Others were appointed to the Assault-resisting [Garrison] or the Courageous Garrison of the Left at the Four Gates.

[48] *Wen-hsien t'ung-k'ao* omits "horns".

[49] An honorific of high prestige.

[50] Whenever the Chinese added "commandery" to a foreign title, it was with the pretense that the foreign country really was a unit of the Chinese local administration.

[51] The year is according to Mathias Tchang, *Synchronismes* p.347.

Huan. T'ai-tsung considered this a good opportunity for attacking Chiao-chih, and, allied with Champa, ordered armies to do so by several routes. Li Huan countered by sending envoys and offering regional objects. This did not halt the war, and the Chinese gained some victories in 981. However, Li Huan had some successes himself and took Champa prisoners. In the 3rd month (Aug./Sep.) of 982 and in 983, envoys from Li Huan again offered regional objects and sought a normalization, to which the emperor agreed. In the 5th month (June/July) of 983, Li Huan informed the court that Champa had attacked Chiao-chih with ships by sea and with elephants and horsemen by land, and that he had repulsed the invaders. In 985 and the autumn of 986, envoys again offered regional objects and letters (*Sung shih* 4:15; 488:2b, 3a, 3b, 4a; *Sung hui-yao kao* 8116:4b; 10122:2a; *Wen-hsien t'ung-k'ao* 330:4b).

In the 10th month (Nov./Dec.) of 986, Sung officially accepted political reality. Li Huan was appointed Acting Grand Guardian, Chief Commandant in charge of all affairs of Chiao-chih, Protector General of Annam, Military Commissioner of the non-existant Army Which Quiets the Sea, and entitled Marquis of Ching-chao commandery[52] and Meritorious Subject.[53] Envoys were sent to confer these honours. In the 4th month (Apr./May) of 988, a Sung envoy appointed Li Huan Acting Grand Commandant and entitled him Dynasty-founding Duke (*Sung shih* 488:5a; *Sung hui-yao kao* 10122:5a; *Wen-hsien t'ung-k'ao* 330: 4b-5a). However, he was not yet recognized as king.

On June 28, 988, a mission from Li Huan brought gifts. In the summer of 990, Sung dispatched envoys to make Li Huan a Specially

[52] It was the custom of the Chinese government to also give nominal land grants which usually were later increased. Thus, Li Huan received a land grant of 3000 households in 986, increased by 1000 households in 990 (*Sung shih* 488:5a). I omit mention of such grants below.

[53] The Sung dynasty was in the habit of conferring on the kings of Chiao-chih/Annam the title of Meritorious Subject, prefixed by a two-character honorific. In the course of time, the title was expanded by additional prefixes, so that the longer the king reigned the longer the title became. For instance, when Li Ch'ien-te died in 1130/31, his title had grown to Meritorious Subject Who Assists Governance, Maintains Integrity, Is Loyal and Trustworthy, Conforms to Virtue, Venerates Benevolence, Displays Strength, Observes Rectitude, Favours Civilization, Cherishes Respect, Aids the Government, Is Content with Sincerity, Is Attentive to the Rules, Supports the Mandate, Completes Good Works, Establishes Loyal Efforts, Follows Righteousness, Esteems Propriety, Raises Prosperity, and Respects Honour. Since these titles are repetitive and tedious, I omit them below.

Advanced.[54] When these envoys returned in the 6th month (Aug./Sep.), the emperor ordered them to itemize the layout of the mountains and rivers, i.e. to provide military intelligence on Chiao-chih's topography. On Dec.22, 990,[55] envoys from Li Huan presented 40 elephant tusks (*Sung shih* 5:8a, 11a; 488:5a; *Sung hui-yao kao* 10122:5a-5b; *Wen-hsien t'ung-k'ao* 330:5a).

In the 2nd month (Feb./Mar.) of 993, Li Huan was finally recognized by Sung as king of Chiao-chih commandery. In the 3rd (Apr./May) and 10th month (Nov./Dec.) of 994, his envoys once more offered gifts (*Sung shih* 5:15b, 18a; *Sung hui-yao kao* 10122:5b; *Wen-hsien t'ung-k'ao* 330:5a).

But relations between Chiao-chih and Sung were not uniformly peaceful. In the spring of 995, more than 100 warships from Chiao-chih raided south China, and in the summer it struck again. T'ai-tsung was unwilling to make an issue of this and instead sent an envoy to Li Huan with a letter and the gift of a beautiful jade belt (*Wen-hsien t'ung-k'ao* 330:5a). Two further imperial communications were brought to Li Huan in 997 (*Sung shih* 488:7b).

When Chen-tsung had ascended the Sung throne on May 8, 997, he immediately recognized Li Huan as king, using the term Nan-p'ing for his state. He also made him a Palace Attendant. Li Huan responded with a mission in the 9th month (Oct./Nov), in which he presented 10 silver vessels, 50 rhinoceros horns and elephant tusks,[56] and 10,000 bolts of silken fabrics. In the 9th month (Sep./Oct.) of 998, envoys from Li Huan offered one tame rhinoceros, two elephants,[57] 27 elephant tusks, and one golden pitcher. The emperor sent a letter. (*Sung shih* 488:8b; *Sung hui-yao kao* 10122:6b; *Wen-hsien t'ung-k'ao* 330:5a).

On Mar.3, 1001, Li Huan presented another tame rhinoceros and a tame elephant. On July 13, 1004, Li Huan's son Ming-t'i offered gifts. On July 28, Emperor Chen-tsung appointed Ming-t'i as Imperial Household Grandee of the Golden Seal and Purple Ribbon, Acting Grand Guardian, and Supreme Pillar of State, confirmed him in an office he already held in Chiao-chih, and entitled him Dynasty-founding Baron. On the New Year's Day of 1005 (Feb.12), Ming-t'i participated

[54] An appellation granted to marquises as a special distinction.

[55] *Sung hui-yao kao* dates this mission in the 10th month (Oct./Nov.).

[56] Since the breakdown is unknown, this figure has been omitted from the statistics below.

[57] *Sung hui-yao kao* says four tame elephants.

in a banquet given for the envoys from Champa and the Arabs and was presented copper cash.[58] In the 2nd month (Mar./Apr.) of 1005, Sung sent envoys to Chiao-chih (*Sung shih* 6:12a; 7:7b; 488:9a; *Sung hui-yao kao* 10122:7a,7b; *Wen-hsien t'ung-k'ao* 330:5a).

In 1006, the Sung learned that Li Huan had died. A Chinese attack on Chiao-chih was proposed, this being an opportune moment, but was rejected by Chen-tsung. This meant no more than that he had been, on the whole, a good neighbour. He was succeeded by his middle son Lung-yüeh, who was promptly killed by his brothers Lung-ch'üan and Lung-t'ing. The latter was enthroned. He proposed sending gifts to the Sung court, i.e. sought recognition. This was accepted by the court, and Sung envoys were sent to Chiao-chih in the 3rd month (Mar.Apr.) of 1007. Lung-t'ing thereupon dispatched a mission, led by his younger brother Ming-ch'ang, which was received at the Sung court on Aug.26. It presented a letter, in which Li Lung-t'ing requested copies of the *Nine Confucian Classics*[59] and the Buddhist *Tripitaka*. These were provided. On Sep.1,[60] the Sung granted Li Huan the posthumous titles of Prefect of the Palace Writers and king of Nan-yüeh. It appointed Lung-t'ing as Acting Grand Commandant, Military Commissioner of the non-existant Army Which Quiets the Sea, Protector General of Annam, Grandee Secretary, and Supreme Pillar of State, recognized him as king of Chiao-chih commandery, gave him the name of Chih-chung (Most Loyal),[61] and presented him with a state seal, banners, and an emblem of authority as king of Annam. On Sep.2, Li Ming-ch'ang was appointed Imperial Household Grandee of the Golden Seal and Purple Ribbon and Concurrent Grandee Secretary, and Supreme Pillar of State, and entitled Dynasty-founding Baron. The other envoys were also given nominal Chinese offices (*Sung shih* 7: 11a-11b, 14b; 488:9a, 10a; *Sung hui-yao kao* 10122:9a-9b; *Hsü Tzu-chih t'ung-chien ch'ang-pien* p.518-519; *Wen-hsien t'ung-k'ao* 330:5b).

On Jan.23, 1009, Li Lung-t'ing offered gifts. He was appointed Jointly Manager of Affairs with the Secretariat-Chancellery (*Sung shih* 7:20b; *Wen-hsien t'ung-k'ao* 330:5b).

---

[58] In the 3rd month (April) of 1006, he passed through Kuang chou on his way home (*Sung hui-yao kao* 10122:7b). He had been in China for some 21 months.

[59] I.e. the *Book of Changes*, the *Book of Documents*, the *Book of Odes*, the *Spring and Autumn Annals*, the *Tso-chuan*, the *Book of Rites*, the *Rites of Chou*, the *Classic of Filial Piety*, and the *Annalects*.

[60] *Sung shih* 7:14b dates this Oct.19.

[61] *Sung shih* and *Sung hui-yao kao* henceforth refer to him by that name.

On Dec.21, 1009, envoys from Li Lung-t'ing presented a tame rhinoceros, 20 rhinoceros horns, 40 elephant tusks, and gold and silver vessels. The rhinoceros had a disagreeable nature. But it had come from far away, and Emperor Chen-tsung did not wish to offend Li Lung-t'ing. He therefore had it released at the seashore. Li Lung-t'ing was given the armour he had requested (*Sung shih* 7:23a; 488:10b; *Sung hui-yao* 10122:10a; *Hsü Tzu-chih t'ung-chien ch'ang-pien* p.638)

Negotiations between Chiao-chih and Sung led to the opening of a joint market on the south coast of present Kuang-tung in 1010 (*Wen-hsien t'ung-k'ao* 330:5b).

By this time, Li Lung-t'ing had fallen out with his brothers and had killed one of them. Ming-ch'ang, the one who had led a mission to Sung in 1006, and others thereupon began to negotiate with Sung on their own authority (*Wen-hsien t'ung-k'ao* 330:5b).

In early 1010, news reached the Sung court that Li Lung-t'ing had died, and that a certain Li Kung-yün had made himself his sucessor. This was not a relative, the Li in both family names being written with different Chinese characters. Li Kung-yün was the founder of the long-lived Li dynasty. On Apr.29, 1010, his envoys offered presents and a letter to the Sung court, no doubt to announce his ascension to the throne. He was immediately appointed Acting Grand Tutor, Protector General of Annam, Military Commissioner of the non-existant Army Which Quiets the Sea, Concurrent Grandee Secretary, and Supreme Pillar of State, recognized as king of Chiao-chih commandery, and entitled Commander Unequalled in Honour and Specially Advanced.[62] Garments, gold and silver belts, [porcelain] vessels, and silk were presented to him, and his envoys received nominal Chinese offices (*Sung shih* 7:23a, 23b; 488:10b-11a; *Sung hui-yao kao* 10122:10b; *Wen-hsien t'ung-k'ao* 330:5b).

In the 12th month (Jan./Feb., 1011) of the Chinese year 1010, envoys from Li Kung-yün brought gifts and congratulated Emperor Chen-tsung on his decision to sacrifice personally to Sovereign Earth (hou-t'u) in Fen-yin[63] in the following year.[64] At the same time, he requested the Buddhist *Tripitaka* and books on ritual and law. These

[62] *Sung hui-yao kao* dates the appointments in the 2nd month (Feb./Mar.).

[63] This prefecture was situated north of the present Jung-ho hsien, Shan-hsi.

[64] This sacrifice was performed on Mar.24, 1011 (*Sung shih* 8:1b). It is possible that envoys of Li Kung-yün attended the sacrifice.

were provided. In the 1st month (Feb./Mar.) of 1011, Li Kung-yün's two chief envoys were appointed to nominal Chinese offices, and each was presented with a purple and gold fish wallet (*Sung shih* 7:26a; *Sung hui-yao kao* 10122:10b-11a).

In the 5th month (June/July) of 1011, Li Kung-yün was appointed Jointly Manager of Affairs with the Secretariat-Chancellery. He offered presents, which were officially accepted by the Sung in the 6th month (July/Aug.). In the 4th month (Apr./May) of 1012, envoys from Li Kung-yün offered 30 rhinoceros horns. In the 5th month (May/June), these envoys were appointed to nominal Chinese offices. In the 11th month (Dec./Jan.1013) of the Chinese year 1012, Li Kung-yün was made a Commander Unequalled in Honour and presented with [porcelain] vessels, silk, and horse trappings (*Sung shih* 8:3a, 4a, 6b; 488: 11b; *Sung hui-yao kao* 10122:11a-11b).

On Aug.15, 1014, Li Kung-yün presented 60 horses and informed the Sung court that he had fought the aboriginals.[65] His envoys received gifts in accordance with their ranks. In the 8th month (Aug./Sep.), another mission offered regional objects. In the 9th month (Sep./Oct.), the two chief envoys were appointed to nominal Chinese offices and ennobled as Dynasty-founding Barons (*Sung shih* 488:11b; *Sung hui-yao kao* 10122:11b, 12a).

On Mar.21, 1017, Li Kung-yün was recognized as king of Nan-p'ing. In 1018, he was presented the collected Taoist works. In the 8th month (September) of 1019, a younger brother of Li Kung-yün offered rhinoceros horns, elephant tusks, and other regional objects. In the 12th month (Dec./Jan., 1020) of the Chinese year 1019, Li Kung-yün was appointed Acting Grand Commandant and presented with [porcelain] vessels, garments, golden belts, and horse trappings (*Sung shih* 8:15b; 488:12a; *Sung hui-yao kao* 10122:12b; 10123:6a; *Wen-hsien t'ung-k'ao* 330:5b).

On May 30, 1022, envoys from Li Kung-yün offered gifts. This was, no doubt, in reponse to Jen-tsung's enthronement on Mar.23. He was appointed Acting Grand Master. In the 7th month (August) of that year, the high Sung officials informed Emperor Jen-tsung that the envoys had brought pewter, red ore, tortoise shells, pitchers, aromatics and other regional objects, and that the merchants had calculated

[65] *Sung hui-yao kao* notes the presence of envoys from Chiao-chih in the Chinese capital, on Aug.8.

their value at 1,682 strings of copper cash. An edict ordered that the repayment should be a liberal 2000 strings of cash. It was furthermore reported that Kuang chou had received from Chiao-chih 5,300 catties of cassia bark. An edict ordered to estimate their value and make a return payment. In 1027, envoys from Li Kung-yün again brought presents. In the 3rd month (Mar.Apr.) of 1028, the high Sung officials informed the emperor that Chiao-chih envoys had sold fragrant drugs at the price of 3,060 strings of copper cash. An edict ordered to pay 4000 strings of cash in return (*Sung shih* 9:1b, 9a; 488:12a, 12b; *Sung hui-yao kao* 10122:12b-13a; 10123:6a; *Wen-hsien t'ung-k'ao* 330:5b).

On May 18, 1028, Li Te-cheng announced to the Sung court that his father Kung-yün had died on Mar.31. As the new ruler, he simultaneously offered gifts. The Sung court dispatched a mission to Chiao-chih to condole and sacrifice. Kung-yün was given the posthumous title of Palace Attendant and king of Nan-yüeh. Te-cheng was recognized as king of Chiao-chih commandery and appointed Acting Grand Commandant. This was followed by a violation of the Chinese border on May 27, 1028 (*Sung shih* 9:10a, 11a; *Sung hui-yao kao* 10122: 13b; *Wen-hsien t'ung-k'ao* 330:5b).

In 1032, Li Te-cheng offered gifts and was appointed Jointly Manager of Affairs with the Secretariat-Chancellery. In 1034, he presented two elephants which were rejected (*Sung shih* 9:13a, 13b; 10:7a 488: 12b, 13a; *Wen-hsien t'ung-k'ao* 330:5b).

Some time between 1034 and 1038, some 600 subjects of Li Te-cheng attempted to defect to China. As had been the case throughout previous Chinese history, governments were always eager to increase their populations and deplored a decrease. A defection of this kind was therefore a sensitive diplomatic matter. The Chinese government decided not to make an issue of it and sent the fugitives back, but it also appealed to Te-cheng not to punish them. Te-cheng sent envoys to offer gifts and was appointed Acting Grand Master (*Wen-hsien t'ung-k'ao* 330:5b).

In 1036, some Chiao-chih chiefs looted Chinese territory. The Sung court protested and asked for the punishment of the culprits. Li Te-cheng sent gifts. He repeated this in 1040. In 1043, he presented five tame elephants, in the 7th month (Aug./Sep.) of 1046 ten tame elephants, and on Dec.25, 1046, one tame elephant. At the last occasion, he was given a purple robe and golden belt. In 1048, he once more offered gifts The envoys of 1040, 1043, and 1046 were appointed to nominal Chinese offices (*Sung shih* 10:9b; 11:6b, 11b, 14b; 488:13a;

Sung hui-yao kao 101223:14a; *Wen-hsien t'ung-k'ao* 330:5b).

In 1050, Li Te-cheng asked for the return of another number of subjects, who had crossed into China, supposedly more than 3000. The Sung agreed (*Wen-hsien t'ung-k'ao* 330:5b).

On Nov.22, 1055, envoys sent by Li Jih-tsun announced the death of his father Te-cheng. They offered testamentary gifts and ten tame elephants. The Sung dispatched a mission to condole and sacrifice and to confer on Te-cheng the posthumous titles of Palace Attendant and king of Nan-yüeh. Jih-tsun was recognized as his successor (*Sung shih* 12:9b-10a; 488:13b-14a; *Sung hui-yao, kao* 10122:14b; *Wen-hsien t'ung-k'ao* 330:5b).

On July 21, 1058, Chiao-chih offered an animal which it claimed to be a *ch'i-lin*.[66] It resembled a water buffalo, had a horn on the tip of its nose, and ate vegetables. The Chinese experts concluded that it was not a *ch'i-lin*, whereupon the court rejected this attribution and merely called it a strange animal (*Sung shih* 12:13b-14a; 488:14a; *Sung hui-yao kao* 10122:15a; *Hsü Tzu-chih t'ung-chien ch'ang-pien* p.1724; *Wen-hsien t'ung-k'ao* 330:5b).[67]

In 1059, Chiao-chih looted Chinese territory. On Aug.5, 1060, local authorities reported to the court that Chiao-chih again had violated the border. The court ordered to mobilize troops against Li Jih-tsun, which was enough to make him back down (*Sung shih* 12:16b; 488:14a *Wen-hsien t'ung-k'ao* 330:5b).

In the 1st month (Feb./Mar.) of 1062, a letter from Li Jih-tsun was presented to the Sung court, and on Feb.8, 1063,[68] he offered nine tame elephants (*Sung shih* 12:20b; *Sung hui-yao kao* 10122:15a-15b).

On Apr.30, 1063, Emperor Jen-tsung of Sung died. In the 4th month (May), his successor Emperor Ying-tsung sent Jen-tsung's testamentary gifts to Li Jih-tsun and appointed him Jointly Manager of Affairs with the Secretariat-Chancellery. On Feb.25, 1067, Ying-tsung recognized Jih-tsun as king of Nan-p'ing and entitled him Commander Unequalled in Honour (*Sung shih* 12:20b; 14:2b; *Wen-hsien t'ung-k'ao* 330:5b).

---

[66] This was the mythical Chinese unicorn, with the body of a deer, tail of an ox, hoofs of a horse, and one horn. It was considered auspicious, rarely seen, and expected to appear only on behalf of sages. The gift was therefore intended to flatter Emperor Jen-tsung of Sung.

[67] *Sung shih* 488:14a and *Hsü Tzu-chih t'ung-chien ch'ang-pien* p.1724 say two strange animals.

[68] By *Sung shih* dated Feb.9.

In the 1st month (Jan./Feb.) of 1067, the Sung court sent one garment, one golden belt, 200 ounces of silver vessels, 300 bolts of pongee,[69] two horses, and gilded silver horse trappings as presents to Li Jih-tsun (*Sung hui-yao kao* 10122:15b).

On Dec.23, 1068, a letter from Li Jih-tsun was presented to the Sung court (*Sung hui-yao kao* 10122:16a)

On Mar.3, 1069, Li Jih-tsun informed the Sung court that he had defeated Champa and captured its king. His envoys were appointed to nominal Chinese offices. Hencefort, Jih-tsun called himself emperor and his state Ta Yüeh (Great Yüeh) (*Sung shih* 14:11a; *Sung hui-yao kao* 10122:16a; *Wen-hsien t'ung-k'ao* 330:5b). The Sung court continued to treat him as a king.

On Nov.2, 1071, the Sung court appointed Li Jih-tsun Military Commissioner of the non-existant Army Which Quiets the Sea, Protector General of Annam, Supreme Pillar of State, and Acting Grand Commandant, and confirmed him as Commander Unequalled in Honour, Jointly Manager of Affairs with the Secretariat Chancellery, and king of Nan-p'ing (*Sung hui-yao kao* 1021:16b-17a).

On Apr.5, 1072, the Kuang-hsi Circuit reported that Li Jih-tsun had died and that his son Ch'ien-te had suceeded him. The Sung court dispatched a mission to condole, contribute to the funeral expenses, confer posthumous titles, and recognize Ch'ien-te as heir. His mother, the Lady Li, was entitled Grand Consort. She and the eunuch Li Shang-chi governed the state in the name of her young son (*Sung shih* 15:7a; *Sung hui-yao kao* 10122:17a; *Wen-hsien t'ung-k'ao* 330:5b).

On Apr.30, 1073, Chiao-chih offered presents. On May 6, Li Ch'ien-te was by the Sung appointed Military Commissioner of the non-existant Army Which Quiets the Sea and Protector General of Annam, recognized as king of Chiao-chih commandery, and presented garments, a silver belt, and vessels (*Sung shih* 15:9a; *Sung shih hui-yao kao* 10122:17a).

In late 1075 and early 1076, Chiao-chih looted three Chinese territories. The first countermeasures were taken on Jan.29, culminating in an alliance with Champa and the Khmer Kingdom. In the 12th month (Dec./Jan, 1077) of the Chinese year 1076, Chiao-chih was defeated. In 1077, envoys brought a letter from Li Ch'ien-te to

69 A thin silk.

propose peace (*Sung shih* 15:15a, 15b; *Sung hui-yao kao* 10122:17a-18a; *Wen-hsien t'ung-k'ao* 330:6a).

On Jan.25, 1078, Chiao-chih communicated with the Sung court. On Oct.10, Chiao-chih offered regional objects and unsuccessfully requested a border adjustment. On Oct.20, Sung responded with a letter. On Aug.4, 1081, a letter from Li Ch'ien-te was received at the court. On July 20, 1082, he presented two tame elephants,[70] 50 rhinoceros horns, and 50 elephant tusks. In the 8th month (Aug./Sep.) of that year, Sung presented Li Ch'ien-te with a collection of "instructive imperial edicts". In 1083, a mission from Li Ch'ien-te arrived at the Sung court. He received robes, belts, and 500 bolts of pongee (*Sung shih* 16:12b; 488:15b; *Sung hui-yao kao* 10122:18a, 19a, 20a-21a; *Wen-hsien t'ung-k'ao* 330:6a).

On Nov.22, 1084, the Sung agreed to redraw the border with Chiao-chih and to cede six prefectures (hsien) to it (*Sung shih* 16:12b).

After Che-tsung had ascended the Sung throne on Apr.1, 1085, Li Ch'ien-te was appointed Jointly Manager of Affairs with the Secretariat-Chancellery (*Sung shih* 488:16a).

On May 9, 1087, envoys from Chiao-chih to the Sung court offered gifts, whereupon Li Ch'ien-te was recognized as king of Nan-p'ing. On June 7, his chief envoy was appointed to a nominal Chinese office. On Apr.26, 1091, Chiao-chih again offered presents, and on May 14 of the same year the Sung court sent robes, belts, brocade, and horse trappings as presents to Li Ch'ien-te. In 1095, Chiao-chih once more offered gifts (*Sung shi* 17:8a, 15b, 17a; 488:16a; *Hsü Tzu-chih t'ung-chien ch'ang-pien* p.3785, 4281; *Wen-hsien t'ung-k'ao* 330:6a).

In c.1101, Sung appointed Li Ch'ien-te Commander Unequalled in Honour and Acting Grand Master (*Wen-hsien t'ung-k'ao* 330:6a).

On Oct.25, 1107, a Sung imperial document refered to Li Ch'ien-te, in addition to his previous titles, as Supreme Pillar of State and king of Nan-p'ing (*Sung hui-yao kao* 10123:1a).

In 1107, envoys from Chiao-chih arrived at the Sung court, wishing to buy books. The hight officials reported to the emperor that the law did not allow it. He overrode their objections on Nov.26 and allowed the envoys to buy books on divination, yin and yang, mathematics, and warfare (*Sung hui-yao kao* 10123:1a; *Wen-hsien t'ung-k'ao* 330:6a).

On June 11, 1111, envoys from Chiao-chih offered presents. On

---

[70] According to *Sung shih* 16:7a, Chiao-chih presented two tame rhinoceroses.

Jan.11, 1119, Li Ch'ien-te was by the Sung appointed Acting Grand Master and Acting Minister of Works, and confirmed as Jointly Manager of Affairs with the Secretariat Chancellery, Protector General of Annam, Military Commissioner of the non-existant Army Which Quiets the Sea, and king of Nan-p'ing (*Sung shih* 20:12b; *Sung hui-yao kao* 10123:1b; *Wen-hsien t'ung-k'ao* 330:6a).

On Dec.5, 1127, Emperor Kao-tsung of Southern Sung ordered the Western Circuit of Kuang-nan not to accept absconding households from Annam (*Sung hui-yao kao* 10123:1b:2a). It is clear from this and preceding entries that there must have been a steady infiltration of the border.

In 1130, Li Ch'ien-te offered gifts. In 1132, Southern Sung learned that he had died[71] and on Mar.26, Kao-tsung granted him the posthumous titles of Palace Attendant and king of Nan-yüeh. His son and successor Li Yang-huan was appointed Military Commissioner of the non-existant Army Which Quiets the Sea, Acting Grand Commandant and Concurrent Grandee Secretary, Protector General of Annam, and Supreme Pillar of State, entitled Specially Advanced, and recognized as king of Chiao-chih commandery (*Sung hui-yao kao* 10123:2a-2b; *Wen-hsien t'ung-k'ao* 330:6a).

On Apr.12, 1138, a mission from Chiao-chih announced that Li Yang-huan had died and that his son T'ien-tso had been enthroned. On Apr.16, Kao-tsung granted Li Yang-huan the posthumous titles of Commander Unequalled in Honour and king of Nan-p'ing. On Apr.24, T'ien-tso was appointed Military Commissioner of the non-existant Army Which Quiets the Sea, Acting Grand Commandant and Concurrent Grandee Secretary, Protector General of Annam, and Supreme Pillar of State, entitled Specially Advanced, and recognized as king of Chiao-chih commandery (*Sung hui-yao kao* 10123:3a; *Wen-hsien t'ung-k'ao* 330:6a).

On July 24, 1139, the Kuang-hsi Circuit reported that previously a son of Li Ch'ien-te by a concubine had fled to the Ta-li State (Nan-chao) in Yün-nan and had changed his name to Chao Chih-chih. When it was learned that Li Yang-huan had died and T'ien-tso had become the king, the Ta-li State had sent him back in an attempt to gain the throne. T'ien-tso had raised troops against him and had

[71] There is a discrepancy in dates. Mathias Tchang, *Synchronismes*, p.359, places Li Ch'ien-te's death in 1127, but in that case he could not have offered gifts in 1130.

foiled the attempt. Later that year, Li T'ien-tso presented the Southern Sung with 50 ounces of gold and one elephant (*Sung hui-yao kao* 10123:3a-3b, 6b).

On July 10, 1144, the Annam State offered gifts. In the 6th month (July/Aug) of 1146, Annam presented ten tame elephants. On Mar.29, 1150, Li T'ien-tso presented another ten tame elephants. On July 10, 1155, the Ministry of Rites informed Kao-tsung that envoys had arrived from Annam with gifts. On Aug.27, Li T'ien-tso was appointed Acting Grand Master, recognized as king of Annam, and presented seven garments, 200 ounces of gold and silver objects, a golden belt, a silver casket, 200 bolts of apparel, and horse trappings. (*Sung shih* 30:7a, 10b; 31:5b; *Sung hui-yao kao* 10123:5a; *Wen-hsien t'ung-k'ao* 330:6a).

On Apr.18, 1156, an imperial edict restricted the number of envoys allowed to enter China from Annam at one time to 50. On June 22, the Ministries of Revenue and War reported to Kao-tsung that envoys had arrived from Annam. On Sep.7, another mission arrived which offered 1,136 ounces of golden vessels, 100 genuine pearls, 1000 catties of gharu wood,[72] 500 kingfisher's feathers, 50 bolts of pongee, ten horses, and nine elephants. On Sep.12, Li T'ien-tso was reconfirmed as Acting Grand Master (*Sung shih* 30:10a; *Sung hui-yao kao* 10123:5a, 6a, 7a).

On Apr.28, 1159, the Southern Sung Ministry of War proposed that the king of Chiao-chih commandery at each great ritual should be presented with one wide garment, one golden belt, a silver casket, 100 bolts of fine clothing, two horses, 200 ounces of silver vessels, 100 bolts of apparel, and gilded silver horse trappings (*Sung hui-yao kao* 10123:7b).

On Sep.30, 1164, envoys from Li T'ien-tso offered 100 ounces of golden vessels, 150 ounces of silver vessels, 30 elephant tusks, and 1,500 catties of two kinds of gharu wood (*Sung shih* 33:15a; *Wen-hsien t'ung-k'ao* 330:6a).

In the 6th month (July/Aug.) of 1173, envoys from Li T'ien-tso offered regional objects. Another mission with gifts was received on Jan.17, 1174. On Feb.25,[73] Emperor Hsiao-tsung gave an audience to the envoys, and on Mar.1 they were invited to a banquet in the Jade

---

[72] An incense. See Hirth and Rockhill, *Chao Ju-kua*, pp.204-206.

[73] According to *Sung hui-yao kao* 10123:9b. *Sung shih* 34:19a dates the audience Feb.21.

Stream Garden. On Mar.5, Hsiao-tsung accepted the name of Annam[74] for their state and recognized Li T'ien-tso as its king. He presented him a wide garment, a golden belt, a silver casket, 100 bolts of fine clothing, two horses, 200 ounces of silver vessels, 100 bolts of apparel, and gilded silver horse trappings.[75] On Aug.24, 1175, the Ministry of Rites reported to Hsiao-tsung that Li T'ien-tso had requested a state seal. This was granted on Sep.2, inscribed "Seal of the King of the Annam State" (*Sung shih* 34:18b, 19a, 21b; 488:17b; *Sung hui-yao kao* 10123:8a, 9b-11a; *Wen-hsien t'ung-k'ao* 330:6b).[76]

In the 5th month (June/July) of 1176, the high Southern Sung officials reported to Hsiao-tsung that Li T'ien-tso had died and requested that his son Lung-kan be recognized as heir. The emperor, sent envoys to condole and sacrifice. On Sep.28 of that year, the Southern Sung gave Annam its calendar. This saved the Annamese tedious calculations but was, in this as in other cases, understood by the Chinese government as confirming its overlordship. On Apr.14 of 1177, Hsiao-tsung appointed Li Lung-kan as Military Commissioner of the non-existant Army Which Quiets the Sea, Acting Grand Commandant and Concurrent Grandee Secretary, and Supreme Pillar of State, entitled him Specially Advanced, and recognized him as king of Annam. This was accompanied by presents (*Sung shih* 34:23b, 25a; 488:17b; *Sung hui-yao kao* 10123:11b, 12b *Wen-hsien t'ung-k'ao* 330:6b).

In 1178, envoys from Li Lung-kan brought a letter and gifts, and in 1180 and 1189 again offered presents (*Sung shih* 35:16b; 488:17b, 18a; *Wen-hsien t'ung-k'ao* 330:6b).

On Dec.2, 1190, the Kuang-hsi Circuit reported that the Annam State had sent a document, congratulating on the enthronement of Emperor Kuang-tsung on Feb.18, 1189 (*Sung shih* 36:7a; *Sung hui-yao kao* 10123:14b).

On Sep.23, 1194, the Southern Sung presented Li Lung-kan a wide garment, a golden belt, 100 bolts of fine clothing, 2 horses, 200 ounces of silver vessels, 100 bolts of apparel, and gilded silver horse trappings (*Sung hui-yao kao* 10123:15a).

On June 2, 1212,[77] the Kuang-hsi Circuit reported to the Southern

---

[74] As has been seen, this name had been used at times before.

[75] I.e. the presents were those agreed on in 1159.

[76] *Wen-hsien t'ung-k'ao* telescopes the recognition and presentation of the seal into the year 1175.

[77] According to *Sung shih* 39:8a, the Southern Sung learned of Li Lung-kan's death on June 28.

Sung court that Li Lung-kan had died on Apr.27, 1211. Emperor Ning-tsung sent envoys to condole and sacrifice. On May 12, he conferred on Li Lung-kan the posthumous title of Palace Attendant. On May 30, 1215, Li Lung-kan's son Hao-ch'ien was appointed Military Commissioner of the non-existant Army Which Quiets the Sea, Acting Grand Commandant and Concurrent Grandee Secretary, and Supreme Pillar of State, entitled Specially Advanced, and recognized as king of Annam. He was presented a wide garment, a golden belt, 100 bolts of fine clothing, a [silver] casket, white pongee, yellow pongee, and horse trappings. Thereafter, relations cooled between the two countries. The king of Annnam sent no further communications, and the Southern Sung conferred no further titles (*Sung shih* 39:8b, 9a; 488:18a; *Sung hui-yao kao* 10123:16a-16b; *Wen-hsien t'ung-k'ao* 330:6b).

The Li dynasty of Annam came to end in the male line in 1224,[78] after having ruled for over two centuries. Li Hao-ch'ien had no sons, so that his daughter Chao-sheng succeeded. She ceded the throne to her husband Ch'en Jih-ching in 1225 (*Sung shih* 488:18a). But relations between Annam and Southern Sung were not restored until Jan.9, 1236, when Ch'en Jih-ching offered gifts. In the 1st month (Feb./Mar.) of 1236, he was presented with garments and a golden belt. On Nov.22, 1236, the Annam State again offered presents. The Southern Sung dispatched a return mission which presented garments and gold and silver belts (*Sung shih* 42:3a, 3b, 6a).

In 1257, the Southern Sung presented the king of Annam golden vessels, silk, aromatics, and tea, and communicated with him again in 1258. In the 11th month (Nov./Dec.) of 1261, the Annam State presented two elephants (*Sung shih* 44:10a; 488:18b).

On July 13, 1262, a letter from Ch'en Jih-ching was presented to Southern Sung. He was appointed Acting Grand Master, Military Commissioner of the non-existant Army Which Quiets the Sea, Acting Grand Commandant, Grandee Secretary, and Supreme Pillar of State, recognized as Great King of the Annam State, and presented with a golden belt, [porcelain] vessels, silk, and horse trappings (*Sung shih* 435:12b, 488:18b).

After Emperor Tu-tsung had ascended the Southern Sung throne on Nov.16, 1264, the Annam State congratulated on his ascension on Sep.24, 1266, and presented regional objects (*Sung shih* 46:6a).

---

[78] Date according to Mathias Tchang, *Synchronismes*, p.392.

In the 11th month (Nov./Dec.) of 1272, the Southern Sung presented horse trappings to Ch'en Jih-ching, who had abdicated in 1258,[79] and his son and sucessor Ch'en Wei-huang (*Sung shih* 46:21b; 488:18b).

In the 6th month (June/July) of 1273, the Annam State presented regional objects, for which it received 500 ounces of gold and 500 bolts of silk (*Sung shih* 46:26a).

All rulers of Chiao-chih/Annam had Chinese or Chinese-style names. The Chinese sources refer to their own rulers from T'ang through Sung by their temple names,[80] while they condescendingly call the rulers of Chiao-chih/Annam and other foreign countries by their given names. Such names would in China have been tabooed, so that their use by the historians was an offensive, sino-centric conceit. The contemporary Chinese diplomatic correspondence was more tactful.[81] The rulers of Chiao-chih/Annam actually conferred on their predecessors temple names according to the Chinese model. For instance, the founder of the Li dynasty, Li Kung-yün, received after his death the temple name of T'ai-tsu (Grand Founder), but these honorifics are never mentioned in the Chinese sources.

Neither were the Chinese generous in granting posthumous titles to the rulers of Chiao-chih/Annam. Li Huan was made a Prefect of the Palace Writers, Li Kung-yün, Li Te-cheng, Li Ch'ien-te, and Li Lung-kan Palace Attendants, and Li Yang-huan a Commander Unequalled in Honour. Only the last of these titles had any prestige.

The Sung is recorded to have recognized seven of the fifteen contemporary rulers of Chiao-chih/Annam, to have congratulated at the enthronement of at least one, to have condoled at the death of five, to have presented testamentary gifts once, and to have received them once. The texts may be deficient. There can be no doubt, however, that the Sung never had official mourning for the rulers of Chiao-chih/Annam.

Relations between Chiao-chih/Annam and China were generally peaceful. The raids of Chinese coastal territories by a fleet of over 100 warships in the spring of 995 and the subsequent one in the summer of the same year were obviously instigated by the king (Li Huan) himself. The responsibility for the border incident of 1028 and the lootings

---

[79] Ibid.

[80] Excepting those, of course, who did not receive any.

[81] For instance, Emperor Hsüan-tsung of T'ang in a letter of 713 to the king of Lin-yi addressed him as "Your Excellency" (*Ts'e-fu yüan-kuei* p.5027).

of 1036, 1059, 1060, 1076, and 1076 may have largely rested with local Annamese chiefs. But in 1076, a brief confrontation took place in which China was allied with Champa and the Khmer Kingdom.

Chiao-chih/Annam was in a peculiar situation. It bordered in the south on the hostile Champa, in the west on the powerful Khmer Kingdom, and in the north on a China which previously for over a millenium had governed it as a colony. While the Sung was not altogether at ease with its southern neighbour, it had lost all aspirations of regaining this former colony. As it did with other countries, it merely incorporated Chiao-chih/Annam into the empire on paper by appointing its rulers as Protector Generals and Military Commissioners of the Army Which Quiets the Sea. This made them Protectors of what they had already and Commanders of Chinese armies which did not exist. In spite of Chinese window-dressing, the Annamese kings were independent, but this does not neccessarily mean that they felt secure. They therefore may have found it useful not to rely exclusively on high levels of diplomacy and trade to benefit politically and profit commercialy from their relations with with the Sung. They made the concession of buying themselves peace, just as Sung did with especially Liao and Chin. It is recorded that in the 12th month (Dec./Jan., 1053) of the Chinese year 1052 an administrator in South China reported to the court that the annual tribute from Chiao-chih had not arrived because an aboriginal rebellion had blocked the road (*Sung hui-yao kao* 10122:14a-14b).[82] On Sep.22, 1081, a local administrator in the Kuang-hsi Circuit reported that Chiao-chih had paid tribute (*Sung hui-yao kao* 10122:20b). It follows that, when all is said and done, there existed some kind of a tributary relationship between Chiao-chih/Annam and Sung, whereby products were brought across China's southern border. When Chao Ju-kua states that Chiao-chih

[82] Another entry is misleading. *Sung hui-yao kao* 10122:14b records that to commemorate his enthronement on Feb.18, 1189, Emperor Kuang-tsung of Southern Sung ordered that only 1/10 of the tribute from Annam should be accepted. There is a similar entry for Champa following the enthronement of Emperor Hsiao-tsung on July 24, 1162. The first recorded mission from Champa to reach the Southern Sung court after that date was on Nov.14, 1174. According to *Wen-hsien t'ung-k'ao* 332:17b, the "tribute" of Champa was at that occasion reduced to 1/10. But Champa never had any tributary relationship with China, so that this is an empty statement. It merely pleased the Chinese court, which considered all presents from all foreign countries as "tribute", to show a disingeneous and entirely meaningless magnanimity after enthronements, while the exchange of goods no doubt went on as before.

annually sent tribute to the Sung court, he may, in fact, have used the right term.[83] This arrangement, which may or may not have been in force throughout the entire period, gave the Annamese rulers freedom to devote their energies toward the south and west. The Sung, on its part, responded to the special relationship between it and Chiao-chih by sending more missions to this state than to any other South Asian or island country, and by conferring on its rulers the titles of Meritorious Subject in their lifetimes and posthumous titles after their deaths, a practice it did not observe toward the rulers of any other states discussed in this chapter.

It is certain that not all missions are recorded from either side. For instance, Chiao-chih/Annam congratulated in 977 on the enthronement of T'ai-tsung, on Dec.2, 1190, on the entronement of Kuang-tsung, and on Sep.24, 1266, on the entronement of Tu-tsung. It is probable, although not recorded, that it congratulated on the ascension of the other Sung emperors as well. On Nov.22, 1055, testamentary gifts from Li Te-cheng were presented to the Sung emperor. On Apr. 30, 1063, testamentary gifts from the Sung emperor Jen-tsung were presented to the king of Chiao-chih, Li Jih-tsun. There is no reason why testamentary gifts should not have been exchanged at the deaths of other rulers also. The ritual missions from Sung for the purpose of congratulations and condolences may well be underrecorded. With three exceptions, it is recorded that the Sung appointed the rulers of Chiao-chih/Annam as Military Commissioners of the non-existant Army Which Quiets the Sea. Ting Hsüan and Li Lung-yüeh were soon overthrown, and the appointments probably could not take place. But it is improbable that Li Te-cheng did not receive the title. There are similar omissions in the granting of the title of Protector General of Annam. In all cases missions would have been involved. On the other hand, according to *Wen-hsien t'ung-k'ao* 330:5b, Chiao-chih after 1010 sent gifts in successive or alternate years. "After" is an ambiguous term, since it could refer to a few years or many. But since missions are recorded for 1011, 1012, 1013, and two for 1014, the coverage may here be complete. In any event, as noted before, the statistics are good enough to reveal general trends.

Missions arrived from Chiao-ch'ih/Annam during every month of the year, but the most preferred seasons seems to have been spring

---

[83] Hirth and Rockhill, *Chau Ju-kua*, p.46.

and summer. The stay in the Chinese capital could be an extended one. Li Huan's son Ming-t'i arrived with a mission in K'ai-feng during July 1004 and did not return until April, 1006 (*Sung hui-yao kao* 10122:7a-7b).

The following table shows the 82 recorded missions by 20-year periods from Chiao-chih/Annam to the Sung:[84]

967- 986:	10
987-1006:	7
1007-1026:	11
1027-1046:	11
1047-1066:	7
1067-1086:	8
1087-1106:	3
1107-1126:	2
1127-1146:	4
1147-1166:	5
1167-1186:	5
1187-1206:	2
1207-1226:	0
1227-1246:	2
1247-1266:	3
1267-1276:[85]	2

The table brings out that for most of the Northern Sung (960-1126), missions arrived regularly and in considerable numbers, with a reduction only in the last forty years. Diplomatic and commercial relations consequently flourished. During the Southern Sung (1127-1276), on the other hand, there was a remarkable decrease in contacts. Whereas 59 missions are recorded for Northern Sung, only 23 are for Southern Sung. This striking phenomenon is not restricted to Southern Sung relations with Chiao-chih/Annam and will be further discussed below.

If the foreign envoys were entrusted with negotiating particular issues, they went to the appropriate Chinese ministry, which then reported to the throne, such as the Ministry of Rites on July 10, 1155,

---

[84] It includes a mission from Li Te-cheng in 1031 in which he thanked for the title of Meritorious Subject (*Sung shih* 9:13b, 488:12b).

[85] 10-year period.

the Ministries of Revenue and War on June 22, 1156, the Ministry of War on Apr.28, 1159, and the Ministry of Rites on Aug.24, 1175. Proper bureaucratic channels had to be observed. But the chief purpose of the missions was trade.

The Chinese historians sometimes make it easy for themselves by recording that Chiao-chih/Annam offered regional objects. But it is not unusual that they specify the gifts and merchandise in detail. These were live rhinoceroses and elephants, rhinoceros horns and elephant tusks, a purported *ch'i-lin*, occasional horses,[86] vessels of gold and silver,[87] pearls, kingfisher's feathers, pongee and other silken fabrics, aromatics, gharu wood, pewter, tortoise shells, and red ore. It is obvious that some of these items were luxury articles for the court. Others, such as ores, were commercial goods. The Chinese government matched gifts for gifts, and also payed in copper cash or precious metals. We have seen that in August of 1022, envoys presented official gifts and merchandise evaluated at 1,682 strings of cash, for which they were paid 2000 strings of cash. In the 3rd month (May/Apr.) of 1028, the high officials memorialized that the envoys, perhaps privately, had sold fragrant drugs at the price of 3,060 strings of copper cash. An edict ordered that they be reembursed with 4000 strings of cash. In the 6th month (June/July) of 1273, the Chinese court paid 500 ounces of gold and 500 bolts of silk for the regional objects presented by Annam. The profit in 1022 was 19%, and in 1028 31%. Even allowing for the possibility that the Chinese authorities and merchants undervalued the foreign goods, the profit was far from low. In any event, it made the Annamese come back for more.

The chief Chinese gifts were garments and precious belts, vessels of gold, silver, and porcelain, silk and brocade, valuable horse trappings, armour, tea, books if requested, and fish wallets for the envoys.

In addition to this official exchange of gifts and trade, there also was regular commerce. A joint market was opened on the south coast of present Kuang-tung in 1010. It has been seen that local officials in that area reported to the court in 1022 that they had received from Chiao-chih a shipment of 5,300 catties of cassia bark, valued at 1,700 strings of copper cash and that the court had ordered its purchase. Chao

[86] This was during Northern Sung, when China got all the horses it needed from its northern neighbours. The horses from Chiao-chih must therefore have been a special and appreciated breed.

[87] Gold and silver objects were not recorded by their number but their weight.

Ju-kua mentions salt among additional Chiao-chih products.[88] That salt was imported to China is proved by the fact that this trade[89] was disallowed by the Southern Sung on Feb.6, 1185 (*Sung shih* 35:16b).

LIN-YI

This state, which comprised most of southern Vietnam, had come into existance in the 3rd century A.D. Its territory had never been part of the Chinese empire. During the Six Dynasties, friendly relations were interspersed with confrontations. Military conflicts are recorded for 399, 407, 405-418, 430 and especially 446. On the other hand, it is recorded that 34 missions from Lin-yi arrived at the southern courts of Eastern Chin, Liu Sung, Southern Ch'i, Liang, and Ch'en between 340 and 572. In 488, a king of Ling-yi even attempted to call on Emperor Ming of Southern Ch'i in Chien-k'ang but drowned en route.[90]

When Emperor Wen of Sui had conquered Ch'en in 589, Lin-yi for the first time in its history found itself the neighbour of a huge and powerful state. It sent a mission to present regional objects. This must be the one which was received on July 20, 595. Thereafter, relations were disrupted (*Sui shu* 2:10a; 82:10b). The ambitious Sui dynasty dispatched an army against Lin-yi in 604. The king resisted with war elephants, was defeated, and abandoned his capital. Subsequently, he sent envoys to seek peace. The state kept its independence (*Sui shu* 53: 9b-10a; 82:2b; *Pei shih* 95:16a).

All texts agree that the first mission from Lin-yi to the T'ang court arrived in the 2nd month (Mar./Apr.) of 623. This was followed by another in the 4th month (May/June) of 625 (*Chiu T'ang shu* 197:1b; *Ts'e-fu yüan-kuei* p.5023; *Tzu-chih t'ung-chien* p.5965; *Wen-hsien t'ung-k'ao* 331:11a).

In 627 or soon thereafter, Lin-yi presented a tame rhinoceros (*Chiu T'ang shu* 197:1b). In the 10th month (November) of 628, a mission from Lin-yi, which also included envoys from Chen-la, paid court and offered presents. In the 10th month (November) of 629, a mission arrived with gifts (*Ts'e-fu yüan-kuei* p.5023).

---

[88] Hirth and Rockhill, *Chau Ju-kua*, p.46.

[89] It conflicted with the Chinese state-monopoly of salt.

[90] See my *Six Dynasties*, vol.I, pp. 99, 113, 129, 136, and vol.II, pp.85-87.

In 630, envoys from the king of Lin-yi, Fan T'ou-li, presented an elephant, gilded objects, court garments, and a fire pearl (burning-lens), as big as a hen's egg. If it was held between the sun and a bit of punk, it set it on fire.[91] According to the Chinese high officials, the king lacked respect, but T'ai-tsung refused to make an issue of it (*Chiu T'ang shu* 197:1b; *Chiu T'ang shu* 197:2b; *Ts'e-fu yüan-kuei* p.5023; *Wen-hsien t'ung-k'ao* 331:11a).

On Nov.30, 631, Fan T'ou-li presented a five-coloured talking parrot and a white cockatoo. Emperor T'ai-tsung ordered the Cadet of the Right of the Heir-apparent to write a *fu* about the parrot. Because the birds suffered from the cold, T'ai-tsung had them released in a forested marsh[92] (*Chiu T'ang shu* 197:1b; *Ts'e-fu yüan-kuei* p.5024; *Tzu-chih t'ung-chien* pp.6089-6090; *Wen-hsien t'ung-k'ao* 331:11a).

In 639, envoys from Lin-yi again presented gifts (*Ts'e-fu yüan-kuei* p.5024).

The king of Lin-yi, Fan T'ou-li, having died, his son Chen-lung succeeded him and in 640 presented to the T'ang ten "heaven-communicating" rhinoceros [horns][93] and various valuables (*Chiu T'ang shu* 197:1b; *T'ang hui-yao* 98:12b; *Wen-hsien t'ung-k'ao* 331:11a).

In the 5th month (June/July) of 642, Lin-yi envoys offered regional gifts (*Ts'e-fu yüan-kuei* p.5024).

In 645, Lin-yi underwent great upheavals. A minister murdered Fan Chen-lung and exterminated his entire clan. This brought the Fan dynasty to an end which had ruled Lin-yi since 336. The assassin enthroned himself but was overthrown and replaced by T'ou-li's son-in-law P'o-lo-men. He was in turn replaced by a daughter of T'ou-li who proved herself incompetent (*Chiu T'ang shu* 197:1b; *Tzu-chih t'ung-chien* p.6282; *Wen-hsien t'ung-k'ao* 331:11a).

---

[91] According to *Ts'e-fu yüan-kuei*, the mission was in 631 and the fire pearl had been obtained by Lin-yi in Lo-ch'a. *Hsin T'ang-shu* 222C:2a states that Lo-ch'a was a great producer of burning-lenses. Cf. Schafer, *Golden Peaches*, p.237, and Needham, *Science and Civiliization*, vol.4:1, p.115.

[92] Cf. Schafer, *Golden Peaches*, p.101. According to *Wen-hsien t'ung-k'ao* 331:11a, the emperor ordered the birds to be returned.

[93] Schafer, *Golden Peaches*, p.83 takes these to be live rhinoceroses. Hirth and Rockhill, *Chao Ju-kua*, p.103, and 108 note 10, identify the term as a precious stone. However, *T'ang hui-yao* uses the numerary adjunct *mei* (staff) for the number ten, which makes it quite clear that the gift consisted of unusually long rhinoceros horns. This is also proved by the fact that during an epidemic in K'ai-feng, a medicine was prepared on Feb.17, 1054, out of pulverized heaven-communicating rhinoceros horns, which was supposed to cure the people (*Hsü Tzu-chih t'ung-chien ch'ang-pien* p.1622).

T'ai-tsung died on July 10, 649. At his order, the features of Fan T'ou-li were carved in stone and placed at his tomb (*Chiu T'ang shu* 197:1b).

In Lin-yi, discontent with the rule of Fan T'ou-li's daughter led to her removal. The powers that be reminded themselves of a certain Chu-ko Ti. His father had married a paternal aunt of Fan T'ou-li but had subsequently been killed by him. Chu-ko Ti had fled to the neighbouring Chen-la State and had remained there. A high dignitary was now sent from Lin-yi to invite him to return and ascend the throne. He did this in early 653. On May 9 of that year, a mission from Chu-ko Ti to the T'ang court presented regional objects and a tame elephant (*Chiu T'ang shu* 4:4b; *Tzu-chih t'ung-chien* p.6282; *Wen-hsien t'ung-k'ao* 331:11a).

In the 5th month (May/June) of 654, the Lin-yi State presented a tame elephant, in the 2nd month (May/June) of 657 gifts, in the 8th month (Sep./Oct.) of 668 regional objects, in 669 gifts, in the 3rd month (Mar./Apr.) of 686 a tame elephant, in the 10th month of 691 a tame elephant, in the 1st month(Jan./Feb.) of 695 a war elephant, in the 4th month of the same year gifts, in the 6th month (July) of 699 a tame elephant, in the 12th month (Dec./Jan., 703) of the Chinese year 702 gifts, in the 1st month of 704 gifts, in the 10th month (November) of the same year gifts, in the 7th month (Aug./Sep.) of 706 gifts, in the 8th month (September) of 707 a tame elephant, in the 11th month (Dec./Jan.,710) of the Chinese year 709 a white elephant and regional objects, in 711 regional objects, and in the 4th month (May/June) of 712 regional objects (*Ts'e-fu yüan-kuei* p.5026).

In the 12th month (Dec./Jan., 714) of the Chinese year 713, the king of Lin-yi presented five elephants. Emperor Hsüan-tsung responded with a letter and the gift of two horses (*Ts'e-fu yüan-kuei* p.5027).

In the 6th month (July/Aug.) of 715, envoys arrived from Lin-yi. In the 10th month (Nov./Dec.) of 731, it presented four elephants, in the 6th month (July/Aug.) of 734 gharu wood and amber, in the 8th month (Aug./Sep.) of 735 a tame elephant, and in the 12th month (Jan./Feb., 736) of that Chinese year a white elephant (*T'ang hui-yao* 98:12b; *Ts'e-fu yüan-kuei* p.5027-5029).

In the 6th month (July) of 748, Lin-yi presented elephant tusks and fancy cotton fabrics. In the 9th month (Oct./Nov.) of 749, envoys from its king Lu-t'o offered 100 precious pearls, 30 catties of black gharu wood, and a quantity of white cotton fabrics. In the 3rd month

(Apr./May) of 750, Lin-yi[94] presented elephant tusks, genuine pearls, and fancy white cotton fabrics (*Ts'e-fu yüan-kuei* p.5030).

In the latter half of the 750's, the name of Lin-yi was changed to Huan-wang. In the 10th month (Nov./Dec.) of 793, the Huan-wang State presented a rhinoceros. Emperor Te-tsung ordered that it be kept at the Imperial Ancestral Temple. In the 12th month (January, 797) of the Chinese year 796, Huan-wang presented another rhinoceros which was highly prized at the T'ang court (*Chiu T'ang shu* 13:13b; *Ts'e-fu yüan-kuei* p.5032).

In the 8th month (Sep./Oct.) of 809, the warlord Chang Chou, who called himself Protector General of Annam, informed the T'ang court that he had crushed Huan-wang and had captured 59 royal sons, military equipment, warships, and war elephants (*Hsin T'ang shu* 222C:1b; *T'ang hui-yao* 98:13a)

Therafter, all relations between Huan-wang and China lapsed (*Hsin T'ang shu* 222C:1b; *Wen-hsien t'ung-k'ao* 332:17a).

The kings of Lin-yi of the Fan dynasty appear in the Chinese sources with sinicized names, as does also Chu-ko Ti. Their ministers do not. After the middle of the 7th century, the names of the kings are transliterated as well, sometimes in abbreviated form. Thus, the Chinese Lu-t'o stands for the Vietnamese Rudravarman II.

The Chinese sources do not record that the Sui and T'ang officially recognized the kings of Lin-yi or conferred any titles on them in their life times or posthumously. Their envoys are not mentioned to have received Chinese nominal titles. Nor do the texts mention congratulations, condolences or testamentary gifts from either side. Apart from the war of 604, relations were correct but apparently not warm.

According to *Sui shu* 82:2b, missions from Lin-yi to Sui arrived after 604 without interruption, yet none is recorded until 623. According to *Chiu T'ang shu* 197:1b, missions arrived after 631 without interruption. But missions are only recorded for 639, 640, 642, 653 etc. It follows that the Chinese sources concentrate on the most important missions. They arrived at all times of the year but the preferred seasons were summer and winter.

The following table shows the 40 recorded missions by 20-year periods from Lin-yi/Huan-wang to the Sui and T'ang:

94 Correcting Pei yi to Lin-yi.

587-606:	2
607-626:	2
627-646:	7
647-666:	3
667-686:	2
687-706:	10
707-726:	5
727-746:	4
747-766:	3
767-786:	0
787-806:	2

It can be seen that, even allowing for omissions, relations hardly survived the rebellion of An Lu-shan in 755. Only two missions are recorded for the period after that event.

The recorded gifts from Lin-yi/Huan-wang were tame elphants, a war elephant, elephant tusks, tame rhinoceroses, rhinoceros horns, gilded objects, a burning-lens, pearls, gharu wood, fabrics, a parrot, and a cockatoo. Nothing is known about the Chinese return gifts or payments other than two horses.

CHAMPA

In the 10th century, a new state came into being in the territory formerly occupied by Lin-yi/Huan-wang. This was Chan-ch'eng or Champa. But whereas its predecessor had bordered on China, Champa did not. The Annamese state of Chiao-chih was situated between them.

The first mission from Champa to the Chinese Later Chou court, is recorded for the 9th month (Sep./Oct.) of 958. The envoy P'u-ho-san[95] from the king Shih-li-yin-te-man, i.e. Sri Indravarman, brought a letter written on palm leaves and offered embroidered robes, long-lasting aromatics, 15 bottles of rose water, 84 opaque glass pitchers, and an unstoppable fierce-burning mineral oil (naphta). If one poured water on it, it burned all the more. The envoys were given an audience in the palace and presented with caps, belts, garments etc. In the 11th

---

[95] According to Schafer, ibid.p.173, this transliterates Abu Hasan. If that is so, the envoy was an Arab acting for Champa.

month (Dec./Jan.959) of the same Chinese year, the envoys were granted silken fabrics, each in accordance with his rank. The king received 1000 ounces of gold and silver vessels, 1000 bolts of silken fabrics, a fine horse, and horse trappings (*Wu-tai hui-yao* 30:14b-15a; *Ts'e-fu yüan-kuei* p.5036; *Wen-hsien t'ung-k'ao* 332:17a).

In the 6th month (July/Aug.) of 959 Champa envoys to the Later Chou court presented a belt of rhinoceros hide and one *p'u-sa* stone[96] (*Ts'e-fu yüan-kuei* p.5036).

In the 12th month (Dec./Jan. 961) of the Chinese year 960, envoys from the king of Champa to the Sung court presented regional objects, including rhinoceros horns and elephant tusks (*Sung hui-yao kao* 8116: 2b).

On Jan.24, 961, Champa envoys brought a letter on palm leaves to congratulate the first Sung emperor, T'ai-tsu. They furthermore presented rhinoceros horns, elephant tusks, aromatic drugs, four peacocks, baroos camphor, and 20 great food vessels. When the envoys returned, they were given presents, each in accordance with his rank. Their king received [porcelain] vessels and silk (*Sung shih* 1:8b; 489:3b; *Sung hui-yao kao* 8116:3a; *Wen-hsien t'ung-k'ao* 332:17a).

On Oct.22, 962, the king of Champa offered 22 elephant tusks and 1000 catties of frankincense. On Apr.2, 966, envoys presented a bull rhinoceros, two elephant tusks, 20 lengths of white cotton fabrics, various kinds of sarongs, *yüeh-no* cloth,[97] and miscelllaneous aromatic drugs. The queen offered rhinoceros horns, elephant tusks, baroos camphor, and tortoise shells. The envoys presented on their own rhinoceros horns and elephant tusks. The Sung court responded with golden belts, silver vessels, horse trappings, and bedding. On Apr.25 of the same year, envoys from the king again brought presents (*Sung shih* 1:13a; 2: 4a; *Sung hui-yao kao* 8116:3a; *Wen-hsien t'ung-k'ao* 332:17a).

At this time, the route of the missions from Champa to the Sung capital passed through the still independent state of Chiang-nan.[98] In the 7th month (July/Aug.) of 966, its ruler, Li Yü, informed the Sung court that he had sent on one rhinoceros horn, two elephant tusks, 30 ounces of white baroos camphor, two catties of green baroos cam-

---

[96] A stone with a white lustruous colour, resembling jade, which reflects the five colours under the rays of the sun.

[97] According to Hirth and Rockhill, *Chao Ju-kua*, p.100 note 7, probably a kind of very fine muslin.

[98] Liu Yü had changed the name of Southern T'ang to Chiang-nan.

phor, 30 catties of frankincense, 30 catties of gharu wood, 70 catties of aromatics, 50 catties of cosmetics, 100 catties of white sandalwood,[99] 50 catties of purple ore, 20,000 cardamoms, 50 catties of betel nuts, and four mats (*Sung hui-yao kao* 8116:3a-3b).

On Oct.25, 966,[100] Champa envoys offered a great elephant, controlled by an aboriginal mahout. It could toss its trunk and kneel, and had a golden saddle. The animal was placed in the Capital Postal Relay Station, where it attracted a great crowd. The envoys presented on their own elephant tusks and aromatic drugs, for which they received [porcelain] vessels, silk, and copper cash (*Sung shih* 2:4b; *Sung hui-yao kao* 8116:3b-4a).

In 967, Champa envoys offered gifts. In 970, they offered regional objects and a female elephant. In 971, the king of Champa, the assistant king, the king's wife, and his son all offered presents. On Apr.27, 972 and on May 15 and July 13, 973, envoys from the king offered regional objects (*Sung shih* 3:1b, 3b; 489:4a; *Wen-hsien t'ung-k'ao* 332:17a).

On Feb.5, 974, Champa envoys presented two peacock parasols and regional objects. In 976, they offered regional objects. On Mar.8, 977, they offered regional objects, including two pieces of *yüeh-no* cloth, two catties of baroos camphor, 1,025 catties of miscellaneous aromatic drugs, and 50 catties of cloves. On June 19, 978, and Dec.23, 979, they offered gifts (*Sung shih* 3:4b; 4:3a, 6b, 12a; 489:4a, 4b; *Sung hui-yao kao* 8116:4a-4b; *Wen-hsien t'ung-k'ao* 332:17a).

In 981, the kingdom of Chiao-chih in northern Vietnam was under attack by Chinese forces allied with Champa. In the 3rd month (Apr./May) of that year, the king of Chiao-chih, Li Huan, presented 93 Champa prisoners to the Chinese authorities in Canton. The Sung emperor requested that they be not sent on, but be provided with clothing and provisions, and returned to Champa (*Sung hui-yao kao* 8116:4b).

In the intercalary month (Jan./Feb.983) of the Chinese year 982, Champa envoys offered a tame elephamt and regional objects. An edict ordered the elephant to be kept in Canton. In the 9th month (Oct./Nov.) of 983, envoys presented a tame elephant which could salute and prostrate itself. An edict ordered to place it in Ning-ling

[99] Used for incense.

[100] *Hsü Tzu-chih t'ung-chien ch'ang-pien* p.68 gives the date of Oct.29.

prefecture[101] of the Metropolitan Region. On Mar.18, 985, envoys offered baroos camphor, tortoise shells, elephant tusks, *yüeh-no* cloth, and limonite. They received in return garments, belts, and horse trappings. The king also informed the Sung court that he was under attack by Chiao-chih (*Sung shih* 5:1a, 4a; 489:4b; *Sung hui-yao kao* 8116: 4b; *Wen-hsien t'ung-k'ao* 332:17a).

In the 3rd month (Apr./May) of 986, Champa envoys offered two rhinoceros horns, ten catties of white baroos camphor, 330 catties of different kinds of gharu wood, and 50 catties of cloves. The chief envoy presented on his own two elephant tusks and ten catties of baroos camphor (*Sung shih* 4:17a; 489:4b; *Sung hui-yao kao* 8116:4b-5a; *Wen-hsien t'ung-k'ao* 332:17a).

In the 1st month (Jan./Feb.) of 988, Champa envoys arrived at the Sung court with regional objects. They were provided with wine and food (*Sung hui-yao kao* 8116:5a).

On Dec.23, 990,[102] Champa envoys presented a tame rhinoceros, ten rhinoceros horns, 15 elephant tusks, one catty of aromatics, and two catties of white baroos camphor etc. Their king announced in a letter that he was under attack by Chiao-chih. Emperor T'ai-tsung advised the king of Chiao-chih, Li Huan, that he and Champa should each guard their borders, i.e. keep peace. The envoys presented on their own rhinoceros horns, elephant tusks, drugs, camphor, cardamoms, and rose water. They were given garments, belts, horse trappings, [porcelain] vessels, and silk, each in in accordance with his rank (*Sung shih* 5:11b; 489:5a; *Sung hui-yao kao* 8111:5a; *Wen-hsien t'ung-k'ao* 332:17a).

On Jan.15, 993, Champa envoys offered ten rhinoceros horns, 20 elephant tusks, 36 catties of aromatics, one catty of white baroos camphor, 6 pieces of cotton, 13 catties of betel nuts, 50 coconuts etc. The envoys presented on their own rhinoceros horns, tortoise shells, aromatics etc. The king was in return presented with two white horses, military implements etc. A Buddhist priest from Champa presented baroos camphor, golden bells, copper incense braziers, and Buddhist sceptres[103] (*Sung shih* 5:15a; *Sung hui-yao kao* 8116:5b).

On Feb.13, 995, envoys from the king of Champa brought gifts and a letter. He was given two fine horses, five banners, five swords

---

[101] The modern Shang-ch'iu *hsien*, situated southeast of K'ai-feng.

[102] *Sung hui-yao kao* dates the arrival in the 10th month (Oct./Nov.) of 990.

[103] This could well have been a private enterprise and is not included in the statistics below.

inlaid with silver, five lances with silver cords, five bows, arrows etc. (*Sung shih* 5:21b; 489:5a; *Wen-hsien t'ung-k'ao* 332:17a).

On Apr.12, 997,[104] Champa envoys offered ten rhinoceros horns, 30 elephant tusks, ten catties of tortoise shells, two catties of baroos camphor, 190 catties of different kinds of gharu wood, 100 catties of sandalwood, 200 catties of pepper, five bamboo mats etc. (*Sung shih* 5:25b; 489:6a ; *Sung hui-yao kao* 8116:6b-7a).

In the 2nd month (Feb.Mar.) of 999, Champa envoys congratulated on the ascension of Emperor Chen-tsung (on May 8, 997) and offered rhinoceros horns, elephant tusks, tortoise shells, and aromatic drugs. On Oct.14, 1004, envoys again brought regional objects, for which their king received two fine horses, armour, military implements, banners etc. On the New Year's Day (Feb.12) of 1005, they were given a banquet together with a royal son from Chiao-chih and Arab envoys. In the 4th month (May/June) of 1005, envoys offered presents. In 1007, envoys brought a letter and received rich gifts (*Sung shih* 6:8b; 7: 7b, 15b; 489:6b; *Sung hui-yao kao* 8116:7a-8a; 10,122:7b; *Hsü Tzu-chih t'ung-chien ch'ang-pien* p.488; *Wen-hsien t'ung-k'ao* 332:17a-17b).

In 1008, Champa envoys offered presents, and the chief envoy was given a nominal Chinese title (*Sung hui-yao kao* 8116:8a).

On May 21, 1010, envoys from the king of Champa offered gifts. He complained that he always was given white horses.[105] On Sep.22, 1010, envoys again offered gifts and were presented with horses and [porcelain] vessels (*Sung shih* 7:25a, 26a; 489:7b; *Sung hui-yao kao* 8116: 8a; *Hsü Tzu-chih t'ung-chien ch'ang-pien* p.645; *Wen-hsien t'ung-k'ao* 332: 17b).

On Nov.28, 1011, Champa envoys presented a golden-maned lion, which had come from India, 62 elephant tusks, 40 rhinoceros horns, 300 catties of tortoise shell, 50 catties of gharu wood, 590 catties of various aromatics, 60 catties of cardamoms, 30 ounces of camphor, 80 catties of myrrh, 470 catties of purple ore, 200 catties of nutmegs, and 200 catties of pepper. An edict ordered that the lion be placed in a park, where it was looked after by two natives of Champa. Subsequently, Emperor Chen-tsung pitied it and on Mar.3, 1012, ordered it to be sent back (*Sung shih* 8:4a; 489:7b; *Sung hui-yao kao* 8116:8b-9a; *Hsü*

[104] By *Sung hui-yao kao* 8116:7a dated Apr.11.

[105] This seems to have arisen through a misunderstanding on the Chinese side. *Sung hui-yao kao* 8116:5b notes that Champa liked white horses, and that therefore such animals were presented.

Tzu-chih t'ung-chien ch'ang-pien p.679; *Wen-hsien t'ung-k'ao* 332:17b).

In the 1st month (Feb./Mar.) of 1014, Champa envoys offered presents. On Aug.8, the Sung responded with a communication. In the 5th month (May/June) of 1015,[106] envoys from the king of Champa brought a letter and offered elephant tusks, tortoise shells, frankincense, cardamoms, betel nuts etc. In the intercalary month (July/Aug.) of that year, the king was given garments ornamented with pearls, banners, bows and arrows, armoured horses, and copper cash (*Sung shih* 8:12b; 489:8a; *Sung hui-yao kao* 8116:9a-9b; 10122:11b; *Wen-hsien t'ung-k'ao* 332:17b).

On Oct.17, 1018, Champa envoys offered 72 elephant tusks, 86 rhinoceros horns, 1000 catties of tortoise shells, 50 catties of frankincense, 80 catties of cloves, 65 catties of cardamoms, 368 catties of different kinds of gharu wood, 100 catties of fennel, and 1,500 catties of betel nuts. They returned to Champa in 1019 with 4,700 ounces of silver, military implements, and horse trappings (*Sung shih* 8:19a; 489: 8a; *Sung hui-yao kao* 8116:9b; *Hsü Tzu-chih t'ung-chien ch'ang-pien* p.818; *Wen-hsien t'ung-k'ao* 332:17b).

In 1020, Champa envoys brought presents, in which context reference is made to a previously offered red cockatoo (*Sung shih* 489: 8a).

In the 5th month (June/July) of 1029, envoys from the king of Champa offered a letter, a live "phoenix", 30 rhinoceros horns, 70 elephant tusks, 245 catties of tortoise shells, 2000 catties of frankincense, and 789 catties of putchuck[107] (*Sung hui-yao kao* 8116:9b-10a).

In the 10th month (Oct./Nov.) of 1030, Champa envoys presented ritual objects, 700 catties of putchuck, more than 40 rhinoceros horns, 80 elephant tusks, more than 400 catties of tortoise shells, and 2000 catties of frankincense. They were received in audience (*Sumg shih* 9: 13a; 489:8b; *Sung hui-yao kao* 8116:10a; *Wen-hsien t'ung-k'ao* 332:17b).

In 1041, the Sung court presented the king of Champa with [porcelain] vessels and silk. In the 11th month (Dec./Jan.1043) of the Chinese year 1042, his envoys offered three tame elephants. On Feb.12, 1050, they offered regional objects, including 201 elephant tusks and 79 rhinoceros horns. On Apr.24, 1053, they offered regional objects. Their king received a silver belt, ten ounces of silver vessels,

[106] *Hsü Tzu-chih t'ung-chien ch'ang-pien* p.739 dates this mission Feb.24.

[107] A root from which was derived a drug used as an ingredient in perfumes. See Hirth and Rockhill, *Chau Ju-kua*, p.121.

20 bolts of clothing, etc. (*Sung shih* 11:4b; 12:2a, 7a; 489:8b-9a; *Sung hui-yao kao* 8116:10a-11a; *Hsü Tzu-chih t'ung-chien ch'ang-pien* p.1606; *Wen-hsien t'ung-k'ao* 332:17b).

In the intercalary month (Apr./May) of 1056, Champa envoys offered regional objects. On Feb.14, 1057, the emperor ordered Canton to pay Champa 1000 ounces of silver. In the 9th month (Oct./Nov.) of 1061, envoys presented a tame elephant (*Sung shih* 12:19a; 489:9a; *Sung hui-yao kao* 8116:11a; *Wen-hsien t'ung-k'ao* 332:17b).

In the 5th month (June/July) of 1062, Champa envoys offered regional objects. In the 6th month (July/Aug.) of that year, their king was presented with [porcelain] tea vessels and a white horse. On July 8, 1068,[108] he offered regional objects and wished to buy mules and horses. He was presented with another white horse and informed that he could buy mules in Canton. In the 9th month (Sep./Oct.) of 1071, a mission from Champa offered gifts. On June 11, 1072, Champa envoys offered opaque glass, coral, wine vessels, baroos camphor, frankincense, cloves, cubebs,[109] purple ore etc. It received for this 2,100 ounces of silver (*Sung shih* 12:20a; 14:6b; 15:17a; 489:9a-9b; *Sung hui-yao kao* 8116: 11a-11b; *Wen-hsien t'ung-k'ao* 332:17b).

On Mar.9, 1076, Sung invited Champa and the Khmer Kingdom to participate in a joint attack on Chiao-chih. On Sept.17 of that year,[110] Champa envoys offered gifts. They stated that their country was one month distant by sea from Chen-la (the Khmer Kingdom). On Jan.6, 1078, Champa envoys offered a tame elephant, and on Sep.19, 1086,[111] gifts. On Jan.10, 1087, envoys offered leggings of rhinoceros hide, for which the Sung paid 2,600 strings of copper cash (*Sung shih* 15:15b, 17a, 19b; 17:17a; 489:9b; *Sung hui-yao kao* 8116:11b-13a).

In the 2nd month (Mar./Apr.) of 1092, Champa envoys offered gifts and proposed a joint attack on Chiao-chih. This was rejected by the Sung court. On Apr.14, the chief envoy was appointed to a nominal Chinese office (*Sung shih*17:18b; 469:10a; *Sung hui-yao kao* 8116:13a; *Wen-hsien t'ung-k'ao* 332:17b).

On July 4, 1104, on Aug.10, 1109, and in 1116, Champa envoys offered presents (*Sung shih* 19:12b; 20:2a, 9b; 21:7b; *Sung hui-yao kao* 8116:134a-13b).

---

[108] By *Sung hui-yao kao* 8116:11b dated July 5.

[109] A kind of pepper. See Hirth and Rockhill, *Chau Ju-kua*, p.224.

[110] By *Sung hui-yao kao* 8116:12a dated Sep.12.

[111] By *Sung hui-yao kao* 8116:13a dated Nov.23.

On Apr.20, 1116, the king of Champa was appointed by the Sung Imperial Household Grandee of the Golden Seal and Purple Ribbon. On Jan.11, 1120, the Sung conferred on him the nominal titles of Acting Minister of Works[112] and Concurrent Grandee Secretary, Military Commissioner of the non-existant Army Which Cherishes the Distance, Surveillance and Supervisory Commissioner and Inspector of the non-existant Lin commandery, and recognized him as king of the Champa State (*Sung shih* 489:10b; *Sung hui-yao kao* 8116:14a; *Wen-hsien t'ung-k'ao* 332:17b).

In the 1st month (Jan./Feb.) of 1129, envoys of the king of Champa offered presents. The Southern Sung appointed him Acting Grand Tutor. Later, it became a constant practice to confer this title on the kings of Champa (*Sung shih* 25:8a; 489:10b; *Wen-hsien t'ung-k'ao* 332: 17b).

On Mar.26, 1132, the king of Champa was appointed by the Southern Sung Military Commissioner of the non-existant Army Which Cherishes the Distance, Surveillance and Supervisory Commissioner and Inspector of the non-existant Lin Commandery in charge of all its military matters, Imperial Household Grandee of the Golden Seal and Purple Ribbon, Acting Grand Tutor and Concurrent Grandee Secretary, and Supreme Pillar of State, and recognized as king of Champa (*Sung hui-yao kao* 8116:15a).

On Sep.19, 1155, envoys from a new king of Champa brought a letter, offered regional objects, and sought recognition. The Southern Sung recognized him in the offices of his father. On Dec.10 of the same year, 28 envoys from the king presented 4,230 catties of different kinds of gharu wood, 168 elephant tusks, 20 rhinoceros horns, 60 catties of tortoise shells, 360 kingfisher's feathers, ten oil lamps, etc. The envoys were received in audience. (*Sung shih* 489:10b; *Sung hui-yao kao* 8116:15a, 16a-16b; *Wen-hsien t'ung-k'ao* 332:17b).

On Jan.3, 1156, the king of Champa was appointed by the Southern Sung Imperial Household Grandee of the Golden Seal and Purple Ribbon, Acting Minister of Works and Concurrent Grandee Secretary, Military Commissioner of the non-existant Army Which Cherishes the Distance, Inspector of the non-existant Lin commandery in charge of all its military matters, and Supreme Pillar of State, and recognized

[112] According to *Sung hui-yao kao*, he was made Acting Minister over the Masses.

as king of Champa (*Sung hui-yao kao* 8116:21b).

On Nov.14, 1167, envoys from the son of the king of Champa offered gifts. On Aug.2, 1174 a Southern Sung communication responded to envoys who had brought a letter from the king of Champa. On Nov.20, 1174, Champa envoys once more offered presents (*Sung shih* 34:3a-3b, 20a; 489:10b; *Sung hui-yao kao* 8116:22a-22b; *Wen-hsien t'ung-k'ao* 332:17b).

In 1175, the Southern Sung disallowed the export of Chinese horses to Champa (*Wen-hsien t'ung-k'ao* 332:18a). This was, no doubt, because the Southern Sung had lost the northern pasture lands for raising horses, had no longer access to horse trade with Central Asian tribes, and had to reserve its diminished livestock for the army.

Before the end of the century, Champa was overrun and annexed by Jayavarman VIII of the Khmer Kingdom.

All kings of Champa appear in the Chinese sources with transliterated names, as also all further kings mentioned in this chapter. It is recorded that kings of Champa congratulated Sung emperors on their enthronements but not the reverse. There is no mention of Chinese condolences or the conferring of posthumous titles. At least toward the end of the period, the Champa kings were officially recognized, and they and some of their envoys were appointed to nominal Chinese offices.

Missions from Champa are recorded to have arived in Sung during all months except the 8th. The spring and autumn were the favoured seasons, followed by the summer. This means that the envoys sailed to China with the summer monsoon and perhaps did not return until the winter monsoon.

The following table shows the recorded 57 missions by 20-year periods from Champa to the Later Chou and Sung:

947- 966:	1
967- 986:	15
986-1006:	8
1007-1026:	9
1027-1046:	3
1047-1066:	5
1067-1086:	5
1087-1106:	3
1107-1126:	2
1127-1146:	1

1147-1166: 2
1167-1186: 3

After a vigorous start, Champa envoys arrived less often. 51 missions are recorded for Northern Sung and, characteristically, only 6 for Southern Sung.

The missions from Champa to the Northern Sung capital of K'ai-feng travelled partially by sea and partially by land. This can be seen from the entry for the 7th month (July/Aug.) of 966,[113] according to which the ruler of Chiang-nan, the former Southern T'ang, delivered to the Sung court a list of the goods which a Champa mission was transporting through his state. Chiang-nan comprised what now is Fu-chien, Chiang-hsi, and An-hui south of the Yangtze. It follows that the Champa missions at that time probably sailed to Ch'üan-chou in present Fu-chien and from there proceeded by land, and that the officials of the then still-independent state of Chiang-nan took an inventory of their goods.

The recorded goods from Champa are rhinoceroses, elephants, peacocks, a red cockatoo, a "phoenix", a lion, rhinoceros horns, a belt of rhinoceros hide, leggings of rhinoceros hide, elephant tusks, tortoise shells, kingfisher's feathers, aromatics, gharu wood, putchuck, sandalwood, frankincense, myrrh, cosmetics, rose water, glass pitchers, opaque glass, wine vessels, coral, baroos camphor, limonite, purple ore, naphta, a *p'u-sa* stone, vessels, cardamoms, cloves, peppers, cubebs, nutmegs, fennel, betel nuts, coconuts, embroidered robes, sarongs, cotton fabrics, *yüeh-no* cloth, parasols, mats, and oil lamps.

Many of these items were not native to Champa. This is true at least for the spices (fennel, cardamons, cloves, nutmegs, pepper, cubebs), frankincense, myrrh, putchuck, sandalwood, baroos camphor, limonite, glass, corals, and rose water. The lion of 1011 is particularly stated to have come from India. Of special interest is the "unstopable fierce-burning mineral oil" of 958, which cannot have been a product of Champa. It has been identified with greek fire or naphta. The Chinese must have been keen to obtain it, since they used it in warfare for incindiary attacks. Also an encyclopaedia of 1044 describes a Chinese flamethrower using naphta.[114] In short, Champa, to a much greater

---

[113] See above.
[114] See Needham, *Science and Civilisation,* vol.4:2, pp.144-147.

extent than Chiao-chih, brought to China goods which it in turn had obtained from abroad. It was situated on the great trade route between the Asian continent and the island archipelago south of it, and also on the route between East and Southeast Asia and the Middle East. It was a flourishing emporium of transit-goods and together with Chiao-chih China's most important trading partner. The importance of this trade to both Champa and the Sung is brought out by the report of the Ministry of Rites to Emperor Che-tsung on Sep.24, 1086, that Champa wished to continue to offer regional objects and that this was immediately accepted (*Hsü Tzu-chih t'ung-chien ch'ang-pien* p.3672).

The Sung repaid the kings of Champa and their envoys with silver, strings of copper cash, caps, golden belts, garments (sometimes adorned with pearls), silk, gold and silver vessels, porcelain vessels, tea vessels (of porcelain), bedding, banners, armour, military equipment, swords, lances, bows, arrows, horses, armoured horses, and horse trappings.

However, the relations between Sung and Champa were not exclusively commercial. Between them was situated the kingdom of Chiao-chih in Northern Vietnam. Champa and Chiao-chih were traditionally on bad terms, in addition to which the latter for much of the period was a not a wholy reliable neighbour of Northern Sung. In 981, Chiao-chih was attacked by Sung forces, allied with Champa. In 985 and 990, Chiao-chih attacked Champa. In 995, 1028, 1036, 1059, 1060, 1075, and 1076, it violated the Chinese border. In 1076, Sung fought a brief war against Chiao-chih, seeking the support of Champa and the Khmer kingdom. In 1092, Champa proposed a joint attack on Chiao-chih. We have here, therefore, a classical example of one country allied with another located behind a potential common enemy, a diplomatic practice which can be observed throughout world history. It should also be noted that among the commodities provided by China to Champa were military equipment, weapons, and armoured horses, whereas Champa supplied China with naphta. In short, China and Champa cooperated for both trade and military advantage.

TO-MIEN

According to *Wen-hsien t'ung-k'ao* 332:16b, representatives of the T'ang reached this country for the first time between 627 and 649. They noted that the people were short and that they practiced polyandry, whereby brothers married the same woman.

In the 8th month (Aug./Sep.) of 661, envoys from the king of

To-mien to the T'ang court offered regional objects (*Ts'e-fu yüan-kuei* p.5015).

WU-HSÜN, P'U-P'O, SAN-MA-LAN

On Mar.25, 1011, Wu-hsün, P'u-p'o, and San-ma-lan offered gifts to the Sung court. Those of Wu-hsün are noted to have been aromatics and elephant tusks, those of San-ma-lan aromatics, elephant tusks, dates, peaches,[115] seeds of schisandra chinensis,[116] rose water, white pebble sweets, opaque glass vessels etc. Apparently, these small countries had combined their resources for a joint mission. In the 6th month (July/Aug.) of that year, the Sung accepted the gifts of Wu-hsün and San-ma-lan, and presumably also of P'u-p'o, i.e. agreed to diplomatic and trade relations. The envoy from San-ma-lan, and no doubt also those from the other two countries, were appointed to nominal Chinese offices (*Sung shih* 8:1b, 3a; *Sung hui-yao kao* ts'e 197; *Wen-hsien t'ung-k'ao* 332:17b).

FU-NAN

Fu-nan had long-standing relations with China, and 20 missions are recorded to the Eastern Chin, Liu Sung, Southern Ch'i, Liang, and Ch'en of the Six Dynasties from 389 to 588.[117]

During the reign of T'ai-tsung (627-649), Fu-nan presented the T'ang court with two men from the State of the White Heads, where all people were white-headed (*T'ung-tien* 188:7a; *Hsin T'ang shu* 222C: 3a; *Wen-hsien t'ung-k'ao* 331:11b).

According to *T'ung-tien* 188:7a, when Sui had reunified China, Fu-nan from 589 to 617 sent envoys with offerings (*T'ung-tien* 188: 70a). None is recorded. According to *T'ung-tien* 188:70a and *Wen-hsien t'ung-k'ao* 331:11a, Fu-nan from 618 to 626 incessantly sent gifts to the T'ang. According to *Hsin T'ang shu* 222C:3a, it twice sent gifts during

[115] In cases like this, it is not possible to decide whether the entry means preserved fruits or seedlings.

[116] A vine or shrub from whose berries a tonic was prepared (*Sung hui-yao kao* 8116:22a-22b).

[117] See my Six Dynasties, vol.II, p.87.

this period. Even though here and below "incessantly" is an overused term which is not to be taken verbatim, the information for Sui and T'ang is nevertheless incomplete.

CHEN-LA

Chen-la was at first a dependency of Fu-nan but sent missions of its own to China. In the 7th century, it succeeded Fu-nan as a kingdom, comprising all of Cambodia and southernmost Vietnam. Its people were the Mon-Khmer whose culture was greatly influenced by Hinduism. Between 705 and 707, Chen-la was divided into two states, Wet Chen-la in the south and Dry Chen-la or Wen-tan in the north (*Chiu T'ang shu* 197:2b; *Wen-hsien t'ung-k'ao* 332:14a). In 802, the two parts were reunited as the Khmer Kingdom. The royal city of Angkor Thom was completed c.900 by Yasovarman. In the 10th century, Buddhism began to rival Hinduism, but the latter reasserted itself. The great Hindu Temple of Angkor Vat can probably be dated to the first half of the 12th century. At the end of that century, Champa was annexed by Jayavarman VIII, at which time the Khmer Kingdom also ruled the larger part of what now is Thailand.

The first recorded mission from Chen-la was to the Sui court in 592, when envoys offered regional objects. In 607, envoys offered presents. On Feb.24, 616, they offered regional objects. Emperor Yang of Sui treated the envoys with great courtesy (*Sui shu* 4:11a; 82:7b; *Wen-hsien t'ung-k'ao* 332:13b).

In 623, envoys from Chen-la to the T'ang court presented regional objects (*Chiu T'ang shu* 1907:2b; *T'ung-tien* 188:71a)[118]

In 625, envoys from Chen-la offered gifts (*Ts'e-fu yüan-kuei* p.5023; *Wen-hsien t'ung-k'ao* 332:14a).[119]

In the 10th month (November) of 628, envoys from Chen-la attached themselves to a mission from Lin-yi to offer presents. T'ai-tsung gave rich presents in return (*Chiu T'ang shu* 197:2b; *T'ang hui-yao* 98:1b; *Ts'e-fu yüan-kuei* p.5023).[120]

---

[118] According to *Hsin T'ang shu* 222C:3 and *Wen-hsien t'ung-k'ao* 332:13b, Chen-la sent four missions during the period 618-700. Seven are actually recorded.

[119] Instead of Chen-la, *Wen-hsien t'ung-k'ao* says Wen-tan, which then was a dependency.

[120] *T'ang hui-yao* dates the mission in the 11th month (December).

In the 4th month (Apr./May) of 635, envoys from Chen-la offered gifts (*Ts'e-fu yüan-kuei* p.5024).

In the 10th month (Nov./Dec.) of 651, the Chen-la State presented a tame elphant (*Ts'e-fu yüan-kuei* p.5025).

In the 5th month (June/July) of 682, in the 1st month (Feb./Mar.) of 698, and in the 5th month (June/July) of 707, envoys from Chen-la offered regional objects (*Ts'e-fu yüan-kuei* p.5026).

During the reigns of Kao-tsung, the Empress Wu, and Hsüan-tsung (650-756), Dry Chen-la (Wen-tan) sent envoys to present regional objects (*Chiu T'ang shu* 197:2b).[121]

In the 1st month (Feb/Mar.) of 710, envoys from [Wet] Chen-la arrived at the T'ang court (*Ts'e-fu yüan-kuei* p.5026).[122]

In the 5th month (June/July) of 717, envoys from Dry Chen-la (Wen-tan) offered regional objects (*Ts'e-fu yüan-kuei* p.5027). In the same month, envoys from [Wet] Chen-la also offered regional objects (*Ts'e-fu yüan-kuei* p.5027). The two missions probably travelled together.

In the 6th month (July/Aug.) of 750, envoys from [Wet] Chen-la offered a rhinoceros (*Ts'e-fu yüan-kuei* p.5030).

In the 9th month (October) of 753, a royal son from Dry Chen-la (Wen-tan) with a mission of 26 men called on Emperor Hsüan-tsung. He was given a nominal Chinese title (*Ts'e-fu yüan-kuei* p.5031; *Wen-hsien t'ung-k'ao* 332:14a).

On Dec.27, 771, the Assistant King of Dry Chen-la (Wen-tan), P'o-mi, and his wife called on Emperor Tai-tsung. He presented 11 tame elephants, was given a nominal Chinese title, and granted the name of Guest of of Han (*Chiu T'ang shu* 11:19a-19b; *Hsin T'ang shu* 222C:3b; *Wen-hsien t'ung-k'ao* 332:14a).[123]

In 813, envoys from the Khmer kingdom offered gifts (*Chiu T'ang shu* 197:2b; *Hsin T'ang shu* 222C:3b; *Ts'e-fu yüan-kuei* p.5032; *Wen-hsien t'ung-k'ao* 332:14a).[124]

---

[121] Kao-tsung died in 683 before the division of Chen-la in 705-707. The earlier missions must therefore have been sent when Dry Chen-la or Wen-tan still was a dependency.

[122] *Ts'e-fu yüan-kuei* throughout does not use the term Wet Chen-la. However, for the two missions of 717, it distinguishes between Chen-la and Wen-tan. This makes it clear that for the period of division it uses Chen-la for Wet Chen-la and Wen-tan for Dry Chen-la.

[123] According to *Chiu T'ang shu*,the king of Wen-tan, P'o-mi, presented 11 tame elephants on Dec.27, 771. There is no mention of his wife.

[124] *Chiu T'ang shu, Hsin T'ang shu*, and *Wen-hsien t'ung-k'ao* say Wet Chen-la which

On Nov.4, 814, envoys from the Khmer Kingdom offered presents (*Chiu T'ang shu* 15:6b; *Ts'e-fu yüan-kuei p.5032*). There followed a period of over two centuries without any diplomatic contacts between the kingdom and China.

In the 12th month (Jan./Feb., 1117) of the Chinese year 1116, the Khmer kingdom resumed relations with a mission and gifts to the Sung court. It consisted of 14 envoys, who were received in audience on Jan.25, 1117, and were presented with court garments. They took leave on Apr.10 in another audience (*Sung shih* 21:7b; 489:11b; *Sung hui-yao kao* ts'e 196; *Wen-hsien t'ung-k'ao* 332:14a).

In 1120, envoys from the Khmer Kingdom brought gifts, on which occasion the Sung recognized their ruler as king. On Dec.25 of that year, the envoys were received in audience and took leave. In 1129, the king was appointed Acting Minister of Works, which later became a constant practice (*Sung shih* 22:4b; 489:11b; *Sung hui-yao kao* ts'e 196; *Wen-hsien t'ung-k'ao* 332:14a).

In 1200, the ruler of the Khmer kingdom had been on the throne for 20 years. His envoys brought a letter and presented two tame elephants and regional objects (*Sung shih* 489:11b; *Wen-hsien t'ung-k'ao* 332:14a).

Missions from the Chen-la/Khmer Kingdom were relatively rare. For 1200, *Wen-hsien t'ung-k'ao* 332:14a makes the curious statement that because of the distance the Khmer Kingdom was excused from "paying tribute". It was not within the power of a Sung emperor to tell the king of the Khmer Kingdom what or what not to do. More probably, the missions ceased to come, and the Chinese tried to put the best light on it. In spite of the visit of the Assistant King of Dry Chen-la in 771, a weak splinter state which preceded the great Khmer Kingdom, relations between what now is Cambodia and China were never close. This may explain the hiatus in relations between 814 and 1117, which is too long to be blamed on incomplete historical entries. It occurred at a time when the Khmer Kingdom stood at the zenith of its power and truly can be called an empire. Its orientation was toward the south, and distant and hard-to-reach China in the north may have been of no interest to the kings.

With the exception of elephants and one rhinoceros, the goods offered by the Chen-la/Khmer kingdom are not specified

---

is an anachronism, or else the term continued to exist as a provincial name. *Ts'e-fu yüan-kuei* says Chen-la State, which I heneforth render as Khmer Kingdom.

SENG-KAO, WU-LING, CHIA-CHA, CHIU-MI

In the 1st month (Jan.Feb.) of 638, envoys from these four states offered gifts to the T'ang court. Soon thereafter, between 650 and 656, they were annexed by Chen-la.

In the 6th month (Sep./Oct.) of 671, envoys from the king of the Chiu-mi State presented regional objects (*Ts'e-fu yüan-kuei* pp.5024, 5026; *Wen-hsien t'ung-k'ao* 331:12b). It follows that he must have ruled his dependency as a vassal of Chen-la.

CHAN-PO or CHAN-P'O

In 657, envoys from Chan-po to the T'ang court offered a tame elephant and a rhinoceros (*Hsin T'ang shu* 222C:4b; *Ts'e-fu yüan-kuei* p.5025)

LO-HU

In the 11th month (Oct./Nov.) of 1155, Lo-hu presented a tame elephant to the Sung court (*Sung shih* 31:6b).

CHEN-LI-FU

On Sep.23, 1200, a local administrator on the south coast of the Bay of Hang-chou in Che-chiang reported to the Southern Sung court that envoys had arrived from the ruler of the Chen-li-fu State to offer two elephants, 20 elephant tusks, 50 rhinoceros horns, and 40 lengths of cotton (*Sung hui-yao kao* ts'e 197).

On Oct.10, 1201, the Chen-li-fu State presented two tame elephants, 11 pieces of cotton, and two pieces of large cotton (*Sung shih* 38:3a; *Sung hui-yao kao* ts'e 197).

On Sep.9. 1205, Chen-li-fu presented another elephant, two elephant tusks, and 10 rhinoceros horns (*Sung shih* 38:11a; *Sung hui-yao kao* ts'e 197).

It is clear that the envoys, from Chen-li-fu, as no doubt all others from the area of Cambodia, arrived by sea and that in Southern Sung times they landed close to the capital of Lin-an.

CH'IH-T'U

It has been noted above that the Master of Affairs of Military Garrisons, Ch'ang Chün, and the Master of Affairs of the Bureau of Forestry and Crafts, Wang Chün-cheng, volunteered in 607 to travel to Ch'ih-t'u, which greatly pleased Emperor Yang of Sui. They embarked in the 10th month (Oct./Nov.) with 5000 gifts from the emperor to the king of Ch'ih-t'u and reached their destination after a voyage of about a month. The king sent a Brahman with 30 boats to welcome them, drumming drums, making music, and presenting golden chains, ornaments, eight golden pitchers of aromatic oils, other fragrant fluids, and four lengths of white cotton. Two elephants carried the envoys to the royal palace, where they presented a letter from Emperor Yang to the king. After the ceremony, they were taken to lodgings. The king sent a Brahman with food, served on leaves. After several days, the envoys were invited to a banquet. When they returned to China, the king sent an envoy of his own to travel with them. On Apr.9, 608, Emperor Yang received Ch'ang Chün and the Ch'ih-t'u envoy.[125] The latter presented golden hibiscus hats and baroos camphor. The emperor was greatly pleased and conferred on the envoy and his attendants nominal offices and rewards, to each in in accordance with his rank (*Sui shu* 3:12b; 82:4a-5a; *Wen-hsien t'ung-k'ao* 331:13a).

On Mar.14, 609, and June 27, 610, envoys from Ch'ih-tu offered regional objects (*Sui shu* 3:12b, 15b).

TO-HO-LO

In the 6th month (June/July) of 638, the 5th month (May/June) of 640,[126] and the intercalary month (July/Aug.) of 643, envoys from the king of To-ho-lo to the T'ang court offered regional objects (*Chiu T'ang shu* 197:3a; *Ts'e-fun yüan-kuei* p.5024).

In the 2nd month (Mar./Apr.) of 649, To-ho-lo together with the states of K'o-ling and To-p'o-teng presented elephant tusks and great pearls.[127] In exchange, the king of To-ho-lo requested good

---

[125] *Sui shu* 82:5b dates the audience 610, which must be wrong.

[126] For 638 and 640, *Ts'e-fu yüan-kuei* p.5024 writes Tu-ho-lo.

[127] *Ts'e-fu yüan-kuei* says a fire pearl, i.e.burning-glas.

horses, which were provided (*Chiu T'ang shu* 197:3a; *Ts'e-fu yüan-kuei* p.5025).

T'OU-HO

The Chinese first learned about this state in Sui times (*Wen-hsien t'ung-k'ao* 332:14b).

Between 627 and 649, envoys from T'ou-ho to the T'ang court presented a letter in an envelope of pure gold. It furthermore offered vases, golden tablets, valuable belts, rhinoceros horns, elephant tusks, and maritime products (*Hsin T'ang shu* 222C:4b; *Wen-hsien t'ung-k'ao* 332:14b).

CHOU-MEI-LIU

On July 25, 1001, nine envoys from the the ruler of Chou-mei-liu to the Sung court offered 1000 catties of putchuck, 100 catties of white copper, 100 catties of hard tin, 35 catties of stems of coptis teeta,[128] 100 catties of lithospermus officiniale,[129] one red felt, four pieces of fancy cottons, 10,000 catties of sapan wood,[130] and 61 elephant tusks. The envoys were given an audience and presented with caps, belts, and garments. They returned with a letter from Emperor Chen-tsung (*Sung shih* 489:24a-24b; *Hsü Tzu-chih t'ung-chien ch'ang-pien* p.411; *Wen-hsien t'ung-k'ao* 332:19b).[131]

On Aug.8, 1014, a Sung edict referred to the arrival of envoys from Chou-mei-liu (*Sung hui-yao kao* 10122:11b).[132]

---

[128] An herb.

[129] A plant yielding a purple dye.

[130] A red soluble wood, yielding a purple dye.

[131] *Sung shih* transliterates the first syllable in the name of Chou-mei-liu with the character for "boat", *Wen-hsien t'ung-k'ao* with the character for "commandery" (chou).

[132] The text miswrites the name Chou-liu-mei. *Sung shih* 490:19b dates this mission 1004.

P'O-LI

During the Six Dynasties, P'o-li had sent four missions to Liu Sung and Liang between 473 and 522.[133]

In 592, envoys from P'o-li to the Sui court offered regional objects. In 616, it sent envoys for the same purpose. Thereafter, communications were cut off (*Sui shu* 82:8a; *T'ung-tien* 188:70b; *Ts'e-fu yüan-kuei* p.5023; *Wen-hsien t'ung-k'ao* 331:12b).

In 630, the king of P'o-li attached envoys to a Lin-yi mission and offered regional objects to the T'ang court (*Chiu T'ang shu* 197:2a; *T'ung-tien* 188:70b; *Ts'e-fu yüan-kuei* p.5023; *Wen-hsien t'ung-k'ao* 331:12b).[134]

LO-CH'A

When Emperor Yang of Sui in 607 sent Ch'ang Chün and others to Ch'ih-t'u, they reached Lo-ch'a (*T'ung-tien* 188:71b; *Wen-hsien t'ung-k'ao* 332:14a). No missions from Lo-ch'a to China are recorded.

ŚRIVIJAYA

The earlier form of the Chinese name for this state was Shih-li-fo-shih, often abbreviated to Fo-shih or Fu-shih. From Sung times, the Chinese called it San-fo-ch'i.

From the 7th century, Śrivijaya became the most powerful Indonesian state under the Shailendra dynasty. Its capital was at Palembang in eastern Sumatra. Śrivijaya developed into an important centre for both Mahayana Buddhism and commerce, and it thrived on the taxes levied on goods shipped or transshipped from and to the Middle and Far East.

The first recorded mission to China was in the 12th month (January, 702) of the Chinese year 701, when envoys from Śrivijaya (Fo-shih) to the T'ang court offered regional objects. In the 3rd month (Mar./Apr.) of 716, envoys again offered presents (*Ts'e-fu yüan-kuei* pp.5026, 5027).

---

133 See my *Six Dynasties*, vol.II, p.89.

134 *Ts'e-fu yüan-kuei* dates this mission 631.

In the 7th month (July/Aug.) of 724, envoys from the king of Śrivijaya (Shih-li-fo-shih) offered two pygmies, one black girl,[135] various musicians, and a five-coloured parrot. The envoy was given a nominal Chinese title and 100 bolts of silk. The king was appointed General-in-chief of the Awesome Guards of the Left and presented with a purple robe and a belt of fine gold (*Hsin T'ang shu* 222C:5a; *Ts'e-fu yüan-kuei* p.5028).

In the 11th month (Nov./Dec.) of 727, envoys from Śrivijaya (Fu-shih) presented a five-coloured parrot (*Ts'e-fu yüan-kuei* p.5028).

In the 12th month (Jan./Feb., 742) of the Chinese year 741, a son of the king of Śrivijaya (Fu-shih) offered regional objects. An edict ordered that he be given a banquet. He was made King Who Submits to Righteousness and appointed to a nominal Chinese office. The last mission during T'ang, presenting regional objects, is recorded for 904, when the chief envoy was appointed to a nominal Chinese office (*Hsin T'ang shu* 222C:5a; *Ts'e-fu yüan-kuei* p.5029; *Wen-hsien t'ung-k'ao* 332:18a).

On Sep.29, 960, envoys from the king of Śrivijaya (San-fo-ch'i[136]) to the Sung court offered regional objects. They came again on June 19, 961, and in the winter of that year (*Sung shih* 1:7b, 10a; 489:13a; *Wen-hsien t'ung-k'ao* 332:18a).

On Apr.11, 962, envoys from the king of Śrivijaya offered regional objects. He received white porcelain vessels, red lacquered vessels, silver vessels, silk brocade, cotton, and horse trappings. On Dec.21 of that year, envoys again offered gifts (*Sung shih* 1:11b, 13; 489:13a; *Wen-hsien t'ung-k'ao* 332:18a).

On Apr.29, 971, envoys from Śrivijaya offered mineral oil (naphta) and crystal. On May 16, 972, envoys offered regional objects (*Sung shih* 2:11b; 3:1b; 489:13a; *Wen-hsien t'ung-k'ao* 332:18a).

On Apr.11, 974, envoys from the king of Śrivijaya offered elephant tusks, frankincense, rose water, dates, granulated sugar, finger rings of rock crystal, opaque glass pitchers, and coral trees (*Sung shih* 3:4b; 489:13a; *Wen-hsien t'ung-k'ao* 332:18a).

On Jan.14, 976, envoys from Śrivijaya presented regional objects. They were given caps, belts, [porcelain] vessels, and silk (*Sung shih* 3: 9a; 489:13a; *Wen-hsien t'ung-k'ao* 332:18a).

---

[135] *Hsin T'ang shu* says two black girls.

[136] Henceforth this name.

In 980, envoys from the king of Śrivijaya were received at the Sung court (*Sung shih* 489:13a; *Wen-hsien t'ung-k'ao* 332:18a).

In the 11th month (Dec./Jan., 984) of the Chinese year 983, envoys from the king of Śrivijaya presented a rock crystal Buddha, cotton, rhinoceros horns,[137] and aromatic drugs. In 988, and in the 12th month (January 990) of the Chinese year 989, envoys offered regional objects (*Sung shih* 5:10a; 489:13b; *Hsü Tzu-chih t'ung-chien ch'ang-pien* p.213; *Wen-hsien t'ung-k'ao* 332:18a).

In 992, Canton informed the Sung court that when the envoy from Śrivijaya, P'u-ya-t'o-li, had reached Canton on the way home in the previous year, he had learned that his country was under attack by She-p'o. He had remained until the spring of 992 and then boarded a ship to Champa. Unfavourable winds had forced the vessel to return. The envoy now requested an imperial certification that he was not responsible for the delays. This was done (*Sung shih* 489:13b).

In 1003, a mission arrived from the king of Śrivijaya. He supposedly informed that a Buddhist temple had been built in his country and requested that the emperor give it a name and a bell. Emperor Chen-tsung chose the name "Long Life Received from Heaven" and presented a bell. The envoys were all appointed to nominal Chinese offices (*Sung shih* 7:2b; 489:13b; *Wen-hsien t'ung-k'ao* 332:18a). This is a most unlikely story. Śrivijaya was full of Buddhist temples, and its powerful king had no need to request a name from the Sung emperor. More likely, the envoys had forwarded the request of a Chinese community in their state.

On Aug.22, 1008, envoys from the king of Śrivijaya offered gifts and congratulated. They received rich presents (*Sung shih* 7:20b; 489:14a; *Hsü Tzu-chih t'ung-chien ch'ang-pien* p.603; *Wen-hsien t'ung-k'ao* 332:18a).

On Aug.8, 1014, a Sung edict edict referred to the arrival of envoys from Śrivijaya (*Sung hui-yao kao* 10122:11b).[138]

In 1017, envoys from the king of Śrivijaya brought a message in golden letters and presented real pearls, elephant tusks, Buddhist sutras etc. They were given presents (*Sung shih* 8:17b; 489:14a; *Wen-hsien t'ung-k'ao* 332:18a).

In 1028, envoys from the king of Śrivijaya offered regional objects.

---

[137] The text says teeth.

[138] *Sung shih* 490:19b dates this mission 1004.

Normally, in the case of distant countries, the emperor presented a belt [ornamented] with gilded silver. This time, he gave a golden belt (*Sung shih* 9:10b; 489:14a; *Wen-hsien t'ung-k'ao* 332:18a).

In 1077, an envoy from Śrivijaya was given a nominal Chinese title (*Wen-hsien t'ung-k'ao* 332:18a).

On Aug.2, 1079, envoys arrived from Śrivijaya with silver, real pearls, *p'o-lü* ointment, and aromatics. For this, they were paid 64,000 copper cash and 10,500 ounces of stringed silver coins. They wished to buy golden belts, silver vessels, and textiles. All was provided in accordance with their request (*Sung shih* 489:14b; *Hsü Tzu-chih t'ung-chien ch'ang-pien* p.2802; *Wen-hsien t'ung-k'ao* 332:18b).

In 1082, envoys from Śrivijaya were received in audience. They presented golden lotus flowers, real pearls, and baroos camphor. All were appointed to nominal Chinese offices. On their return trip, perhaps in 1083, one of the envoys fell ill and died not far south of K'ai-feng. The emperor contributed 50 bolts of pongee toward the funeral expenses (*Sung shih* 489:14b-15a; *Wen-hsien t'ung-k'ao* 332:18a).

In the 9th month (October) of 1084, Śrivijaya offered gifts. On Jan.19, 1089, it presented golden lotus flowers, real pearls, and baroos camphor. In the 12th month (Dec./Jan., 1091) of the Chinese year 1090, in 1091, in the 10th month (Nov./Dec.) of 1094, and in 1095 it offered presents (*Sung shih* 16:12b; 17:11b, 15a, 17a; 18:3b, 5b; *Hsü Tzu-chih t'ung-chien ch'ang-pien* p.4246; *Wen-hsien t'ung-k'ao* 332:18b).

On Mar.11, 1156, and Feb.6, 1157, envoys from the king of Śrivijaya to the Southern Sung court offered presents (*Sung shih* 31:8a, 11a; 489:15a; *Wen-hsien t'ung-k'ao* 332:18b).

In 1172, the king of Śrivijaya wrote and requested [to buy] copper for building ships. The Southern Sung court agreed but later no longer allowed such purchases (*Wen-hsien t'ung-k'ao* 332:18b). Shortage of copper was a persistent problem for the Sung, since this metal was needed for coinage.

The last recorded mission from Śrivijaya to Southern Sung was in the 12th month (Jan./Feb., 1179) of the Chinese year 1178, when envoys offered regional objects (*Sung shih* 35:3b; 489:15a; *Wen-hsien t'ung-k'ao* 332:18b).

In a single instance, for 1008, it is recorded that a king of Śrivijaya congratulated, but the text does not say why. If it was on Chen-tsung's enthronement on May 8, 997, eleven years had elapsed between the event and the congratulation. It could be that the mission of 1003 brought the news to Śrivijaya, and that the next mission, which was in 1008, conveyed the congratulations. Only one ruler of Śrivijaya is stated to have received a Chinese title. This was in 724, when the king was made a General-in-chief. That was not an impressive title for a man who governed a powerful state.

The Chinese, being obsessed with rank, presented belts of different value to foreign envoys. The fact that the envoys from Śrivijaya, except in 1028, received silver belts and not golden belts, shows that the Sung court did not realize the importance of this state.

Envoys from Śrivijaya were appointed to nominal Chinese offices, but that was a standard practice of the Chinese to impress and flatter foreigners and themselves. That the government felt responsible for envoys while they were on Chinese territory is shown by the fact that it assumed the expenses for a deceased envoy in 1082 or 1083.

It is hard to say whether all missions from Śrivijaya to China are recorded in the sources. *Hsin T'ang shu* 222C:5a states that envoys arrived frequently between 713 and 741. The actual missions listed are three. That is hardly frequent. Some missions must therefore have been omitted.

Missions from Śrivijaya are recorded for most months of the year, but the preferred time of arrival was the winter. This means that the envoys sailed to China with the end of the summer monsoon and returned with the end of the winter monsoon.

The following table shows the recorded 38 missions from Śrivijaya to T'ang and Sung by 20-year periods:

687-706:	1
707-726:	2
727-746:	2
747-766:	0
767-786:	0
787-806:	0
807-826:	0
827-846:	0
847-866:	0
867-886:	0
887-906:	1
907-926:	0
927-946:	0
947-966:	5
967-986:	7

987-1006:	3
1007-1026:	3
1027-1046:	1
1047-1066:	0
1067-1086:	4
1097-1106:	5
1107-1126:	0
1127-1146:	0
1147-1166:	2
1167-1186:	2

The missions from Śrivijaya come to an abrupt end after An Lu-shan's rebellion in 755, with but a single mission in 904. 27 missions are recorded for Northern Sung but only 4 for Southern Sung.

The recorded offerings from Śrivijaya were pygmies, one or two black girls, musicians, five-coloured parrots, elephant tusks, rhinoceros horns, golden lotus flowers, silver, crystal, a rock crystal Buddha, finger rings of rock crystal, pearls, coral trees, opaque glass pitchers, frankincense, aromatic drugs, ointments, rose water, dates, sugar, baroos camphor, and mineral oil (naphta). These were mostly luxury articles of no great bulk and high value. Some of the goods, such as opaque glass, frankincense, camphor, etc. were themselves imported by Śrivijaya.[139] The mention of naphta is particularly interesting, since it has been seen that the Sung in 958 had also received it from Champa, presumably for military experimentation.

The Chinese, as usual, matched gifts for gifts or paid in silver and copper cash. The chief Chinese offerings were caps, robes, belts, porcelain vessels, lacquered vessels, silver vessels, silk and cotton fabrics, horse trappings, and copper.

In addition to this government trade, there also was private trade by merchants and shipmasters from Śrivijaya. In 980, Ch'ao commandery on the northeast coast of Kuang-tung reported to the Sung court that the foreign merchant Li Fu-hui from Śrivijaya had arrived by ship after a stormy voyage of 60 days with aromatic drugs, rhinoceros horns, and elephant tusks. His goods had been sent to Canton. In 985, the shipmaster Chin Hua-ch'a came from Śrivijaya with regional objects

[139] Hirth and Rockhill, *Chau Ju-kua*, p.150 note 2, suggest that the black girl or girls may have been from Africa.

(*Sung shih* 489:13a-13b). Both entrepeneurs had Chinese names, so that at least the first and perhaps both were overseas Chinese. It must be noted, however, that since the ancient historians found it worthwhile actually to record both arrivals, such events must have been rare.

TO-P'O-TENG

In the 6th month (July/Aug.) of 647, envoys from To-p'o-teng to the T'ang court offered cotton, elephant tusks, and white sandalwood. T'ai-tsung responded with a letter stamped with the inperial seal and presented miscellaneous objects (*Chiu T'ang shu* 3:11a; 197:3b; *T'ung-tien* 188:72a; *T'ang hui-yao* 100:3a; *Ts'e-fu yüan-kuei* p.5025).

In the 2nd month (Mar./Apr.) of 649, joint envoys from To-p'o-teng and K'o-ling offered gifts. This was shortly before T'ai-tsung's death on July 10. He again responded with a letter stamped with the imperial seal (*Hsin T'ang shu* 222C:3b; *Wen-hsien t'ung-k'ao* 332:16a).

K'O-LING

In the 5th month (May/June) of 640, envoys from K'o-ling to the T'ang court offered regional objects (*Chiu T'ang shu* 197:3a; *Ts'e-fu yüan-kuei* p.5024).

In the 2nd month (Mar./Apr.) of 649, joint envoys from K'o-ling, To-ho-lo, and To-p'o-teng presented golden flowers etc. T'ai-tsung responded with a letter stamped with the imperial seal (*Hsin T'ang shu*222C:3b; *T'ung-tien* 188:72b; *Wen-hsien t'ung-k'ao* 332:16a).

In the 7th month (Aug./Sep.) of 666, envoys from the K'o-ling State offered regional objects (*Ts'e-fu yüan-kuei* p.5025)

In the 4th month (May/June) of 768, the 1st month (Feb.Mar.) of 769, and the 12th month (Dec./Jan., 770) of the same Chinese year, envoys from the K'o-ling State offered gifts (*Chiu T'ang shu* 197:3a; *Ts'e-fu yüan-kuei* p.5031).

At this time (766-779), the T'ang learned that a woman had become the ruler of K'o-ling (*Wen-hsien t'ung-k'ao* 332:16a).

On Oct.4, 815, envoys from the K'o-ling State presented five black youths, a five-coloured parrot, cockatoos, a *p'in-chia* bird,[140] rare aro-

---

[140] Schafer, *Golden Peaches*, pp.103-104, identifies the *p'in-chia* bird as a paradise dorgon.

matics, and valuables of various kinds. The emperor appointed the chief envoy to the Courageous Garrison of the Left at the Four Gates. He yielded this title to his younger brother, whereupon the emperor appointed both to nominal Chinese offices (*Chiu T'ang shu* 15:9a; *Hsin T'ang shu* 222C:4a; *Ts'e-fu yüan-kuei* p.5033; *Wen-hsien t'ung-k'ao* 332: 16a).[141]

In 818, envoys from the K'o-ling State presented two black girls, cockatoos, tortoise shells, and a live rhinoceros (*Chiu T'ang shu* 15:16a; 197:3a; *Ts'e-fu yüan-kuei* p.5033).

At some time between 860-874, K'o-ling presented female musicians (*Hsin T'ang shu* 222C:4a; *Wen-hsien t'ung-k'ao* 332:16a).

According to *Hsin T'ang shu* 222C:4a and *Wen-hsien t'ung-k'ao* 332: 16a, K'o-ling sent three missions between 766-779 and two missions between 827 and 835. No missions are recorded by exact dates for the earlier period and three for the later. Of the 11 recorded missions, 8 arrived after the rebellion of An Lu-shan in 755.

SHE-P'O

She-p'o on Java had been known to the Chinese well before the T'ang. In 433 and 435, it had sent missions to the Liu Sung of the Six Dynasties[142]

During T'ang, the first recorded mission from She-p'o was received at the court on Nov.10, 820, when envoys offered gifts. They came again in the 2nd month (Mar./Apr.) of 831, and on Mar.14, 839 (*Chiu T'ang shu* 16:5a; 17B:26b; *Ts'e-fu yüan-kuei* p.5033.[143]

After a hiatus of over 150 years, relations were resumed in 992, when the king of the She-p'o State sent envoys to Sung. These arrived on a large ship in the Bay of Hang-chou in Che-chiang, which event was reported to the government by the local authorities on Sep.18. The envoys were received at the court in the 12th month (Dec./Jan., 993) and offered ten elephant tusks, rhinoceros horns, two catties of real pearls, 100 pieces of various textiles, gilded objects, 4,423 catties

---

[141] *Hsin T'ang shu* and *Wen-hsien t'ung-k'ao* date this mission 813. Furthermore, *Hsin T'ang shu* gives the number of black youths as four.

[142] See my *Six Dynasties*, vol.II, p.88. At that time, the state was referred to as She-p'o-po-ta.

[143] I emend 1st month, *mou-shen*, of 839 to 1st intercalary month.

of sandalwood, two betel nut trays, 12 swords adorned with gold and silver, seven white cockatoos,[144] 40 bamboo mats with woven patterns, and valuable ornaments. The envoys on their own offered 67 catties of large tortoise shells, five catties of white baroos camphor, 10 catties of cloves, and 20 bamboo mats with woven patterns. When they returned to She-p'o after a long stay, they were given gold, silk, fine horses, and military implements (*Sung shih* 5:14b; *Sung hui-yao kao* ts'e 197; *Wen-hsien t'ung-k'ao* 332:14b-15a).

On Aug.8, 1014, an edict referred to the arrival of envoys from She-p'o (*Sung hui-yao kao* 10122:11b).

In the 6th month (July) of 1109, envoys from the She-p'o State offered gifts. An edict ordered that the protocol for these envoys should be the same as for those from Chiao-chih (*Sung shih* 20:9b; 489:17b; *Wen-hsien t'ung-k'ao* 332:15a).

On Jan.21, 1129, the Southern Sung appointed the ruler of She-p'o Military Commissioner of the non-existant Army Which Cherishes the Distance, Surveillance and Supervisory Commissioner and Inspector of the non-existant Lin commandery,[145] in charge of all its military matters, Imperial Household Grandee of the Golden Seal and Purple Ribbon, Acting Minister of Works and Concurrent Grandee Secretary, and Supreme Pillar of State, and recognized him as king of She-p'o. Subsequently, he was made Acting Minister over the Masses (*Sung shih* 489:17b-18a; *Sung hui-yao kao* ts'e 197; *Wen-hsien t'ung-k'ao* 332:15a).

On Aug.14, 1131, the Maritime Trade Commissioner of Kuang-nan in present Kuang-tung reported to the court that the She-p'o barbarians wished to trade locally. An edict did not allow it (*Sung hui-yao kao* ts'e 197).

Three missions are recorded from She-p'o to the T'ang, three to the Northern Sung, and none to the Southern Sung.

PO-NI

On Nov.3, 977, the first mission from the king of Po-ni arrived at the Sung court. It included a deputy named P'u-ya-li. The envoys presented a letter and offered large-sliced baroos camphor, green

[144] *Sung hui-yao kao* says one cockatoo.

[145] Note that the various offices concerned with the non-existant Lin commandery had almost simultaneously been conferred on also kings of Champa.

dragon camphor, tortoise shells, sandalwood, and six elephant tusks. The camphor was graded by the Chinese according to quality. Emperor T'ai-tsung made rich bestowals on the envoys, i.e. payed a good price (*Sung shih* 489:19a-19b; *Hsü Tzu-chih t'ung-chien ch'ang-pien* p.157; *Wen-hsien t'ung-k'ao* 332:18b).

In the 2nd month (March) of 1082, envoys from the king of Po-ni offered regional objects. They begged to return to their country by ship from Ch'üan chou. This was allowed (*Sung shih* 489:20a; *Wen-hsien t'ung-k'ao* 332:18b).

Hirth and Rockhill, *Chau Ju-kua*, p.157, read P'u-ya-li as a transliteration of Abu Ali. This would mean that Po-ni made use of an Arab intermediary, just as Champa may had done in 958. In fact, the letter of the king stated that he had asked the help of a stranger. In 1082, the envoys must have come as passengers on a ship, since they needed permission to return on a vessel not their own. That vessel could have been Arabian.

T'O-HUAN

In 644, envoys from T'o-huan to the T'ang court offered gifts (*Chiu T'ang shu* 197:2b).[146]

In 647, envoys from T'o-huan presented a white-feathered cockatoo with several ten red-coloured feathers on its head,[147] a five-coloured parrot, and *p'o-lü* ointment. They requested in exchange horses and copper vessels. This was agreed to (*Chiu T'ang shu* 197:2b; *T'ung-tien* 188:72b; *Ts'e-fu yüan-kuei* p.5025; *Wen-hsien t'ung-k'ao* 332:16a).

The last recorded mission from T'o-huan was in 651, when envoys offered gifts (*Ts'e-fu yüan-kuei* p.5025).

MO-YI

Men with valuable goods from this country reached Canton in 982 (*Sung shih* 489:17b; *Wen-hsien t'ung-k'ao* 332:15a). It is not recorded that

[146] *Ts'e-fu yüan-kuei* p.5024 dates this mission 643. It may have arrived that year and departed in 644.

[147] Schafer, *Golden Peaches*, pp.101-102, identifies this bird as the rose-crested cockatoo of Ceram and Amboina (Kokatoë moluccensis).

they were sent on to the Sung capital. This may have been a private venture, rather than an official mission.

KO-LO-SHE

Between 650 and 656, Ko-lo-she offered a five-coloured parrot to the T'ang court (*Hsin T'ang shu* 222C:2b).

In the 5th month (May/June) of 660, envoys from Ko-lo-she were received at the T'ang court and offered regional objects (*T'ung-tien* 188:72b; *T'ang hui-yao* 100:15a; *Ts'e-fu yüan-kuei* p.5025; *Wen-hsien t'ung-k'ao* 332:16b).

KAN-T'ANG

In 635, envoys from Kan-t'ang were received at the T'ang court (*Hsin T'ang shu* 222C:2a; *Wen-hsien t'ung-k'ao* 331:12b).

The second and last recorded mission from Kan-t'ang arrived in the 12th month (January, 637) of the Chinese year 636 (*Ts'e-fu yüan-kuei* p.5024).

CHU-NA or SHU-NA

A single mission is recorded for 628, when envoys presented regional objects to the T'ang court (*Hsin T'ang shu* 222C:2a; *Wen-hsien t'ung-k'ao* 331:12b).

TO-MO-CH'ANG

In the 2nd month (Feb./Mar.) of 659, envoys from To-mo-ch'ang offered gifts to the T'ang court (*Hsin T'ang shu* 222C:5a; *T'ang hui-yao* 100:14b; *Wen-hsien t'ung-k'ao* 332:16b). No other mission is recorded.

P'AN-P'AN

Twelve missions from P'an-p'an to Liu Sung, Liang, and Ch'en of the Six Dynasties are recorded for 424-584.[148]

---

[148] See my *Six Dynasties*, vol.II, p.89.

In 616, envoys from P'an-p'an to the Sui court offered regional objects and congratulated (*Sui shu* 82:8a; *T'ung-tien* 188:70b). It is not clear what the congratulations were for.

Between 627 and 649, two missions from P'an-p'an arrived at the T'ang court (*Hsin T'ang shu* 222C:2b). Four further missions were received in the 9th month (Oct./Nov.) of 633, the 9th month (Oct./Nov.) of 635, the 2nd month (Mar./Apr.) of 641, and the 6th month (June/July) of 648 (*Chiu T'ang shu* 197:2a; *Ts'e-fu yüan-kuei* p.5024).

TAN-TAN

Seven missions from Tan-tan to Liang and Ch'en of the Six Dynasties are recorded for 530-585.[149]

In the 7th month (Aug./Sep.) of 616, Tan-tan offered regional objects to the Sui court (*Sui shu* 82:8a; *Ts'e-fu yüan-kuei* p.5026).

A single mission is recorded for T'ang. In 669, envoys to the court offered regional objects (*Hsin T'ang shu* 222C:5b; *Ts'e-fu yüan-kuei* p.502; *Wen-hsien t'ung-k'ao* 332:15b).

P'IAO

P'iao in eastern Burma had relations with China only at the end of T'ang. On Feb.13, 802, a younger brother of the king presented 12 songs[150] of their national music and 35 musicians (*Chiu T'ang shu* 13: 19b; *T'ang hui-yao* 100:18b-19a; *Ts'e-fu yüan-kuei* p.5032).

In the 12th month (Jan./Feb., 807) of the Chinese year 806, and in the 2nd month (Mar./Apr.) of 862, P'iao offered regional objects (*T'ang hui-yao* 100:19a; *Ts'e-fu yüan-kuei* p.5032).

P'U-TUAN or P'U-KAN

The kingdom of Pagan was a great Buddhist centre in central Burma which flourished in the 11th and 12th centuries. It was destroyed by the Mongols.

---

[149] See my *Six Dynasties*, vol.II, pp.89-90.

[150] *Chiu T'ang shu* says 12 songs, *T'ang hui-yao* 22 songs, and *Ts'e-fu yüan-kuei* 10 songs.

On Sep.30, 1003, Pagan (P'u-tuan) presented to the Sung court regional objects and a red cockatoo. The envoys stayed through the New Year and were in the 1st month (Jan./Feb.) of 1004 invited to a lantern banquet and granted copper cash (*Sung shih* 7:2a; *Sung hui-yao kao* 3997).

In the 5th month (May/June) of 1004, another mission from Pagan (P'u-tuan) offered regional objects.[151] In the 9th month (Sep./Oct.) of that year, the high officials reported to the court that the envoys from Pagan (P'u-tuan) often bought Chinese objects such as gold, silver, banners, and pennants and took them back to their country. People who came from far away did not know that such private trade was forbidden. The market people should be instructed that foreigners were not allowed to trade privately. This was approved (*Sung shih* 7: 3b, 7b; 490:19b; *Sung hui-yao kao* 3997).

In the 6th month (July/Aug.) of 1007, envoys from the the king of Pagan (P'u-tuan) offered tortoise shells, baroos camphor, cloves and regional objects. The envoys were given caps, belts, garments, embroidered sashes, vessels, and strings of copper cash, each in in accordance with his rank. In the 8th month (Sep./Oct.), the envoys were received in audience and given horse trappings and two large banners. The high officials objected on the grounds that, since Pagan ranked below Champa, it should be given five small banners. This was rejected by Emperor Chen-tsung (*Sung shih* 7:15b; *Sung hui-yao kao* 3997).

In early March, 1011, envoys arrived from the ruler of Pagan (P'u-tuan). Emperor Chen-tsung had at that time proceeded to Fen-yin in order to sacrifice to Sovereign Earth. The envoys were ordered to follow him there. They were received on Mar.25, one day after the sacrifice, and presented a letter engraved on a golden tablet. The envoys offered cloves, white baroos camphor, tortoise shells, a red cockatoo, and a black slave. The gifts were officially accepted in the 6th month (July/Aug.), with one exception. The black slave was returned because the emperor pitied his "strange vulgarity". The chief envoy was appointed to a nominal Chinese office. The king requested in exchange textiles and five small banners "in order to dazzle distant regions". The Sung court agreed to this and presented them in the

---

[151] This is the mission which according to Chao Ju-kua came from P'u-kan. See Hirth and Rockhill, *Chau Ju-kua*, p.58.

7th month (August) (*Sung shih* 8:1b, 3a; *Sung hui-yao kao* 3997; *Wen-hsien t'ung-k'ao* 332:17b).

On Aug.8, 1014, an edict referred to the arrival of envoys from Pagan (P'u-tuan) (*Sung hui-yao kao* 10122:11b).

In the 6th month (July) of 1106, envoys from Pagan (P'u-kan) were received at the Sung court. An edict ordered that the protocol should be the same as for Chu-lien. The Imperial Secretariat objected. Chu-lien was a dependency of Śrivijaya. An imperial communication addressed to it during the *hsi-ning* period (1068-1077) had been written on plain white paper.[152] Pagan on the other hand was a big state and should not be treated like a small state. The protocol for Pagan should be the same as for the Ta-shih (Arabs) and Chiao-chih. Emperor Hui-tsung accepted this (*Sung shih* 489:11b-12a; *Wen-hsien-t'ung-k'ao* 332:19b).[153]

SHIH-TZU

Shih-tzu or Ceylon sent six missions from c.405 to527 to Eastern Chin, Liu Sung, and Liang of the Six Dynasties.[154]

During T'ang, Shih-tzu supposedly had the largest ships trading with China. They were up to 200 feet long and carried 600-770 men. Many had life boats and homing pigeons.[155] It was on vessels like these that the missions arrived.

The first mission from Shih-tzu to the T'ang court is recorded for 669, when envoys offered gifts.[156] At the end of 711, they offered regional objects (*Ts'e-fu yüan-kuei* p.5026).

In the 1st month (Jan./Feb.) of 746, envoys from the king of the Shih-tzu State, Shih-lo-mi-chia,[157] presented big pearls, necklaces of fine gold, 40 sheets of fine cotton fabrics, and Buddhist texts of the Mahayana School on palm leaves (*Hsin T'ang shu* 222C:9a; *T'ang hui-yao* 100:16a; *Ts'e-fu yüan-kuei* p.5030).

In the 3rd month (Apr./May) of 750, the Shih-tzu State presented

---

152 Instead of a more valuable material.

153 Hirth and Rockhill, *Chau Ju-kua*, p.59 note 1, confuse missions from Champa with those from Pagan.

154 See my *Six Dynasties*, vol.II, p.88.

155 See Schafer, *Golden Peaches*, p.13.

156 By *Hsin T'ang shu* 222C:9a dated 670. This probably means that the envoys remained in Ch'ang-an through the New Year.

157 By Schafer, *Goldern Peaches*, p.222, identified as Sīlamegha.

elephant tusks and real pearls. In the 6th month (June/July) of 762, it again offered gifts (*Hsin T'ang shu* 222C:9a; *Ts'e-fu yüan-kuei* p.5030, 5031). No further missions are recorded.[158]

INDIA

The Chinese historians of T'ang and Sung times had only vague knowledge of the political borders of India (T'ien-chu, from Sung onward called Yin-tu). They were usually content to divide it schematically into Northern, Southern, Eastern, Western, and Central India, which stood in no relation to real conditions.

Five missions from India to Eastern Chin, Liu Sung, and Liang are recorded for the Six Dynasties from 357-503,[159] but no missions arrived from India in Sui times. Relations were only restored during T'ang (*Sung shih* 490:1b).

In 641, envoys from the king of Mo-chia-t'o (Magadha),[160] Shih-lo-yi-to (Harsa), arrived at the T'ang court with a letter and gifts. Emperor T'ai-tsung ordered the Commandant of the Cavalry Fleet as Clouds, Liang Huai-ching,[161] to go to Magadha as a return envoy and present a letter stamped with the imperial seal (*Chiu T'ang shu* 198:12a; *Hsin T'ang shu* 221A:12a; *T'ung-tien* 193:19a; *Ts'e-fu yüan-kuei* p.5024; *Wen-hsien t'ung-k'ao* 338:50a).

In the 5th month (June/July) of 646, envoys from an unspecified Indian state offered presents (*Ts'e-fu yüan-kuei* p.5014).

In the 3rd month (Apr./May) of 647, Liang Huai-ching returned from Magadha. King Harsa had attached an envoy of his own to him, who presented Emperor T'ai-tsung with a fire pearl (burning-glas), curcoma longa,[162] and [seedlings of] the Bodhi tree, jackfruit tree, and white poplar. The emperor sent the Assistant of the Commandant of

---

[158] *Liao shih* 12:5a and 70:8a-8b record that on Mar.12, 989, the Shih-tzu State offered gifts to the Liao court. Wittfogel, *Liao*, pp.51-52, considers it within the realm of possibility that contacts were established between Liao and Ceylon, but also suggests that the Shih-tzu State could have been a Central Asian country, governed by a "shih-tzu wang" or "lion king" (Arslan). I believe this mission to have come from Turfan. See under that heading.

[159] See my *Six Dynasties*, p.90.

[160] Situated in northern India, south of Nepal.

[161] *Ts'e-fu yüan-kuei* gives his name as Li Yi-piao, but in the sequence of events, as set out in *Hsin T'ang shu*, Li Yi-piao, must have been sent in 647.

[162] A perfume or incense.

the Guards, Li Yi-piao, as an envoy in response (*Chiu T'ang shu* 198: 12a; *Hsin T'ang shu* 221A:12a; *Ts'e-fu yüan-kuei* p.5025; *Wen-hsien t'ung-k'ao* 338:50a, 51b).

In 648, T'ai-tsung dispatched the Chief Clerk of the Guard Commandant of the Right [of the Heir-apparent], Wang Hsüan-ts'e to Central India (>Magadha). The often quoted account of his exploits there is based on the self-serving report he gave on his return. As he tells it, he found on arriving in Central India that king Harsa had died and that his minister A-lo-na-shun (Aryuna) had enthroned himself. Various local princes paid Hsüan-ts'e "tribute", i.e. offered gifts. But Aryuna attacked Hsüan-ts'e, defeated his small suite of 30 horsemen, and captured the gifts. Hsüan-ts'e fled alone to the Tibetans. These reenforced him with 1,200[163] men and the Nepalese with more than 7000 cavalry. He then defeated Aryuna's forces at the capital of Central India in a battle lasting for three days,[164] cutting off more than 3,000 heads. 10,000 enemy soldiers drowned. 12,000 men and women were captured,[165] as well as 20,000 heads of various livestock. 580 towns surrendered. Aryuna attempted to flee but was taken prisoner. A local prince sent 30,000 cattle, bows, and swords to supply Hsüan-ts'e's army. Another presented rare objects and a geographical map[166] and requested an image of Lao-tzu and the *Tao-te ching*[167] (*Chiu T'ang shu* 198:12b; *T'ung-tien* 193:19a; *Tzu-chih t'ung-chien* pp. 6257-6258; *Wen-hsien t'ung-k'ao* 338:50a).

When this account is shorn of its obvious exaggerations in which all figures are ludicrously inflated, it says no more than that Aryuna was hostile and turned on Hsüan-ts'e. The latter received help from the Tibetans and Nepalese in defeating and capturing Aryuna.

Wang Hsüan-ts'e returned to China with Aryuna as his captive. He also brought with him an Indian Master of Recipes, who claimed to

[163] *Wen-hsien t'ung-k'ao* says 1,000.

[164] The report of Wang Hsüan-ts'e gives June 16 as the date of the battle. That, however, is a later insert by the dynastic historian. *Chiu T'ang shu* 3:11b records that in the 5th month (May/June) of 648, messengers arrived from the Central Indian State to report a victory. That was the victory of Wang Hsüan-ts'e. June 16 is therefore the date when the news reached the T'ang court.

[165] *Wen-hsien t'ung-k'ao* says 22,000.

[166] Presenting a map of one's territory was to the Chinese a symbol of surrender. That would not have occurred to the Indian king.

[167] O.Franke, *Geschichte*, vol.III, p.368, agrees with Pelliot that this request was made to Li Yi-piao in 647.

know the art of long life. T'ai-tsung was inclined to believe him and ordered him to mix the drug of long life.[168] Hsüan-ts'e was appointed a Supernumerary Grandee at the Court.[169] When, in spite of the elixir, T'ai-tsung died soon thereafter on July 10, 649, the image of Aryuna was at his orders carved in stone and placed at his tomb (*Chiu T'ang shu* 198:12b-13a; *Tzu-chih t'ung-chien* p.6258; *Wen-hsien t'ung-k'ao* 338: 50a).

In the 8th month (September) of 658, envoys from the kings of the Ch'ien-ssu-fo, She-li-chün, and Mo-la States brought regional objects. All three are stated to have been dependencies of Southern India which had never yet had any relations with China. They stated that they had sailed for several months and had arrived via Chiao commandery[170] (*Ts'e-fu yüan-kuei* p.5025).

In 668, envoys arrived from five Indian states (*Hsin T'ang shu* 221A: 12b; *Wen-hsien t'ung-k'ao* 338:50a).

In the 3rd month (Apr./May) of 672, and in the 12th month (Jan., 683) of the Chinese year 682, envoys from Southern India offered regional objects (*Ts'e-fu yüan-kuei* p.5026).

In the 3rd month (Mar./Apr.) of 692, envoys from Northern, Southern, Eastern, Western, and Central India simultaneously offered presents (*Chiu T'ang shu* 6:4b; 198:13a; *T'ang hui-yao* 100:9b; *Ts'e-fu yüan-kuei* p.5026; *Sung shih* 490:1b).[171]

In the 1st month (Feb./Mar.) of 710, in the 9th month (Sep./Oct.) of the same year, and in the 1st month (February) of 713, envoys from the Southern Indian State brought regional objects (*Chiu T'ang shu* 198: 13a; *Ts'e-fu yüan-kuei* p.5026, 5027).

On Sep.16, 714, the Western Indian State presented regional objects (*Chiu T'ang shu* 8:4a; 198:13a; *Ts'e-fu yüan-kuei* p.5027).

In the 2nd month (Mar./Apr.) of 715, an envoy from an unspecified Indian state offered regional objects (*Ts'e-fu yüan-kuei* p.5027).

In the 5th month (June/July) of 717, envoys from Central India offered regional objects. In the 6th month (June/July) of 719, envoys

[168] According to *Tzu-chih t'ung-chien* p.6303, the Indian was on the point of returning home in 657. Someone advised Kao-tsung that if this man really could mix the drug of long life, he ought not be sent home. In the end, he died in Ch'ang-an.

[169] According to *Hsin T'ang shu* 221A:13a, Emperor Kao-tsung (r.650-683) sent Wang Hsüan-ts'e on a second mission to Magadha, where he set up a stele.

[170] I.e. the area of Hanoi in northern Vietnam which then was a Chinese possession.

[171] By *Chiu T'ang shu* 198:13a dated 691.

from the Southern Indian State brought gifts (*Ts'e-fu yüan-kuei* p.5027).

In the 1st month (Feb./Mar.) of 720, envoys arrived from the Central Indian State. In the 5th month (June/July), a mission from the king of the Southern Indian State presented a leopard fur and a five-coloured parrot who could talk. He proposed to attack the Arabs with war elephants, infantry, and cavalry. If he hoped for cooperation from the Chinese, he did not receive any. Emperor Hsüan-tsung merely conferred on his army the name of Army Which Cherishes Virtue. The envoys requested belts and robes. They were given brocade robes, gilded leather belts, and wallets for fish tallies (*Chiu T'ang shu* 8:9b; 198:13a; *Ts'e-fu yüan-kuei* p.5027; *Wen-hsien t'ung-k'ao* 338:50b). *Chiu T'ang shu* 198:13a makes the unlikely claim that the Indian king had requested a name for his army. It is more probable that Hsüan-tsung conferred it unilaterally, thereby felt that he had incorporated the Indian army into the Chinese military organization, and thus had done his part against the Arabs.

In the 9th month of the same year 720, the king of Southern India supposedly requested "Attachment to Civilization" as the name for a temple he had built. Emperor Hsüan-tsung granted it (*Chiu T'ang shu* 198:13a). This is a parallel case to the one in Śrivijaya of 1003. The Indian king had no need to request a name from the Chinese emperor. More probably, this was a temple built by a Chinese community in his state which asked for a name and perhaps a contribution via an Indian mission.

In the 11th month (Dec./Jan., 721) of the same Chinese year 720, a mission sent by the king of the Southern Indian State arrived at the T'ang court. Emperor Hsüan-tsung responded with a mission of his own in the same month to recognize the king (*T'ang hui-yao* 100:9b; *Ts'e-fu yüan-kuei* p.5027).

In the 6th month (July) of 729, a Buddhist priest from Northern India presented *chih-han* and other drugs[172] (*Ts'e-fu yüan-kuei* p.5028).

In the 11th month (Dec./Jan.731) of the Chinese year 730, envoys from Central India brought gifts. In the 4th month (May/June) of 737, a Buddhist priest from the Eastern Indian State presented foreign drugs, Pali sutras, and a text on astrology (*Ts'e-fu yüan-kuei* pp.5028, 5029). In the 3rd month (Mar./Apr.) of 741, a son of the king of Central India

[172] Cf. ibid., p.184. Schafer refers to the *chih-han* drug as citragandha.

came to the T'ang court and was appointed to a nominal Chinese office (*Chiu T'ang shu* 198:13a).[173]

After c.760, Indian envoys no longer came (*Wen-hsien t'ung-k'ao* 338: 50b; *Sung shih* 490:1b).[174]

In 953, 16 Buddhist priest and others from Western India presented fine horses to the Later Chou court (*Sung shih* 490:1b; *Wen-hsien t'ung'kao* 338:50b).

In the winter of 975, a son of the king of Eastern India arrived with gifts at the Sung court (*Sung shih* 490:2a; *Wen-hsien t'ung-k'ao* 338: 50b).

Between 984 and 987, a Buddhist priest returned from the Western Region together with a foreign priest and presented to Emperor T'ai-tsung of Sung letters from the king of Northern India and from the king of the Diamond Throne[175]

Wen-hsien t'ung-k'ao 338:50a states that from 713 to 741, Central India sent three missions and Northern India two. The texts actually record six missions from Central India (720, 725, 730, 731, 741) and one from Northern India (729). According to *Chiu T'ang shu* 198:134a, Indian envoys arrived repeatedly from 742 to 756, but no missions are recorded Nevertheless, the information for T'ang is probably fairly complete for the major missions. It can be seen that these came to an abrupt halt after the rebellion of An Lu-shan in 755.

According to *Sung shih* 490:2a and *Wen-hsien t'ung-k'ao* 338:50b, presents from India to the Sung were uninterrupted after the period 968-976, but only one mission is recorded. The information for Sung is therefore incomplete. Buddhist priests arrived, but apparently returned from pilgrimages or had purposes of their own.[176]

---

[173] His name is given as Li Ch'eng-en which is not a transliteration but Chinese. The prince was probably granted the imperial surname (Li) and a Chinese given name.

[174] However, according to *Hsin T'ang shu* 221A:13a, Te-tsung (r.780-785) presented an engraved goblet to the king of Magadha. That could have been in response to a mission.

[175] I.e. Vajrāsana, Buddhgaya. See Hirth and Rockhill, *Chau Ju-kua*, p.114 note 5.

[176] In 965, a Buddhist priest returned via the Western Region and presented a Buddhist relic, rock crystal vessels, and Pali sutras on palm leaves. He had been away for 12 years (*Sung shih* 490:1b).

In 982, a Chinese Buddhist priest arrived from India (*Sung shih* 490:2b). During the same year, a Brahman priest and a Persian heretic arrived in the capital (*Sung shih* 490:3b). Cf. Hirth and Rockhill, *Chau Ju-kua*, pp.112-113 note 1, who propose

It cannot be determined how the missions travelled from India to China. The one in 658 went by ship. That may have been the case with all missions coming from the sourthern part of the subcontinent. But missions from Northern India could well have travelled through the Khyber Pass, across the Pamir Mountains, and then continued on one of the Silk Routes. That was a way well-known to the Buddhist monks.

CHU-LIEN

This country had so far had no relations with China (*Wen-hsien t'ung-k'ao* 332:19a). The first recorded mission of 52 envoys from the king of Chu-lien was received at the Sung court on Oct.17, 1015. They had travelled by sea via Śrivijaya and claimed that the voyage to Canton had taken 1,150 days. The envoys brought a letter and gifts which they spread out in front of the imperial throne. The king's letter supposedly stated that there had been no storms for ten years, which according to an obscure text, called the *Ku lao chuan*, meant that there was a sage in China. Therefore he had sent the envoys.[177] They said through interpreters that they wished to evince the respect of their distant nation for China. The king's offerings were one robe and one cap adorned with real pearls, 21,000 ounces of real pearls, 60 elephant tusks, 60 catties of frankincense, jade, glass, and cotton fabrics. The envoys presented on their own 6,600 ounces of pearls and 3,300 catties of aromatic drugs. They were invited to participate in the festivities of Emperor Chen-tsung's birthday on Jan.14, 1016,

---

that the Brahman and Persian heretic were, in fact, Malabar Christians.

In the 8th month (Aug./Sep.) of 985, a Buddhist priest from India arrived with sacred objects ((*Sung shih* 490:4a).

On Oct.23, 1024, Buddhist priests from Western India presented Pali sutras. Each was given a purple robe and silk (*Sung shih* 490:4b; *Hsü Tzu-chih t'ung-chien ch'ang-pien* p.909).

In the 2nd month (Mar./Apr.) of 1027, a Buddhist priest and others, five men, came with Pali Texts. Each was bestowed a purple robe (*Sung shih* 490:4b; *Wen-hsien t'ung-k'ao* 338:51a).

In 1036, a Buddhist monk and others, nine men, presented to the court Pali sutras, a bone of the Buddha, and the image of a Bodhisatva. They were given silk (*Sung shih* 490:2b).

[177] This is the "memorial" which Ma Tuan-lin admits to have been a Chinese composition. Cf. supra p. 6, note 1.

and then returned with rich gifts. One of the envoys died en route while still in China (*Sung shih* 489:23a; *Hsü Tzu-chih t'ung-chien ch'ang-pien* pp.752; *Wen-hsien t'ung-k'ao* 332:19a).[178]

On Nov.16, 1033, envoys from the king of Chu-lien presented a letter, one robe and one cap adorned with real pearls, 105 ounces of real pearls, and 100 elephant tusks. The envoys stated that they had frequently attempted to come to the court, but that the sea and wind had crushed their ships. In the 2nd month (Feb./Mar.) of 1034, the chief envoy was appointed to a nominal Chinese office (*Sung shih* 489:23b; *Hsü Tzu-chih t'ung-chien ch'ang-pien* p.1012; *Wen-hsien t'ung-k'ao* 332:19b).

On June 26, 1077, a mission of 27 men sent by the king of Chu-lien presented pea-sized pearls, a large wash basin of opaque glass, white plum blossom camphor, cotton, rhinoceros horns,[179] frankincense, rose water, golden lotus flowers, putchuck, asafoetida,[180] borax,[181] and cloves. The envoys knelt in the throne hall and spread out their offerings. The chief envoy was appointed to a nominal Chinese office. All received garments, [porcelain] vessels, and silk, each in accordance with his rank. The king was paid 81,800 copper cash and 52,000 ounces of stringed silver coins (*Sung shih* 15:19a; 489:23b-24a; *Wen-hsien t'ung-k'ao* 332:19b).

WU-CH'A or WU-CH'ANG or WU-TU

This country had so far had no relations with China (*Ts'e-fu yüan-kuei* p.5024). The first recorded mission was in 642 to the T'ang court, when the king 's envoys presented baroos camphor. Emperor T'ai-tsung responded with a letter stamped with the imperial seal (*Hsin T'ang shu* 221A:13a; *T'ung-tien* 188:72a; *Wen-hsien t'ung-k'ao* 332:16a; 338:51b).

On Jan.30, 648, envoys offered gifts (*Ts'e-fu yüan-kuei* p.5025).

In the 4th month (May/June) of 720, Emperor Hsüan-tsung recog-

---

[178] According to Chao Ju-kua, the envoys were given a banqet by the Audience Ushers, the protocol being equal to that for Chiao-chih, and subsequently invited to the court congratulations on the emperor's birthday. See Hirth and Rockhill, *Chau Ju-kua*, p.96.

[179] Correcting the "teeth" of the texts to "horns".

[180] The gum resin of certain oriental plants used in medicine.

[181] A mineral used for glass manifacture, as a flux, cleansing agent, etc.

nized the king (*Hsin T'ang shu* 221A:13a; *T'ang hui-yao* 99:23b).

NA-CHIEH

In 646, envoys from Na-chieh to the T'ang court offered regional objects (*Hsin T'ang shu* 221A:13a; *Wen-hsien t'ung-k'ao* 338:51b).

NEPAL

In 647, envoys from Nepal to the T'ang court presented spinach and onions (*T'ang hui-yao* 100:11b).

In 650 and 651, envoys from the king of Nepal to the T'ang court offered gifts (*Chiu T'ang shu* 198:1b; *T'ung-tien* 190:9b; *Wen-hsien t'ung-k'ao* 335:34b).

TS'ENG-T'AN

The first recorded mission from Ts'eng-t'an was to the Sung court in 1071. It had travelled by sea to Canton via Śrivijaya, and the voyage had taken 160 days. The envoys stated that the name of their king was A-mei-lo A-mei-lan.[182] He was the tenth ruler of his dynasty, which had lasted for 500 years. The language of the people resembled Arabic. Springs and winters were warm. Important people rode elephants and horses. Of cereals, they had rice, millet, and wheat. Of animals, they had sheep, goats, buffalos, water buffalos, camels, horses, rhinoceroses, and elephants. In commercial transactions, they used coins made by the government. Private coining was forbidden (*Sung shih* 490:21b; *Wen-hsien t'ung-k'ao* 332:20a).

In 1083, the envoy Ts'eng-chia-ni arrived a second time.[183] In consideration of the very great distance he had come, Emperor Shen-tsung gave him the same presents which he had received at the previous occasion, with an additional 2000 ounces of silver (*Sung shih* 490:22a; *Wen-hsien t'ung-k'ao* 332:20a).

---

[182] Hirth and Rockhill, *Chau Ju-kua*, p.127 note 4 read this as the Persian Amir-i-amirân.

[183] He is referred to as the Gentleman Who Maintains Obedience, which title he must have received as one of the envoys in 1071.

The total number of datable missions from the countries of continental South Asia and the islands to Sui, T'ang, Later Chou, and the Sung dynasties between 589 and 1276 was 338. The following table shows them by 20-year periods:

587- 606:	5
607- 626:	11
627- 646:	31
647- 666:	23
667- 686:	15
687- 706:	14
707- 726:	21
727- 746:	11
747- 766:	7
767- 786:	4
787- 806:	4
807- 826:	4
827- 846:	2
847- 866:	1
867- 886:	1
887- 906:	1
907- 926:	0
927- 946:	0
947- 966:	7
967- 986:	34
987-1006:	3
1007-1026:	33
1027-1046:	15
1047-1066:	12
1067-1086:	21
1087-1106:	11
1107-1126:	7
1127-1146:	5
1147-1166:	12
1167-1186:	10
1187-1206:	6
1207-1226:	0
1227-1246:	2

1247-1266:	3
1267-1276:[184]	2

It can be seen that the early T'ang was a truly international period, with the largest numbers of missions arriving during the reigns of Emperor T'ai-tsung (627-649) and his successors until the end of the reign of Hsüan-tsung (712-756). Then the missions fell off sharply. After a hiatus for most of the Five Dynasties, government trade revived forcefully during the Northern Sung and flourished even more than in the early T'ang. But after the establishment of the Southern Sung in 1127, the missions again became fewer and fewer. A little over 1/6 of all missions to the T'ang arrived after 755, and only a little over 1/4 of all missions to the Sung arrived after 1127. And yet, in both dynasties the periods before and after 755 and before and after 1127 respectively were of roughly equal length.

In the case of the T'ang, the decrease was due to the rebellion of An Lu-shan in 755 and its aftermath. This decrease was surely not the wish of the court. But the central government was weakened, the emperors became figureheads, power shifted to the regional commanders, and communications within China became probably less safe. Under the circumstances, the foreign countries would have concluded that missions were not worth the investment.

In the case of the Southern Sung, the decrease after 1127 is particularly striking, since Lin-an, the capital of Southern Sung , was situated near Hang-chou Bay and therefore, in contrast to the Northern Sung capital of K'ai-feng, easily accessible by ship. Also, northern China had been lost and an opening toward South Asia and the islands should have been advantageous. Why then the drastic reduction of trade, not only on the government level but on the private one as well?

This has been blamed i.a. on the gradual decline of Śrivijaya and on the disruptions caused by the crusades. If that were true, a country like Chiao-chih/Annam should not have been affected. Foreign goods brought to the Sung court from the spice islands and further west came in larger volume via Champa than Chiao-chih, and events in the Middle East and Sumatra were of little consequence to the latter. Chiao-chih relied for its foreign trade chiefly on its own products, especially elephant tusks, which were in high demand in China. Yet, as

[184] 10-year period.

has been seen, the missions from Chiao-chih declined from 58 before 1127 to 23 after that date. The reason for that decline must therefore be sought in Southern Sung and not abroad.

I consequently agree with the view that it was the Chinese themselves who curtailed foreign trade. They may not have wished to be distracted from the urgent need to defend themselves militarily and diplomatically against first the Jurchen and then the Mongols in the north. But a stronger reason must have been the pervasive hostility of Neo-Confucianism toward foreigners and foreign trade. This xenophobia led to an isolationism which cut China off from foreign goods, ideas, and technology, and did not serve it well.

In conclusion, it has been seen that almost the only motif for the foreign relations discussed in this chapter was trade. Sung and Champa had an additional interest in curbing the aggressive tendencies of Chiao-chih, and in 1076 Sung invited the Khmer Kingdom to join in that endeavor. Some missions to and from Chiao-chih and China served the purpose of improving relations. There was an occasional exchange of sacred and secular books. But otherwise, all dealings between China and the countries of South Asia and the islands were commercial.

Let us now arrange the foreign goods brought to China from these countries[185] under categories similar to those of Schafer in his splendid book on *The Golden Peaches of Samarkand*.[186]

Humans

627-649: 2 white-headed men from Fu-nan.
724: 2 pygmies, 1 or 2 black girls, and musicians from Śrivijaya.
802: 35 musicians with songs of their national music from P'iao.
815: 5 black youths from K'o-ling.
818: 2 black girls from K'o-ling.
860-874: female musicians from K'o-ling.
1011: 1 black slave from Pagan (rejected).

---

[185] This includes all goods, whether brought by the envoys on behalf of their rulers or for their own profit.

[186] Occasionally, Schafer has entries for which I cannot find the source. On the other hand, since Schafer did not intend to be exhaustive, my listings have numerous entries ignored by him.

Animals and Animal Products

Elephants

630: one elephant from Lin-yi.
651: one elephant from Chen-la.
653: one elephant from Lin-yi.
654: one elephant from Lin-yi.
657: one elephant from Chan-po.
686: one elephant from Lin-yi.
691: one elephant from Lin-yi.
695: one war elephant from Lin-yi.
699: one elephant from Lin-yi.
707: one elephant from Lin-yi.
709: one white elephant from Lin-yi.
713: 5 elephants from Lin-yi.
731: 4 elephants from Lin-yi.
735: one elephant and one white elephant from Lin-yi.
750: one elephant from Wet Chen-la.
771: 11 elephants from Dry Chen-la.
966: one elephant from Champa.
970: one elephant from Champa.
983: one elephant from Champa.
998: 2 elephants from Chiao-chih.
1001: one elephant from Chiao-chih.
1034: 2 elephants from Chiao-chih (rejected).
1042: 3 elephants from Champa.
1043: 5 elephants from Chiao-chih.
1046: 11 elephants from Chiao-chih.
1055: 10 elephants from Chiao-chih.
1061: one elephant from Champa.
1063: 9 elephants from Chiao-chih.
1078: one elephant from Champa.
1082: 2 elephants from Chiao-chih.
1139: one elephant from Chiao-chih.
1146: 10 elephants from Chiao-chih.
1150: 10 elephants from Chiao-chih.
1155: one elephant from Lo-hu.
1156: 9 elephants from Chiao-chih.
1200: 2 elephants from the Khmer Kingdom.

1201: 2 elephants from Chen-li-fu.
1205: one elephant from Chen-li-fu.
1261: 2 elephants from Chiao-chih.

Elephant tusks

627-649: elephant tusks from T'ou-ho.
647: elephant tusks from To-p'o-teng.
649: elephant tusks from To-ho-lo.
748: elephant tusks from Lin-yi.
750: elephant tusks from Lin-yi and Shih-tzu.
960: elephant tusks from Champa.
961: elephant tusks from Champa.
962: 22 elephant tusks from Champa.
966: elephant tusks from Champa.
974: elephant tusks from Śrivijaya.
975: elephant tusks from Chiao-chih.
985: elephant tusks from Champa.
986: 2 elephant tusks from Champa.
990: 40 elephant tusks from Chiao-chih, more than 15 from Champa.
992: 10 elephant tusks from She-p'o.
993: more than 20 elephant tusks from Champa.
997: 30 elephant tusks from Champa, elephant tusks from Chiao-chih.
998: 27 elephant tusks from Chiao-chih.
999: elephant tusks from Champa.
1001: 61 elephant tusks from Chou-mei-liu.
1009: 40 elephant tusks from Chiao-chih.
1011: elephant tusks from Wu-hsün and San-ma-lan, 62 from Champa.
1015: elephant tusks from Champa, 60 from Chu-lien.
1017: elephant tusks from Śrivijaya.
1018: 72 elephant tusks from Champa.
1019: elephant tusks from Chiao-chih.
1029: 70 elephant tusks from Champa.
1030: 80 elephant tusks from Champa.
1033: 100 elephant tusks from Chu-lien.
1050: 201 elephant tusks from Champa.
1082: 50 elephant tusks from Chiao-chih.
1155: 168 elephant tusks from Champa.

1164: 30 elephant tusks from Chiao-chih.
1200: 20 elephant tusks from the Khmer Kingdom.
1205: 2 elephant tusks from Chen-li-fu.

Rhinoceroses

c.627: one rhinoceros from Lin-yi.
657: one rhinoceros from Chan-po.
703: one rhinoceros from Lin-yi.
793: one rhinoceros from Lin-yi.
796: one rhinoceros from Lin-yi.
818: one rhinoceros from K'o-ling.
966: one rhinoceros from Champa.
990: one rhinoceros from Champa.
998: one rhinoceros from Chiao-chih.
1001: one rhinoceros from Chiao-chih.
1009: one rhinoceros from Chiao-chih (released).

Rhinoceros horns

627-649: rhinoceros horns from T'ou-ho.
640: 10 rhinoceros horns from Lin-yi.
960: rhinoceros horns from Champa.
961: rhinoceros horns from Champa.
966: rhinoceros horns from Champa.
975: rhinoceros horns from Chiao-chih.
983: rhinoceros horns from Śrivijaya.
986: 2 rhinoceros horns from Champa.
990: more than 10 rhinoceros horns from Champa.
992: rhinoceros horns from She-p'o.
993: more than 10 rhinoceros horns from Champa.
997: 10 rhinoceros horns from Champa, rhinoceros horns from Chiao-chih.
999: rhinoceros horns from Champa.
1009: 20 rhinoceros horns from Chiao-chih.
1011: 40 rhinoceros horns from Champa.
1012: 30 rhinoceros horns from Chiao-chih.
1018: 86 rhinoceros horns from Champa.
1019: rhinoceros horns from Chiao-chih.
1029: 30 rhinoceros horns from Champa.
1030: more than 40 rhinoceros horns from Champa.

1050: 79 rhinoceros horns from Champa.
1077: rhinoceros horns from Chu-lien.
1082: 50 rhinoceros horns from Chiao-chih.
1155: 20 rhinoceros horns from Champa.
1200: 50 rhinoceros horns from the Khmer Kingdom.
1205: 10 rhinoceros horns from Chen-li-fu.

Felines and feline products

720: one leopard fur from the Southern Indian State.
1011: one lion from Champa.

Strange animals

1058: one or two strange animals from Chiao-chih, claimed to be *ch'i-lins*.

Horses

953: fine horses from the Western Indian State.
1014: 60 horses from Chiao-chih.
1156: 10 horses from Chiao-chih.

Birds and feathers

631: one five-coloured parrot and one cockatoo from Lin-yi.
647: one rose-crested cockatoo from T'o-huan.
720: one five-coloured parrot from the Southern Indian State.
650-656: one five-coloured parrot from Ko-lo-she.
724: one five-coloured parrot from Śrivijaya.
727: one five-coloured parrot from Śrivijaya.
815: one five-coloured parrot, cockatoos, and one *p'in-chia* bird from K'o-ling.
961: 4 peacocks from Champa.
992: 7 white cockatoos from She-p'o.
1003: one red cockatoo from Pagan.
1011: one red cockatoo from Pagan.
Before1020: one red cockatoo from Champa.
1029: one live "phoenix" from Champa.
1155: 360 kingfisher's feathers from Champa.

Tortoise shells:

818: from K'o-ling.
966: from Champa.
977: from Po-ni.
985: from Champa.
992: 67 catties of large shells from She-p'o.
993: from Champa.
997: 10 catties from Champa.
999: from Champa.
1007: from Pagan.
1011: 300 catties from Champa.
1015: from Champa.
1018: 1000 catties from Champa.
1029: 245 catties from Champa.
1030: more than 400 catties from Champa.
1155, 60 catties from Champa.

Aromatics

The Chinese made no clear distinction between drugs, incenses, perfumes, cosmetics etc.[187] It means that this section brings together a somewhat heterogeneous collection of items. For instance, sandalwood was a fragrant wood but also used for carving. Camphor was used a a medicinal agent but also as an insect repellent.

Aromatic and medical drugs, aromatic oils

607: aromatic oils and other fragrant fluids from Ch'ih-t'u.
647: *p'o-lü* ointment from T'o-huan.
729: *chih-han* drug from the Northern Indian State.
737: foreign drugs from the Eastern Indian State.
815: rare aromatics from K'o-ling.
958: long-lasting aromatics from Champa.
961: aromatic drugs from Champa.
966: 70 catties of aromatics from Champa.

---

[187] Cf. Schafer, *Golden Peaches*, p.155.

975: aromatic drugs from Chiao-chih.
977: 1,025 catties of aromatic drugs from Champa.
983: aromatic drugs from Śrivijaya.
990: 1 catty of aromatics from Champa.
993: 36 catties of aromatics from Champa.
999: aromatic drugs from Champa.
1011: aromatics from Wu-hsün.
1011: aromatics from San-ma-lan.
1011: 590 catties of aromatics and 80 catties of myrrh from Champa.
1015: 3,300 ounces of aromatic drugs from Chu-lien.
1022: aromatics from Chiao-chih.
1028: fragrant drugs from Chiao-chih.
1077: asafoetida from Chu-lien.
1078: *p'o-lü* ointment and aromatics from Śrivijaya.

Frankincense

962: 1000 catties of frankincense from Champa.
966: 30 catties of frankincense from Champa.
974: frankincense from Śrivijaya.
1015: frankincense from Champa.
1015: 60 catties of frankincense from Chu-lien.
1018: 50 catties of frankincense from Champa.
1029: 2000 catties of frankincense from Champa.
1030: 2000 catties of frankincense from Champa.
1072: frankincense from Champa.
1077: frankincense from Chu-lien.

Rose water

958: 15 bottles of rose water from Champa.
974: rose water from Śrivijaya.
990: rose water from Champa.
1011: rose water from San-ma-lan.
1077: rose water from Chu-lien.

Fragrant woods

647: white sandalwood from To-p'o-teng.
734: gharu wood from Lin-yi.
749: 30 catties of black gharu wood from Lin-yi.
992: 4,423 catties of sandalwood from She-p'o.

966: 100 catties of sandalwood from Champa.
986: 330 catties of gharu wood from Champa.
997: 190 catties of gharu wood and 100 catties of sandalwood from Champa.
1011: schisandra chinensis from San-ma-lan.
1011: 50 catties of gharu wood from Champa.
1018: 368 catties of gharu wood from Champa.
1155: 4,230 catties of gharu wood from Champa.
1156: 1000 catties of gharu wood from Chiao-chih.
1164: 1,500 catties of gharu wood from Chiao-chih.

Camphor

607: baroos camphor from Ch'ih-t'u.
642: baroos camphor from Wu-ch'a.
961: camphor from Champa.
966: 30 ounces of white baroos camphor and 2 catties of green baroos camphor from Champa.
977: 2 catties of baroos camphor from Champa.
977: large-sliced baroos camphor and green dragon camphor from Po-ni.
985: baroos camphor from Champa.
986: 10 catties of baroos camphor and 10 catties of white baroos camphor from Champa.
990: 2 catties of white baroos camphor from Champa.
992: 5 catties of white baroos camphor from She-p'o.
993: 1 catty of white baroos camphor from Champa.
997: 2 catties of baroos camphor from Champa.
1007: baroos camphor from Pagan.
1011: white baroos camphor from Pagan.
1011: 30 ounces of camphor from Champa.
1072: baroos camphor from Champa.
1077: white plum blossom camphor from Chu-lien.
1082: baroos camphor from Śrivijaya.
1088: baroos camphor from Śrivijaya.

Cosmetics

647: curcoma longa from Maghada.
966: 50 catties of cosmetics from Champa.
1001: 1000 catties of putchuck from Chou-mei-liu.

1029: 789 catties of putchuck from Champa.
1030: 700 catties of putchuck from Champa.
1077: putchuck from Chu-lien.

Spices

966: 20,000 cardamoms from Champa.
977: 50 catties of cloves from Champa.
986: 50 catties of cloves from Champa.
990: cardamoms from Champa.
992: 10 catties of cloves from She-p'o.
997: 200 catties of pepper from Champa.
1007: cloves from Pagan.
1011: cloves from Pagan.
1011: 60 catties of cardamom, 200 catties of nutmeg, and 200 catties of pepper from Champa.
1015: cardamoms from Champa.
1018: 80 catties of cloves, 65 catties of cardamom, and 100 catties of fennel from Champa.
1022: cassia bark from Chiao-chih.
1072: cloves and cubebs from Champa.
1077: cloves from Chu-lien.

Trees, Plants, and Fruits

647: [seeds of] a Bodhi tree, a jackfruit tree, and a white poplar from Magadha.
966: 50 catties of betel nuts from Champa.
974: dates from Śrivijaya.
993: 12 catties of betel nuts and 50 coconuts from Champa.
1001: 35 catties of stems of coptis teeta, 100 catties of lithospermus officiniale, 10,000 catties of sapan wood from Chou-mei-liu.
1011: dates from San-ma-lan.
1015: betel nuts from Champa.
1018: 1,500 catties of betel nuts from Champa.

Minerals, Ores, Metals, and Naphta

958: naphta from Champa.

966: 50 catties of purple ore from Champa.
971: crystal and naphta from Chou-mei-liu.
985: limonite from Champa.
1001: 100 catties of white copper and 100 catties of hard tin from Chou-mei-liu.
1011: 470 catties of purple ore from Champa.
1022: pewter and red ore from Chiao-chih.
1072: purple ore from Champa.
1077: borax from Chu-lien.
1078: silver from Śrivijaya.
1139: 50 ounces of gold from Chiao-chih.

Manufactured Objects

Of metal

607: golden chains, 8 golden pitchers, ornaments, and golden hibiscus hats from Ch'ih-t'u.
627-649: vases and golden tablets from T'ou-ho.
630: gilded objects from Lin-yi.
649: golden flowers from K'o-ling.
746: necklaces of fine gold from Shih-tzu.
992: gilded objects and 12 swords adorned with gold and silver from She-p'o.
993: golden bells, copper incense braziers, and Buddhist sceptres from Champa.
997: 10 silver vessels from Chiao-chih.
998: one golden pitcher from Chiao-chih.
1009: gold and silver vessels from Chiao-chih.
1077: golden flowers from Chu-lien.
1082: golden lotus flowers from Śrivijaya.
1088: golden lotus flowers from Śrivijaya.
1156: 1,136 ounces of gold vessels from Chiao-chih.
1164: 150 ounces of silver vessels and 100 ounces of gold vessels from Chiao-chih.

Of crystal

983: one rock crystal Buddha from Śrivijaya.

Of glass

630: one fire pearl (burning-lens) from Lin-yi.
647: one fire pearl from Magadha.
958: 84 opaque glass pitchers from Champa.
974: opaque glass pitchers from Śrivijaya.
1011: opaque glass vessels from San-ma-lan.
1015: glass from Chu-lien.
1072: opaque glass from Champa.
1077: one large wash basin of opaque glass from Chu-lien.

Of leather or feathers

627-649: valuable belts from T'ou-ho.
959: one belt of rhinoceros hide from Champa.
974: 2 peacock parasols from Champa.
1087: leggings of rhinoceros hide from Champa.

Other

961: 20 great food vessels from Champa.
966: 4 mats from Champa.
992: 2 betel nut trays, 60 bamboo mats with woven patterns, and valuable ornaments from She-p'o.
997: 5 bamboo mats from Champa.
1022: pitchers from Chiao-chih
1072: wine vessels from Champa.
1155: 10 oil lamps from Champa.

Textiles

Cottons

607: 4 lengths of white cotton from Ch'ih-t'u.
647: cotton fabrics from To-p'o-teng.
748: fancy cotton fabrics from Lin-yi.
749: white cotton fabrics from Lin-yi.
750: white fancy cotton fabrics from Lin-yi.
764: 40 sheets of fine cotton fabrics from Shih-tzu.
966: 20 lengths of white cotton fabrics and *yüeh-no* cloth from Champa.

977: 2 pieces of *yüeh-no* cloth from Champa.
983: cotton fabrics from Śrivijaya.
985: *yüeh-no* cloth from Champa.
993: 6 pieces of cotton fabrics from Champa.
1001: 4 pieces of fancy cotton fabrics from Chou-mei-liu.
1015: cotton fabrics from Chu-lien.
1077: cotton fabrics from Chu-lien.
1200: 40 lengths of cotton fabrics from the Khmer Kingdom.
1201: 11 pieces of cotton fabrics and 2 pieces of large cotton fabrics from Chen-li-fu.

Silks

990: 10,000 bolts of silken fabrics from Chiao-chih.
1156: 50 bolts of pongee from Chiao-chih.

Other

992: 100 pieces of various textiles from She-p'o.

Garments

630: court garments from Lin-yi.
958: embroidered robes from Champa.
966: sarongs from Champa.
1001: one red felt from Chou-mei-liu.
1015: one robe and cap ornamented with pearls from Chu-lien.
1033: one robe and cap ornamented with pearls from Chu-lien.

Jewels

649: pearls from To-ho-lo.
715: amber from Lin-yi.
746: pearls from Shih-tzu.
749: 100 pearls from Lin-yi.
750: pearls from Lin-yi.
750: pearls from Shih-tzu.
959: one *p'u-sa* stone from Champa.
974: finger rings of rock crystal and coral trees from Śrivijaya.
992: 2 catties of pearls from She-p'o.
1015: 27,600 catties of pearls and jade from Chu-lien.
1017: pearls from Śrivijaya.

1033: 105 ounces of pearls from Chu-lien.
1078: pearls from Śrivijaya.
1072: coral from Champa.
1077: pearls from Chu-lien.
1082: pearls from Śrivijaya.
1088: pearls from Śrivijaya.
1156: 100 pearls from Chiao-chih.

Sweets

974: white granulated sugar from Śrivijaya.
1011: white pebble sweets from San-ma-lan.

Texts

737: Pali sutras and a work on astrology from the Eastern Indian State.
746: Buddhist texts from Shih-tzu.
1017: Buddhist sutras from Śrivijaya.

Fu-nan had presented musicians to the Wu State of the Six Dynasties.[189] in 243. But that was an isolated case, the interest in foreign music being much greater during T'ang. The blacks were, of course, curiosities to the Chinese.

Elephants had been rare gifts during the Six Dynasties, and rhinoceroses even more so. Lin-yi had presented one elephant to the Eastern Chin in 340 and another in 417, Fu-nan one elephant in 357 to the same dynasty. P'an-p'an had offered one elephant to the Liang in 551. Fu-nan presented one rhinoceros to the Liang in 539.[190] This adds up to only four elephants and one rhinoceros to the southern courts of the Six Dynasties.

In contrast, no less than 122 elephants are recorded to have been presented to the T'ang and Sung between 618 and 1276. These are the offering countries arranged in numerical sequence:

Chiao-chih 74 elephants

---

[189] See my *Six Dynasties*, vol.II, p.83.
[190] See my *Six Dynasties*, vol.II, p.83.

Lin-yi	20
Chen-la[191]	15
Champa	8
Chen-li-fu	3
Chan-po	1
Lo-hu	1

Northern and southern Vietnam were the chief providers. Chiao-chih in the north shows the highest number with 74. Lin-yi and its successor state Champa in the south come second with a combined total of 28. Chiao-chih was closest to China and had a land border with it. The elephants could therefore have been brought by land, although sea transport to the Yangtze is not out of the question. The animals from all other states must have ben brought by sea, which was no mean shipping achievement.

It can be seen that the T'ang and even more so the Sung courts were awash with elephants. Some attempts were made to reduce their numbers. When Emperor Te-tsung of T'ang had ascended the throne on June 12, 779, he set free precious birds and rare beasts. 32 elephants from the imperial parks were released on the north side of the Ching Mountain (*Chiu T'ang shu* 11:19a-19b; *Wen-hsien t'ung-k'ao* 332:14a). This was probably in the wild area between the lower Han River and the Yangtze. The lifetime of an elephant is from 45 to 60 years, and according to the above table no 32 gift elephants existed in China in 779. Either the texts omit the presentation of some elephants, or, more probably, the elephants reproduced in the imperial parks. It has been seen that in 970, and surely at other times as well, female elephants had been among those offered. In 1034, two elephants from Chiao-chih were rejected by the Sung. In 1182, a Southern Sung edict stated that the elephants presented by Annam (Chiao-chih) were useless and a trouble for the people. They should no longer be accepted (*Sung shih* 488:18a; *Wen-hsien t'ung-k'ao* 330:6b). However, they kept coming.

For the T'ang, the sources do not record the number of elephant tusks offered. For the Sung, they more often do so than not. Where figures are given, they add up to 1,182 tusks, which is, of course, well below the real number. The offering countries in numerical sequence

[191] Chen-la (1), Dry Chen-la (11), Wet Chen-la (1) and the Khmer Kingdom (2).

were:

Champa	742
Chiao-chih	187
Chu-lien	160
Chou-mei-liu	61
Khmer Kingdom	20
She-p'o	10
Chen-li-fu	2

Northern and southern Vietnam were again the chief providers. But this time, Champa is well ahead of Chiao-chih. Because of the longer distance, it preferred to ship ivory rather than live elephants, while Chiao-chih took the opposite approach.

The total figure of 1,182 tusks does not necessarily mean that 591 elephants were killed for the Chinese market, since the tusks could be sawed off from live animals.

The rhinoceros was then as now a rarer animal than the elephant, and apparently highly appeciated by the Chinese. Of the 11 animals offered during T'ang and Sung, only one was released in 1009, and that was not out of pity but because of its bad temper. The countries presenting live rhinoceroses were in numerical sequence:

Lin-yi	4
Chiao-chih	3
Champa	2
Chan-po	1
K'o-ling	1

Chiao-chih in northern Vietnam and Lin-yi and its successor state Champa in southern Vietnam provided nine. One was brought alive from K'o-ling in probably far-away Java.

Rhinoceros horns were in great demand for Chinese medicine because they were believed to be aphrodisiacs and also a cure for illnesses. Where figures are given, they add up to 497 horns presented to the T'ang and Sung, which again is below the real number. The countries offering them were in numerical sequence:

Champa	327
Chiao-chih	100
Khmer Kingdom	50
Lin-yi	10
Chen-li-fu	10

Champa and Chiao-chih in Vietnam are once more the chief providers. To obtain the horns, the animals had to be killed, which adds up to a sizable population of rhinoceroses destroyed for a superstition.

During T'ang, China received 22 elephants before the rebellion of An Lu-shan in 755 and 11 thereafter. The figures for Northern and Southern Sung are 50 and 38 respectively. 6 rhinoceroses were offered to the T'ang, 3 before and 3 after the rebellion of An Lu-shan. All 5 rhinoceroses presented to China thereafter were brought during Northern Sung.

Rare birds were rated higly by the Chinese courts. During the Six Dynasties, red and white cockatoos had been presented by Lin-yi to the Eastern Chin in 417, by the Indian Chia-p'i-li State to the Liu Sung in 428, by Ho-lo-tan to the Liu Sung in 430, by P'o-huang to the Liu Sung in 459, and by P'o-li to the Liang in 522.[192] More than 24 were brought to China from 631 to 1029.

As to the other items listed above, some were luxuries or curiosities intended to please the emperor and his court, or medicines to cure ills. But most were commercial goods pure and simple, and not necessarily from the countries presenting them. In most cases, it is useless to add up the numbers and weights, as these are not systematically given. It can be seen, however, that they would have come to respectable figures. For instance, the noted weight of frankincense, recorded for 6 deliveries out of 10 is 5,140 catties = 3,067.6 kilograms or 6,748.3 pounds. If the price of frankincense at that time was anywhere near its present level, that amount represented a fortune.

The Chinese paid for these goods chiefly with gold, silver, silver coins, copper cash, silk, brocade, garments, caps, belts ornamented with gold, silver or jade, gold and silver vessels and objects, copper vessels, porcelain vessels, lacquered vessels, horses, horse trappings, tea, armour, precious swords, lances, bows, arrows and other military implements, banners, and Buddhist and Taoist texts.

Sung shih 186:19b lists goods exchanged between Sung China and the Arabs, Champa, Śrivijaya, She-p'o, Po-ni, Mo-yi etc. These are gold, silver, copper cash, lead, tin, piece goods of various colours, por-

---

192 See my *Six Dynasties*, vol.II, pp.83-84.

celain vessels, aromatics, rhinoceros horns, elephant tusks, coral, amber, pearls, steel, tortoise shells, carnelian, *chü-chü*,[193] rock crystal, foreign cottons, ebony, sapan wood etc. This list mingles together imports and exports and refers to trade in general. It is interesting, however, that with the exception of lead, steel, *chü-chü*, and ebony, all items also were part of the goods exchanged on the government level.

Garments, caps, and belts were frequent Chinese exchange gifts. The starchy Confucianists took the view that the only right way to dress was the Chinese way. The court therefore did the foreigners a service by providing them with the right apparel.

Information on the rate of exchange is scant, only two previously quoted instances being recorded for the entire period. But judging from its 19% profit in 1022 and 31% profit in 1028, Chiao-chih did well in its government trade with Sung.

---

[193] According to Hirth and Rockhill, *Chau Ju-kua*, p.19 note 3, probably a large white shell of the cockle kind.

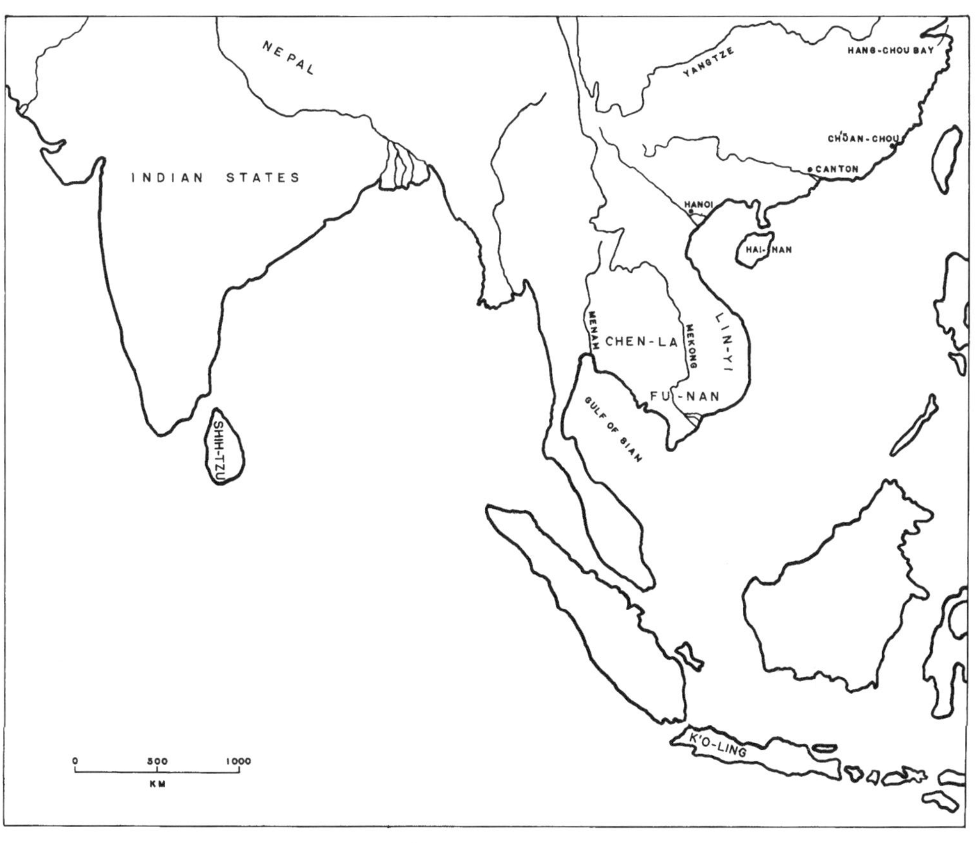

Map 1. Continental South Asia and the Islands in the Chinese sources, 7th century.

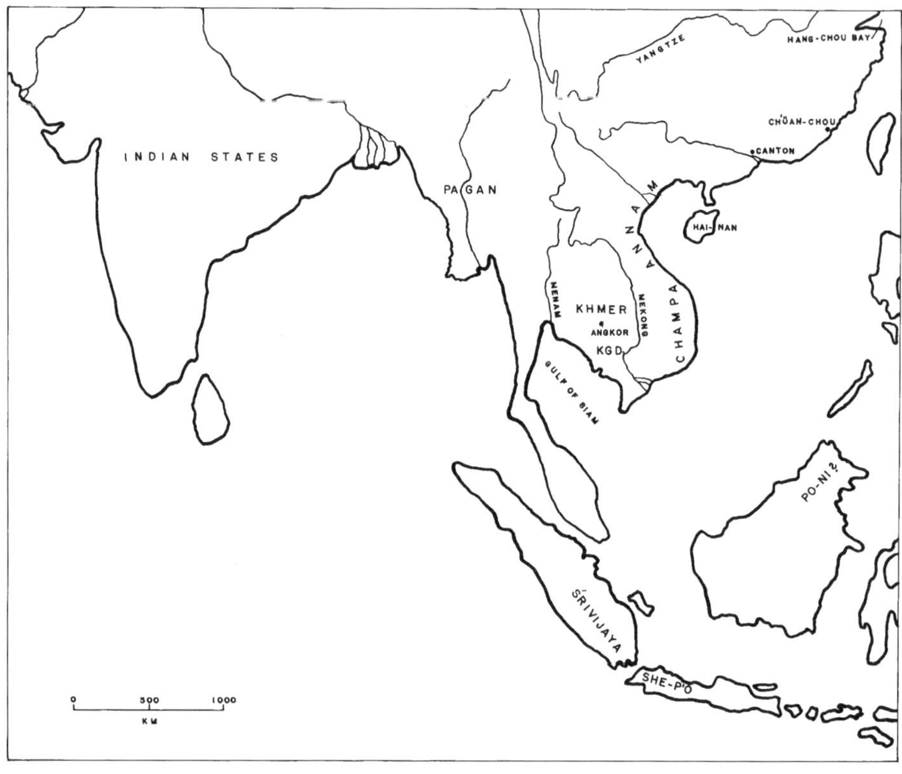

Map 2. Continental South Asia and the Islands in the Chinese sources, 11th century.

JAPAN

During the first centuries of their mutual acquaintance, the Chinese referred to Japan as the *Wo kuo* or "Country of the Dwarfs" and to its inhabitants as the "Dwarf Slaves". Only from 702 do the Chinese sources adopt the name of Jih-pen (Nippon). According to *T'ang hui-yao* 99:13a, the Japanese had requested this change of name themselves. The Chinese historians did not at first realize that Wo and Jih-pen were the same country, because *Chiu T'ang shu* 199A:14a has consecutive entries for them and states that the Jih-pen were a separate tribe of the Wo.

Trade between the Japanese and Chinese had been lively as early as Former Han times, but no official missions are recorded. The first mission from the "king of the Wo slaves" is recorded for A.D.57. The next mission arrived in 107, presenting 160 slaves.[1] During the Six Dynasties, Japan sent ten missions to Eastern Chin and Liu Sung from 413 to 478.[2] The Chinese sources throughout refer to the Japanese emperor as king.

In 600, envoys from the "king" of the Wo State arrived at the Sui court.[3] The letter they brought addressed the Chinese emperor as "my younger brother". Emperor Wen ordered the responsible authorities to question the envoys about their customs. They stated that their king considered Heaven as his elder brother and the sun as his younger brother. Emperor Wen remarked: "This is utterly improper". He had the envoys admonished and "ordered" them to change the terminology (*Sui shu* 81:13b; *Wen-hsien t'ung-k'ao* 324:46a). This naturally had no effect.

In 607, envoys from the "king" of the Wo State led by Ono-no-Imoko again brought gifts to the Sui court. The envoys were received on Apr.9, 608. They supposedly stated that they had been sent because China was ruled by a Son of Heaven who was a Bodhisattva uphold-

---

1 See my *Restoration*, vol.III, pp. 145, 148.

2 See my *Six Dynasties*, vol.II, pp.91-92. The entry for "460, 12th month" is there inadvertently given twice.

3 This mission is not mentioned in the Japanese accounts. For Chinese-Japanese relations see Tsunoda and Goodrich, *Japan in the Chinese Dynastic Histories*, pp.31-82.

ing the dharma. Several tens of monks accompanied this mission to study Buddhism in China. The letter addressed to the Chinese ruler said: "The Son of Heaven of the place where the sun rises sends this letter to the Son of Heaven of the Place where the sun sets. May you have no illness". Emperor Yang was displeased and said to the Herald: "The letter of the barbarian is impolite". He ordered that such a letter should not again be presented to him (*Sui shu* 3:11b; 81:15a; *Pei shih* 12:11a-11b; 94:28a-28b; *T'ung-tien* 185:56a).

The letters of 600 and 607, presumably written at the behest of Prince Shōtoku, are of unusual interest. They obviously are originals, composed at the Japanese court, and not translated and suitably rephrased at the Chinese court, and they allow us to see how a self-conscious foreign ruler or his deputy addressed his Chinese counterpart. It can also be seen that the Herald, the official in charge of envoys, read the letter before submitting it to the emperor, since he otherwise could not withhold one which was deemed to be improper. The flattering comparison of Emperor Yang to a Bodhisattva, on the other hand, is no doubt a sino-centric embroidery of the interview with the envoys.

When Ono-no-Imoko returned to Japan in 608, Emperor Yang, sent with him the Gentleman of the Forest of Literature P'ei Ch'ing as Chinese envoy. They sailed via Paekche. On arrival in Japan, Ch'ing was welcomed by several 100 men with drums and horns. He was conveyed to the palace by 200 horsemen and received in audience by the "king". According to Ch'ing's report to Emperor Yang, the "king" was greatly pleased and said:"I have heard that to the west of the sea there is the Great Sui, a country of propriety and righteousness. Therefore, I have sent [envoys] to pay court and tribute. We are barbarians and live secluded at a cove of the sea, and we have not learned about propriety and righteousness. Therefore, we have been kept within our borders and have not been able to call on you..." Ch'ing said in his response:"The virtue of our emperor combines Heaven and Earth, and his kindness overflows the Four Seas. Because of Your Majesty's desire for civilization, [the emperor] has sent an envoy to come here." Subsequently, Ch'ing was given a banquet. The "king" then sent envoys to follow Ch'ing back to China and present regional objects (*Sui shu* 3:11b; 81:15a-15b; *T'ung-tien* 185:56a). P'ei Ch'ing's report cannot have any basis in facts. If by "king" he meant Shōtoku, it is perfectly possible that the latter expressed a wish that the Japanese should learn from China, but certainly not in the terms used by the envoy. Ch'ing gave a sino-centric report on his return, and did not miss the opportunity to flatter Emperor Yang. It is significant, however, that he used the term "Your Majesty" (wang). With few exceptions (one to be mentioned presently), the Chinese envoys were tactful enough to conform to foreign etiquette, and this carried over into Ch'ing's report.

On Feb.25, 610, a new mission arrived from the Wo State to offer regional objects to the Sui court (*Sui shu* 3:14b).

The first mission from the Wo State to the T'ang court arrived with regional objects in the 11th month (Nov./Dec.) of 631.[4] Since the envoys came from far away, Emperor T'ai-tsung made the empty gesture of freeing them from "annual tribute". He then sent the Inspector of Hsin commandery, Kao Piao-jen,[5] as his envoy to Japan. This man had no talent for diplomacy, being the arrogant and unbending type of Chinese who insisted on the priority of his country and rejected foreign conventions. He wrangled about the protocol, was not satisfied, and returned to China without having delivered T'ai-tsung's letter. The result was a temporary break in relations (*Chiu T'ang shu* 199A: 14a; *T'ung-tien* 185:56a; *Ts'e-fu yüan-kuei* p.5024; *Tzu-chih t'ung-chien* p.6090; *Wen-hsien t'ung-k'ao* 324:46b).

Contacts were resumed in 649, when a communication from the Wo State reached the T'ang court via Silla (*Chiu T'ang shu* 199:14a; *Wen-hsien t'ung-k'ao* 324:46b).

Two Japanese missions with student priests in 653 and 654 are recorded in the *Nihongi* but not in Chinese sources.[6]

On Jan.24, 655, envoys from the Wo State presented amber, carnelian, and baroos camphor. The amber was as big as a peck, and the carnelian was half that size.[7] The same year, Silla was attacked by Koguryŏ and Paekche, whereupon Emperor Kao-tsung proposed in a letter that the Japanese should give it military help (*Chiu T'ang shu* 4:5a; *Hsin T'ang shu* 220:12a; *T'ang hui-yao* 99:13a; *Ts'e-fu yüan-kuei* p.5025; *Wen-hsien t'ung-k'ao* 324:46b).

---

[4] By *T'ang hui-yao* 99:12b dated 11th month (Dec./Jan.,642) of the Chinese year 641.

[5] *T'ung-tien* and *Wen-hsien t'ung-k'ao* write Kao Jen-piao.

[6] See Tsunoda and Goodrich, *Japan in the Chinese Dynastic Histories*, p.50 note 17.

[7] A peck (*tou*) consisted of 10 *sheng*, the carnelian of the offering being evaluated at 5 *sheng*.

In the 10th month (Oct./Nov.) of 659, envoys from Wo State were received at the T'ang court together with Ainus. The Ainu envoys had four-feet long beards. Being superb archers, they could unfailingly hit a gourd on the head of a man standing several ten paces away (*Hsin T'ang shu* 220:12a; *Ts'e-fu yüan-kuei* p.5025; *Wen-hsien t'ung-k'ao* 324: 46b; 326:58b).

663 saw a brief clash between the Chinese and Japanese, when Japanese troops supported an uprising in Paekche and were defeated (*Tzu-chih t'ung-chien* p.6337).

On Feb.10, 666, Emperor Kao-tsung performed the *feng* sacrifice and on Feb.12 the *shan* sacrifice at Mount T'ai. Envoys from the Wo State, Koguryŏ, Silla, and Paekche were present (*Chiu T'ang shu* 5:1a; *Tzu-chih t'ung-chien* p.6344; *Wen-hsien t'ung-k'ao* 325:50b).

In the 11th month (Dec./Jan.,669) of the Chinese year 668, envoys from the Wo State offered gifts. In the 3rd month (Mar/Apr.) of 670, envoys from the Wo State congratulated on the defeat of Koguryŏ (in 668) (*Hsin T'ang shu* 220:12a; *T'ang hui-yao* 99:13a; *Ts'e-fu yüan-kuei* p.5026; *Wen-hsien t'ung-k'ao* 324:46b).

In the 10th month (Oct./Nov.) of 702, the high official Mabito Awada arrived with regional objects from the Jih-pen State. The Empress Wu gave him a banquet and appointed him to the nominal office of Supernumerary Gentleman in Charge of Provisions (*Chiu T'ang shu* 6:8a; 199:14a; *T'ung-tien* 185:56a; *Ts'e-fu yüan-kuei* p.5026; *Wen-hsien t'ung-k'ao* 324:46b).[8]

In the 2nd month (Mar./Apr.) of 706, envoys arrived from the Jih-pen State (*Ts'e-fu yüan-kuei* p.5026).

In the 10th month (Nov./Dec.) of 717, Mabito Awada from Jih-pen came on a second mission to the T'ang court. Emperor Hsüan-tsung ordered a Secretarial Receptionist to call on him at the guest quarters of the Herald. The envoy requested instruction in the Confucian classics, whereupon a teacher was provided. The assistant envoy Nakamura did not return to Japan with the mission. He changed his family and given names to the Chinese Chao Heng and was successively appointed to the nominal offices of Rectifier of Omissions of the Left and Companion of a son of Hsüan-tsung. After a long stay, he temporarily went back to Japan (*Hsin T'ang shu* 220:12a; *Ts'e-fu yüan-kuei* p.5026; *Wen-hsien t'ung-k'ao* 324:46b).

[8] By *Chiu T'ang shu* 199A:14a and *Ts'e-fu yüan-kuei* dated 703, and by *Wen-hsien t'ung-k'ao* 701.

In the 8th month (Sep./Oct.) of 733, a flotilla of Japanese ships with a congratulatory envoy from the Japanese court was blown off course by a storm and landed in Su commandery in southern Chiang-su. The local authorities reported this, whereupon Emperor Hsüan-tsung sent a Secretarial Receptionist to Su commandery to call on the envoy (*Ts'e-fu yüan-kuei* p.5029).

In 734, envoys from the Jih-pen State offered 400 bolts of silken fabrics, and in 735 they presented regional objects (*Ts'e-fu yüan-kuei* p.5029).

In the 3rd month (Apr./May) of 753, envoys from Jih-pen offered presents and congratulated. In the 6th month (July/Aug.) of the same year, envoys arrived again (*Chiu T'ang shu*199A:14b; *Ts'e-fu yüan-kuei* p.5030; *Wen-hsien t'ung-k'ao* 324:46b). Chao Heng (Nakamura) accompanied one of these missions and remained in China. He was appointed a Regular Cavalier Attendant of the Left and Protector General of Annam (*Hsin T'ang shu* 220:12a).

In the 1st month (Feb./Mar.) of 778, envoys from the Jih-pen State offered gifts. In the 2nd month (Mar./Apr.) of 780, another mission offered regional objects (*Hsin T'ang shu* 220:12a-12b; *Ts'e-fu yüan-kuei* p.5032; *Wen-hsien t'ung-k'ao* 324:46b).

In the12th month (Jan./Feb., 805) of the Chinese year 804, a mission from the Jih-pen State included the student Tachibana Hayanari and the Buddhist monk Kūkai. They wished to remain in China for study and stayed for over 20 years. Hayanari and others only went back to Japan after a later envoy named Takashima Mabito urged their return. The mission of 804 took leave in the 2nd month (Mar./Apr.) of 805 and was given presents (*Chiu T'ang shu* 13:21b; 14:1b; 199A: 14b; *Hsin T'ang shu* 220:12a-12b; *Ts'e-fu yüan-kuei* p.5032; *Wen-hsien t'ung-k'ao* 324:46b-47a).

In 806, envoys from the Jih-pen State brought a letter. In the 12th month (Dec./Jan., 839) of the Chinese year 838, they presented real pearls and pongee (*Chiu T'ang shu* 17B:26a; 199A:14b; *Ts'e-fu yüan-kuei* p.5033).

In the intercalary month (Feb./Mar.) of 839, envoys from Jih-pen offered gifts (*Chiu T'ang shu* 199A:14b; *Ts'e-fu yüan-kuei* p.5033; *Wen-hsien t'ung-k'ao* 324:47a).

In the 3rd month (Apr./May) of 848, a mission from the Jih-pen State, led by a prince, offered regional objects. In the 4th month (May/June) of 853, another prince presented valuable vessels and music[9] (*Chiu T'ang shu* 18B:5b; *Ts'e-fu yüan-kuei* p.5033).

The missions of 848 and 853 are the last ones recorded for the T'ang. There followed a long period without any recorded official contacts between Japan and China.[10] However, on Jan.9, 926, Jih-pen opened diplomatic relations with the Khitan by offering gifts (*Liao shih* 2:5b; 70:2b). This was followed by a mission of 28 men, which was received by the Liao court of the Khitan in the 9th month (Oct./Nov.) of 1091 (*Liao shih* 70:22b).

Official missions from Japan to Sung China were relatively few. Like the Indian kings, the Japanese at this time occasionally employed Buddhist priests for diplomatic purposes, while other priests travelled on their own and had no official standing. The difference is not always easy to see.[11]

In 1026, Ming[12] on the southern coast of Hang-chou Bay reported that a Japanese mission had arrived with regional objects but without official documents. The court rejected the gifts (*Sung shih* 491:11a; *Wen-hsien t'ung-k'ao* 324:47b). This was obviously an attempt by smart merchants to pose as an official mission.

In 1072, the Buddhist priest Jōjin reached Che-chiang and stayed

---

[9] This must be understood to have included performers. Cf.Schafer, *Golden Peaches*, p.51.

[10] During the Five Dynasties period, the state of Wu-yüeh had commercial contacts with Japan from 935 to 959. See Worthy, Jr., in Rossabi ed., *China among Equals*, pp.35-36.

[11] I have assumed that two of the Buddhist priests were private travellers. (I omit all references to the many nameless monks who came to study in China.):

In 984, the Japanese monk Chōnen with five or six disciples crossed the sea and on Apr.8 presented more than ten bronze vessels and other objects, two Japanese texts, and Buddhist sutras. He could not speak Chinese but was able to answer questions in Chinese writing and to give a detailed account of Japanese conditions, administration, and history. He was received in audience by Emperor T'ai-tsung, was presented with a purple robe, obtained a number of Chinese books, including the *Tripitaka* and *Classic of Filial Piety*, visited Mount Wu-t'ai, and returned to Japan on a merchant ship in 985 (*Sung shih* 491:4b-9a; *Hsü Tzu-chih t'ung-chien ch'ang-pien* pp.218-219; *Wen-hsien t'ung-k'ao* 324:46b-47a). Several years later, Chōnen sent a disciple to the Sung court with a fulsome letter, dated Feb.27, 988. He also presented through this disciple a great many presents which were enumerated in a second letter (*Sung shih* 491:9a-10b). These obviously were not official gifts at the government level but an effort at private trading by Chōnen and perhaps his monastery and patrons.

In 1004, the Japanese monk Jaku Shō arrived with others, eight men in all. He could not speak Chinese but knew the characters and could communicate in writing (*Sung shih* 491:11a; *Wen-hsien t'ung-k'ao* 324:47b).

[12] Modern Ning-po.

at a temple of the T'ien-t'ai sect. He was ordered to proceed to the Sung court, where he presented a silver incense brazier, a Buddhist rosary made of sapindus seeds, white opaque glass, rock crystal, red sandalwood, amber, and silken fabrics (*Sung shih* 491:11a-11b; *Wen-hsien t'ung-k'ao* 324:47b).

On Dec.26, 1077, Ming reported that the Buddhist priest Chūkai and others, six men, had arrived from the Jih-pen State. In 1078, they presented 200 bolts of thin silk and 5000 ounces of mercury (*Sung shih*491:11b; *Hsü Tzu-chih t'ung-chien ch'ang-pien* p.2698; *Wen-hsien t'ung-k'ao* 324:47b).

Meanwhile, the Japanese kept their communications open with Liao. On Oct.28, 1091, a mission of 28 men from Jih-pen, including Teigen, Teishin, the Buddhist priest Ohan, and others offered gifts to the Liao. On Oct.30, 1092, envoys from the Jih-pen State again offered gifts to Liao (*Liao shih* 25:4b).

In 1169, unnamed Japanese envoys offered regional objects to the Southern Sung (*Wen-hsien t'ung-k'ao* 324:48a).

The Japanese missions sailed to China on small flotillas of ships, with crews and personnels of hundreds of individuals. They either navigated along the Korean coast or, especially later, made directly for the Yangtze delta. The sea captains preferred the winter and spring for the voyage to China, since during these seasons the winds from Japan and Korea blow in a southwesterly direction. But losses could be heavy. The mission returning from China in 778, consisted of four ships. Some 65 dignitaries and their attendants were washed overboard. One of the ships was wrecked. Another broke into two halves which both drifted to Kyūshū with few survivors.[13] The Chinese sources mention wrecks and forced landings of Japanese merchant vessels in 1176, 1183, 1190, 1193, and safe landings in 1200, and 1202. (*Sung shih* 491:12a; *Wen-hsien t'ung-k'ao* 324:48a).

From the Japanese point of view, the most important aim of the missions was to seek knowledge. This is why students, scholars, Buddhist priests, persuers of statecraft, and artisans were attached to the missions and why they brought back books on religious and secular subjects. This contrasts sharply with the relations to China of the countries of continental South Asia and the islands. With the exception of Chiao-chih, these showed no interest in Chinese culture. Chiao-chih

[13] See Sansom, *Japan*, pp.87-88.

bordered directly on China and was open to influence from its splendid civilization. It has been seen that in 1007 Chiao-chih requested copies of the *Nine Confucian Classics* and the Buddhist *Tripitaka*, and that in 1176 it adopted the Sung calendar. But no other countries of continental South Asia and the islands had any wish to learn from the Chinese.[14]

From the Chinese point of view, however, their civilization was ipso facto higher than any other, so that the Japanese thirst for knowledge cannot have been any cause of suprise, only of mild flattery. To the Chinese, the commercial side of the missions must therefore have been more important than to the Japanese, until xenophobia brought the missions to and end during Southern Sung. Private trade continued, of course and was so brisk and lucrative that it led to a Chinese drain of copper. This forced the Southern Sung government on Aug.17, 1199, to prohibit merchants from Japan and Koryŏ to depart with copper cash they had obtained for their goods (*Sung shih* 37:13a).

This is the distribution by 20-year periods of the 29 recorded missions from Japan to Sui, T'ang, and Sung:

587- 606:	1
607- 626:	2
627- 646:	1
647- 666:	6
667- 686:	2
697- 706:	2
707- 726:	1
727- 746:	2
747- 766:	1
767- 786:	2
787- 806:	2
807- 826:	0
827- 846:	2
847- 866:	1
867- 886:	1
887- 906:	0
907- 926:	0

[14] Except for the curious case in Wang Hsüan-ts'e's report that in 648 an Indian prince requested an image of Lao-tzu and the *Tao-te-ching*.

927- 946:	0
947- 966:	0
967- 986:	0
987-1006:	0
1007-1026:	0
1027-1046:	0
1047-1066:	0
1067-1086:	2
1087-1106:	0
1107-1126:	0
1127-1146:	0
1147-1166:	0
1167-1186:	1

The closest relations between Japan and China were during the reign of Kao-tsung (650-683) of T'ang with seven or almost 1/4 of all recorded missions. In addition to the missions to China, the texts also record four missions from Japan to the Khitan/Liao court.

Unfortunately, the sources do not normally enumerate the goods brought by the Japanese and content themselves by stating that these were regional objects. The few specified items fall into the following categories:

Humans

853: Musicians.

Aromatics

Fragrant woods

1072: red sandalwood.

Camphor

655: baroos camphor.

Minerals and Metals

1072: rock crystal.
1078: 5000 ounces of mercury.

Manufactured Objects

Of metal

1072: one silver incense brazier.

Of glass:

1072: white opaque glass.

Other:

853: valuable vessels.
1072: one Buddhist rosary of sapindus seeds.

Textiles

Silks:

734: 400 bolts of silken fabrics.
838: pongee.
1072: silken fabrics.
1078: 200 bolts of thin silk.

Jewels

654: amber and carnelian.
838: pearls.
1072: amber.

It is not recorded what the Chinese offered in response.

KOREA

Emperor Wu of Former Han conquered northwestern Korea in 198 BC. and established a number of commanderies. These were eventually reduced to one, named Lo-lang. It comprised the lowlands to the mountains in the east and to just north of present Seoul in the south. The capital was at present P'yŏngyang. In the early 3rd century A.D., Lo-lang was subdivided, and its southernmost part and adjoining territory to the south became the Tai-fang commandery.

In the 1st century B.C., the Tungusic Koguryŏ people had established themselves in northeastern Korea and soon expanded into southern Manchuria. In the early 4th century A.D., they overran Lo-lang and Tai-fang, and in 427 made P'yŏngyang their capital. Han tribes inhabited southwestern Korea and in the late 3rd century evolved into the state of Paekche. From 538, its capital was Puyŏ. The tribes of southeastern Korea were gradually federated into the state of Silla with its capital near modern Kyŏngju. All three kingdoms were under Chinese cultural influence. Silla was destined to unify Korea in the 7th century (map 3).

KOGURYŎ

During the Six Dynasties, Koguryŏ was a sizable state, comprising not only northern Korea but also the Liao-tung Peninsula and Manchuria northward beyond the latitude of modern Mukden. In the west, it reached the Sea of Japan. For that period, 38 missions by sea are recorded from Koguryŏ to Eastern Chin, Liu Sung, Southern Ch'i, Liang, and Ch'en from 336 to 585. But Koguryŏ between 425 and 583 also sent no less than 100 missions by land to Northern Wei, Eastern Wei, Northern Ch'i, Northern Chou, and Sui (before the reunification of 589). It therefore had much closer relations to the northern dynasties than to the southern ones.[1]

---

[1] See my *Six Dynasties*, vol.II, pp.92-97.

The reunification of China in 589 posed an immediate threat to Koguryŏ, since it could be assumed that the Sui would attempt to restore the borders of the Han empire. In fact, Emperor Wen did not recognize Kao Yang[2] (P'yŏng-wŏn Wang) as the king of Koguryŏ, only as duke of Liao-tung commandery (*Sui shu* 2:6b). This title was intended to reduce him to the dignitary of a Chinese territorial unit.

News of Kao Yang's death reached the Sui court on Aug.31, 590. He was succeeded by his son Kao Yüan (Yŏng-yang Wang). Emperor Wen sent envoys to appoint him as Supreme Commander Unequalled in Honour and as duke of Liao-tung commandery and to present him with garments. Kao Yüan, on his part, congratulated the Sui emperor on auspicious omens and requested recognition as king. Emperor Wen complied (*Sui shu* 2:6b; 81:4a; *Wen-hsien t'ung-k'ao* 325:49b).

On Feb.17 and June 10 of 591, envoys from Koguryŏ to the Sui court offered regional objects (*Sui shu* 2:7a).

In 597, Emperor Wen, in a letter stamped with the imperial seal, demanded annual tribute-bearing envoys from Koguryŏ (*Sui shu* 81: 2b-3a; *Wen-hsien t'ung-k'ao* 325:49b).

But relations between Sui and Koguryŏ did not develop to the satisfaction of the Sui court. After a violation of the Chinese border, Sui went to war in 598. The Chinese sources state that on Aug.4 of that year, Emperor Wen stripped Kao Yüan of office and rank, that the latter became fearful and sent envoys with a "memorial" to "apologize",[3] and that Emperor Wen thereupon halted the attack (*Sui shu* 2:12b, 13a; 81:4a-4b; *Wen-hsien t'ung-k'ao* 325:49b). The truth behind these fine words is that the Chinese assault by land and sea failed and that the war ended with a status quo.

On Jan.21, 600, Koguryŏ envoys offered regional objects (*Sui shu* 2:13b-14a).

After Emperor Yang had ascended the Sui throne on Aug.13, 604,

---

[2] The Chinese texts refer to the Korean rulers by their sinicised family and given names, the latter of which would have been tabooed in China. This discourtesy toward foreign rulers, which has been noted before, was intended to stress the gulf between an emperor and his potential subjects, and was observed not only by the Chinese histories but also by those devoted to e.g. the Northern Wei, Liao, and Chin. The Korean texts naturally refer to the kings by their posthumous titles. I will follow the Chinese practice, but at the first mention of the family and given name of a ruler will give his Korean posthumous title in parenthesis.

[3] He would not have referred to himself as a "shit", as claimed by *Pei shih* 94: 9b.

he attempted to take a strong line with Koguryŏ and invited its king, Kao Yüan, to come to his court. The king naturally refused, but hardly out of fear as claimed by the texts (*Sui shu* 81:4b; *Wen-hsien t'ung-k'ao* 325:49b).

In the 8th month (Aug./Sep.) of 607, Emperor Yang, to no avail, reminded Koguryŏ envoys that he expected their king to arrive at his court (*Sui shu* 3:11a).

On May 14, 609, a mission from Koguryŏ called on Emperor Yang in northwestern China while he was preparing for an attack on the T'u-yü-hun (*Pei shih* 12:13a).

Emperor Yang's foiled expectations led to a new conflict of arms, conducted in three campaigns. The first, in 612, supported by Paekche, led to a small territorial gain for Sui in which the Liao River became the border between China and Koguryŏ. The second, in 613, had to be aborted because of a rebellion in China. In the third, in 614, Sui troops reached P'ŏngyang but were unable to take it. The war ended in another standoff and was worth neither the investment nor the result. Another attempt by Emperor Yang to bring Kao Yüan to his court failed, as it was bound to do (*Sui shu* 81:5a; *Wen-hsien t'ung-k'ao* 325:49b).

In Koguryŏ, Kao Yüan was in 618 succeeded by his brother Kao Chien-wu (Yŏngnyu Wang).[4] In 619, his envoys came to the T'ang court (*Chiu T'ang shu* 199A:1b; *Ts'e-fu yüan-kuei* p.5023).

In the 7th month (July/Aug.) of 621, Koguryŏ envoys offered gifts. They furthermore requested instruction in Taoism, whereupon Chinese Tao masters were dispatched to their country (*Chiu T'ang shu* 199A:1b; *Ts'e-fu yüan-kuei* p.5023; *Tzu-chih t'ung-chien* p.5923; *Wen-hsien t'ung-k'ao* 325:50a).

In 622, envoys from Koguryŏ arrived again at the T'ang court (*Ts'e-fu yüan-kuei* p.5023). That same year, T'ang and Koguryŏ reached an agreement to exchange nationals. Many Chinese, including warriors of the defeated Sui armies, were living in Koguryŏ, while Koreans from Koguryŏ stayed in various parts of China. These were to be repatriated (*Chiu T'ang shu* 199A:1b; *Tzu-chih t'ung-chien* p.5964).

In the 12th month (Dec./Jan., 624) of the Chinese year 623, Koguryŏ envoys offered presents (*Ts'e-fu yüan-kuei* p.5023).

On Mar.1, 624,envoys from the king of Koguryŏ, Kao Chien-

[4] The Imperial Annals of *Chiu T'ang shu* refer to him throughout as Kao Wu.

wu, asked for a calendar. As has been noted before, such a request meant to the Chinese, but not to the foreigners, recognition of their suzerainity. On Mar.3,[5] Emperor Kao-tsu ordered a Master of Writing of the Ministry of Punishments to go as his envoy to Koguryŏ, appoint Kao Chien-wu as Supreme Pillar of State, and recognize him as king of Liao-tung commandery and Koguryŏ (*Chiu T'ang shu* 1:8a; 199A:1b; *Tzu-chih t'ung-chien* p.5976). Presumably, he also brought the calendar.

In the 12th month (Jan.Feb., 625) of the Chinese year 624, Koguryŏ again offered regional objects (*Ts'e-fu yüan-kuei* p.5023). But relations between Koguryŏ and the T'ang were uneasy, and Emperor Kao-tsu complained about it to his officials on Apr.14, 625. In 626, Silla and Paekche accused Koguryŏ of blocking the roads for their missions to China (*Chiu T'ang shu* 199A:2a, 7b; *T'ang hui-yao* 95:6a-6b; *Wen-hsien t'ung-k'ao* 325:50a).

Later in 626, Silla, Paekche, and Koguryŏ attacked each other. The T'ang court sent a Supernumerary Cavalier Attendant as a mediator, whereupon all three states made peace and informed the T'ang court (*Chiu T'ang shu* 2:8a; 199A:2b; *Ts'e-fu yüan-kuei* p.5023; *Tzu-chih t'ung-chien* p.6030).

In the 9th month (Oct./Nov.) of 628, envoys from Kao Chien-wu congratulated Emperor T'ai-tsung on having defeated the Hsieh-li Qaghan of the Eastern Turks. At the same time, he offered a map of his state (*Chiu T'ang shu* 199A:2b; *Ts'e-fu yüan-kuei* p.5023). As remarked before, presenting a map of one's territory was to the Chinese a symbol of submission. Nothing could have been further from the mind of the Koguryŏ king. He and the Chinese had no doubt diverging views on the calendar of 624 and the map of 628. What the king had in mind was probably to make a gesture in order to forestall an alliance against his state by T'ang, Paekche, and Silla.

In the 9th month (Sep./Oct.) of 629, Koguryŏ envoys offered gifts (*Ts'e-fu yüan-kuei* p.5023).

On Sep.18, 631, T'ai-tsung sent a Garrison Major to Koguryŏ to collect the bones of the fighting men who had fallen there in Sui times,

---

[5] This is the sequence of events as given by *Tzu-chih t'ung-chien*. *Chiu T'ang shu* 1: 8a reverses it and places the mission of Kao-tsu ahead of the request for a calendar. However, the text dates the mission 1st month, *chi-yu*, which date did not exist. This makes it clear that 1st month, *chi-yu*, must be emended to 2nd month, *chi-yu* (Mar.3).

bury them, and sacrifice to them. This was an act which, according to the Chinese sources, worried the Korean king and made him improve his defenses (*Chiu T'ang shu* 199A:2b; *Tzu-chih t'ung-chien* p.6087).

In 639, envoys from Koguryŏ offered gifts. In the 12th month (Jan./Feb., 641) of the Chinese year 640, the king's heir-apparent brought regional objects (*Chiu T'ang shu* 3:6b, 7a; 199A:2b; *Ts'e-fu yüan-kuei* p.5024). Kao Chien-wu was obviously anxious to improve relations.

In the 5th month (June/July) of 641, T'ai-tsung sent a Gentleman-of-the-Palace of the Bureau of Operations on a spying mission to Koguryŏ. At his return on Sep.20, 641, he reported on the topography and customs of Koguryŏ (*Tzu-chih t'ung-chien* p.6169).

In the 1st month (Feb./Mar.) of 642, a Koguryŏ mission presented regional objects (*Ts'e-fu yüan-kuei* p.5024).

On Dec.2, 642, the Military Governor of Ying commandery[6] reported to the T'ang court that the Koguryŏ dignitary Yŏn Kae-so-mun had personally murdered Kao Chien-wu and enthroned the latter's nephew Kao Tsang (Pojang Wang). Henceforth, Yŏn Kae-so-mun controlled the government. T'ai-tsung commenced mourning for Chien-wu and sent an envoy to condole and sacrifice. The emperor was advised to use this opportunity for an attack on Koguryŏ, but rejected it on the grounds that during Chien-wu's reign "tribute had been uninterrupted" (*Chiu T'ang shu* 3:8a; 199A:2b; *Tzu-chih t'ung-chien* p.6181; *Wen-hsien t'ung-k'ao* 325:50a). The real reason was inadequate resources.

On Jan.26, 643, Koguryŏ presented regional objects (*Ts'e-fu yüan-kuei* p.5024). This was the first day of the year, so that the mission must have been sent to congratulate on the New Year's Day. On Aug.10 of the same year,[7] T'ai-tsung sent an envoy to appoint Kao Tsang as Supreme Pillar of State and recognize him as king of Liao-tung commandery and Koguryŏ (*Chiu T'ang shu* 199 A:2b; *Tzu-chih t'ung-chien* p.6202).

On Oct.21, 643, envoys from Silla informed the T'ang court that it was under attack from Paekche and Koguryŏ, that it had lost more than 40 of its towns, and that the route was cut on which its envoys travelled to the T'ang court. It asked for support. T'ai-tsung sent an Assistant of the Minister of Agriculture, carrying a letter stamped with

---

[6] Ying commandery bordered on Koguryŏ and like all border commanderies routinely reported on events abroad.

[7] Correcting 6th month to 6th intercalary month.

the imperial seal. It urged the king of Koguryŏ not to attack Silla. "You and Paekche must cease hostilities, otherwise I will attack your country next year" (*Chiu T'ang shu* 199A:2b, 7b, 11a; *Tzu-chih t'ung-chien* p.6204; *Wen-hsien t'ung-k'ao* 326:54b, 55b).[8]

On Feb.14, 644, the New Year's Day, Koguryŏ envoys offered regional objects (*Ts'e-fu yüan-kuei* p.5024). On Oct.30 of the same year, the Herald reported that Koguryŏ had presented silver (*Tzu-chih t'ung-chien* p.6212).

On Jan.17, 645, T'ai-tsung ordered an attack on Koguryŏ by land and sea, in which the Chinese were allied with Silla, Paekche, the Hsi, and the Khitan, and also used auxiliary Turkish troops (*Chiu T'ang shu* 199A:2b, 8a; *Tzu-chih t'ung-chien* p.6215; *Wen-hsien t'ung-k'ao* 325:50a; 54b). Although the Chinese won some victories in Liao-tung, this war ended in 647 as inconclusively as the previous ones.

In spite of the war, Koguryŏ sent envoys in the 1st month (Jan./Feb.) of 646, probably on the New Year's Day (Feb.10). They presented two beautiful women, whom T'ai-tsung rejected (*Ts'e-fu yüan-kuei* p.5014).

On Jan.30, 648, the New Year's Day, Koguryŏ sent envoys with gifts (*Ts'e-fu yüan-kuei* pp.5024-5025).

After T'ai-tsung had died on July 10, 649, Kao Tsang sent an envoy to condole (*Wen-hsien t'ung-k'ao* 325:50b).

In 651, Emperor Kao-tsung warned Paekche not to attack Koguryŏ and Silla (*Chiu T'ang shu* 199A:8a; *Tzu-chih t'ung-chien* p.6277).

On Feb.15, 652, the New Year's Day, a mission from Koguryŏ offered gifts (*Ts'e-fu yüan-kuei* p.5025; *Tzu-chih t'ung-chien* p.6277)

In the 1st month (Feb./Mar.) of 655, Koguryŏ, Paekche and the Mo-ho joined forces and attacked Silla. Envoys from the king of Silla to the T'ang court requested support. In the 2nd month (Mar./Apr.), T'ang conducted a raid into Koguryŏ which, in spite of claims to the contrary, seems to have been a minor one (*Chiu T'ang shu* 199A:8b; *Tzu-chih t'ung-chien* pp.6287-6288; *Wen-hsien t'ung-k'ao* 326:54b). Another raid in 658 was equally unsuccessful.

In the 12th month (Dec./Jan., 657) of the Chinese year 656, envoys from the king of Koguryŏ, Kao Tsang, presented a letter and

[8] *Chiu T'ang shu* and *Wen-hsien t'ung-k'ao* date the attack of Paekche and Koguryŏ 642, in which case the report from Silla would have been rather late.

congratulated on the investiture of the imperial heir-apparent (*Ts'e-fu yüan-kuei* p.5025).[9]

In 660, T'ang allied with Silla attacked Paekche. A Chinese amphibian force landed on its coast, while a Silla army invaded it from the east. Paekche was destroyed and occupied by Chinese troops (*Chiu T'ang shu* 199A:8b; *Wen-hsien t'ung-k'ao* 326:54b). This was followed by a brief clash between T'ang and Koguryŏ in the 12th month (Jan./Feb., 661) of the Chinese year 660 (*Tzu-chih t'ung-chien* p.6321).

On Dec.7, 665, a son of the king of Koguryŏ was received at the T'ang court. On Feb.10, 666, he attended Emperor Kao-tsung's *feng* sacrifice and on Feb.12 his *shan* sacrifice at Mount T'ai. Envoys from Japan, Silla, and the occupied Paekche were also present (*Chiu T'ang shu* 5:1a; *Tzu-chih t'ung-chien* p.6344; *Wen-hsien t'ung-k'ao* 325:50b).

On July 14, 666, news reached the T'ang court that Koguryŏ's strong-man Yŏn Kae-so-mun had died. His three sons contested the succession, and one of them, as well as a brother of Yŏn Kae-so-mun, sought Chinese support. Meanwhile, the king, Kao Tsang, sent a son to the T'ang court (*Chiu T'ang shu* 5:1b; 199A:5b; *Wen-hsien t'ung-k'ao* 325:50b).

Taking advantage of the dissention in Koguryŏ, T'ang, again allied with Silla, launched in 667 a large and coordinated attack against Koguryŏ from the north and south. This included a Chinese army from the former Paekche. P'yŏngyang was taken on Oct.22, 668. Kao Tsang and his high officials surrendered and Koguryŏ ceased to exist and was made into the An-tung Protectorate (*Chiu T'ang shu* 5:2a, 2b; *Tzu-chih t'ung-chien* p.6356).

At this time, the attitude of Silla changed. It could not be in its interest to concur in a Chinese occupation of the major part of Korea, in addition to which it had ambitions of its own. When a Chinese general in the 12th month (Dec./Jan.673) of the Chinese year 672 was fighting Koguryŏ loyalists who had attempted to restore the kingdom, the king of Silla sent troops to their aid and received those who fled to his state. In 673 and 674, he continued to accept Koguryŏ refugees. In 677, he took P'yŏngyang, and subsequently unified Korea under his dynasty (*Chiu T'ang shu* 5:5a; *Tzu-chih t'ung-chien* pp.6370, 6372, 6383).

The former king of Koguryŏ, Kao Tsang, was by the T'ang appointed a Master of Writing of the Ministry of Works. On Apr.2,

---

[9] Kao-tsung had changed his heir-apparent on Feb.6, 656 (*Chiu T'ang shu* 4:6a).

677, he was made Military Governor of Liao-tung commandery and, reviving an ancient name from Former Han times, king of Ch'ao-hsien (Chosŏn) commandery (*Tzu-chih t'ung-chien* p.6382; *Wen-hsien t'ung-k'ao* 325:51a). This was an attempt to attract at least some of his former subjects to a tiny principality, established as a buffer between Silla and the Chinese Liao-tung. It did not work out as planned. On arrival, Kao Tsang secretely communicated with the Mo-ho in the north, planning to rise against the T'ang. When this was discovered, he was exiled to Ssu-ch'uan (*Tzu-chih t'ung-chien* pp.6382, 6383; *Wen-hsien t'ung-k'ao* 325:51a).

In 686, the T'ang enfeoffed Kao Ts'ang's grandson Pao-yüan as king of Ch'ao-hsien commandery and in 698 made him a General-in-chief of the Guards Who Soar Like Hawks of the Left (*Chiu T'ang shu* 199A:5b). In 699, Kao Ts'ang's son Te-wu was appointed Chief Commandant of the no longer existing An-tung Protectorate (*T'ang hui-yao* 95:13a).

Like Chiao-chih/Annam, and Japan, the three Korean states were under the influence of Chinese civilization and actively sought to learn from their neighbour, both in the cultural and administrative spheres. It has been seen that Koguryŏ in 621 requested Tao masters, and that in 624 it asked for the T'ang calendar. Students from Koguryŏ, Paekche, and Silla studied at the National Academy in Ch'ang-an (*Tzu-chih t'ung-chien* pp.6152-6153). But this does not mean that any of the states were vassals of China or that they paid tribute to it. Koguryŏ fought three great wars for its independence, in 598, 612-614, and 645-647, which is not the behavior of a tributary. Yŏn Kae-so-mun who controlled Koguryŏ from 642 to 666 was not a friend of China. Because of the hostility of the three Korean states to each other, which offered a leverage to the Chinese, Koguryŏ was vulnerable. The kings found it useful to be recognized by China. They were willing to make some concessions, such as presenting the map in 628 and sending princes as envoys in 640, 663, and 666. That Koguryŏ repeatedly congratulated on New Year's Days, condoled on the death of T'ai-tsung in 649, and congratulated on the investiture of a new heir-apparent in 656 proves nothing, since such acts were part of standard diplomatic etiquette between states with close relations.

The division of Korea into three states was to China's advantage. In 612, Paekche was opposed to Koguryŏ. In 626, Silla and Paekche were opposed to Koguryŏ, as well as hostile to each other. In 643, Koguryŏ and Paekche were opposed to Silla. In 645-647, Silla and

Paekche were opposed to Koguryŏ. In 648, Paekche was opposed to Silla. In 651, Paekche was opposed to Koguryŏ and Silla. In 668, Silla was opposed to Koguryŏ. This enabled China to act as a mediator and, by shifting its support, influence events. But the chief ally of the T'ang was Silla. This is another classical case of two states co-operating against a potential or real enemy situated between them. It was with the help of Silla that the T'ang was able in 660 to destroy Paekche and in 668 Koguryŏ. This proved to be a serious mistake as it enabled Silla to unify Korea and thereby politically to shut out China from Korea.

Sui shu 81:4b claims that after the war of 598, Kao Yüan sent missions annually to the Sui court, yet only one is recorded for the rest of the Sui dynasty. The historian may have exaggerated in order to put the best face on the Chinese defeat of 598, but we cannot be sure. By the same token, New Year congratulations by Koguryŏ are recorded for 643, 644, probably 646, 648, and 652. Did it not congratulate at other times? Probably yes. In 20 cases, the months are recorded when the Koguryŏ missions were received at the Chinese courts. 5 of these were in the 12th month and 8 in the 1st month. Those who were received in the 12th month surely stayed over the New Year, and those who were received in the 1st month surely had arrived in the 12th. That adds up to 13 New Year congratulations. It should also be noted that the numbers of missions by 20-year periods show a very even distribution, indicating routine. The statistics may therefore be reasonably correct.

The following table shows the recorded 26 missions by 20-year periods from Koguryŏ to Sui and T'ang:

587-606:	5
607-626:	7
627-646:	9
647-666:	5

Apart from ceremonial functions, the envoys from Koguryŏ had no doubt many sensitive matters to discuss which concerned them and the Chinese, but, as all other envoys, they also engaged in high-level government, and no doubt also private, trade. Unfortunately the sources only twice give specific information. In 644, Koguryŏ offered silver and in 646 two beautiful women (rejected). For the rest, the sources simply state that the missions brought regional objects.

PAEKCHE

For the Six Dynasties, 26 missions are recorded from Paekche to Eastern Chin, Liu Sung, Liang, and Ch'en between 372 and 586.[10]

Early in the 580's, before the reunification of China in 589, envoys from the king of Paekche, Fu-yü Ch'ang (Widŏk Wang), to the Sui court offered regional objects. Emperor Wen appointed him Supreme Commander Unequalled in Honour, entitled him duke of Tai-fang commandery, and recognized him as king of Paekche (*Sui shu* 81: 5b).

In 589, Paekche congratulated Sui on the conquest of Ch'en (*Wen-hsien t'ung-k'ao* 325:54b).

In the 7th month (Aug./Sep.) of 590, Paekche envoys to the Sui court offered regional objects (*Ts'e-fu yüan-kuei* p.5023).

In 598, a Chief Clerk of the king of Paekche presented regional objects. The king subsequently sent other envoys and requested to be given a military rank (*Sui shu* 81:7a).

In 607, envoys of the king of Paekche, Fu-yü Chang (Mu Wang)[11] offered gifts to the Sui court. The same year, he dispatched another envoy with presents, urging the Sui to take action against Koguryŏ. Emperor Yang was not yet ready to do so (*Sui shu* 81:7a; *Wen-hsien t'ung-k'ao* 326:54b).

On Apr.9, 608, Paekche envoys offered regional objects. On June 26, 610, envoys again offered gifts (*Sui shu* 3:11b, 15b; *Pei shih* 12: 11a-11b).

When Emperor Yang in 611 made preparations for his first attack on Koguryŏ, Fu-yü Chang sent an envoy to coordinate the war effort. Emperor Yang responded by dispatching a Gentleman of the Bureau of Public Construction of the Masters of Writing to Paekche to complete the negotiations. When the war began, the king of Paekache placed troops at his border, no doubt in the hope of weakening Koguryŏ by drawing some of its forces against himself (*Sui shu* 81:7a-7b).

In 614, the last mission from Paekche to Sui arrived at the court with offerings. Thereafter, missions ceased because of the disorders in China (*Sui shu* 81:7b; *Wen-hsien t'ung-k'ao* 326:54b).

---

[10] See my *Six Dynasties*, vol.II, pp.95-96. Note that on p.96 above the date of 567, 9th month, Nov.5, the word "Ch'en" has dropped out.

[11] Widŏk Wang had in 598 been succeeded by Hye Wang, followed by Pŏp Wang in 599, and Mu Wang in 600.

In the 7th month (July/Aug.) of 621, envoys from Fu-yü Chang to the T'ang court presented horses. These were classified by the Chinese as inferior (*Chiu T'ang shu* 199A:7a; *Ts'e-fu yüan-kuei* p.5023; *Wen-hsien t'ung-k'ao* 326:54b).

On Feb.8,[12] 624, a high Paekche official with a letter and presents was received at the T'ang court. Emperor Kao-tsu sent an envoy to recognize Fu-yü Chang as king of Tai-fang commandery and recognize him as king of Paekche (*Chiu T'ang shu* 1:8a; 199A:7b; *Tzu-chih t'ung-chien* p.5976).

In the 5th (May/June) and 7th (July/Aug.) month of 624, Paekche envoys offered gifts, and in the 9th month (Oct./Nov.) they presented armour (*Ts'e-fu yüan-kuei* p.5023).

In the 11th month (Dec./Jan., 626) of the Chinese year 625, Paekche envoys again offered gifts (*Ts'e-fu yüan-kuei* p.5023).

In 626, Paekche and Silla accused Koguryŏ of blocking the roads for their missions to China (*Chiu T'ang shu* 199A:2a, 7b). This makes clear that Paekche at that time used the land route through Koguryŏ rather than the sea route.

Later in 626, Silla, Paekche, and Koguryŏ attacked each other. The T'ang court sent a Supernumerary Cavalier Attendant as a mediator, whereupon all three state made peace and informed the court (*Chiu T'ang shu* 2:8a; 199A:2b, 7b; *Ts'e-fu yüan-kuei* p.5023; *Tzu-chih t'ung-chien* p.6030; *Wen-hsien t'ung-k'ao* 326:54b).

In the 12th month (Dec./Jan., 627) of the Chinese year 626, a Paekche mission brought offerings. The T'ang court advised the envoys that Paekche should control its resentment against Koguryŏ and Silla, and a letter stamped with the imperial seal repeated this advice to the king. But the hostilities did not cease (*Chiu T'ang shu* 2: 8a; 199A :7b; *Ts'e-fu yüan-kuei* p.5023; *Wen-hsien t'ung-k'ao* 326:54b).

In the 9th month (Sep./Oct.) of 629, in the 9th month (Oct.) of 631, in 632, and in the 2nd month (Mar./Apr.) of 636, Paekche envoys offered regional objects (*Ts'e-fu yüan-kuei*, pp.5023, 5024).

On Jan.1, 638, a mission from Paekche, led by a prince, was received at the T'ang court. He offered iron armor and engraved axes. T'ai-tsung presented him with 8000 pieces of silken fabrics, brocade robes, etc. (*Chiu T'ang shu* 3:5b; 199A:7b; *Ts'e-fu yüan-kuei* p.5024).

On Dec.5, 638, envoys from Paekche offered golden armour and

---

[12] Correcting *chi-yu* to *yi-yu*.

engraved axes (*Chiu T'ang shu* 3:6a; *Ts'e-fu yüan-kuei* p.5024).

On June 29, 641, envoys from Fu-yü Yi-tz'u informed the T'ang court that his father, the king of Paekche, Chang, had died. T'ai-tsung wore mourning and shed (diplomatic) tears for him. He contributed 200 items to the funeral expenses and sent envoys to recognize Fu-yü Yi-tz'u (Ŭija Wang) as king of Tai-fang commandery and Paekche (*Chiu T'ang shu* 3:7b; 199A:7b; *Tzu-chih t'ung-chien* p.6168).

In the 1st month (Feb./Mar.) of 642, envoys from Paekche offered regional objects (*Ts'e-fu yüan-kuei* p.5024).

On Oct.21, 643, envoys from Silla to the T'ang court announced that it was under attack from Paekche and Koguryŏ, that it had lost more than 40 of its towns, and that the route was cut on which it's envoys travelled to China. It asked for support. T'ai-tsung sent an Assistant of the Minister of Agriculture, urging the kings of Paekche and Koguryŏ not to attack Silla (*Chiu T'ang shu* 199A:2b, 7b, 11a; *Tzu-chih t'ung-chien* p.6204; *Wen-hsien t'ung-k'ao* 326:54b; 55b).[13]

On the New Year's Days of 643 (Jan.26) and 644 (Feb.14), envoys from Paekche presented regional objects. On the New Year's Day of 645 (Feb.3), envoys from the heir-apparent of Paekche, Fu-yü K'ang, congratulated and offered regional objects (*Ts'e-fu yüan-kuei* p.5024).

When T'ai-tsung in 645 attacked Koguryŏ, Paekche and Silla were his allies (*Tzu-chih t'ung-chien* p.6215).

In 648, Paekche attacked Silla and took more than ten of its towns (*Chiu T'ang shu* 199A:8a; *Wen-hsien t'ung-k'ao* 326:54b).

After Kao-tsung had been enthroned on July 10, 649, Paekche sent envoys and the emperor answered with a letter (*Wen-hsien t'ung-k'ao* 326:54b).

In 650, Paekche was attacked by Silla (*Chiu T'ang shu* 199A:11a-11b; *Wen-hsien t'ung-k'ao* 326:55b).

In 651, Paekche envoys to the T'ang court offered gifts. Kao-tsung rejected the mission, blaming the political tensions in Korea on Paekche. He sent a letter, warning Paekche not to attack Silla and Koguryŏ. "Otherwise, I will mobilize troops and punish you" (*Chiu T'ang shu* 199A:8a; *Tzu-chih t'ung-chien* p.6277).

On Feb.15, 655, the New Year's Day, Paekche envoys presented gifts (*Ts'e-fu yüan-kuei* p.5025; *Tzu-chih t'ung-chien* p.6277).

---

[13] *Chiu T'ang shu* and *Wen-hsien t'ung-k'ao* date the attack of Paekche and Koguryŏ 642.

In the 1st month (Feb./Mar.) of 655, Koguryŏ, Paekche and the Mo-ho joined forces and attacked Silla. The king of Silla sent envoys to the T'ang court and requested support (*Chiu T'ang shu* 199A:8b; *Tzu-chih t'ung-chien* pp.6287; *Wen-hsien t'ung-k'ao* 326:54b).

In September of 660, China, allied with Silla, destroyed Paekche in an amphibian operation. The king, Fu-yü Yi-tz'u, his heir-apparent, Lung, and others, including 59 generals, were taken prisoners and brought to Ch'ang-an. Several days after reaching the Chinese capital, the king died. He was given the posthumous titles of Imperial Household Grandee of the Golden Seal and Purple Ribbon and of Commandant of the Guards, and his former subjects were allowed to mourn for him. Paekche was annexed (*Chiu T'ang shu* 199A:8b, 11b; *T'ang hui-yao* 95:14a-14b; *Wen-hsien t'ung-k'ao* 325:54b).

An uprising broke out in Paekche almost immediately. A prince of the royal house, Fu-yü Feng, was brought from Japan and enthroned as king (P'ungjang Wang). A Japanese navy arrived in his support but was defeated by the Chinese in 663. The king fled to Koguryŏ, and Paekche surrendered (*Tzu-chih t'ung-chien* p.6337).

On Nov.17, 665, a peace conference was held in Paekche by representatives of T'ang, Silla, Paekche, and Japan. Thereafter, all followed the Chinese envoy by sea to Shan-tung, where on Feb.10, 666 they attended Emperor Kao-tsung's *feng* sacrifice and on Feb.12 his *shan* sacrifice at Mount T'ai (*Chiu T'ang shu* 5:1a; *Tzu-chih t'ung-chien* p.6344; *Wen-hsien t'ung-k'ao* 325:50b).

In 674, Silla occupied the old territory of Paekche. Kao-tsung made one last attempt to regain a foothold. The former heir-apparent of Paekche, Lung, son of Fu-yü Yi-tz'u, had previously been given the nominal title of Minister of Agriculture. On Oct.2, 677, he was invested as king of Tai-fang commandery with the expectation that he should return to Paekche and rally the people. However, he did not dare to go back to his homeland (*Tzu-chih t'ung-chien* pp.6372, 6382-6383). Paekche was thereby lost to China forever.

Paekche, like Koguryŏ, had been an independent state, influenced by Chinese culture but not its vassal. One king of Paekche (Fu-yü Chang) is recorded to have received Chinese posthumous titles, versus none in Koguryŏ.

During the Six Dynasties, envoys from Paekche to the southern courts had travelled by sea. In T'ang times, they preferred to go by land via Koguryŏ. Again, it is difficult to say how complete the statistics are. According to *T'ung-tien* 185:55a, Paekche incessantly sent envoys between 618-649. The recorded missions are 19. That comes on the average to about one mission every 1½ years, which can be called incessant. On the other hand, Paekche congratulated in 643, 644, 645, and 652 on the New Year's Day. Two missions in the 11th month and one in the 12th probably stayed through the New Year reception. Were these the only congratulations? Perhaps not. In numbers, the missions of Paekche are compatible with those of Koguryŏ, 31 compared to 26. This is their distribution by 20-year periods:

587-606:	4
607-626:	13
627-646:	11
647-666:	3

The middle period was obviously the most active.

As in the case of Koguryŏ, the goods exchanged are rarely mentioned, other than in general terms. In 621, Paekche offered inferior horses, and in 624 and 638 gold and iron armour and axes. The people of this state must have been skilled metal workers. The T'ang gave in exchange silk and brocade robes.

LATER PAEKCHE

When rebellions broke out toward the end of the Silla rule of Korea, the kingdom of Paekche was restored as Later Paekche in 892. In 935, it absorbed Silla, only to be destroyed by Koryŏ in 936.

A single mission from Later Paekche is recorded to the Later T'ang of the Five Dynasties, which offered regional objects on Jan.31, 936 (*Chiu Wu-tai shih* 48:1a; *Ts'e-fu yüan-kuei* p.5035).[14]

SILLA

During the Six Dynasties, Silla's relations with foreign countries were much more limited than those of Koguryŏ and Paekche. Only five

[14] According to the *Samguk sagi*, Later Paekche presented horses to Wu-yüeh in 918. See Worthy, Jr. in Rossaby ed., *China among Equals*, p.34.

missions are recorded to the Liang and Ch'en from 521-578, and two to the Northern Ch'i in 564 and 572.[15] This changed dramatically in T'ang times.

In 594, Silla envoys offered regional objects to the Sui court. Emperor Wen appointed its king, Chin Chen-p'ing (Chinp'yŏng Wang) as Supreme Commander Unequalled in Honour, entitled him duke of Lo-lang commandery, and recognized him as king of Silla (*Sui shu* 81:8a; *Wen-hsien t'ung-k'ao* 325:55a).

On Feb.4, 615, the New Year's Day, envoys from Silla offered presents and participated in a great banquet at the Sui court (*Sui shu* 4:9b).

In the 7th month (July/Aug.) of 621, Silla envoys offered gifts to the T'ang court. Emperor Kao-tsu dispatched a Cavalier Gentleman-in-Attendance for Comprehensive Duty as his envoy to Silla with a letter stamped with the imperial seal and 300 items of painted movable door screens and brocades (*Chiu T'ang shu* 199A:10b; *Ts'e-fu yüan-kuei* p.5023).

In the 10th month (Oct./Nov.) of 623, Silla envoys offered gifts (*Ts'e-fu yüan-kuei* p.5023).

On Feb.8,[16] 624, Kao-tsu sent envoys and appointed Chin Chen-p'ing as Pillar of State, entitled him king of Lo-lang, and recognized him as king of Silla (*Chiu T'ang shu* 1:8a; 199A:10b; *Tzu-chih t'ung-chien* p.5976; *Wen-hsien t'ung-k'ao* 326:55b).[17]

In the 11th month (Dec./Jan., 626) of the Chinese year 625, and in the 7th month (July/Aug.) of 626, Silla envoys brought offerings (*Chiu T'ang shu* 2:8a; *Ts'e-fu yüan-kuei* p.5023).

In 626, Silla, Paekche, and Koguryŏ attacked each other. The T'ang court sent a Supernumerary Cavalier Attendant as a mediator, whereupon all three states made peace and informed the court (*Chiu T'ang shu* 2:8a; 199A:2b, 7b; *Ts'e-fu yüan-kuei* p.5023; *Tzu-chih t'ung-chien* p.6030; *Wen-hsien t'ung-k'ao* 326:54b).

In the 6th month (July/Aug.) of 626, in the 11th month (Dec./Jan., 628) of the Chinese year 627, and in the 9th month (Sep./Oct.) of 629, Silla envoys offered gifts (*Ts'e-fu yüan-kuei* p.5023).

---

[15] See my *Six Dynasties*, vol.II, p.96.

[16] Correcting *chi-yu* to *yi-yu*.

[17] *Tzu-chih t'ung-chien* dates the appointments Mar.1.

On Dec.10, 631, Silla offered two female musicians with beautiful hair. They pined for their homes. This was shorthly after Lin-yi had presented a five-coloured parrot and a white cockatoo on Nov.30, 631. Emperor T'ai-tsung's trusted counsellor Wei Cheng (581-643) considered it improper to accept the girls. T'ai-tsung said:"While the parrot from Lin-yi can talk, it suffers from the cold and thinks of returning home. How much more is this true for the two women, who are separated from their relatives far away!" He rejected the girls and released the birds (*Chiu T'ang shu* 199A:11a; *Tzu-chih t'ung-chien* p.6090; *Wen-hsien t'ung-k'ao* 326:55b).

In 631, it became known at the T'ang court that the king of Silla, Chin Chen-p'ing, had died. He had no sons, so that his daughter Chin Shan-te (Sŏndŏk Yŏwang) was enthroned. T'ai-tsung bestowed on Chin Chen-p'ing the posthumous title of Imperial Household Grandee of the Left and contributed 200 items of objects toward the funeral expenses (*Chiu T'ang shu* 199A:11a; *Tzu-chih t'ung-chien* p.6092; *Wen-hsien t'ung-k'ao* 326:55b).

In 632, Silla offered gifts (*Ts'e-fu yüan-kuei* p.5024).

In 635, T'ai-tsung sent envoys to appoint Chin Shan-te as Pillar of State, entitle her queen of Lo-lang commandery, and recognize her as queen of Silla (*Chiu T'ang shu* 199A:11a).

In 639 and in the 1st month (Feb./Mar.) of 642, Silla envoys brought regional objects (*Chiu T'ang shu* 3:6b; *Ts'e-fu yüan-kuei* p.5024).

On Jan.26, 643, the New Year's Day, Silla offered regional objects (*Ts'e-fu yüan-kuei* p.5024).

On Oct.21, 643, envoys arrived from Silla and announced that it was under attack from Paekche and Koguryŏ, that it had lost more than 40 of its towns, and that the route was cut on which its envoys travelled to the T'ang court. It asked for support. T'ai-tsung sent an Assistant of the Minister of Agriculture, urging the kings of Paekche and Koguryŏ not to attack Silla (*Chiu T'ang shu* 199A:2b, 7b, 11a; *Tzu-chih t'ung-chien* p.6204; *Wen-hsien t'ung-k'ao* 326:54b, 55b).[18]

In the 11th month (Dec./Jan.) of 643 and on Feb.14, 644, the New Year's Day, Silla envoys offered regional objects (*Ts'e-fu yüan-kuei* p.5024).

On Jan.17, 645, T'ai-tsung ordered an attack on Koguryŏ by land

[18] *Chiu T'ang shu* and *Wen-hsien t'ung-k'ao* date the attack of Paekche and Koguryŏ 642.

and sea, in which Silla, as an ally, was to attack from the south (*Chiu T'ang shu* 199A:11a). It has been seen that this war ended inconclusively in 647.

On Feb.2, 645, the New Year's Day, Sillas envoys congratulated and offered regional objects (*Ts'e-fu yüan-kuei* p.5024).

On Jan.30, 648, the New Year's Day, Silla envoys offered gifts (*Ts'e-fu yüan-kuei* p.5025). That year, it became known at the T'ang court that Chin Shan-te had died and had been succeeeded by her younger sister Chin Chen-te (Chindŏk Yŏwang). T'ai-tsung conferred on the deceased queen the posthumous title of Imperial Household Grandee, appointed her sister as Pillar of State, entitled Chen-te queen of Lo-lang commandery, and recognized her as queen of Silla (*Chiu T'ang shu* 3:11b; 199A:11a; *Tzu-chih t'ung-chien* p.6252; *Wen-hsien t'ung-k'ao* 326:55b).

Chin Chen-te sent her younger brother Chin Ch'un-ch'iu and his son Wen-wang[19] to the T'ang court, where they were received on Jan.25, 649. Ch'un-ch'iu announced that Silla was adopting Chinese court dress,[20] and expressed the wish to attend a discussion at the National Academy. T'ai-tsung appointed him a Specially Advanced and gave his son the nominal title of General of the Martial Guards of the Left. He presented precious garments to both (*Chiu T'ang shu* 3: 11b; 199A:11a; *T'ung-tien* 185:55b; *Wen-hsien t'ung-k'ao* 326:55b).

In 650, Silla attacked Paekche. Chin Chen-te sent Chin Ch'un-ch'iu's son Fa-min to the T'ang court to announce it. He was given the nominal appointment of Grand Treasurer (*Chiu T'ang shu* 199A: 11a-11b; *Wen-hsien t'ung-k'ao* 326:55b).

In 651, Emperor Kao-tsung, blaming the tensions in Korea on Paekche, warned it not to attack Silla and Koguryŏ (*Tzu-chih t'ung-chien* p.6277).

On Feb.15, 652, the New Year's Day, Silla envoys offered gifts. In the 11th month (Nov./Dec.) of 653, its envoys presented textiles (*Ts'e-fu yüan-kuei* p.5025; *Tzu-chih t'ung-chien* p.6277).

In the intercalary month (June/July) of 654, news reached the T'ang court that Chin Chen-te had died and had been succeeded by Chin Ch'un-ch'iu (Muryŏl Wang). Kao-tsung commenced mourning for

[19] By *Chiu T'ang shu* 199A:11a called Wen-cheng.

[20] *Wen-hsien t'ung-k'ao* 326:55b claims that he "begged" to change the ceremonial dress of Silla in accordance with the Chinese regulations. Naturally, no permission was needed.

her, conferred on her the posthumous title of Commander Unequalled in Honour, and presented 200 pieces of silken fabrics [toward the funeral expenses]. He sent envoys to condole and sacrifice, appoint Ch'un-ch'iu as Commander Unequalled in Honour, entitle him king of Lo-lang commandery, and recognize him as king of Silla (*Chiu T'ang shu* 199A:11b; *T'ang hui-yao* 95:15*a;Tzu-chih t'ung-chien* p.6285; *Wen-hsien t'ung-k'ao* 326:55b).

In the 1st month (Feb./Mar.) of 655, Koguryŏ, Paekche and the Mo-ho joined forces and attacked Silla. Chin Ch'un-ch'iu sent envoys to the T'ang court and requested support (*Chiu T'ang shu* 199A:8b; *Tzu-chih t'ung-chien* pp.6287; *Wen-hsien t'ung-k'ao* 326:54b).

In the 3rd month (April) of 656, Silla envoys announced a victory over the troops of Paekche. In the10th month (Oct./Nov.) of the same year, Chin Ch'un-ch'iu's son, the General of the Martial Guards of the Right,[21] Wen-wang, arrived as his envoy at the T'ang court (*T'ang hui-yao* 95:15a; *Ts'e-fu yüan-kuei* p.5025).

In September, 660, Paekche was destroyed in a joint operation by T'ang and Silla (*Chiu T'ang shu* 199A:8b, 11b; *T'ang hui-yao* 95:14a-14b; *Wen-hsien t'ung-k'ao* 325:54b). 199SA:11b).

On Sep.29, 661, it became known at the T'ang court that the king of Silla, Chin Ch'un-ch'iu, had died and had been succeeded by his son, the Grand Treasurer,[22] Fa-min (Munmu Wang). Kao-tsung appointed him Commander Unequalled in Honour, and Supreme Pillar of State, entitled him king of Lo-lang commandery, and recognized him as king of Silla (*Chiu T'ang shu* 4:9b; 199A:11a; *Tzu-chih t'ung-chien* p.6325; *Wen-hsien t'ung-k'ao* 326:55b).

In 663, Kao-tsung attempted to incorporate Silla into the Chinese imaginary world empire. He created out of Silla the non-existant Chi-lin Area Command and appointed Fa-min its Military Governor. (*Chiu T'ang shu* 199A:11b; *Wen-hsien t'ung-k'ao* 326:55b). This looked fine on paper but from a practical point of view meant nothing.

On Nov.17, 665, a peace conference was held in Paekche by representatives of T'ang, Silla, Paekche, and Japan.[23] Thereafter, all

---

[21] During his visit to the T'ang court in 649, Chin Wen-wang had been given the nominal Chinese title of General of the Martial Guards of the Left. "Right" is therefore probably an error for "Left".

[22] Fa-min had been given this nominal Chinese title during his visit to Ch'ang-an in 650.

[23] *T'ang hui-yao* 95:15b dates the conference in the 8th month (Sep./Oct.) and adds that the text of the covenant was stored in the Ancestral Temple of Silla.

followed the Chinese envoy by sea to Shan-tung, where on Feb.10, 666 they attended Emperor Kao-tsung's *feng* sacrifice and on Feb.12 his *shan* sacrifice at Mount T'ai (*Chiu T'ang shu* 5:1a; *Tzu-chih t'ung-chien* p.6344; *Wen-hsien t'ung-k'ao* 325:50b).

In 668, Koguryŏ was destroyed by China, in alliance with Silla (*Chiu T'ang shu* 5:2b; *Tzu-chih t'ung-chien* p.6356). Thereafter, Silla's relations with China began to cool, since a permanent Chinese occupation of Paekche and Koguryŏ could not be to Silla's benefit. From 673 onward, Silla began to receive loyalists and refugees from the old Koguryŏ. In 674, it annexed what had been Paekche. At that time, Fa-min's younger brother Jen-wen was in Ch'ang-an. He had been given the nominal Chinese title of Supernumerary General-in-chief of the Resolute Guards and had been entitled duke of Lin-hai commandery. Kao-tsung now took recourse to the old Chinese policy of causing dissention by recognizing Jen-wen as king of Silla and sending him back to his state (*Chiu T'ang shu* 5:5a; *Tzu-chih t'ung-chien* pp.6370, 6372; *Wen-hsien t'ung-k'ao* 326:55b).

In the 2nd month (March) of 675, the Chinese attacked Silla. They were allied with the Mo-ho who raided the southern coast of Silla by sea. Silla thereupon sent envoys to the T'ang court, offering gifts and seeking peace. The Chinese texts state that Kao-tsung "pardoned" Silla, abandoned Chin Jen-wen, and again recognized its king Chin Fa-min. In the 9th month (Sep./Oct.) of the same year, envoys from Chin Fa-min offered regional objects (*Chiu T'ang shu* 5:6a; *Ts'e-fu yüan-kuei* p.5026; *Tzu-chih t'ung-chien* p.6375; *Wen-hsien t'ung-k'ao* 326:55b). The "pardon" of the texts is, of course, mere window dressing. Chin Fa-min, undeterred, took P'yŏngyang in 677, and unified Korea under his dynasty (*Tzu-chih t'ung-chien* p.6383).

On Dec.7, 681, it became known at the T'ang court that Chin Fa-min had died and had been succeeded by his son Cheng-ming[24] (Sinmun Wang). He dispatched a mission to the T'ang court. Kao-tsung sent envoys to recognize him as king of Silla and appointed him to the offices of his father (*Chiu T'ang shu*5:10b; 199A:11b; *T'ang hui-yao* 95:16a; *Wen-hsien t'ung-k'ao* 326:55b).

In 686, envoys from Cheng-ming brought a letter and requested the *Rites of T'ang* and other texts. The Empress Wu presented the king 50 chapters (chüan) of books (*Chiu T'ang shu* 199A:11b-12a).

---

[24] *Chiu T'ang shu* 5:10b calls him Chin Cheng.

In 692, Chin Cheng-ming died and was succeeded by his son Li-hung (Hyoso Wang). The empress Wu commenced mourning for Cheng-ming and sent envoys to condole and sacrifice. On Mar.28, 693, she appointed Li-hung as General-in-chief Who Supports the State, General-in-chief of the Leopard Bow-case Guards, and Military Governor of the non-existant Chi-lin Area Command, and recognized him as king of Silla (*Chiu T'ang shu* 199A:12a; *Tzu-chih t'ung-chien* p.6490).

In the 2nd month (Mar./Apr.) of 699, envoys from Chin Li-hung offered regional objects (*Ts'e-fu yüan-kuei* p.5026).

In 702, Li-hung died and was succeedeed by a younger brother (Sŏngdŏk Wang). The Empress Wu commenced mourning for Li-hung and suspended the court for two days. She sent envoys to confer on the new king the titles of his brother and recognize him as king of Silla. Since his original given name, from the Chinese point of view, violated an imperial taboo, the Empress Wu changed it to Hsing-kuang in 712 (*Chiu T'ang shu* 199A:12a; *T'ang hui-yao* 95:16b). The only purpose of this high-handed and sino-centric measure must have been for Chinese domestic use. It would have been ignored in Silla.

In the 1st month (Feb./Mar.) of 704, in the 3rd (Mar./Apr.) and 9th month (Sep./Oct.) of 705, in early 706, and in the 8th (Sep./Oct.) and 10th month (Nov.Dec.) of the same year, Silla envoys offered regional objects (*Ts'e-fu yüan-kuei* p.5026)

In 707, Emperor Chung-tsung appointed the king of Silla as General-in-chief of Agile Cavalry (*T'ang-hui-yao* 95:16b).

In the 12th month (Dec./Jan., 708) of the Chinese year 707, in the 6th month (July/Aug.) of 709, in the 1st month (Feb./Mar.) of 710, in the 12th month (Jan./Dec., 712)[25] of the Chinese year 711, in the 2nd month (Mar.Apr.) of 712, and in the 12th month (January, 713) of the Chinese year 712, Silla envoys offered regional objects (*Ts'e-fu yüan-kuei* pp.5026, 5027).

According to *Hsin T'ang shu* 220:10a and *Wen-hsien t'ung-k'ao* 326:55b, Silla between 713 and 741 frequently sent envoys to offer fruits and inferior horses. It also presented two women. Emperor Hsüan-tsung remarked that these were the paternal aunts or sisters of the king, and that he did not have the heart to keep them. He sent them home with

[25] *Ts'e-fu yüan-kuei* p.5026 says 11th month, but the entry is preceded by another which is also dated 11th month. The second "11th" should therefore be emended to "12th".

rich gifts. Hsüan-tsung presented Chin Hsing-kuang with brocade, gauze in five colours, purple embroidered robes, and fine vessels of gold and silver. Hsing-kuang offered dogs, horses, real gold, and beautiful false hair. *Ts'e-fu yüan-kuei* gives more detailed information:

In the 2nd (March) and 6th month (June/July) of 713, Silla envoys offered gifts (*Ts'e-fu yüan-kuei* p.5027). In the 3rd month (Mar./Apr.) of 716, a high official congratulated on the New Year's Day of 717 (Feb.16) (*Ts'e-fu yüan-kuei* p.5027).

In the 3rd (Apr./May) and 5th month (June/July) of 717, and in the 2nd month (Mar.Apr.) of 718, Silla offered regional objects (*Ts'e-fu yüan-kuei* p.5027).

On Jan.26, 719, Silla envoys congratulated on the New Year's Day (*Ts'e-fu yüan-kuei* p.5027).

On Nov.20, 722, a high official from Silla congratulated on the New Year's Day of 723 (Feb.10) (*Ts'e-fu yüan-kuei* p.5027).

In the 4th month (May/June) of 723, the king of Silla, Chin Hsing-kuang, sent envoys to present one inferior horse (*Ts'e-fu yüan-kuei* p.5027).

In the 2nd month (March) of 724, a high official from Silla congratulated on the New Year's Day of 725 (Feb.18). He was bestowed 50 bolts of silk (*Ts'e-fu yüan-kuei* p.5028).

At some time in 724, Hsing-kuang's nephew Chih-lien arrived with a letter and offered two small inferior horses, three dogs, 100 ounces of gold, 2,000 ounces of silver, 60 bolts of cotton, 20 ounzes of cow bezoar,[26] 200 ounces of ginseng, 100 ounces of human hair, and 16 seal ("sea leopard") skins, court garments, and engraved bells for the tailfeathers of falcons, etc. Chih-lien was appointed to the nominal Chinese office of Junior Herald (*T'ang hui-yao* 95:16b; *Ts'e-fu yüan-kuei* p.5029).

In the 12th month (Dec./Jan., 725) of the Chinese year 724, envoys from the king of Silla, Chin Hsing-kuang, offered regional objects (*Ts'e-fu yüan-kuei* p.5028).

In the 4th month (May/June) of 726, Silla envoys congratulated on the New Year's Day of 727 (Jan.27). In the 5th month (June/July) of the same year, a younger brother of the king of Silla came to the T'ang court (*Ts'e-fu yüan-kuei* p.5028).

---

[26] A concretion in the alimentary organs, used in Chinese medicine, and believed to have magical powers.

In 727, Silla envoys presented regional objects (*Ts'e-fu yüan-kuei* p.5028).

On Sep.24, 728, envoys from the king of Silla, Chin Hsing-kuang, offered regional objects. The king also proposed that men from his state study the classics in China. Emperor Hsüan-tsung accepted this (*Chiu T'ang shu* 8:15b; 199A:12a).

On Jan.23, 730, the New Year's Day, envoys from Silla congratulated. In the 9th month (Oct./Nov.) of the same year, envoys from Silla offered gifts (*Ts'e-fu yüan kuei* p.5028).

In the 2nd month (Mar/Apr.) of 731, Silla envoys congratulated on the New Year's Day of 732 (Feb.1) (*Ts'e-fu yüan-kuei* p.5028).

In 732, Hsüan-tsung presented Hsing-kuang one male and one female white cockatoo, embroidered robes of purple thin silk, embroidered silk in five colours, and other silken fabrics, in all more than 300 pieces, and vessels of gold and silver filigree. In 733, Hsing-kuang's nephew Chih-lien arrived with a letter of thanks and presented a painting of a Long Life Plant (*T'ang hui-yao* 95:17a).

In 732, Po-hai forces raided Teng[27] on the northern coast of Shan-tung by sea. At this time, Chin Hsing-kuang's clan member Ssu-lan was in the T'ang capital. Emperor Hsüan-tsung appointed him Supernumerary Grand Coachman and sent him back to Silla to attack Po-hai from the south in early 733. He also appointed Chin Hsing-kuang as Commander Unequalled in Honour and Military Commissioner of the non-existant Army Which Brings Repose to the Sea. The attack had to be called off because of an unusually cold winter (*Chiu T'ang shu* 199A:12a; 199B12b; *Tzu-chih t'ung-chien* p.6799; *Wen-hsien t'ung-k'ao* 326:55b).

In the 4th month (May/June) of 734, a high Silla official arrived at the T'ang court to congratulate on the New Year's Day of 735 (Jan.29). Subsequently Hsing-kuang sent a first paternal cousin to the T'ang court, but he died en route in the 11th month (Nov./Dec.) of 735. He was given the nominal Chinese title of Commandant of the Guards. In the 12th month (Jan./Feb., 736) of the same Chinese year 735, Silla envoys offered regional objects (*Chiu T'ang shu* 8:20b; *T'ang hui-yao* 95:17a; *Ts'e-fu yüan-kuei* p.5029).

In the 6th month (July/Aug.) of 736, envoys from Chin Hsing-kuang arrived to present a letter and congratulate [on the New Year's Day

---

[27] Modern P'eng-lai *hsien*.

of 737 (Feb.4)] In the 2nd month (Mar./Apr.) of 737, Silla envoys arrived to congratulate on the New Year's Day of 738 (Jan.25) and offer regional objects (*Ts'e-fu yüan-kuei* p.5029). The latter mission was probably recalled because of the death of the king. As will be seen below, a new mission arrived in the 12th month.

On Mar.29, 737, envoys arrived from Silla, announcing that Chin Hsing-kuang had died and that his son Ch'eng-ch'ing (Hyosŏng Wang) had succeeded to the throne. Emperor Hsüan-tsung sent an Admonisher Grandee as Acting Junior Herald to condole and sacrifice. Hsing-kuang was granted the posthumous title of Grand Guardian of the Heir-apparent, while Ch'eng-ch'ing was appointed Commander Unequalled in Honour and recognized as king of Silla (*Chiu T'ang shu* 9:1a; 199A:12a; *Tzu-chih t'ung-chien* p.6826; *Wen-hsien t'ung-k'ao* 326:55b).

In the 12th month (Dec./Jan., 738) of the Chinese year 737, envoys from the new king of Silla, Chin Ch'eng-ch'ing, arrived to offer regional objects (*Ts'e-fu yüan-kuei* p.5029).

In the 2nd month (Feb./Mar.) of 738, a high Silla official arrived to congratulate on the New Year's Day of 739 (Feb.13) (*Ts'e-fu yüan-kuei* p.5029).

In 743, it became known at the T'ang court that the king of Silla, Chin Ch'eng-ch'ing had died and had been succeeded by his younger brother Hsien-ying (Kyŏngdŏk Wang). Emperor Hsüan-tsung sent an Admonisher Grandee to condole and sacrifice. Hsien-ying was appointed to his elder brother's titles and recognized as king of Silla. Hsien-ying responded with a mission of his own. Hsüan-tsung was at that time in Ssu-ch'uan. The Silla envoys went up the Yangtze to Ch'eng-tu and congratulated there on the New Year's Day of 744 (Jan.20) (*Chiu T'ang shu* 119A:12b; *Wen-hsien t'ung-k'ao* 3426:55b).

In the intercalary month (Mar.Apr.) of 744, Silla envoys arrived to congratulate on the New Year's Day of 745 (Feb.6) and offer regional objects. This must have been an aborted mission since a new one arrived in the 12th month for the same purpose (*Ts'e-fu yüan-kuei* p.5030).

In the 4th month (May/June) of 744, Silla envoys were received at the court. In the 12th month (Jan./Feb., 745), a younger brother of the king of Silla arrived to congratulate on the New Year's Day of 745 (Feb.6) (*Ts'e-fu yüan-kuei* p.5030).

In the 4th month (May/June) of 745, Silla envoys brought gifts. In the 10th month (Oct./Nov.) of the same year, Silla envoys arrived to congratulate on the New Year's Day of 746 (Jan.26). The chief envoy was given the nominal Chinese office of Supernumerary Chief Clerk of the Police Patrol Guard Command of the Left and presented with a green robe and a silver belt (*T'ang hui yao* 95:17b; *Ts'e-fu yüan-kuei* p.5030).

In the 2nd month (Feb./Mar.) of 746, Silla envoys arrived to congratulate on the New Year's Day of 747 (Feb.14) and present regional objects (*Ts'e-fu yüan-kuei* p.5030).

In 748, the king of Silla presented gold, silver, cotton, court garments, cow bezoar, human hair, ginseng etc (*T'ang hui-yao* 95:17b).

In the 8th month (September) of 753, and in the 9th month (Sep./Oct.) of 762, Silla envoys were received at the court (*Ts'e-fu yüan-kuei* p.5031).

In 763, envoys from Chin Hsien-ying offered presents. The chief envoy was given the nominal Chinese title of Master of Writing of the Ministry of Rites. In the 3rd month (Apr./May) of 766, Silla envoys brought gifts (*T'ang hui-yao* 95:17b; *Ts'e-fu yüan-kuei* p.5031).

In 767, it became known at the T'ang court that Chin Hsien-ying had died and been succeeded by his son Ch'ien-yün (Hyegong Wang). He dispatched a mission that year with a letter and regional objects and requested recognition. In the 2nd month (Feb./Mar.) of 768, Emperor Su-tsung sent a Gentleman-of-the Palace of the Ministry of Granaries and Concurrent Palace Assistant Secretary to condole and sacrifice, appoint Chin Ch'ien-yün as Commander Unequalled in Honour, and recognize him as king of Silla. On Feb.11, the new king's mother was entitled Grand Consort. In the 9th month (Oct./Nov.) of the same year, Silla envoys offered gifts (*Chiu T'ang shu* 11:13b; 199A:12b; *T'ang hui-yao* 95:17b-18a; *Ts'e-fu yüan-kuei* p.5031; *Wen-hsien t'ung-k'ao* 326:55b).

In the 5th month (June/July) of 772, a Silla envoy arrived to congratulate on the New Year's Day of 773 (Jan.28). He was received in audience and appointed to the nominal office of Supernumerary Junior Commandant of the Guards (*Chiu T'ang shu* 199A:12b; *Ts'e-fu yüan-kuei* p.5031).

In the 4th month (Apr./May) of 773, Silla envoys arrived to congratulate on the New Year's Day of 774 (Feb.15). They presented gold, silver, cow bezoar, court garments, silken fabrics etc. In the 6th month (June/July) of the same year, another mission arrived from Silla, whose envoys were received in audience (*Chiu T'ang shu* 199A:12b; *T'ang hui-yao* 95:18a; *Ts'e-fu yüan-kuei* p.5032).

In the 4th month (May/June) of 774, Silla envoys offered gifts. In the 10th month (Nov./Dec.) of the same year, envoys arrived from Silla to congratulate on the New Year's Day of 775 (Feb.5). They were received in audience (*Ts'e-fu yüan-kuei* p.5032).

In the 1st (Feb./Mar.) and 6th month (July) of 775, Silla envoys offered gifts. In the 7th (July/Aug.) and 10th ((Nov./Dec.) month of 776, and in the 12th month (Jan., 778) of the Chinese year 777, they again offered presents (*Ts'e-fu yüan-kuei* p.5032).

Immediately after Te-tsung had ascended the T'ang throne on June 12, 779, he ordered that falcons were no longer to be accepted from Silla and Po-hai (*Chiu T'ang shu* 12:1a-1b). He may not have approved of hunting or conspicuous consumption or simply have wished to impress his contemporaries by his frugality.[28]

In the intercalary month (Feb./Mar.) of 782, Silla envoys offered gifts (*Ts'e-fu yüan-kuei* p.5032).

In 783, it became known at the T'ang court that Chin Ch'ien-yün had been killed. He had no sons and was succeeeded by his chancellor Chin Liang-hsiang (Sŏndŏk Wang) (*Chiu T'ang shu*199A:12b; *Wen-hsien t'ung-k'ao* 326:56a). In the 2nd month (Mar./Apr.) of 785, Emperor Te-tsung dispatched a Gentleman-of-the-Palace of the Ministry of Households to appoint Liang-hsiang as Acting Grand Commandant, Military Governor of the non-existant Chi-lin Area Command, and Military Commissioner of the non-existant Army Which Brings Repose to the Sea, and to recognize him as king of Silla. However, Chin Liang-hsiang died that very year of 785. His paternal uncle Chin Ching-hsin (Wŏnsŏng Wang) was enthroned and succeeded to his titles (*Chiu T'ang shu* 12:19a; 199A:12b; *Wen-hsien t'ung-k'ao* 326:58a).

In 798, Chin Ching-hsin died. He was succeeded by Chin Chün-yung (Sosŏng Wang), a grandson through his legitimate wife. On May 19, 800, Te-tsung sent a Gentleman-of-the-Palace of the Ministry of Honours and Concurrent Palace Assistant to appoint Chün-yung as Commander Unequalled in Honour and Acting Grand Commandant and to recognize him as king of Silla. En route, the Chinese envoy learned that the new king had died. With that, his commission had become void, and he returned. The T'ang court sent another mission to posthumously recognize Chün-yung as king of Silla, and to entitle his mother as Grand Consort and his widow as Consort (*Chiu*

[28] Cf. Schafer, *Golden Peaches*, pp.59, 93.

T'ang shu 199A:12b, 13a; *Tzu-chih t'ung-chien* p.7587; *Wen-hsien t'ung-k'ao* 326:56a).

In the 11th month (Dec./Jan., 805) of the Chinese year 804, a mission arrived from Silla (*Ts'e-fu yüan-kuei* p.5032).

In the 2nd month (Mar./Apr.) of 805, Emperor Shun-tsung sent a Gentleman-of-the-Palace of the Ministry of Arms to recognize Chin Chün-yung's son Chung-hsing (Aejang Wang) as king of Silla. His mother was entitled Grand Consort and his wife Consort (*Chiu T'ang shu* 14:1b; 199A:13a; *Wen-hsien t'ung-k'ao* 326:56a).

In the 8th month (Sep./Oct.) of 806, Silla envoys offered presents. In the 11th month (Dec./Jan., 807) of the same Chinese year 806, a royal Silla prince who had served in the imperial guards returned home. He was given the nominal title of Probationary Inspector of the Imperial Library (*Chiu T'ang shu* 199A:13a; *T'ang hui-yao* 95:18b; *Ts'e-fu yüan-kuei* p.5032

On Feb.8, 807, in 808, and in 809, Silla envoys offered gifts (*Chiu T'ang shu* 14:10a, *Ts'e-fu yüan-kuei* p.5032; *Wen-hsien t'ung-k'ao* 326: 56a).

In the 10th month (November) of 810, a son of the king of Silla presented gold and silver, an image of the Buddha, Buddhist sutras, pennants etc. in memory of Shun-tsung[29] (*Chiu T'ang shu* 199A:13a; *Ts'e-fu yüan-kuei* p.5032).

In 812,[30] Chin Chung-hsin died and was suceeded by his chancellor Chin Yen-sheng (Hŏndŏk Wang). In the 4th month (May/June) of the same year, a mission of 54 men from Chin Yen-sheng arrived at the T'ang court to congratulate on the New Year's Day of 813 (Feb.5) and at the same time to announce the death of his predecessor. The envoys were received in audience *Chiu T'ang shu* 199A:13a; *Ts'e-fu yüan-kuei* p.5032; *Wen-hsien t'ung-k'ao* 326:56a). On Sep.2, 812,[31]

---

[29] Who had abdicated in 805 and died in 806.

[30] *Chiu T'ang shu* says unequivocably that Chung-hsing died in 812. *Wen-hsien t'ung-k'ao* states that Chung-hsing died after a reign of seven years. If counted from the year of China's recognition (805) this would give 812. *Ts'e-fu yüan-kuei* agrees that the death was announced in 812. This conflicts with the Korean chronology as given by Marcus, *Korean Studies Guide*, p.181, according to which Chung-hsing died in 809. But if Chung-hsing had died in 809, Silla would have had opportunity to announce it in the mission of 810.

[31] *Chiu T'ang shu* 15:2a gives the date as 6th month, *chi-mou*, *Chiu T'ang shu* 199A: 13a and *T'ang hui-yao* 95:19a as 7th month without cyclical characters. The 6th month had no day with the cyclical characters *chi-mou*, so that 7th month is correct.

Emperor Hsien-tsung sent envoys to Silla to condole and sacrifice. Chin Yen-sheng was appointed Commander Unequalled in Honour, Acting Grand Commandant, Grand Chief Commandant in charge of all military matters of the non-existant Chi-lin Area Command, Military Commissioner of the non-existant Army Which Brings Repose to the Sea, and Supreme Pillar of State. He was recognized as king of Silla and his wife was entitled Consort. On Sep.10, titles and gifts were conferred on three high Silla officials (*Chiu T'ang shu* 15:2a; 199A:13a; *Wen-hsien t'ung-k''ao* 326:56a).

In the 3rd month (Mar./Apr.) of 817, Silla envoys arrived with gifts (*Chiu T'ang shu* 15:9b; *Ts'e-fu yüan-kuei* p.5033).

In 818, the T'ang court ordered that missions from Silla were not to exceed 20 members (*T'ang hui-yao* 97:12b).

In the 11th month (Dec./Jan.821) of the Chinese year 820, and in the 12th month (Jan./Feb., 823) of the Chinese year 822, envoys from Silla offered gifts (*Chiu T'ang shu* 199A:13a; *Ts'e-fu yüan-kuei* p.5033).

In 825, a royal son from Silla was received at the T'ang court. He was appointed to the imperial guards (*Chiu T'ang shu* 199A:13a-13b; *T'ang hui-yao* 95:19b).

On June 22, 826, envoys from Silla offered falcons. In the 4th month (May) of 827, in the 12th month (Dec./Jan., 830) of the Chinese year 829, and in the 12th month (Dec./Jan., 831) of the Chinese year 830, Silla envoys offered presents (*Chiu T'ang shu* 17:9a; 199A:13b; *Ts'e-fu yüan-kuei* p.5033).

In the 2nd month (Mar./Apr.) of 831, a son of the king of Silla and nine Buddhist priests brought offerings (*Ts'e-fu yüan-kuei* p.5033).

In 831 the T'ang court learned of the death of Chin Yen-sheng (*Chiu T'ang shu* 199A:13b).[32] His son Ching-hui succeeded (Hŭngdŏk Wang). The emperor ordered the Adviser of the Left of the Heir-apparent and Concurrent Assistant Palace Secretary to appoint Ching-hui as Commander Unequalled in Honour, Acting Grand Commandant, Grand Chief Commandant of all military matters of the non-existant Chi-lin Area Command, and Military Commissioner of the non-existant Army Which Brings Repose to the Sea. Ching-hui was recognized as king of Silla, his mother was entitled Grand Consort, and his wife as Consort

[32] T'ang hui-yao 95:19b gives the year as 830. Both dates conflict with the Korean chronology as given by Marcus, *Korean Studies Guide*, p.181, according to which the Hŏndŏk Wang died in 826. If he had died in 826, Silla would have had ample opportunity to announce it in the misssions of 627, 629, and perhaps 630.

(*Chiu T'ang shu* 199A:13b; *Wen-hsien t'ung-k'ao* 326:56a).

In the 11th month (Dec./Jan.,832) of the Chinese year 831, Silla envoys offered gifts (*Ts'e-fu yüan-kuei* p.5033).

In the 12th month (Jan./Feb., 837) of the Chinese year 836, a royal prince from Silla arrived with gifts. He stayed in the Chinese capital as a member of the imperial guards until he returned to his state on May 19, 837 (*Chiu T'ang shu* 199A:13b; *Ts'e-fu yüan-kuei* p.5033; *Wen-hsien t'ung-k'ao* 325:56a).

In the 4th month (May/June) of 840, the Sung ministry of the Herald announced to Silla that Emperor Wen-tsung had died (on Feb.10) (*Chiu T'ang shu* 199A:13b).

On Mar.26, 846, the last recorded mission from Silla to T'ang was received at the court. Thereafter, they no longer came (*Wen-hsien t'ung-k'ao* 326:56a).

In the 10th month (Nov./Dec.) of 915, Silla envoys offered regional objects to the Khitan court (*Liao shih* 1:8b).

On Dec.28, 923, Silla envoys with regional objects were received at the Later T'ang court. The chief envoy was appointed to the nominal office of Grandee for Court Discussion. All were given presents, each in accordance with his rank (*Chiu Wu-tai shih* 30:9b; *Hsin Wu-tai shih* 5:6b; *Wu-tai hui-yao* 30:10b; *Ts'e-fu-yüan-kuei* p.5033; *Wen-hsien t'ung-k'ao* 326:56a).

On Feb.18, and in the 6th month (July/Aug.) of 924, Silla envoys offered presents to the Later T'ang court (*Chiu Wu-tai shih* 31:2a; *Hsin Wu-tai shih* 5:6b; *Ts'e-fu-yüan-kuei* p.5034).

On Dec.8, 925, Silla offered gifts to the Khitan court (*Liao shih* 2:5b; 70:2b).

In 926 or earlier, Silla sent envoys to the king of Wu-yüeh,[33] Ch'ien Liu (*Chiu Wu-tai shih* 133:16a).

On Mar.26, 927, Silla envoys offered regional objects to the Later T'ang court. In the 3rd month (Apr./May), the Later T'ang conferred the title of General-in-chief Who Cherishes Civilization on a Silla dignitary. In the 4th month (May/June), Silla envoys again arrived at the Later T'ang court. They were received in audience and given presents, each in accordance with his rank (*Chiu Wu-tai shih* 38:3a, 5b; *Wu-tai hui-yao* 30:10b, 11a; *Ts'e-fu-yüan-kuei* p.5034; *Wen-hsien t'ung-k'ao* 326:56a).

[33] Comprising the coastal part of central China.

On May 16, 932, Silla offered regional objects to the Later T'ang court. The chief envoy was given the nominal title of Master of Writing of the Ministry of Works, and his deputy that of Junior Inspector of the Court Architect (*Hsin Wu-tai shih* 6:10b; *Wu-tai hui-yao* 30:11a-11b; *Ts'e-fu yüan-kuei* p.5035).[34]

It can be seen that during its last enfeebled years, Silla reached out to Later T'ang, Wu-yüeh, and the Khitan, but all to no avail. In 935, it was overrun by Later Paekche, and the last king fled to Koryŏ.

Like Koguryŏ and Paekche, Silla was deeply influenced by the Chinese civilization. Students enroled at the National Academy in Ch'ang-an. In 840 alone, 105 students returned to Silla (*T'ang hui-yao* 95:20a). Chin Ch'un-chiu, the future Muryŏl Wang, attended a discussion at the National Academy in 649. In 686, Silla requested and received the *Rites of T'ang* and other texts. In 728, it arranged for Korean scholars to study the classics in China. In the middle of the 7th century, Silla adopted T'ang court dress. And these are only the instances mentioned in the Chinese sources. There must have been many others.

Also, like Koguryŏ and Paekche, Silla was not a Chinese vassal. It was, in fact, an ally, against Paekche in 660 and against Koguryŏ in 645-747 and in 668. Even after Silla had unified Korea in the 670's, common interests still forced the two states to cooperate, now against Po-hai, and the Khitan.

The Chinese historians liked to believe that Silla princes were in the Chinese capital as hostages. The commentator of the *Tzu-chih t'ung-chien* (p.6799) Hu San-hsing (1230-1287) claims that the Chin Ssu-lan, who in 733 was to attack Po-hai on behalf of the T'ang, had come to Ch'ang-an as a hostage.The *T'ang hui-yao* (95:19a; 20a) refers to hostages in 812 and 840. It is a fact that Silla princes were at times in the capital, in addition to those just mentioned another in 674, another in 806, another in 816, another in 825, and still another in 837. But to call them hostages must surely be wishful thinking, certainly by the ancient historians and perhaps by the T'ang government. China did not have the power to demand nor Silla the need to provide hostages. The princes came to Ch'ang-an on their own initiative or at the behest of their fathers; they were given nominal appointments to the imperial guards and may have done some studying, but they must have been

---

[34] By *Wu-tai hui-yao* dated 933.

in the Chinese metropolis chiefly for their own amusement.

Relations between T'ang and Silla, except for the brief war in 675, were generally cordial. The Chinese court conferred no posthumous titles on the kings of Koguryŏ and only one on a king of Paekche. Condolences were rendered for a single king of Koguryŏ and none of Paekche. Mourning was held for a single king of Koguryŏ and Paekche each. In contrast, posthumous titles are recorded for Silla's Chinp'yŏng Wang, Sŏndŏk Yŏwang, Chindŏk Yŏwang, and Sŏngdŏk Wang. The T'ang condoled and sacrificed at the death of Chindŏk Yŏwang, Sinmun Wang, Sŏngdŏk Wang, Hyosŏng Wang, Kyŏngdŏk Wang, and Aejang Wang, and it held mourning for the Sinmun Wang and Hyoso Wang. This list may not be complete. Why, for instance, is no action of the T'ang court recorded after the death of the Muryŏl Wang, Munmu Wang, Hyegong Wang, Sosŏng Wang, Hŏndŏk Wang, and Hŭngdŏk Wang?[35] But even allowing for omissions in the records for Silla, as also in those for Koguryŏ and Paekche, it is still true beyond question that Silla was diplomatically closer to China than the other two states.

During the Six Dynasties, the missions from Silla to the southern courts had by necessity come by sea, since the land route was blocked. In T'ang times, Silla could make use of the land route. The preferred times of travel where the winter and spring. The envoys might stay in the Chinese capital for extended periods of time. Six missions for the New Year congratulations are recorded to have arrived in the preceding 2nd months, one in the 3rd, two in the 4th, and one in the 5th. It means that on each occasion the envoys stayed in Ch'ang-an for the better part of the year, which gave them ample opportunity for commerce and enjoyment.

The statistics are, as usual, not entirely, but nearly, complete. *Sui shu* 81:8b states that from 605, Silla annually sent missions, but only one for 615 is recorded. *Chiu T'ang shu* 199A:10b says that from 621 the missions were uninterrupted. In fact, missions are recorded for 623, 625, 626, 627 (2), 629, 631, and 632. According to *T'ang hui-yao* 95:17b, Silla incessantly sent envoys from 745. Missions are recorded for 746, 748, and 753. *Wen-hsien t'ung-k'ao* 326:56a records that from

[35] It should be noted, however, that all but the first two of these kings ruled after An Lu-shan's rebellion in 755, when relations between T'ang and Silla became less intimate and the Chinese attitude may have changed.

the mid 760's Silla annually sent envoys. Missions are recorded for 767, 768, 772, and 773 (2). *Chiu T'ang shu* 199A:12b says that from 774 to 777 Silla annually sent envoys. No less than seven missions are recorded for that period. Congratulations on the New Year Days are either directly mentioned or can be surmised from the arrival times of the missions; but obviously not all of them were recorded or they were not a regular feature throughout the period under discussion.

This is the distribution by 20-year periods of the 122 recorded missions from Silla to Sui, Tang, Later T'ang, and Wu-yüeh:

587-806:	1
607-626:	6
627-646:	11
647-666:	8
667-686:	4
687-706:	7
707-726:	20
727-746:	21
747-766:	5
767-786:	13
787-806:	2
807-826:	10
827-846:	7
847-866:	0
867-886:	0
887-906:	0
907-926:	4
927-946:	3

For the period 587 to 666, the figures are compatible with those for Koguryŏ and Paekche, 26 in comparison to 27 and 31. After the unification of Korea the missions at first became fewer, presumably because China was unhappy with Silla's achievement, but then reached their highest level in the reign of Hsüan-tsung (712-756). After the rebellion of An Lu-shan in 755, the missions continued to come, but they again became fewer, and eventually ceased altogether. This was not only due to the disruptions in China but also the disintegration of Silla. In addition to the 122 Silla missions to China, the texts also record two to the Liao.

The purpose of the missions was diplomacy concerning war and peace, courtesy calls on ceremonial occasions, and trade. The envoys exchanged goods on the government level, as well as, no doubt, privately. In contrast to Koguryŏ and Paekche, the merchandise is at times described by the sources. They fall into the following categories:

Humans and Human Products

631: 2 female musicians (rejected), hair.
713–741: 2 women (rejected).
724: 100 ounces of human hair.
748: human hair.

Animals and Animal Products

Horses

723: 1 inferior horse.
724: 2 small inferior horses.

Dogs

724: 3 dogs.

Furs

724: 16 seal skins.

Birds

826: falcons.

Medical Drugs

724: 20 ounces of cow bezoar.
748: cow bezoar.
774: cow bezoar.

Plants and Fruits

713-741: fruits.
724: 200 ounces of ginseng.
748: ginseng.

Metals

724: 100 ounces of gold, 2000 ounces of silver.
748: gold and silver.
774: gold and silver.
810: gold and silver.

Manufactured Objects

Of metal

724: engraved bells for the tailfeathers of falcons.

Other

733: a painting of a Long Life Plant.
810: an image of the Buddha, pennants.

Textiles

Cottons

724: 60 bolts of cotton.

Silks

774: silken fabrics.

Garments:

724: court garments.
748: court garments.
774: court garments.

Texts

810: Buddhist sutras.

The recorded Chinese offerings were brocades, gauzes and other silken fabrics, embroidered robes, belts, vessels of gold and silver, door screens, books, and cockatoos.

KORYŎ

During Sui and T'ang, Chinese relations with Korea had been relatively simple. Koguryŏ, Paekche, and Silla fought each other in varying combinations, while China attempted to restore the borders of Han times or even go beyond them. When this proved unsucessful, the T'ang learned to coexist peacefully with Silla, in which process the unified Korea continued to be inspired by the splendid T'ang culture, and Silla and T'ang benefited from political and commercial relations.

From the 10th century, the situation changed. China and the new state of Koryŏ (916-1392) had not only to deal with each other but also with two consecutive great powers in the north, the Khitan/Liao (907-1125) and the Jurchen/Chin (1115-1234). In the process, diplomatic relations became more complicated and at the same time also more sophisticated.

In 901, the Buddhist monk Kung-yi (Kungye) founded a state in the central part of northern Korea, proclaiming himself king and calling his domain Ta-feng (T'aebong) (*Tzu-chih t'ung-chien* p.8848). The state has also been known as Later Koguryŏ.

In the 10th month (Nov./Dec.) of 915, envoys from Kung-yi to the Khitan court presented a precious sword (*Liao shih* 1:8b). In 918 Kung-yi was overthrown by his officer Wang Chien (Wang Kŏn) and subsequently killed. Wang Chien (T'aejo) made himself king and shortened the name of the state to Koryŏ (*Tzu-chih t'ung-chien* p.8861).

Wang Chien immediately opened relations with neighbouring states. In the 2nd month (Mar./Apr.) of 918, his envoys offered a precious sword to the Khitan court. In the 3rd month (Apr./May) of the same year, another Koryŏ mission was received at the Khitan court (*Liao shih* 1:10a-10b; 70:1b; 115:1a). In the 7th month (July/Aug.) of 919, envoys from Koryŏ arrived in the Chinese state of Wu[-yüeh] (*Tzu-chih t'ung-chien* p.8848). In 923, a Koryŏ mision was received at the court of the Later Liang[36] (*Wen-hsien t'ung-k'ao* 325:51a).

In 924, Wang Chien sent envoys to the Khitan court (*Liao shih* 115:1a). On Dec. 6, 925,[37] his envoys presented regional objects to the Later T'ang court. In the 1st month (Feb./Mar.) of 926, the Later T'ang appointed the head of the Koryŏ mission as Gentleman for Closing Court and his deputy Probationary Gentleman of the Imperial Library (*Hsin Wu-tai shih* 5:8b; *Wu-tai hui-yao* 30:4b; *Ts'e-fu yüan-kuei* p.5034).

On Nov.10, 925, on Apr.5, 926, and in 927, Koryŏ missions were received at the Khitan court (*Liao shih* 2:5b, 6b; 115:1a).

On Sep.28, 929, a mission of 53 men[38] from Wang Chien was received at the Later T'ang court. It presented censers for aromatics, gilded lances, swords, textiles, human hair, ginseng, fragrant oils, silver-engraved scissors etc (*Hsin Wu-tai shih* 6:8a; *Ts'e-fu yüan-kuei* p.5034).

In the 3rd month (Apr./May) of 932,[39] a mission from Wang Chien, led by a high official, offered gifts to the Later T'ang court. On July 6, Emperor Ming-tsung of that dynasty appointed Wang Chien as Specially Advanced, Acting Grand Guardian, Chief Commandant of Hsüan-t'u commandery,[40] Military Commissioner of the non-existant Army of Great Righteousness, Concurrent Grandee Secretary, and Supreme Pillar of State, and recognized him as king of Koryŏ. In the 7th month (Aug./Sep.), Wang Chien's wife was entitled Consort (*Chiu wu-tai shih* 43:4a; *Hsin Wu-tai shih* 6:10b; *Wu-tai hui-yao* 30:4b-5a; *Ts'e-fu yüan-kuei* p.5035; *Wen-hsien t'ung-k'ao* 325:51a). In the 7th month (Aug./Sep.) of the same year, Wang Chien presented a communication to Ming-tsung (*Chiu wu-tai shih* 43:6b).

In the 8th month (Sep./Oct.) of 934, local officials in northern Shan-tung[41] reported to the Later T'ang court that a mission had arrived from Koryŏ (*Ts'e-fu yüan-kuei* p.5035).

In the 10th month (Oct./Nov.) of 935, envoys from Wang Chien to the Later T'ang court offered gifts. Another mission arrived in the 12th month (Dec./Jan.936) of the Chinese year 935. In the 1st month (Jan./Feb.) of 936, its chief envoy was by the Later T'ang appointed

[36] Or possibly Later T'ang. The last Later Liang emperor committed suicide on Nov.18.

[37] By *Ts'e-fu yüan-kuei* p.5034 dated 10th month (Oct./Nov.) instead of 11th.

[38] *Wu-tai hui-yao* 30:4b says 52 men.

[39] By *Wu-ta hui-yao* 30:4b dated 2nd month (Mar./Apr.). *Hsin Wu-tai shih* 74:13b dates the mission 931, which must be an error.

[40] The name of an administrative unit during Han and Western Chin.

[41] Probably in the port of Teng.

Probationary Junior Inspector of the Court Architect, and his deputy Probationary Master of Records of the Inspector of the Privy Treasurer (*Wu-tai hui-yao* 30:5a; *Ts'e-fu yüan-kuei* p.5035).

In the 1st month (Jan./Feb.) of 936, a royal son of Koryŏ with a mission of 30 men offered regional objects to the Later T'ang court. He was made an Acting Supervisor of the Right of the Masters of Writing, and his deputy a Probationary Inspector of the Court Architect. The other members of the mission were appointed to lesser offices (*Wu-tai hui-yao* 30:5a; *Ts'e-fu yüan-kuei* p.5035).

In the 12th month (Jan./Feb., 937) of the Chinese year 936, it became known in Later Chin that Wang Chien had conquered Later Paekche, which in 935 had absorbed Silla, and thereby had reunited Korea (*Tzu-chih t'ung-chien* p.9166). The Later Chin recognized Wang Chien as king of Koryŏ, of which he in turn informed the Khitan court in 939 (*Liao shih* 115:1a).

On Nov.2, 939, a Koryŏ mission of 92 men[42] to the Later Chin court offered regional objects (*Chiu wu-tai shih* 78:8a; *Ts'e-fu yüan-kuei* p.5035).

On July 14, 941, the Later Chin entitled Wang Chien Commander Unequalled in Honour, Chief Commandant of Hsüan-t'u commandery, and Military Commissioner of the non-existant Army of Great Righteousness, and recognized him as king of Koryŏ. An Erudite of the National University was sent to Koryŏ to confer these titles (*Chiu wu-tai shih* 79:11a; *Wu-ta hui-yao* 30:5b).

On Dec.26, 943, a Koryŏ envoy was received at the Later Chin court (*Hsin Wu-tai shih* 9:4a).

On Jan.8, 944, a Koryŏ mission was received at the Later Chin court. Its chief envoy was appointed Acting Prefect of the Granary Bureau and Supreme Pillar of State and presented with a purple and gold fish wallet. The lesser envoys were made Acting Supervisor of the Masters of Writing, Acting Master of Writing in the Ministry of Rites, Probationary Commandant of the Guards, Probationary Junior Commandant of the Guards, Probationary Grand Treasurer, Probationary Junior Grand Treasurer, Probationary Master of Records of the Inspector of the Court Architect, and Acting Master of Writing in the Ministry of Works, and all were given golden fish wallets (*Hsin Wu-tai shih* 9:4a; *Wu-tai hui-yao* 30:5b-6a).

---

[42] *Wu-tai hui-yao* 30:5b says 72 men.

On Nov.21, 945, Koryŏ envoys to the Later Chin court announced that Wang Chien had died [in 943] and had been succeeded by his son Wu (Hyejong). Another mission was received on Dec.2. On Dec.12., the Later Chin appointed Wang Wu as Specially Advanced, Acting Grand Guardian, Chief Commandant of Hsüan-t'u commandery, Military Commissioner of the non-existant Army of Great Righteousness, and Concurrent Grandee Secretary, and recognized him as king of Koryŏ. In the 12th month (Jan./Feb., 946) of the same Chinese year 945, the Later Chin sent envoys to Koryŏ for the formal recognition (*Chiu wu-tai shih* 84:5a, 6a; *Hsin Wu-tai shih* 9:6b, 7a; *Wu-tai hui-yao* 30:6a-6b; *Ts'e-fu yüan-kuei* p.5036; *Tzu-chih t'ung-chien* p.9298; *Wen-hsien t'ung-k'ao* 325:51a).The Chinese court was obviously unaware that Wang Wu had died earlier in 945.

Wang Wu was suceeded by Yao (Chŏngjong), who is not mentioned in the Chinese sources and died in 949. Yao's successor was Chao (Kwangjong). There seems to have been a hiatus in Koryŏ's relations with China, since *Chiu wu-tai shih* 112:3b as late as 952 refers to Chao as "probationary" ruler. This simply means that he had not yet been recognized.

On Feb.11, 952, a 97-men mission from Wang Chao to the Later Chou court offered gifts. On Mar.5, the Later Chou appointed him as Specially Advanced, Acting Grand Guardian, Chief Commandant of Hsüan-t'u commandery, Military Commissioner of the non-existant Army of Great Righteousness, and Concurrent Grandee Secretary, and recognized him as king of Koryŏ. The Commandant of the Guards and a Secretarial Receptionist were sent to confer these titles. The former died en route of an undisclosed illness and the latter drowned (*Chiu wu-tai shih* 112:3b, 4b; *Wu-tai hui-yao* 30:6b; *Ts'e-fu yüan-kuei* p.5036; *Wen-hsien t'ung-k'ao* 325:51a).[43]

In the 7th month (July/Aug.) of 952, a Buddhist priest from Koryŏ presented regional objects to the Later Chou court (*Ts'e-fu yüan-kuei* p.5036). It is difficult to know whether the priest acted for his church or the state.

In the 9th month (Sep./Oct.) of 952, the Later Chou sent a new mission to the Koryŏ court in order to recognize Wang Chao. It was led by the Junior Grand Coachman, who for that purpose was made

---

[43] *Wu-tai hui-yao* dates these events 951. *Chiu wu-tai shih* 115:10b dates the appointments 11th month (Dec./Jan., 956) of the Chinese year 955. It also says Acting Grand Commandant instead of Grand Guardian.

an Acting Commandant of the Guards. His deputy, a member of the Defense Guard Command of the Right, was made a Junior Inspector of the Court Architect (*Wu-tai hui-yao* 30:7a).

Emperor Shih-tsung of Later Chou (r.954-959) sent a Supernumerary Gentleman of the Bureau of Waterways and Irrigation of the Masters of Writing to Koryŏ to buy copper for casting cash, for which he paid with several 1000 bolts of silk (*Hsin Wu-tai shih* 74:14a).

In the 10th month (Oct./Nov.) of 954, a high official from Koryŏ offered regional objects to the Later Chou court (*Ts'e-fu yüan-kuei* p.5036).

On Nov.30, 955, Koryŏ envoys to the Later Chou court presented regional objects and congratulated on the ascension of Emperor Shih-tsung (on Feb.22, 954) (*Chiu wu-tai shih* 115:9a; *Ts'e-fu yüan-kuei* p.5036).[44]

In the 12th month (January, 956) of the Chinese year 955, Shih-tsung of Later Chou appointed Wang Chao as Commander Unequalled in Honour and Acting Grand Master and once more recognized him as king of Koryŏ (*Wu-tai hui-yao* 30:7a).

In the 7th month (July/Aug.) of 958, the Later Chou sent a Supernumerary Gentleman of the Bureau of Waterways and the Chief Steward of the Imperial Hand-drawn Carriage Service as envoys to the Koryŏ court, where they presented 1000 bolts of silk (*Wu-tai hui-yao* 30:7a).

On Feb.16, 959, Wang Chao's envoys to the Later Chou court offered fine horses, woven robes, bows, swords, armour, 2000 pieces each of purple and white rock crystals, and 50,000 catties of yellow copper. On Oct.4, Koryŏ presented four different editions of the *Classic of Filial Piety*. On Oct.28, the Later Chou sent a General-in-chief of the Resolute Guards of the Left as envoy to the Koryŏ court (*Chiu wu-tai shih* 119:1a; 138:6b; *Hsin Wu-tai shih* 12:6b; 74:14a; *Ts'e-fu yüan-kuei* p.5036).

On Oct.17, 959, the last Later Chou emperor, Kung, reconfirmed Wang Chao as Acting Grand Master (*Chiu wu-tai shih* 120:5b).

In the 11th month (December) of 959, envoys from Koryŏ to the Later Chou court offered 50,000 catties of copper etc. (*Ts'e-fu yüan-kuei* p.5036).[45] This was the last recorded mission from Koryŏ to China

[44] *Ts'e-fu yüan-kuei* wrongly dates this mission in the 11th month. The 11th did not have the cyclical characters *mou-yin*.

[45] According to *Wu-tai hui-yao* 30:7b the copper and rock crystals were all presented in the 11th month.

before the establishement of the Sung Dynasty in 960.

In 962, envoys from Wang Chao arrived at the Sung court. He was granted the title of Meritorious Subject Who Is Righteous (*Sung shih* 487:1b-2a; *Wen-hsien t'ung-k'ao* 325:51a). In the 9th month (October) and 11th month (December) of 962, Wang Chao again offered regional objects (*Sung shih* 1:13a; 487:2a).

In the 1st month (Feb./Mar.) of 965, Koryŏ envoys to the Sung court offered gifts (*Sung shih* 2:1a).

In 972,[46] envoys from Wang Chao to the Sung court presented regional objects. His title was expanded to Meritorious Subject Who Extends Sincerity, Obeys Civilization, Maintains Integrity, and Guards Righteousness. Chinese envoys were sent in response (*Sung shih* 3:2a; 487:2a-2b; *Wen-hsien t'ung-k'ao* 325:51a).

When Wang Chao died in 975, he was succeeded by his son Chou (Kyŏngjong). On Oct.2, 976, his envoys to the Sung court offered presents. He was appointed Acting Grand Guardian, Military Governor of Hsüan-t'u subcommandery, and Military Commissioner of the non-existant Army of Great Righeousness, and recognized as king of Koryŏ. After T'ai-tsung had ascended the Sung throne on Nov.14, 976, he confirmed Wang Chou as Acting Grand Guardian and made him a Meritorious Subject. The Army of Great Righteousness was changed to the equally non-existant Army of Great Obedience. Chinese envoys were dispatched to Koryŏ, while Wang Chou sent a native of his state to study under the aegis of the Sung Directorate of Education. On Dec.6, Wang Chou was again recognized as king of Koryŏ (*Sung shih* 3:12a; 4:2a; 487:2b; *Wen-hsien t'ung-k'ao* 325:51a).

On Nov.5, 978, a son of Wang Chou congratulated on the enthronement of T'ai-tsung and presented fine horses, military implements, and regional objects (*Sung shih* 4:5a; 487:2b; *Hsü Tzu-chih t'ung-chien ch'ang-pien* p.166).

On July 25, 980,[47] envoys from Wang Chou to the Sung court presented regional objects. He was appointed Acting Grand Master. On May 25, 981, Koryŏ envoys again offered gifts (*Sung shih* 4:12b, 14a; 487:3a).

---

[46] *Sung shih* 3:2a dates this mission 7th month, *keng-yin*, but the 7th did not have these cyclical characters.

[47] *Hsü Tzu-chih t'ung-chien ch'ang-pien* p.180 erroneously gives the cyclical characters of *jen-tzu* instead of *jen-wu*.

On Jan.7, 983, a Koryŏ mission was received at the Sung court, announcing that Wang Chou had died and that his younger brother Ch'ih (Sŏngjong) had succeeded him.[48] The envoys presented gold and silver threaded mats, brocade garments, bedding, knives, bows, and arrows ornamented with silver and gold, fine horses, and aromatic drugs. T'ai-tsung sent envoys in response and appointed Ch'ih as Grand Guardian, Military Governor of Hsüan-t'u subcommandery, and Military Commissioner of the non-existant Army of Great Obedience, and recognized him as king of Koryŏ (*Sung shih* 4:17a; 487:3a; *Wen-hsien t'ung-k'ao* 325:51a).

On Dec.1, 984, envoys from Wang Ch'ih to the Sung court offered gifts. In 985, T'ai-tsung made him Acting Grand Tutor and sent a mission in response (*Sung shih*) 487:3a).

In the 7th month (July/Aug.) of 985, Sheng-tsung of Liao ordered that preparations be made for an attack on Koryŏ (*Liao shih* 115:1a). This was, however, postponed. During the same year, a Sung mission to the Koryŏ court proposed an alliance against Liao. This came to nothing.[49]

In 986, Wang Ch'ih attacked the Jurchen and simultaneously sent a mission to the Sung court. Emperor T'ai-tsung showed the envoys the document in which the Jurchen had informed him about the emergency. He demanded that Koryŏ should return the prisoners it had taken (*Sung shih* 5:5a; 487:3a-3b; *Wen-hsien t'ung-k'ao* 325: 51a). The Jurchen in question must have been those living in the Yalu River valley, whom the Sung hoped to mobilize against Liao.[50] A conflict between the Jurchen and Koryŏ was therefore not in Sung's interest.

On Nov.21, 986, another mission from Koryŏ offered gifts to the Sung court. It included two natives who were to study under the aegis of the Directorate of Education (*Sung shih* 487:5a; *Wen-hsien t'ung-k'ao* 325:51b).

On Apr.21, 988, T'ai-tsung appointed Wang Ch'ih Acting Grand Commandant and Military Commissioner of the non-existant Army Which Quiets the Sea. On May 12, the emperor sent a Supernumerary

---

[48] *Hsü Tzu-chih t'ung-chien ch'ang-pien* p.200 dates this mission 982, 8th month, *kuei-ch'ou*, but that date did not exist.

[49] See Rogers, "Factionalism and Koryŏ Policy", p.16 note 4.

[50] See *The Cambridge History of China*, vol.6, p.102.

Gentleman [of the Bureau of] Evaluations and Concurrent Attending Secretary for General Purpose together with two Members of the Suite to inform the king of these honours (*Sung shih* 5:8a; 487:5a; *Hsü Tzu-chih t'ung-chien ch'ang-pien* p.250).

On Dec.12, 988, and some time in 989, Koryŏ envoys to the Sung court offered gifts. It also sent a Buddhist priest to beg for the *Tripitaka.* This was provided (*Wen-hsien t'ung-k'ao* 325:51b).

On Jan.2, 991, Koryŏ envoys to the Sung court offered gifts. Later that year, Wang Ch'ih sent another mission with offerings and requested printed Buddhist sutras. These were provided. On Nov.25, 992, a mission with gifts from Koryŏ was received at the Sung court, and in the 1st month (Jan./Feb.) of 993 another mission offered regional objects and thanked for the sutras (*Sung shih* 5:15a, 15b; 487:6a-6b).

In the 12th month (Jan./Feb., 993) of the Liao year 992, war broke out between Liao and Koryŏ (*Liao shih* 13:3b). A large Liao army crossed the Yalu River but met with determined Korean defense.

On Mar.2, 993, T'ai-tsung sent envoys to Koryŏ to confer on its king, Wang Ch'ih, the title of Acting Grand Master, to confirm him as Military Commissioner of the non-existing Army Which Quiets the Sea, and to present him with garments, golden belts, several 100 ounces of gold and silver vessels, and more than 30,000 lengths of cotton. The round trip of this mission took 70-odd days. Wang Ch'ih responded with envoys who expressed his thanks and requested the *Nine Confucian Classics* for the instruction of Korean scholars. The envoys were given 200 bolts of clothing, 200 ounces of silver vessels, and 50 sheep (*Sung shih* 487:8a; *Wen-hsien t'ung-k'ao* 325:51b).

In the 3rd month (Mar./Apr.) of 993, envoys from Wang Ch'ih arrived at the Liao court for peace negotiations, which by the *Liao shih* is phrased as an "apology". The Liao made concessions in the territory east of the Yalu River (*Liao shih* 13:4a; 115:1a-1b).

On Mar.21, 994, Koryŏ envoys to the Liao court offered gifts. On Apr.18, another mission from Koryŏ requested that the Korean prisoners taken by Liao in the war of 993 be cared for. Sheng-tsung of Liao agreed that the prisoners be ransomed and returned to their country (*Liao shih* 13:4b; 70:9a; 115:1b).

On Aug.9, 994, Koryŏ envoys to the Sung court informed it about border violations by Liao and proposed a joint military action against it. But the Sung wished to avoid military engagements. The emperor merely made a soothing statement and showered the envoys with gifts (*Sung shih* 5:19b; 487:8a; *Hsü Tzu-chih t'ung-chien ch'ang-pien* p.303; *Wen-hsien t'ung-k'ao* 325:51b).

In the 12th month (Jan./Feb., 995) of the Liao year 994, Wang Ch'ih offered singing girls to Sheng-tsung of Liao. He rejected them (*Liao shih* 13:5b).

On Mar.31, 995, Koryŏ offered gifts to the Liao court. On June 7, 995, another mission presented falcons. On Nov.6, still another mission offered gifts (*Liao shih* 13:6a, 6b; 70:9a; 115:1b).

On Dec.13, 995, Sheng-tsung of Liao sent envoys to recognize Wang Ch'ih as king of Koryŏ (*Liao shih* 13:6b; 115:1b).

On Dec.20, 995, ten lads from Koryŏ arrived in Liao to learn the Khitan language (*Liao shih* 13:7a; 115:1b).

On Mar.23, 996, Wang Ch'ih requested a marriage with the imperial Liao house. This was agreed to, and a daughter of the Princess of Yüeh, who was the third daughter of Emperor Ching-tsung, was married to him (*Liao shih* 13:7a; 115:1b).

On Mar.31, 996, another ten lads from Koryŏ arrived in Liao to learn the Khitan language (*Liao shih* 13:7a).

On July 8, 996, Koryŏ envoys inquired about the "Activity and Repose", i.e. well-being, of the Liao emperor (*Liao shih* 13:7b; 115: 1b).

On Aug.19, 997, Koryŏ envoys to the Liao court offered silk and condoled on the death of the Princess of Yüeh, i.e. the mother-in-law of Wang Ch'ih (*Liao shih* 13:8b-9a; 115:1b).

In the 11th month (December) of 997, Koryŏ envoys informed the Liao court that Wang Ch'ih had died and had been succeeded by his nephew Sung (Mokchong). Koryŏ also announced this to the Sung court (*Liao shih* 13:9a; 115:1b; *Sung shih* 487:8a; *Wen-hsien t'ung-k'ao* 325:51b).

On Jan.24, 998, envoys from Sheng-tsung of Liao to the Koryŏ court sacrificed to the late Wang Ch'ih and recognized Wang Sung as king (*Liao shih* 13:9b; 14:1b; 115:1b).

In the 11th month (Nov./Dec.) of 998, a mission from Sheng-tsung again formally recognized Wang Sung as king of Koryŏ (*Liao shih* 14: 1b; 115:1b).

In 1000, Koryŏ envoys landed in Teng on the northern coast of Shan-tung. The local officials reported this to the Sung capital. Chen-tsung summoned the envoys to an audience and presented Wang Sung with hairpins and a filigree armour (*Sung shih* 6:8b; 487:8a-8b; *Wen-hsien t'ung-k'ao* 325:51b).

In the 2nd month (Mar./Apr.) of 1002, Koryŏ envoys congratulated Liao on a successful attack on Sung. On Aug.18 of the same year,[51] Koryŏ envoys offered the Liao court a map of their state (*Liao shih* 14:3b; 70:11a; 115:1b). As has been seen, such an act was a not seriously-meant symbol of surrender.

In 1003, Koryŏ envoys to the Sung court informed it that attacks by Liao had not ceased (*Sung shih* 487:8b; *Wen-hsien t'ung-k'ao* 325:51b).

On Sep.24, 1004, Sheng-tsung of Liao sent envoys to inform the Koryŏ court that he was attacking the Sung State (*Liao shih* 14:5a; 115:2a).

On June 28, 1005, Koryŏ envoys congratulated Liao on having made peace with Sung (*Liao shih* 14:6b; 115:2a).

On June 12, 1008, Koryŏ presented to the Liao court mats made of Lung-hsü plants[52] and congratulated on the walling of the Central Capital (*Liao shih* 14:7b; 70:12b; 115:2a).

On Jan.6, 1010, Sheng-tsung sent envoys to Koryŏ to announce the death of his mother, the Empress Dowager, on Dec.29, 1009. On Mar.7, 1010, Koryŏ envoys to the Liao court sacrificed. Another mission arrived from Koryŏ in the 3rd month (Apr./May), whose members attended the burial of the Empress Dowager on May 31 (*Liao shih* 14:8a; 15:1a-1b; 115:2a).

In 1010 it became known in Sung and Liao that the king of Koryŏ, Wang Sung, had been murdered and been replaced by Wang Hsün (Hyŏnjong). Sheng-tsung supposedly resented the coup and the fact that he had not been subsequently informed. He ordered an attack on Koryŏ. Wang Hsün sent envoys to the Sung court, asking it to act as an intermediary for peace with Liao. In the 8th month (Sep./Oct.), Sheng-tsung took personal command and dispatched envoys to inform the Sung court. On Nov.9, the Jurchen offered the Liao 10,000 fine horses for the campaign. They also wished to actively participate in it, which was rejected. A subsequent appeal by Wang Hsün to cease hostilities was refused by Sheng-tsung (*Liao shih* 15:1b, 2a; 115:2a; *Sung shih* 487:8b; *Wen-hsien t'ung-k'ao* 325:51b).

On Dec.18, 1010, the Liao army crossed the Yalu River, whereafter the Koryŏ capital of Kaegyŏng was captured and burned. But the

---

[51] 70:11a gives the wrong date of 6th month. The cycical characters *hsin-ch'ou* did not occur in that month.

[52] According to Wittfogel, *Liao*, p.355, note 49, a kind of a rush, probably *juncus effusus*.

Liao forces soon faltered, which made Sheng-tsung willing to discuss peace. On Dec.24, Wang Hsün's envoys proposed that he personally would come to the Liao court. This was accepted. In the 1st month (Feb./Mar.) of 1011, the Liao army withdrew from Koryŏ, and its conquests were lost (*Liao shih* 15:2a, 2b; 115:2a; *Wen-hsien t'ung-k'ao* 325:51b).

Wang Hsün did not keep his promise to visit to the Liao court. Instead he sent an envoy, who was received on Apr.26, 1012. The *Liao shih* claims that Wang Hsün through this envoy "declared himself a subject as of old". Sheng-tsung insisted that Wang Hsün come personally. A Koryŏ envoy informed the Liao court on Sep.12 that the king was too ill to make the journey (*Liao shih* 15:4a; 115:2b). This was a standard excuse which deceived no one and yet had to be accepted.

On July 29, 1013, Sheng-tsung sent the Palace Assistant Secretary, Yeh-lü Tzu-chung, to the Koryŏ court, requesting a border adjustment. This envoy returned without results on Oct.7 (*Liao shih* 15:6a, 6b; 115:2b). On Nov.13, Sheng-tsung questioned the Jurchen on the best way to attack and defeat Koryŏ and accepted their advice (*Liao shih* 15:7a).

On Mar.11, 1014, Sheng-tsung sent Yeh-lü Tzu-chung, now promoted to Vice Regent of the Supreme Capital, on another mission to the Koryŏ court with the same errand (*Liao shih* 15:7b; 115:2b). This was not only unsuccessful but Tzu-chung was detained by the Koreans. Being under pressure from Liao, Wang Hsün made new overtures to Sung. On Jan.8, 1015, a mission of his, consisting of 78 members, was received at the Sung court and offered two saddles ornamented with dragons and phoenixes and 12 horses. He was presented with garments, belts, horse trappings etc. (*Sung shih* 8:10b; *Hsü Tzu-chih t'ung-chien ch'ang-pien* p.736; *Wen-hsien t'ung-k'ao* 325:51b).

On Dec.30, 1015, Koryŏ envoys together with the Eastern Jurchen offered gifts to the Sung court. On Jan.9, 1016, they requested the Sung calendar. The envoys also informed that the Khitan had built a floating bridge across the Yalu and had erected fortifications east of the river. They proposed that these be burned (*Sung shih* 8:12b; 487:9a; *Hsü Tzu-chih t'ung-chien ch'ang-pien* p.756; *Wen-hsien t'ung-k'ao* 325:51b).

In the 1st month (Feb./Mar.) of 1016, Liao engaged a Koryŏ army (*Liao shih* 15:10a; 70:15b). That same year, the Sung presented Wang Hsün of Koryŏ with the calendar, garments, golden belts, [porcelain] vessels, silk, and horse trappings (*Sung shih* 487:10a; *Hsü Tzu-chih t'ung-chien ch'ang-pien* p.756).

On Dec.19, 1017, Koryŏ envoys to the Sung court presented a communication and regional objects (*Hsü Tzu-chih t'ung-chien ch'ang-pien* p.805; *Wen-hsien t'ung-k'ao* 325:51b).

In the 9th month (Sep./Oct.) of the same year 1017, the Liao forces withdrew from Koryŏ but attacked again in the 10th month (Nov./Dec.). In the 12th month (Jan./Feb., 1019) of the Liao year 1018, a Liao army was defeated by the Koreans (*Liao shih* 15:11b; 16:2a, 2b).

In 1019, envoys from Wang Hsün to the Liao court proposed to offer regional objects. This was an attempt to restore peace. But in the 8th month (September), the Liao attacked Koryŏ once more (*Liao shih* 16:3b-4a; 115:3b).

In the 9th month (September) of 1019, Teng on the northern coast of Shan-tung reported to the Sung court that a Koryŏ mission had been shipwrecked and had lost some of the objects it had brought. The emperor sent a palace official to take care of the envoys. In the 11th month (Nov./Dec.) these envoys and a Jurchen chief were received in audience and presented mats, brocade garments, long knives ornamented with gold, horse trappings, and 2000 bolts of middling quality cotton. They requested Buddhist sutras. The cotton was rejected, and the sutras were provided. Because of their shipwreck, the envoys were given garments and silken fabrics (*Sung shih* 8:20a, 20b; 487:10a; *Wen-hsien t'ung-k'ao* 325:51b-52a).

Having been unable to win decisive victories, Liao was in 1020 ready to make peace with Koryŏ. When on Jan.26, 1020 Wang Hsün repeated his offer to present regional objects, this was accepted. The Koreans released Yeh-lü Tzu-chung after a detention of six years, and he returned to Liao on June 13. He brought with him a letter from Wang Hsün in which, according to *Liao shih,* the latter "surrendered" and "begged to call himself a vassal and offer tribute". The following day, June 14, Sheng-tsung sent envoys "to pardon Wang Hsün's crimes" (*Liao shih* 16:4a, 4b; 115:3b).

In the 6th month (July/Aug.) of 1021, Koryŏ offered gifts to the Sung court (*Hsü Tzu-chih t'ung-chien ch'ang-pien* p.864).

In the 9th month (Oct./Nov.) of 1021, a mission of 179 men from Wang Hsün was received at the Sung court.[53] The envoys announced

---

[53] *Hsü Tzu-chih t'ung-chien ch'ang-pien* says 170 men.

that Koryŏ had made peace with Liao and requested books on geomancy and geography. These were provided. In the 2nd month (Mar./Apr.) of 1022, this mission returned to Koryŏ with gifts for Wang Hsün (*Sung shih* 8:23b; 487:10b, 11b; *Hsü Tzu-chih t'ung-chien ch'ang-pien* p.867; *Wen-hsien t'ung-k'ao* 325:52a).

In the 11th month (Dec./Jan., 1022) of the Liao year 1021, Koryŏ offered gifts to the Liao court (*Liao shih* 16:6b).

On Feb.24, 1029, Liao envoys offered gifts to the king of Koryŏ (*Liao shih* 17:6a; 115:3b).[54]

When Ta Yen-lin in the 8th month (Sep./Oct.) of 1029 rose in the former Po-hai against the Liao, he received some support from the Southern and Northern Jurchen. Koryŏ remained neutral but briefly suspended diplomatic relations with Liao (*Liao shih* 17:7a).

In 1030, a mission of 293 men from Wang Hsün of Koryŏ was received at the Sung court. The envoys were given an audience and presented a communication as well as golden vessels, silver [-embroidered] mats, knives, swords, horse trappings, and aromatic oils. The envoys departed in the 2nd month (Feb./Mar.) of 1031, each with gifts in accordance with his rank (*Sung shih* 9:13a; 487:11b; *Wen-hsien t'ung-k'ao* 325:52a).

On June 30, 1031, Emperor Hsing-tsung sent envoys to the Koryŏ court to announce the death of his father Sheng-tsung on June 25. In the 7th month (July/Aug.), Koryŏ envoys condoled at the Liao court (*Liao shih* 18:1b; 115:3b).

In 1031, the king of Koryŏ, Wang Hsün, died and was succeeded by his son Ch'in (Tŏkjong). The latter announced his ascension by envoys to the Liao court on Jan.7, 1033, whereupon Hsing-tsung recognized him as king of Koryŏ (*Liao shih* 16:7b; 115:3b).[55]

No diplomatic relations between Koryŏ and Sung are recorded from 1031 to 1070,[56] while those with Liao continued. Koryŏ mis-

---

[54] *Liao shih* gives the name of the king as Ch'in, which is an error for Hsün. See next note.

[55] The chronology in *Liao shih* is here garbled. Marcus, *Korean Studies Guide*, p.182, and Mathias Tchang, *Synchronismes*, p.352, both place the death of Wang Hsün in 1031. This must be correct, since Wang Hsün according to *Sung shih* was alive in 1030. The statement of *Liao shih* 115:3b, that Wang Hsün died in 1021 should therefore be emended to 1031. Furthermore, if the date of the announcement in *Liao shih* 16: 7b is emended from 1022, 12th month, *hsin-ch'ou*, to 1032, 12th month, *hsin-ch'ou*, it would have been made on Jan.7, 1033.

[56] According to *Sung shih* 487:11b, Koryŏ had no relations with China from

sions were received at the Liao court on Mar.18, 1038, May 6, 1043, Apr.25 and July 13, 1044, Jan.2, 1045, in the 4th month (Apr./May) of 1045, and on Apr.25, 1046 (*Liao shih* 18:7b; 19:4a, 5a, 6a, 6b, 7a, 7b; 70:16b, 17b, 18a; 115:3b).

On Sep.8, 1046, Koryŏ envoys announced the death of their king at the Liao court. Wang Hui (Munjong) inherited the throne (*Liao shih* 19:8a, 115:3b; *Sung shih* 487:11b).[57]

On Jan.10, 1047, May 23, 1048, in the 3rd month (Apr./May) of 1049, and on May 21, 1050, Koryŏ envoys to the Liao court offered gifts. In the 6th month (June/July) of 1050, they congratulated Liao on the victorious campaign against Hsia. On July 3, 1053, and May 19, 1054, they again offered presents to the Liao court (*Liao shih* 20: 1b, 2a, 4b, 7b, 8a; 70:18b, 19a, 19b; 115:3b, 4a).

On July 17, 1054, a son of Wang Hui of Koryŏ was by Liao appointed Acting Grand Commandant. Wang Hui had supposedly requested this (*Liao shih* 20:8b; 115:4a).[58]

On Sep.1, 1055, Emperor Tao-tsung of Liao sent envoys to Koryŏ to announce the death of his father Hsing-tsung on Aug.28. On Oct.20 he ordered envoys to present the late emperor's testamentary gifts to the Koryŏ court, and on Dec.1 envoys from Koryŏ attended Hsing-tsung's burial (*Liao shih* 21:1b, 2a; 115:4a).

On July 31, 1056, and Dec.26, 1057, Koryŏ envoys to the Liao court offered gifts (*Liao shih* 21:3b, 5a, 115:4a).

In the spring of 1058, Liao sent envoys to Koryŏ to announce the death of the Grand Empress Dowager, widow of Sheng-tsung, on Jan.24. On May 28, envoys from Koryŏ attended her burial (*Liao shih* 21:5b; 115:4a).

In 1061, 1062, 1063, and 1064, Koryŏ envoys to the Liao court offered gifts (*Liao shih* 115:4a).

In 1070, a mission of 110 men from Wang Hui of Koryŏ was received at the Sung court. Shen-tsung ordered that the protocol

---

1031 for 43 years. 39 is the correct figure. *Wen-hsien t'ung-k'ao* 325:52a merely states that there was a disruption.

[57] According to *Liao shih*, it was Wang Ch'in who died. That is again a garbled account. Wang Ch'in died in 1034 and was succeeded by Hsiang (Chŏngjong). It was Wang Hsiang who died in 1046 and was succeeded by Wang Hui.

The ascension of Wang Hui is recorded in *Sung shih*. The Sung had learned about this either second-hand or directly from Koryŏ. In the latter case, the hiatus in diplomatic relations would have been briefer.

[58] 115:4a dates the appointment in the 4th month (May/June).

should be the same as for the envoys from Hsia. On June 22 and Aug.28, 1071, Koryŏ envoys offered gifts to the Sung court (*Sung shih* 15:5b, 6a; 487:12b).[59]

On Dec.19, 1071, July 17, 1072, and Jan.26, 1073,[60] Koryŏ envoys were received at the Liao court. At the last occasion, Tao-tsung presented Koryŏ with the Buddhist *Tripitaka* (*Liao shih* 22:7b, 23:1b, 2a; 70:20b, 21a; 115:4a).

On Jan.23, and Dec.15, 1074, Koryŏ envoys to the Liao court offered gifts (*Liao shih* 23:2b, 3a; 70:21a).

On Jan.25,1074, a Koryŏ envoy and his deputy were received in audience by Shen-tsung of Sung. They requested a change in the route taken by the envoys from Koryŏ to the Sung capital in order to avoid the Khitan. On Oct.31, 1076, the Sung government approved Ming on the sourthern shore of Hang-chou Bay as the new port of entry. Wang Hui furthermore requested Chinese physicians, pharmacists, painters, and sculptors to teach the people of his state (*Sung shih* 15: 13a; 487:12b; *Hsü Tzu-chih t'ung-chien ch'ang-pien* p.2334, 2618; *Wen-hsien t'ung-k'ao* 325:52a).

On Apr.13, 1076, Tao-tsung of Liao sent envoys to Koryŏ to announce the death of the Empress Dowager, widow of Hsing-tsung, on Apr.11. On July 7, envoys from Koryŏ condoled and sacrificed (*Liao shih* 23:4a; 115:4a).[61] During the same year of 1076, Koryŏ envoys also arrived at the Sung court (*Sung shih* 487:12b-13a).[62]

In 1078, for the first time in decades, Sung sent a goodwill mission to Koryŏ. It was led by a Grandee Remonstrant and Consultant, who for that purpose was appointed Acting Prefect of the Imperial Diarists. Two ships were built for the mission in Ming. Wang Hui received the envoy and, being ill, asked for physicians and medicine (*Sung shih* 487: 13a; *Wen-hsien t'ung-k'ao* 325:52a).[63] *Sung shih* 487:15b interprets Wang Hui's actions as surrender to the Sung.

---

[59] Rogers, "Factionalism and Koryŏ Policy", pp.16-17, shows from Korean sources that the Sung resumed relations with Koryŏ in 1071 at the initiative of Wang An-shih. Koryŏ took this earlier initiative in 1070.

[60] 115:4a dates this event 1062, but the historians have probably misread *hsien-ning* 8th year as *ch'ing-ning* 8th year.

[61] 115:4a misdates these events 1075.

[62] On Dec.4 (correcting *mou-tzu* to *mou-wu*), 1076, Shen-tsung allowed three Buddhist priests from Koryŏ to visit a shrine in Che-chiang (*Hsü Tzu-chih t'ung-chien ch'ang-pien*, p.2633). This was not an official mission.

[63] Rogers, "Sung-Koryŏ Relations: some inhibiting Factors", p.196, quotes Korean

On Feb.10, 1078, a Sung mission was sent to the Koryŏ court (*Hsü Tzu-chih t'ung-chien ch'ang-pien* p.2707).

On May 21, 1078, Koryŏ envoys requested a border adjustment, whereby the Liao would cede territory east of the Yalu River to Koryŏ. This was rejected (*Liao shih* 23:6b; 70:21a-21b; 115:4a).

In 1079, Sung sent a physician to Koryŏ to attend its king. Wang Hui responded with a mission to express his thanks but the ships encountered a storm at sea, and all gifts were lost (*Sung shih* 487:13a; *Wen-hsien t'ung-k'ao* 325:52a).

In the 1st month (Jan./Feb.) of 1080, Shen-tsung of Sung approved that each time the king of Koryŏ offered gifts, he should receive in return 10,000 bolts of pongee (*Hsü Tzu-chih t'ung-chien ch'ang-pien* p.2834).

On Feb.18, 1080, a mission of 121 men from Koryŏ was received in audience by Shen-tsung. Each received gifts in accordance with his rank. Although some of their gifts had been lost in a stormy sea voyage, the envoys were able on Mar.8 to present eight carriages constructed in Koryŏ. The emperor inquired whether the medicines provided for the Korean king had been beneficial (*Sung shih* 16:1a; *HsüTzu-chih t'ung-chien* p.2834, 2835, 2837, 2841).

On Dec.19, 1081, Koryŏ envoys to the Liao court offered gifts (*Liao shih* 24:3b; 70:21b).

In 1083, Wang Hui died and was succeeded by his son Hsün (Sunjong).[64] The Sung ordered the local authorities in Ming to send envoys, condole, and offer libations. Hsün died the same year[65] and was succeeded by his younger brother Yün (Sŏnjong) (*Sung shih* 487: 14a; *Wen-hsien t'ung-k'ao* 325:52a; *Liao shih* 24:5a; 115:4a).

On Dec.24, 1083, Tao-tsung of Liao ordered a Buddhist priest to collate and publish the Buddhist sutras which Koryŏ had presented (*Liao shih* 24:5b).

In 1085, Wang T'ung, a younger brother of the king of Koryŏ, Wang Yün, arrived at the Sung court with gifts. He inquired about the Buddhist dharma. (*Sung shih* 17:4b; 487:14a; *Wen-hsien t'ung-k'ao* 325:52a).

---

sources to the effect that the Sung envoys received a tumultuous welcome, but that their visit was seriously harmed by their mercenary behaviour.

[64] Not to be confused with the king of Koryŏ Wang Hsün who died in 1031. The names are written with different Chinese characters.

[65] He is by *Liao shih* refered to as the duke of San-han.

On Dec.15, 1085, Tao-tsung sent envoys to recognize Wang Yün as king of Koryŏ (*Liao shih* 24:6b; 115:7a).

After Che-tsung had ascended the Sung throne on Apr.1, 1085, Koryŏ envoys congratulated on Dec.20. They wished to buy books on penal law, the encyclopaedia *T'ai-p'ing yü-lan*, and the anthology *Wen-yüan ying-hua*.[66] The Sung only allowed the sale of the *Wen-yüan ying-hua*, for which Koryŏ paid with fine horses and brocade (*Sung shih* 487:14a; *Hsü Tzu-chih t'ung-chien ch'ang-pien* p.3334; *Wen-hsien t'ung-k'ao* 325:52a).[67]

On Feb.4, 1086, Sung sent horse trappings, garments, belts, vessels, and silk as gifts to the king of Koryŏ (*Sung shih* 17:5b).[68]

On Jan.1, 1087, Koryŏ envoys thanked Tao-tsung for the recognition of Wang Yün. On Apr.8 of the same year, envoys from Koryŏ to the Liao court offered gifts (*Liao shih* 24:8a; 25:1a; 70:22a; 115:4a).

On Mar.7, 1089, Koryŏ envoys to the Liao court offered gifts (*Liao shih* 25:3a; 70:22b; 115:4a).[69]

In 1090, Koryŏ envoys to the Sung court offered gifts. They received in return 5000 ounces of silver vessels (*Sung shih* 17:15a; 487:14b; *Wen-hsien t'ung-k'ao* 325:52a).

On Nov.25, 1090, Koryŏ envoys offered gifts to the Liao court (*Liao shih* 25:3b-4a; 70:22b; 115:4a).

On Feb.28, 1091, Koryŏ envoys offered gifts to the Sung court (*Sung shih* 17:17a).

On Dec.6, 1092, envoys from Koryŏ were received in audience at the Sung court. They presented the *Huang-ti hsien-ching*[70] and wished to buy books, including the dynastic histories and the *Ts'e-fu yüan-kuei*, as well as gold foil.[71] On Feb.20, 1093, an edict made the *Huang-ti hsien-ching* known to the empire. On Mar.3, 1093, the great Su Shih

[66] Both compiled under the direction of Li Fang (925-996).

[67] On Feb.21, 1093, the sale of the *T'ai-p'ing yü-lan* was again rejected (*Hsü Tzu-chih t'ung-chien ch'ang-pien* p.4486). The Koreans were only able to buy the *T'ai-p'ing yü-lan* in 1101. See Rogers, "Sung-Koryŏ Relations: some inhibiting factors", p.201.

[68] In the intercalary month (Mar./Apr.) of 1086, 18 Buddhist priests from Koryŏ had an audience with Che-tsung of Sung (*HsüTzu-chih t'ung-chien* p.3439). This was hardly an official mission.

[69] The same year, a Buddhist priest sent by a son of the Koryŏ king, arrived in Hang subcommandery in Che-chiang to sacrifice to deceased Buddhist priests (*Sung shih* 487:14a; *Wen-hsien t'ung-k'ao* 325:52a). This obviously was not an official mission.

[70] *The Needle Classic of the Yellow Lord*, a book on acupuncture.

[71] Attached to Buddhist statues as acts of piety.

(Su Tung-p'o 1036-1101), leader of an anti-Koryŏ faction, advised that books offered by the Koreans did not have the value of silk and hair, and that the Koreans should not be allowed to purchase books and gold foil. In other words, he wanted straightforward business transactions in commercial goods. An edict allowed the gold foil, and, in the end, the envoys were able to buy the *Ts'e-fu yüan-kuei* (*Sung shih* 17:18b, 19a; 487:14b; *Hsü Tzu-chih t'ung-chien ch'ang-pien* p.4472; *Wen-hsien t'ung-k'ao* 325:52a-52b).

On Aug.21, 1093, Tao-tsung sent envoys to present sheep to Koryŏ (*Liao shih* 25:5b; 115:4a).

In 1094, the king of Koryŏ, Wang Yün, died. His son and successor Yü (Hŏnjong) sent envoys to announce this to the Liao court. Tao-tsung dispatched envoys to contribute to the funeral expenses and to recognize Yü as king. On Mar.15, 1095, envoys from Wang Yü offered gifts to the Liao court. Yü abdicated on Nov.6, 1095, in favour of his uncle Wang Yung (Sukjong).[72] (*Liao shih* 25:7a; 26:1a, 2a, 2b; 70:24b; 115:4a-4b)

On Nov.11, 1096, envoys from Wang Yung offered gifts to the Liao court,[73] and in 1098 to the Sung court (*Liao shih* 16:2b; 70:24b; 115:4b; *Sung shih* 18:12b; 487:14b).[74]

On Nov.15, 1099, envoys from Koryŏ to the Liao court requested that their king, Wang Yung, be recognized (*Liao shih* 26:4b; 115:4b).

After Hui-tsung had ascended the Sung throne on Feb.23, 1100, Koryŏ envoys congratulated and condoled on the death of his brother, Che-tsung (*Sung shih* 487:14b; *Wen-hsien t'ung-k'ao* 325:52b).

On Sep.18, 1100, envoys from Koryŏ were received at the Sung court with a communication from Wang Yung (*Sung shih* 19:4a).

At some time during the same year of 1100, Tao-tsung enfeoffed Wang Yung as duke of San-han (*Liao shih* 26:6a; 115:4b).

On Mar.5, 1101, Emperor T'ien-tso of Liao sent envoys to Koryŏ to announce the death of his grandfather Tao-tsung on Feb.12. On May 5, Koryŏ envoys condoled at the Liao court. On Jan.1, 1102,

---

[72] Yü died on Apr.4, 1097. The Liao was not informed of his death. Cf. Rogers, "Studies in Korean History", pp. 31-32.

[73] According to the *Koryŏ-sa*, Wang Yung did not inform the Liao of his ascension until 1098, i.e. after Yü's death. See Rogers, op.cit., p.33 note 1.

[74] A Sung edict of Feb.28, 1099, refers to visiting Korean scholars in China (*Sung shih* 18:13a).

other envoys from Koryŏ congratulated on the ascension of T'ien-tso (*Liao shih* 27:1b, 2a; 115:4b).

In 1103, Sung sent a Gentleman-in-Attendance of the Ministry of Households and a Serving within the Palace as envoys to the Koryŏ court (*Sung shih* 487:14b; *Wen-hsien t'ung-k'ao* 325:52b).

On Dec.30, 1105, envoys from Wang Yu (Yejong) to the Liao court announced the death of his father Yung (*Liao shih* 27:4b; 115:4b). Soon thereafter, he sent five men to attend the Sung Academy. The Sung court appointed Erudites as teachers for them. Yu also requested physicians from Sung. Two were sent to Koryŏ and stayed there for two years. The protocol for Koryŏ was raised by Sung above that of the Hsia State, meaning that Koryŏ had precedence (*Sung shih* 487: 14b, 15a; *Wen-hsien t'ung-k'ao* 325:52b).

On May 28, 1108, T'ien-tso recognized Wang Yu as duke of San-han and his father Yung posthumously as king of the Koryŏ State.[75] On Jan.6, 1109,[76] envoys from Wang Yu conveyed his thanks the Liao court. On Jan.6, 1110, Koryŏ envoys offered gifts (*Liao shih* 27: 5a, 5b; 70:26a, 26b; 115:4b).

In 1112, Koryŏ offered presents to the Sung court (*Sung shih* 21: 2a).

On Nov.18, 1112, Koryŏ envoys announced at the Liao court that the mother of the duke of San-han, Wang Yu, had died. T'ien-tso immediately sent envoys to sacrifice. On Jan.11, 1113, Koryŏ envoys thanked for the sacrifice. On Jan.24, 1114, envoys from Wang Yu thanked T'ien-tso that, after the mourning period for his mother, he had been recognized at his previous rank (*Liao shih* 27:7a, 7b; 70:26b-27a; 115:4b). This was the last recorded routine exchange of missions between Koryŏ and Liao. The war between Liao and the Jurchen had begun, which led to the foundation of the Jurchen Chin empire in 1115 and the collapse of the Liao empire in 1124.

In the intercalary month (Feb./Mar.) of 1116, Koryŏ envoys to the Chin court congratulated on its victory over Liao. During the same year, Koryŏ also offered gifts to the Sung court (*Chin shih* 2:11a; 135: 4a; *Sung shih* 21:7b).

On Sep.5, 1117, Koryŏ requested a territorial adjustment from Chin (*Chin shih* 2:11b).

---

[75] 115:4b dates this 1105, 8th month. For 8th month, read 8th year = 1108.

[76] 70:26a says 11th month, but the 11th did not have the cyclical characters *chi-mou*.

In 1118, Koryŏ offered gifts to the Sung court (*Sung shih* 21:11a).

On Nov.17, 1118, Hui-tsung of Sung received Koryŏ envoys in audience. On Dec.1 of the same year, the port of Ming reported to the Sung court that a Koryŏ mission had landed (*Sung hui-yao kao*, ts'e 197).

In early 1119, Chin proposed a border demarkation to Koryŏ (*Chin shih* 2:13b; 135:4a).

In 1120, T'ien-tso of Liao begged for troops from Koryŏ in his last stand against Chin. This was refused (*Liao shih* 115:4b).

On Oct.15, 1122, envoys from Koryŏ announced at the Sung court that Wang Yu had died. Sung sent a mission to condole and sacrifice. After a struggle, Yu's son K'ai (Injong) was enthroned in Koryŏ (*Sung shih* 22:7a; 487:15a; *Wen-hsien t'ung-k'ao* 325:52b).

In the 9th month (Oct./Nov.) of 1124, Koryŏ offered gifts to the Sung court (*Sung shih* 22:11a).

After Ch'in-tsung had ascended the Sung throne on Jan.19, 1126, Koryŏ envoys landed in Ming to congratulate (*Sung shih* 487:15a; *Wen-hsien t'ung-k'ao* 325:52b).

On June 23, 1126, Wang K'ai of Koryŏ "presented a memorial [to Chin] and declared himself a vassal" (*Chin shih* 3:8a; 135:5a).

On July 23, 1126, Chin sent a mission to the Koryŏ court (*Chin shih* 3:8a; 135:5a).

On Nov.11, 1126, Koryŏ's last recorded mission to Northern Sung was received at the court (*Sung shih* 23:13b).

On Jan.14, 1127,[77] Chin sent envoys to congratulate the king of Koryŏ on his birthday (*Chin shih* 3:9a).

On Feb.13, 1127, the New Year's Day, Koryŏ envoys congratulated at the Chin court (*Chin shih* 3:9b).

When Kao-tsung had ascended the throne on June 12, 1127, and founded the Southern Sung Dynasty, he was worried about a diplomatic rapprochement between Chin and Koryŏ. He sent a mission to Koryŏ, led by an Acting Junior Director of the Imperial Clan, while Chin simultaneously sent envoys to recognize Wang K'ai as king (*Sung shih* 487:15b; *Wen-hsien t'ung-k'ao* 325:53a).

On Sep.28, 1127, Emperor T'ai-tsung of Chin sent envoys to Koryŏ to announce his victory over [Northern] Sung (*Chin shih* 3:10a).

---

[77] Emending 11th month to 11th intercalary month.

On Nov.20, 1127, Koryŏ envoys to the Chin court congratulated on the birthday of T'ai-tsung (*Chin shih* 3:10b).[78]

On Feb.3, 1128, the New Year's Day, Koryŏ envoys congratulated at the Chin court (*Chin shih* 3:11a).

In the 3rd month (April) of 1128,[79] the Southern Sung sent Yang Ying-ch'eng as envoy to both Chin and Koryŏ. He had an audience with Wang K'ai. The Southern Sung was at that time at war with Chin and no doubt sought support from Koryŏ. K'ai rejected this but entrusted a letter to the envoy. In the 10th month (Oct./Nov.), Yang Ying-ch'eng returned to the Sung court and reported his cool reception in Koryŏ. Emperor Kao-tsung was furious, but a Master of Documents pointed out that Koryŏ, as a neighbour of Chin and separated from the Southern Sung by sea, could hardly act otherwise (*Sung shih* 25:3b, 6a; 487:16a-16b; *Wen-hsien t'ung-k'ao* 325:53a, 53b).

On Nov.9, 1128, Koryŏ envoys to the Chin court congratulated on the birthday of T'ai-tsung (*Chin shih* 3:12a).

In the 11th month (Nov./Dec.) of 1128, a high official from Wang K'ai of Koryŏ was received in audience by Kao-tsung of Southern Sung. He was presented with wine and food, treated with courtesy, and sent back (*Sung shih* 25:6b; 487:16b-17a; *Wen-hsien t'ung-k'ao* 325: 53b).

On Jan.22, 1129, the New Year's Day, Koryŏ envoys congratulated at the Chin court (*Chin shih* 3:12a).

On Nov.28, 1129, Koryŏ envoys to Chin congratulated on the birthday of T'ai-tsung. On Dec.23 of the same year, envoys from Koryŏ offered gifts to the Chin court (*Chin shih* 3:13a).[80]

On Feb.10, 1130, the New Year's Day, Koryŏ envoys congratulated at the Chin court (*Chin shih* 3:13a; 135:5b).

On Nov.17, 1130, Koryŏ envoys to the Chin court congratulated on the birthday of T'ai-tsung (*Chin shih* 3:14b).

On Jan.31, 1131, the New Year's Day, Koryŏ envoys congratulated at the Chin court (*Chin shih* 3:15a).

---

[78] Birthdays were dated according to the lunar calendar. T'ai-tsung's birthday fell on the 15th day of the 10th lunar month and was celebrated accordingly. This means that the date translated to the solar calendar was different each year: Nov.20, 1127, Nov.9, 1128, Nov.28, 1129, Nov.17, 1130, Nov.6, 1131, Nov.24, 1132, Nov.13, 1133, and on Nov.2, 1134.

[79] *Wen-hsien t'ung-k'ao* 325:53a says 6th month (July).

[80] For a Chin mission to Koryŏ in 1129 see Rogers in Rossabi, ed., *China among Equals*, p.161.

In the 10th month (Oct./Nov.) of 1131, Koryŏ offered gifts to Southern Sung court (*Sung shih* 487:14b).

On Nov.6, 1131, Koryŏ envoys to the Chin court congratulated on the birthday of T'ai-tsung (*Chin shih* 3:15b).

On Jan.20, 1132, the New Year's Day, Koryŏ envoys congratulated at the Chin court (*Chin shih* 3:16b).

On May 19, 1132, envoys from Wang K'ai of Koryŏ to the Southern Sung court presented 100 ounces of gold, 1000 ounces of silver, 200 bolts of silk gauze, and 50 catties of ginseng. Kao-tsung received the envoys in audience and presented K'ai with two golden belts (*Sung shih* 27:4a; 487:17b; *Wen-hsien t'ung-k'ao* 325:53b).

On Nov.24, 1132, Koryŏ envoys to the Chin court congratulated on the birthday of T'ai-tsung (*Chin shih* 3:16a).

In the 12th month (Jan./Feb., 1133) of the Chinese year 1132, a mission of 65 men from Wang K'ai of Koryŏ, arriving via Ming, offered gifts to the Southern Sung court (*Sung shih* 487:17b-18a; *Wen-hsien t'ung-k'ao* 325:53b).

On Feb,7, 1133, the New Year's Day, Koryŏ envoys congratulated at the Chin court (*Chin shih* 3:16b).

On Nov.13, 1133, Koryŏ envoys to the Chin court congratulated on the birtday of T'ai-tsung (*Chin shih* 3:17a).

At some time during 1133, a temple in the temporary Southern Sung capital was given the new name of the Lodge of Shared Culture to house visitors from Koryŏ (*Wen-hsien t'ung-k'ao* 325:53b).

On Jan.27, 1134, the New Year's Day, Koryŏ envoys congratulated at the Chin court (*Chin shih* 3:17a).

On Nov.2, 1134, Koryŏ envoys to the Chin court congratulated on the birthday of T'ai-tsung (*Chin shih* 3:17a).

On Feb.13, 1135, Emperor Hsi-tsung of Chin sent envoys to Koryŏ to announce the death of his granduncle T'ai-tsung on Feb.9. On Apr.20, Koryŏ envoys condoled at the Chin court. On May 29, Koryŏ envoys congratulated Hsi-tsung on his enthronement (*Chin shih* 4:1b, 2a).

On Jan.29, 1136, Chin for the first time established a protocol for the missions from Koryŏ and Hsia (*Chin shih* 4:2a).

On Feb.4, 1136, the New Year's Day, Koryŏ envoys congratulated at the Chin court (*Chin shih* 4:2b).

On Feb.8, 1136, Chin presented its calendar to Koryŏ (*Chin shih* 4:2b).

On Feb.20, 1136, Koryŏ envoys to the Chin court congratulated on the birthday of Hsi-tsung (*Chin shih* 4:2b).

On May 2, 1136, Koryŏ envoys to the Chin court condoled on the death of the Grand Empress Dowager on Feb.12 (*Chin shih* 4:2b).[81]

On Nov.15, 1136, Hsi-tsung of Chin appointed envoys to congratulate the king of Koryŏ on his birthday (*Chin shih* 4:2b).

At some time during 1136, a Koryŏ envoy to the Southern Sung court landed in Ming. He was presented silver and silk but sent back out of fear that he might be a Jurchen spy. Thereafter, diplomatic relations between Southern Sung and Koryŏ were interrupted for a long time (*Sung shih* 487:18a; *Wen-hsien t'ung-k'ao* 325:53b).

On Jan.23, 1137, the New Year's Day, Koryŏ envoys congratulated at the Chin court (*Chin shih* 4:3a).

On Feb.8, 1137, Koryŏ envoys to the Chin court congratulated on the birthday of Hsi-tsung (*Chin shih* 4:3a).

On Feb.12, 1138, the New Year's Day, Koryŏ envoys congratulated at the Chin court (*Chin shih* 4:3b).

On Feb.28, 1138, Koryŏ envoys to the Chin court congratulated on the birthday of Hsi-tsung (*Chin shih* 4:3b).

On Jan.24, 1139, Koryŏ envoys offered gifts to the Chin court (*Chin shih* 4:4b).

On Feb.1, 1139, the New Year's Day, Koryŏ envoys congratulated at the Chin court (*Chin shih* 4:3b).

On Feb.17, 1139, Koryŏ envoys to the Chin congratulated on the birthday of Hsi-ts'ung (*Chin shih* 4:4b).

On Jan.22, 1140, the New Year's Day, Koryŏ envoys congratulated at the Chin court (*Chin shih* 4:4b).

On Feb.7, 1140, Koryŏ envoys to the Chin court congratulated on the birthday of Hsi-tsung (*Chin shih* 4:6a).

On Feb.9, 1141, the New Year's Day, Koryŏ envoys congratulated at the Chin court (*Chin shih* 4:6b).

On Feb.25, 1141, Koryŏ envoys to the Chin court congratulated on the birthday of Hsi-tsung (*Chin shih* 4:7a).

On Dec.14, 1141, the Koryŏ State offered congratulations to the Chin court (*Chin shih* 4:8a).

On Jan.29, 1142, the New Year's Day, Koryŏ envoys congratulated at the Chin court (*Chin shih* 4:8a).

Having made peace with the Southern Sung in 1141, Hsi-tsung

[81] She was the widow of Emperor T'ai-tsu, founder of the dynasty.

of Chin ordered an attack on Koryŏ on Feb.8, 1142 (*Chin shih* 4:8a). Nothing came of it.

On Feb.14, 1142, Koryŏ envoys to the Chin court congratulated on the birthday of Hsi-tsung (*Chin shih* 4:8a).

On Dec.25, 1142, envoys from the king of Koryŏ to the Chin court thanked for his recognition (*Chin shih* 4:9a). Since Hsi-tsung had been emperor since 1135, this had obviously come late.

On Jan.18, 1143, the New Year's Day, Koryŏ envoys congratulated at the Chin court. On Feb.3, Hsi-tsung ordered that the protocol for his birthday and for the New Year's Day should be the same (*Chin shih* 4:9a).

On Feb.6, 1144, the New Year's Day, Koryŏ envoys congratulated at the Chin court (*Chin shih* 4:9b).

On Feb.22, 1144, Koryŏ envoys to the Chin court congratulated on the birthday of Hsi-tsung (*Chin shih* 4:9b).

On Jan.25, 1145, the New Year's Day, Koryŏ envoys congratulated at the Chin court (*Chin shih* 4:10b).

On Feb.10, 1145, Koryŏ envoys to the Chin court congratulated on the birthday of Hsi-tsung (*Chin shih* 4:10b).

On Feb.13, 1146, the New Year's Day, Koryŏ envoys congratulated at the Chin court (*Chin shih* 4:10b).

On Mar. 1, 1146, Koryŏ envoys to the Chin court congratulated on the birthday of Hsi-tsung (*Chin shih* 4:11a).

On June 14, 1146, it became known at the Chin court that the king of Koryŏ, Wang K'ai, had died. On Aug.6, Hsi-tsung sent envoys to condole and sacrifice (*Chin shih* 4:11a). K'ai was succeeded by Wang Hsien (Ŭijong).

On Feb.2, 1147, the New Year's Day, Koryŏ envoys congratulated at the Chin court (*Chin shih* 4:11b).

On Feb.18, 1147, Koryŏ envoys to the Chin court congratulated on the birthday of Hsi-tsung (*Chin shih* 4:11b).

On Apr.15, 1147, Koryŏ envoys to the Chin court thanked Hsi-tsung for the condolence (*Chin shih* 4:11b).

On Jan.23, 1148, the New Year's Day, Koryŏ envoys congratulated at the Chin court (*Chin shih* 4:12a).

On Feb.8, 1148, Koryŏ envoys to the Chin court congratulated on the birthday of Hsi-tsung (*Chin shih* 4:12a).

On Mar.15, 1148, Hsi-tsung appointed envoys for presenting gifts to the Koryŏ court (*Chin shih* 4:12a).

On Mar.17, 1148, Hsi-tsung dispatched a mission, headed by the

Grand Judge, to recognize Wang Hsien as king of Koryŏ. In the 6th month (June/July), envoys from Wang Hsien to the Chin court thanked for the recognition (*Chin shih* 4:12a, 12b).

On Feb.10, 1149, the New Year's Day, Koryŏ envoys congratulated at the Chin court (*Chin shih* 4:13a).

On Feb.26, 1149, Koryŏ envoys to the Chin court congratulated on the birthday of Hsi-tsung (*Chin shih* 4:13b).

In the 1st month (January) of 1150, the Dismissed Emperor[82] of Chin sent the Commander-in-chief of the Imperial Bodyguard to inform the Koryŏ court of his ascension (*Chin shih* 5:3b-4a). Emperor Hsi-tsung had been murdered on Jan.9. The Dismissed Emperor was his elder brother and instigator of the assassination.

Koryŏ congratulated the Dismissed Emperor twice on his enthronement, on Apr.8 and June 27, 1150 (*Chin shih* 5:4a, 4b-5a).

On Jan.20, 1151, the New Year's Day, Koryŏ envoys congratulated at the Chin court (*Chin shih* 5:6a).

On Feb.4, 1151, Koryŏ envoys to the Chin court congratulated on the birthday of the Dismissed Emperor (*Chin shih* 5:6a).

In the 6th month (July/Aug.), the Dismissed Emperor of Chin sent a mission to congratulate the king of Koryŏ on his birthday (*Chin shih* 5:7a).

On Feb.8, 1152, the New Year's Day, Koryŏ envoys congratulated at the Chin court (*Chin shih* 5:7b).

On Feb.23, 1152, Koryŏ envoys to the Chin court congratulated on the birthday of the Dismissed Emperor (*Chin shih* 5:8a).

In the 9th month (October) of 1152, the Dismissed Emperor of Chin sent a mission headed by the Commissioner of Waterways to congratulate the king of Koryŏ on his birthday (*Chin shih* 5:8b).

On Jan.27, 1153, the New Year's Day, the Dismissed Emperor of Chin did not hold court. He ordered the high officials to receive the envoys from Koryŏ and to acccept their gifts (*Chin shih* 5:9a)

On Feb.11, 1153, Koryŏ envoys to the Chin court congratulated on the birthday of the Dismissed Emperor (*Chin shih* 5:9a).

On Sep.20, the Dismissed Emperor of Chin appointed a Gentleman-of-the-Palace of the the Ministry of Personnel as envoy to congratulate the king of Koryŏ on his birthday (*Chin shih* 5:10a).

---

[82] Also known as the king of Hai-ling. He was murdered in 1161 and never received a posthumous title.

On Feb.14, 1154, the New Year's Day, the Dismissed Emperor of Chin was unwell and did not give the usual reception. The envoys from Koryŏ took up lodgings in Yen (Peking, capital since 1183) (*Chin shih* 5:11a).

On Mar.1, Koryŏ envoys to the Chin court congratulated on the birthday of the Dismissed Emperor (*Chin shih* 5:11a).

In the 11th month (Dec./Jan., 1155) of the Chin year 1154, envoys from the king of Koryŏ to the Chin court thanked for the birthday gifts (*Chin shih* 5:12a).

On Feb.4, 1155, the New Year's Day, Koryŏ envoys congratulated at the Chin court (*Chin shih* 5:12a).

On Feb.19, 1155, Koryŏ envoys to the Chin court congratulated on the birthday of the Dismissed Emperor (*Chin shih* 5:12a).

On Jan.24, 1156, the New Year's Day, Koryŏ envoys congratulated at the Chin court (*Chin shih* 5:14a).

On Feb.8, 1156, Koryŏ envoys to the Chin court congratulated on the birthday of the Dismissed Emperor (*Chin shih* 5:14a).

On Feb.12, 1157, the New Year's Day, Koryŏ envoys congratulated at the Chin court (*Chin shih* 5:15a).

On Feb.17, 1157, Koryŏ envoys to the Chin court congratulated on the birthday of the Dismissed Emperor (*Chin shih* 5:15b).

On Apr.11, 1157, Koryŏ envoys offered congratulations at the Chin court (*Chin shih* 5:15b).

In the 3rd month (Apr./May) of 1157, the Dismissed Emperor of Chin sent a member of the Court Ceremonial Institute with presents to the Koryŏ court (*Chin shih* 5:15b).

On Feb.1, 1158, the New Year's Day, Koryŏ envoys congratulated at the Chin court (*Chin shih* 5:16b).

On Feb.15, 1158, Koryŏ envoys to the Chin court congratulated on the birthday of the Dismissed Emperor (*Chin shih* 5:16a).

On Oct.7, 1158, the Dismissed Emperor of Chin sent the Superintendent of the Music Office to congratulate the king of Koryŏ on his birthday (*Chin shih* 5:16b).

On Jan.21, 1159, the New Year's Day, Koryŏ envoys congratulated at the Chin court (*Chin shih* 5:17a).

On Feb.5, 1159, Koryŏ envoys to the Chin court congratulated on the birthday of the Dismissed Emperor (*Chin shih* 5:17b).

On Feb.9, 1160, the New Year's Day, Koryŏ envoys congratulated at the Chin court (*Chin shih* 5:18b).

On Feb.24, 1160, Koryŏ envoys to the Chin court congratulated on the birthday of the Dismissed Emperor (*Chin shih* 5:18b).

On Jan.21, 1161, the New Year's Day, Koryŏ envoys congratulated at the Chin court (*Chin shih* 5:19b).

On Feb.12, 1161, Koryŏ envoys to the Chin congratulated on the birthday of the Dismissed Emperor (*Chin shih* 5:20a).

In the 8th month (Sep./Oct.) of 1161, the Dismissed Emperor of Chin sent an Erudite of the Grand Master of Ceremonies to congratulate the king of Koryŏ on his birthday (*Chin shih* 5:22a).

In the 11th month (Nov./Dec.) of 1161, Emperor Shih-tsung of Chin sent a Supernumerary Gentleman of the Right Office of the Masters of Writing to Koryŏ to announce that he had ascended the throne on Oct.27 (*Chin shih* 6:3b-4a). His brother, the Dismissed Emperor, was murdered by his officers on Dec.15, while campaigning against the Southern Sung (*Chin shih* 5:24a).

In the 3rd month (Apr./May) of 1162, a Koryŏ envoy landed in Ming and stated that his country wished to resume diplomatic relations with the Southern Sung. This was reported to the court by the local officials. The Attending Secretary Wu Fei warned that, since Koryŏ and Chin adjoined each other, the request was suspect. The proposal was thus rejected out of fear that the envoy might be a Jurchen spy (*Sung shih* 487:18a; *Wen-hsien t'ung-k'ao* 325:53b).

On Feb.5, 1163, the New Year's Day, Koryŏ envoys congratulated at the Chin court (*Chin shih* 6:10a).

On Apr.4, 1163, Koryŏ envoys arrived at the Chin court to congratulate on the birthday of Shih-tsung[83] A separate mission at about the same time congratulated on his enthronement (*Chin shih* 6:10b).

On May 23, 1163, Shih-tsung sent the Commissioner of Presentations with gifts to the Koryŏ court (*Chin shih* 6:11a).

On Nov.6, 1163, Shih-tsung sent an envoy to congratulate the king of Koryŏ on his birthday (*Chin shih* 6:12b).

On Jan.26, 1164, the New Year's Day, Koryŏ envoys congratulated at the Chin court (*Chin shih* 6:13a).

On Mar.25, 1164, Koryŏ envoys to the Chin court congratulated on the birthday of Shih-tsung (*Chin shih* 6:13b).

On May 6, 1164, Ming reported to the Southern Sung court that Koryŏ had offered gifts. These were rejected (*Chin shih* 33:13b; 487: 18a; *Wen-hsien t'ung-k'ao* 325:53b).

---

[83] It fell on Apr.6.

On Oct.16, 1164,[84] Shih-tsung sent the Junior Supervisor of the Household of the Heir-apparent to congratulate the king of Koryŏ on his birthday (*Chin shih* 6:15a).

On Feb.13, 1165, the New Year's Day, Koryŏ envoys congratulated at the Chin court. Shih-tsung gave them "instructions" (*Chin shih* 6: 15a; 135:5b).

On Apr.13, 1165,[85] Koryŏ envoys to the Chin court congratulated on the birthday of Shih-tsung (*Chin shih* 6:15b).

On Nov.10, 1165, Shih-tsung sent an Assistant of the Grand Director of the Imperial Clan to congratulate the king of Koryŏ on his birthday (*Chin shih* 6:16a).

On Feb.3, 1166, the New Year's Day, Koryŏ envoys congratulated at the Chin court (*Chin shih* 6:16b).

On Apr.6, 1166,[86] envoys to the Chin court congratulated on the birthday of Shih-tsung (*Chin shih* 6:16b).

On May 26, 1166, Shih-tsung sent a Gentleman-of-the-Palace of the Right Office of the Masters of Writing with gifts to the Koryŏ court (*Chin shih* 6:17a).

On Nov.3, 1166, Shih-tsung sent a Gentleman-in-Attendance of the Ministry of Arms to congratulate the king of Koryŏ on his birthday (*Chin shih* 6:17b).

On Jan.23, 1167, the New Year's Day, Koryŏ envoys congratulated at the Chin court (*Chin shih* 6:18a).

On Mar.23, 1167, Koryŏ envoys to the Chin court congratulated on the birthday of Shih-tsung (*Chin shih* 6:18a).

On Oct.31, 1167, Shih-tsung sent the Inspector of Water Ways to congratulate the king of Koryŏ on his birthday (*Chin shih* 6:18b).

On Feb.11, 1168, the New Year's Day, Koryŏ envoys congratulated at the Chin court (*Chin shih* 6:19b).

On Apr.10, 1168, Koryŏ envoys to the Chin court congratulated on the birthday of Shih-tsung (*Chin shih* 6:20b).

---

[84] Emending 8th month to 9th. The 8th did not have the cyclical characters of *hsin-hai*.

[85] The text says 3rd month, *mou-shen*, but these cyclical characters did not occur in that month. We know, however, from *Chin shih* 6:13a that Shih-tsung's birthday was celebrated on the 1st day of the 3rd month. The entry can therefore be emended to Apr.13.

[86] The text says 3rd month, *jen-yin*, but these cyclical characters did not occur in that month. In accordance with the preceding note, the date can be emended to Apr.6.

On Nov.10, 1168, Shih-tsung of Chin sent an Edict Attendant of the Han-lin Academy to congratulate the king of Koryŏ on his birthday (*Chin shih* 6:22a).

On Jan.30, 1169, the New Year's Day, Koryŏ envoys congratulated at the Chin court (*Chin shih* 6:22a).

On Mar.30, 1169, Koryŏ envoys to the Chin court congratulated on the birthday of Shih-tsung (*Chin shih* 6:22b).

On May 28, 1169, Shih-tsung sent a Gentleman for Tallies and Seals with gifts to the Koryŏ court (*Chin shih* 6:23a).

On Sep.23, 1169, Shih-tsung sent the Superintendant of the Office of Astronomy to congratulate the king of Koryŏ on his birthday (*Chin shih* 6:23b).

On Jan.19, 1170, the New Year's Day, Koryŏ envoys congratulated at the Chin court (*Chin shih* 6:24b).

On Mar.20, 1170, Koryŏ envoys to the Chin court congratulated on the birthday of Shih-tsung (*Chin shih* 6:24b).

On Nov.12, 1170, Shih-tsung sent an Assistant of the Grand Director of the Imperial Clan to congratulate the king of Koryŏ on his birthday (*Chin shih* 6:25b).

Having overthrown his brother Wang Hsien in 1170, Wang Hao (Myŏngjong) informed Chin in the 4th month (May/June)[87] of 1171 that Wang Hsien had "abdicated" (he was murdered in 1173) and that he had succeeded him. Shih-tsung sent a Gentleman-in-Attendance of the Ministry of Personnel to Koryŏ to find out the facts (*Chin shih* 6:27a; 135:6a).

In the 12th month (Dec./Jan.1172) of the Chin year 1171, the king of Koryŏ, Wang Hao, sent a Gentleman-in-Attendance of the Ministry of Rites to the Chin court and asked for recognition (*Chin shih* 135:6b).

On Jan.27, 1172, the New Year's Day, Koryŏ envoys congratulated at the Chin court (*Chin shih* 7:1a).

On Mar.26, 1172, Koryŏ envoys to the Chin court congratulated on the birthday of Shih-tsung (*Chin shih* 7:1b).

On Apr.3, 1172, Shih-tsung sent an Auxiliary General to Koryŏ to recognize Wang Hao as king *Chin shih* 7:1b).

On May 23, 1172, Koryŏ envoys offered congratulations to the Chin court (*Chin shih* 7:2a).

[87] 135:6a says 3rd month (Apr./May).

In the 10th month (Oct./Nov.) of 1172, envoys from the king of Koryŏ, Wang Hao, to the Chin court thanked for the recognition (*Chin shih* 7:2b).

On Jan.16, 1173, the New Year's Day, Koryŏ envoys congratulated at the Chin court (*Chin shih* 7:4a).

On Apr.14, 1173, Koryŏ envoys to the Chin court congratulated on the birthday of Shih-tsung (*Chin shih* 7:4a).

In the 11th month (Dec./Jan.1174) of the Chin year 1173, Shih-tsung sent the Commissioner of Presentations to congratulate the king of Koryŏ on his birthday (*Chin shih* 7:5b).

On Feb.4, 1174, the New Year's Day, Koryŏ envoys congratulated at the Chin court (*Chin shih* 7:6a).

On Apr.4, 1174, Koryŏ envoys to the Chin court congratulated on the birthday of Shih-tsung (*Chin shih* 7:6a).

On Dec.20, 1174, Shih-tsung sent the Commissioner of the Imperial Regalia Office to congratulate the king of Koryŏ on his birthday (*Chin shih* 7:7b).[88]

On Jan.25, 1175, the New Year's Day, Koryŏ envoys congratulated at the Chin court

On Mar.24, Koryŏ envoys to the Chin court congratulated on the birthday of Shih-tsung.

On Sep.29, 1175, the Regent of Koryŏ's Western Capital, Chao Wei-ch'ung, appealed to the Chin. He had risen against the king, Wang Hao, and wished to surrender with more than 40 towns west of the Tz'u-pei Range and east of the Yalu River. This was rejected (*Chin shih* 7:7b).

On Oct.29, 1175,[89] a mission of 96 men from Wang Hao of Koryŏ to the Chin court requested the execution of Chao Wei-ch'ung (*Chin shih* 7:8a; 135:7a).

On Dec.15, 1175, Shih-tsung sent an Auxiliary General to congratulate the king of Koryŏ on his birthday (*Chin shih* 7:8b).

On Feb.13, 1176, the New Year's Day, Koryŏ envoys congratulated at the Chin court (*Chin shih* 7:8b).

The birthday of Sheng-tsung of Chin in 1176 fell on Apr.11. Because

[88] Here follows a lacuna until the 9th month of 1175. However, Koryŏ's congratulations on the New Year's Day and the Chin emperor's birthday can be reconstituted.

[89] Emending 9th month to 9th intercalary month.

of an eclipse of the sun on that day, the celebration was postponed to the following day. Consequently, the Koryŏ envoys offered their congratulations on Apr.12 (*Chin shih* 7:9a).

In the 11th month (December) of 1176, Shih-tsung sent a Gentleman-of-the-Palace to congratulate the king of Koryŏ on his birthday (*Chin shih* 7:10b).

On Feb.1, 1177, the New Year's Day, Koryŏ envoys congratulated at the Chin court. They brought a letter from the king, Wang Hao, in which he announced that order had been restored in Koryŏ and thanked the Chin for not having supported Chao Wei-ch'ung (*Chin shih* 7:10b).

On Apr.1, 1177, Koryŏ envoys to the Chin court congratulated on the birthday of Shih-tsung (*Chin shih* 7:11b).

On May 18, 1177, Shih-tsung sent an envoy with gifts to the Koryŏ court (*Chin shih* 7:12a).

In the 12th month (Dec./Jan.1178) of the Chin year 1177, Shih-tsung of Chin sent an Auxiliary General to congratulate the king of Koryŏ on his birthday (*Chin shih* 7:14a).

On Jan.21, 1178, the New Year's Day, Koryŏ envoys congratulated at the Chin court (*Chin shih* 7:14b).

On Mar.21, 1178, Koryŏ envoys to the Chin court congratulated on the birthday of Shih-tsung (*Chin shih* 7:15a).

On May 14, 1178, Shih-tsung sent the Admonisher of the Left of the Heir-apparent to the Koryŏ court with gifts (*Chin shih* 7:15a).

On Jan.6, 1179, Shih-tsung sent the Commissioner of the Palace Audience Gate of the East to congratulate the king of Koryŏ on his birthday (*Chin shih* 7:16b).

On Feb.9, 1179, the New Year's Day, Koryŏ envoys congratulated at the Chin court (*Chin shih* 7:17a).

On Apr.9, 1179, Koryŏ envoys to Chin court congratulated on the birthday of Shih-tsung (*Chin shih* 7:17a).

On Dec.14, 1179, Shih-tsung sent the Commissioner of the Palace Audience Gate of the West to congratulate the king of Koryŏ on his birthday (*Chin shih* 7:18b).

On Jan.29, 1180, the New Year's Day, Koryŏ envoys congratulated at the Chin court (*Chin shih* 7:18b).

On Mar.28, 1180, Koryŏ envoys to the Chin court congratulated on the birthday of Shih-tsung (*Chin shih* 7:18b).

In the 4th month (Apr./May) of 1180, Shih-tsung Chin sent the

Commissioner of the Palace Audience Gate of the West[90] to the Koryŏ court with gifts (*Chin shih* 7:19a).

On Dec.5, 1180, Shih-tsung sent the Junior Grand Master of Ceremonies to congratulate the king of Koryŏ on his birthday (*Chin shih* 7:20a).

On Jan.17, 1181, the New Year's Day, Koryŏ envoys congratulated at the Chin court (*Chin shih* 8:1a).

On Mar.17, 1181, Koryŏ envoys to the Chin court congratulated on the birthday of Shih-tsung (*Chin shih* 8:1b-2a).[91]

On Feb.5, 1182, the New Year's Day, Koryŏ envoys congratulated at the Chin court.

On On Apr.5, 1182, Koryŏ envoys to the Chin court congratulated on the birthday of Shih-tsung.

On Apr.5, 1182, Koryŏ envoys to the Chin court congratulated on the birthday of Shih-tsung (*Chin shih* 8:3b).

On Dec.14, 1182, Shih-tsung sent an Auxiliary General to congratulate the king of Koryŏ on his birthday (*Chin shih* 8:4a).

On Jan.26, 1183, the New Year's Day, Koryŏ envoys congratulated at the Chin court (*Chin shih* 8:4b).

On Mar.26, 1183, Koryŏ envoys to the Chin congratulated on the birthday of Shih-tsung (*Chin shih* 8:4b).

In the 3rd month (Mar./Apr.) of 1183, Shih-tsung sent the Director of the Grand Judge with gifts to Koryŏ (*Chin shih* 8:5a).

On Feb.8, 1184, envoys from the king of Koryŏ to the Chin court announced the death of his mother (*Chin shih* 8:7a).

On Dec.13, 1184, Shih-tsung announced that because the distance to the Supreme Capital (in central Manchuria) was great and its weather cold, Koryŏ and Hsia were exempted from congratulating him on his birthday and Southern Sung from congratulating on the New Year's Day (*Chin shih* 8:9a).

On Dec.21, 1184, Shih-tsung sent a Supernumerary Gentleman of the Ministry of Rites to congratulate the king of Koryŏ on his birthay. Because of the death of his mother, Wang Hao declined the gifts. This

---

[90] Not the same man who was sent in 1179.

[91] From here on, entries are missing until the 3rd month of 1182, including Koryŏ's congratulations to Chin on the New Year's Day of 1182, as well as Chin's congratulations on the birthday of the king of Koryŏ in 1181, and perhaps a mission with gifts to Koryŏ earlier that year. However, the dates for the New Year and birthday congratulations can be reconstituted.

was in turn approved by the Chin court (*Chin shih* 8:11b).

On Jan.23, 1186, the New Year's Day, Koryŏ envoys congratulated at the Chin court (*Chin shih* 8:12a).

On Mar.23, 1186, Koryŏ envoys to the Chin court congratulated on the birthday of Shih-tsung (*Chin shih* 8:12a).[92]

In the 4th month(May/June) of 1186, Shih-tsung sent the Commissioner of the Visitors Bureau with gifts to Koryŏ (*Chin shih* 8:13b).

On Feb.10, 1187, the New Year's Day, Koryŏ envoys congratulated at the Chin court (*Chin shih* 8:17b).

On Apr.11, 1187, Koryŏ envoys to the Chin court congratulated on the birthday of Shih-tsung (*Chin shih* 8:18b).

On Jan.3, 1188, Shih-tsung sent an Edict Attendant of the Hanlin Academy to congratulate the king of Koryŏ on his birthday (*Chin shih* 8:20a).

On Jan.30, 1188, the New Year's Day, Koryŏ envoys congratulated at the Chin court (*Chin shih* 8:20b).

On Mar.30, 1188, Koryŏ envoys to the Chin court congratulated on the birthday of Shih-tsung (*Chin shih* 8:21a).

On Dec.13, 1188,[93] Shih-tsung sent the Director of the Grand Judge to congratulate the king of Koryŏ on his birthday (*Chin shih* 8: 23b-24a).

On Jan.19, 1189, the New Year's Day, Shih-tsung was ill with a great sweat and could not hold court. The envoys from Koryŏ were sent home (*Chin shih* 8:24a).

On Jan.31, 1189, Chin sent envoys to the Koryŏ court to announce the death of Emperor Shih-tsung on Jan.20 (*Chin shih* 9:2b). He was succeeded by his grandson Chang-tsung.

On Aug.10, envoys from the king of Koryŏ to the Chin court condoled and sacrificed. That month, the high officials of Chin informed Koryŏ that Chang-tsung's birthday would be celebrated on the 1st day of the 9th month (*Chin shih* 9:4a-4b).

On Aug.26, 1189,[94] Koryŏ envoys to the Chin court congratulated Chang-tsung on his enthronement (*Chin shih* 9:4b).

On Oct.10, 1189, Koryŏ envoys arrived at the Chin court to con-

---

[92] Shih-tsung had left the Supreme Capital on May 27, 1185 (*Chin shih* 8:10a).

[93] Emending 11th month to 12th month. The 11th did not have the cyclical characters *ping-yin*.

[94] Emending 6th month to 7th month. The 6th did not have the cycical characters *hsin-wei*.

gratulate on the birthday of Chang-tsung. On Oct.12 was the imperial birthday, but because of the mourning for Shih-tsung, Chang-tsung did not hold court (*Chin shih* 9:5a).

On Oct.24, 1189, Chang-tsung sent the Commissioner of the Service Overseeing the Imperial Hand-drawn Carriage with gifts to Koryŏ court (*Chin shih* 9:5b).

On Dec.14, 1189, Chang-tsung sent the Commissioner of the Palace Audience Gate of the West to congratulate the king of Koryŏ on his birthday (*Chin shih* 9:6b).

On Feb.5, 1190, Koryŏ envoys arrived at the Chin court to congratulate on the New Year's Day. On Feb.7, the New Year's Day, Chang-tsung did not accept congratulations because of the mourning for Shih-tsung (*Chin shih* 9:7a).

On Sep.28, 1190, Koryŏ envoys arrived at the Chin court to congratulate on the birthday of Chang-tsung. On Oct.1 was the imperial birthday, but because of the mourning for Shih-tsung, Chang-tsung did not hold court (*Chin shih* 9:9b).

In the 11th month (December) of 1190, Chang-tsung sent the Commissioner of the Palace Audience Gate of the West to congratulate the king of Koryŏ on his birthday (*Chin shih* 9:10a).

On Jan.12, 1191, Koryŏ envoys arrived at the Chin court to congratulate on the New Year's Day. On Jan.27, the New Year's Day, Chang-tsung did not hold court because of the mourning for Shih-tsung (*Chin shih* 9:10b).

On Feb.12, 1191, Chang-tsung sent envoys to Koryŏ to announce the death of his mother, the Empress Dowager, on Jan.7 (*Chin shih* 9:10b).

On Apr.22, 1191, Koryŏ envoys condoled and sacrificed at the Chin court (*Chin shih* 9:11b).

On Sep.9, 1191, Koryŏ envoys arrived at the Chin court to congratulate on the birthday of Chang-tsung. On Sep.21 was the imperial birthday, but because of the mourning for the Empress Dowager, Chang-tsung did not hold court (*Chin shih* 9:12b).

On Dec.9, 1191, Chang-tsung sent the Vice Commissioner of the Court Attendant Service to congratulate the king of Koryŏ on his birthday (*Chin shih* 9:13a).

On Jan.15, 1192, Koryŏ envoys arrived at the Chin court to congratulate on the New Year's Day. On Jan.17, the New Year's Day, Chang-tsung did not hold court because of the mourning for the Empress Dowager (*Chin shih* 9:13b).

On June 12, 1192, Chang-tsung sent a Supernumerary Gentleman of the Ministry of Rites with gifts to Koryŏ (*Chin shih* 9:15b).

On Oct.5, Koryŏ envoys arrived at the Chin court to congratulate on the birthday of Chang-tsung. On Oct.8 was the imperial birthday but because of the mourning for the Empress Dowager, Chang-tsung did not hold court (*Chin shih* 9:17a).

On Jan.9, 1193, Chang-tsung sent the Commissioner of the Palace Audience Gate of the East to congratulate the king of Koryŏ on his birthday (*Chin shih* 9:19a).

On Feb.2, 1193, Koryŏ envoys arrived at the Chin court to congratulate on the New Year's Day. On Feb.4, the New Year's Day, Chang-tsung did not hold court because of the mourning for the Empress Dowager (*Chin shih* 9:19b; 10:1a).

On Sep.27, 1193, on his birthday, Chang-tsung received the kings who were related to him, the officials, and the foreign envoys, including those from Koryŏ, in the Hall of Great Peace (*Chin shih* 10:4a).

In the 12th month (Dec./Jan., 1194) of the Chin year 1193, Chang-tsung sent an envoy to congratulate the king of Koryŏ on his birthday (*Chin shih* 10:4b).

On Jan.24, 1194, the New Year's Day, Koryŏ envoys congratulated at the Chin court (*Chin shih* 10:5a).

On Sep.16, 1194, Koryŏ envoys to the Chin court congratulated on the birthday of Chang-tsung (*Chin shih* 10:6b).

In the 12th month (Jan./Feb., 1195) of the Chin year 1194, Chang-tsung sent a Gentleman-of-the Palace of the Ministry of Households to offer gifts on the birthday of the king of Koryŏ (*Chin shih* 10:8a).

On Feb.12, 1195, the New Year's Day, Koryŏ envoys congratulated at the Chin court (*Chin shih* 10:8b).

On Oct.5, 1195, Koryŏ envoys to the Chin court congratulated on the birthday of Chang-tsung (*Chin shih* 10:10b).

In the 12th month (January 1196) of the Chin year 1195, Chang-tsung sent the Administrator of the Public Petitioners Review Office to congratulate the king of Koryŏ on his birthday (*Chin shih* 10:11a).

On Feb.1, 1196, the New Year's Day, Koryŏ envoys congratulated at the Chin court (*Chin shih* 10:11b).

On Aug.3, 1196, envoys from Koryŏ were received in audience by Chang-tsung of Chin and presented letters (*Chin shih* 10:13a).

On Sep.24, 1196, Koryŏ envoys to the Chin court congratulated on the birthday of Chang-tsung (*Chin shih* 10:13a).

On Dec.26, 1196, Chang-tsung sent the Associate Administrator of the Public Petitioners Review Office to congratulate the king of Koryŏ on his birthday (*Chin shih* 10:14a).

On Jan.20, 1197, the New Year's Day, Koryŏ envoys congratulated at the Chin court (*Chin shih* 10:14a).

On Oct.13, 1197, Koryŏ envoys to the Chin court congratulated on the birthday of Chang-tsung (*Chin shih* 10:16a).

On Nov.21, 1197, the Imperial Chancellery of Chin reported to Chang-tsung that, according to information received, the king of Koryŏ, Wang Cho (Sinjong), had taken over the government from his old and sick elder brother Wang Hao (*Chin shih* 10:16b).[95]

On Feb.8, 1198, the New Year's Day, there was an eclipse of the sun. Chang-tsung postponed the festival until Feb.10, when he received the envoys from Sung and Hsia (*Chin shih* 11:1a). None are mentioned from Koryŏ.

On May 6, 1198, envoys from Koryŏ to the Chin court announced officially that Wang Cho had taken over the government (*Chin shih* 11:1b).

In the 4th month (May/June) of 1198, Chang-tsung of Chin sent an Attending Secretary to Koryŏ to make inquiries (*Chin shih* 11:2a).

In the 12th month (Dec./Jan., 1199) of the Chin year 1198, envoys from Wang Cho of Koryŏ were received at the Chin court (*Chin shih* 11:2b).

In the 3rd month (Mar./Apr.) of 1199, Chang-tsung sent envoys to the Koryŏ court to recognize Wang Cho as king (*Chin shih* 11:3b).

On Sep.22, 1199, Koryŏ envoys to the Chin court congratulated on the birthday of Chang-tsung (*Chin shih* 11:5a-5b).

On Jan.18, 1200, the New Year's Day, Koryŏ envoys congratulated at the Chin court (*Chin shih* 11:6a).

On Oct.10, 1200, Koryŏ envoys to the Chin court congratulated on the birthday of Chang-tsung (*Chin shih* 11:7b).

On Feb.5, 1201, the New Year's Day, Koryŏ envoys congratulated at the Chin court (*Chin shih* 11:8b).

In the 5th month (June) of 1201, Chang-tsung sent the Auxiliary [Commissioner] of the Palace Audience Gate of the East to the Koryŏ court with gifts (*Chin shih* 11:9b).

On Sep.29, 1201, Koryŏ envoys to Chin congratulated on the birthday of Chang-tsung (*Chin shih* 11:10a).

[95] Wang Hao had been overthrown in a coup. He died on Dec.3, 1202.

On Nov.18, 1201, Chang-tsung sent the Disciplinarian of Attendants of the Commander-in-chief of the Army of the Martial Guards to congratulate the king of Koryŏ on his birthday (*Chin shih* 11:10b).

On Jan.26, 1202, the New Year's Day, Koryŏ envoys congratulated at the Chin court (*Chin shih* 11:11a).

On Sep.18, 1202, Koryŏ envoys to the Chin court congratulated on the birthday of Chang-tsung (*Chin shih* 11:12a).

On Nov.7. 1202,[96] Chang-tsung sent the Vice Commissioner of the Service Directing the Imperial Hand-drawn Carriage to congratulate the king of Koryŏ on his birthday (*Chin shih* 11:12a).

On Feb.14, 1203, the New Year's Day, Koryŏ envoys congratulated at the Chin court (*Chin shih* 11:12b).

On Oct.7, 1203, Koryŏ envoys to the Chin court congratulated on the birthday of Chang-tsung (*Chin shih* 11:14a).

In the 10th month (Nov./Dec.) of 1203, Chang-tsung sent the Commissioner of Food Service to congratulate the king of Koryŏ on his birthday (*Chin shih* 11:14a).

On Feb.3, 1204, the New Year's day, Koryŏ envoys congratulated at the Chin court (*Chin shih* 12:1a; 135:7b).

On Feb.29, 1204, envoys from Wang Ying (Hŭijong) of Koryŏ to Chin court announced that his father Wang Cho had died and that he had succeeded him (*Chin shih* 12:1a).

On Apr.26, 1204, Chang-tsung sent the Commissioner of the Palace Audience Gate of the West and others to sacrifice to the late king of Koryŏ, Wang Cho. He also sent the Commissioner of the Palace Audience Gate of the East to inquire about the well-being of the new king, Wang Ying, and to offer gifts (*Chin shih* 12:2a).

On Sep.25, 1204, Koryŏ envoys to the Chin court congratulated on the birthday of Chang-tsung (*Chin shih* 12:3b).

On Jan.22, 1205, the New Year's Day, Koryŏ envoys congratulated at the Chin court (*Chin shih* 12:4a).

On Oct.14, 1205, Koryŏ envoys to the Chin court congratulated on the birthday of Chang-tsung (*Chin shih* 12:5b).

On Nov.19, 1205, Chang-tsung sent a Supernumerary Gentleman of the Ministry of Punishments to congratulate the king of Koryŏ on his birthday (*Chin shih* 12:6a).

---

[96] Emending 9th month to 10th month. The 9th did not have the cyclical characters *jen-ch'en*.

On Feb.10, 1206, the New Year's Day, Koryŏ envoys congratulated at the Chin court (*Chin shih* 12:6b).

On Oct.4, 1206, Koryŏ envoys to the Chin court congratulated on the birthday of Chang-tsung (*Chin shih* 12:11a).

On Jan.30, 1207, the New Year's Day, Koryŏ envoys congratulated at the Chin court (*Chin shih* 12:13b; 135:8a).

On May 23, 1207, Chang-tsung sent the Vice Inspector of Palace Accounts to the Koryŏ court with gifts (*Chin shih* 12:4b).

On Sep.24, 1207, Koryŏ envoys to Chin court congratulated on the birthday of Chang-tsung (*Chin shih* 12:15b; 135:8a).

On Oct. 31, 1207, Chang-tsung sent the Prefect of the Arsenal to congratulate the king of Koryŏ on his birthday (*Chin shih* 12:16a).

On Jan.19, 1208, the New Year's Day, Koryŏ envoys congratulated at the Chin court (*Chin shih* 12:16b).

On July 9, 1208, the birthday celebration of Chang-tsung of Chin was moved from the 1st day of the 9th month to the 15th day of the 10th month (*Chin shih* 12:18a).

On Nov.14, 1208, Chang-tsung sent a Gentleman-of-the-Palace to congratulate the king of Koryŏ on his birthday (*Chin shih* 12:18b).

On Nov.24, 1208, Koryŏ envoys to Chin court congratulated on the birtday of Chang-tsung (*Chin shih* 12:18b).

In the 5th month (June/July) of 1209, Koryŏ envoys congratulated the King of Wei-shao on his enthronement as emperor of Chin (*Chin shih* 13:2b).[97]

On Jan.17, 1211, the New Year's Day, Koryŏ envoys congratulated at the Chin court (*Chin shih* 13:4a).

In the 8th month (Aug./Sep.) of 1213, it became known at the Chin court that the king of Koryŏ, Wang Ying, had died. In the 9th month (Sep./Oct.), Koryŏ officially announced the death. Chin sent envoys to condole and sacrifice and to recognize Wang Ying's successor (Kangjong) (*Chin shih* 135:8a).

In 1214, Emperor Hsüan-tsung of Chin attempted to send an envoy to the Koryŏ court, but the roads were blocked [by the Mongols] (*Chin shih* 135:8a).[98]

---

[97] Chang-tsung had died on Dec.29, 1208, and his uncle was enthroned. Since the latter was overthrown, he never received a posthumous title and is known as the king of Wei-shao.

[98] The King of Wei-shao had been overthrown in a coup on Sep.10, 1213, by his nephew (a brother of Chang-tsung), who then ascended the throne as Emperor Hsüan-tsung.

On Mar.25, 1219, Koryŏ envoys for the first time in Hsüan-tsung's reign reached the Chin court and offered presents. Hsüan-tsung thereupon attempted to send envoys in return. But the roads were blocked [by the Mongols], and there were no further relations between the two states (*Chin shih* 15:19a; 135:8a-8b).

The Five Dynasties, Sung, Liao, and Chin all liked to pretend that Koryŏ was a tributary vassal. Nothing could be more wrong. The Five Dynasties and Sung had no common border with Koryŏ and no way, even if they had possessed the military resources, to assert any supremacy over it. The Liao invasions of Koryŏ from 993 to1020 were successfully repelled by the Koreans. The Chin made no serious attempts against Koryŏ. The dynastic historians accepted nevertheless the official fiction and referred to Koryŏ by an unrealistic terminology. Let us look at the instances.

When peace negotiations between Koryŏ and Liao were conducted in 993, these are by *Liao shih* expressed as a Korean "apology". They were nothing of the sort, and, in fact, Liao made concessions to Koryŏ.

When in 994 Koryŏ envoys to Sung proposed a joint military action against Liao, they met with refusal. Henceforth, Koryŏ "accepted the decrees of the Khitan", and missions to China ceased (*Wen-hsien t'ung-k'ao* 325:51b). This means no more than that Koryŏ realized the weakness of the Sung and, without losing its independence, adjusted itself to coexistence with its powerful neighbour in the north.

In 1002, Koryŏ envoys offered the Liao a map of their state. It has been seen that such a symbol of surrender was hardly ever seriously meant.

When Sheng-tsung of Liao in 1010 ordered an attack on Koryŏ on the grounds that Wang Sung had been murdered and that he had not been informed of Wang Hsün's succession, he did not act as a piqued overlord but because this gave him a pretext to resume the war.

When Wang Hsün in 1010 sent envoys to the Liao court "to hand up a memorial and beg to pay court" and this was "allowed" (*Liao shih* 15:2a), the phraseology simply means that he was willing to negotiate peace.

When the *Liao shih* claims that Wang Hsün in 1012 "declared himself a subject as of old", this is hyperbole. Wang Hsün had never been a subject but an independent ruler and continued to be so, whatever the rhetoric.

When in 1020 Liao realized that a conquest of Koryŏ was beyond its powers, *Liao shih* claims that Wang Hsün "surrendered" and "begged to call himself a vassal and offer tribute", and that Sheng-tsung of Liao "pardoned Wang Hsün's crimes". Shorn of its dynastic language, this means no more than that the two states concluded peace as equal partners (formalized in 1022). In fact, Wang Hsün kept his own reign title and continued his diplomatic relations with Sung.

When in 1078 a Sung mission was received by Wang Hui of Koryŏ, *Sung shih* interprets this as Koryŏ's surrender to Sung. But it adds disapprovingly that Hui also accepted recognition from the Liao and used its calendar (*Sung shih* 487:15b). In reality, Koryŏ attempted to make use of Sung to preserve its independence from Liao.[99]

When Wang Yu of Koryŏ in 1114 thanked Liao for having been recognized at his previous rank after the mourning period for his mother, this was an empty diplomatic gesture which changed nothing in practice.

When Wang K'ai of Koryŏ in 1126 "presented a memorial [to Chin] and declared himself a vassal", the terminology meant no more than it had done in Liao times. It is a fact that on Dec.24, 1130, Wang K'ai sent envoys to Chin with his oath of allegiance.[100] But he felt, no doubt, that the independence of Koryŏ was worth an oath, and he also kept his own reign title.

When Chin in 1136 presented its calendar to Koryŏ, its acceptance was another symbolic gesture.

When Wang Hao in 1170 had overthrown his brother Hsien and made himself king of Koryŏ, Shih-tsung of Chin sent an envoy to Koryŏ to look into the matter. This may have satisfied Shih-tsung's ego but served no practical purpose, since he recognized Wang Hao as king in 1171.

When Shih-tsung announced in 1184 that because of special circumstances Southern Sung was not expected to congratulate on the New Year's Day and the imperial birthday, and that Koryŏ and Hsia were not expected to do so on his birthday, *Chin shih* states that these

[99] In 938, Koryŏ used the Later Chin calendar, in 948 the Later Han calendar, in 952 the Later Chou calendar, and in 963 the Sung calendar. In 994 it adopted the Liao calendar, in 1016 the Sung calendar, and in 1022 the Liao calendar (Wittfogel, p.353, note 37). To this can be added that Koryŏ in 1136 was presented with the Chin calendar. It is even possible that Koryŏ used different calendars simultaneously, depending on which country it dealt with.

[100] See Rogers in Rossabi, ed., *China among Equals*, p.161.

states were not "allowed" to congratulate. This is dynastic vocabulary without any relation to reality.

When Wang Hao of Koryŏ had been overthrown by his younger brother Cho, Chang-tsung of Chin sent an envoy in 1198 to make inquiries. This is no more significant than the Chin mission of 1170, since Chang-tsung recognized Wang Cho before the end of 1198.

There are two further entries which require consideration. In the 8th month (Aug./Sep.) of 938, local authorities on the northern cost of the Shan-tung peninsula informed the Later Chin court that the hostage Wang Jen-ti, who served in the Imperial Bodyguards, wished to be released so that he could return home to Koryŏ. He was allowed to do so (*Wu-tai hui-yao* 30:5a-5b). This account is as misleading as the previous ones discussed for Silla. Hostages, usually sons of foreign kings or chiefs, served as guarantors for the good faith of their countries and risked execution if this faith was broken. They were therefore kept in the capital in case of future need, not in the countryside. Furthermore, Koryŏ was on excellent terms with the Later Chin and had no reason whatsoever to provide hostages. Judging from the name, Wang Jen-ti could have been a member of the new royal Koryŏ house. He had probably, as had so many other foreign princes, come to China to to take up a sinecure appointment in the guards, perhaps to do some studying, and certainly to amuse himself. Wishing to return, he had proceeded to a port in northern Shan-tung. He needed a permit to board a ship, and this was requested by the local Chinese authorities. The rest is imagination.

The other entry is to the effect that on Apr.12, 1088, Liao remitted Koryŏ's "annual tribute" (*Liao shih* 25:2a; 115:4a). This tribute is in the beholder's eye. Koryŏ, in exchange for proper payment, offered gifts to Liao on an almost annual basis. A more likely explanation for the cancelation of what Liao preferred to call tribute is therefore that it did not expect any gifts that year or rationalized the fact that it did not receive any.

To repeat, Koryŏ was not a vassal with tributary duties to the Five Dynasties, Sung, Liao, and Chin. In spite of its smaller size, it was able to stand up to Liao and Chin, and did not have to buy peace. This required clever diplomacy and a minimum of appeasement. In spite of window-dressing, rhetorics, and even a pinch of nostalgia for the good old times of Korean-Chinese friendship, Koryŏ succeeded in keeping its autonomy until the advent of the Mongols.

The attitudes of China, Liao, and Chin to Koryŏ differed. All recognized its kings and none conferred posthumous titles on them or held official mourning. But China appointed the kings to honourary offices[101] and gave titles to their envoys, while Liao and Chin are not recorded to have done so.[102] Liao married a princess to a king of Koryŏ, China and Chin did not.

Like its Korean predecessors Koguryŏ, Paekche, and Silla, Koryŏ was deeply influenced by Chinese culture. One purpose of its missions to the Five Dynasties and Sung was to seek knowledge in such fields as Confucianism, Buddhism, history, literature, law, the plastic arts, medicine, pharmacy and geomancy, and, at times, even to make contributions in return. Koreans were sent with missions to Sung to stay there for study in 976, 986, and soon after 1105. A brother of a Koryŏ king inquired about the Buddhist dharma in 1085. Koryŏ requested printed Buddhist sutras in 991, the *Nine Confucian Classics* in 993, again Buddhist sutras in 1019, books on geomancy and geography in 1021, the Buddhist *Tripitaka* in 1073, physicians, pharmacists, painters, and sculptors in 1074, books on penal law and the *Wen-yüan ying-hua* in 1085, the dynastic histories and the *Ts'e-fu yüan-kuei* in 1092, and again physicians soon after 1105. On its part, Koryŏ presented four different editions of the *Classic of Filial Piety* to the Later Chou in 959, and the *Huang-ti hsien-ching* to Sung in 1092. And these are only the recorded cases.

Other purposes of the Koryŏ missions to China were to announce the death of a king and the name of his successor, to congratulate on an enthronement, to request a resumption of diplomatic relations, to seek a change of route for arrival, to request mediation for peace, to announce a peace, and to inform about border violations. Koryŏ and Sung also had a common interest in restraining the Liao of the Khitan and later the Chin of the Jurchen, in the classical pattern of a joint enemy situated between them, but although alliances and combined military actions were repeatedly proposed and explored, nothing ever came of it.

The Koryŏ missions to Liao and Chin had the same purposes, as well as to announce the death of a royal mother, to condole and sacrifice after the death of an emperor or empress dowager, to attend an imperial burial, to thank for condolence, to congratulate on the

[101] In 932, the Later T'ang also conferred a title on Wang Chien's queen.

[102] Only a son of the king Wang Hui was given a title by Liao.

walling of the Central Capital, to congratulate on having attacked Sung and Hsia, to congratulate on having made peace with Sung, to seek the release of Korean prisoners, and to seek border adjustments. In addition, starting in 1127, the missions from Koryŏ to Chin had a new function. This was to congratulate on the New Year's Day and on the emperor's birthday.[103] The Chin did not congratulate Koryŏ on the New Year's Day, but it did congratulate its kings on their birthdays, rarely before 1161 and almost consistently thereafter.

But in all Koryŏ missions to the Five Dynasties, Sung, Liao, or Chin, trade was an additional and important aspect. The evidence for that is not far to seek. It has been seen that Su Shih (Su Tung-p'o) suggested in 1093 that the Koryŏ envoys should not offer books but keep to straightforward business transactions in commercial goods such as silk and hair.

Furthermore, Koryŏ missions were sent even though it was known that they would not be received. On Jan.31, 1189, Chin sent envoys to Koryŏ to announce the death of Emperor Shih-tsung. On Oct.10, Koryŏ envoys arrived in Chin for the birthday celebration of Emperor Chang-tsung on Oct.12, knowing fully well that this would be cancelled because of the mourning for Shih-tsung. On Feb.5, 1190, Koryŏ envoys arrived in Chin for the New Year reception on Feb.7, knowing fully well that this would be cancelled because of the mourning for Shih-tsung. On Sep.28, 1190, Koryŏ envoys arrived in Chin for the birthday celebration of Emperor Chang-tsung on Oct.1, knowing fully well that this would be cancelled because of the mourning for Shih-tsung. On Jan.12, 1191, Koryŏ envoys arrived in Chin for the New Year reception on Jan.27, knowing fully well that this would be cancelled because of the mourning for Shih-tsung. On Feb.12, Emperor Chang-tsung of Chin sent envoys to Koryŏ to announce that his mother had died. On Apr.12, Koryŏ envoys condoled and sacrificed to the Empress Dowager in Chin. On Sep.9, Koryŏ envoys arrived in Chin for the birthday celebration of Emperor Chang-tsung on Sep.21, knowing fully well that this would be cancelled because

---

[103] Twice, the festivals were postponed because of an eclipse of the sun, the imperial birthday in 1176 and the New Year's reception in 1198. It is interesting that the superstition of solar eclipses being baleful events lingered, since Chinese astronomers had been able to predict them, including those invisible in China, for a millenium and therefore knew that they were natural phenomena. See my *Six Dynasties*, vol.II, pp. 143-144.

of the mourning for the Empress Dowager. On Jan.15, 1192, Koryŏ envoys arrived in Chin for the New Year reception on Jan.17, knowing fully well that this would be cancelled because of the mourning for the Empress Dowager. On Oct.5, Koryŏ envoys arrived in Chin for the birthday celebration of Emperor Chang-tsung on Oct.8, knowing fully well that this would be cancelled because of the mourning for the Empress Dowager. On Feb.2, 1193, Koryŏ envoys arrived in Chin for the New Year reception on Feb.4, knowing fully well that this would be cancelled because of the mourning for the Empress Dowager.

Why did Koryŏ send missions which would not be received? They were costly, but for the home country only to the border. Thereafter, their upkeep was paid by the host country. It was the latter which had reason to object to the expense of what, at first sight, looks like unnecassary missions. These may have been required by protocol and the wish of the host country to enhance its prestige. But even if that were the case, another potent reason was trade. Government exchange of goods could take place in spite of mourning, and the envoys profited from private trade. In fact, the *Chin shih* 9:10b is quite unequivocal on this point. It records that Emperor Chang-tsung, because of the cancellation of the New Year reception in 1191, allowed the envoys from Hsia to remain in their guest lodge for one day to trade. The Department of State Affairs pointed out that, according to precedent, the envoys should be permitted to stay for three days. The emperor accepted this. While this entry is for Hsia, it obviously also applies to Koryŏ and other states. In fact, the Koryŏ envoys remained on that occasion for at least 15 days.

Since the land route from Koryŏ to China was blocked by the Liao and later the Chin, the missions had to travel by sea. They could not land wherever they wished in China but had to call at certain ports. In the earlier period, this was chiefly Teng on the northern coast of the Shan-tung Peninsula. It was a stormy voyage in which ships could be wrecked. In 1074, Koryŏ requested a change of route, to put a greater distance between itself and the Khitan, and on Oct.31, 1076, the Sung government approved Ming on the southern coast of Hang-chou Bay as the new port of entry. The preferred seasons for sailing to China were the fall and winter.

Again the question arises how complete the records are on missions from Koryŏ to China. *Chiu wu-tai shih* 138:6b states that from 923 to 930 Koryŏ frequently sent envoys. Missions are recorded for 923, 925, and 930, which perhaps can be considered as frequent.

According to *Wen-hsien t'ung-k'ao* 325:51a, Koryŏ sent envoys from 936 to 944. Missions are recorded for 936, 939, and 943. The text does not say annually so that three missions may be the truth or close to it. In short, while there must be omissions, the statistics are complete enough to reveal trends.

This is the distribution by 20-year periods of the 82 missions recorded from Koryŏ to Wu-yüeh, the Later Liang, Later T'ang, Later Chin, Later Chou, and Sung, the 80 missions from Koryŏ to Liao, and the 190 missions from Koryŏ to Chin:

Missions from Koryŏ

	To China	To the Khitan/Liao	To Chin
907- 926:	3	6	
927- 946:	11	2	
947- 966:	11	0	
967- 986:	7	0	
987-1006:	11	14	
1007-1026:	7	9	
1027-1046:	1	10	
1047-1066:	0	15	
1067-1086:	8	8	
1087-1106:	7	11	
1107-1126:	9	5	2
1127-1146:	5		45
1147-1166:	2		43
1167-1186:	0		47
1187-1206:	0		45
1207-1226:	0		8

Before the Liao became a great power, the Koreans preferred to send missions to China. While this never led to a formal alliance, close political relations could be an advantage for both sides. Thereafter, the majority of the Koryŏ missions went to Liao, which had become a dangerous neighbour. The great number of missions from Koryŏ to Chin was not only necessitated by the need to negotiate and trade with another strong state, but also because diplomatic protocol by that time required congratulations on the New Year Days and the birthdays of the emperors. At the New Year and birthday congratulations, trade was, of course not overlooked.

As to Southern Sung, the rapid drop in missions from Koryŏ and their eventual diappearance follows the usual pattern. One reason was Southern Sung xenophobia and morbid fear of Jurchen spies, another Koryŏ disenchantment with Southern Sung as a possible ally against the Jurchen. This, however, did not affect private trade between Koryŏ and both Sung dynasties. In fact, the Northern Sung found it necessary to establish a trade law for Koryŏ on Feb.10, 1079 (*Sung shih* 15:22a). The Southern Sung decreed on Aug.17, 1199, that merchants from Koryŏ and Japan were not allowed to accept copper cash for their goods, and that Chinese merchants were not allowed to purchase goods for copper cash in Koryŏ (*Sung shih* 37:13a; 487:18a-18b). This shows that the great volume of private trade had brought on an acute copper shortage in Southern Sung.

Unfortunately, the goods brought by the Koryŏ missions to China are usually referred in the sources as regional objects. Those which are specified fall into the following categories:

Human Products

929: human hair.

Animals

Horses

959: fine horses.
978: fine horses.
983: fine horses.
1014: 12 horses.
1085: fine horses.

Aromatics

Aromatic and medical drugs, aromatic oils

929: fragrant oils.
983: aromatic drugs.
1030: aromatic oils.

Plants

929: ginseng.
1132: 50 catties of ginseng.

Minerals and Metals

959: 2000 pieces each of purple and white rock crystals, 50,000 catties of copper.
1132: 100 ounces of gold, 1000 ounces of silver.

Manufactured Objects

Of metals

929: censers for aromatics, lances, swords, scissors.
959: swords, armour.
978: military implements.
983: knives.
1019: long knives ornamented with gold.
1030: golden vessels, knives, swords.

Of leather

1014: saddles.
1019: horse trappings.
1030: horse trappings.

Other

959: bows.
983: bows and arrows.
1080: 8 carriages.

Textiles

Cottons

1019: 2000 bolts of middling quality cotton (rejected).

Silks

1085: brocade.
1132: 200 bolts of silk gauze.

Other

929: unspecified textiles.
983: mats, bedding.
1019: mats.
1030: mats.

Garments

959: robes.
983: brocade garments.
1019: brocade garments.

Texts

959: four different editions of the *Classic of Filial Piety*.
1092: the *Huang-ti hsien-ching*.

The Chinese offered in return garments, golden belts, silken fabrics, cotton, gold, silver, and porcelain vessels, gold foil, armour, horse trappings, hairpins, Buddhist sutras, the *Wen-yüan ying-hua*, the *Ts'e-fu yüan-kuei*, and perhaps also the dynastic histories, and books on penal law, geomancy, and geography.

The value of the goods brought by foreign missions to the imperial courts was assessed immediately, obviously so that appropriate return offerings or payments could be made through the missions to their own courts. There is no case on record for the Five Dynasties or Sung, but there is one for Chin. On Feb.5, 1177, the high officials of Chin presented a memorial to Emperor Shih-tsung, stating that the jade belt which the Koryŏ envoys had presented on the New Year's Day was only stone resembling jade, and requested an inquiry. Shih-tsung replied that there were no experts in a small state like Koryŏ, and that he considered this an honest mistake (*Chin shih* 7:10b-11a). The belt had been presented on Feb.1, so that only four days had elapsed.

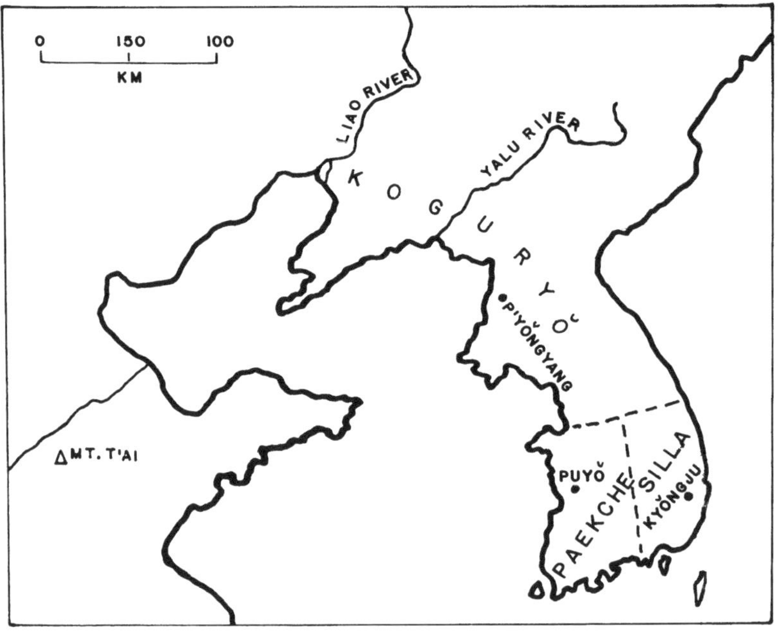

Map. 3. Korea c. 650.

THE NORTHEAST

Between 589 and the beginning of the 10th century, the chief tribes of Manchuria and adjoining parts of Jehol were the two Hsi, Mo-ho, Shih-wei, Khitan, and Jurchen. Their relations with China will be discussed here, except for the Khitan (Liao) and Jurchen (Chin) who have chapters of their own (map 4).

THE HSI

The Hsi were a pastoral people with little agriculture in southern Jehol. The Chinese originally called them the K'u-mo-hsi (*T'ung-tien* 200: 48a). But from the Sui onward, they appear in the Chinese sources only under the abbreviated form. They were probably linguistically related to the Khitan.[1]

On Feb.11, 593, Hsi envoys to the Sui court offered gifts (*Sui shu* 2:8b).

In 629 and in the 11th month (Dec./Jan., 630) of the Chinese year 631, Hsi were received at the T'ang court (*Ts'e-fu yüan-kuei* p.5024; *Wen-hsien t'ung-k'ao* 344:14b).

In the intercalary month (Sep./Oct.) of 632 and in the 1st month (Feb./Mar.) of 633, Hsi envoys offered gifts (*Ts'e-fu yüan-kuei* p.5024).

On Feb.2, 645, the New Year's Day, Hsi envoys congratulated and offered regional objects (*Ts'e-fu yüan-kuei* p.5024).

On Feb.16, 645, Emperor T'ai-tsung issued orders for his war against Koguryŏ, in which Silla, Paekche, the Hsi, and the Khitan were expected to attack by several routes (*Tzu-chih t'ung-chien* p.6215).

In 648, T'ai-tsung established the imaginary Jao-lo Area Command and appointed the Hsi chief K'o-tu-che as its Military Governor and

[1] See e.g. Wittfogel, *Liao*, p.95. According to Twichett, *Cambridge History of China*, vol.3:1, p.364, the Hsi were Turkish. They are not to be confused with the much less important Hsi of the next section. The names of both Hsi tribes have the same transliteration in English but are written with different characters in Chinese. Wherever Hsi are mentioned in this work other then in the brief account below, they are the Hsi of this section.

Concurrent General of the Right Commanding the Army. He also entitled him a duke and conferred on him the imperial surname of Li. Soon after 656, K'o-tu-che was made General-in-chief of the Right Inspecting the Gates (*Chiu T'ang shu* 199B:8a).

After a long hiatus, a mission from the Hsi chief Li Ta-fu[2] arrived in 710 with regional objects. Emperor Jui-tsung invited the envoys to a banquet and gave them rich presents (*Chiu T'ang shu* 199B:8a; *Ts'e-fu yüan-kuei* p.5026).

In 712, a T'ang army attacked the Hsi and was defeated (*Chiu T'ang shu* 199B:8a).

In 713, a high dignitary sent by Li Ta-fu proposed peace. The imaginary Jao-lo Area command was reestablished by Emperor Hsüan-tsung, and Li Ta-fu was made its Military Governor. He was also entitled king of Jao-lo commandery and appointed a Supernumerary General-in-chief of the Gilded Mace of the Left (*Chiu T'ang shu* 199B: 8b; *T'ang hui-yao* 96:4b).[3]

In the 2nd month (Mar./Apr.) of 717, Li Ta-fu paid a personal visit to the T'ang court. A daughter of an imperial daughter, the Lady Hsin, was enfeoffed as Princess of Ku-an and married to him. He was also presented with 1,500 objects. A General of the Right Commanding the Army was ordered to escort the couple back to the Hsi territory (*T'ung-tien* 200:48a; *Chiu T'ang shu* 199B:8b).

On Jan.26, 719, the New Year's Day, envoys from Li Ta-fu congratulated. In the 2nd month (Feb./Mar.) of the same year, his envoys offered regional objects (*Ts'e-fu yüan-kuei* p.5027).

In 720, Li Ta-fu fell in battle in support of the Khitan and was succeeded by his younger brother Lu-su. In the 11th month (Dec./Jan., 721) of the same Chinese year 720, Hsüan-tsung appointed Lu-su Military Governor of the non-existant Jao-lo Area Command (*T'ung-tien* 200:48a; *Chiu T'ang shu* 199B:8b; *Tzu-chih t'ung-chien* p.6743).

On May 16, 722, Li Lu-su personally came to the T'ang court. Hsüan-tsung recognized him as king of Jao-lo commandery and appointed him Supernumerary General-in-chief of the Gilded Mace of the Right and Concurrent Commissioner of the Army Which Pro-

---

[2] *Chiu T'ang shu* and *T'ang hui-yao* (96:4b) render the name as Li Ta-fu, *T'ung-tien* and *Ts'e-fu yüan-kuei* as Li Ta-p'u, i.e. the first writes the phonetic of the last character with radical 159, and the others with radical 164. Note that the imperial T'ang surname is used by the Chinese sources.

[3] *T'ang-hui-yao* dates the enfeoffment as king and appointment as general 717.

tects the Border. He was presented with 1000 objects and "ordered" in turn to marry the Princess of Ku-an (*T'ung-tien* 200:48a; *Chiu T'ang shu* 199B:8b). In China, a man could not marry a widowed sister-in-law. That was a custom prevalent in Central and North Asia. Hsüan-tsung therefore merely accepted a marriage which surely already had taken place.

On his return, Li Lu-su barely survived a conspiracy against him by a party in support of the Turks. But the resourceful Princess of Ku-an invited the plotters to a banquet and had them killed (*T'ung-tien* 200:48a).

In the 2nd month (March) of 724, a Hsi mission of ten men arrived at the court. The envoys returned to their homeland with 50 bolts of silk. In the 5th month (May/June) of the same year, the Jao-lo Area Command, i.e. the Hsi, presented musk (*Ts'e-fu yüan-kuei* p.5028).

On Feb.10, 726,[4] Hsüan-tsung entitled Li Lu-su as King Who Upholds Sincerity and appointed him Supernumerary General of the Army of the [Feathered] Forest of the Right (*Chiu T'ang shu* 8:14a; 199B:8b-9a; *Tzu-chih t'ung-chien* p.6770).

The Princess of Ku-an had meanwhile fallen victim to an intrigue. The legal wife of her father, the imperial princess, claimed that the Princess of Ku-an was not her daughter, i.e. had been born by a concubine, and proposed (in vain) that her own daughter be married to Li Lu-su. Hsüan-tsung "ordered" Lu-su to divorce his wife, enfeoffed a daughter of a daughter of Emperor Chung-tsung, the Lady Wei, as Princess of Tung-kuang, and sent her to Li Lu-su (*T'ung-tien* 200:48a; *Chiu T'ang shu* 199B:8b; *Tzu-chih t'ung-chien* p.6770). Nothing is known about the fate of Princess of Ku-an.

In the 11th month (Nov./Dec.) of 726, Hsi envoys were received at the T'ang court (*Ts'e-fu yüan-kuei* p.5028).

In the 5th month (May/June) of 730, the Hsi were under attack by the Turks. Li Lu-su and the Princess of Tung-kuang fled to T'ang (*Chiu T'ang shu* 8:17a; 199B:9a; *Tzu-chih t'ung-chien* p.6789). In the fall of the same year, the Chinese used the opportunity to attack the Hsi themselves (*Chiu T'ang shu* 199B:9a).

In the 11th month (Dec./Jan., 731) of the Chinese year 730, Hsi envoys offered gifts (*Ts'e-fu yüan-kuei* p.5028).

[4] *Chiu T'ang shu* 8:14a has 1st month, *kuei-hai*, which date did not exist. *Tzu-chih t'ung-chien* p.6770 has 1st month, *kuei-wei* = Feb.10.

On Feb.1, 732, the New Year's Day, Hsi envoys congratulated at the T'ang court (*Ts'e-fu yüan-kuei* p.5028). Later in the same year, envoys from the Hsi chief Li Shih and others were received at the T'ang court. Hsüan-tsung entitled Li Shih King Who has Attached Himself to Righteousness, Military Governor of the imaginary Kuei-yi Area Command (Area Command Attached to Righteousness), General-in-chief of the Feathered Forest of the Left, and Specially Advanced, and presented him with 100,000 objects (*Chiu T'ang shu* 199B:9a). There followed a period of hostility from 736 to 740.

On Apr.20, 745, Hsüan-tsung enfeoffed his sister's daughter, the Lady Yang, as Princess of Yi-fang, and married her to the Hsi king, Li Yen-ch'ung (*Tzu-chih t'ung-chien* p.6864).

The marriage was brief. In the 9th month (October) of 745, Li Yen-ch'ung killed the princess and began hostilities against the T'ang. He was defeated by An Lu-shan (*Chiu T'ang shu* 9:7a; *Tzu-chih t'ung-chien* p.6868).

On Apr.26, 746, Hsüan-tsung entitled the Hsi king, So-ku, King Who Displays Sincerity and appointed him Military Governor of the non-existant Jao-lo Area Command (*Chiu T'ang shu* 199B:9a; *Tzu-chih t'ung-chien* p.6871).

On Jan.23, 749, the New Year's Day, Hsi envoys congratulated at the T'ang court (*Ts'e-fu yüan-kuei* p.5030).

In the 1st month (Jan./Feb.) of 760, 12 men sent by the Hsi king, Chu-lo, were received at the T'ang court (*Ts'e-fu yüan-kuei* p.5031). This was presumably on the New Year's Day of Jan.23.

In the 8th month (Sep./Oct.) of 762, the Hsi offered gifts (*Ts'e-fu yüan-kuei* p.5031).

In the 11th month (Dec./Jan., 772) of the Chinese year 771, Hsi envoys were received at the T'ang court (*Ts'e-fu yüan-kuei* p.5031).

In the autumn of 772, Hsi envoys offered gifts. In the 12th month (Dec./Jan., 773) of the same Chinese year 772, envoys again offered presents (*Chiu T'ang shu* 11:20b; *Ts'e-fu yüan-kuei* p.5031).

In the 12th month (January 774) of the Chinese year 773, in the 12th month (January, 775) of the Chinese year 774, and in the 12th month (Dec./Jan., 776) of the Chinese year 775, Hsi envoys offered gifts (*Ts'e-fu yüan-kuei* p.5032).

In the 4th month (May/June) of 777, Hsi envoys offered regional objects (*Chiu T'ang shu* 11:26a; *Ts'e-fu yüan-kuei* p.5032).

In the 12th month (January, 778) of the Chinese year 777, Hsi envoys offered regional objects (*Ts'e-fu yüan-kuei* p.5032).

In the 9th month (Oct./Nov.) of 785, Hsi envoys were received at the T'ang court (*Chiu T'ang shu* 12:21a).

In the 7th month (Aug./Sep.) of 788, the Hsi and Shih-wei looted Chinese territory (*Chiu T'ang shu* 199B:9a).

On Feb.9, 793,[5] Hsi envoys were received at the T'ang court (*Chiu T'ang shu* 13:8a).

In 801, Hsi envoys were given an audience by Emperor Te-tsung (*Ts'e-fu yüan-kuei* p.5032).

In 806, the Hsi king, Military Governor of the non-existant Jao-lo Area Command, and King Who Has Attached Himself to Truthfulness, Mei-lo, came personally to the T'ang court. He was appointed Acting Minister of Works and then returned to his home land (*Chiu T'ang shu* 199B:9a).

In the 2nd month (Mar./Apr.) of 807, Hsi envoys offered gifts (*Chiu T'ang shu* 14:13a; *Ts'e-fu yüan-kuei* p.5032).

In 808, Emperor Hsien-tsung made the Hsi chief So-ti a General of the Majestic Guards of the Right and conferred on him the imperial surname of Li (*Chiu T'ang shu* 199B:9a).

In the 11th month (December) of 810, in 813, and in 815, the Hsi presented offerings (*Chiu T'ang shu* 199B:9a, 9b; *Ts'e-fu yüan-kuei* p.5032).

In the 1st month (Feb./Mar.) of 816, Hsi chiefs presented fine horses (*Chiu T'ang shu* 15:11b; 199B:9a; *Ts'e-fu yüan-kuei* p.5033).

In 818, the 12th month (Jan./Feb., 823) of the Chinese year 822, on Jan.1, 825, in the 12th month (Jan./Feb., 826) of the Chinese year 825, in the 12th month (Dec./Jan., 831) of the Chinese year 830, in the 11th month (Dec./Jan., 832) of the Chinese year 831, and in 834, Hsi envoys offered gifts (*Chiu T'ang shu* 15:16a; *T'ang-hui-yao* 96:5b; *Ts'e-fu yüan-kuei* p.5033).

In the 12th month (Dec./Jan., 836) of the Chinese year 835, the Hsi chief No-lang and others, 30 men in all, were received at the T'ang court (*Ts'e-fu yüan-kuei* p.5033).

In the 12th month (Jan./Feb.), 840) of the Chinese year 839, the Hsi chief Wen-na-ku offered gifts (*Ts'e-fu yüan-kuei* p.5033).

In 923, the Later T'ang conferred on the Hsi king, Sao-tz'u, the imperial surname of Li and the given name of Shao-wei (*Wu-tai hui-yao* 28:13b).

[5] Correcting 12th month to 12th intercalary month.

In the 12th month (Jan./Feb., 924) of the Chinese year 923, the Hsi chief Li Shao-wei (Sao-tz'u) sent envoys with offerings to the Later T'ang (*Ts'e-fu yüan-kuei* p.5034).

On Apr.2, 924, the Hsi king Li Shao-wei (Sao-tz'u) offered racehorses to the Later T'ang court (*Chiu Wu-tai shih* 31:6b-7a).

In the 11th month (Nov./Dec.) of 924, the Hsi king Li Shao-wei (Sao-tz'u) presented racehorses to the Later T'ang (*Ts'e-fu yüan-kuei* p.5034).

In the 9th month (Sep./Oct.) of 925, Hsi envoys arrived at the Later T'ang court to congratulate on the birthday of Emperor Chuang-tsung.[6] Another mission was received on Nov.11 (*Hsin Wu-tai shih* 5: 8b; *Wu-tai hui-yao* 28:13b).

On Mar.10, 926, the Hsi offered horses to the Later T'ang (*Chiu wu-tai shih* 34:2a).

In the 6th month (July/Aug.) of 929, Li Su-ku, son of the former Hsi king Sao-tz'u (Li Shao-wei), presented his father's horse trappings, garment, and armour [as testamentary gifts] to the Later T'ang (*Wu-tai hui-yao* 28:13b; *Ts'e-fu yüan-kuei* p.5034).

In the 11th month (Nov./Dec.) of 933, the Hsi chief Li Su-ku came personally to the Later T'ang court (*Ts'e-fu yüan-kuei* p.5035).

During the 10th century, the Hsi were absorbed into the Liao empire, but as late as 1001, a Hsi mission with gifts was received at the Sung court (*Sung shih* 6:14b).

The Hsi consisted of several tribes. They were not united into a cohesive state but ruled by chiefs whose lineages cannot be reconstructed. The fact that imperial surnames were conferred on three chiefs in 648, 808, and 923 proves that the latter did not descend from the earlier. In the course of time, some chiefs became more powerful than others, and it was these whom the Chinese recognized as kings and whom they appointed to nominal offices. The imperial courts did not, however, confer posthumous titles on any of them.

The Hsi were in no way vassals of the T'ang or Five Dynasties. Military conflicts are recorded for 712 and 788. The killing of a Chinese princess by her husband in 745, within months after her mariage, was not a friendly act. A pro-Turkish party existed among the Hsi in

---

[6] According to *Chiu Wu-tai shih* 27:1a, Chuang-tsung was born in 885, 10th month, *kuei-hai*. That was the 12th day of the month (not the 22nd as claimed by the text). In 925, the birthday consequently fell on Oct.31.

722. Later, the Hsi were dominated by the Uighurs, which led to the wholesale killing of Uighur tax collectors in the 9th month (Oct./Nov.) of 842 (*Tzu-chih t'ung-chien* p.7967). In short, the Chinese held no sway over the Hsi. Their value to the Chinese was the buffer they formed against Po-hai, the Khitan, Turks, and Uighurs.

It follows that the missions from the Hsi to China were never for the purpose of paying "tribute". In 713, they came to negotiate peace. They frequently congratulated on the New Year's Day[7] and at least once on an imperial birthday. But the missions chiefly served the purpose of trade. They normally consisted of several hundred men. At the Chinese border, 35 men were selected to proceed to the court, from which they were sent back with gold and silk (*T'ang hui-yao* 96: 5b).

According to *Chiu T'ang shu* 199B:8a, the Hsi sent envoys with gifts to the T'ang State between 618 and 626. None is recorded. According to *Chiu T'ang shu* 199B:9a, the Hsi sent missions without interruption from 816, sometimes arriving two to three times a year. The actual number of missions recorded from 816 to 840 is 10. The statistics are therefore incomplete, only the most important missions being recorded.

This is the distribution by 20-year periods of the 53 missions recorded from the Hsi to Sui, T'ang, and Later T'ang:

587- 606: 1
607- 626: 1
627- 646: 5
647- 666: 0
667- 686: 0
687- 706: 0
707- 726: 8
727- 746: 3
747- 766: 3
767- 786: 9
787- 806: 3
807- 826: 7
827- 846: 5
847- 866: 0

[7] The missions arriving in the 11th, 12th, and 1st months must be included among the New Year congratulations.

867- 886: 0
887- 906: 0
907- 926: 6
927- 946: 1
947- 966: 0
967- 986: 0
987-1006: 1

The number of recorded missions before the rebellion of An Lu-shan in 755 is 19, and after it, until the end of T'ang, 26. In spite of the disruptions caused by that uprising, the missions not only kept coming but increased in number. This must have been due to the proximity of the Hsi which facilitated trade and even more so by China's chronic need for horses. The drop at the end of T'ang from 847 to 906 must have been due to unsettled conditions, dangerous journeys, and an impoverished T'ang court.

The commodities brought by the Hsi missions are rarely mentioned, but musk is recorded for 724, and horses for 816, 924, and 926. The Chinese paid with gold and silk.

THE HSI

These Hsi are not to be confused with the Hsi of the preceding section. The tribes are in the Chinese written with different characters. According to Wittfogel (*Liao*, p.149 note 8), they lived in late T'ang times at the Western Liao River or Shira Muren in northeastern Jehol. Their language may have been related to that of the Khitan.

On Feb.11, 593, Hsi envoys to the Sui court offered regional objects (*Sui shu* 2:8b; *T'ung-tien* 200:49b).

In 629, Hsi envoys to the T'ang court offered regional objects (*Chiu T'ang shu* 199B:13b; *Ts'e-fu yüan-kuei* p.5023; *Wen-hsien t'ung-k'ao* 344: 14b).

PO-HAI

The Mo-ho were a Tungusic people, which in Northern Wei times had been known as the Wu-chi. They were divided into a number of tribes, occupying the area from central Manuchuria around the

Sungari River eastward to the Sea of Japan. The eastern Mo-ho became expert sailors.[8]

On Dec.29, 591, Jan.21, 593,[9] and Aug.12, 593, Mo-ho envoys were received at the Sui court (*Sui shu* 2:7b, 8a, 8b). At one of these occasions, Emperor Wen supposedly announced "I look on you as my sons, and you should honour me as your father", which is possible, to which the envoys supposedly replied "Your subjects ... have heard that in China there is a sage. Therefore we have come to pay court and salute", which is impossible. Emperor Wen then "ordered" that the Mo-ho and Khitan should not attack each other, whereupon the Mo-ho "apologized". In reality, the Mo-ho envoys had come on trading missions, which Emperor Wen, no doubt, approved of. He gave a banquet, at which the envoys rose and danced. They received brocade and silk (*Pei shih* 94:1b-18a; *Wen-hsien t'ung-k'ao* 326:57a)

On Feb.4, 615, the New Year's Day, Mo-ho envoys were received at the Sui court and offered presents (*Sui shu* 4:9b).

In 621, Mo-ho envoys, together with Khitan envoys, were received at the T'ang court (*Chiu T'ang shu* 199B:5b).

In the 11th month (Dec./Jan., 623) of the Chinese year 622, and again in the 7th month (July/Aug.) of 624, the Mo-ho chief A-ku-lang personally came to the court (*Ts'e-fu yüan-kuei* p.5023).

In the 4th month (May) of 626, Mo-ho envoys arrived with gifts (*Ts'e-fu yüan-kuei* p.5023).

On Jan.4, 630, Mo-ho envoys offered gifts (*Tzu-chih t'ung-chien* p.6067).

In the 11th month (Dec./Jan., 633) of the Chinese year 632, Mo-ho offered gifts. In the 4th month (May) of 634, Mo-ho chiefs were received at the T'ang court (*Ts'e-fu yüan-kuei* p.5024).

On Feb.3, 645, the New Year's Day, Mo-ho envoys congratulated at the T'ang court and offered regional objects (*Ts'e-fu yüan-kuei* p.5024).

When the Chinese attacked Silla in the 2nd month (March) of 675, their Mo-ho allies raided the southern coast of Silla by sea (*Tzu-chih t'ung-chien* p.6375).

---

[8] In the survey below, I exclude those Mo-ho who had willingly or unwillingly accomodated themselves to China and semi-autonomously lived on Chinese territory. For the chief T'u Ti-chi and his son Chin-hsing see *Chiu T'ang shu* 199B:10b, 11a; *Ts'e-fu yüan-kuei* p.5023; *Wen-hsien t'ung-k'ao* 326:57a.

[9] Correcting *chi-yu* to *yi-yu*.

Soon thereafter, an important kingdom came into being in Manchuria. It was founded by the former Koguryŏ general Ta Tso-jung. After the destruction of Koguryŏ in 668, he and other refugees from that state had moved to Manchuria, where he defeated Chinese forces in 696 or 697. Between 698 and 700, he proclaimed himself king of the Chen State[10] and sent envoys to the Turks (*Chiu T'ang shu* 199B:11b; *Tzu-chih t'ung-chien* p.6680; *Wen-hsien t'ung-k'ao* 326:57b). At its height, this state was to comprise the Liao-tung Peninsula and eastern Manchuria to the upper Sungari River, bordering in the east on the Sea of Japan. Its subject people were chiefly the Mo-ho, except the hostile Black River Mo-ho at the Amur River, and some of the Jurchen.

Emperor Chung-tsung (r.705-710) of T'ang sent an Attending Secretary as an envoy to Tso-jung, and the latter sent a son to the T'ang court (*Chiu T'ang shu* 199B:11b; *Tzu-chih t'ung-chien* p.6680).

In the 11th month (Dec./Jan., 712) of the Chinese year 711, Mo-ho envoys offered regional objects (*Ts'e-fu yüan-kuei* p.5026).[11]

In 712, Emperor Jui-tsung sent a General of the Gentlemen [-of-the-Household] to appoint Tso-jung as [General-in-chief of the] Resolute Guards of the Left and Supernumerary General-in-chief, and recognize him as king of Po-hai commandery. His territory was made into the fictitious Hu-han Area Command, and he was appointed its nominal Military Governor (*Chiu T'ang shu* 199B:11b; *Tzu-chih t'ung-chien* p.6680; *Wen-hsien t'ung-k'ao* 326:57b).[12]

In the 12th month (Dec./Jan., 714) of the Chinese year 713, a son of the Mo-ho king (i.e. of Ta Tso-jung of Po-hai) was received at the T'ang court He wished to engage in private trade, which was allowed (*Ts'e-fu yüan-kuei* p.5027).

In the 2nd month (Feb./May) of 714 and in the intercalary month

---

[10] The Empress Wu had earlier enfeoffed his father as duke of Chen (*Wen-hsien t'ung-k'ao* 326:57b). *Chiu T'ang shu* and *Tzu-chih t'ung-chien* write the phonetic of the name with radical 64, *Wen-hsien t'ung-k'ao* with radical 173.

[11] All sources distinguish between the Mo-ho (occasionally with the tribal prefixes T'ieh-li or Yüeh-hsi) and the Black River Mo-ho. One must therefore assume that the former, although subjects of the new state, still had their own chiefs and, at times, sent envoys of their own.

[12] *Chiu T'ang shu* and *Tzu-chih t'ung-chien* date the mission 713, which is repeated by some Western historians. But *Wen-hsien t'ung-k'ao* states explicitly that the envoy was sent by Jui-tsung. That emperor abdicated in the 8th month (Sep./Oct.) of 712, so that 713 must be wrong.

(Jan./Feb., 717) of the Chinese year 716, Mo-ho chiefs were received at the T'ang court (*Ts'e-fu yüan-kuei* p.5027).

In the 3rd (Apr./May) and 5th month (June/July) of 717, Mo-ho envoys offered regional objects (*Ts'e-fu yüan-kuei* p.5027).

In the 2nd month (Mar./Apr.) of 718, Mo-ho envoys were received at the T'ang court (*Ts'e-fu yüan-kuei* p.5027).

In the 1st month (Jan./Feb.) of 719, envoys from the Mo-ho, the T'ieh-li Mo-ho, and the Yüeh-hsi Mo-ho were received at the T'ang court. In the 2nd month (Feb./Mar.) of the same year, Mo-ho envoys presented regional objects (*Ts'e-fu yüan-kuei* p.5027).

In the 3rd month (Mar./Apr.) of 719, it became known at the T'ang court that Ta Tso-jung had died. In the 6th month (June/July), Emperor Hsüan-tsung sent envoys to condole and sacrifice, to appoint Wu-yi, Tso-jung's son by his legitimate wife, as General-in-chief of the Resolute Guards of the Left and Military Governor of the non-existing Hu-han Area Command, and to recognize him as king of Po-hai (*Chiu T'ang shu* 199B:11b-12a; *Tzu-chih t'ung-chien* p.6735; *Wen-hsien t'ung-k'ao* 326:57b).

In the 8th month (Sep./Oct.) of 719, Mo-ho envoys presented maritime products, sable furs, and white hare furs (*Ts'e-fu yüan-kuei* p.5027).

On Nov.29, 721, a Mo-ho chief from Po-hai was received at the T'ang court and was appointed an officer of the Asssault-resisting Garrison. In 722, another Mo-ho chief came to the court (*Ts'e-fu yüan-kuei* p.5027; *Wen-hsien t'ung-k'ao* 326:57a).

In the 11th month (Dec./Jan., 723) of the Chinese year 722, a high Po-hai official offered falcons (*Ts'e-fu yüan-kuei* p.5027).

In the 2nd month (Mar./Apr.) of 724, a high official of the Po-hai Mo-ho was received at T'ang court. He was presented with 50 bolts of silk (*Ts'e-fu yüan-kuei* p.5028).

In the 12th month (Dec./Jan.,725) of the Chinese year 724, an envoy from the Yüeh-hsi Mo-ho arrived at the T'ang court to congratulate on the New Year's Day and offer regional objects (*Ts'e-fu yüan-kuei* p.5028).

On Feb.18, 725, the New Year's Day, a Po-hai chief congratulated at the T'ang court and offered regional objects (*Ts'e-fu yüan-kuei* p.5028).

In 726, the Black River Mo-ho sent envoys to the T'ang court. Hsüan-tsung responded with envoys of his own and named their territory the Black River Area Command. The king of Po-hai, Ta Wu-yi, considered this a hostile act. To forestall a possible attack by the Black River Mo-ho, he decided to take the offensive himself. He placed his full younger brother Ta Men-yi and his maternal uncle Jen-ya in command of troops and ordered them to march against the Black River Mo-ho. Men-yi had stayed in the T'ang capital and had returned from there soon after 713. He was friendly to China and advised against the war. Wu-yi replaced him and summoned him to his court. Fearing for his life, Men-yi fled to Ch'ang-an, where Hsüan-tsung appointed him General of the Resolute Guards of the Left. Wu-yi dispatched envoys to the T'ang court and demanded Men-yi's execution. Hsüan-tsung secretely sent Men-yi to Central Asia. He detained the Po-hai envoys, informed Wu-yi through the Junior Herald that, since Men-yi had attached himself to China, he could not be killed, and stated falsely that Men-yi had been banished to the far south. Wu-yi repeated his demand, which infuriated the emperor (*Chiu T'ang shu* 199B:12a-12b; *Tzu-chih t'ung-chien* pp.6774-6775; *Wen-hsien t'ung-k'ao* 326:57b).

In the 11th month (Nov.,/Dec.) of the same year 726, a son of the king of the Po-hai Mo-ho (i.e. of Wu-yi) offered regional objects (*Chiu T'ang shu* 8:14b; *Ts'e-fu yüan-kuei* p.5028).

In the 10th month (Nov./Dec.) of 727, Mo-ho envoys offered regional objects (*Ts'e-fu yüan-kuei* p.5028).

In the 2nd month (Mar./Apr.) of 729, the Po-hai Mo-ho presented falcons and mullets (*Ts'e-fu yüan-kuei* p.5028).

On Jan.23, 730, the New Year's Day, a younger brother of a Mo-ho chief congratulated at the T'ang court and presented regional objects (*Ts'e-fu yüan-kuei* p.5028).

In the 2nd month (Feb./Mar.) of 730, a Po-hai Mo-ho chief presented regional objects and 30 horses (*Ts'e-fu yüan-kuei* p.5028).

In the 5th month (May/June) of 730, a Po-hai Mo-ho envoy offered five seal skins, three leopard furs, one cup of carnelian, and 30 horses (*Ts'e-fu yüan-kuei* p.5028).

In the 9th month (Oct./Nov.) of 730, Mo-ho envoys offered gifts (*Ts'e-fu yüan-kuei* p.5028).

In the 2nd month (Mar./Apr.) of 731, Po-hai Mo-ho envoys were received at the T'ang court. In the 10th month (Nov./Dec.) of the same year, a mission from the king of the Po-hai Mo-ho, consisting of 120 men, arrived at the T'ang court (*Ts'e-fu yüan-kuei* p.5028).

In spite of the subsequent missions, the relations between Po-hai and T'ang had been strained since 726. This led to a naval raid by Po-hai on the important port of Teng on the northern coast of Shan-tung in the 9th month (Sep./Oct.) of 732. Hsüan-tsung now planned a double-pronged attack on Po-hai. Men-yi was to invade it with a Chinese army from the southwest, while Silla agreed to do so from the south. The war commenced in the 1st month (Jan./Feb.) of 733 but had to be abandoned because of a harsh winter. Wu-yi retaliated by attempting to have Men-yi murdered. His agents stabbed him at the T'ien-chin Bridge of Lo-yang. Men-yi resisted and survived. The assassins were arrested and executed (*Chiu T'ang shu* 199A:12a; 199B: 12b; *Tzu-chih t'ung-chien* p.6799; *Wen-hsien t'ung-k'ao* 326:58a).

Relations between Po-hai and T'ang thereafter returned to normal, and in the 3rd month (Mar./Apr.) of 735 a younger brother of the king of the Po-hai Mo-ho arrived at the T'ang court (*Ts'e-fu yüan-kuei* p.5029).

In the 9th month (Oct./Nov.) of 736, the Yüeh-hsi Mo-ho presented regional objects (*Ts'e-fu yüan-kuei* p.5029).

In the 1st month (Feb./Mar.) of 737, a Po-hai Mo-ho chief was received at the T'ang court. In the 4th month (May/June) of the same year, a Po-hai official presented falcons (*Ts'e-fu yüan-kuei* p.5029).

In the intercalary month (Sep./Oct.) of 738, Po-hai Mo-ho envoys offered 1000 leopard furs and 100 dried striped fish (*Ts'e-fu yüan-kuei* p.5029).

During 738, the king of the Po-hai Mo-ho, Ta Wu-yi, fell ill and died,[13] and his son Ch'in-mao inherited the throne. Hsüan-tsung dispatched a Palace Attendant to condole and sacrifice, to appoint Ch'in-mao as General-in-chief of the Resolute Guards of the Left, General-in-chief of the Golden Mace of the Left, and Military Governor of the non-existant Hu-han Area Command, and to recognize him as king of Po-hai. Ch'in-mao sent envoys to follow the Palace Attendant back to the T'ang court and offer gifts (*Chiu T'ang shu* 9: 2b; 199B:12b).

In the 2nd month (Mar./Apr.) of 739, envoys from the king of the Po-hai Mo-ho presented falcons. In the 10th month (Nov./Dec.) of the same year, a high Po-hai official thanked [for the recognition] (*Ts'e-fu yüan-kuei* p.5029).

In the 2nd month (March) of 740, high officials of the Yüeh-hsi Mo-ho and T'ieh-li Mo-ho offered regional objects. In the 10th month

---

[13] The date is according to *Chiu T'ang shu* 9:2b. 199B:12b states that Wu-yi died in 737.

(Oct./Nov) of the same year, Po-hai Mo-ho envoys presented sable furs and fabrics (*Ts'e-fu yüan-kuei* p.5029).

In the 2nd month (Feb./Mar.) of 741, a high official of the Po-hai Mo-ho and a chief of the Yüeh-hsi Mo-ho were received at the T'ang court. In the 4th month (Apr./May) of the same year, Po-hai Mo-ho envoys presented falcons (*Ts'e-fu yüan-kuei* p.5029).

At some time between 742 and 756, Hsüan-tsung made Ch'in-mao a Specially Advanced and Supervisor for Guests of the Household of the Heir-apparent (*Chiu T'ang shu* 199B:13a).

In the 3rd month (Mar./Apr.) of 746, Po-hai envoys arrived at the court (*Ts'e-fu yüan-kuei* p.5030).

On Feb.14, 747, the New Year's Day, Po-hai envoys congratulated at the T'ang court and offered regional objects (*Ts'e-fu yüan-kuei* p.5030).

In the 3rd month (Mar./Apr.) of 749, Po-hai envoys presented falcons. In the 3rd month (Apr./May) of 750, they again presented falcons (*Ts'e-fu yüan-kuei* p.5030).

In the 3rd month (Apr./May) of 753, Po-hai envoys arrived at the court (*Ts'e-fu yüan-kuei* p.5030).

On Jan.28, 754, the New Year's Day, Po-hai envoys congratulated at the T'ang court (*Ts'e-fu yüan-kuei* p.5031).

In 762, the Chinese emperor[14] "promoted" Ch'in-mao to King of State. Between 766 and 779, Tai-tsung appointed Ch'in-mao [Acting] Minister of Works and Acting Grand Commandant (*Chiu T'ang shu* 199B:13a; *Wen-hsien t'ung-k'ao* 326:58a).[15]

In the 7th month (July/Aug.) of 767, Po-hai envoys were received at the T'ang court (*Ts'e-fu yüan-kuei* p.5031).

On Sep.6, 767, Po-hai envoys were received at the T'ang court (*Ts'e-fu yüan-kuei* p.5031).

In the 9th (Sep./Oct.), 11th (Nov./Dec.), and 12th month (Dec./Jan., 768) of the Chinese year 767, Po-hai envoys offered gifts (*Ts'e-fu yüan-kuei* p.5031).

In the 3rd (Apr./May) month of 769, Po-hai Mo-ho envoys offered presents, and in the 12th month (Jan., 770) of the same Chinese year, Po-hai envoys again offered gifts (*Ts'e-fu yüan-kuei* p.5031).

In the autumn of 772, Po-hai and Mo-ho envoys offered gifts, and

---

[14] Probably Tai-tsung who ascended the throne on May 17 of that year.

[15] *Wen-hsien t'ung-k'ao* dates the appointment as Acting Grand Commandant 762.

in the 12th month (Jan., 773) of the same Chinese year, Po-hai Mo-ho envoys offered presents (*Chiu T'ang shu* 11:20b; *Ts'e-fu yüan-kuei* p.5031).

In the 4th (Apr./May), 6th (June/July), 11th (Nov./Dec.), intercalary (Dec./Jan., 774), and 12th month (Jan./Feb., 774) of the Chinese year 773, Po-hai and Po-hai Mo-ho envoys offered regional objects (*Ts'e-fu yüan-kuei* p.5031, 5032).

In the 1st (Feb./Mar.) and 12th month (Jan./Feb., 775) of the Chinese year 774, Po-hai envoys were received at the T'ang court (*Ts'e-fu yüan-kuei* p.5032).

In the 1st (Feb./Mar.), 5th (June/July), 6th (July), and 12th (Dec/Jan., 776) month of the Chinese year 775, Po-hai and Mo-ho envoys offered gifts (*Ts'e-fu yüan-kuei* p.5032).

In the 1st month (Feb./Mar.) of 777, Po-hai envoys presented 11 Japanese dancing girls and regional objects (*Chiu T'ang shu* 11:25b; 199B:12b; *Ts'e-fu yüan-kuei* p.5032; *Wen-hsien t'ung-k'ao* 326:58a).

In the 2nd month (Mar./Apr.) of 777, Po-hai envoys presented falcons (*Ts'e-fu yüan-kuei* p.5032).

In the 4th (May/June) and12th month (Jan., 778) of the Chinese year 777, Po-hai and Po-hai Mo-ho envoys offered regional objects (*Chiu T'ang shu* 11:26a, 199B:12b; *Ts'e-fu yüan-kuei* p.5032).

Immediately after Te-tsung had ascended the T'ang throne on June 12, 779, he ordered, out of conviction or to make a show of his modesty, that falcons were no longer to be received from Silla and Po-hai (*Chiu T'ang shu* 12:1a-1b).

In the 10th month (November) of 780, Po-hai envoys offered gifts (*Ts'e-fu yüan-kuei* p.5032).

In the 5th month (June/July) of 782, Po-hai envoys offered presents (*Ts'e-fu yüan-kuei* p.5032).

In the 1st month (Feb./Mar.) of 791, Po-hai envoys were received at the T'ang court (*Ts'e-fu yüan-kuei* p.5032).

In the 8th month (Sep./Oct.) of 791, a royal son from Po-hai was received at the T'ang court (*Chiu T'ang shu* 199B:12b).

In the intercalary month (Jan./Feb., 793) of the Chinese year 792, a mission of 35 Mo-ho offered gifts (*Chiu T'ang shu* 13:8a; *T'ang hui-yao* 196:11b; *Ts'e-fu yüan-kuei* p.5032).

In the 1st month (Feb./Mar.) of 794, a mission from Po-hai, led by a royal son and consisting of more than 30 men, was received at the T'ang court. The prince was made a General of the Guards of the Right. His subordinates were appointed to offices, each in accordance with his rank (*Chiu T'ang shu* 199B:12b-13a; *T'ang hui-yao* 196:11b).

On Mar.2, 795, a Regular Palace Attendant was sent by Te-tsung to appoint Ta Ch'in-mao's son Sung-lin as General-in-chief of the Resolute Guards of the Right and Military Governor of the non-existant Hu-han Area Command, and to recognize him as king of Po-hai commandery.[16] A mission of 32 men from Sung-lin protested against the term "commandery". All envoys were given Chinese titles and sent back in the 12th month (Jan./Feb., 796) of the Chinese year 795 (*Chiu T'ang shu* 13:11a; 199B:13a; *T'ang hui-yao*196:11b, 12a).

In the 3rd month (Mar./Apr.) of 798, Te-tsung appointed Sung-lin as Imperial Household Grandee of the Silver Seal and Blue Ribbon and Acting Minister of Works, and "promoted" him to king of Po-hai (*Chiu T'ang shu* 199B:13a; *T'ang hui-yao* 11b-12a; *Wen-hsien t'ung-k'ao* 326:58a).[17]

In the 11th month (Dec,/Jan., 799) of the Chinese year 798, Te-tsung appointed a nephew of Sung-lin as General of the Gentlemen-of-the Household of the Resolute Guards of the Left (*Chiu T'ang shu* 199B:13a).

In the 11th month (Dec./Jan., 805) of the Chinese year 804, Po-hai envoys were received at the T'ang court (*Ts'e-fu yüan-kuei* p.5032).

In 805, an envoy from Sung-lin was received at the T'ang court. Emperor Shun-tsung appointed the king as Imperial Household Grandee of the Golden Seal and Purple Ribbon and confirmed him as Acting Minister of Works (*Chiu T'ang shu* 199B:13a).

On Dec.10, 806, Emperor Hsien-tsung appointed Sung-lin as Acting Grand Commandant (*Chiu T'ang shu* 14:9b; 199B:13a).[18]

On Feb.8, 807, Po-hai envoys offered gifts (*Chiu T'ang shu* 14:10a; 199B:13a; *Ts'e-fu yüan-kuei* p.5032).

---

[16] According to *Tzu-chih t'ung-chien* p.7565 and *Wen-hsien t'ung-k'ao* 326:58a, at Ta Ch'in-mao's death [in 784] his son Hung-lin was no longer alive. The relative Ta Yüan-yi was enthroned but killed after one year, and Hung-lin's son Hua-hsü became king [in 786]. When Hua-hsü died, Ch'in-mao's youngest son Sung-lin was enthroned in the 12th month (Dec./Jan., 795) of the Chinese year 794. *Chiu T'ang shu* 13:11a wrongly gives Ta Sung-lin's name as Ta Sung.

[17] According to *Chiu T'ang shu*, Sung-lin was promoted to king of Po-hai commandery. But "commandery" must be an error, since he had been given that title already in 795. In short, the T'ang reversed itself and recognized Sung-lin as king of Po-hai.

[18] *Chiu T'ang shu* 14:9b has 9th month, *ping-hsü*, 199B:13a has 10th month. The 9th month did not have the cyclical characters *ping-hsü* so that 10th month is correct.

In the 2nd month (Mar./Apr.) of 807, Po-hai envoys offered gifts (*Chiu T'ang shu* 14:13a; *Ts'e-fu yüan-kuei* p.5032).

In the 1st month (Jan./Feb.) of 809, it became known at the T'ang court that the king of Po-hai, Ta Sung-lin, had died and that his son Yüan-yü had been enthroned. Hsien-tsung appointed Yüan-yü as Imperial Household Grandee of the Silver Seal and Blue Ribbon, Inspector of the Imperial Library, and Military Governor of the non-existant Hu-han Area Command, and recognized him as king of the Po-hai State (*Chiu T'ang shu* 199B:13a; *Tzu-chih t'ung-chien* p.7656; *Wen-hsien t'ung-k'ao* 326:58a).[19]

In the 1st month (Feb./Mar.) of 810, Po-hai envoys were received at the T'ang court (*Chiu T'ang shu* 199B:13a; *Ts'e-fu yüan-kuei* p.5032).

In the 11th month (December) of 810, a son of the king of Po-hai presented regional objects (*Chiu T'ang shu* 199B:13a; *Ts'e-fu yüan-kuei* p.5032).

In the 12th month (Jan./Feb., 813) of the Chinese year 812, Pohai envoys were received at the T'ang court (*Chiu T'ang shu* 199B:13a; *T'ang hui-yao* 196:12a).

When Ta Yüan-yü died [in 812], he was succeeded by his younger brother Yen-yi. On Feb.20, 813, Hsien-tsung appointed him as Imperial Household Grandee of the Silver Seal and Blue Ribbon, Acting Inspector of the Imperial Library, and Military Governor [of the non-existant Hu-han Area Command], and recognized him as king of the Po-hai State. A Palace Assistant was sent to him as an envoy (*Chiu T'ang shu* 15:3a; 199B:13a).

In the 12th month (Dec./Jan., 814) of the Chinese year 813, a royal son from Po-hai was received at the T'ang court (*Ts'e-fu yüan-kuei* p.5032).

In the 1st month (Jan./Feb.) of 814, a Po-hai mission of 37 men presented two images of the Buddha, one of gold and one of silver (*Ts'e-fu yüan-kuei* p.5032).

In the 11th month (Dec./Jan., 815) of the Chinese year 814, Po-hai envoys presented falcons (*Ts'e-fu yüan-kuei* p.5032).

In the 12th month (Jan./Feb., 815) of the Chinese year 814, a Po-hai mission of 59 men was received at the T'ang court (*Ts'e-fu yüan-kuei* p.5033).

In the 7th month (Aug./Sep.) of 815, a Po-hai mission of 101 men,

[19] *T'ang hui-yao* 196:12a dates these appointment 806.

led by a royal son, offered presents (*Chiu T'ang shu* 15:9b; *Ts'e-fu yüan-kuei* p.5033).

When Ta Yen-yi died [in 816], his younger brother Ming-chung was enthroned (*Wen-hsien t'ung-k'ao* 326:58a).

In the 3rd month (April) of 816, Po-hai Mo-ho envoys were received at the T'ang court. The 20 members of the mission were appointed to Chinese offices (*T'ang hui-yao* 196:12a-12b; *Ts'e-fu yüan-kuei* p.5033).

In the 11th month (Nov./Dec.) of 816, Mo-ho and Po-hai offered gifts (*Chiu T'ang shu* 15:11b; *Ts'e-fu yüan-kuei* p.5033).

In the 2nd month (Feb./Mar.) of 817, Po-hai envoys offered gifts (*Ts'e-fu yüan-kuei* p.5033).

When Ta Ming-chung died [in 817], he was succeeded by his paternal uncle Jen-hsiu (*Wen-hsien t'ung-k'ao* 326:58a).

In 818, Po-hai envoys announced the death of Ta Ming-chung (*Chiu T'ang shu* 15:16a; 199B:13a).

On June 25, 818, Hsien-tsung appointed Ta Jen-hsiu as Imperial Household Grandee of the Silver Seal and Blue Ribbon, Acting Inspector of the Imperial Library, and Military Governor [of the non-existant Hu-han Area Command], and recognized him as king of the Po-hai State (*Chiu T'ang shu* 15:14b; 199B:13a; *Tzu-chih t'ung-chien* p.7751).

In the intercalary month (Feb./Mar.) of 820, Po-hai envoys offered presents. Emperor Mu-tsung appointed Jen-hsiu as Imperial Household Grandee of the Golden Seal and Purple Ribbon and Acting Minister of Works (*Chiu T'ang shu* 199B:13a; *Ts'e-fu yüan-kuei* p.5033).

In the 12th month (Jan./Feb., 821) of the Chinese year 820, Po-hai envoys offered gifts (*Chiu T'ang shu* 199B:13a; *Ts'e-fu yüan-kuei* p.5033).

In the 1st month (Jan./Feb.) of 822, Po-hai envoys offered gifts (*Chiu T'ang shu* 199B:13a; *Ts'e-fu yüan-kuei* p.5033).

In the 2nd month (Mar./Apr.) of 824, Po-hai envoys offered gifts (*Ts'e-fu yüan-kuei* p.5033).

In the 3rd month (Mar./Apr.) of 825, five Po-hai envoys offered gifts (*Chiu T'ang shu* 199B:13b; *Ts'e-fu yüan-kuei* p.5033).

In the 1st month (Feb./Mar.) of 826, Po-hai envoys offered gifts (*Ts'e-fu yüan-kuei* p.5023).

In the 4th month (May) of 827, Po-hai envoys were received at the T'ang court (*Chiu T'ang shu* 199B:13b; *Ts'e-fu yüan-kuei* p.5033).

In the 12th month (Dec./Jan., 830) of the Chinese year 829, Po-hai envoys offered gifts (*Ts'e-fu yüan-kuei* p.5033).

In 830, it became known at the T'ang court that the king of Po-hai, Ta Jen-hsiu, had died and that, since his son Hsin-te had died earlier, his grandson Yi-chen had succeeded (*Wen-hsien t'ung-k'ao* 326:58a).

In the 12th month (Dec./Jan., 831) of the Chinese year 830, Po-hai envoys offered gifts (*Ts'e-fu yüan-kuei* p.5033).

In 831, Emperor Wen-tsung appointed Ta Yi-chen as Imperial Household Grandee of the Silver Seal and Blue Ribbon, Acting Inspector of the Imperial Library, and Military Governor [of the non-existant Hu-han Area Command], and recognized him as king of Po-hai (*Chiu T'ang shu* 199B:13b).

In the 11th month (Dec./Jan., 832) of the Chinese year 831, Po-hai envoys offered gifts (*Ts'e-fu yüan-kuei* p.5033).

In the 3rd month (Apr./May) of 832, a son of the king of Po-hai was received at the T'ang court (*Chiu T'ang shu* 199B:13ab; *Ts'e-fu yüan-kuei* p.5033).

In the 1st month (Jan./Feb.) of 833, the Joint Manager of Affairs of the Right of the Palace Writers of the king of Po-hai thanked for the recognition. Three students were attached to the mission (*Chiu T'ang shu* 199B:13b; *Ts'e-fu yüan-kuei* p.5033).

On Mar.16, 833, a mission of six men from Po-hai, led by a royal son, was received at the T'ang court (*Chiu T'ang shu* 17B:18a; 199B: 13b)

In the 12th month (Jan./Feb., 837) of the Chinese year 836, Po-hai envoys offered gifts (*Ts'e-fu yüan-kuei* p.5033).

In the 12th month (Jan./Feb., 840) of the Chinese year 839, a son of the king of Po-hai offered gifts (*Ts'e-fu yüan-kuei* p.5033).

On Feb.16, 846, Po-hai envoys were received at the T'ang court (*Chiu T'ang shu* 18A:16b; *Ts'e-fu yüan-kuei* p.5033).

In the 2nd month (Feb./Mar.) of 858, it became known at the T'ang court that the king of Po-hai, Ta Yi-chen, had died and that his younger brother Ch'ien-huang had been enthroned. On Mar.9 of that year, Emperor Hsüan-tsung[20] recognized Ch'ien-huang as king (*Wen-hsien t'ung-k'ao* 326:58a; *Tzu-chih t'ung-chien* p.8069).

On June, 15, 907, a son of the Po-hai king Ta Yin-chuan[21] offered

---

[20] This Emperor Hsüan-tsung reigned from 847 to 859. He is not to be confused with the earlier famous Hsüan-tsung, who reigned from 712 to756. The *Hsüan* in both names is written with different Chinese characters.

[21] According to *Hsin T'ang shu* 219:10a and *Wen-hsien t'ung-k'ao* 326:58a, Ch'ien-

"products from east of the sea" to the Later Liang court (*Hsin Wu-tai shih* 2:1b; *Ts'e-fu yüan-kuei* p.5033, *Wen-hsien t'ung-k'ao* 326:58a).

On Feb.29, 908, Po-hai envoys to the Later Liang court offered gifts (*Hsin Wu-tai shih* 2:2b; *Wu-tai hui-yao* 30:8b; *Wen-hsien t'ung-k'ao* 328:58a).

On Mar.29, 909, a high official of the king of Po-hai offered men and women, sable furs, and bear skins to the Later Liang court (*Hsin Wu-tai shih* 2:3b; *Ts'e-fu yüan-kuei* p.5034; *Wen-hsien t'ung-k'ao* 326:58a).

In the 5th month (May/June) of 912, royal sons from Po-hai offered regional objects to the Later Liang court. Emperor T'ai-tsu gave them rich gifts (*Wu-tai hui-yao* 30:8b; *Ts'e-fu yüan-kuei* p.5034; *Wen-hsien t'ung-k'ao* 328:58a).

In the 2nd month (Mar./Apr.) of 918, Po-hai envoys to the Khitan court offered gifts (*Liao shih* 1:10a-10b).

On Feb.24, 924, a son of the king of Po-hai, offered gifts to the Later T'ang court. Emperor Chuang-tsung paid with gold and silk. In the 8th month (Sep./Oct.), a nephew of the king of Po-hai arrived to study at the Later T'ang Academy. He was made a Probationary Assistant at the Directorate of Education (*Chiu Wu-tai shih* 31:3a; *Wu-tai hui-yao* 30:8b; *Ts'e-fu yüan-kuei* p.5034; *Wen-hsien t'ung-k'ao* 325:58a).

In the 5th month (June/July) of 924, envoys from the king of Po-hai to the Later T'ang court offered gifts (*Chiu wu-tai shih* 32:2a; *Ts'e-fu yüan-kuei* p. 5034).

On Mar.15, 925, envoys from the king of Po-hai to the Later T'ang court offered fabrics, a coverlet of sable fur, six hoes and delicate women. In the 5th month (May/June), the chief envoy was presented with a purple and gold fish wallet (*Hsin Wu-tai shih* 5:8a; *Wu-tai hui-yao* 30:9a; *Ts'e-fu yüan-kuei* p.5034; *Wen-hsien t'ung-k'ao* 326:58a).

In 925 and in the 4th month (May/June) of 926, Po-hai envoys to the Later T'ang court offered gifts (*Hsin Wu-tai shih* 6:4a; *Wen-hsien t'ung-k'ao* 326:58a).

At some time before 926, Po-hai also sent a mission to the king of Wu-yüeh, Ch'ien Liu (*Chiu wu-tai shih* 133:16a).

On Feb.28, 926, Ta Yin-chuan surrendered to the Khitan, and the kingdom of Po-hai came to an end. A Po-hai mission of 116 men, which was received by the Later T'ang court in the 4th month (May/June) of

---

huang was succeeded by Hsüan-hsi. The relationship is unknown, and no dates are given. The last king of Po-hai was Ta Yin-chuan.

926, must have set out before the surrender. It presented three males and three females, fabrics, and tiger skins (*Ts'e-fu yüan-kuei* p.5034; *Wen-hsien t'ung-k'ao* 326:58a).

Nevertheless, envoys kept coming, namely on Aug.16, 926, in the 5th month (June/July) of 929, on Jan.28, 932, on Mar.6, 932, in 933, on Aug.24, 935, in the 11th month (Nov./Dec.) of 935, and in 936. All claimed to be from Po-hai (*Chiu Wu-tai shih* 36:7b; 47:11b; *Hsin Wu-tai shih* 6:10a, 10b; 7:5a; *Ts'e-fu yüan-kuei* p.5034, 5035; *Wen-hsien t'ung-k'ao* 326:58a-58b). They may have been sent by Mo-ho tribes in the former Po-hai who opposed the Khitan.

Like the Korean states and Japan, Po-hai was influenced and impressed by Chinese culture. *Wen-hsien t'ung-k'ao* 326:58a states that its kings frequently sent students to attend the Academy in China. Actually recorded cases are three students in 833 and a royal nephew in 924, but the real number was, of course, very much higher.

In the earlier years, the Po-hai State was a mixture of a royal bureaucracy and semi-autonomous Mo-ho tribes under their own chiefs. Tribal prefixes disappear after 741, proof of a trend toward greater but never complete integration. As far as can be judged, the royal Po-hai administration was modeled on that of China.

The Chinese imperial courts recognized the kings of Po-hai and conferred official but not posthumous titles on them. Whatever the Chinese liked to believe, Po-hai was an entirely independent state and not always friendly to China. Tensions rose from 726 and culminated in the Po-hai raid of Teng in 732 and the abortive Chinese war against Po-hai in 733. Thereafter, relations became amicable.

The claim by the dynastic historians that Ta Tso-jung sent a son to "attend" at the T'ang court, a term synonymous with hostage, and that Ta Wu-yi's younger brother Men-yi had been a hostage in Ch'ang-an must be rejected. Po-hai had as little reason as Silla and Koryŏ to provide hostages, and the T'ang had no way to enforce their being rendered. If princes went to Ch'ang-an, it was for their education or amusement, and the initiative rested with Po-hai.

Po-hai's location beyond the Hsi and Khitan could be a diplomatic asset to China, while the Black River Mo-ho at the Amur River could be hoped to be a counterweight to Po-hai. But the view from Po-hai was different. Few of the missions were concerned with diplomacy. They might congratulate on a New Year's Day, announce the death of a king, or thank for Chinese recognition, but the chief purpose was trade on the government level and private trade by the envoys on the market. The latter was explicitly allowed by the Chinese government in 713. Evidence that trade flourished is the fact that during some years Po-hai missions arrived repeatedly, three in 719, four in 730, two in 731, two in 732, two in 739, three in 740, three in 741, five in 767, two in 769, two in 772, five in 773, two in 774, three in 775, four in 777, two in 791, two in 810, three in 814, two in 816, two in 820, two in 833, and two in 924. There were not enough diplomatic issues between Po-hai and China to justify such a plethora of missions. The motive was commerce.

According to *Chiu T'ang shu* 199B:11b, the Po-hai State sent annual missions to the T'ang court from 713. The sources record missions from 713 to 725 for all years except 715, 720, and 723. According to *Wen-hsien t'ung-k'ao* 326:58a, Po-hai sent 25 missions from 766 to 779. 25 are, in fact, recorded. According to *Wen-hsien t'ung-k'ao* 326: 58a, four missions were sent from 780 to 805. No less than eight are recorded. According to *Wen-hsien t'ung-k'ao* 326:58a, Po-hai sent 16 missions from 806 to 820. 17 are recorded. According to *Wen-hsien t'ung-k'ao* 326:58a, four missions were sent from 821 to 824. Two are recorded. According to *Chiu T'ang shu* 199B:13b, Po-hai sent missions every year from 825-827, according to *Wen-hsien t'ung-k'ao* 326:58a twice. Two missions are recorded. According to *Wen-hsien t'ung-k'ao* 326: 58a, 12 Po-hai missions arrived from 827 to 840. Nine are recorded. According to *Wen-hsien t'ung-k'ao* 326:58a, four missions were sent from 841 to 846. One is recorded. According to *Wen-hsien t'ung-k'ao* 326: 58a, Po-hai sent three missions from 860 to 874. None is recorded. Clearly, the dated entries are almost complete for the earlier period, whereas summary entries prevail for the end of T'ang.

The missions from Po-hai to T'ang arrived by sea, with probably Teng on the northern shore of the Shan-tung peninsula as the main port. The preferred seasons were the winter and spring. This is the distribution by 20-year periods of the 132 recorded Mo-ho/Po-hai missions to Sui, T'ang, Later Liang, Later T'ang, and Wu-yüeh until 924:

587-606:	4
607-626:	4
627-646:	4
647-666:	0
667-686:	0
687-706:	1

707-726:	16
727-746:	21
747-766:	5
767-786:	28
787-806:	7
807-826:	20
827-846:	10
847-866:	0
867-886:	0
887-906:	0
907-926:	12

After T'ang had recognized the state of Po-hai in 712, missions arrived in large numbers until the middle of the 9th century. The lower figure for 747-766 was due to the rebellion of An Lu-shan in 750. The other for 787-806 is unexplained. Perhaps it was due to unsettled conditions, following the uprising of the Military Governors from 781 to 786. No missions are recorded by date from 847 to 906, although it is known from *Wen-hsien t'ung-k'ao* that three arrived between 860 and 874. The decline during that period is characteristic, and has been observed also for Silla and the Hsi. It probably was not worth the trouble for Po-hai and the others to send missions through unsafe countryside to an impoverished court. With the Five Dynasties, the missions revived.

The specified goods brought by the Po-hai missions fall into the following categories:

Humans

777: 11 Japanese dancing girls.
909: men and women.
925: delicate women.
926: 3 males and 3 females.

Animals and Animal Products

Horses

730: 60 horses.

Birds

722: falcons.
729: falcons.
737: falcons.
739: falcons.
741: falcons.
749: falcons.
750: falcons.
777: falcons.
814: falcons

Furs

719: sable furs, white hare furs.
730: 5 seal skins, 3 leopard furs.
738: 1000 leopard furs.
740: sable furs.
909: sable furs, bear skins.
926: tiger skins.

Fish

719: maritime products.
729: mullets.
738: 100 dried striped fish.

Manufactured Objects

Of metal

814: One image of the Buddha in gold and one in silver.
925: 6 hoes.

Of precious stone

730: One cup of carnelian.

Textiles

740: fabrics.
925: fabrics, one coverlet of sable fur.

Most of the goods were local products. Falcons were apparently in particular demand at the T'ang court, until Emperor Te-tsung in 779 disallowed their import. But after had he died in 805, they were brought again. Other products had been imported by Po-hai itself before it offered them to China. It had a lively trade with Japan, and the 11 dancing girls obviously came from there, as probably also the images of the Buddha, the cup of carnelian, and perhaps the fabrics.

China paid for the Po-hai goods with gold, brocade, and silk.

TING-AN

After the surrender of Po-hai to the Khitan in 926, some of the Mo-ho established a small kingdom, centred on modern Kirin and called Ting-an (Chŏngan). It fought the Khitan in 975, the 980's, and from 994, the resistance ending in 999. Ting-an was poor state and not able to send missions of its own. At all four occasions, when Ting-an envoys arrived at the Sung court, they were attached to Jurchen missions. Needless to say, the envoys had no other purpose than trade.

In 970, envoys from the king of Ting-an offered regional objects (*Sung shih* 491:1b; *Wen-hsien t'ung-k'ao* 327:61b).

In the winter of 981, Ting-an envoys presented a letter from their king (*Sung shih* 491:2a; *Wen-hsien t'ung-k'ao* 327:61b).

In 989, the king of Ting-an offered whistling arrows ((*Sung shih* 491:3a; *Wen-hsien t'ung-k'ao* 327:61b).

In 991, Ting-an envoys presented a letter from their king. This was the last communication (*Sung shih* 491:3a; *Wen-hsien t'ung-k'ao* 327:61b).

THE BLACK RIVER MO-HO

The Black River Mo-ho were independent tribes at the lower Amur River, unfriendly to the Mo-ho of Po-hai.

In the 11th month (Nov./Dec.) of 631, envoys of the Black River Mo-ho offered gifts to the T'ang court (*Ts'e-fu yüan-kuei* p.5024).

In 640, envoys of the Black River Mo-ho offered gifts (*T'ang hui-yao* 96:10a).

On Feb.18, 725, the New Year's Day, the Black River Mo-ho congratulated at the T'ang court and presented regional objects (*Ts'e-fu yüan-kuei* p.5028).

In 726, envoys from the Black River Mo-ho were received at the T'ang court. Emperor Hsüan-tsung created out of their territory the fictitious Black River Area Command and appointed a chief as Military Governor. He sent envoys to confer further titles. It has been seen that the king of Po-hai, Ta Wu-yi, suspected that the ultimate aim of the Black River Mo-ho and T'ang was an attack on his state, and that he launched a preemptive and unsuccessful strike against the former. This soured relations between Po-hai and T'ang for the next decade (*Chiu T'ang shu*199B:12a-12b; *Tzu-chih t'ung-chien* pp.6774-6775; *Wen-hsien t'ung-k'ao* 326:57b).

On Mar.12, 728, envoys of the Black River Mo-ho offered gifts (*Chiu T'ang shu* 8:15b). During the same year, the Military Governor of the non-existant Black River Area Command was granted the T'ang imperial surname of Li and appointed General of the Cloud Flags (*Chiu T'ang shu* 199B:11a).

In the 5th month (May/June) of 730, envoys of the Black River Mo-ho offered regional objects (*Ts'e-fu yüan-kuei* p.5028).

In the 2nd month (Feb./Mar.) of 741, envoys of the Black River Mo-ho were received at at the T'ang court (*Ts'e-fu yüan-kuei* p.5029).

On Feb.14, 747, the New Year's Day, envoys of the Black River Mo-ho congratulated at the T'ang court and presented regional objects (*Ts'e-fu yüan-kuei* p.5030).

In the 1st month (Feb./Mar.) of 748, envoys of the Black River Mo-ho offered gifts. In the 3rd month (Apr./May) of the same year, envoys of the Black River Mo-ho, together with envoys from four Shih-wei tribes, presented gold, silver, textiles, silken fabrics, cow bezoar, human hair, and ginseng (*Ts'e-fu yüan-kuei* p.5030).

On Feb.11, 750, the New Year's Day, envoys of the Black River Mo-ho congratulated at the T'ang court (*Ts'e-fu yüan-kuei* p.5030).

In the 12th month (Dec./Jan., 752) of the Chinese year 751, envoys of the Black River [Mo-ho] were received at the T'ang court (*Ts'e-fu yüan-kuei* p.5030).

In the 2nd month (Mar./Apr.) of 815, a chief of the Black River [Mo-ho], heading a mission of 11 men, offered gifts (*Chiu T'ang shu* 15:9b); *Ts'e-fu yüan-kuei* p.5033).

In 924, envoys of the Black River [Mo-ho] to the Later T'ang court offered gifts. The chief envoy was made a General of the Gentlemen-of-the Household Who Cherishes Civilization. Another mission from the Black River Barbarians is recorded for the same year (*Chiu wu-tai shih* 32:7a; *Wu-tai hui-yao* 30:12a; *Ts'e-fu yüan-kuei* p.5034; *Wen-hsien t'ung-k'ao* 326:57b).

On June 11, 925, envoys of the Black River Barbarians to the Later T'ang court offered presents (*Chiu wu-tai shih* 32:14b; *Ts'e-fu yüan-kuei* p.5034).

In the 8th month (Aug./Sep.) of 928, envoys of the Black River Mo-ho to the Later T'ang court offered regional objects (*Wu-tai hui-yao* 30:12a).

On Sep.14, 929, envoys of the Black River [Mo-ho] to the Later T'ang court offered regional objects (*Hsin Wu-tai shih* 6:8a; *Ts'e-fu yüan-kuei* p.5034).

On Mar.7, 930, envoys of the Black River [Mo-ho] to the Later T'ang court offered regional objects (*Chiu wu-tai shih* 41:1b; *Ts'e-fu yüan-kuei* p.5035).[22]

In the 5th month (May/June) of 931, local officials informed the Later T'ang court that Black River Mo-ho had arrived in Teng on the north coast of Shan-tung to sell horses (*Wu-tai hui-yao* 30:12a).

The last recorded mission from the Black River Mo-ho was to the Later T'ang court in 932. Thereafter contacts ceased (*Hsin Wu-tai shih* 74:1b; *Wen-hsien t'ung-k'ao* 326:57b) because the Black River Mo-ho were absorbed into the Liao empire.

The Black River Mo-ho and the Chinese had a mutual interest in restraining Po-hai situated between them, which led to close relations of the classical kind. The other and dominant reason for the missions was exchange of goods. It has been seen that the mission to sell horses in 931 arrived in Teng by sea, as no doubt all other missions before it had done, since it is not probable that Po-hai allowed transit through its territory. The Black River Mo-ho ships must have departed from a port on the Sea of Japan and sailed around the Korean Peninsula. The preferred season was the spring.

This is the distribution by 20-year periods of the 21 recorded Black River Mo-ho missions to T'ang and Later T'ang:

627-646: 2
647-666: 0
667-686: 0

[22] *Ts'e-fu yüan-kuei* dates the mission 2nd month, *Chiu wu-tai shih* 1st month, *chi-hai*. The 1st month did not have a day with the cyclical characters *chi-hai*, so that *Ts'e-fu yüan-kuei* is correct. However, *Hsin Wu-tai shih* 6:8a dates the reception Mar.6.

687-706:	0
707-726:	2
727-746:	3
747-766:	5
767-786:	0
787-806:	0
807-826:	1
827-846:	0
847-866:	0
867-886:	0
887-906:	0
907-926:	3
927-946:	5

The high point was during the reign of Emperor Hsüan-tsung (712-756). Then follows the decline which is characteristic for the end of the T'ang dynasty and the revival during the Five Dynasties.

Very little is known about the goods brought by the Black River Mo-ho, gold, silver, textiles, cow bezoar, human hair, and ginseng being presented by them and Shih-wei tribes in 748, and horses in 931.

THE SHIH-WEI

The Shih-wei were linguistically related to the Khitan and inhabited the area of northwestern Manchuria. They consisted of several tribes which usually in the sources are collectively called the Shih-wei and rarely are distinguished from each other by prefixes.

On Feb.11, 593, and June 27, 610, Shih-wei envoys to the Sui court offered regional objects (*Sui shu* 2:8b; 3:15b).

In 625, Shih-wei envoys to the T'ang court offered gifts (*T'ang hui-yao* 96:8b).

In 629, Shih-wei envoys presented leopard and sable furs (*Chiu T'ang shu* 199B:9b; *Ts'e-fu yüan-kuei* p.5023).

In the 7th month (Aug./Sep.) of 630, Shih-wei envoys offered regional objects (*Ts'e-fu yüan-kuei* p.5023).

In the 11th month (Nov./Dec.) of 631, Shih-wei envoys offered sable furs (*Ts'e-fu yüan-kuei* p.5024; *Wen-hsien t'ung-k'ao* 347:27a).

In the 11th month (Dec./Jan., 633) of the Chinese year 632, Shih-wei offered gifts (*Ts'e-fu yüan-kuei* p.5024).

In the 4th month (May) of 634, Shih-wei chiefs were received at the T'ang court (*Ts'e-fu yüan-kuei* p.5024).

In the 9th month (Oct./Nov.) of 635, Shih-wei envoys offered regional objects (*Ts'e-fu yüan-kuei* p.5024).

In the 11th month (Nov./Dec.) of 707, envoys from Shih-wei chiefs arrived with presents. It may have been at this occasion that they offered the T'ang an alliance against the Turks[23] (*Ts'e-fu yüan-kuei* p.5026; *Wen-hsien t'ung-k'ao* 347:27a).

In the 10th month (Nov./Dec.) of 709, Shih-wei envoys offered regional objects (*Ts'e-fu yüan-kuei* p.5026).

In the 11th month (Dec./Jan., 712) of the Chinese year 711, Shih-wei envoys presented regional objects (*Ts'e-fu yüan-kuei* p.5026).

In the 2nd month (March) of 713, Shih-wei envoys offered presents (*Ts'e-fu yüan-kuei* p.5027).

In the 7th month (Aug./Sep.) of 725, Shih-wei envoys offered presents (*Ts'e-fu yüan-kuei* p.5028).

In the 2nd (Mar./Apr.) and 10th month (Nov./Dec.) of 731, Shih-wei envoys were received at the T'ang court (*Ts'e-fu yüan-kuei* p.5028).

In the 2nd month (Mar./Apr.) of 745, envoys of the Yellow-headed Shih-wei offered regional objects (*Ts'e-fu yüan-kuei* p.5030).

On Feb.14, 747, the New Year's Day, envoys of the Yellow-headed Shih-wei congratulated at the T'ang court and offered regional objects (*Ts'e-fu yüan-kuei* p.5030).

In the 12th month (Jan./Feb., 948) of the Chinese year 747, Shih-wei presented 60 horses (*Ts'e-fu yüan-kuei* p.5030).

In the 1st month (Feb./Mar.) of 748, envoys of the Yellow-headed Shih-wei offered gifts (*Ts'e-fu yüan-kuei* p.5030).

In the 3rd month (Apr./May) of 748, envoys of the Yellow-headed Shih-wei, Ho-chieh Shih-wei, Ju-che Shih-wei, and Lu-tan Shih-wei, together with the Black River Mo-ho, presented gold, silver, textiles, silken fabrics, cow bezoar, human hair, and ginseng (*Ts'e-fu yüan-kuei* p.5030).

On Feb.11, 750, the New Year's Day, envoys of the Yellow-headed Shih-wei congratulated at the T'ang court (*Ts'e-fu yüan-kuei* p.5030).

In the 9th (Sep./Oct.) and 12th month (Dec./Jan., 768) of the Chinese year 767, Shih-wei envoys offered presents (*Ts'e-fu yüan-kuei* p.5031).

---

[23] *Wen-hsien t'ung-k'ao* dates the offer 707-710.

In the 12th month (January, 770) of the Chinese year 769, Shih-wei envoys offered gifts (*Ts'e-fu yüan-kuei* p.5031).

In the autumn and 12th month (Dec./Jan., 773) of the Chinese year 772, Shih-wei envoys offered presents (*Chiu T'ang shu* 11:20b; *Ts'e-fu yüan-kuei* p.5031).

In the intercalary (Dec./Jan., 774) and 12th month (Jan./Feb., 774) of the Chinese year 773, Shih-wei envoys offered gifts (*Ts'e-fu yüan-kuei* p.5032).

In the 1st (Feb./Mar.) and 12th month (Jan./Feb., 775) of the Chinese year 774, Shih-wei envoys weren received at the T'ang court (*Ts'e-fu yüan-kuei* p.5032).

In the 1st (Feb./Mar.) and 12th month (Dec./Jan.,776) of the Chinese year 775, Shih-wei envoys offered gifts (*Ts'e-fu yüan-kuei* p.5032).

In the 4th (May/June) and 12th month (January 778) of the Chinese year 777, Shih-wei envoys offered regional objects (*Chiu T'ang shu* 11: 26a; *Ts'e-fu yüan-kuei* p.5032).

In the 7th month (July/Aug.) of 788, Shih-wei and Hsi looted Chinese territory (*Chiu T'ang shu* 199B:9a; *Wen-hsien t'ung-k'ao* 347:27a).

In the intercalary month (Jan./Feb., 793) of the Chinese year 792, a mission of ten men, led by the Military Governor of Shih-wei, was received at the T'ang court (*Ts'e-fu yüan-kuei* p.5032).

In the 12th month (Jan./Feb., 794) of the Chinese year 793, a mission of 30 men, led by the Grand Military Governor of Shih-wei, offered gifts (*Ts'e-fu yüan-kuei* p.5032).

In the 1st month (Feb./Mar.) of 826, Shih-wei envoys offered gifts (*Ts'e-fu yüan-kuei* p.5033).

In the 12th month (Dec./Jan., 830) of the Chinese year 829, Shih-wei envoys offered presents (*Ts'e-fu yün-kuei* p. 5033).

In the 12th month (Dec./Jan., 836) of the Chinese year 835, a mission of 30 Shih-wei led by the Grand Military Governor presented 50 horses (*Chiu T'ang shu* 199B:10a).

In the 12th month (Jan./Feb., 837) of the Chinese year 836, the Grand Military Governor of Shih-wei and others were received at the T'ang court (*Ts'e-fu yüan-kuei* p.5033).

In the 12th month (January, 838) of the Chinese year 837, Shi-wei offered gifts (*Ts'e-fu yüan-kuei* p.5033).

In the 12th month (Jan./Feb., 840) of the Chinese year 839, the Grand Military Governor of Shih-wei offered presents (*Ts'e-fu yüan-kuei* p.5033).

In the 2nd month (Mar./Apr.) of 842, a Shih-wei mission of 15 men, led by the Military Governor, arrived at the T'ang court. All were received in audience in the 12th month (Jan./Feb., 843) of the same Chinese year, given a banquet, and presented with gifts, each in accordance with his rank (*T'ang hui-yao* 96:9a; *Ts'e-fu yüan-kuei* p.5033).

In the 1st month (February) of 846, Shih-wei envoys were received at the T'ang court (*Chiu T'ang shu* 18A:16b; *Ts'e-fu yüan-kuei* p.5033).

In the 1st month (Jan./Feb.) of 860, Shih-wei envoys were received at the T'ang court. Thereafter, the Office of History had no information (*T'ang hui-yao* 96:9a; *Wen-hsien t'ung-k'ao* 347:27a).

The fact that the T'ang conferred on some of the Shih-wei chiefs the title of Military Governor or Grand Military Governor shows that it attempted to set up another fictitious Area Command. Its name is not recorded. But the diplomatic value of the Shih-wei to the Chinese cannot have been great. They could have been a counterweight to the Hsi, but, as far as can be judged, the Shih-wei and Hsi were on good terms with each other. Together they looted Chinese border lands in 788. Furthermore, the Shih-wei missions to the T'ang must have passed through Hsi territory, which required a fair degree of amity. The Turks were a common danger to the Shih-wei and Chinese, but there is no evidence of serious cooperation against them. While to the Chinese the Shih-wei may have been a minor pawn in the complicated diplomatic game of balancing foreign countries and tribes against each other, China was to the Shih-wei chiefly a trading partner. This is also proved by the fact that the missions might stay in China for the better part of a year, as in 842.

Chiu T'ang shu 199B:10a states that from 713 to 756, Shih-wei envoys arrived each year or each second year. According to *Wen-hsien t'ung-k'ao* 347:27a, they arrived during that period ten times. The texts record exactly ten missions. According to *Wen-hsien t'ung-k'ao* 347: 27a, 11 missions arrived from 766 to779. 13 are actually recorded. According to *Wen-hsien t'ung-k'ao* 347:27a, missions arrived three times from 827 to 835. Two missions are recorded. According to *Chiu T'ang shu* 199B:10a, missions arrived three times from 831 to 834. None is recorded. According to *Wen-hsien t'ung-k'ao* 347:27a, one mission arrived between 847 and 860. One is recorded. The statistics are therefore almost complete.

The prefered times of arrival were the 11th, 12th, and 1st months, when 3/4 of the missions were received at the Chinese courts. The envoys obviously combined New Year congratulations with commerce.

This is the distribution by 20-year periods of the 47 recorded Shih-wei missions to the Sui and T'ang:

587-606:	1
607-626:	2
627-646:	6
647-666:	0
667-686:	0
687-706:	0
707-726:	5
727-746:	3
747-766:	5
767-786:	13
787-806:	2
807-826:	1
827-846:	8
847-866:	1

22 missions arrived before the rebellion of An Lu-shan in 755 and 25 thereafter. After a hiatus until 766, missions not only kept coming but actually increased. The statistics are similar to those for the Hsi. As in their case, the Chinese chronic need for horses may have kept the Shih-wei envoys coming. No missions are recorded by date or otherwise after 860. This must again have been due to unsettled conditions and an impoverished T'ang court.

The goods brought by the envoys are rarely specified, leopard and sable furs in 629, sable furs in 631, 60 horses in 747, gold, silver, textiles, silken fabrics, cow bezoar, human hair, and ginseng together with the Black River Mo-ho in 748, and 50 horses in 836.

THE WU-LO-HUN

This tribe was in Northern Wei times known as the Wu-lo-hou. During T'ang times, they were at times called the Wu-lo-hun. Their territory bordered in the east on the Mo-ho (Po-hai), in the west on the Turks, and in the south on the Khitan (*Chiu T'ang shu* 199B:13b). That would place them in central Manchuria. They were probably linguistically related to the Khitan.

In 632, envoys from a Wu-lo-hun chief to the T'ang court presented sable furs (*Chiu T'ang shu* 199B:13b; *T'ung-tien* 200:49a; *Wen-hsien t'ung-k'ao* 347:27a).

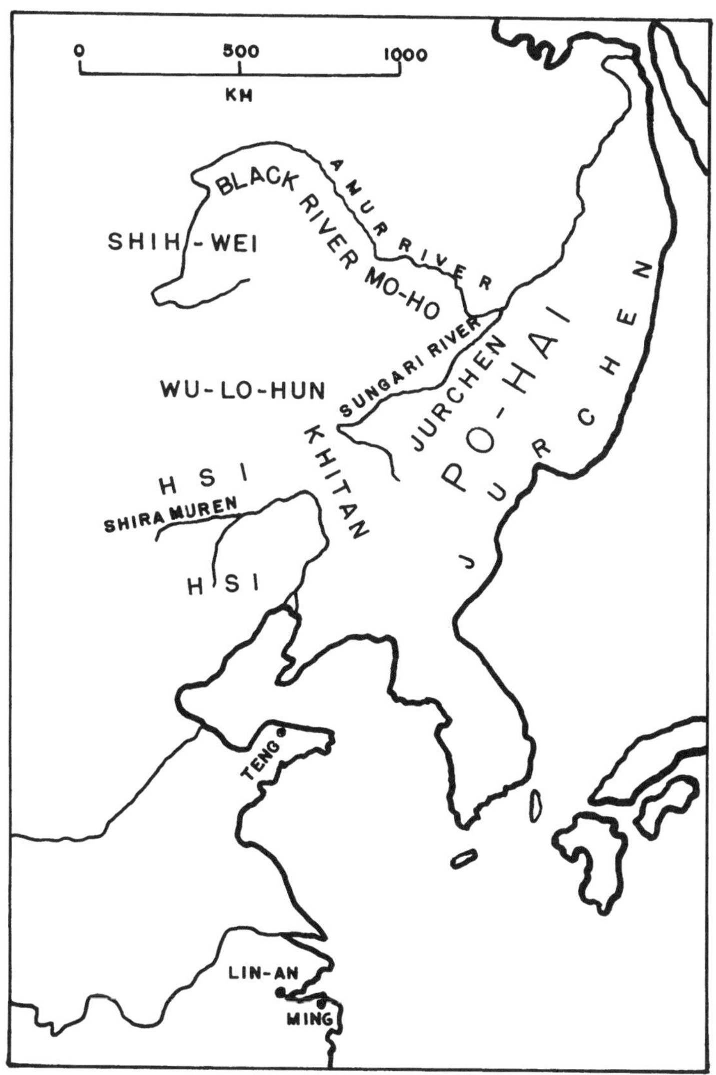

Map 4. The Northeast.

THE SOUTHWEST

TIBET

In the earlier days, the Chinese distinguished between two kinds of Tibetans, the Ti and the Ch'iang. The former, among whom the White Horse Ti were best known, lived during Han times in the valleys of the western part of the Ch'in Range and were culturally more advanced than the Ch'iang in what now is Tibet. Some of the Ti subsequently infiltrated northwestern China. During the Period of Division, they founded two northern dynasties, the Former Ch'in (351-394) and the Later Liang (386-404). A Ch'iang, formerly in Chinese service, founded the Later Ch'in Dynasty (384-417).

By T'ang times, the Ti had disappeared, and the Ch'iang were by that dynasty, the Five Dynasties, and the Sung usually referred to as T'u-fan. These T'u-fan or Tibetans were in the 630's for the first time in their history united into a kingdom by Gnam-ri-srong-btsan and his son Srong-btsan-sgam-po. It lasted for a little over two centuries and then disintegrated (map.6).

On Dec.11, 634, envoys from Srong-btsan-sgam-po were received at the T'ang court. This was his first mission to China after the unification of Tibet, although Emperor T'ai-tsung had sent letters to Tibet from 627. T'ai-tsung dispatched an Usher on a return mission (*Chiu T'ang shu* 3:3b; 196A:2a; *Ts'e-fu yüan-kuei* p.5024; *Tzu-chih t'ung-chien* pp.6107-6108, 6791).

In the 12th month (Jan./Feb., 636) of the Chinese year 635, Tibetan envoys returned with the Usher to the T'ang court. They presented gold and other valuables with a letter from their king, seeking a marriage with a Chinese princess. T'ai-tsung rejected this. Srong-btsan-sgam-po repeated his demand at the risk of war and then attacked the upper reaches of the Min River in Ssu-ch'uan. Marching down along the river, he approached the great city of Ch'eng-tu, but he was defeated on Nov.3, 638, and withdrew. This experience changed T'ai-tsung's mind (*Chiu T'ang shu* 196A:2a-2b; *Ts'e-fu yüan-kuei* p.5024; *Tzu-chih t'ung-chien* p.6139, 6140).

When on Dec.11, 640, Srong-btsan-sgam-po's envoys presented vessels of real gold with a combined weight of 1000 catties and again requested a marriage, T'ai-tsung agreed and enfeoffed a lady of the imperial house as Princess of Wen-ch'eng to become the bride of Srong- btsan-sgam-po. On Feb.20, 641, the king's Chancellor of State, whose name in the Chinese sources is transliterated as Lu Tung-tsan, arrived in Ch'ang-an to meet the lady and presented 5000 ounces of gold and several 100 other kinds of valuables. T'ai-tsung appointed him General-in-chief of the Guards of the Right and offered him the Senior Princess of Lang-ya in marriage. She was a daughter of one of his daughters who had married a member of the Tuan clan. The Chancellor rejected this on the grounds that he had a wife already. On Mar.2, the Master of Writing of the Ministry of Rites, the king of Chiang-hsia, Li Tao-tsung, set out from Ch'ang-an to escort the Princess of Wen-ch'eng to Tibet. He was a distant relative of T'ai-tsung. Srong-btsan-sgam-po met the princess at the border (*Chiu T'ang shu* 3:7a; 196A:2b, 3a-3b; *T'ung-tien* 190:8a; *Tzu-chih t'ung-chien* p.6140, 6164; *Wen-hsien t'ung-k'ao* 334:28b). Subsequently, Srong-btsan-sgam-po founded Lhasa as the Tibetan capital.

In the 1st month (Feb./Mar.) of 642, Tibetan envoys offered regional objects (*Ts'e-fu yüan-kuei* p.5024).

On Feb.14, 644, the New Year's Day, Tibetan envoys offered regional objects (*Ts'e-fu yüan-kuei* p.5024).

On Feb.2, 645, the New Year's Day,[1] Tibetan envoys congratulated at the T'ang court and offered regional objects (*Ts'e-fu yüan-kuei* p.5024).

In the 4th month (May) of 645, the Tibetans presented a vessel of real gold which was 7 feet high. It could be filled with 3 *hu* (59 quarts, 55.9 litres) of wine (*Ts'e-fu yüan-kuei* p.5024).

In the 1st month (Feb./Mar.) of 647, the Tibetans offered regional objects (*Ts'e-fu yüan-kuei* p.5024).

In the 12th month (January, 648) of the Chinese year 647, T'ai-tsung invited the Tibetans, T'ieh-le, Turks, and T'u-yü-hun to join the Chinese in an attack on Kucha (*Tzu-chih t'ung-chien* p.6251).

On Jan.30, 648, the New Year's Day, Tibetan envoys offered gifts (*Ts'e-fu yüan-kuei* p.5025). Later that year, Tibetans assisted the Chinese envoy, Wang Hsüan-ts'e, in his attack on the Indian state of Magadha (*Chiu T'ang shu* 196A:3a; *Tzu-chih t'ung-chien* 6257-6258).

After Kao-tsung had ascended the T'ang throne on July 10, 649, he appointed Srong-btsan-sgam-po as Chief Commandant of Attendant

---

[1] Correcting *keng-tzu* to *keng-wu*.

Cavalry, entitled him king of Hsi-hai commandery, and presented him with 2000 items of objects. Srong-btsan-sgam-po responded with 3000 items of gold (*Chiu T'ang shu* 196A:3a; *Tzu-chih t'ung-chien* p.6268).

In the 1st month (Feb./Mar.) of 650, Tibetan envoys offered gifts (*Ts'e-fu yüan-kuei* p.5025).

At some time in early 650, Kao-tsung entitled Srong-btsan-sgam-po "Guest King" (*Wen-hsien t'ung-k'ao* 334:28b).

On June 28, 650, it became known at the T'ang court that Srong-btsan-sgam-po had died. Kao-tsung commenced mourning for him. He sent the General of the Martial Guards of the Right with a letter stamped with the imperial seal to condole and sacrifice. Since Srong-btsan-sgam-po's sons had died before him, he was succeeded by a grandson. The latter was not yet of age, and the affairs of state were managed by the above-mentioned Chancellor, Lu Tung-tsan (*Chiu T'ang shu* 4:2b; 196A:3a; *Tzu-chih t'ung-chien* p.6271; *Wen-hsien t'ung-k'ao* 334:28b).

In the 8th month (Sep./Oct.) of 654, Tibetan envoys presented 100 wild horses and large asses (*Chiu T'ang shu* 4:5a; *Ts'e-fu yüan-kuei* p.5025).

In the 12th month (Jan./Feb., 658) of the Chinese year 657, envoys from the king of Tibet presented a town made of gold. On it were images of a lion, a camel, a horse, a ram etc. each with a rider (*Ts'e-fu yüan-kuei* p.5025).

In the 10th month (November) of 659, the new Tibetan king unsuccessfuly requested a marriage (*Tzu-chih t'ung-chien* p.6310).

In the 6th month (July/Aug.) of 660, the Tibetans attacked the T'u-yü-hun at Ch'ing-hai (Kokonor). In the 6th month (July/Aug.) of 663, Tibetan envoys to the T'ang court complained about the T'u-yü-hun and again asked for a marriage. Kao-tsung rejected this. He sent a General of the Gentlemen of the Guards of the Left to take a critical letter stamped with the imperial seal to the Tibetans. On Feb.14, 665, he received Tibetan envoys in audience. They again requested a marriage and a border adjustment in their favour. The emperor refused. In the 7th month (July/Aug.) of 670, the Tibetans renewed their attack on the T'u-yü-hun and defeated a Chinese army sent to their rescue. The king of the T'u-yü-hun fled and sought Chinese protection in the eastern Kan-su Corridor, while his old territory was annexed by by the Tibetans. Henceforth, the relations between the Tibetans and T'ang were tense, and the Tibetans looted Chinese border lands (*Chiu T'ang shu* 5:3b; 196A:3b; 198:8a; *Tzu-chih t'ung-chien* pp.6321, 6336, 6343).[2] From 670 to 692, they controlled the Tarim Basin.

In the 4th month (May) of 672, Tibetan envoys offered gifts. Kao-tsung questioned them about their customs (*Ts'e-fu yüan-kuei* p.5026; *Tzu-chih t'ung-chien* p.6368).

On May 24, 672, Kao-tsung sent the Commissioner of Waterways as his envoy to Tibet (*Tzu-chih-t'ung-chien* p.6369).

On Feb.26, 675, a high official of the Tibetans was received at the T'ang court. He asked for peace and a marriage alliance, and for Chinese mediation between them and the T'u-yü-hun. Kao-tsung rejected this (*Chiu T'ang shu* 5:6a; *Tzu-chih t'ung-chien* p.6375).

In 676, the Tibetans looted Chinese border lands and occupied a swath of territory from present Lan-chou south (*Tzu-chih t'ung-chien* p.6380). This was followed by a great Chinese defeat near Ch'ing-hai in 678.

On Mar.28, 679 it became known at the T'ang court that the king of Tibet had died. He was succeeeded by his 8-year-old son (*Chiu T'ang shu* 5:8a; 196A:4b).

On Nov.24, 679, a high official sent by the Princess of Wen-ch'eng from Tibet to the T'ang court officially announced the death of the king. She also requested peace and a marriage alliance, which was rejected. Kao-tsung sent a General of the Gentlemen[-of-the-Household] to condole and sacrifice (*Chiu T'ang shu* 5:8b; 196A:4b; *Tzu-chih t'ung-chien* p.6393).

In 680, it became known at the T'ang court that the Princess of Wen-ch'eng had died. Kao-tsung sent envoys to condole and sacrifice (*Chiu T'ang shu* 196A:4b).

In the 7th month (August) of 680 and in the 7th month (Aug./Sep.) of 682, the Tibetans looted Chinese border lands (*Tzu-chih t'ung-chien* pp.6395, 6412).

In 689 and 690, the Chinese attacked the Tibetans (*Chiu T'ang shu* 196A:4b).

In the 5th month (May/June) of 692, the chief of a Tibetan tribe attempted on his own initiative to make peace with China but was exposed and arrested by his own men. Another chief succeeded in the same endeavour. The Chinese endowed his tribal territory with

[2] For a detailed discussion of these events see the section on the T'u-yü-hun.

the name of a commandery, which changed nothing in practice. (*Chiu T'ang shu* 196A:4b; *Tzu-chih t'ung-chien* p.6482). Nevertheless, the T'ang was able to reestablish the An-hsi Protectorate in Kucha that year and to regain some control over the Tarim Basin.

In 696 and 697, Tibetan envoys requested peace. Negotiations were attempted but proved fruitless (*Chiu T'ang shu* 196A:5a; *Wen-hsien t'ung-k'ao* 334:29a).

In 699, the king of Tibet, successfully asserted himself against the members of the mGar clan who had been regents during his minority (*Tzu-chih t'ung-chien* p.6539; *Wen-hsien t'ung-k'ao* 334:29a). The previously all-powerful mGar Khri-'bring committed suicide. His brother, whose name in the Chinese sources is transliterated as Lun Tsan-p'o and others deserted to the Chinese side. The Chinese attempted to exploit the situation. Tsan-p'o was made a Specially Advanced and King Who Attaches Himself to Virtue. A son of Khri-'bring, whose name in the Chinese sources is transliterated as Lun Kung-jen, was appointed General of the Guards of the Jade Bells of the Left. On Nov.3, 699, Tsan-p'o was received in Ch'ang-an and appointed General-in-chief of the Guards of the Right. Thereafter, he departed and was expected to protect the Chinese border (*Tzu-chih t'ung-chien* p. pp.6539-6540, 6542; *Wen-hsien t'ung-k'ao* 334:29a).

On Oct.10, 702, Tibetan envoys requested peace and were given a banquet by the Empress Wu (*Chiu T'ang shu* 196A:5a-5b; *Hsin T'ang shu* 4:11b).

In the 4th month (Apr./May) of 703, Tibetan envoys presented 1000 horses and 2000 ounces of gold and requested a marriage. The Empress Wu agreed. However, the king of Tibet fell against the Nepalese and was succeeded by his 7-year old son Tsuk-tsen (*Chiu T'ang shu* 196A:5b; *Hsin T'ang shu* 4:11b; *Tzu-chih t'ung-chien* pp.6562, 6569; *Wen-hsien t'ung-k'ao* 334:29a).

In the 1st month (Feb./Mar.), of 704, Tibetan envoys offered gifts (*Ts'e-fu yüan-kuei* p.5026).

In 705, Tibetan envoys officially announced the death of their king. Emperor Chung-tsung commencenced mourning and suspended the court for one day. Subsequently, Tsuk-tsen's grandmother sent a high official to present 2000 ounces of gold and request a marriage on behalf of her grandson (*Chiu T'ang shu* 196A:5b; *T'ang hui-yao* 97:6a; *Wen-hsien t'ung-k'ao* 334:29a).

On Mar.15, 707, high officials sent by the Tibetan king offered regional objects (*Chiu T'ang shu* 7:6a; *Ts'e-fu yüan-kuei* p.5026; *Tzu-chih t'ung-chien* p.6610).[3]

On May 19, 707, Emperor Chung-tsung selected a great-granddaughter of Kao-tsung as the bride of Tsuk-tsen and made her the Princess of Chin-ch'eng. She had been brought up by Chung-tsung (*Chiu T'ang shu* 7:6a; 196A:5b-6a; *T'ung-tien* 190:8a; *Tzu-chih t'ung-chien* p.6610).

In the 2nd (Mar./Apr.) and 8th month (Sep./Oct.) of 709, Tibetan envoys offered regional objects (*Ts'e-fu yüan-kuei* p.5026).

In the 11th month (Dec./Jan., 710) of the Chinese year 709, a delegation of more than 1000 men, led by a high official, arrived from Tibet to welcome the Princess of Chin-ch'eng. Chung-tsung gave them a banquet at a boll field in an imperial park and then watched a ball game played by the Chinese against the Tibetans (*Chiu T'ang shu* 7: 8b; 196A:6a; *Tzu-chih t'ung-chien* p.6637).

On Feb.28, 710, the General-in-chief of the Resolute Guards of the Right and Military Commissioner of the Ho-yüan Army received orders to escort the Princess of Chin-ch'eng to Tibet. On Mar.2, the emperor followed the princess to Shih-p'ing prefecture,[4] where a tent was set up and the emperor gave a banquet for the kings, dukes, Grand Councilors, and Tibetan envoys (*Chiu T'ang shu* 7:9a; 196A:6b).

After Jui-tsung had ascended the T'ang throne on July 25, 710, war broke out again (*Chiu T'ang shu* 196A:6b). This did not prevent the coming and going of missions.

In the 9th (Sep./Oct.) and 12th month (Dec./Jan., 711) of the Chinese year 710, Tibetan envoys offered regional objects (*Ts'e-fu yüan-kuei* p.5026).

In the 5th (June/July) and 8th month (Sep./Oct.) of 712, Tibetan envoys to the T'ang court were received in audience, and in the 12th month (January, 713) of the same Chinese year, Tibetans again came to the court (*Ts'e-fu yüan-kuei* p.5026).

In the 2nd month (March) of 713, Tibetan envoys offered gifts (*Ts'e-fu yüan-kuei* p.5027).

---

[3] *Tsu-chih t'ung-chien* dates this mission in the 3rd month, but that month did not have the cyclical characters *ping-tzu*.

[4] About 50 miles or 80 km west of Ch'ang-an, north of the Wei River, the modern Hsing-p'ing. The name was in T'ang times changed to Chin-ch'eng, presumably in honour of the princess.

On Dec.16, 713, a high Tibetan official requested that peace be restored (*Tzu-chih t'ung-chien* p.6692).

On July 9, 714, a Tibetan Chancellor wrote to a Grand Councilor in Ch'ang-an and suggested that the border between the two countries should be delineated. Emperor Hsüan-tsung ordered the Grand Councilor to write a reply (*Tzu-chih t'ung-chien* p.6699; *Wen-hsien t'ung-k'ao* 334:29a).

On July 26, 714, a Tibetan Chancellor brought a covenant for peace. Hsüan-tsung did not accept it. Subsequently, the Tibetans looted Chinese border lands (*Chiu T'ang shu* 196A:7a; *Tzu-chih t'ung-chien* p.6701, 6704).

On Nov.25, 714, Hsüan-tsung was informed that while the Yellow River[5] had been considered the border for a long time, the Tibetans had now gone across it and built fortifications. These should be destroyed. The emperor approved (*Tzu-chih t'ung-chien* p.6705).

On Dec.12, 714, Hsüan-tsung sent a Gentleman of the Resolute Guards of the Left as his envoy to the Tibetans. He was met at the T'ao River[6] by Tibetan envoys who requested peace. The emperor rejected it (*Tzu-chih t'ung-chien* p.6706).

On July 26, and in the 8th month (Aug./Sep.) of 716, in the 11th month (Nov./Dec.) of 718,[7] on May 11, 717, in the 1st month (Jan./Feb.) of 719, on July 2, 719, and in the 11th (Dec./Jan., 721) and 12th month (January, 721) of the Chinese year 720, Tibetan envoys were received at the T'ang court, mostly asking for peace. Nothing came of it (*Chiu T'ang shu* 8:9a; *Hsin T'ang shu* 5:6a; *Ts'e-fu yüan-kuei* p.5027; *Tzu-chih t'ung-chien* pp.6720, 6734, 6736).

In 725, Tibetan envoys wished to congratulate at the T'ang court but were not received (*T'ang hui-yao* 97:6a).

In 726, peace was finally achieved. The Tibetans had requested it again and Hsüan-tsung had agreed. He sent gifts to the Princess of Chin-ch'eng, whereupon envoys of her husband promised that he would observe a treaty. He also presented valuables. The emperor received the envoys with courtesy. He then dispatched his Grandee Secretary to respond with a goodwill mission. Agreement was reached on the delineation of the border, and the peace covenant was carved

[5] At Lan-chou in Kan-su.

[6] It enters the Yellow River from the south just above Lan-chou.

[7] *Tzu-chih t'ung-chien* p.6734 says 11th month, *mou-ch'en*, but the 11th month did not have these cyclical characers.

on a large stele. The imperial library was ordered to copy the *Five Confucian Classics* which the Tibetans had requested, whereupon the Tibetans sent envoys with thanks (*Wen-hsien t'ung-k'ao* 334:29b).[8]

In 727, the Tibetans presented several 100 valuable vessels (*Wen-hsien t'ung-k'ao* 334:29b).

In 729, the Tibetans sent envoys "to request peace". Hsüan-tsung responded with an envoy of his own to the Princess of Chin-ch'eng, and this envoy subsequently made a covenant with the king. In the winter, an envoy of the princess arrived at the T'ang court (*Chiu T'ang shu* 196A:8a-8b).

In the 4th month (Apr./May) of 730, Tibetan envoys offered gifts (*Ts'e-fu yüan-kuei* p.5028).

In the 5th month (May/June) of 730, Tibetan envoys presented a letter at the border and "requested peace" (*Tzu-chih t'ung-chien* p.6789).

In the 9th month (Oct./Nov.) and on Nov.21 of 730, the Tibetans "requested peace" and a marriage alliance. Hsüan-tsung sent two envoys to the king, who showed them Chinese imperial letters which had been received in Tibet from 627. The king then ordered officials to follow the Chinese envoys back to Ch'ang-an and offer regional objects. Hsüan-tsung received them in audience, gave them a banquet, and presented the head of the mission with a purple robe, a golden belt, and a wallet for a fish token. The envoy rejected the wallet on the grounds that it was unknown in his country. He also requested on behalf of the princess copies of the *Mao Odes*, the *Spring and Autumn Annals*, the *Book of Rites*, the anthology of literarture called the *Wen-hsüan*, and the *Cheng-tzu*, a dictionary of correct characters. The emperor ordered these works to be copied and provided, even though an official protested that they contained information which should be reserved for the Chinese and not be dissiminated to barbarians (*Chiu T'ang shu* 8:17b; 196A:9a; *Hsin T'ang shu* 5:10a; *Ts'e-fu yüan-kuei* p.5028; *Tzu-chih t'ung-chien* pp.6790-6791).[9]

In the 12th month (Jan./Feb., 731) of the Chinese year 730, an official of the king of Tibet presented regional objects (*Ts'e-fu yüan-kuei* p.5028).

---

[8] For the following years, the sources repeatedly state that Tibetans "requested peace", even when covenants should still have been in force. This may not have been as odd as it seems and will be further discussed below.

[9] *Tzu-chih t'ung-chien* dates the book request 1st month (Feb./Mar.) of 731.

On Mar.4, 731,[10] Hsüan-tsung ordered the Herald to go on a good-will mission to the Tibetans. He departed on Apr.11[11](*Chiu T'ang shu* 8:17b; *Tzu-chih t'ung-chien* p.6794).

In 731, the Tibetans sent a high official, who was met at the border by the Chinese Junior Herald. On Oct.30,[12] this envoy had an audience, at which he requested a joint border market. Hsüan-tsung agreed (*Chiu T'ang shu* 8:17b; *Ts'e-fu yüan-kuei* p.5028; *Tzu-chih t'ung-chien* p.6796).

On Aug.5, 731, the Tibetans "requested peace" (*Hsin T'ang shu* 5: 10a).

On Feb.9, 733, Hsüan-tsung ordered a Master of Writing of the Ministry of Works to go as an envoy to the Tibetans (*Chiu T'ang shu* 8:19a).

In the 2nd month (Feb./Mar.) of 733, the T'ang court agreed to a proposal by the Princess of Chin-ch'eng to set up a stele as a border marker on Oct.13 (*T'ang hui-yao* 97:6b; *Tzu-chih t'ung-chien* p.6799).

In the 1st month (Feb./Mar.) of 734, Tibetan envoys were received at the T'ang court, probably on the New Year's Day of Feb.9 (*Ts'e-fu yüan-kuei* p.5029).

On July 10, 734, Hsüan-tsung sent the General of the Golden Mace of the Left to delineate the border together with the Tibetans and to set up stone markers (*Chiu T'ang shu* 8:20a; 196A:9b-10a).

In the 2nd month (Feb./Mar.) of 735, an envoy sent by the king of Tibet congratulated (belatedly) on the New Year's Day (Jan.29) and offered regional objects (*Ts'e-fu yüan-kuei* p.5029).

In the 1st month (Feb./Mar.) of 736, probably on the New Year's Day on Feb.16, Tibetan envoys presented several 100 gold and silver vessels of rare shapes. Hsüan-tsung ordered that they be displayed to the officials (*Chiu T'ang shu* 8:20b; *Ts'e-fu yüan-kuei* p.5029).

In 736, the Tibetans destroyed the border markers (*Chiu T'ang shu* 196A:10a-10b; *Tzu-chih t'ung-chien* p.6827). T'ang was at this time fighting the Tibetans over Gilgit (Po-lü), situated north of Kashmir.[13]

---

[10] *Tzu-chih t'ung-chien* has *hsin-wei* = Mar.4. *Chiu T'ang shu* gives the cyclical characters *hsin-mao*, which did not occur in the 1st month.

[11] Correcting *yi-yu* to *chi-yu*.

[12] *Chiu T'ang shu* and *Tzu-chih t'ung-chien* have 9th month, *hsin-wei* = Oct.30. *Ts'e-fu yüan-kuei* has 8h month, but the cyclical characters *hsin-wei* did not occur in that month.

[13] For details see infra under the heading of Gilgit.

In 738, Tibetans invaded Chinese border lands, and the Chinese counterattacked (*Chiu T'ang shu* 196A:10b; *Wen-hsien t'ung-k'ao* 334:29b).

In the spring of 740, Tibetan envoys informed the T'ang court that the Princess of Chin-ch'eng had died.[14] Hsüan-tsung ordered three days of mourning. The envoys also proposed to make peace, which the emperor rejected (*Chiu T'ang shu* 9:4a; 196A:11b; *T'ang hui-yao* 97:7a; *Tzu-chih t'ung-chien* p.6843).

In the 3rd month (Mar./Apr.) of 741, in spite of the war, Tibetan envoys were received at the T'ang court. In the 8th month (Sep./Oct.) of the same year, they offered regional objects (*Chiu T'ang shu* 9:4a; *Ts'e-fu yüan-kuei* p.5029).

In 755, it became known at the T'ang court that the king of Tibet had died and had been succeeded by his son Khri-sron lde-brtsan. He sent envoys to the T'ang court to restore good relations. Hsüan-tsung dispatched the Junior Governor of the Capital to recognize him and to condole and sacrifice. When that envoy returned, the rebellion of An Lu-shan had broken out (*Chiu T'ang shu* 196A:11b; *Wen-hsien t'ung-k'ao* 334:30a).

In the 3rd month of (Feb./Mar.) of 757, Tibetan envoys requested peace. Emperor Su-tsung ordered that they be given a banquet, and dispatched a Serving Within the Palace on a return goodwill mission. In spite of raids, Tibetan envoys continued to argue for peace. In the 2nd month (Mar./Apr.) of 758, a covenant was concluded in a Buddhist temple in which the Grand Councilor Kuo Tzu-yi presided on the Chinese side (*Chiu T'ang shu* 196A:12a; *T'ang hui-yao* 97:7a; *Wen-hsien t'ung-k'ao* 334:30a).[15]

On Dec.24, 761, Tibetan envoys "requested peace" (*Tzu chih t'ung-tien* p.7118).

In the 5th month (May/June) of 762, Tibetan envoys offered gifts (*Ts'e-fu yüan-kuei* p.5031).

In the 6th month (June/July) of 762, two Tibetan envoys presented regional objects. They received gifts, each in accordance with his rank (*Chiu T'ang shu* 196A:12b; *Ts'e-fu yüan-kuei* p.5031).

In the 3rd month (Apr./May) of 763, Emperor Tai-tsung sent the Regular Cavalier Attendant of the Left and Concurrent Grandee Sec-

---

[14] *T'ang hui-yao* places her death in 741, *T'ung-tien* in 755.

[15] *Chiu T'ang shu* dates all events 756 and *Wen-hsien t'ung-k'ao* 757.

retary, Li Chih-fang, and the Cadet of the Left and Concurrent Palace Assistant Secretary, Ts'ui Lun, as envoys to the Tibetans. When they reached the border, they were detained by the Tibetans (*Chiu T'ang shu* 196A:12b). The reason was that the Tibetans were preparing for a huge attack on China.

On Nov.18, 763, remarkably it happened that the Tibetans took the T'ang capital of Ch'ang-an. They there enthroned the king of Kuang-wu, Li Ch'eng-hung, as emperor. He was a great-grandson of Emperor Kao-tsung, and no doubt was chosen because he was a brother of the Princess of Chin-ch'eng. But the Tibetans had no way of holding on to the city. They looted it for fifteen days and then withdrew, whereupon Tai-tsung was able to return to his capital. Ch'eng-hung, who probably had been coerced by the Tibetans, was banished but not executed (*Hsin T'ang shu* 81:5a; *Tzu-chih t'ung-chien* pp.7151-7153, 7157; *Wen-hsien t'ung-k'ao* 334:30a).

In 764, the Tibetans released Li Chih-fang and Ts'ui Lun, and in the 3rd month (Mar./Apr.) of 765, their envoys requested peace. At the advice of Kuo Tzu-yi, Tai-tsung accepted, and a covenant was concluded in a Buddhist temple (*Chiu T'ang shu* 196A:12b; *Tzu-chih t'ung-chien* p.7174; *Wen-hsien t'ung-k'ao* 334:30a).

War broke out again immediately, and on Oct.4, 765, a large Tibetan army reached Feng-t'ien prefecture, situated north of the Wei River 50 miles (80 km) northwest of Ch'ang-an (map 5). The Tibetans advanced on Oct.5. On Oct.26, they joined forces with Uighurs and attacked Ching-yang prefecture, situated only 27 miles (43 km) north of Ch'ang-an. They then withdrew (*Chiu T'ang shu* 196A:12b; *Tzu-chih t'ung-chien* pp.7177, 7180).

In the 2nd month (Mar./Apr.) of 766, Tai-tsung sent the Junior Judge and Concurrent Palace Assistant Secretary to seek renewed good relations with the Tibetans. These attached a mission of over 100 men, led by a chief, to the Chinese envoy to follow him back to Ch'ang-an (*Chiu T'ang shu* 196B:1a).

In the 7th month (July/Aug.) of 767, Tibetan envoys were received at the T'ang court (*Ts'e-fu yüan-kuei* p.5031).

In the 10th month (Oct./Nov.) of 767, Chinese troops stationed in what now is called the Ning-hsia Oasis defeated a Tibetan army (*Chiu T'ang shu* 196B:1a).

In the 11th month (Nov./Dec.) of 767, a Master of Writing of the Ministry of Households and Concurrent Grandee Secretary returned from a mission to the Tibetans. A Tibetan chief followed him back to

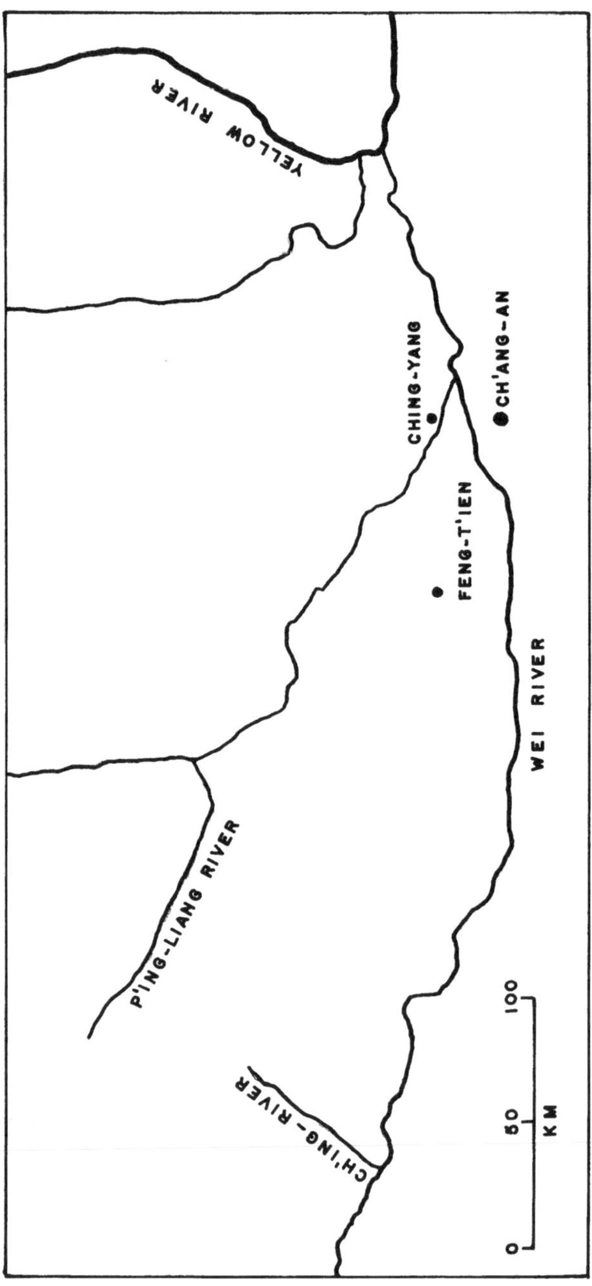

Map 5. Ch'ang-an and environs.

the court (*Chiu T'ang shu* 196B:1a; *Ts'e-fu yüan-kuei* p.5031).

In 768, the Tibetans again fought the Chinese and looted border lands (*Chiu T'ang shu* 196B:1a).

In the 12th month (January, 770) of the Chinese year 769, Tibetan envoys offered gifts (*Ts'e-fu yüan-kuei* p.5031).

In the autumn and in the 12th month (Dec./Jan., 773) of the Chinese year 772, Tibetan envoys offered presents (*Chiu T'ang shu* 11:20b; *Ts'e-fu yüan-kuei* p. p.5031).

In 773, the Tibetans raided the Ning-hsia Oasis (*Wen-hsien t'ung-k'ao* 334:30a).

In 774, Tai-tsung dispatched a Grandee Remonstrant and Consultant to the Tibetans in the hope of restoring good relations (*Wen-hsien t'ung-k'ao* 334:30a). In the 6th (July/Aug.) and 7th month (Aug./Sep.), the Tibetans responded by sending envoys of their own to the T'ang court (*Ts'e-fu yüan-kuei* p.5032).

In 775, the Tibetans attacked again. In the 1st month (Feb./Mar.) of 778, they looted the Ning-hsia Oasis (*T'ang hui-yao* 97:7a; *Wen-hsien t'ung-k'ao* 334:30b).

In the 8th month (Sep./Oct.) of 779, Emperor Te-tsung, who had ascended the throne on June 12, sent the Junior Grand Master of Ceremonies, Wei Lun, to the Tibetans, no doubt to open communications. This did not prevent the Tibetans from looting Chinese border lands in the 10th month (Nov./Dec.) (*Chiu T'ang shu* 196B:2a).

In the 4th month (May/June) of 780, envoys from the Tibetan king offered gifts (*Tzu-chih t'ung-chien* p.7279). On June 11, Te-tsung sent Wei Lun on a second mission to the Tibetans, this time with the rank of Grand Master of Ceremonies, and also ordered the release of Tibetan prisoners of war. Wei Lun returned with a Tibetan mission of 55 men, headed by a Chancellor, which presented regional objects in order to restore good relations (*Chiu T'ang shu* 12:5a, 6a; 196B:2b; *Wen-hsien t'ung-k'ao* 334:30b).

In 781, Te-tsung dispatched the Junior Palace Inspector as envoy to the Tibetan king. There followed negotiations which lasted until the 10th month (Nov./Dec.) of 782, and in which the Tibetans successfully protested against the sinocentric terminology of the proposed treaty (*Chiu T'ang shu* 196B:2b-3a; *Wen-hsien t'ung-k'ao* 334:30b). It was agreed to conclude a covenant on the 15th day of the 1st month of the following year at the Ch'ing River. This was a northern affluent of the upper Wei River. On Feb.18, 783, the delegates met at the appointed place. The T'ang was represented by a Military Commissioner, Tibet by a Chancellor. On Feb.20 (the 15th day), the covenant was agreed upon (*Chiu T'ang shu* 12:11a; 196B:2b-3a; *Wen-hsien t'ung-k'ao* 334:30b). In this treaty, T'ang ceded territory between the upper Min and Wei Rivers and the Yellow River to the Tibetans.

In the 2nd month (Feb./Mar.) of 784, Tibetan envoys were received at the T'ang court, and a Grandee Secretary was sent as a Chinese envoy in return. The latter was in the 4th month (Apr./May) followed by the Junior Grand Master of Ceremonies and Concurrent Palace Assistant Secretary (*Chiu T'ang shu* 12:14b; 196B:4b).

In the 9th month (Oct./Nov.) of 785, Te-tsung sent a General of the Guards Inspecting the Gates of the Left as envoy to the Tibetans in order to delineate the border (*T'ang hui-yao* 97:8b).

In the 10th month (Nov./Dec.) of 785, Chinese troops made a suprise attack on the Tibetans (*T'ang hui-yao* 97:8b).

In 786, the T'ang court sent a Gentleman-of-the-Palace of the Bureau of Granaries and Concurrent Grandee Secretary as an envoy to the Tibetans. In the 8th (Aug./Sep.), 9th (Sep./Oct.), and 11th month (Nov./Dec.) the Tibetans made deep inroads into Chinese border lands (*Chiu T'ang shu* 196B:4b; *T'ang hui-yao* 97:9a-9b).

On Apr.5, 787, Te-tsung sent an Acting Cadet of the Left and Concurrent Palace Assistant Secretary to the Tibetans and simultaneously made a military demonstration. The Tibetan Chancellor Shan-rgyal-btsan thereupon proposed through three envoys that the two states should conclude a covenant of peace and restore good relations. Te-tsung did not believe that the Tibetans acted in good faith but wished peace in order to have a free hand against the Uighurs. When the envoys repeated the request in an audience, he therefore agreed. On May 25, the Palace Attendant Hun Chen was appointed chief Chinese negotiator, with the Master of Writing of the Ministry of Arms Ts'ui Han-heng as his deputy. The meeting was again to be held at the Ch'ing River but at the request of Shan-rgyal-btsan was moved to the P'ing-liang River, some 62 miles (100 km) northeast of the former. On July 13, the covenant was concluded but ended in disarray.[16] Hun Chen was robbed by the Tibetans, Ts'ui Han-heng was temporarily arrested, and another imperial envoy was returned at the border. In the 8th month (Sep./Oct.), Shan-rgyal-btsan sent Ts'ui

[16] According to *Chiu T'ang shu* 196B:5b, it was concluded at the Ch'ing River, which is an error for P'ing-liang River.

Han-heng back with an escort and repeated his wish for peace, but this time his envoys were stopped and sent back (*Chiu T'ang shu* 12: 24a, 24b; 196B:5a, 5b; *Tzu-chih t'ung-chien* p.7482, 7483, 7488, 7496). For the next ten years, there was uninterrupted fighting and no diplomatic exchange between the two countries. In 790, the Tibetans overran the Chinese protectorate of Pei-t'ing (Besbalïq) in Zungharia (*Chiu T'ang shu* 195:10a),[17] whereafter the Tarim Basin again came under Tibetan domination.

On Feb.16, 797, envoys from the Tibetan king were received at the T'ang court, proposing peace and a marriage alliance. But when Te-tsung was informed, he refused to receive the envoys because so many covenants had been broken. The king died, and his son unsuccessfully repeated the request (*Chiu T'ang shu* 13:13b; 196B:11a; *Tzu-chih t'ung-chien* p.7576; *Wen-hsien t'ung-k'ao* 334:31a).

Renewed fighting lasted until 803, when a Tibetan envoy was received at the T'ang court in the 5th month (May/June). In the 6th month (June/July), Te-tsung made the General-in-chief Who Is Martial as a Dragon a Concurrent Grandee Secretary and sent him as his envoy to the Tibetans (*Chiu T'ang shu* 196B:12b; *Wen-hsien t'ung-k'ao* 334:31a).[18] Henceforth, relations improved.

In early 804, Tibetan envoys announced that the king of Tibet had died and had been succeeded by his younger brother.[19] On Apr.22, Te-tsung suspended the court for three days and ordered the civilian and military officials from the 3rd rank up to condole with the envoys (*Chiu T'ang shu* 13:21a; 196B:12b; *Tzu-chih t'ung-chien* p.7605; *Wen-hsien t'ung-k'ao* 334:31a).

On June 3, 804, a Tibetan mission of 54 men offered gifts (*Chiu T'ang shu* 13:21b; 196B:12b).

On June 12, 804, Te-tsung appointed a Senior Compiler of the Historiography Institute as Gentleman-in-Attendance and Concurrent Grandee Secretary and sent him to Tibet to condole and sacrifice (*Chiu T'ang shu* 13:21b; 196B:12b; *Tzu-chih t'ung-chien* p.7605; *Wen-hsien t'ung-k'ao* 334:31a).

In the 12th month (Jan./Feb., 805) of the Chinese year 804, Tibetan

---

17 Cf. Mackerras, *Uighur Empire*, p.162 note 191.

18 The events of 803 are by *Wen-hsien t'ung-k'ao* dated 802.

19 According to *Chiu T'ang shu* 196B:12b, following the *Shih-lu*, the king was succeeded by his eldest son, who died within a year and was succeeded by his younger brother. This is rejected by Ssu-ma Kuang in his *K'ao-yi*.

envoys offered presents (*Chiu T'ang shu* 13:21b; 196B:12b; *Ts'e-fu yüan-kuei* p.5032).

In the 2nd month (Mar./Apr.) of 805, Emperor Shun-tsung ordered the General of the Guards of the Golden Mace of the Left and Concurrent Palace Assistant Secretary to announce the death of Te-tsung on Feb.25 to the Tibetans. A Supernumerary Gentleman of the Bureau of Storehouses and Concurrent Palace Assistant Secretary was his deputy (*Chiu T'ang shu* 196B:12b; *Wen-hsien t'ung-k'ao* 334:31a).

On July 30, 805, Tibetan envoys offered regional objects (*Chiu T'ang shu* 14:2b; 196B:12b; *Ts'e-fu yüan-kuei* p.5032).

In the 10th month (Oct./Nov.) of 805, envoys from the king of Tibet offered gifts and presented gold, silver, silk, cattle, and horses toward the construction of Te-tsung's tomb. These gifts were displayed in the Hall of the Grand Ultimate, i.e. the main audience hall (*Chiu T'ang shu* 196B:12b; *T'ang hui-yao* 97:11b; *Wen-hsien t'ung-k'ao* 334:31a).

In the 11th month (Nov./Dec.) of 805, a Junior Commandant of the Guards and Concurrent Palace Assistant Secretary was sent as envoy to the Tibetans (*Chiu T'ang shu* 196B:13a).

In the intercalary month (July/Aug.) of 806, and in the 2nd month (Mar./Apr.) of 807, the Tibetans offered gifts (*Chiu T'ang shu* 14:9a; 196B:13a; *Ts'e-fu yüan-kuei* p.5032).

In 808, the Tibetans requested peace (*Hsin T'ang shu* 7:13a).[20]

On June 26, 810, a Tibetan envoy offered presents and requested peace and at the same time returned the coffins of two Chinese envoys who had died in Tibet. In the 6th month (July/Aug.),[21] Emperor Hsien-tsung ordered the Grand Councilor Tu Yu[22] and others to discuss the question of peace with the envoy (*Chiu T'ang shu* 14:17a; 196B:13a; *Tzu-chih t'ung-tien* p.7676).

In the 7th month (Aug./Sep.) of 810, Hsien-tsung sent the Junior Herald and Acting Palace Assisant Secretary as envoy to the Tibetans. A Chief Clerk was his deputy (*Chiu T'ang shu* 196B:13a).

In the 2nd month (Mar./Apr.) of 812, Tibetan envoys were received at the T'ang court (*Ts'e-fu yüan-kuei* p.5032).

On Dec.26, 816, the T'ang court agreed to joint border markets with the Tibetans (*Tzu-chih t'ung-chien* p.7720; *Wen-hsien t'ung-k'ao* 334:31a).

---

[20] The text gives the date of 7th month, *kuei-hai*, which did not exist.

[21] *T'ang hui-yao* 97:12a says 5th month (June/July).

[22] Author of the *T'ung-tien*.

On Mar.9, 816, Tibetan envoys announced that their king had died. In the 4th month (May/June) of 817, Hsien-tsung sent the General of the Guards of the Right to condole and sacrifice. The same month, Tibetans presented ten horses, two jade belts, ten golden vessels, and one yak (*Chiu T'ang shu* 15:10a; 196B:13a; *Ts'e-fu yüan-kuei* p.5033; *Wen-hsien t'ung-k'ao* 334:31a).

In 818, Tibetan envoys offered gifts and were given a banquet. When they were taking leave in the 8th month (Sep./Oct.6), Tibetans once more had opened hostilities. In retaliation, the envoys were detained but then released on Feb.9, 819 (*Chiu T'ang shu* 15:16a; *T'ang hui-yao*, 97:12a-12b; *Tzu-chih t'ung-chien* p.7757; *Wen-hsien t'ung-k'ao* 334: 31a).

At this time, the T'ang court ordered that missions from the Tibetans were not to exceed 30 members, and that no more than ten of them were to be appointed to nominal Chinese offices (*T'ang hui-yao* 97:12b).

In 819, after further looting, Tibetan envoys offered gifts (*T'ang hui-yao* 97:12b).

In the 2nd month (Mar./Apr.) of 820, Emperor Mu-tsung sent the Junior Inspector of the Imperial Library and Concurrent Palace Assistant Secretary to the Tibetans to announce the death of his father Hsien-tsung on Feb.14, and his own enthronement on Feb.20 (*Chiu T'ang shu* 196B:13b-14a).

In the 3rd month (Apr./May of 820, the Tibetans looted Chinese border lands. In the 7th month (Aug./Sep.), their envoys to the T'ang court condoled and sacrificed. In the 10th month (Nov./Dec.), they again raided. The T'ang sent the Junior Privy Treasurer and Concurrent Palace Assistant Secretary as envoy to the Tibetans (*Chiu T'ang shu* 196B:14a; *Tzu-chih t'ung-chien* p.7785).

In the 4th month (May/June) of 821, Tibetan envoys were received at the court, although the fighting and looting continued (*Chiu T'ang shu* 196B:14a; *T'ang hui-yao* 97:13b; *Tzu-chih t'ung-chien* p.7791).

At last, in the 9th month (October) of 821,[23] there was a breakthrough in the negotiations. Tibetan envoys proposed a covenant, the Chinese agreed, and this finally led to a real peace treaty. It was solemnly concluded on the Western Suburban Altar of Ch'ang-an on Nov.8, 821, and later ratified in Lhasa. The Chinese were represented

[23] *T'ang hui-yao* 97:13b says 8th month (September).

by the General-in-chief of the Guards of the Left. It was a treaty among equals, and the peace held.[24] Henceforth, the Tibetans regularly sent missions and presented rhinoceroses and deer fashioned in gold and silver, valuable vessels, jade belts, woolen fabrics, otter skins, horses, camels, sheep, yaks, and yak tails (*Chiu T'ang shu* 196B:14a; *Wen-hsien t'ung-k'ao* 334:31a).

In the 11th month (Nov./Dec.) of 821, Tibetan envoys were received at the T'ang court (*T'ang hui-yao* 97:14a).

In the 2nd month (Feb./Mar.) of 822, Tibetan envoys requested that the border be delineated. In the 6th month (June/July),[25] they offered 60 horses, 200 sheep, silver vessels, and jade belts (*Chiu T'ang shu* 196B:15a; *T'ang hui-yao* 97:14a; *Ts'e-fu yüan-kuei* p.5033).

On Aug.13, 822, the Grand Judge returned from a mission to the Tibetans and reported that the king of Tibet, Khri-gtsug lde brtsan had confirmed the peace treaty on May 30 (*T'ang hui-yao* 97:14a; *Tzu-chih t'ung-chien* p.7820).

In the 12th month (Jan./Feb., 823) of the Chinese year 822, Tibetan envoys offered gifts (*Ts'e-fu yüan-kuei* p.5033).

On Feb.15, 823, the New Year's Day, Tibetan envoys congratulated at the T'ang court and presented 600 sheep (*Chiu T'ang shu* 196B:15-16a; *T'ang hui-yao* 97:114b).

In the 2nd month (Mar./Apr.) of 824, Tibetan envoys offered presents and requested a painting of Wu-t'ai Mountain with its famous Buddhist shrines in northern Shan-hsi. On Nov.20 of the same year, they presented a rhinoceros, bull, sheep, and deer made of silver, and yaks (*Chiu T'ang shu* 17A:4a, 196B:16a; *T'ang hui-yao* 97:14b). *Ts'e-fu yüan-kuei* p.5033).

In the 12th month (Dec./Jan., 825) of the Chinese year 824, Tibetan envoys offered gifts (*Chiu T'ang shu* 17A:4b; *Ts'e-fu yüan-kuei* p.5033).

In the 3rd month (Mar./Apr.) of 825, Tibetan envoys offered presents. In the 9th month (Oct./Nov.) of the same year,[26] Emperor Ching-tsung sent the Superintendent of the Imperial Household as envoy in response (*Chiu T'ang shu* 196B:16a; *Ts'e-fu yüan-kuei* p.5033).

In the 8th month (Aug./Sep.) of 827 Tibetan envoys presented gold

---

[24] The text of the treaty in Tibetan and Chinese was engraved on a stele which to this day is preserved in Lhasa.

[25] *T'ang hui-yao* says 5th month (May/June).

[26] *T'ang hui-yao* 97:14b dates this mission 11th month (December) 826.

and silver vessels, a jade belt, and horses (*Ts'e-fu yüan-kuei* p.5033).

In the 12th month (Dec./Jan., 831) of the Chinese year 830, Tibetan envoys offered gifts (*Ts'e-fu yüan-kuei* p.5033).

In the 1st month (Feb./Mar.) of 831, Tibetan envoys were received at the T'ang court (*T'ang hui-yao* 97:14b).

In the 11th month Dec./Jan., 832) of the Chinese year 831, Tibetan envoys offered presents (*Ts'e-fu yüan-kuei* p.5033).

On Mar.16, 833, Tibetan envoys were received at the T'ang court (*Chiu T'ang shu* 17B:9a).

In the 1st month (Feb./Mar.) of 835, Tibetan envoys were received at the T'ang court (*T'ang hui-yao* 97:14b).

On Jan.22, 836, the New Year's Day, Tibetan envoys congratulated at the T'ang court and presented horses (*T'ang hui-yao* 97:14b).

In the 12th month (Jan./Feb., 837) of the Chinese year 836, Tibetan envoys offered gifts (*Chiu T'ang shu* 196B:16a; *Ts'e-fu yüan-kuei* p.5033).

In 837, Tibetan envoys presented gold and silver vessels, jade belts, otter skins, yak tails, court garments, cotton fabrics, various drugs, horses, cattle, and camels to the T'ang court (*Chiu T'ang shu* 196B: 16a; *T'ang hui-yao* 97:15a).

In the 5th month (June/July), of 837, a Chinese mission returned from Tibet (*T'ang hui-yao* 97:15a).

In 838, the king of Tibet, Ral-pa-chen, died and was succeeded by his younger brother Dar-ma. He lacked support, and the state disintegrated (*Tzu-chih t'ung-chien* p.7983). In 839, Emperor Wen-tsung sent the Supervisor of the Household of the Heir-apparent as envoy to the Tibetans. The Tibetans, on their part, presented jade vessels, horses, and sheep to the T'ang court (*Wen-hsien t'ung-k'ao* 334:31a).

On Jan.11, 842, Tibetan envoys announced that their king Darma had died. Emperor Wu-tsung suspended the court for three days and ordered the civilian and military officials from rank 4 and up to condole with the Tibetan envoys at the Office of the Herald. He sent the Junior Inspector of the Court Architect and Concurrent Palace Asssistant Secretary to condole and sacrifice. This envoy returned on the 1st month (Feb./Mar.) of 843. Under the following chaotic conditions, Tibet dissolved into chiefdoms, and diplomatic relations with China ceased for the rest of T'ang (*Chiu T'ang shu* 18A:7a; 196B:16a; *T'ang hui-yao* 97:15a, 16a; *Tzu-chih t'ung-chien* pp.7969-7970; *Wen-hsien t'ung-k'ao* 334:31a).

In the 1st month (Feb./Mar.) of 908, Tibetan envoys to the Later Liang court offered gifts. The chief envoy and his deputy were appointed to nominal Chinese offices (*Wu-tai hui-yao* 30:2a; *Ts'e-fu yüan-kuei* p.5033; *Wen-hsien t'ung-k'ao* 335:32a).

In the 12th month (Dec./Jan., 912)[27] of the Chinese year 911, a Tibetan and a Uighur chief were received in audience at the Later Liang court. The two chiefs and their 122 attendants prostrated themselves and presented letters and regional objects. They received gold and silk (*Wu-tai hui-yao* 30:2a; *Ts'e-fu yüan-kuei* 5034).

During the reign of Emperor Ming-tsung (926-933) of Later T'ang, envoys of the Tibetan chief Sun Ch'ao brought gifts and were received in audience. Ch'ao was given the empty titles of Inspector of Liang commandery and Military Commissioner of the Army West of the [Yellow] River. Each of the envoys was presented with a tiger skin (*Chiu wu-tai shih* 138:3a; *Wen-hsien t'ung-k'ao* 335:32a). Liang was the name of the easternmost part of the Kan-su Corridor, a territory which Ch'ao and his tribe inhabited, so that he became Inspector of what was his already. The Army West of the [Yellow] River did not exist.

In the 11th month (Nov./Dec.) of 927,[28] Tibetan envoys to the Later T'ang court offered gifts. With them were four Buddhist monks who had brought two Tibetan texts. None at the Chinese court could read the Tibetan script. In the 1st month (Jan./Feb.) of 928, each envoy was appointed a general (*Wu-tai hui-yao* 30:2a; *Wen-hsien t'ung-k'ao* 335:32a).

On Jan,7, 928 Tibetans offered gifts to the Later T'ang court (*Hsin Wu-tai shih* 6:6a; *Ts'e-fu yüan-kuei* p.5034).

In the intercalary month (Sep./Oct.) of 928, Tibetans offered presents to the Later T'ang court (*Ts'e-fu yüan-kuei* p.5034).

In the 9th month (Oct./Nov.) of 928, Tibetan envoys to the Later T'ang court offered gifts. They were appointed Managers of Lances (*Wu-tai hui-yao* 30:2a; *Ts'e-fu yüan-kuei* p.5034).

In the 11th month (Dec./Jan., 929) of the Chinese year 928,[29] Tibetans offered gifts to the Later T'ang court. The chief envoy was appointed General of the Gentlemen Who Has Attached Himself to

---

[27] *Wu-tai hui-yao* has 11th month (Nov./Dec.).

[28] By *Wen-hsien t'ung-k'ao* dated 922.

[29] By *Wu-tai hui-yao* dated 12th month (Jan./Feb., 929) of the Chinese year 928.

Virtue. 18 chiefs were made Managers of Lances (*Wu-tai hui-yao* 30: 2a-2b; *Ts'e-fu yüan-kuei* p.5034).[30]

In the 9th month (Oct./Nov.) of 929, a Tibetan chief was received at the Later T'ang court. In the 10th month (Nov./Dec.), another chief came to the court. Both were appointed Managers of Lances (*Wu-tai hui-yao* 30:2b; *Ts'e-fu yüan-kuei* p.5034).

In the 4th month (May) of 930, a Tibetan chief presented two yaks to the Later T'ang (*Ts'e-fu yüan-kuei* p.5035).

On Sep.26, 930, two Tibetan chiefs and their attendants, 30 men in all, presented 80 horses and one jade lump to the Later T'ang court (*Hsin Wu-tai shih* 6:9a; *Ts'e-fu yüan-kuei* p.5035).

On Jan.5, 932, Tibetan envoys were received at the Later T'ang court (*Hsin Wu-tai shih* 6:10a).

In the 1st (Feb./Mar.) and 2nd month (Mar./Apr.) of 932, Tibetan envoys to the Later T'ang court offered gifts. In the 3rd month (Apr./May), these envoys were appointed to the nominal offices of General-in-chief, General of the Gentlemen, Chief of Attendants, and Guard of the Stairs (*Wu-tai hui-yao* 30:2b; *Ts'e-fu yüan-kuei* p.5035).

On Sep.8, 932, Tibetan envoys to the Later T'ang court were received in audience by Ming-tsung (*Chiu wu-tai shih* 43:7b; *Ts'e-fu yüan-kuei* p.5035).

In the 11th month (Nov./Dec.) of 933, Tibetan envoys to the Later T'ang court offered gifts. They were given gold and silk and one tiger skin each (*Wu-tai hui-yao* 30:3a; *Ts'e-fu yüan-kuei* p.5035).

In the 10th month (Nov./Dec.) of 939, a Tibetan chief presented gifts to the Later Chin court (*Ts'e-fu yüan-kuei* p.5035).

In 942, Tibetan envoys from the westernmost part of the Kan-su Corridor to the Later Chin court offered uncut gems, antelope horns, Persian brocade, white cotton fabrics from An-hsi in Central Asia, metallic salts, large borax, and dull jade lumps (*Chiu wu-tai shih* 138: 3a).

On Nov.12, 948, Tibetan envoys to the Later Han presented regional objects (*Chiu wu-tai shih* 101:9b).

In 952, Che-pu Chia-shih, who had succeeded Sun Ch'ao as chief, sent men to the Later Chou to sell horses in the capital (*Chiu wu-tai shih* 138:2a).

---

[30] *Chiu wu-tai shih* 138:3a records a joint Tibetan Uighur mission in 928, without giving the month. It is therefore unclear whether this joint mission was in the intercalary, 9th, or 11th month.

In the 9th month (Sep./Oct.) of 952, Tibetan chiefs were by the Later Chou court appointed Imperial Household Grandee of the Silver Seal and Blue Ribbon, Acting Master of Writing of the Ministry of Works, and Generals-in-chief (*Wu-tai hui-yao* 30:3a-3b).

In the 8th month (Sep./Oct.) of 953, Tibetan envoys to the Liao court offered gifts (*Liao shih* 6:2b; 70:6a).

In 961, the Ling-wu Tibetans in the Ning-hsia Oasis offered camels and fine horses to the Sung court. Sung presented Tibetan chiefs at the upper Wei River with brocade robes and silver belts (*Sung shih* 492:2a-2b; *Wen-hsien t'ung-k'ao* 335:32a).

In 967, a Tibetan delegation of six men offered horses to the Sung court (*Sung shih* 492:3a).

In 973, Tibetans offered gifts to the Sung court (*Sung shih* 492:3a).

In 977, various Tibetan tribes at the upper Wei River looted the Chinese (*Wen-hsien t'ung-k'ao* 335:32a).

On Oct.26, 983, Tibetan tribes offered horses to the Sung court. Emperor T'ai-tsung summoned their chiefs and presented them with silk. He remarked that the language of the Tibetans was unintelligable and their clothes strange (*Sung shih* 492:3b; *Hsü Tzu-chih t'ung-chien ch'ang-pien* p.211; *Wen-hsien t'ung-k'ao* 335:32a).

In 984, local authorities reported to the Sung court that Tibetans at the upper Wei River had presented horses and sheep. The emperor ordered that they be paid with tea and silk (*Wen-hsien t'ung-k'ao* 335: 32a).

On Mar.31, 989, Tibetans offered gifts to the Liao court (*Liao shih* 12:5a).[31]

In 994, the Tibetans of the Six Valleys in eastern Kan-su presented 1000 horses to the Sung court (*Sung shih* 492:4b).

In 995, the Tibetans of Liang offered fine horses to the Sung court. T'ai-tsung rewarded them (*Sung shih* 492:4b; *Wen-hsien t'ung-k'ao* 335: 32a).

In the 7th month (July/Aug.) of 996, the Tibetans of the Six Valleys presented fine horses to the Sung court (*Sung shih* 492:5a).

In the 11th month (Nov./Dec.) of 998, Tibetans offered regional objects and more than 2000 horses to the Sung court (*Sung shih* 492: 5a; *Wen-hsien t'ung-k'ao* 335:32a).

---

[31] *Liao shih* 70:8b dates this the 3rd month, but that month did not have the cyclical, characters *kuei-yu*.

In 1000, Tibetans offered 5000 horses to the Sung court. Emperor Chen-tsung ordered that they be paid well for them, and in addition presented them with tea and silk (*Wen-hsien t'ung-k'ao* 335:32a-32b).

In the 11th month (Dec./Jan., 1003) of the Chinese year 1002, Tibetans presented 5000 horses to the Sung court. They were given 100 items of textiles and 100 catties of tea (*Sung shih* 492:6b).

In 1003, Tibetans presented gifts and a letter to the Sung court (*Sung shih* 492:6b; *Wen-hsien t'ung-k'ao* 335:32b).

In the 8th month (Aug./Sep.) of 1003, Tibetans presented fine horses to the Sung court (*Sung shih* 492:7a; *Wen-hsien t'ung-k'ao* 335:32b).

In 1004,[32] Tibetans presented fine horses to the Sung court. They were given objects covered with gold foil and silk (*Sung shih* 492:7b; *Wen-hsien t'ung-k'ao* 335:32b).

In 1005, Tibetans offered gifts to the Sung court (*Sung shih* 492: 8b).

In 1006, two different tribes of Tibetans offered presents to the Sung court (*Wen-hsien t'ung-k'ao* 335:32b).

In 1007, Tibetans envoys were received at the Sung court. They were given bells, tea, drugs, garments, and golden belts (*Sung shih* 492: 9b-10a; *Wen-hsien t'ung-k'ao* 335:32b).

On Mar.25, 1011, a Tibetan chief presented gifts to the Sung court. He was given a purple robe (*Sung shih* 8:1b; 492:10a).

In 1012, Tibetans offered gifts to the Sung court. During the same year, the chief of the Tibetan Lung tribe sent envoys to present horses (*Sung shih* 492:10a).

On June 12, 1018, a Tibetan king informed the Liao court that he wished to pay tribute to i.e. trade with it, and proposed to avail himself of a route through the Hsia State. This was accepted (*Liao shih* 16:1b).

In the 2nd month (Mar./Apr.) of 1051, Tibetan envoys were received at the Liao court (*Liao shih* 70:19a).

In the 6th month (July/Aug.) of 1054, Tibetan envoys to the Liao court offered gifts (*Liao shih* 70:19b).

On July 21, 1055, Tibetans offered gifts to the Liao court (*Liao shih* 20:8b).

---

[32] Correcting *ching-te* 6th year to 1st year (1004). That reign title had no 6th year, in addition to which this entry is followed by one for 1005.

On July 2, 1069, Tibetan envoys to the Liao court offered gifts (*Liao shih* 22:6a; 70:20a).

On July 25, 1071, Tibetan envoys to the Liao court offered gifts (*Liao shih* 22:7b; 70:20b).

On Aug.9, 1075, Tibetans offered gifts to the Liao court (*Liao shih* 23:3b; 70:21a).

On Nov.14, 1103, Tibetan envoys to the Liao court offered gifts (*Liao shih* 27:3a; 70:26a).

On July 15, 1104, Tibetans offered gifts to the Liao court (*Liao shih* 27.3b; 70:26a).

The Tibetan culture was never heavily influenced by the Chinese, as were those of Japan, the Korean states, and Po-hai. On the contrary, Tibet was a truly alien country to the Chinese. Ssu-ma Kuang claims that the Princess of Wen-ch'eng hated the custom of the Tibetans of smearing their faces red and persuaded her husband, Srong-btsan-sgam-po, to prohibit this. It is also claimed that the princess changed the suspicious and cruel attitude of the Tibetans and aranged for the sons and younger brothers of chiefs to study at the Academy in Ch'ang-an and learn the *Book of Odes* and *Book of Documents* (*Tzu-chih t'ung-chien* pp.6164-6165). The same text states that T'ai-tsung had increased the student lodgings at the Academy to 12,000 units, and that among the students were sons and younger brothers of Tibetan chiefs (*Tzu-chih t'ung-chien* p.6153). This account overlooks the fact that Srong-btsan-sgam-po also had a Nepalese wife, and that the Indian influence on Tibet was much greater than the Chinese.

In spite of allegations by the dynastic historians that the Tibetans offered "tribute" and presented "memorials", they and their kings were not only independent but frequently at war with China. Chinese claims of suzerainity over Tibet are therefore absurd. When a Chinese envoy in 729 arrived in Tibet for a covenant, he supposedly ordered the king to kowtow and declare himself a subject (*Chiu T'ang shu* 196A: 8b). This preposterous lie was obviously concocted in the self-serving report of the Chinese envoy and then, via the archives, found its way into the *Chiu T'ang shu*.

The Chinese did what they could to neutralize Tibet as a threat. They conferred titles on Srong-btsan-sgam-po and perhaps also on his successors. They twice married princesses to its kings, the Princess of Wen-ch'eng in 641 and the Princess of Chin-ch'eng in 710. These marriages were diplomatic coups for the Tibetans but brought no lasting benefits to the Chinese. In 705, the T'ang emperors suspended the court for one day and in 804 and 842 for three days after the deaths of Tibetan kings. In 650, 679, 755, 804, 816, and 842, they sent envoys to condole and sacrifice. In 680, they condoled and sacrificed after the death of the Princess of Wen-ch'eng. In 740, they suspended the court for three days after the death of the Princess of Chin-ch'eng. These ceremonies were probably regular features, although they are not recorded after the death of every king.

In spite of all these efforts, relations between China and Tibet were bad. This is proved by the fact that covenants had to be concluded over and over, in 726, 729, 758, 765, 783, abortively in 787, and in 821. Only the last of these was successful. All others were soon broken, mostly by the Tibetans.

It is an interesting feature that Tibetan kings "requested peace" in 729, thrice in 730, in 731, and in 761, when the two countries were technically at peace already. The reason can perhaps be sought in the form of Tibetan government. The kings did not control all the tribes, and some of them looted Chinese territories on their own initiative. This created a fluid situation, in which some kings attempted to restore peace in the face of tribal hostility, and in which the Chinese were frustrated by the lack of authoritative negotiating partners.

In their relations to the Tibetans, the Chinese were therefore throughout at a disadvantage. They took recourse to their old habit of fostering rivals in the enemy camp, which led to the titles conferred on Lun Tsan-p'o in 699 as a possible counterweight to the king. Nothing came of it. As a rule, the Tibetans had the initiative, and until 821 there always was a political distance between the two countries. The Chinese did not even bother to recognize the Tibetan kings, and no posthumous titles were conferred on any of them.

It is clear from the above that the Tibetan missions to the T'ang courts had substantial matters to discuss, and that they arrived both in peace and war. Covenants were often on the agenda, as was the drawing of the border, congratulations and condolences. But, as always, trade formed part of the missions, and after 821 almost exclusively so.

According to *Chiu T'ang shu* 196A:6a, the Tibetans sent annual missions after 707. Those recorded are three for 709, two for 710, three for 712, two for 713, one for 714, and one for 716. According to *T'ang hui-yao* 97:6a, the Tibetans sent eight missions from 717-722. Six are recorded. According to *T'ang hui-yao* 97:7a, the Tibetans congratulated on the New Year's Day each year from 734. Such congratulations are recorded for 734, 735, and 736. According to *T'ang hui-yao* 97:7a, the Tibetans sent seven missions from 766 to 775. Eight are recorded. According to *Chiu T'ang shu* 196B:13a, the Tibetans sent envoys from 811 to 815 without interruption. The recorded missions are one for 812 and one for 815. According to *Wen-hsien t'ung-k'ao* 334:31a, the Tibetans twice sent envoys from 827 to 835. Four missions are actually recorded. According to *Chiu T'ang shu* 196B:16a, the Tibetans sent envoys without interruption from 831 to 834. The recorded missions are for 831, 832, and 833. According to *Wen-hsien t'ung-k'ao* 334:31a, the Tibetans sent envoys each fifth year after 835. The recorded missions are for 836, 837, 839, and 842. According to *Wen-hsien t'ung-k'ao* 335:33a, Tibetan envoys arrived each year or each second year after 1016. The only further missions to the Sung are recorded for 1077, 1086, 1088, 1094. The statistics are therefore fairly complete, except for the Sung in the 11th century.

The Tibetans preferred the seasons of winter and spring for the arrival of their missions in Ch'ang-an, which means that they departed from their homeland in the fall and returned in the spring and summer, thus avoiding the harsh winters.

This is the distribution by 20-year periods of the 166 recorded Tibetan missions to T'ang, Later Liang, Later T'ang, Later Chin, Later Han, Later Chou, and Sung:

647- 666:	9
667- 686:	3
687- 706:	6
707- 726:	22
727- 746:	17
747- 766:	8
767- 786:	10
787- 806:	11
807- 826:	20
827- 846:	11
847- 866:	0
867- 886:	0
887- 906:	0
907- 926:	2
927- 946:	16
947- 966:	3
967- 986:	3

987-1000: 12
1007-1026: 5

Missions were most frequent from 707 to 846, with 747 to 766 as the lowest point. This was the time of An Lu-shan's rebellion and its aftermath and also of the deepest Tibetan inroads into China. Then followed the period of chaos in Tibet, with, however, increased tribal missions to the Five Dynasties and early Sung. The statistics for the 11th century may be incomplete. In addition, 12 missions from the Tibetans to the Liao are recorded for 953 to 1104.

The specified goods brought by the Tibetan missions to China fall into the following categories:

Animals and Animal Products

Horses

654: 100 wild horses.
703: 1000 horses.
805: horses.
817: 10 horses.
822: 60 horses.
827: horses.
836: horses.
837: horses.
839: horses.
930: 80 horses.
961: fine horses
967: horses.
983: horses.
984: horses.
994: 1000 horses.
995: fine horses.
998: 2000 horses.
1002: 5000 horses.
1003: fine horses.
1004: fine horses.
1012: horses.

Asses

654: large asses.

Camels

827-835: camels.
837: camels.
961: camels.

Cattle

805: cattle.
837: cattle.

Sheep

822: 200 sheep.
823: 600 sheep.
827-835: sheep.
839: sheep.
984: sheep.

Yaks

817: 1 yak.
824: yaks.
930: 2 yaks.

Furs

827-835: otter skins.
837: otter skins.

Horns

942: antelope horns.

Other

827-835: yak tails.
837: yak tails.

Aromatics

837: various drugs.

Minerals and Metals

635: gold.
641: 5000 ounces of gold.
703: 2000 ounces of gold.
705: 2000 ounces of gold.
805: gold, silver.
930: one jade lump.
942: metalic salts and large borax, dull jade lumps.

Manufactured Objects

Of metal

638: 1000 catties of vessels of real gold.
645: one 7 feet high vessel of real gold.
649: 3000 items of real gold.
657: one town made of gold, with images of a lion, a camel, a horse, a ram etc., each with a rider.
736: gold and silver vessels of rare shapes.
817: 10 golden vessels.
822: silver vessels.
824: a rhinoceros, bull, sheep, and deer made of silver.
827: gold and silver vessels.
837: gold and silver vessels.
Undated: rhinoceroses and deer of gold and silver.

Of jade

817: 2 jade belts.
822: jade belts.
827: jade belts
837: jade belts.
839: jade vessels.

Other

641: 100 items of valuables.
727: Several 100 valuable vessels.

Textiles

Cottons

837: cotton fabrics.
942: white cotton fabrics from An-hsi.

Silks

805: silk.
942: Persian brocade.

Garments:

837: court garments.

Jewels

942: uncut gems.

It can be seen that the majority of these goods came from Tibet, that horses were a favourite item of sale, and that the Tibetans were fine gold and silversmiths. But some of the items reached China in transit, such as Persian brocade and cotton fabrics from An-hsi.

The Chinese paid with silks, garments, belts, gold, vessels, drugs, tiger skins, and, beginning with Sung, tea.

In addition to the state founded by Srong- btsan-sgam-po, the Chinese sources mention six[33] other Tibetan principalities which existed for a while and had relations with China:

[33] Five are discussed here, the sixth in the chapter on Ch'ing-hai.

THE EASTERN KINGDOM OF WOMEN

Albert Herrmann in his *Atlas of China*, p.39, places this kingom at the upper Mekong River. According to *Chiu T'ang shu* 197:5a, it was commonly ruled by a woman and was called "Eastern" to distinguish it from the Kingdom of Women in the west.

In 625 or early 626, envoys from the queen arrived for the first time at the T'ang court and offered regional objects. Emperor Kao-tsu sent them back with rich presents. Travelling through Kan-su, they were looted by Turks and returned to the court. T'ai-tsung had meanwhile ascended the throne on Sep.3 and had them escorted back to their state with a letter stamped with the imperial seal (*Chiu T'ang shu* 197: 5b-6a; 5a; *Wen-hsien t'ung-k'ao* 339:55a).

In 630, envoys from the same queen came to the court. T'ai-tsung presented her with a letter stamped with the imperial seal (*Wen-hsien t'ung-k'ao* 339:55a).

In the 1st month (Feb./Mar.) of 633, a female envoy together with a son of the ruler arrived at the court (*T'ang hui-yao* 99:9b).

In 656 or soon thereafter, another mission arrived (*Wen-hsien t'ung-k'ao* 339:55a).

In 686, a high envoy from the ruler was received at the T'ang court and supposedly requested an official title. That is possible, since such titles carried some prestige. The Empress Wu made the ruler a General of the Jade Bell Guards and presented silk garments made in barbarian stile (*Chiu T'ang shu* 197:6a).

In 692, the ruler personally came to the court (*Chiu T'ang shu* 197: 6a).

In 696, the ruler sent envoys to the court (*T'ang hui-yao* 99:9b-10a).

In the 12th month (Jan./Feb., 742) of the Chinese year 741, a son of the ruler presented regional objects *(Chiu T'ang shu* 197:6a). In the 5th month (June/July) of 742, Emperor Hsüan-tsung ordered the Grand Councilors and other high officials to give a banquet for the prince. He entitled the ruler Queen Who Has Attached Herself to Prosperity and General-in-chief of the Guards of the Golden Mace of the Left, and presented the prince with 80 bolts of silk (*Chiu T'ang shu* 197:6a;*T'ang hui-yao* 99:10a; *Wen-hsien t'ung-k'ao* 339:55a).

FU

Placed by Herrmann, *Atlas of China*, p.35, north of the Brahmaputra in southern Tibet.

In 608, eight envoys of the king of Fu were received at the Sui court (*Sui shu* 83:17a).

In 609, a mission of 60 men, led by a younger brother of the king of Fu, was received at the Sui court. Because the fine horses they had intended to present had been lost through the hardships of travel, envoys proposed the building of a road. This was rejected by Emperor Yang (*Sui shu* 83:17a).

GREATER YANG-T'UNG

There also existed a Lesser Yang-t'ung, but this has no entries in its own right in the dynastic histories and encyclopaedias. According to Herrmann, *Atlas of China*, p.39, Yang-t'ung was situated in central Tibet, north of the Transhimalayas.

In the 12th month (Dec./Jan., 632) of the Chinese year 631, envoys from Greater Yang-t'ung brought gifts to the T'ang court (*T'ang hui-yao* 99:13b).

In the 11th month (Dec./Jan., 642) of the Chinese year 641, envoys from Greater Yang-t'ung offered regional objects (*T'ung-tien* 190:9b; *Ts'e-fu yüan-kuei* p.5024; *Wen-hsien t'ung-k'ao* 335:34a).

In the 1st month (Feb./Mar.) of 647, Yang-t'ung presented regional objects (*Chiu T'ang shu* 3:11a; *Ts'e-fu yüan-kuei* p.5024).

Not later than 649, Greater Yang-t'ung was destroyed by Srong-btsan-sgam-po (*T'ang hui-yao* 99:13b-14a).

SU-P'I

The Su-p'i were a tribe of the western Tibetans (Hsi-ch'iang) (*Wen-hsien t'ung-k'ao* 335:35a).

In 632, Su-p'i envoys offered gifts to the T'ang court. Subsequently, the territory was annexed by Srong-btsan-sgam-po (*Wen-hsien t'ung-k'ao* 335:35a).

THE KINGDOM OF WOMEN

Herrmann, *Atlas of China*, pp. 34-35, places this kingom north of the upper course of the Indus in Tibet. *Wen-hsien t'ung k'ao* 339:55b calls it the Western Kingdom of Women. It was ruled by queens (*Sui shu* 83:10a; *T'ung-tien* 193:22a).

Between 590 and 600, envoys from the Kingdom of Women to the Sui court offered presents (*T'ung-tien* 193:22a).

Between 605 and 617, envoys from the Kingdom of Women were received at the T'ang court and offered gifts (*Pei shih* 96:23b).

In 634, envoys from the Kingdom of Women offered gifts (*Chiu T'ang shu* 3:3b; *Wen-hsien t'ung-k'ao* 339:55b).

On Jan.26, 643, the New Year's Day, the Kingdom of Women presented regional objects (*Ts'e-fu yüan-kuei* p.5024).

In the 1st month (February) of 656, probably on the New Year's Day on Feb.1, a female envoy from the Kingdom of Women and three sons of its ruler, were received at the T'ang court (*Ts'e-fu yüan-kuei* p.5025).

In the late 680's,[34] envoys from the Kingdom of Women offered presents (*Ts'e-fu yüan-kuei* p.5026).

In the 12th month (Jan./Feb., 742) of the Chinese year 741, a son of the ruler of the Kingdom of Women was received at the T'ang court (*Chiu T'ang shu* 9:4a).

In the 12th month (January, 797) of the Chinese year 796, envoys from the Kingdom of Women offered gifts (*Chiu T'ang shu* 13:13b; *Ts'e-fu yüan-kuei* p.5032).

NAN-CHAO

The ruling tribe of the Nan-chao State claimed descent from the Ai-lao (*Chiu T''ang shu* 197:6b). The Ai-lao appeared for the first time in Chinese history during Later Han times. Large numbers of them submitted in A.D.51 and 69. During the latter year, Emperor Ming created two new prefectures and the Yung-ch'ang commandery in what now is western Yün-nan to settle them. These aboriginals, and

---

[34] The text says *ch'ui-kung* 9th year, which date did not exist.

others who followed them, kept their tribal organisations with a high degree of autonomy, and thereby formed an unstable and unabsorbed element within the Chinese border. It ensured that Yün-nan remained predominantly aboriginal, and the emergence of Nan-chao in the 7th century as an independent state was the logical conclusion.[35]

To assign a date to the foundation of Nan-chao is arbitrary. One could chose 629, when the chief Hsi-nu-lo began his rule or 730 when P'i-lo-ko united the tribes. Little is known about the early history of the tribes and their rulers. In 639, envoys from the K'un-ming tribe offered gifts to the T'ang court (*Chiu T'ang shu* 3:6b). During the reign of Kao-tsung (650-683), another mission arrived, probably sent by Hsi-nu-lo (*Chiu T'ang shu* 197:7a).

Hsi-nu-lo was succeeded by his son Lo-sheng,[36] who visited Ch'ang-an in the reign of the Empress Wu (684-704). He was presented with a brocade robe and a golden belt and then returned. Lo-sheng was succeeded by his son Sheng-lo-p'i, and the latter by his son P'i-lo-ko (*Chiu T'ang shu* 197:7a). P'i-lo-ko is the first Nan-chao ruler who is not a shadowy figure.

After the unification of the tribes in 730, P'i-li-ko in 738 called on Hsüan-tsung in Ch'ang-an. The emperor acknowledged his status by appointing him as Specially Advanced and duke of the Yüeh State. He also confered on him the name of Kuei-yi (Attached to Righteousness).[37] Subsequently, Hsüan-tsung recognized him as king of Yün-nan and presented him with a brocade robe and golden belt (*Chiu T'ang shu* 197:7a; *Wen-hsien t'ung k'ao* 329:70b).

In 739, P'i-lo-ko moved his capital to Ta-ho, just south of the present Ta-li in Yün-nan (*Chiu T'ang shu* 197:7a; *Wen-hsien t'ung-k'ao* 329:70b).

In 745, P'i-lo-ko sent his grandson Feng-chia-yi to Ch'ang-an, where he entered the imperial guards and received the nominal title of Herald. He returned with rich presents (*Chiu T'ang shu* 197:7a; *Wen-hsien t'ung-k'ao* 329:70b).

In 748, P'i-lo-ko died and was succeeded by his son Ko-lo-feng. Hsüan-tsung recognized him as king of Yün-nan and conferred on his son Feng-chia-yi the nominal title of Inspector of Kua commandery

[35] See my *Restoration*, vol.III, pp.77-78, 85.
[36] Or Lo-sheng-p'i.
[37] The sources henceforth refer to him by that name.

in Kan-su (*Chiu T'ang shu* 197:7a; *Wen-hsien t'ung-k'ao* 329:70b).

In 750, Nan-chao and China had their first military encounter. The Grand Administrator of Yün-nan commandery, southeast of Nan-chao, abused and insulted Ko-lo-feng, whereupon the latter attacked and killed him (*Chiu T'ang shu* 197:7a-7b).

In 751, Hsüan-tsung ordered the Military Commissioner of Chien-nan, whose territory adjoined Nan-chao north of the Yangtze, to lead troops against Ko-lo-feng. Ko-lo-feng sent envoys to offer peace and promised the return of the Chinese prisoners he had taken. He also pointed out that Yün-nan did not belong to the T'ang, and that great bodies of Tibetan troops were standing at his northern border. Unless the Chinese withdrew their armies, he would be forced to ally himself with Tibet. This was rejected by Hsüan-tsung, and the envoys were detained. The war continued and turned into a military and diplomatic disaster for the Chinese. Their armies were utterly defeated, and Ko-lo-feng allied himself with the Tibetans. These conferred on him the Tibetan name for king, also called him the Eastern Emperor, and presented him with a golden seal. A second Chinese attack in 753 ended in another great defeat (*Chiu T'ang shu* 197:7b; *Wen-hsien t'ung-k'ao* 329:70b).

When An Lu-shan rose in 755, Ko-lo-feng took advantage of the opportunity and conquered Sui commandery, situated northwest of Nan-chao east of the upper course of the Yangtze. He there captured the Prefect of Hsi-lu,[38] Cheng Hui, who held the degree of Understanding the Classics. Ko-lo-feng came to respect him highly and made him the tutor of his son Feng-chia-yi (*Chiu T'ang shu* 197:7b-8a; *Wen-hsien t'ung-k'ao* 329:71a).

Ko-lo-feng died in 778 and, since his son Feng-chia-yi had preceded him, was succeeded by the latter's son Yi-mou-hsün. Cheng Hui was kept at the court and ordered to tutor the sons of Yi-mou-hsün (*Chiu T'ang shu* 197:7b; *Wen-hsien t'ung-k'ao* 329:71a).

Yi-mou-hsün greatly expanded his state to comprise all what now is Yün-nan province and used from 787 Ta-li as his capital.

Displeased with his Tibetan alliance and supposedly influenced by Cheng Hui, Yi-mou-hsün decided to seek a reprochement with China. He secretly sent three envoys to Ch'ang-an, where Te-tsung received

---

[38] Situated 25 *li* W of the present Hsi-ch'ang *hsien*, Ssu-ch'uan.

them in audience in the 4th month (May/June) of 788. The emperor was obviously pleased with this diplomatic overture and gave a banquet for the envoys on June 16. They received enfeoffments and rich presents (*Chiu T'ang shu* 197:8a; *Tzu-chih t'ung-chien* p.7513).

In 791, Te-tsung sent a secret envoy of his own to Yi-mou-hsün. The Tibetans learned about this, became suspicious, and demanded hostages from Nan-chao. There is no record that Yi-mou-hsün complied (*Chiu T'ang shu* 197:8a).

In 793, Yi-mou-hsün sent envoys by three different routes to the T'ang court, via Ssu-ch'uan, Kuei-chou, and Annam. All arrived in Ch'ang-an and presented unwrought gold and cinnabar. Te-tsung ordered Ts'ui Tso-chih to go as his envoy to Nan-chao and review the situation (*Chiu T'ang shu* 197:8a; *Tzu-chih t'ung-chien* p.7547).

At the end of 793,[39] Ts'ui Tso-chih reached the court of Yi-mou-hsün, where he was received in secrecy by night. In the 1st month (Feb./Mar.) of 794, a covenant was concluded, presumably also in secrecy, in a spirit temple on a nearby mountain, in which Nan-chao was represented by a son of Yi-mou-hsün and a Chancellor. Yi-mou-hsün relinquished the title of emperor, and the T'ang agreed to resume the name of Nan-chao instead of Yün-nan. The agreement was carved on gold and presented to the Chinese envoy (*Chiu T'ang shu* 197:8b; *Tzu-chih t'ung-chien* p. 7552).

The Tibetans had been defeated by the Uighurs in 791 and had requested military assistance from their then ally Nan-chao. This was used as a ruse by Yi-mou-hsün in 794. He informed the Tibetans that he only could contribute 3000 men, but at their insistance raised the number to 5000. With these 5000 men he made a suprise attack on the Tibetans and defeated them. Subsequently, he sent an envoy to the T'ang court to announce this victory (*Chiu T'ang shu* 197:8b-9a; *Wen-hsien t'ung-k'ao* 329:71a).

In the 6th month (July) of 794,[40] a younger brother of Yi-mou-hsün and others presented at the T'ang court a geographical map, regional objects, swords, and eight Tibetan seals, including the golden one of 751. All envoys received nominal Chinese offices, each in accordance

[39] According to *Tzu-chih t'ung-chien*, Ts'ui Tso-shih reached the capital of Nan-chao in the 1st month (Feb./Mar.) of 794.

[40] *T'ang hui-yao* 99:5b dates this mission 9th month (Sep./Oct.) which in the sequence of events cannot be right.

with his rank[41] (*Chiu T'ang shu* 197:9a; *Ts'e-fu yüan-kuei* p.5032; *Tzu-chih t'ung-chien* p.7561; *Wen-hsien t'ung-k'ao* 329:71a).

On July 13, 794,[42] Te-tsung dispatched the Gentleman-of-the-Palace Yüan Tzu to recognize Yi-mou-hsün as king of Nan-chao. He presented him with a golden seal engraved with silver, inscribed "Seal of Nan-chao, invested during *chen-yüan*".[43] The king gave a banquet, during which he showed the envoy two silver plates which had been presented by Emperor Hsüan-tsung (r.712-756). He also pointed at an old flutist and a singing girl and said that of the musicians from Kucha, whom Hsüan-tsung had presented, only these two were still alive (*Chiu T'ang shu* 197:9a; *Tzu-chih t'ung-chien* pp.7561-7562; *Wen-hsien t'ung-k'ao* 329:71a).

When the Chinese envoy returned to Ch'ang-an, Yi-mou-hsün attached a Chancellor to the mission, who in the 3rd month (Mar./Apr.) of 795 presented 100 Tibetan prisoners of war and regional objects to the T'ang court. He was appointed Supervisor of the Household of the Heir-apparent and Concurrent Palace Assistant Secretary and was given letters to Yi-mou-hsün, his heir, and others. A younger brother of Yi-mou-hsün, who in the previous year had led a mission to Ch'ang-an, started back to Nan-chao in 795, probably together with the Chancellor. He died en route. Te-tsung posthumously entitled him Regular Cavalier Attendant of the Right (*Chiu T'ang shu* 197:9a-9b; *Wen-hsien t'ung-k'ao* 329:71a).

In the 9th month (Oct./Nov.) of 795, envoys from Nan-chao presented 60 horses (*Chiu T'ang shu* 197:9b; *Ts'e-fu yüan-kuei* p.5032).

In the 12th month (January 797) of the Chinese year 796, envoys from Nan-chao offered gifts (*Chiu T'ang shu* 13:13b; *Ts'e-fu yüan-kuei* p.5032).

On Feb.3, 799, a General-in-chief sent by Yi-mou-hsün arrived at the T'ang court to congratulate on the New Year's Day of Feb.10 (*Chiu T'ang shu* 13:15b; 197:9b; *Ts'e-fu yüan-kuei* p.5032).

In the 1st month (Jan./Feb.) of 800, musicians and dancers presented by Nan-chao performed a sacred musical dance play for Te-tsung in front of the Hall of Unicorn Virtue (*Chiu T'ang shu* 13:17b).

---

[41] According to *Tzu-chih t'ung-chien* and *Wen-hsien t'ung-k'ao*, the T'ang resumed the name of Nan-chao at this occasion.

[42] Ssu-ma Kuang corrects *Chiu T'ang shu* and *Hsin T'ang shu* on the basis of the *Shih-lu*.

[43] This was the current reign title in T'ang.

In the 1st month (Feb./Mar.) of 802, Nan-chao envoys were received in audience at the T'ang court (*Ts'e-fu yüan-kuei* p.5032).

On Jan.27, 803, the New Year's Day, Te-tsung received the congratulations of a Nan-chao mission. The chief envoy was made a Probationary Junior Grand Coachman (*Chiu T'ang shu* 107:9b).

In the 12th month (Jan./Feb., 805) of the Chinese year 804, Nan-chao envoys offered gifts (*Chiu T'ang shu* 13:21b; 197:9b; *Ts'e-fu yüan-kuei* p.5032).

In 805, a Nan-chao envoy [sacrificed] at the tomb of Te-tsung[44] (*T'ang hui-yao* 99:6a).

In the 8th (Sep./Oct.) and 12th month (Jan./Feb., 807) of the Chinese year 806, Nan-chao envoys offered presents (*Ts'e-fu yüan-kuei* p.5032).

In the 2nd month (Mar./Apr.) of 807, Nan-chao envoys offered gifts. In the 8th month (Sep./Oct.), a new mission arrived at the T'ang court, whose head was appointed Probationary Palace Inspector. In the 12th month (January, 808) of the Chinese year 807, Nan-chao envoys arrived at the T'ang court to congratulate [on the New Year's Day of Jan.31, 808] (*Chiu T'ang shu* 14:13a; 197:9b; *T'ang hui-yao* 99: 6a; *Ts'e-fu yüan-kuei* p.5032).

In 808, Yi-mou-hsün died, whereupon Emperor Hsien-tsung on Jan.6, 809,[45] suspended the court for three days. On Jan.8,[46] the emperor ordered a Grandee Remonstrant and Consultant and Concurrent Palace Assistant Secretary to condole and sacrifice in Nan-chao and to recognize Yi-mou-hsün's son Hsün-ko-ch'üan as king. But it was then decided that the envoy's rank was too low, and he was in the 1st month (Jan./Feb.) of 809 replaced by the Junior Grand Master of Ceremonies (*Chiu T'ang shu* 14:13b; 197:9b; *T'ang hui-yao* 99:6; *Tzu-chih t'ung-chien* p.7656; *Wen-hsien t'ung-k'ao* 329:71a).

In the 12th month (Jan./Feb., 810) of the Chinese year 809, Nan-chao envoys offered gifts. It may have been this embasasy which informed the T'ang court that Hsün-ko-ch'üan had died that year and been succeeded by his son Ch'üan-lung-sheng (*Ts'e-fu yüan-kuei* p.5032; *Tzu-chih t'ung-chien* p.7668; *Wen-hsien t'ung-k'ao* 329:71b).

---

[44] He had died on Feb.25.

[45] 806, 12th month, *chia-tzu*. *T'ang-hui-yao* 99:6a has 11th month, but the cyclical characters *chia-tzu* did not occur in that month.

[46] Emending the 11th month of *T'ang-hui-yao* 99:6a to 12th month, in accordance with the preceding note.

In the 10th month (Nov./Dec.) of 812,[47] Nan-chao envoys offered presents (*Chiu T'ang shu* 197:9b).

In the 11th month(Dec./Jan., 816) of the Chinese year 815, 29 Nan-chao envoys offered gifts (*Chiu T'ang shu*15:9b; *T'ang hui-yao* 99: 6b; *Ts'e-fu yüan-kuei* p.5033).

On May 7, 816, Hsien-tsung dispatched a Military Commissioner to Nan-chao to announce the death of his mother, the Empress Dowager (widow of Shun-tsung), on Apr.5 (*Chiu T'ang shu* 15:10a).

In 816, Ch'üan-lung-sheng was murdered and succeeded by his younger brother Ch'üan-li.[48] Nan-chao envoys requested recognition of their new king. In the 5th month (May/June), Hsien-tsung suspended the court for three days. He sent the Junior Inspector of the Privy Treasurer with a Grandee Admonisher of the Left as his deputy to condole and sacrifice and to recognize Ch'üan-li (*Chiu T'ang shu* 197: 9b; *Wen-hsien t'ung-k'ao* 329:71b).

In the 12th month (Dec./Jan.817) of the Chinese year 816, Nan-chao envoys offered gifts (*Ts'e-fu yüan-kuei* p.5033).

In the 12th month (Jan./Feb., 818) of the Chinese year 817, Nan-chao envoys offered presents (*Ts'e-fu yüan-kuei* p.5033).

In the 4th month (May/June) of 818, Nan-chao envoys presented slaves and sheep (*Chiu T'ang shu* 15:16a; *T'ang hui-yao* 99:6b).

In the 8th month (Sep./Oct.) of 818, the T'ang court ordered that missions from Nan-chao were not to exceed 30 envoys. No more than 5 envoys were to be appointed to nominal offices (*T'ang hui-yao* 97:12b).

In 820, Nan-chao envoys offered gifts (*Ts'e-fu yüan-kuei* p.5033).

In 823, the king of Nan-chao was presented with a Chinese seal (*Wen-hsien t'ung-k'ao* 329:71b).

In the 7th month (Aug./Sep.) of 823, Nan-chao envoys informed the T'ang court that Ch'üan-li had died and had been succeeded by his younger brother Feng-yu. Emperor Mu-tsung sent the Junior Governor of the Capital to recognize Feng-yu (*Ts'e-fu yüan-kuei* p.5033; *Tzu-chih t'ung-chien* p. 7827; *Wen-hsien t'ung-k'ao* 329:71b).

In the 9th month (Oct./Nov.) of 823, envoys of the king of Nan-chao were received at the T'ang court (*Ts'e-fu yüan-kuei* p.5033).[49]

---

47 *T'ang hui-yao* 99:6b dates this mission 12th month (Jan./Feb., 813) of the Chinese year 812.

48 Or Ch'üan-li-sheng.

49 The text gives the name of the king as Ch'üan-li. Ssu-ma Kuang rejects this

In the 1st month of (Feb./Mar.) of 826 and in 827, Nan-chao envoys offered gifts (*Chiu T'ang shu* 197:9b; *Ts'e-fu yüan-kuei* p.5033).

In 829, war broke out between Nan-chao and T'ang. In the 11th month (December), the Nan-chao forces defeated a Chinese army and subsequently raided the Min and Fou River valleys of Ssu-ch'uan. In the 1st month (Jan./Feb.) of 830, they looted Ch'eng-tu. In the same month, the king of Nan-chao offered peace, and normal relations were restored (*Chiu T'ang shu* 197:9b-10a; *Tzu-chih t'ung-chien* p.7869; *Wen-hsien t'ung-k'ao* 329:71b).

In the 12th month (Dec./Jan., 831) of the Chinese year 830, and in the 11th month (Dec./Jan., 832) of the Chinese year 831, Nan-chao envoys offered regional objects (*Chiu T'ang shu* 197:10a; *Ts'e-fu yüan-kuei* p.5033).[50]

In 834, the 12th month (Jan./Feb., 837) of the Chinese year 836, and in the 12th month (January, 838) of the Chinese year 837, Nan-chao envoys offered presents (*Chiu T'ang shu* 18A:16b; 107:10a; *Ts'e-fu yüan-kuei* p.5033).

On Jan.19, 839, the New Year's Day, Emperor Wen-tsung received congratulations from a Nan-chao mission of 37 men. He appointed the envoys to nominal offices and presented them with gold, silk, silver vessels, gold and silver belts, and garments, to each in accordance with his rank (*T'ang hui-yao* 99:7a).

In the intercalary month (Feb./Mar.) of 839, Nan-chao envoys offered presents (*Chiu T'ang shu* 197:10a; *Ts'e-fu yüan-kuei* p.5033).

In the 12th month (Dec./Jan., 841) of the Chinese year 840, Wen-tsung received a Nan-chao mission of 16 men in audience (*Chiu T'ang shu* 197:10a; *T'ang hui-yao* 99:7a; *Ts'e-fu yüan-kuei* p.5033).

In the 1st month (Feb./Mar.) of 842, Emperor Wu-tsung received a Nan-chao mission of 25 men in audience (*Chiu T'ang shu* 197:10a; *T'ang hui-yao* 99:7a-7b).

On Feb.16, 846, Nan-chao envoys offered gifts (*Chiu T'ang shu* 18A: 16b; *Ts'e-fu yüan-kuei* p.5033).

In the 2nd month (March) of 854, Nan-chao envoys offered a rhi-

---

in his *K'ao-yi* and points out that the error has arisen from the *Shih-lu* (*Tzu-chih t'ung-chien* p.7827). The mission was sent by Feng-yu. It was probably the same as the one recorded by *Wen-hsien t'ung-k'ao* 329:71b for 823 in which Feng-yu thanked the T'ang for the recognition.

[50] For Mar.16, 833, *Chiu T'ang shu* 17B:9a mentions the presence of envoys from K'un-ming in the capital. These were probably not sent by the king of Nan-chao.

noceros to the T'ang court. It was rejected (*T'ang hui-yao* 99:7b).

In 859, T'ang envoys to Nan-chao announced that Emperor Hsüan-tsung had died on Sep.7. At this time, the king of Nan-chao, Feng-yu, also died and was succeeded by Ch'iu-lung. He resented the fact that the T'ang court had not condoled on the death of his predecessor, adopted the title of emperor, and called his state Ta-li (Great Propriety).[51] He discontinued the missions to the T'ang, and war broke out (*Wen-hsien t'ung-k'ao* 329:71b).

In 869, an envoy from Nan-chao set out to give thanks for the release of prisoners of war. He never reached Ch'ang-an but was killed en route by a Military Commissioner. Although the court dismissed the culprit, the war continued. In the 11th month (Dec./Jan., 870) of the Chinese year 869, Nan-chao forces looted western Ssu-ch'uan. In the 12th month (Jan./Feb., 870) of the same Chinese year 869, a mission of ten men from Nan-chao to the T'ang court sought peace in vain. Envoys from the T'ang to Ch'iu-lung were equally unsuccessful (*T'ang hui-yao* 99:7b-8a; *Tzu-chih t'ung-chien* p.8150; *Wen-hsien t'ung-k'ao* 329:71b).

In the 12th month (Jan./Feb., 875) of the Chinese year 874, Nan-chao again looted western Ssu-ch'uan (*T'ang-hui-yao* 99:8a).

In the 3rd month (Mar./Apr.) of 876, Nan-chao envoys proposed peace. They reached no further than Ssu-ch'uan, where they were decapitated. But in spite of the hostility of local Chinese officials, the T'ang court also wished peace. It sent envoys who concluded a covenant in Nan-chao. Ch'iu Lung responded with a mission of his own. Emperor Hsi-tsung appointed the chief envoy Herald and Acting Regular Cavalier Attendant (*Tzu-chih t'ung-chien* p.8183; *Wen-hsien t'ung-k'ao* 329:71b).

Ch'iu-lung died in 877. He was succeeded as emperor of Nan-chao by his son Fa.[52] In the 11th month (Nov./Dec.) of the same year,[53] four envoys of his to a Military Commissioner in Kuang-hsi reaffirmed peace. Hsi-tsung ordered the acceptance of this. The Military Commissioner consequently sent an envoy to Nan-chao, who on his

[51] Yi-mou-hsün had in 779 changed the name of Nan-chao to Ta-li (Great Principle), but the T'ang sources, and presumably the government, accepted neither term and refered to it as Nan-chao until the end of the dynasty. The name of Ta-li (Great Principle) was resumed in 937 and was acknowledged by the Sung.

[52] Or Lung-shun.

[53] *T'ang hui-yao* says 876.

return in the 7th month (August) of 878 brought a *Nan-chao lu* (*Record of Nan-chao*) in 3 chapters. Subsequently, in spite of some looting of Chinese lands, Nan-chao envoys proposed a marriage alliance (*T'ang hui-yao* 99:8b; *Wen-hsien t'ung-k'ao* 329:72a).

In the 7th month (Feb./Mar.) of 882, Nan-chao envoys repeated the request for a marriage. Hsi-tsung agreed and for that purpose enfeoffed a lady of the imperial house as Princess of An-hua (*Tzu-chih t'ung-chien* p.8273; *Wen-hsien t'ung-k'ao* 329:329:72a).

In the 7th month (Aug./Sep.) of 883, three high-ranking official arrived from Nan-chao to welcome the princess. The well-known retired Chinese official Kao P'ing (d.887), who at one point had been stationed in Ssu-ch'uan, advised the court that the three men were the "stomach and heart" of Nan-chao and that they should be poisoned. Hsi-tsung accepted this. The envoys were informed that the marriage should be postponed because, due to the emperor's absence from the capital on a tour of inspection, the protocol could not be prepared. The three envoys did not accept the explanation but started their voyage home. When they reached Ch'eng-tu, all were murdered (*Tzu-chih t'ung-chien* p.8297; *Wen-hsien t'ung-k'ao* 329:72a).

Fa died in 897 and was succeeded as emperor of Nan-chao by his son Shun-hua.[54] He wished to restore good relations with the T'ang and sent envoys to Chinese border officials. Emperor Chao-tsung wished to respond. But a Chinese official memorialized that the Nan-chao were lesser barbarians who should be ignored. Chao-tsung accepted this, after which there were no further relations between China and Nan-chao until the end of T'ang (*Tzu-chih t'ung-chien* pp.8511-8512; *Wen-hsien t'ung-k'ao* 329:72a).

In the 10th month (Nov./Dec.) of 926, envoys [from Nan-chao] were received in audience by Emperor Ming-tsung of Later T'ang. The chief envoy was made a General Who Brings Repose to the Distance and his deputy a General Who Consolidates the Distance (*Wu-tai hui-yao* 30:12b-13a; *Wen-hsien t'ung-k'ao* 329:72a).

In the 7th month (August) of 927, Ming-tsung of Later T'ang sent a General-in-chief of the Guards of the Left as envoy to the barbarians [of Nan-chao] (*Wu-tai hui-yao* 30:13a; *Wen-hsien t'ung-k'ao* 329:72a).

On June 13, 1076, envoys from the Ta-li State (Great Principle) to the Sung court presented gems set in gold, mats, swords, and horse

[54] Or Shun-hua-chen.

trappings of rhinoceros hide. Thereafter, missions did not come regularly (*Wen-hsien t'ung-k'ao* 329:72a).

In the 4th month (May/June) of 1116, the Sung "ordered the Ta-li State to pay tribute", i.e. it expressed the wish to resume relations and trade. That year, envoys arrived (*Sung shih* 488:19a; *Sung hui-yao, chüan* 10,353).

On Jan.23, 1117, envoys from the Ta-li State offered 380 horses, musk, cow bezoar, fine mats, and gems. They wished to pay homage to the image of Confucius, which was arranged (*Sung shih* 21:7b; 488:19b; *Sung hui-yao, chüan* 10,353; *Wen-hsien t'ung-k'ao* 329:72a).

On May 6, 1117, envoys of the Ta-li State offered gifts. On June 1, the envoys were received in audience by Emperor Hui-tsung. That day, the ruler of the Ta-li State, Tuan Ho-yü,[55] was by the Sung appointed Imperial Household Grandee of the Golden Seal and Purple Ribbon, Military Commissioner of the non-existant Yün-nan Area Command, Acting Minister of Works, and Supreme Pillar of State, and recognized as king of the Ta-li State. On June 10, the envoys took leave (*Sung shih* 21:7b; *Sung hui-yao, chüan* 10,353; *Wen-hsien t'ung-k'ao* 329:72a).

On Nov.12, 1133, local officials reported to the Southern Sung court that the Ta-li State wished to offer gifts and sell horses. This was repeated in 1136. Both offers were rejected (*Sung shih* 488:19b-20a; *Sung hui-yao, chüan* 10,353; *Wen-hsien t'ung-k'ao* 329:72a). Henceforth, the Southern Sung and Nan-chao simply ignored each other. In 1254, Nan-chao was conquered by the Mongols.

Nan-chao was not only an independent state, but its rulers called themselves emperors from 751 to 794 and permanently from 859. Yet, the accounts of the Chinese dynastic historians ignore Nan-chao's sovereign statehood and provide striking examples of sinocentric arrogance, untruthful diplomatic reporting, and false claims of Chinese suzerainity. They fail to understand that Nan-chao first allied itself with Tibet and later intermittently with China for the very purpose of guarding its independence, and that it never submitted to either of them.

Tzu-chih t'ung-chien p.7552 gives the following account of the behaviour of the Chinese envoy Ts'ui Tso-shih to Nan-chao in 793: At this time, there were several hundred Tibetan envoys in the capital. Yi-mou-hsün did not wish them to know that he was negotiating with the

---

[55] Or Tuan Cheng-yen. His dynasty had ruled since 937.

Chinese and requested Tso-shih to disguise himself as an aboriginal. Tso-shih refused, saying:"I am an envoy of the great T'ang. How could I wear the garments of lesser barbarians?" He was then smuggled into the palace by night, where he loudly proclaimed the imperial edict. Yi-mou-hsün became afraid, looked to the left and right, and paled. He wept, prostrated himself, and accepted the edict. Tso-shih then persuaded him to kill all the Tibetan envoys.

This account fails by its own preposterousness. It is barely possible that Tso-shih, with not unusual Chinese tactlessness, refused to disguise himself, but it is out of the question that Yi-mou-hsün weepingly prostrated himself. It is equally impossible that Yi-mou-hsün killed the Tibetan envoys, since in that case the subsequent attack on the Tibetans in 794 would not have been the suprise the sources insist it was. It is obvious that Tso-shih wrote a fraudulent report in order to flatter Emperor Te-tsung and advance his own career, and that this report was later found in the archives and quoted by the dynastic historian.

The same applies to the claim that when Yüan Tzu in 794 presented a golden seal to Yi-mou-hsün, the latter knelt facing north,[56] accepted the seal, kotowed, and saluted twice. During the following banquet, Tzu supposedly urged Yi-mou-hsün to be entirely loyal to the T'ang, whereupon the latter answered:"Do I dare not to receive the orders of the envoy with respect?" (*Tzu-chih t'ung-chien* pp.7561-7562). This account also comes from a self-serving and false report.

Ch'iu-lung supposedly at some times was not willing to salute Chinese envoys and at others times he was (*Wen-hsien t'ung-k'ao* 329:71b). The first reports were true, the second were not.

The geographical map of 794, as other cases examined, was no more than a symbolic gesture.

According to *Wen-hsien t'ung-k'ao* 329:71a, 71b, Yi-mou-hsün in 799 sent the sons and younger brothers of his high officials as hostages to Ch'ang-an, and Ch'iu-lung sent 20 hostages in 876. Nan-chao had no need to render hostages, so that the purpose must have been some other. It so happens that the T'ang normally did not accept students from Nan-chao at the Academy in Ch'ang-an and instead referred

---

[56] Subjects of the Chinese emperor, in his presence or that of his representatives, faced north.

them to the institutions in Ch'eng-tu.[57] It is probable, therefore, that in the negotiations of 799 and 876 the T'ang made exceptions, and that the students in Ch'ang-an either by the governments of that time or later by the dynastic historians were wishfully or wilfully misrepresented as hostages.

Especially toward the end of T'ang, its diplomacy could be blundering or outright disthonest. In 818, the court decreed that Nan-chao missions were not to exceed 20 members, yet for 839 there is reference to one with 37. It was more serious that in 869 and 876 Nan-chao envoys were killed by local officials en route to the capital. In 883, three important Nan-chao envoys were murdered with the connivance of Hsi-tsung. The same emperor acted with extraordinary clumsiness when in 882 he agreed to the marriage of a Chinese princess with Fa and then in 883 avoided it by transparent deceit. In 897, Emperor Chao-tsung accepted the view that the people of Nan-chao were "lesser barbarians" who should be ignored.

In short, the relations between China and Nan-chao were those between two independent states and alternated between war and peace. The T'ang emperors twice (809, 816) suspended the court for three days after the death of Nan-chao rulers and condoled at both occassions. Most Nan-chao rulers were recognized by China (738, 748, 794, 809, 816, 823, and 1117). Chinese titles were conferred on them in 738 and 1117, but posthumous titles never. Relations were therefore ambivalent. The inhabitants and officials of Ssu-ch'uan had special reasons to fear Nan-chao, but the Chinese aggrevated matters by tactlessness and brutality. Yet missions to the T'ang court were frequent in peace times, and the magnet which drew them was trade.

According to *Chiu T'ang shu* 197:9b and *Ts'e-fu yüan-kuei* p.5033, Nan-chao envoys arrived annually from 817 to 820, sometimes two or three times a year. Only two missions are recorded. *Wen-hsien t'ung-k'ao* 329:71b says, under the heading of 830, that envoys arrived every year. Five missions are recorded from 830 to 836. According to *Wen-hsien t'ung-k'ao* 329:71b, envoys arrived twice between 836 and 846. Six missions are recorded. It follows that the statistics are fairly complete.

Nan-chao missions arrived at the Chinese court throughout the year. But they came most often in the 12th and 1st months in order to attend the New Year festivals.

---

[57] See O.Franke, *Geschichte*, II, pp. 450-451.

This is the distribution by 20-year periods of the 53 recorded Nan-chao missions after the unification of the tribes in 730 to T'ang, Later T'ang, and Sung:

730- 746:[58]	1
747- 766:	1
767- 786:	0
787- 806:	15
807- 826:	14
827- 846:	9
847- 866:	1
867- 886:	7
887- 906:	0
907- 926:	1
927- 946:	0
947- 966:	0
967- 986:	0
987-1006:	0
1007-1026:	0
1027-1046:	0
1047-1066:	0
1067-1086:	1
1087-1106:	0
1107-1126:	3

From 750 to 794, Nan-chao and T'ang were at war, which included the time of An Lu-shan's uprising. Then came a peaceful period with many missions from 794 to 846, only interrupted by a brief war from 829 to 830. Another war followed from 859 to 876. After a brief increase, missions ceased for the rest of T'ang, and only one is recorded for the Five Dynasties. Relations revived slightly at the end of Northern Sung and at the express wish of that dynasty in 1116. The Southern Sung withdrew from 1127 into isolationism and xenophobia.

The specified goods brought by the Nan-chao missions are rarely mentioned and fall into the following categories:

[58] 17-year period.

Humans

795: 100 Tibetan prisoners of war.
800: musicians and dancers.
818: slaves.

Animals

Rhinoceroses

854: one rhinoceros (rejected).

Horses

795: 60 horses.
1117: 380 horses.
1133: horses (rejected).

Sheep

818: sheep.

Aromatics

Aromatics and medical drugs:

1117: musk, cow bezoar.

Ores and Metals

793: unwrought gold, cinnabar.

Manufactured Objects

Of metal::

794: swords.
1076: swords.

Of leather:

1076: horse trappings of rhinoceros hide.

Other:

1076: mats.
1117: mats.

Jewels

1076: gems set in gold.
1117: gems.

The Chinese paid with musicians, singing girls, gold, silver vessels, brocade robes and other garments, and gold and silver belts.

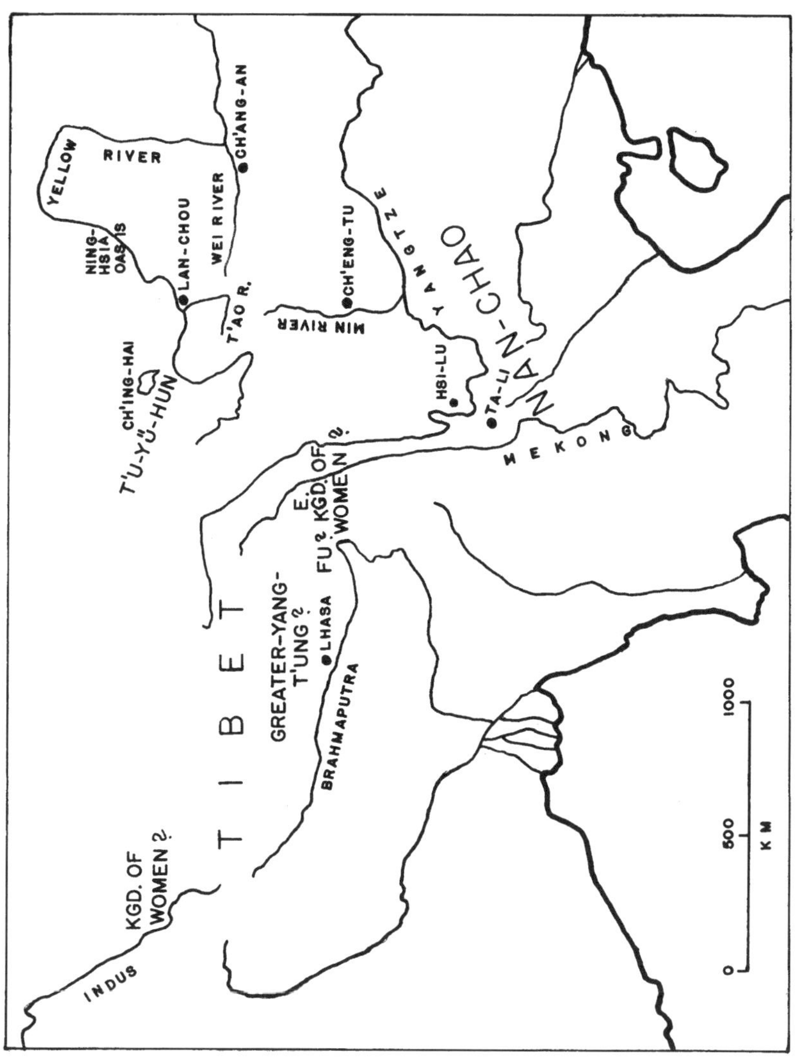

Map 6. The Southwest and Ch'ing-hai.

CH'ING-HAI

THE T'U-YÜ-HUN

The T'u-yü-hun state was founded by a branch of the Mu-jung clan of the Hsien-pi and came gradually into existance after about A.D.300. The people of this state seem to have been a mixture of Mongols, Tibetans, and some Turks. They inabited the area of the great lake now called Ch'ing-hai or Kokonor and were Buddhists. From 423 to 540, 29 missions are recorded from the T'u-yü-hun to the Liu Sung, Southern Ch'i, and Liang dynasties of the south, and 75 to the Northern Wei, Eastern Wei, Northern Ch'i, Western Wei, Northern Chou, and Sui[1] dynasties of the north. The kings of the T'u-yü-hun were never vassals of the Chinese emperors, and one of them even executed a Southern Ch'i envoy in 490 for his insolence.[2]

From having prospered through the caravan trade which passed through their territory and from their lively commerce with the northern and southern dynasties in China, the T'u-yü-hun fell on hard times during the T'ang and disappeared from history after the 10th century. From 925, the sources occasionally refer to them by the abbreviated name of T'u-hun.

On Sep.1, 590, T'u-yü-hun envoys were received at the Sui court (*Sui shu* 2:6b).

In 591, it became known at the Sui court that the king of the T'u-yü-hun, K'ua-lü,[3] had died and that his son Shih-fu had succeeded him (*Sui shu* 83:4a; *Pei shih* 96:18b).

On Mar.2, 591, Shih-fu's elder brother's son Wu-su presented regional objects and a letter to the Sui court. In this letter, the new king offered a daughter to Emperor Wen. This was rejected (*Sui shu* 2:7a; 83:4a; *Pei shih* 96:18b-19a).

On Mar.30, 591,[4] Emperor Wen sent a Secretarial Receptionist as envoy to the T'u-yü-hun. In 592, he dispatched a Master of Writing

---

[1] Before the unification of 589.

[2] See my *Six Dynasties*, vol.I, p.122 and passim, vol.II, pp. 81,82, 99-101.

[3] Correcting Lü-k'ua to K'ua-lü. Cf. my *Six Dynasties*, vol.I, p.201 note 36.

[4] The text has 3rd month, *jen-wu*, but that was the last day of the 2nd month.

of the Ministry of Punishments on the same errand (*Sui shu* 2:7a; 83: 4a).

At the end of 592,[5] T'u-yü-hun envoys presented regional objects (*Sui shu* 2:8a).

On June 28, 595, T'u-yü-hun envoys offered gifts (*Sui shu* 2:10a).

In 596, Emperor Wen married the Princess of Kuang-hua to Shih-fu. The latter proposed that she be called Heavenly Queen, which was not to the liking of the Chinese court (*Sui shu* 83:4a; *Pei shih* 96:19a).

In 597, T'u-yü-hun envoys to the Sui court announced that Shih-fu had been killed and been replaced by his younger brother Yün-fu.[6] According to custom, he married his elder brother's widow, the Princess of Kuang-hua (*Sui shu* 83:4a-4b; *Pei-shih* 96:19a).

After Emperor Yang had ascended the Sui throne on Aug.13, 604, Yün-fu's son Shun was received at the court. Yang detained him and appointed him an Imperial. Household Grandee of the Golden Seal and Purple Ribbon (*Sui shu* 83:4b; *Chiu T'ang shu* 198:7a; *Wen-hsien t'ung-k'ao* 334:26a).

With Emperor Yang, the political climate changed from the peaceful coexistance of China and the T'u-yü-hun in the time of his father to confrontation. After a brief war with the Turkic T'ieh-le, Emperor Yang formed an alliance with them against the T'u-yü-hun (*Sui shu* 83:4b; *Wen-hsien t'ung-k'ao* 334:26a).

Two more T'u-yü-hun missions are recorded before the outbreak of hostilities. The first was received at the Sui court on July 21, 607, the second in northwestern China on May 14, 609, where Emperor Yang was making preparations for the war (*Sui shu* 3:10b, 13a; *Pei shih* 12:13a).

In the summer of 609, the Chinese and T'ieh-le attacked, and Yün-fu was forced to flee. Emperor Yang enthroned Yün-fu's son Shun as ruler of the T'u-yü-hun but did not send him back (*Sui shu* 3:13b; 83: 4b-5a; *Tzu-chih t'ung-chien* p.5841).[7]

The Chinese victory was ephemeral. With the collapse of the Sui empire, Yün-fu regained his old territory and in retaliation looted

---

[5] The text has 12th month, *chi-yu*, but these cyclical characters did not occur in that month.

[6] The name is by the sources variously given as Yün-fu and Fu-yün. But since his elder brother's name was Shih-fu, *fu* was obviously the second part of a generational name. Yün-fu is therefore correct, and I have adjusted the entries accordingly.

[7] *Tzu-chih t'ung-chien* refers to Yün-fu and his sucessors throughout as qaghan.

Chinese border lands without meeting any resistance (*Sui shu* 83:5a; *Chiu T'ang shu*198:6a).

After Kao-tsu had ascended the throne on June 18, 618, and had founded the T'ang dynasty, he made peace with the T'u-yü-hun and allied himself with them in 619. Yün-fu, on his part, requested the return of his son Shun. The latter had remained in the entourage of Emperor Yang, and after Yang's murder in 618 had returned from Chiang-tu to Ch'ang-an. Kao-tsu sent him to his father, the year not being recorded (*Sui shu* 83:5a; *Chiu T'ang shu* 198:6a; *Tzu-chih t'ung-chien* p.5841).

In the 2nd (Feb./Mar.), 9th (Oct./Nov.), and 11th month (Dec./Jan., 620) of the Chinese year 618, T'u-yü-hun envoys offered gifts (*Ts'e-fu yüan-kuei*, p.5023).

In 621, 622, and 623 the T'u-yü-hun looted Chinese border lands (*T'ang hui-yao* 94:17a; *Tzu-chih t'ung-chien* pp.5951, 5966). But in the 6th (July/Aug.), 9th (October), and 12th month (Dec./Jan., 624) of the Chinese year 623, and the 6th month (June/July) of 624 their envoys again offered presents (*Ts'e-fu yüan-kuei* p.5023).

In the 10th month (Nov./Dec.) of 624, the T'u-yü-hun looted the Chinese northwest (*Tzu-chih t'ung-chien* p.5993).

In the 1st month (Feb./Mar.) of 625, the T'u-yü-hun and Chinese agreed on joint border markets. In the 3rd month (Apr./May), T'u-yü-hun envoys offered gifts (*Ts'e-fu yüan-kuei* p.5023; *Tzu-chih t'ung-chien* p.5994).

After T'ai-tsung had ascended the T'ang throne on Sep.3, 626, Yün-fu sent an envoy and proposed peace But even before this envoy had departed from Ch'ang-an on his voyage home, Yün-fu looted again. T'ai-tsung invited him to his court, but Yün-fu refused on the pretext of illness (*Chiu T'ang shu* 198:6b; *Tzu-chih t'ung-chien* pp.6017, 6106).

Even though no formal treaty was concluded, peace held until 634. T'u-yü-hun envoys offered gifts in the intercalary month (Apr./May) of 627, the 2nd month (Mar./Apr.) of 630, the 5th month (May/June) of 632, thc 5th month (Junc/July) of 633, and thc 4th month (May) of 634 (*Ts'e-fu yüan-kuei* pp. 5023, 5024).

In the 5th month (June) of 634, Yün-fu requested that one of his sons marry a Chinese princess. T'ai-tsung agreed, but Yün-fu proceeded to loot Chinese lands and also arrested a T'ang envoy. The emperor sent an envoy to dissuade him, and also summoned Yün-fu's envoys in Ch'ang-an to warn him. This had no result. The marriage was consequently cancelled (*Chiu T'ang shu* 3:3a-3b).

In the 5th month (June/July) of 635, the Chinese went on the attack, and in a campaign lasting for several months defeated the T'u-yü-hun. Among the captives were Yün-fu's wives and children. He escaped but then hanged himself.[8] Yün-fu was succeeded by his son Shun, the one who had been detained in China from 604 to 618. Because of his long absence, his father had selected another son as heir-apparent. But being the son of Yün-fu's legal wife, Shun had a geater right to the throne than the heir-apparent and replaced him either by consensus or force. He made peace with the T'ang and was by it recognized as king of Hsi-p'ing. Shun was not popular, however, because of his extended stay in China, and he was murdered before the end of 635. His young son No-ho-po was entroned. Since the new king was still young, various dignitaries struggled for power at the T'u-yü-hun court (*Chiu T'ang shu* 198:7a, 7b; *Tzu-chih t'ung-chien* pp.6113, 6117; *Wen-hsien t'ung-k'ao* 334:26a).

In Shun, the Chinese had lost a potentially friendly ruler. In the 12th month (Jan./Feb., 636) of the Chinese year 635, T'ai-tsung ordered a military demonstration in favour of No-ho-po, presumably in the hope of winning him over. But he also demanded the release of Chinese envoys who had been detained by the T'u-yü-hun (*Chiu T'ang shu* 198: 7b; *Tzu-chih t'ung-chien* p.6117). The outcome is not recorded.

On Apr.17, 636, envoys from No-ho-po were received at the T'ang court. They requested the T'ang calendar, which was provided. On Apr.27, T'ai-tsung entitled No-ho-po king of the imaginary Ho-yüan commandery ("Commandery at the Source of the Yellow River") and recognized him as qaghan (*Chiu T'ang shu* 198:7b; *Tzu-chih t'ung-chien* p.6119).

In the 11th month (Nov./Dec.) of 637, No-ho-po presented 13,000 head of cattle and sheep (*Ts'e-fu yüan-kuei* p.5024).

In the 8th month (Sep./Oct.) of 638, T'u-yü-hun envoys offered regional objects (*Ts'e-fu yüan-kuei* p.5024).

On Jan.20, 640, No-ho-po was personally received at the T'ang court. T'ai-tsung enfeoffed a lady of the imperial house as Princess of Hung-hua, married her to him, and gave him rich presents. On Mar.10, the General of the Resolute Guards of the Left and king of Huai-yang, a distant relative of T'ai-tsung, set out from Ch'ang-an

[8] According to *Tzu-chih t'ung-chien* and *Wen-hsien t'ung-k'ao*, he was killed by his attendants.

to escort the Princess of Hung-hua and presumably No-ho-po to the T'u-yü-hun territory (*Chiu T'ang shu* 3:6b; 198:7b; *Tzu-chih t'ung-chien* p.6150).

This rapprochement between No-ho-po and T'ai-tsung did not please the conservative T'u-yü-hun and led to an attempt by the chancellor to attack the cortège. No-ho-po fled to Shan-shan (Lob-nor) in the Tarim Basin and was well received by its king. In the following year, 641, No-ho-po with auxiliary Shan-shan and Chinese troops defeated the chancellor and killed him and two of his brothers. He sent envoys to inform T'ai-tsung. The latter responded by dispatching a Master of Writing of the Ministry of Households (*Chiu T'ang shu* 198: 8a; *Tzu-chih t'ung-chien* p.6167).

In the 1st month (Feb./Mar.) of 642, 1st month (Jan./Feb.) of 643, and 1st month (Feb./Mar.) of 644, presumably on the respective New Year Days of Feb.5, Jan.26, and Feb.14, T'u-yü-hun envoys offered regional objects (*T'se-fu yüan-kuei* p.5024).

On Feb.2, 645, the New Year's Day, T'u-yü-hun envoys congratulated at the T'ang court and offered gifts (*Ts'e-fu yüan-kuei* p.5024).

In the 1st month (Jan./Feb.) of 646 and 1st month (Feb./Mat.) of 647, presumably on the resepective New Year Days of Jan.22 and Feb.10, the T'u-yü-hun offered regional objects (*Ts'e-fu yüan-kuei* p.5024).

In the 12th month (January, 648) of the Chinese year 647, T'ai-tsung invited the T'ieh-le, Turks, Tibetans, and T'u-yü-hun to join in a Chinese attack on Kucha in East Turkestan (*Tzu-chih t'ung-chien* p.6251).

On Jan.30, 648, the New Year's Day, T'u-yü-hun envoys offered gifts (*Ts'e-fu yüan-kuei* p.5025).

In the 12th month (Jan./Feb., 649) of the Chinese year 648, T'u-yü-hun envoys offered presents (*Ts'e-fu yüan-kuei* p.5025).

After T'ai-tsung's death on July 10, 649, the image of No-ho-po was carved in stone and placed at his tomb. T'ai-tsung's son and successor Kao-tsung appointed No-ho-po as Chief Commandant of Attendant Cavalry and presented him with 40 items of objects (*Chiu T'ang shu* 198:8a).

In their war during the following years with the Tibetans, the T'u-yü-hun requested Chinese support but never received it (*Chiu T'ang shu* 198:8a).

In the 8th month (Sep./Oct.) of 649, No-ho-po presented horses and cattle (*Ts'e-fu yüan-kuei* p.5025).

On Feb.15, 652, the New Year's Day, T'u-yü-hun envoys offered gifts. In the 8th month (Sep./Oct.), they presented fine horses (*Ts'e-fu yüan-kuei* p.5025).

In the 11th month (Dec./Jan., 653) of the Chinese year 652, No-ho-po's wife, who meanwhile had been promoted by theT'ang to Senior Princess of Hung-hua, paid a visit to the T'ang court (*Chiu T'ang shu* 4:4a).

In the 7th month (August) of 653, the T'u-yü-hun presented fine horses (*Ts'e-fu yüan-kuei* p.5025).

In the 9th month (Oct./Nov.) of 654, T'u-yü-hun envoys offered gifts (*Ts'e-fu yüan-kuei* p.5025).

From 660, the attacks by the Tibetans on the T'u-yü-hun increased in ferocity, culminating in 670 with their final assault. The T'u-yü-hun were routed, and No-ho-po fled with the [Senior] Princess of Hung-hua north to the eastermost part of the Kan-su Corridor. Kao-tsung finally sent an army to his rescue, but this was utterly defeated. The state of the T'u-yü-hun ceased to exist, and its territory was annexed by Tibet. In 672, Kao-tsung moved No-ho-po and his followers to what now is the Ning-hsia Oasis. This area was renamed the An-lo commandery, and No-ho-po was appointed its Inspector (*Chiu T'ang shu* 5:3b; 198: 8a; *Tzu-chih t'ung-chien* p.6321; *Wen-hsien t'ung-k'ao* 334:26a).

Thus the state of the T'u-yü-hun came to its end. It had existed for almost 400 years. Henceforth, their kings became clients of the T'ang. Their subsequent dynasty in Ning-hsia can be traced until the end of the 8th century and then petered out. When No-po-ho died in 688, he was succeeded by his son Chung. When Chung died in 698, he was succeeded by his son Hsüan-chao. In the 3rd month (Mar./Apr.) of 700, the T'ang recognized his empty titles as king and qaghan of Ch'ing-hai, and appointed him Supernumerary General-in-chief of the Guards of the Leopard Bow-cases of the Left. Hsüan-chao sent envoys to the T'ang court in the 1st month (Jan./Feb.) of 708, probably for the New Year's Day of Jan.28. When he died in about 709, he was succeeded by his son Hsi-hao. When Hsi-hao died in about 738, he was succeeded by his son Chao. He was the last of the old dynasty. After Chao's death, a certain Mu-jung Fu, judging from the name a relative, was in 798 given by the T'ang the empty titles of king and qaghan of the Ch'ing-hai State. He had no successors. No further official missions are recorded until the end of T'ang (*Chiu T'ang shu* 198:8a; *Tzu-chih t'ung-chien* p.6546; *Wen-hsien t'ung-k'ao* 334:26a, 26b).

This does not mean that the T'u-yü-hun as a people immediately disappeared from history. There are references to them until 997. Tribes under lesser chiefs survived in the old homeland, and some of these sent missions to the Later T'ang, Later Chin, Later Han, Later Chou, and the Khitan/Liao.

On Apr.2, 924, the T'u-hun offered race horses to the Later T'ang court (*Chiu Wu-tai shih* 31:6b-7a).

In the 2nd month (Feb./Mar.) of 925, a T'u-hun chief presented horses to the Later T'ang court. Another mission offered sheep and horses. On Nov.11th, a T'u-hun chief offered regional objects (*Hsin Wu-tai shih* 5:8b; *Ts'e-fu yüan-kuei* p.5034).

On Mar.7, 926, T'u-hun envoys to the Later T'ang court presented horses (*Chiu wu-tai shih* 34:2a).

On Feb.28, 928, a T'u-hun chief presented 120 horses to the Later T'ang court. Emperor Ming-tsung conferred on him the nominal titles of Meritorious Subject, Imperial Household Grandee of the Golden Seal and Purple Ribbon, and Acting Grand Guardian (*Hsin Wu-tai shih* 6:6b; *Wu-tai hui-yao* 28:11a).

On Dec.25, 928, the T'u-hun presented 53 horses to the Later T'ang court (*Hsin Wu-tai shih* 6:7a; *Ts'e-fu yüan-kuei* p.5034).

On Sep.16, 929, a T'u-hun chief came to the Later T'ang court and offered gifts (*Hsin Wu-tai shih* 6:8a; *Wu-tai hui-yao* 28:11a).

In the 3rd month (April) of 930, Emperor Ming-tsung of Later T'ang conferred on a T'u-hun chief the nominal title of Inspector and gave him a Chinese name. On Sep.19 of that year, a T'u-hun mission arrived at the Later T'ang court (*Hsin Wu-tai shih* 6:9a; *Wu-tai hui-yao* 28:11a-11b).

On Mar.1, 931, a T'u-hun chief presented horses to the Later T'ang court (*Ts'e-fu yüan-kuei* p.5045; *Hsin Wu-tai shih* 6:9b).

On Mar.3, 933, the T'u-yü-hun offered gifts to the Khitan court (*Liao shih* 3:6b).

In the 1st month (Feb./Mar.) of 935, a T'u-hun chief came to the Later T'ang court and presented horses (*Ts'e-fu yüan-kuei* p.5035).

On Juy 2, 935, the T'u-yü-hun offered gifts to the Khitan court (*Liao shih* 3:8a).

On July 19 and Aug.29, 936, the T'u-yü-hun offered gifts to the Khitan court (*Liao shih* 3:8b).

On June 30 and Sep.22, 938, the T'u-yü-hun offered gifts to the Khitan court (*Liao shih* 4:1b).

On July 29, 939, the T'u-yü-hun offered gifts to the Khitan court (*Liao shih* 4:3b).

In the 1st month (Jan./Feb.) of 941, a T'u-hun chief was received at the Later Chin court. In the 5th month May/June), another chief arrived. On Oct.18, still another T'u-hun chief led a mission of 118 men and offered gifts to the Later Chin court (*Hsin Wu-tai shih* 8:8b; *Wu-tai hui-yao* 28:12a; *Ts'e-fu yüan-kuei* p.5035).

In the 3rd month (Mar./Apr.) of 942, a T'u-hun mission of 14 men presented 10 horses to the Later Chin court (*Ts'e-fu yüan-kuei* p.5035).

In the 4th month (May/June) of 942, Khitan envoys to the Later Chin court objected to the fact that that Emperor Kao-tsu had given refuge to the T'u-hun chief Po-ch'eng-fu[9] and his tribe. Kao-tsu consequently expelled them from Chinese territory (*Hsin Wu-tai shih* 74: 2b; *Tzu-chih t'ung-chien* p.9236).

On July 19, 942, the T'u-hun offered gifts to the Later Chin court (*Hsin Wu-tai shih* 8:9a-9b; *Ts'e-fu yüan-kuei* p.5035).

On July 18, 945, the T'u-yü-hun offered gifts to the Khitan court (*Liao shih* 4:12a; 70:5b).

On Apr.13, 946, the T'u-yü-hun presented 1000 households to the Khitan court (*Liao shih* 4:12b).

In 949, T'u-hun envoys arrived at the the Later Han court (*Hsin Wu-tai shih* 74:3b).

In the 8th month (Sep./Oct.) of 953, T'u-yü-hun envoys to the Liao court of Khitan offered gifts (*Liao shih* 6:2b).

In the 9th month (Oct./Nov.) of 953, a T'u-hun mission was received at the Later Chou court (*Hsin Wu-tai shih* 11:6b).

On Nov.14, 971, the T'u-yü-hun offered gifts to the Liao court (*Liao shih* 8:3a).

On Oct.10, 994, the T'u-yü-hun offered gifts to the Liao court (*Liao shih* 13:5a).

In the 7th month (Aug./Sep.) of 997, the Liao attempted to stop the T'u-hun from selling horses to the Sung court (*Liao-shih* 70:9b).

Chinese terminology notwithstanding, the T'u-yü-hun formed an

[9] Emperor Chuang-tsung of Later T'ang (r.923-926) had previously appointed this chief as Chief Commandant of two commanderies (fu) and had bestowed on him the imperial surname of Li and the given name of Shao-lu. When the Last Emperor of Later Chin (r.942-946) broke with the Khitan, he summoned Po-ch'eng-fu (Li Shao-lu) to reenter China and appointed him a Military Commissioner. He was subsequently killed by Liu Chih-yüan, the future founder of the Later Han dynasty (Hsin Wu-tai shih 74:2b-3a).

independent state until their destruction by the Tibetans in 670. It has been seen that according to *Sui shu* 83:4a, their king Shih-fu offered a daughter to Emperor Wen in 591. The text claims that she was intended for the imperial harem, which would have been an insult to her father. He would not have been satisfied with such an inferior position for a T'u-yü-hun princess. What he must have had in mind was marriage among equals to a prince of the Sui house.[10] This in turn looked like arrogance to Emperor Wen, and that is why he rejected the proposal. When Yün-fu in 597 married his elder brother's widow, the Chinese Princess of Kuang-hua, he certainly did not ask Emperor Wen's permission, as claimed by *Pei shih* 96:19a.

Chiu T'ang shu 198:7a, 7b and *Tzu-chih t'ung-chien* p.6117 state that Shun had been a hostage in China for a long time. But, as has been seen, he was detained in China against his will from 604 to 618 and consequently was not a hostage in the traditional sense. This makes the claim of *Tzu-chih t'ung-chien* p.6119 highly improbable that No-ho-po in 636 offered to send a son or younger brother as hostage to the T'ang court. He had no need to do so, but the visit of a relative to Ch'ang-an could easily have been misinterpreted or misrepresented by the Chinese historians as the rendering of a hostage.

When the same king in 636 requested the T'ang calendar, this was, as always, understood by the Chinese court to mean submission. In actual fact, the T'u-yü-hun may simply have needed a calendar, which it was beyond their ability to construct, and they probably were not even aware of the Chinese implications.

T'ang policy toward the T'u-yü-hun had the aim of regularizing relations for the sake of a peaceful. border, as well as the usual exchange of goods. For that purpose, Chinese princesses were married to T'u-yü-hun rulers in 596 and 640. At least two rulers received nominal but not posthumous titles before 670. Their is no evidence that the T'ang emperors suspended the court as a token of mourning for T'u-yü-hun kings. The most favoured of them was No-ho-po, but he was also the one most friendly to China.

According to *Sui shu* 83:4b, T'u-yü-hun missions arrived annually from 597. Only one mission in 604 is recorded. According to *Tzu-chih-t'ung-chien* p.5841, the T'u-yü-hun frequently sent missions from

[10] Emperor Wen's empress was still alive, and Fu would not have aimed that high in any event.

618. Ten are recorded from 619 to 626. According to *Hsin Wu-tai shih* 74:3a, T'u-hun missions arrived frequently from 936 to 942. Five are recorded. The statistics may therefore be better for the T'ang and Five Dynasties than for the Sui.

T'u-yü-hun missions arrived at the Chinese courts throughout the year, but they had a preference for the 12th and 1st months in order to attend the New Year ceremonies.

This is the distribution by 20-year periods of the 62 recorded T'u-yü-hun missions to Sui, T'ang, Later T'ang, Later Chin, Later Han, and Later Chou:

Period	Missions
587-606:	7
607-626:	12
627-646:	16
647-666:	8
667-686:	0
687-706:	0
707-726:	1
727-746:	0
747-766:	0
767-786:	0
787-806:	0
807-826:	0
827-846:	0
847-866:	0
867-886:	0
887-906:	0
907-926:	5
927-946:	11
947-966:	2

The figure for 587 to 606 may be too low. During T'ang, relations were close until the death of T'ai-tsung in 649. Only five missions are recorded for the reign of Kao-tsung (650-683). He had no understanding of his father's policy to maintain an alliance with the T'u-yü-hun as a counterweight to the Tibetans. After the collapse of the T'u-yü-hun state in 670, only the mission of 708 is recorded before the end of T'ang. During Later T'ang and Later Chin, T'u-yü-hun chiefs resumed relations with China. Since great diplomatic matters no longer needed to be discussed, the single purpose was obviously commerce. At that time, the T'u-yü-hun also traded with the Liao, with 12 missions recorded from 933 to 994.

The chief export of the T'u-yü-hun was livestock. These are the recorded items:

637: 13,000 head of cattle and sheep.
649: horses and cattle.
652: fine horses.
653: fine horses.
924: race horses.
925: sheep and horses.
926: horses.
928: 53 horses.
931: horses.
935: horses.
942: 10 horses.

It is not recorded what the Chinese paid for these goods.

THE TIBETANS OF TSONG-KHA

Sung shih has a special section for this tribe. The only other source, the *Wen-hsien t'ung-k'ao*, has entries for it only under the heading of Tibet.

This Tibetan tribe lived in the Huang River Valley east of lake Ch'ing-hai or Kokonor, an area which in Tibetan was called Tsong-kha (map.7). The tribe does not appear in the sources until the year 1008. It is probable, therefore, that it had moved into the former territory of the T'u-yü-hun after their destruction in 670. The first documented chief, Chüeh-ssu-lo, descended from the Tibetan royal house, i.e. ultimately from Srong-btsan-sgam-po[11] (*Sung shih* 492:11b).

In the 11th month (December) of 1008, the Tsong-kha Tibetans offered gifts to the Sung court (*Sung shih* 492:10a).

In 1015, envoys from Chüeh-ssu-lo to the Sung court offered 7000 ounces of gold and fine horses. He received in return brocade robes,

[11] According to R.Stein, Chüeh-ssu-lo was a transliteration of the Tibetan rgyal-sras, meaning prince. See Petech in Rossabi, ed., *China among Equals*, p.195 note 8.

golden belts, [porcelain] vessels, silk, tea, and drugs (*Sung shih* 492:12a; *Wen-hsien t'ung-k'ao* 335:32b).[12]

In 1016, Chüeh-ssu-lo presented 582 horses, for which he received 12,000 items of [porcelain] vessels and silk (*Sung shih* 492:12b; *Wen-hsien t'ung-k'ao* 335:33a).

On Jan.3, 1036, Emperor Jen-tsung appointed Chüeh-ssu-lo Military Commissioner of the non-existing Army Which Guarantees Obedience (*Sung shih* 10:8b; 492:13a).

In 1037, Chüeh-ssu-lo offered gifts (*Sung shih* 10:10b).

In 1038, Jen-tsung presented Chüeh-ssu-lo with 20,000 bolts of silk (*Sung shih* 492:13a; *Wen-hsien t'ung-k'ao* 335:33a).

On Feb.12, 1041, Jen-tsung appointed Chüeh-ssu-lo Military Commissioner of the non-existing Army West of the [Yellow] River (*Sung shih* 11:1a).

In 1046, 1050, and 1059, Chüeh-ssu-lo offered gifts (*Sung shih* 11: 11b; 12:2a, 15b).

In the winter of 1065, it became known at the Sung court that Chüeh-ssu-lo had died and had been succeeded by his third son, Tung-chan. Emperor Ying-tsung appointed him Military Commissioner of the non-existant Army Which Guarantees Obedience and Acting Minister of Works. Tung-chan sent envoys to offer gifts (*Sung shih* 492:14a-15b).

After Shen-tsung had ascended the Sung throne on Jan.25, 1067, he promoted Tung-chan to Grand Guardian and Grand Tutor ((*Sung shih* 492:16b).

In 1068, Shen-tsung entitled Tung-chan's mother, the Lady Ch'iao,[13] Grand Lady of An-k'ang commandery, and appointed his son Lin-pu as Inspector of Chin subcommandery (*Sung shih* 492:15b).[14]

In the summer of 1070, Shen-tsung sent a letter stamped with the imperial seal to thank Tung-chan for having won a victory over Hsia (*Sung shih* 492:15b).

In 1077, Tung-chan presented real pearls, jade, elephant tusks, frankincense, and horses. He received silver, silk, garments, and tea (*Sung shih* 492:16a; *Wen-hsien t'ung-k'ao* 335:33b).

On Apr.5, 1079, an envoy from Tung-chan offered regional objects. Tung-chan received a garment, a golden belt, 10,000 cash, 1000 items

[12] See also Petech, op.cit., p.176.

[13] She was the third wife of Chüeh-ssu-lo (Sung shih 492:14b).

[14] An-k'ang and Chin existed only on paper.

of silver, and silk (*Sung shih* 15:22b; 492:16a).

In 1081, Shen-tsung entitled Tung-chan king of Wu-wei commandery (*Sung shih* 492:16b).

In the 3rd (Apr./May) and 9th month (Oct./Nov.) of 1081, envoys from Tung-chan offered gifts (*Sung shih* 16:3b, 4b).

After Che-tsung had ascended the Sung throne on Apr.1, 1085, he promoted Tung-chan to Acting Grand Commandant (*Sung shih* 492:17a).

In 1086, it became known at the Sung court that Tung-chan had died and had been succeeded by his fosterson A-li-ku. The latter sent envoys with gifts. Che-tsung appointed him General-in-chief Who Surpasses the Army, Acting Minister of Works, and Military Commissioner of the non-existant Army West the [Yellow] River, and entitled him duke of Ning-sai (*Sung shih* 492:17a; *Wen-hsien t'ung-k'ao* 335:33b).

After a brief period of tension, A-li-ku presented a letter on Feb.19, 1088 and offered gifts. Che-tsung agreed to continued trade. He made A-li-ku an Imperial Household Grandee of the Golden Seal and Purple Ribbon and Acting Grand Guardian, entitled his wife as Lady of An-hua commandery, appointed A-li-ku's son Pang-ch'u-ch'ien as Defense Commissioner of Shan subcommandery, and the latter's younger brother as Inspector of Hsi subcommandery (*Sung shih* 17:10a; 492:17b; *Wen-hsien t'ung-k'ao* 335:33b).

On May 14 and Aug.23, 1088, A-li-ku offered gifts (*Sung shih* 17:10b).

On Apr.18, 1094,[15] A-li-ku presented a lion for which he received rich gifts (*Sung shih* 18:1b; 492:17b; *Wen-hsien t'ung-k'ao* 335:33b).

In 1095, A-li-ku offered gifts (*Sung shih* 18:5b).

In 1096, it became known at the Sung court that A-li-ku had died and had been succeeded by his son Hsia-cheng (alias Pang-ch'u-ch'ien) (*Sung shih* 492:18a; *Wen-hsien t'ung-k'ao* 335:33b).

Hsia-cheng had a rival in Lung-tsa, son of Mu-cheng and great-grandson of Chüeh-ssu-lo by his legitimte wife (*Sung shih* 492:19a). His brief reign was filled with dissention, and the Sung government knew how to take advantage of it. Mu-cheng had surrendered to the Chinese and had been granted the imperial surname and given name of Chao Ssu-chung. Seven of his relatives were also granted names beginning

---

[15] *Sung shih* 18:1b says 1st day of the 4th month = Apr.18. However, the cyclical characters of that day were not *yi-chi* as claimed by the text but *jen-yin*.

with Chao. He and these relatives were appointed to Chinese offices. His mother was entitled Grand Consort of Sui-ning commandery, and his wife Lady of Hsien-ning commandery (*Sung shih* 492:20a-20b).

On Jan.20, 1097, Che-tsung appointed Hsia-cheng Military Commissioner of the non-existant Army West of the [Yellow] River and Acting Minister of Works, and entitled him duke of Ning-sai commandery (*Sung shih* 18:7b; 492:18a).

In 1099, first Hsia-cheng and then Lung-tsa surrendered to the Sung after internal troubles. This caused resentment among the conservative tribesmen, who refused to accept Chinese rule (*Sung shih* 492:18b).

On Apr.28, 1100, Che-tsung appointed Hsia-cheng Military Commissioner of the non-existant Army Which Cherishes the Distance. He appointed Lung-tsa Military Commissioner of the non-existant Army West of the [Yellow] River and granted him the imperial surname and given name of Chao Huai-te (*Sung shih* 19:2b).

Hsia-cheng found a refuge in China and died there in 1102. Lung-tsa arrived in K'ai-feng in 1104 and was appointed Military Commissioner of the non-existant Army Which Induces Virtue and enfeoffed as king of An-hua (*Sung shih* 492:19b).

The Tibetans here discussed were, to the Chinese, peaceful neighbours and trading partners, whose rulers were friendly to China. The Sung emperors did not formally recognize the chiefs, did not suspend the court at their deaths for a mourning period, and did not grant them any posthumous titles. But they knew how to please them, their mothers, and wives by nominal Chinese titles and rich gifts. While the rulers became sinicized, the tribesmen did not, and this for the better part of a century kept the Chinese at bay. The principality was, of course, much weaker than the T'u-yü-hun State had been, but, brief though it existance, it was not a tributary dependency of the Sung.

This is the distribution by 20-year periods of the 16 dated missions from Tsong-kha to Sung:

1007-1026: 2
1027-1046: 2
1047-1066: 3
1067-1086: 3
1097-1106: 6

Judging from these statistics, the Tibetans were drawn into a steadily closer contact with the Chinese.

The specified goods brought by the Tibetan missions fall into the following categories:

Animals and Animal Products

Elephant tusks

1077: elephant tusks.

Felines

1094: one lion.

Horses

1015: fine horses.
1016: 582 horses.

Aromatics

Frankincense

1077: frankincense.

Minerals and Metals

1015: 7000 ounces of gold.
1077: jade.

Jewels

1077: pearls.

Horses were a native product. Jade came from Central Asia. The lion and elephant tusks could have been from India via Tibet or Pamir, although the lion might have been from West Asia. Frankincense was a product of East Africa and the Middle East and had been brought to Tsong-kha on the Silk Routes. These goods witness eloquently of the far-flung commercial contacts of this small Tibetan principality.

The Chinese paid with silver, copper cash, brocade robes, golden belts, porcelain vessels, silk, tea, and drugs.

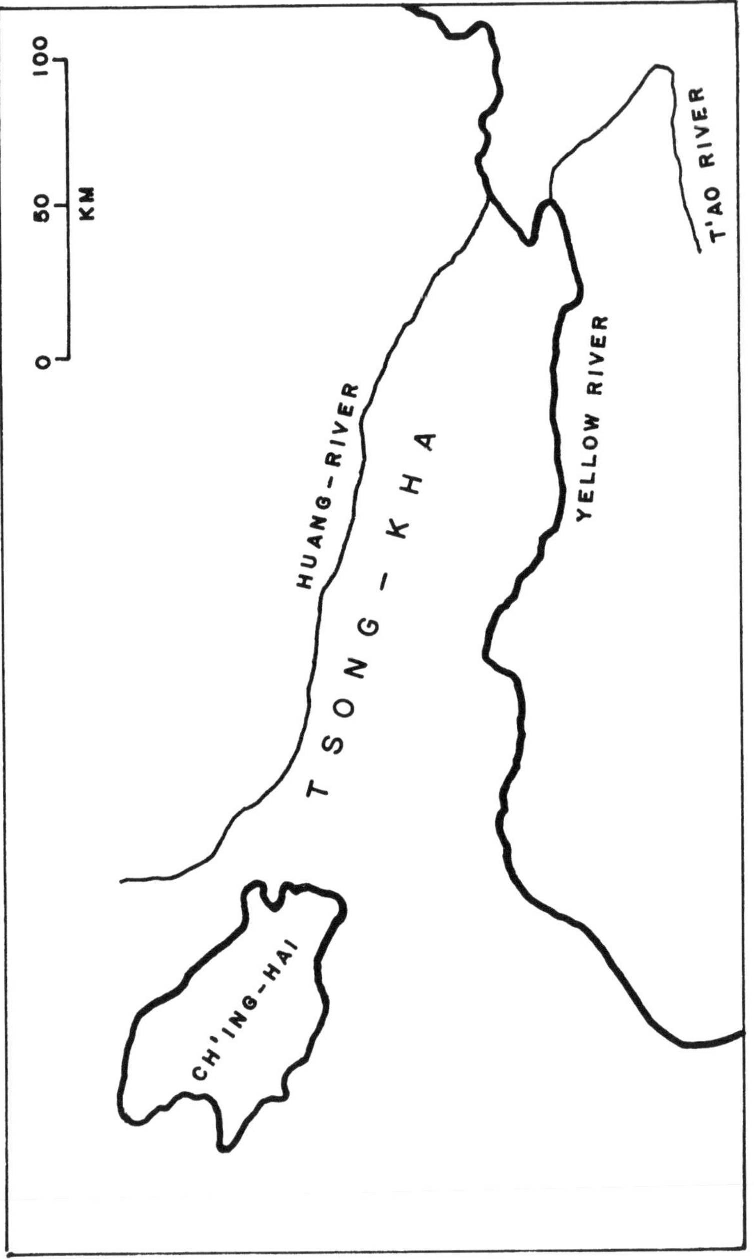

Map 7. Tsong-kha.

EAST TURKESTAN

THE NORTHERN SILK ROUTE

TURFAN

Travelling west on the Northern Silk Route through the Tarim Basin, Turfan was the first great oasis after Hami (map.8).[1] In Han times, it was called Chü-shih, thereafter Kao-ch'ang. For the Six Dynasties, the sources record one mission from Turfan to the Liang and 17 to the Northern Wei and Northern Chou.[2]

On July 21, 607, Turfan envoys to the Sui court offered regional objects (*Sui shu* 3:10b).

In 608, Turfan envoys offered gifts (*Sui shu* 83:7a).

On May 14, 609, envoys from Turfan were received at the Sui court (*Sui shu* 3:13a).

On July 23, 609, the king of Turfan, Ch'ü Po-ya, called on Emperor Yang of Sui in person. Po-ya had recently succeeded his father, his mother being the daughter of a Turkish qaghan. The emperor was at that time in northwestern China. He gave a banquet for the king and appointed him an Imperial Household Grandee of the Left and Grand Administrator of Chü-shih. This revived the Han Dynasty name for the kingdom of Turfan and turned it into an imaginary commandery. Po-ya was also entitled duke of Pien. He accompanied Emperor Yang's attack on Koguryŏ in 612. On their return, the emperor enfeoffed a lady of the Yü-wen clan as Princess of Hua-jung and married her to him. Before the end of 612, Po-ya went back to Turfan (*Sui shu* 3:13a; *Chiu T'ang shu* 198:3b; *Wen-hsien t'ung-k'ao* 325:49b; 336:38b).

On Sep.2, 619, envoys from Ch'ü Po-ya to the T'ang court offered gifts. Later that year envoys announced that Po-ya had died and had been succeeded by his son Wen-t'ai. Kao-tsu sent an Inspector to condole (*Chiu T'ang shu* 1:6a; 198:3b-4a; *Ts'e-fu yüan-kuei* p.5023; *Tzu-chih t'ung-chien* p.5859).

---

[1] Hami has no section of of its own in the dynastic histories and encyclopaedias.

[2] See my *Six Dynasties*, vol.II, p.102.

On Apr.17, 620, envoys from Ch'ü Wen-t'ai offered gifts (*Chiu T'ang shu* 1:6a; *Ts'e-fu yüan-kuei* p.5023).[3]

In the 8th month (Sep./Oct.) of 624,[4] the king of Turfan, Ch'ü Wen-t'ai , presented a male and a female dog, each 6 inches high and over a foot long. Both were trained to lead a horse or to carry a candle in its mouth. The breed came supposedly from Fu-lin (Syria) (*Chiu T'ang shu* 198:4a; *Ts'e-fu yüan-kuei* p.5023; *Wen-hsien t'ung-k'ao* 336:38b).

In the intercalary month (Apr./May) of 627, Turfan envoys offered garments of black fox fur. Emperor T'ai-tsung sent gifts to Ch'ü Wen-t'ai's wife, the Lady Yü-wen,[5] who in turn presented a jade plate (*Chiu T'ang shu* 198:4a; *Ts'e-fu yüan-kuei* p.5023).

In the 2nd month (March) and on Nov.29 of 629, Turfan envoys offered gifts (*Ts'e-fu yüan-kuei* p.5023).

On Jan.31, 631, the king of Turfan, Ch'ü W'en-t'ai and his wife personally called on Emperor T'ai-tsung in Ch'ang-an and received rich gifts. The Lady Yü-wen requested favours for her relatives, whereupon T'ai-tsung enfeoffed the Lady Li as Princess of Ch'ang-lo (*Chiu T'ang shu* 3:2a; 198:4a; *Tzu-chih t'ung-chien* p.683; *Wen-hsien t'ung-k'ao* 336:38b).

While Ch'ü Wen-t'ai was in the capital, T'ai-tsung decided to establish closer relations with other states of the Tarim Basin, supposedly at their own request. For that purpose, he dispatched a high official in the entourage of Ch'ü Wen-t'ai as his envoy. T'ai-tsung's famous councilor Wei Cheng protested. He quoted the precedent of Emperor Kuang-wu (r.A.D.25-57), founder of Later Han, who had refused to establish a protectorate over the Tarim Basin.[6] It would now as then be a burden for China. Border trade should be enough. T'ai-tsung accepted this and sent a messenger to overtake and bring back the envoy (*Tzu-chih t'ung-chien* pp.6083-6084).

On Feb.20, 631, Ch'ü Wen-t'ai was given a banquet (*Tzu-chih t'ung-chien* p.6086). The date of his return to Turfan is not recorded.

---

[3] Both texts say Ch'ü Po-ya which, unless his death date of 619 in *Chiu T'ang shu* is wrong, must be an error for Ch'ü Wen-t'ai.

[4] The month is only given by *Ts'e-fu yüan-kuei*, but it says 6th month. Since the preceding entry is dated 7th month and the following 9th month, 6th must be emended to 8th.

[5] In accordance with local custom, Wen-t'ai must have married his father's widow.

[6] See my *Restoration*, vol.III, p.133.

T'ai-tsung's change of heart was, however, brief, and he entered into diplomatic relations with Karashahr, further west from Turfan on the Northern Silk Route. Since Turfan greatly profited from the caravan trade through its territory, to the detriment of travellers, the king of Karashahr decided to bypass it and open a route through the desert in a southeasterly direction, linking up with the Southern Silk Route west of lake Lob-nor This was resented by Ch'ü Wen-t'ai. He therefore attacked Karashahr in 632 and looted its territory (*Tzu-chih t'ung-chien* p.6096; *Wen-hsien t'ung-k'ao* 336:40b).

There was no immediate reaction to this from T'ai-tsung, and missions from Turfan were received at the T'ang court in the 7th month (Aug./Sep.) of 633 and in 634 (*Chiu T'ang shu* 3:3b; *Ts'e-fu yüan-kuei* p.5024).

In 638, Ch'ü Wen-t'ai, allied with the Western Turks, again attacked Karashahr, burned settlements, kidnapped men and women, and withdrew. The king of Karashahr complained to T'ai-tsung, who sent a Gentleman-of-the-Palace of the Bureau of Forestry to find out the facts (*Chiu T'ang shu* 198:4a; *Tzu-chih t'ung-chien* p.6142).

T'ai-tsung had several grievances against Ch'ü Wen-t'ai, that he had allied himself with the Western Turks, had attacked Karashar, had threatened Hami, and had detained Chinese refugees who wished to return to their homeland. When Turfan envoys arrived at the T'ang court in 639, T'ai-tsung informed them that he intended to attack their country in the following year (*Chiu T'ang shu* 3:6b; 198:4a; *Tzu-chih t'ung-chien* 6146; *Wen-hsien t'ung-k'ao* 336:38b).

In the 3rd month (Apr./May) of 639, the Turkish Hsüeh-yen-t'o, a tribe of the T'ieh-le, proposed a joint attack on Turfan. T'ai-tsung sent a Master of Writing of the Ministry of Common People and the General-in-chief Who Commands the Army of the Right to present silk to the Hsüeh-yen-t'o and discuss the campaign. In the 7th month (Aug.Sep.), he also sent the Minister of Agriculture with a letter stamped with the imperial seal to the Hsüeh-yen-t'o (*Chiu T'ang shu* 198:4b; *Tzu-chih t'ung-chien* pp.6146-6147, 6148).

In the 11th month (December) of 639, T'ai-tsung sent another letter stamped with the imperial seal to Ch'ü Wen-t'ai, threatening him, and summoning him to his court. Wen-t'ai refused to come under the pretext of illness (*Chiu T'ang shu*198:4b; *Tzu-chih t'ung-chien* p.6150).

On Jan.2, 640, T'ai-tsung ordered the attack on Turfan by combined Chinese and Turkish forces, over the fervent protests of Wei Cheng and other advisers. While this army was approaching, Ch'ü

Wen-t'ai fell ill and died. He was succeeded by his son Chih-sheng. The latter wrote to the attacking general, trying in vain to stop the war by blaming it on his late father. In the 8th month (Aug./Sep.), Chih-sheng surrendered. In the 9th month (Sep./Oct.), T'ai-tsung annexed Turfan with the new name of Hsi commandery. It became the seat the An-hsi Protectorate from 640 to 649 (*Chiu T'ang shu* 198:4b, 5a; *Tzu-chih t'ung-chien* p.6150, 6155; *Wen-hsien t'ung-k'ao* 336:38b).

In the 12th month (Jan./Feb., 641) of the Chinese year 640, Ch'ü Chih-sheng was presented as a prisoner to T'ai-tsung in the Hall of Beholding Virtue. The emperor treated him with generosity. He appointed him General of the Martial Guards of the Left and entitled him duke of Chin-ch'eng commandery. His younger brother Chih-chan was made General of the Gentlemen-of-the-Household of the Martial Guards of the Left and entitled duke of T'ai-shan prefecture.[7] The prominent families of Turfan were transferred to China. After T'ai-tsung had died on July 10, 649, the features of Chih-sheng were carved in stone and placed at the emperor's tomb (*Chiu T'ang shu* 3: 7a; 198:5b).

Turfan having lost its independence, there were no further missions until the Sung dynasty. By that time, Turfan was ruled by Uighurs, a branch of whom had moved into East Turkestan after their defeat by the Kirghiz in 840.

In the 12th month (Jan./Feb., 908) of the Chinese year 907, the Uighurs of Turfan[8] offered gifts to the Khitan court (*Liao shih* 70: 1b).

On Nov.10, 913, the Uighurs of Turfan[9] offered gifts to the Khitan court (*Liao shih* 1:7a).

On July 14, 933, the Arslan Uighurs[10] offered gifts to the Khitan court (*Liao shih* 3:6b).

On May 19, 951, an envoy from the Uighurs of Turfan[11] to the Later Chou court offered six big and small jade lumps, nine catties of jade and amber, 1329 pieces of white cotton fabrics, 280 pieces of

[7] His son Ch'ung-shui was between 690 and 692 made General-in-chief of the Martial Guards of the Left and entitled king of Chiao-ho commandery. He was the last of his line (*T'ang hui-yao* 195:6a).

[8] Here called Ho chou.

[9] Here called Ho chou.

[10] The "Lion Uighurs". See note 14.

[11] Here called Hsi chou.

white coarse woolen stuffs, six corals, 2632 sable furs, 250 black sable furs, 503 blue sable furs, four old sable robes, one ring of white jade, one ring of blue-green jade, two iron mirrors, 69 jade belt buckles, one jade belt, and aromatic drugs (*Chiu Wu-tai shih* 111:2a; 138:5b; *Ts'e-fu yüan-kuei* p.5036).

In the 4th month (May/June) of 962, a Uighur mission of 42 men from Turfan[12] to the Sung court, offered regional objects (*Sung shih* 490:8b; *Wen-hsien t'ung-k'ao* 336:38b).

In the 11th month (Nov./Dec) of 965, the Uighur qaghan of Turfan[13] presented a tooth of the Buddha, opaque glass vessels, and amber cups to the Sung court (*Sung shih* 490:8b; *Wen-hsien t'ung-k'ao* 336:38b).

On Mar.15, ·971, Emperor Ching-tsung of Liao sent an envoy to the Arslan Uighurs (*Liao shih* 8:2b).

On June 29, 973, the Arslan Uighurs offered gifts to the Liao court (*Liao shih* 8:3b).

On Mar.26, 978, the Arslan Uighurs offered gifts to the Liao court (*Liao shih* 9:1b).

On Apr.26, 981, an envoy from the king of Turfan, who had assumed the titles of Shih-tzu wang and Assu-lan (Arslan),[14] offered gifts to the Sung court. In the 5th month (June/July), Emperor T'ai-tsung dispatched a Palace Servitor in response. He returned in 984 (*Sung shih* 4:14a; 490:8b; *Hsü Tzu-chih t'ung-chien ch'ang-pien* p.186; Wen-hsien t'ung-k'ao 336:38b).

In 983, Turfan envoys to the Sung court offered gifts (Sung shih 490:8b).

---

[12] Here called Hsi chou.

[13] Here called Hsi chou.

[14] Shih-tzu in Chinese means lion. A-ssu-lan, more commonly transliterated A-sa-lan (with various transscriptions in Chinese characers), renders the Turkish Arslan, also meaning lion. The ruler of Turfan therefore called himself Lion King in 981. According to Wittfogel, *Liao*, p.102, this designation was used by the rulers of Turfan, Kucha, and Kan-chou and often but not always referred to Turfan. It will be seen that at least one Uighur ruler of Kucha did, in fact, use the title of shih-tzu wang. I can, however, find no evidence that the qaghans of Kan-chou did the same. The term Lion King, or at times Arslan Uighurs, without reference to any political unit, would therefore in the present context (it was also used by the Qarluqs) seem to refer to Kucha or Turfan. I have listed all instances under Turfan, even though this may not always be correct.

In 984, the Uighurs of Turfan[15] offered gifts to the Sung court (*Sung shih* 490:13b; *Wen-hsien t'ung-k'ao* 347:30b).

In the intercalary month (June/July) of 988, Arslan Uighurs were received at the Liao court (*Liao shih* 70:8a).

On Mar.12, 989, envoys of the the Arslan Uighurs to the Liao court offered gifts (*Liao shih* 12:5a).[16]

In the 6th month (June/July) of 990, envoys of the the Arslan Uighurs to the Liao court offered gifts (*Liao shih* 13:1b).

On Nov.10, 991, the Arslan Uighurs offered gifts to the Liao court (*Liao shih* 13:3a).

On Nov.27, 995, envoys of the the Arslan Uighurs to the Liao court offered gifts (*Liao shih* 13:6b).

In the 11th month (Dec./Jan., 997) of the Liao year 996, [the king] of the Arslan Uighurs sought a marriage for his son with the imperial house of Liao. Emperor Sheng-tsung rejected it (*Liao shih* 13:7b).

In 1004, envoys from Turfan to the Sung court offered fine jade, fine horses, and other regional objects (*Sung shih* 490:12b; *Sung hui-yao kao*, chüan 6291; *Wen-hsien t'ung-k'ao* 336:38b).

On May 19, 1005, envoys of the Arslan Uighurs to the Liao court offered gifts. In the 7th month (Aug./Sep.) of that year, envoys of the Arslan Uighurs requested the return of envoys who previously had been detained by Liao. All were sent back (*Liao shih* 14:6b; 70:11b).

On Dec.11, 1045, envoys of the the Arslan Uighurs to the Liao court offered gifts (*Liao shih* 19:7a).

On Apr.17, 1049, envoys from Turfan to the Liao court offered gifts (*Liao shih* 20:3a).

On Dec.16, 1052, envoys of the the Arslan Uighurs presented Emperor Hsing-tsung of Liao with fine horses and leopards (*Liao shih* 20:7a; 70:19b).

On Feb.26, 1053, the Arslan Uighurs informed the Liao court that they were attacked by a neighbouring country and requested help (*Liao shih* 20:7b).

On May 20, 1068, envoys of the Arslan Uighurs to the Liao court offered gifts (*Liao shih* 22:5b).

On June 29, 1112, the Uighurs of Turfan[17] offered gifts to the Liao court (*Liao shih* 27:6b).

---

[15] Here called Hsi chou.

[16] By 70:8b dated 3rd month (Apr./May).

[17] Here called Ho chou.

It is evident that during the Five Dynasties and Sung, Turfan had much closer relations to the Khitan than to the Chinese, 19 recorded missions against 7.

KARASHAHR

Karashahr was the next great oasis on the Northern Silk Route west of Turfan. Its Chinese name since Han times was Yen-ch'i. There were no documented relations between Karashahr and the Six Dynasties.

During the reign of Emperor Yang (605-617), envoys from the king of Karashahr to the Sui court offered regional objects (*Sui shui* 83:10b; *Ts'e-fu yüan-kuei* p.5023; *Wen-hsien t'ung-k'ao*336:40b).

In the 7th month (July/Aug.) of 632, envoys from the king of Karashahr to the T'ang court offered regional objects (*Chiu T'ang shu* 198:8b; *Ts'e-fu yüan-kuei* p.5024; *Wen-hsien t'ung-k'ao* 336:40b).

Until this time, Turfan had become wealthy through the caravan trade on the Northern Silk Route passing through its territory. The king of Karashahr therefore decided to bypass Turfan by developing a route through the desert in a southeasterly direction, linking up with the Southern Silk Route west of lake Lob-nor. He informed Emperor T'ai-tsung and presented fine horses. The king of Turfan resented this development, attacked Karashahr in 632 and looted its territory (*Chiu T'ang shu* 198:8b; *Tzu-chih t'ung-chien* p.6096; *Wen-hsien t'ung-k'ao* 336:40b).

In the 2nd month (Feb./Mar.) of 635 and in the 2nd month (Mar./Apr.) of 636, envoys from Karashahr to the T'ang court offered gifts (*Ts'e-fu yüan-kuei* p.5024).

In 638, Karashahr was again attacked by Turfan, allied with the Western Turks. The enemy burned settlements, and kidnapped men and women. The king of Karashahr complained to T'ai-tsung, who sent a Gentleman-of-the-Palace of the Bureau of Forestry to find out the facts (*Chiu T'ang shu* 198:4a; *Tzu-chih t'ung-chien* p.6142).

In 639, Karashahr allied itself with the Western Turks. But it also sent envoys with gifts to the T'ang (*Chiu T'ang shu* 3:6b; *Tzu-chih t'ung-chien* p.6151).

In the 1st month (Jan./Feb.) of 640, envoys from Karashahr to the T'ang court offered regional objects (*Ts'e-fu yüan-kuei* p.5024). That year, the T'ang destroyed Turfan and annexed its territory. The commanding Chinese general sent an agent to Karashahr, proposing an alliance. The king of Karashahr responded with another mission to the T'ang court, offering regional objects (*Chiu T'ang shu* 198:8b).

Karashahr found itself in a difficult position, with both China and the Western Turks bringing pressure on it. The latter arranged a marriage between one of their dignitaries and a daughter of the king of Karashahr. T'ai-tsung, on his part, sent an army which captured the king, Lung Ch'üeh-chi-chih, and his family, and in the 10th month (Nov./Dec.) of 644 brought them to Ch'ang-an. Karashahr meanwhile enthroned a new king, who allied himself with the Western Turks but also sent missions to the T'ang court (*Tzu-chih t'ung-chien* pp.6211-6212, 6213).

In the 3rd month (Mar./Apr.) of 648, envoys from Karashahr offered gifts (*Ts'e-fu yüan-kuei* p.5025).

After T'ai-tsung's death on July 10, 649, the image of the still living Lung Ch'üeh-chi-chih was carved in stone and placed at his tomb (*Chiu T'ang shu* 198:9a).

In 651, the throne of Karashahr fell vacant, and its people requested the return of their former king, Lung Ch'üeh-chi-chih. Emperor Kao-tsung approved. In the 4th month (Apr./May) of that year, he appointed Ch'üeh-chi-chih as General of the Martial Guards of the Right and sent him back to Karashahr (*Tzu-chih t'ung-chien* p.6274).

In the 1st month (Feb./Mar) of 710, envoys from Karashahr were received at the T'ang court (*Ts'e-fu yüan-kuei* p.5026).

In the 2nd month (March) of 713, envoys from Karashahr offered gifts (*Ts'e-fu yüan-kuei* p.5027).

In the 1st month (Feb/Mar.) of 737, a chief from Karashahr was received at the T'ang court (*Ts'e-fu yüan-kuei* p.5029).

On Feb.14, 747, the New Year's Day, envoys from Karashahr congratulated at the T'ang court and offered regional objects (*Ts'e-fu yüan-kuei* p.5030).

In the 3rd month (Apr./May) of 748, envoys from Karashahr presented regional objects (*Ts'e-fu yüan-kuei* p.5030).

KUCHA

Kucha was situated on the Northern Silk Route west of Karashahr. Its Chinese name since Han times was Chiu-tz'u. For the Six Dynasties, two missions are recorded from Kucha to the Liang and 12 to the Northern Wei and Northern Chou.[18]

[18] See my *Six Dynasties*, vol.II, p.103.

On Feb.4, 615, the New Year's Day, Kucha envoys offered gifts to the Sui court (*Sui shu* 4:9b; 83:11a; *Wen-hsien t'ung-k'ao* 336:40a).

After Kao-tsu had founded the T'ang dynasty on June 18, 618, envoys from the king of Kucha were received at the T'ang court (*Chiu T'ang shu* 198:9a; *Ts'e-fu yüan-kuei* p.5023; *Wen-hsien t'ung-k'ao* 336:40a).

In 626, Kucha envoys offered gifts (*Chiu T'ang shu* 2:8a).

In 630, envoys from the king of Kucha presented horses (*Chiu T'ang shu* 198:9b; *Ts'e-fu yüan-kuei* p.5024; *Wen-hsien t'ung-k'ao* 336:40a).

In 634, Kucha envoys offered gifts (*Chiu T'ang shu* 3:3b).

Subsequently, Kucha allied itself with the Western Turks, but it did not break off relations with the T'ang, and its envoys presented regional objects in the 1st month (Feb./Mar.) of 642 (*Ts'e-fu yüan-kuei* p.5024; *Tzu-chih t'ung-chien* p.6151; *Wen-hsien t'ung-k'ao* 336:40a).

In 644, Kucha sent troops to aid Karashahr against the T'ang (*Chiu T'ang shu* 198:9b; *Wen-hsien t'ung-k'ao* 336:40a).

In the 1st month (Feb./Mar.) of 647, Kucha again offered regional objects to the T'ang court (*Ts'e-fu yüan-kuei* p.5024).

Having annexed Turfan in 640 and defeated Karashahr in 644, T'ai-tsung turned against Kucha in 648. When the Chinese army, augmented by allies, approached, Kucha surrendered and its king, Ho-li-pu-shih-pi, and his chancellor were subsequently taken prisoners. After a brief reverse, the Chinese took control of Kucha and installed a new king. In 649, they moved the seat of the An-hsi Protectorate from Turfan to Kucha. This protectorate eventually, but only temporarily, came to comprise Kucha, Karashahr, Kashgar, Khotan, and Tokmak west of lake Issyk-Kul (*Chiu T'ang shu* 198:10a-10b; *Tzu-chih t'ung-chien* pp.6251, 6271; *Wen-hsien t'ung-k'ao* 336:40a).

On Feb.22, 649, the captured king of Kucha, Ho-li-pu-shih-pi, his chancellor, and other prisoners were presented in the Temple to the Gods of the Soils and Crops in Ch'ang-an. The king was appointed a General of the Gentlemen-of-the-Household of the Martial Guards of the Left. The chancellor and lesser officials received nominal offices, each in accordance with his rank. After T'ai-tsung's death on July 10, 649, the features of the still-living Ho-li-pu-shih-pi were carved in stone and placed at the emperor's tomb (*Chiu T'ang shu* 3:11b; 198: 10a; *Tzu-chih t'ung-chien* p.6265).

In the 8th month (September) of 650, Emperor Kao-tsung appointed Ho-li-pu-shih-pi as General-in-chief of the Resolute Guard of the Right, subsequently restored him as king of Kucha, and sent him back to his state with 1000 items of gifts (*Chiu T'ang shu* 198:10a; *Tzu-chih t'ung-chien* p.6271).

On Sep.7,[19] 656, the king of Kucha. Ho-li-pu-shih-pi personally visited the T'ang court (*Tzu-chih t'ung-chien* p.6298).

On Feb.4, 675, the king of Kucha offered gifts and received silk in return (*Chiu T'ang shu* 5:6a; *Ts'e-fu yüan-kuei* p.5026).[20]

On Jan.8, 676, the king of Kucha presented fine horses to the T'ang court, even though the Tibetans loosely controlled East Turkestan from 670 to 692 (*Chiu T'ang shu* 5:6b; 198:10b; *Ts'e-fu yüan-kuei* p.5026).

In the 3rd month (Mar./Apr.) of 692, Kucha offered gifts (*Ts'e-fu yüan-kuei* p.5026)

In the 1st month (Feb./Mar.) of 709, Kucha envoys offered regional objects (*Ts'e-fu yüan-kuei* p.5026).

In the 6th month (July) of 721, envoys from the king of Kucha presented horses and dogs (*Ts'e-fu yüan-kuei* p.5026).

In 730, the king of Kucha sent a younger brother on a visit to the T'ang court (*Wen-hsien t'ung-k'ao* 330:40a).

On Feb.14, 747, the New Year's Day, Kucha envoys congratulated at the T'ang court and presented regional objects (*Ts'e-fu yüan-kuei* p.5030).

In the 3rd month (April) of 748, envoys from Kucha presented regional objects (*Ts'e-fu yüan-kuei* p.5030). This is the last recorded mission from Kucha in T'ang times.

In the 5th month (June) of 976, envoys from Kucha offered gifts to the Sung court. This state was henceforth under Uighur rulers (*Sung hui-yao kao* 1076:1a).

In the 2nd month (Feb./Mat.) of 1001, envoys from Kucha presented fine horses, dromedaries, camels without humps, jade horse trappings, a precious sword, an iron sword, opaque glass vessels, pitchers of *t'ou* stone[21] etc. They received brocade garments, golden belts, 200 ounces of silver wine vessels, and 200 bolts of brocade and thin silk (*Sung hui-yao kao* 1076:1a-2a).

On Dec.15, 1001, Kucha envoys offered gifts (*Sung shih* 6:14a, 14b; *Wen-hsien t'ung-k'ao* 336:40a).[22]

---

[19] Correcting *chi-ssu* to *yi-ssu*.

[20] According to *Ts'e-fu yüan-kuei*, this king also had the Chinese title of General-in-chief of the Resolute Guards of the Right.

[21] A copper-coloured mineral.

[22] On July 7, 1003, a Buddhist priest from Kucha presented leaves from the

In the 11th month (Nov./Dec.) of 1003, Kucha envoys offered gifts (*Sung hui-yao kao* 1076:2a).

In the 5th month (May/June) of 1004, Kucha envoys offered gifts (*Sung shih* 7:7b; *Sung hui-yao kao* 1076:2a).

In the 6th month (June/July) of 1004, Kucha envoys offered gifts (*Sung hui-yao kao* 1076:2a).

In the intercalaray month (Mar./Apr.) of 1010, a mission from the king and qaghan of Kucha, headed by a certain Li Yen-sheng, with Li An-fu as his deputy, presented 249 catties of frankincense, two bolts of flowered cotton, 371 catties of uncut gems, one dromedary, and 15 big-tailed white sheep. In addition to these royal goods, the envoys traded on their own. Li Yen-sheng offered ten horses, horsetrappings, and 212 catties of gold and jade. Li An-fu offered 40 catties of amber and 12 catties of jade. Another envoy offered 69 catties of frankincense, two catties of jade, and 14 catties of barbarian (hu) *huang-lien.*[23] Another envoy offered 76 catties of frankincense. Still another envoy offered 39 catties of frankincense. A Buddhist priest attached to the mission offered 45 catties of amber and 46 catties of jade (*Sung shih* 7:26a; 490: 15a; *Sung hui-yao kao* 1076:2a-2b; *Wen-hsien t'ung-k'ao* 336:40a).

In 1011, the mission of the preceding year was still in K'ai-feng, and the chief envoy, Li Yen-sheng, was appointed General of the Garrison Guards of the Left (*Sung hui-yao kao* 1076:2b).

On Jan.1, 1014, a mission from the king of Kucha, consisting of 36 men, offered camels, fine horses, horse trappings, 60 jade lumps, bows and arrows, aromatic drugs, etc. An edict ordered payment for these goods (*Sung shih* 8:8a; 490:15a; *Sung hui-yao kao* 1076:2b-3a; *Hsü Tzu-chih t'ung-chien ch'ang-pien* p.716).

In the 4th month (Apr./May) of 1017, envoys from the king of Kucha offered horses, jade, and aromatic drugs (*Sung hui-yao kao* 1076: 3a).

In the 6th month (June/July) of 1017, a Kucha envoy presented one horse, jade horse trappings, and one jade lump (*Sung shih* 8:16a, 17b; *Sung hui-yao kao* 1076:3a).

On Dec.27, 1020, envoys from the qaghan and Lion King (Arslan or shih-tzu wang) of Kucha and of the Uighurs of Kan chou offered

---

Bodhi tree. He was presented with a purple robe and belt (*Sung-hui yao-kao* 1076:2a). This was not an official mission.

[23] A bitter plant used for medicine.

big-tailed white sheep (*Sung shih* 8:20b; 490:16a; *Sung hui-yao kao* 1076: 3a).

In the 7th month (Aug./Sept.) of 1021, a palace eunuch informed Emperor Chen-tsung that envoys from Kucha had requested the *Tripitaka* and golden images (*Sung hui-yao kao* 1076:3a).[24]

In the 4th month (May/June) of 1024, envoys from the qaghan and king of Kucha offered camels, horses, and frankincense (*Sung shih* 9: 5b; *Sung hui-yao kao* 1076:3a).[25]

In 1025, 1029, 1030, on Feb.5, 1031, and the 6th month (July/Aug.) of 1037, Kucha offered gifts. At the last occasion, Sung presented the ruler with Buddhist sutras (*Sung shih* 9: 6b, 12a, 13b-14a; 10:10b; 490: 22b; *Sung hui-yao kao* 1076:3a-3b; *Hsü Tzu-chih t'ung-chien ch'ang-pien* p.979; *Wen-hsien t'ung-k'ao* 336:40a).

In the 4th month (May/June) of 1040, Kucha envoys offered gifts (*Sung hui-yao kao* 1076:3b).

In the 9th month (Sep./Oct.) of 1071, a Kucha envoy offered gifts (*Sung shih* 490:22b; *Sung hui-yao kao* 1076:3b; *Wen-hsien t'ung-k'ao* 336: 40a).

On Feb.23, 1072, a Kucha envoy offered gifts (*Sung shih* 15:7a; *Wen-hsien t'ung-k'ao* 336:40a).

In 1096, a great chief of Kucha, heading a mission of three men, presented a letter and a jade Buddha (*Sung shih* 18:7a; 490:22b; *Wen-hsien t'ung-k'ao* 336:40a).

KASHGAR

Kashgar, situated in the westernmost part of the Tarim Basin, was the oasis where, if one travelled west, the Northern and Southern Silk Routes met. Kashgar therefore can be assigned to either of them. Its Chinese name since Han times was Su-le.[26] No missions are recorded from Kashgar to the Six Dynasties.

On Feb.4, 615, the New Year's Day, Emperor Yang of Sui gave a

---

[24] In 1022, a Buddhist priest from Kucha arrived at the Sung court from Western India with bones of the Buddha (*Sung-hui-yao* 1076:3a). This was not an official mission.

[25] The reception of this mission is by *Hsü Tzu-chih t'ung-chien ch'ang-pien* p.903 dated Apr.16.

[26] The first character of the name is written by the sources in three variants.

great banquet for the envoys from Kashgar and other states (*Sui shu* 4:9b; 83:11b; *Wen-hsien t'ung-k'ao* 337:42b).

In the intercalary month (May/June) of 635, envoys from Kashgar to the T'ang court presented fine horses (*Chiu T'ang shu* 198:10b; *Ts'e-fu yüan-kuei* p.5024; *Wen-hsien t'ung-k'ao* 337:42b).

In the 2nd month (Mar./Apr.) of 636, envoys from Kashgar were received at the T'ang court (*Ts'e-fu yüan-kuei* p.5024).

In the 12th month (Dec./Jan., 637) of the Chinese year 636, envoys from Kashgar were received at the T'ang court (*Ts'e-fu yüan-kuei* p.5024).

In 639, envoys from Kashgar offered gifts (*Chiu T'ang shu* 3:6b; *Wen-hsien t'ung-k'ao* 337:42b).

In the 9th month (Sep./Oct.) of 659, Emperor Kao-tsung gave the unrealistic order to establish Chinese commanderies and prefectures out of Kashgar, Tashkent, Kabūdhān, Kish, Māimargh, Bukhara, Tokharia, Yi-ta, etc. (*Tzu-chih t'ung-chien* p.6317).

In 698, envoys of the king of Kashgar offered gifts (*Ts'e-fu yüan-kuei* p.5026).

In 728, Emperor Hsüan-tsung sent the Director of the Grand Judge to recognize the king of Kashgar (*Chiu T'ang shu* 198:10b; *Wen-hsien t'ung-k'ao* 337:42b).

On Feb.8, 753, the New Year's Day, a chief from Kashgar congratulated at the T'ang court and was presented with a purple robe and a fish wallet (*Ts'e-fu yüan-kuei* p.5030; *Wen-hsien t'ung-k'ao* 337:42b).

THE SOUTHERN SILK ROUTE

CHU-CHÜ-PO

Chu-chü-po was situated on the Southern Silk Route southeast of Kashgar. According to *Hsin T'ang shu* 221A:10b, its first mission to China was to the Northern Wei between 435 and 440. There were no documented relations between Chu-chü-po and the Six Dynasties.

In 635, Chu-chü-po envoys were received at the T'ang court (*Hsin T'ang shu* 221A:11a).

On Jan.23, 637, Chu-chü-po envoys were received at the T'ang court (*Ts'e-fu yüan-kuei* p.5024; *Tzu-chih t'ung-chien* p.6123).

In the 12th month (Dec./Jan., 638) of the Chinese year 637, Chu-chü-po envoys were received at the T'ang court (*T'ang hui-yao* 99: 19b).

In 639, Chu-chü-po envoys, together with Kashgar, offered regional objects (*Wen-hsien t'ung-k'ao* 337:42b).

Between 713 and 741, Chu-chü-po was annexed by the T'ang (*Hsin T'ang shu* 221A:11a).

KHOTAN

Khotan was the next great oasis on on the Southern Silk Route, travelling east from Chu-chü-po. Its Chinese name since Han times was Yü-t'ien. For the Six Dynasties, four missions are recorded from Khotan to Liang and 13 to Northern Wei.[27]

On Feb.4, 615, the New Year's Day, Emperor Yang of Sui gave a great banquet for the envoys from Khotan and other states (*Sui shu* 4:9b; 83:11b; *Wen-hsien t'ung-k'ao* 337:42b).

In 632, envoys from the king of Khotan to the T'ang court presented a jade belt. Emperor T'ai-tsung responded with a letter (*Chiu T'ang shu* 198:11a; *Ts'e-fu yüan-kuei* p.5024; *Wen-hsien t'ung-k'ao* 337:41a).

In the 2nd (Feb./Mar.) and 9th month (Oct./Nov.) of 635, envoys from the king of Khotan offered regional objects (*Ts'e-fu yüan-kuei* p.5024).

In the 2nd month (Mar./Apr.) of 636, Khotan envoys were received at the T'ang court (*Ts'e-fu yüan-kuei* p.5024).

In 639, Khotan envoys offered gifts (*Chiu T'ang shu* 3:6b).

In the 1st month (Feb./Mar.) of 642, Khotan envoys offered regional objects (*Ts'e-fu yüan-kuei* p.5024).

On Feb.2, 645, the New Year's Day, Khotan envoys congratulated at the T'ang court and offered regional objects (*Ts'e-fu yüan-kuei* p.5024).

On Jan.30, 648, the New Year's Day, Khotan envoys offered gifts (*Ts'e-fu yüan-kuei* p.5025).

At the end of 648, a son of the king of Khotan presented 300 camels (*Wen-hsien t'ung-k'ao* 337:41a).

In the intercalary month (Jan./Feb., 649) of the Chinese year 648, the king of Khotan, Fu-she-hsin, paid a personal visit to the T'ang court. One of his sons entered the imperial bodyguards. After T'ai-tsung had died on July 10, 649, the image of the still-living Fu-she-hsin was carved in stone and placed at the grave mound. Kao-tsung

[27] See my *Six Dynasties*, vol.II, pp.103-104.

appointed Fu-she-hsin General-in-chief of the Resolute Guards of the Right and one of his sons General of the Resolute Guards of the Right. Both were presented with golden belts and 60 items of brocade robes and textiles. On Aug.19, 649, Fu-she-hsin was still in Ch'ang-an (*Chiu T'ang shu* 3:11b; 4:2a; 198:11a; *Wu-tai hui-yao* 29:13a; *Tzu-chih t'ung-chien* p.6266).

On Jan.14, 674, the king of Khotan, with sons, younger brothers, and chiefs, 70 men in all, visited the T'ang court, in spite of the Tibetan presence in East Turkestan from 670-692 (*Tzu-chih t'ung-chien* p.6374; *Wen-hsien t'ung-k'ao* 337:41a).

In the 4th month (May/June) of 677, Khotan offered regional objects (*Ts'e-fu yüan-kuei* p.5026).

In the 12th month (Jan./Feb., 683) of the Chinese year 682, Khotan presented regional objects (*Ts'e-fu yüan-kuei* p.5026).

Somewhere around this time, Emperor Kao-tsung (d.Dec.27, 683), established the fictitious P'i-sha Area Command with the king of Khotan as its Military Governor (*Wen-hsien t'ung-k'ao* 337:41b).

The king of Khotan having died, the Empress Wu recognized his successor in 687 (*Chiu T'ang shu* 198:11a; *Wen-hsien t'ung-k'ao* 337:41b).

In the 2nd month (March) of 713, Khotan envoys offered gifts (*Ts'e-fu yüan-kuei* p.5027).

In the 6th month (July/Aug.) of 717, Khotan envoys presented four horses and camels (*Ts'e-fu yüan-kuei* p.5027; *Wen-hsien t'ung-k'ao* 337:41b).

In 728, envoys from the new king of Khotan offered gifts (*Chiu T'ang shu* 198:11a).

On Feb.14, 747, the New Year's Day, Khotan envoys congratulated at the T'ang court and offered regional objects (*Ts'e-fu yüan-kuei* p.5030).

In the 3rd month (Apr./May) of 748, Khotan envoys offered regional objects (*Ts'e-fu yüan-kuei* p.5030).

For reasons which are not entirely clear, a certain Yao became king of Khotan and was recognized by Emperor Su-tsung on Feb.15, 760. Meanwhile, Yao's elder brother Sheng was in Ch'ang-an. In 764, Emperor Tai-tsung attempted to send Sheng back to Khotan to claim his throne, but Sheng objected on the grounds that the people of the state had accepted his younger brother Yao. Tai-tsung gave in and appointed Sheng as Commander Unequalled in Honour and conferred on him the nominal title of king of Wu-tu (*Tzu-chih t'ung-chien* pp.7090, 7171; *Wen-hsien t'ung-k'ao* 337:41b).

The question of legitimacy arose again in 785, when Yao wished to make Sheng's son Chih his successor. Sheng was still alive and lived with Chih in Ch'ang-an. Emperor Te-tsung appointed Chih as Acting Superintendent of the Imperial Household and prepared to send him to Khotan. But Sheng objected on the grounds that his brother and presumably that branch of the family were popular in Khotan, and that Chih had been born and had grown up in China without knowing the customs of Khotan. This ended the matter. Chih remained in China and was appointed Adviser of the king of Shao[28] (*Tzu-chih t'ung-chien* p.7467; *Wen-hsien t'ung-k'ao* 337:41b).

When Khotan reemerged in history in the 10th century, it was ruled by Uighurs.

In the 9th month (Sep./Oct.) of 938, envoys from the king of Khotan to the Later Chin court presented jade lumps, white cotten fabrics, yak tails, red salt, curcoma longa,[29] uncut gems, jade horse trappings etc. The king gave his name as Li Sheng-t'ien and claimed to be a relation of the T'ang imperial house. This means that, according to him, one of his ancestors had been conferred the imperial surname of that dynasty. On Nov.22, Emperor Kao-tsu of Later Chin appointed the chief envoy as General-in-chief Who Maintains the State in Peace, enfeoffed him as Dynasty-founding Duke of Fu-feng commandery, and appointed his deputy as State Courier-envoy. He also sent a Palace Servitor, an Acting Grand Herald, and an Administrative Assistant to entitle Li Sheng-t'ien as Greatly Valued King of Khotan. It took the Chinese envoys two years to reach Khotan, and they did not return until 942. At that occasion, the king of Khotan presented 1000 catties of jade and a jade seal (*Wu-tai hui-yao* 29:13b; *Hsin Wu-tai shih* 8:6b; 74:11a, 13a; *Ts'e-fu yüan-kuei* p.5035; *Wen-hsien t'ung-k'ao* 337:41b).

On Feb.4, 943, envoys from the Uighurs of Khotan to the Later Chin court offered regional objects (*Chiu wu-tai shih* 81:9a).

In the 6th month (June/July of 947, Khotan envoys were received at the Later Han court (*Hsin Wu-tai shih* 10:4a).

In the 5th month (June/July) of 948, Khotan envoys to the Later Han court offered gifts. The chief envoy was appointed Acting Minister of Works (*Wu-tai hui-yao* 29:13b; *Ts'e-fu yüan-kuei* p.5036; *Wen-hsien t'ung-k'ao* 337:41b).

[28] He was a half brother of Te-tsung.

[29] A fragrant herb.

In 959, envoys from Khotan were received at the Later Chou court (*Sung shih* 490:1b).

In the 12th month (Jan./Feb., 962) of the Chinese year 961, envoys from the king of Khotan to the Sung court offered one *kuei* tablet[30] in a jade envelope, two pitchers of opaque glass, and barbarian (hu) brocade. The envoys told that in their state people collected jade in the rivers (*Sung shih* 490:4b; *Wen-hsien t'ung-k'ao* 337:41b).[31]

On Jan.16, 966, envoys from the king of Khotan, the qaghan of the Uighurs of Kan chou, and others presented 1000 horses, 500 camels, 500 jade lumps, and 500 catties of amber (*Sung shih* 2:2b-3a; *Wen-hsien t'ung-k'ao* 337:41b).

On Mar.15, 966, a son of the king of Khotan offered regional objects (*Sung shih* 2:4a; 490:5a; *Wen-hsien t'ung-k'ao* 337:41b).

In the 11th month (Nov./Dec.) of 968, Khotan envoys offered camels and regional, objects (*Sung hui-yao kao* ts'e 197:2a).

In 969,[32] an envoy of the Khotan Uighurs told the Sung court that in his state there was a jade lump weighing 237 catties and proposed that the Sung should send for it. Emperor T'ai-tsu appointed him Grand Master Who Displays Civilization and requested him to bring the jade to China (*Sung shih* 2:9a; 490:5b; *Wen-hsien t'ung-k'ao* 337:41b).

In 971, a Buddhist priest presented a letter to the Sung court in which the king of Khotan informed that he had defeated Kashgar and had captured a dancing elephant, which he wished to present. Emperor T'ai-tsu accepted it (*Sung shih* 490:5b; *Wen-hsien t'ung-k'ao* 337:41b).

On Mar.12 and Apr.5 of 989, Khotan envoys to the Liao court offered gifts (*Liao shih* 12:5a).[33]

On Feb.28, 990, Khotan envoys to the Liao court offered gifts (*Liao shih* 13:1a).

In 1009, a Uighur envoy from Khotan to the Sung court offered regional objects. He observed Chinese court protocol by kneeling and wishing Long Life (*Sung shih* 7:23a; 490:5b; *Wen-hsien t'ung-k'ao* 337: 41b-42a).

---

[30] A symbol of authority.

[31] In the 5th month (June) of 965, Bhuddist priests from Khotan and two other places were received at the Sung court (*Sung shih* 490:5a; *Wen-hsien t'ung-k'ao* 337:41b). This was not an official mission.

[32] *Sung shih* 2:9a says 11th month, *keng-yin*, which date did not exist.

[33] Both dates fall into the 2nd month. *Liao shih* 70:8a-8b lists a mission from Khotan in the 3rd month. That is probably an error for 2nd.

On Feb.22, 1015, the Khotan State offered gifts to the Liao court (*Liao shih* 15:8b).

In the 12th month (Dec./Jan., 1020) of the Chinese year 1019, Khotan envoys to the Sung court offered jade horse trappings, a white jade belt, barbarian (hu) brocade, dromedaries, frankincense, and uncut gems. An edict ordered that they be repaid for the value of their goods and additionally be presented with 200 garments, golden belts, and 100 ounces of silver vessels (*Wen-hsien t'ung-k'ao* 337:42a).

In 1025, Khotan offered gifts (*Sung shih* 9:6b).

In the 8th month (Aug./Sep.) of 1063, Khotan envoys offered regional objects. In the 11th month (Nov./Dec.), the newly enthroned Sung Emperor Ying-tsung appointed the king as Specially Advanced, recognized him as king and qaghan of Khotan, and ordered that he be paid 5000 strings of cash for his goods (*Sung shih* 490:6b-7a; *Wen-hsien t'ung-k'ao* 337:42a).

According to *Wen-hsien t'ung-k'ao* 337:42a, among the goods brought from Khotan at this time are listed pearls, jade, corals, kingfisher's feathers, elephant tusks, frankincense, putchuck, opaque glass, flowered cotton, uncut gems, dragon salt, western brocade, jade horse trappings, castoreum,[34] star quartz, and chicken tongue aromatics.

On Mar.18, 1071, the Khotan State offered gifts (*Sung shih* 15: 5a).

On Mar.27, 1074, Khotan offered gifts (*Sung shih* 15:10b).

On May 2, 1077, Khotan offered gifts (*Hsü Tzu-chih t'ung-chien ch'ang-pien* p.2657).

On July 20, 1078, Khotan envoys sought to buy tea (*Sung hui-yao kao* ts'e 197)

On Nov.29, 1078, Khotan offered regional objects (*Sung shih* 15: 21b).[35]

In the 1st month (Feb./Mar.) of 1079, Khotan offered gifts (*Sung-hui-yao kao* ts'e 197)[36]

---

[34] According to Webster, a creamy orange-brown substance with a strong penetrating odor and bitter taste which consists of the dried perineal glands of the beaver and their secretion or an extract of this and is used by perfumers as a fixative. The Chinese term could also stand for civet, a similar substance obtained from the civet cat and used in perfumes as well.

[35] By *Sung hui-yao kao* ts'e 197 dated Dec.5, 1078.

[36] This and the next entry in *Sung hui-yao kao* are dated 1081. But the preceding entry is dated 1078 and the following 1080. 1081 should therefore be emended to 1079.

On Jan.19, 1080, Emperor Shen-tsung ordered that missions from Khotan were not to exceed 50 men, and that China would only accept regional objects, horses, and donkeys. Frankincense was to be rejected because of its uselessness (*Sung shih* 490:7a; *Sung hui-yao kao* ts'e 197; *Wen-hsien t'ung-k'ao* 337:42a).

On Feb.20, 1080,[37] a great chief from Khotan offered gifts (*Sung shih* 16:1a; *Sung hui-yao kao* ts'e 197).

On Nov.22, 1080, border officials reported to the Sung court that envoys from Khotan had arrived with 100,000 catties of frankincense and miscellaneous goods. Because of the imperial decree, they had not dared to pass them through. An edict ordered the frankincense to be returned (*Sung hui-yao kao* ts'e 197).

On Mar.6, 1081, another chief from Khotan brought a letter and gifts (*Sung shih* 16:3a; 490:7a; *Wen-hsien t'ung-k'ao* 337:42a).

On May 20, 1083, Khotan offered gifts (*Sung shih* 16:10a).

On Oct.9, 1085, Khotan envoys offered gifts (*Sung hui-yao kao* ts'e 197).

On Dec.1, 1085, Khotan offered horses for which they were paid 1,200,000 cash (*Sung hui-yao kao* ts'e 197).

On Dec.21, 1085, Khotan presented a lion. It was rejected, but on Dec.25 the king was paid 1,000,000 cash, presumably for other goods (*Sung shih* 17:4a; 490:7b; *Sung hui-yao kao* ts'e 197; *Wen-hsien t'ung-k'ao* 337: 337:42a).

On Apr.8, 1086,[38] Emperor Che-tsung, who had ascended the throne on Apr.1 of the preceding year, presented the king of Khotan with garments, belts, vessels, and silk. On Dec.29, envoys from Khotan offered gifts (*Sung shih* 17:5b, 7a; *Sung hui-yao kao* ts'e 197).

On Feb.17, 1087, Sung paid the king of Khotan 300,000 cash (*Sung hui-yao kao* ts'e 197).

On Mar.21, 1087, Che-tsung presented the king of Khotan with a golden belt, brocade robes, vessels, and silk (*Sung-shih* 17:7b; *Sung hui-yao kao* ts'e 197).

On June 24, 1087, Apr.19, 1088, July 8,[39] 1089, Mar.24, 1090, July

---

[37] In accordance with *Sung hui-yao kao*, the *ting-mao* of *Sung shih* must be corrected to *hsin-mao*.

[38] By *Sung hui-yao kao* dated Mar.23.

[39] *Hsü Tzu-chih t'ung-chien ch'ang-pien* p.4003 gives the date of 4th month, *yi-ssu*, which did not exist.

10, 1091,[40] Jan.18, 1092, and Dec.8, 1092, Khotan offered gifts (*Sung shih* 17:8b, 11b, 12b, 15a,, 18b; *Sung hui-yao kao* ts'e 197; *Hsü Tzu-chih t'ung-chien ch'ang-pien* p.4127).

In 1093, Khotan offered the Sung an alliance against the Hsia State, which was rejected (*Sung shih* 490:7b-8a; *Wen-hsien t'ung-k'ao* 337:42a).

On Aug.4, 1096, envoys from Khotan offered regional objects (*Sung hui-yao kao* ts'e 197).

On Feb.22, 1097, Dec.28, 1108, Feb.11, 1117, Aug.26, 1118, and Nov.4, 1124, Khotan offered gifts (*Sung shih* 18:10b; 20:8b; 21:7b, 11a; 22:11a; *Sung hui-yao kao* ts'e 197).

The oasis states of East Turkestan were rich through the caravan trade on the Silk Routes but poor in the size of their populations. They were also weakened by fighting each other. This made them vulnerable to the aggression of the Chinese, Tibetans, Turks, and Uighurs. Survival against these powerful neighbours could be not by force of arms but only by diplomacy.

Emperor Wu of Former Han had succeeded in establishing a protectorate over East Turkestan from the end of the 1st century B.C. onward. This lasted until the beginning of Later Han, when Emperor Kuang-wu (r.A.D.25-57) refused military involvement in Central Asia.[41] With the Chinese victories over the Northern Hsiung-nu in A.D.73 and 89, East Turkestan was again brought under Chinese control until the protectorate disintegrated after 150.

In the following centuries, the oasis states maintained their independence but again lost it in T'ang times. Over the protests of his chief advisers, T'ai-tsung annexed Turfan in 640 and defeated Karashahr in 644. In 640, he established the An-hsi Protectorate in Turfan, which was moved to Kucha in 649. Subsequently, Kashgar and Khotan were brought under Chinese control by diplomatic means, Chu-chü-po as late as 713-741. From 670, the Tibetans controlled East Turkestan, but they were defeated in 692 by armies sent by the Empress Wu, and the An-hsi Protectorate was reestablished (*Chiu T'ang shu* 198:10b). From 790, East Turkestan again fell to the Tibetans.

The Five Dynasties were too weak to assert themselves in Central

[40] *Hsü Tzu-chih t'ung-chien ch'ang-pien* p.4269 gives the date of Mar.3, but that refers to the reception of the mission from Fu-lin.

[41] See my *Restoration*, vol.III, pp.131-134.

Asia, and the Sung was blocked from that region by the Hsia State. The oasis states of East Turkestan, now ruled by Uighurs, were therefore once more independent. But the goods they traded were actively sought by the Sung. For instance, an edict of Nov.4, 1087, "ordered" Khotan annually to "offer tribute" (*Hsü Tzu-chih t'ung-chien ch'ang-pien* p.3840), i.e. requested trade missions.

During the times when East Turkestan was a Chinese protectorate, the Chinese rarely mixed into the internal affairs of the states. They maintained the peace, and the states governed themselves under their own rulers. China recognized some and perhaps all of them. One Chinese princess was married to the king of Turfan in 612. The T'ang is recorded to have condoled on the death of the king of Turfan in 619, but no official mourning was held and no posthumous titles were conferred. During T'ang, as they had done in Han times, rulers in East Turkestan sent hostages to the Chinese court. Of all the cases examined in this work, this is the only one where the rendering of hostages cannot be in doubt. The only cases recorded concern the king of Khotan in 635 and 639 (*Chiu T'ang shu* 3:6b; *Wen-hsien t'ung-k'ao* 337:41a).), but there must have been others. This does not mean that the Indo-European oasis states of T'ang times welcomed the presence and cultural influence of the Chinese. It has been seen that a Khotan prince, residing in Ch'ang-an, refused in 785 to let his son become king of Khotan because he was too sinified.

According to *Sui shu* 83:8a, Turfan offered annual gifts from 609. Only one further mission is recorded for Sui. According to *Chiu T'ang shu* 198:9a, Karashahr offered goods from 649 without interruption. Five missions are recorded until 737. According to *Wen-hsien t'ung-k'ao* 336:40b, Karashahr frequently offered gifts from 742 to 753. Two missions are recorded. According to *Chiu T'ang shu* 198:9b and *Ts'e-fu yüan-kuei* p.5024, Kucha offered gifts from 630 without interruption. Three missions are recorded until 642. According to *Sung shih* 490: 22b and *Wen-hsien t'ung-k'ao* 336:40a, Kucha sent five missions from 1023 to 1037. Six are actually recorded. According to *Chiu T'ang shu* 198:10b, Kashgar sent missions from 635 without interruption. Four missions are recorded until 639. According to *T'ung-tien* 193:21a, Chu-chü-po continuously sent envoys from early T'ang. Two missions are recorded until 636. According to *Wen-hsien t'ung-k'ao* 337:42a, missions from Khotan arrived from the late 1060's to1085 every year or every second year, sometimes twice a year. Seven missions are recorded for that period, but never two in one year. In about 1086, the Sung court restricted missions from Khotan to one a year (*Wen-hsien t'ung-k'ao*337: 42a). Missions are recorded for 1087, 1088, 1089, 1090, 1092, and 1093. The conclusion must be that for Sui and T'ang, the statistices are incomplete. The caravan traffic to China on the Silk Routes must have been so intense that the historians only noted the most important arrivals. For Sung, on the other hand, the statistics seem to be relatively comprehensive.

Missions from East Turkestan arrived at the Chinese courts throughout the year, but the preference was for the 11th, 12th and 1st months in order to attend the New Year ceremonies. The 2nd month also had a high frequency, whereas the 3rd to the 10th months had the lowest.

This is the distribution by 20-year periods of the 150 recorded missions from Turfan, Karashahr, Kucha, Kashgar, Chu-chü-po, and Khotan to Sui, T'ang, Later Chin, Later Han, Later Chou and Sung:

	Northern Silk Route	Southern Silk Route
587- 606:	0	0
607- 626:	14	1
627- 646:	24	10
647- 666:	3	3
667- 686:	2	3
687- 706:	2	0
707- 726:	4	3
727- 746:	2	0
747- 766:	5	2
767- 786:	0	0
787- 806:	0	0
807- 826:	0	0
827- 846:	0	0
847- 866:	0	0
867- 886:	0	0
887- 906:	0	0
907- 926:	0	0
927- 946:	0	3
947- 966:	3	6
967- 986:	4	3
987-1006:	6	0
1007-1026:	8	3

1027-1046:	5	0
1047-1066:	0	1
1067-1086:	2	14
1087-1106:	1	9
1107-1126:	0	4

It can be seen that although the Western Turks excerted general control over the Tarim Basin until the 640's, the oasis states had no trouble in pursuing their own relations with the Sui and T'ang. During the Tibetan occupation from 670-692, a few missions got through to the T'ang (from Kucha, Kashgar, and Khotan). But after the return of the Tibetans in 790, government trade ceased altogether while private trade of course continued. It is also clear that, incomplete though the statistics may be for the T'ang, missions from Turfan, Karashahr, Kucha, and Kashgar along the Northern Silk Route to China by far outstripped those from Chu-chü-po and Khotan along the Southern Silk Route,[42] 56 for the north and 22 for the south. In the second half of the 11th century, however, the situation was reversed. Khotan then only competed with Kucha, and the southern missions became far more numerous than the northern, 28 against 3. From 1127, all relations between East Turkestan and the distant Southern Sung came to an end.[43]

The almost exclusive purpose of the missions from the oasis states to the Chinese court was trade, and the envoys dealt with Chinese merchants as well as the government. According to *Wen-hsien t'ung-k'ao* 337:42a, they sold their goods either to merchants or the Outer Treasury, depending on where they got the better price.

The specified goods brought by the missions from East Turkestan to China fall into the following categories:

Human Products

965: a tooth of the Buddha from Turfan.

[42] Yarkand (So-chü), situated between Kashgar and Khotan, did not have the importance of its neighbours.

[43] Note that Turfan also sent one and Khotan three missions to the Liao court.

Animals and Animal Products

Elephants

971: one dancing elephant from Khotan.

Elephant tusks

Undated: elephant tusks from Khotan.

Felines

1052: leopards from Turfan.
1085: one lion from Khotan (rejected).

Horses

630: horses from Kucha.
632: fine horses from Karashahr.
635: fine horses from Kashgar.
675: fine horses from Kucha.
721: horses from Kucha.
717: 4 horses from Khotan.
966: 1000 horses from Khotan (with Kan-chou).
1001: fine horses from Kucha.
1004: fine horses from Turfan.
1010: 10 horses from Kucha.
1013: fine horses from Kucha.
1017: horses from Kucha.
1024: horses from Kucha.
1052: fine horses from Turfan.
1085: horses from Khotan.

Camels

648: 300 camels from Khotan.
717: camels from Khotan.
966: 500 camels from Khotan (with Kan chou).
1001: dromedaries and camels without humps from Kucha.
1010: one domedary from Kucha.
1013: camels from Kucha.
1019: dromedaries from Khotan.
1024: camels from Kucha.

Sheep

1010: 15 big-tailed white sheep from Kucha.
1020: big-tailed white sheep from Kucha.

Dogs

624: two miniature male and female dogs from Turfan.
721: dogs from Kucha.

Furs and feathers

951: 2632 sable furs, 250 black sable furs, and 503 blue sable furs from Turfan.
Undated: kingfisher's feathers from Khotan.

Other

938: yak tails from Khotan.

Aromatics

Aromatic and medical drugs

951: aromatics from Turfan.
1010: barbarian (hu) *huang-lien* from Kucha.
1013: aromatic drugs from Kucha.
1017: aromatic drugs from Kucha.
Undated: chicken tongue aromatics from Khotan.

Frankincense

1010: 393 catties of frankincense from Kucha.
1019: frankincense from Khotan.
1024: frankincense from Kucha.
1080: frankincense from Khotan.

Fragrant herbs

938: curcoma longa from Khotan.

Cosmetics

Undated: putchuck from Khotan, castoreum from Khotan.

Spices

938: red salt from Khotan.
Undated: dragon salt from Khotan.

Minerals and Metals

938: jade lumps from Khotan.
951: 6 big and small jade lumps and a quantity of jade from Turfan.
966: 500 jade lumps from Khotan (with Kan chou).
1004: jade from Turfan.
1010: 60 catties of jade from Kucha.
1013: 60 jade lumps from Kucha.
1017: jade from Kucha.
1010: 212 catties of gold and jade from Kucha.
Undated: star quartz from Khotan.

Manufactured Objects

Of metal

1001: one precious sword and an iron sword from Kucha.
951: 2 iron mirrors from Turfan.

Of glass

965: opaque glass vessels from Turfan.
961: 2 opaque glass pitchers from Khotan.
1001: opaque glass vessels from Kucha.

Of precious stone

627: one jade plate from Turfan.
938: jade horse trappings from Khotan.
951: 2 rings of white jade, 2 rings of blue-green jade, 69 jade belt buckles, and one jade belt from Turfan.

961: one *kuei* tablet in a jade envelop from Khotan.
1001: jade horse trappings and pitchers of *t'ou* stone from Kucha.
1010: jade horse trappings from Kucha.
1017: jade horse trappings from Kucha.
1019: jade horse trappings and a white jade belt from Khotan.
1096: one jade Buddha from Kucha.

Of amber

965: amber cups from Turfan.

Of fur

627: garments of black fox fur from Turfan.
951: 4 old sable robes from Turfan.

Of leather

1013: horse trappings from Kucha.

Other

1013: bows and arrows from Kucha.

Textiles

Cottons

938: white cotton fabrics from Khotan.
951: 1329 pieces of white cotton fabrics and 280 pieces of white coarse woolen stuffs from Turfan.
1010: 2 bolts of flowered cotton from Kucha.
Undated: flowered cotton from Khotan.

Silks

961: barbarian (hu) brocade from Khotan.
1019: barbarian (hu) brocade from Khotan.
Undated: western brocade from Khotan.

Jewels

938: uncut gems from Khotan
951: 6 corals and a quantity of amber from Turfan.
966: 500 catties of amber from Khotan (with Kan chou).
1010: 371 catties of uncut gems from Kucha.
1017: uncut gems from Khotan.
Undated: pearls and corals from Khotan.

Of these items, very few were native to East Turkestan, chiefly horses, camels, sheep, dogs, yak tails, jade, and some textiles. The vast majority had been brought to the oasis states on the caravan routes. Such items as the elephant, ivory, kingfisher's feathers, frankincense, glass, amber, western brocade, and corals had been passed along over vast distances, first to the oasis states and then to China.

The Chinese paid for the goods received with copper cash, silver, silver vessels, [porcelain] vessles, silk, brocade, golden belts, garments, tea, and Buddhist sutras.

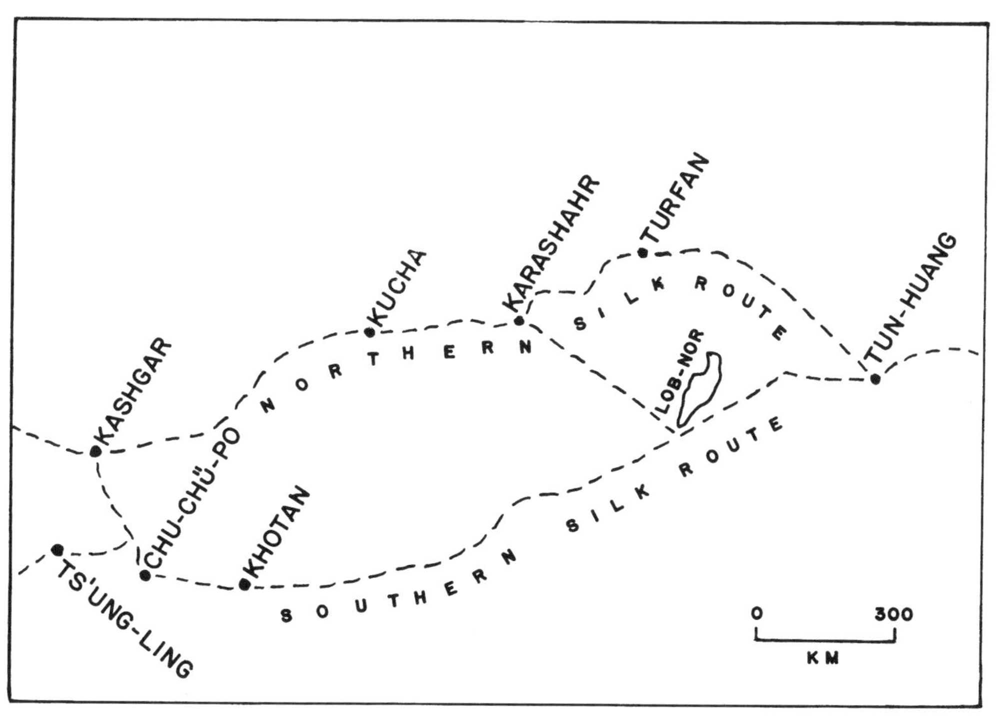

Map 8. East Turkestan.

WEST TURKESTAN

On May 23, 743, Emperor Hsüan-tsung requested information on the location of foreign countries. Part of the report of the Herald concerned with West Turkestan is preserved in the *T'ang hui-yao* 100: 21a-22b. It mentions seven of the seventeen states which have sections of their own in the histories and encyclopaedias, as well as others which are now obscure. Distances are given in day journeys or in Chinese miles (*li*), based on contemporary maps.

The Chinese sources refer to the states of West Turkestan by Chinese names. While their locations, with two exceptions, can be established with a fair degree of certainty, their equivalent West Asian names are a different matter. Some of the towns have existed under changing names until today. Some have disappeared, but their ancient names are known. In other cases, only the Chinese names are preserved. If their ancient territories were situated between modern places, it is a matter of conjecture by which names they should be referred to. It is nevertheless better, wherever possible, to attempt rough West Asian correlations so that the geography can be more easily visualized (map.9).

Emperor Yang of Sui (r.605-618), eager to establish relations with foreign countries and doing just as he had done in the maritime south, sent two envoys to West Turkestan. These were the Attending Secretary Wei Chieh and the Attendant of the Director of the Retainers Tu Hsing-man. When they returned to Ch'ang-an, they brought carnelian cups, Buddhist sutras, ten dancing girls, and asbestos (*Pei shih* 97:3a-3b).

FERGHANA

The Chinese name for this state was P'o-han.[1] It was situated at the upper Syr-Darya, between Kokand and Andizhan, with Ferghana between them (map 9).

Between 605 and 617, envoys from Ferghana to the Sui court offered

[1] *Wen-hsien t'ung-k'ao* 338:47b calls it Chin-han.

regional objects (*Sui shu* 83:12b; *Wen-hsien t'ung-k'ao* 338:47b).

In 656 or 657, envoys from the king of Ferghana to the T'ang court offered gifts. In 658, Emperor Kao-tsung created the imaginary Hsiu-hsün Area command and appointed the king of Ferghana as its Military Governor (*Wen-hsien t'ung-k'ao* 338:47b).

In 738, Emperor Hsüan-tsung entitled the ruler of Ferghana King Who Upholds Civilization (*Wen-hsien t'ung-k'ao* 338:47b).

In 744, Emperor Hsüan-tsung changed the name of the state to Ning-yüan (Pacifying the Distance), by which it henceforth appears in the Chinese sources. He also granted the king the epithet Valued, enfeoffed a lady of the imperial house as Princess of Ho-yi,[2] and married her to him (*Tzu-chih t'ung-chien* p.6862; *Wen-hsien t'ung-k'ao* 338:47b).

In the 11th month (Dec./Jan., 750) of the Chinese year 749, envoys from the king of Ferghana arrived at the T'ang court to congratulate on the New Year's Day of Jan.23, 750 (*Ts'e-fu yüan-kuei* p.5030).

In the 2nd month (March) of 751, envoys from the king of Ferghana presented 22 horses, one leopard, and one "heavenly" dog. In the 9th month (Sep./Oct.), envoys presented 20 horses and later that month 40 horses (*Ts'e-fu yüan-kuei* p.5030).[3]

In the 12th month (Jan./Feb., 753) of the Chinese year 752, envoys from Ferghana were received at the T'ang court (*Ts'e-fu yüan-kuei* p.5030).

In the 8th month (Sep./Oct.) of 753, envoys from Ferghana offered gifts (*Ts'e-fu yüan-kuei* p.5031).

In the 4th month (Apr./May) of 754, envoys from Ferghana were received at the T'ang court. In the 9th month (Sep./Oct.), its king presented barbarian (hu) horses and regional objects (*Ts'e-fu yüan-kuei* p.5031). A son of the king of Ferghana visited the T'ang court at one of these two occasions and requested to be enrolled in the imperial bodyguards. He was appointed General of the Martial Guards of the Left (*Wen-hsien t'ung-k'ao* 338:47b).

In the 3rd month (Apr./May) of 759, an envoy from Ferghana was received at the T'ang court (*Ts'e-fu yüan-kuei* p.5031).

In the 6th (June/July), 8th (Aug./Sep.), and 12th month (Dec./Jan., 763) of the Chinese year 762, Ferghana offered gifts (*Ts'e-fu yüan-kuei* p.5031).

---

[2] *Wen-hsien t'ung-k'ao* says Princess of An-wei.

[3] The mission had probably set out with 60 horses, but stragglers with 40 horses had fallen behind.

TASHKENT

The Chinese name for this state was Shih.[4] It was situated on the right shore of the Syr-Darya, northwest of Ferghana, and its territory corresponded to modern Tashkent.[5]

In 609, envoys from Tashkent to the Sui court offered gifts (*Sui shu* 83:9b; *T'ung-tien* 193:21b; *Wen-hsien t'ung-k'ao* 339:54b).

In the 12th month (Dec./Jan., 635) of the Chinese year 634, envoys from Tashkent to the T'ang court offered gifts (*Chiu T'ang shu* 3:3b; *T'ung-tien* 193:21b).

In the 1st month (Jan./Feb.) of 646, envoys from Tashkent offered gifts (*Ts'e-fu yüan-kuei* p.5024).

In the 1st month (Feb./Mar.) of 647, envoys from Tashkent offered gifts (*Chiu T'ang shu* 3:11a; *Ts'e-fu yüan-kuei* p.5024).

In the 1st month (Jan./Feb.) of 648, envoys from Tashkent offered gifts (*Ts'e-fu yüan-kuei* p.5025).

In the 6th month (July/Aug.) of 655, envoys from Tashkent offered gifts (*Ts'e-fu yüan-kuei* p.5025).

In 658, Emperor Kao-tsung created the imaginary Ta-wan Area Command and appointed the king of Tashkent as its Military Governor (*Wen-hsien t'ung-k'ao* 339:54b).

In the 9th month (Sep./Oct.) of 659, Emperor Kao-tsung gave the unrealistic order to establish Chinese commanderies and prefectures out of Kashgar, Tashkent, Kabūdhān, Kish, Māimargh, Bukhara, Tokharia, Yi-ta, etc. (*Tzu-chih t'ung-chien* p.6317).

In the 9th month (Oct./Nov.) of 682, envoys from Tashkent offered regional objects (*Ts'e-fu yüan-kuei* p.5026).

In c.713, Emperor Hsüan-tsung recognized the king of Tashkent and appointed him a Specially Advanced (*T'ang hui-yao* 99:15a; *Wen-hsien t'ung-k'ao* 339:54b).

In the 2nd month (Mar./Apr.) of 718, envoys from Tashkent were received at the T'ang court (*Ts'e-fu yüan-kuei* p.5027).

In the 12th month (January 721) of the Chinese year 720, envoys from Tashkent offered gifts (*Ts'e-fu yüan-kuei* p.5027).

In the 2nd month (March) of 721, envoys from the king of Tashkent offered gifts (*Ts'e-fu yüan-kuei* p.5027).

---

[4] Written with the Chinese character for "stone".

[5] Schafer, *Golden Peaches*, p.64, prefers Chāch, and Herrmann, *Atlas*, p.37, Chāsh.

In the 5th month (May/June) of 727, Tashkent presented barbarian (hu) twirling girls[6] and grape wine (*Ts'e-fu yüan-kuei* p.5028).

In the 4th month (Apr./May) of 730, envoys from Tashkent offered gifts (*Ts'e-fu yüan-kuei* p.5028).

In 740, Hsüan-tsung conferred on the king of Tashkent the title of King Who Obeys Righteousness (*Wen-hsien t'ung-k'ao* 339:54b).

In 741, the king of Tashkent sought help against the Arabs. This was rejected by Hsüan-tsung (*Wen-hsien t'ung-k'ao* 339:54b-55a).

In the 3rd month (Apr./May) of 742, Tashkent presented horses and regional objects (*Ts'e-fu yüan-kuei* p.5029).

In the 12th month (Dec./Jan., 744) of the Chinese year 743, the son-in-law of a high official in Tashkent presented objects (*Ts'e-fu yüan-kuei* p.5030).

In the 7th month (Aug./Sep.) of 744, envoys from Tashkent presented horses (*Ts'e-fu yüan-kuei* p.5030).

In the 7th month (August) of 745, envoys from a high official of the king of Tashkent offered gifts (*Ts'e-fu yüan-kuei* p.5030).

In the 3rd month (Mar./Apr.) of 746, envoys from the king of Tashkent presented 15 horses, and from the assistant king regional objects. That year, Emperor Hsüan-tsung conferred on a royal son of Tashkent the title of King Who Cherishes Civilization (*T'ang hui-yao* 99:15a; *Ts'e-fu yüan-kuei* p.5030; *Wen-hsien t'ung-k'ao* 339:55a).

In the intercalary month (Nov./Dec.) of 746, envoys from Tashkent offered presents (*Ts'e-fu yüan-kuei* p.5030).

In the 5th month (June/July) of 747, envoys from the king of Tashkent offered horses (*Ts'e-fu yüan-kuei* p.5030).

In the 8th month (Dep/Oct.) of 749, a son of the king of Tashkent was received at the T'ang court (*Ts'e-fu yüan-kuei* p.5030).

In 750, the Military Commissioner of the An-hsi Protectorate, Kao Hsien-chih, a Korean in Chinese service, overran Tashkent, apparantly without provocation, and captured its king. In the 1st month (Feb./Mar.) of 751, he presented the king of Tashkent, and the king of Chieh-shih, a Turkish qaghan, and Tibetan chiefs whom he had also captured to the T'ang court.[7] In the 4th month (Apr./May), the king and his son escaped and returned to Tashkent (*Tzu-chih t'ung-chien* p.6904, 6907).

---

[6] Dancers.

[7] See also infra note 27.

In the 12th month (Dec./Jan., 757) of the Chinese year 756, Tashkent offered regional objects (*Ts'e-fu yüan-kuei* p.5031).

In the 12th month (Dec./Jan., 763) of the Chinese year 762, Tashkent offered gifts (*Ts'e-fu yüan-kuei* p.5031).

In 763,[8] envoys from Tashkent offered gifts (*Wen-hsien t'ung-k'ao* 339:55a).

In 772, envoys from Tashkent offered gifts (*T'ang hui-yao* 99:15b).

In the autumn of 777, envoys from Tashkent offered gifts (*Chiu T'ang shu* 11:10b).

SAMARKAND

The T'ang sources consider Samarkand (K'ang) as a sucessor of Sogdiana (K'ang-chü) of Han times (*Sui shu* 83:8a; *Chiu T'ang shu* 198: 13b; *Tzu-chih t'ung-chien* p.6091).[9]

Between 605 and 617, envoys from Samarkand once offered regional objects to the Sui court (*Sui shu* 83:9a).

In the 6th month (June/July) of 624, envoys from Samarkand offered fine horses to the T'ang court (*T'ang hui-yao* 99:18a; *Ts'e-fu yüan-kuei* p.5023).

In the 12th month (Dec./Jan., 627 of the Chinese year 626, envoys from the king of Samarkand presented fine horses (*Ts'e-fu yüan-kuei* p.5023).

In the 5th month (June/July) of 627, envoys from Samarkand offered gifts (*Ts'e-fu yüan-kuei* p.5023; *Wen-hsien t'ung-k'ao* 338:47a).

In 628, envoys from the king of Samarkand presented fine horses (*Chiu T'ang shu* 198:14a).

In the 12th month (Dec./Jan., 632) of the Chinese year 631, Samarkand offered the T'ang an alliance.[10] Emperor T'ai-tsung rejected it (*Tzu-chih t'ung-chien* p.6091).

On Apr.28, 635,[11] Samarkand presented a lion. T'ai-tsung ordered the Inspector of the Imperial Library to write a *fu* about it (*Chiu T'ang shu* 3:3b; 198:14a; *Ts'e-fu yüan-kuei* p.5024).

---

[8] *T'ang hui-yao* 99:15b erroneously writes *pao-li* instead of *pao-ying* 2nd year.

[9] *T'ung-tien* 193:18a and *Wen-hsien t'ung-k'ao* 338:47a continue to call Samarkand K'ang-chü.

[10] The text says that Samarkand "begged to attach itself to China" which is, of course, preposterous.

[11] By *T'ang hui-yao* 99:18a dated 7th month (July/Aug.) of 626.

In 637,[12] Samarkand presented [seedlings of] gold and silver peach trees. T''ai-tsung ordered that they be planted in a park (*Chiu T'ang shu* 198:14a; *Ts'e-fu yüan-kuei* p.5024).

In the 2nd month (Mar./Apr.) of 639, envoys from Samarkand offered gifts (*Chiu T'ang shu* 3:6b; *Ts'e-fu yüan-kuei* p.5024).

In the 1st month (Feb./Mar.) of 642, envoys from Samarkand offered regional objects (*Ts'e-fu yüan-kuei* p.5024).

On Jan.26, 643, the New Year's Day, envoys from Samarkand to the T'ang court presented regional objects (*Ts'e-fu yüan-kuei* p.5024).

On Feb.14, 644, the New Year's Day, envoys from Samarkand to the T'ang court presented regional objects (*Ts'e-fu yüan-kuei* p.5024).

On Feb.2, 645, the New Year's Day, envoys from Samarkand congratulated at the T'ang court and offered regional objects (*Ts'e-fu yüan-kuei* p.5024).

In the 1st month (Feb./Mar.) of 647, Samarkand offered regional objects (*Ts'e-fu yüan-kuei* p.5024). In the 3rd month (Apr./May), Samarkand presented yellow peaches, as big as goose eggs. The colour was like gold. They were also called golden peaches[13] (*T'ung-tien* 193:18a; *Ts'e-fu yüan-kuei* p.5025). On Sep.21, envoys from the king of Samarkand offered gifts (Chiu T'ang shu 3:10b-11a).

On Jan.30, 648, the New Year's Day, envoys from Samarkand to the T'ang court offered gifts (*Ts'e-fu yüan-kuei* p.5025).

In the 4th month (Apr./May) of 654, envoys from Samarkand offered gifts (*Ts'e-fu yüan-kuei* p.5026).

In 658,[14] Emperor Kao-tsung established the imaginary K'ang-chü Area Command and appointed the king of Samarkand as its Military Governor (*T'ang hui-yao* 99:18a-18b; *Wen-hsien t'uing-k'ao* 338:47a).

In the 10th month (Nov./Dec.) of 679, envoys from Samarkand offered gifts (*Ts'e-fu yüan-kuei* p.5026).

In 696, the Empress Wu recognized the king of Samarkand and appointed him General-in-chief of the Resolute Guards of the Left (*Chiu T'ang shu* 198:14a).

[12] By *T'ang hui-yao* 99:18a dated 11th month (Dec./Jan., 627) of the the Chinese year 626.

[13] These are the golden peaches of Schafer's title.

[14] The date is according to *T'ang hui-yao*. *Wen-hsien t'ung-k'ao* has 650-656. However, Emperor Kao-tsung established other Area Commands in 658, so that this date should be correct.

Between 705 and 707, Emperor Chung-tsung recognized a king of Samarkand (*T'ang hui-yao* 99:18b).

In the 6th month (July) of 707, envoys from Samarkand presented regional objects (*Ts'e-fu yüan-kuei* p.5026).

In the 3rd month (Apr./May) of 717, envoys from Samarkand presented textiles and indigo (*Ts'e-fu yüan-kuei* p.5027).

In 718, envoys from Samarkand offered a pygmy, barbarian (hu) twirling girls, a leopard, dogs, chain armour, a rock crystal bowl, a carnelian pitcher, ostrich eggs, and *yüeh-no* cloth (*Chiu T'ang shu* 198:14a; *Ts'e-fu yüan-kuei* p.5027; *Wen-hsien t'ung-k'ao* 338:47b).

In the 2nd (Feb./Mar.) month of 719, the kings of Samarkand and Bukhara informed the T'ang court that they had been under attack by the Arabs (*Tzu-chih t'ung-chien* p.6735). In the 6th month (June/July), envoys from Samarkand offered gifts (*Ts'e-fu yüan-kuei* p.5027).

In the 4th month (Apr./May) of 724, envoys of the king of Samarkand presented one pygmy, two horses, and two dogs (*Ts'e-fu yüan-kuei* p.5028).

In the 11th month (Nov./Dec.) of 726, envoys from the king of Samarkand presented a leopard and regional objects (*Ts'e-fu yüan-kuei* p.5028).

In the 5th month (May/June) of 727, Samarkand presented barbarian (hu) twirling girls and a leopard (*Ts'e-fu yüan-kuei* p.5028).

In 731, the king of Samarkand requested recognition of one of his sons as king of Kabūdhān and of another as king of Māimargh.[15] Emperor Hsüan-tsung complied (*Chiu T'ang shu* 198:14a-14b; *Wen-hsien t'ung-k'ao* 338:47b).

In 739, it became known at the T'ang court that the king of Samarkand had died. Hsüan-tsung recognized his successor (*Chiu T'ang shu* 198:14b).

In the 10th month (Oct./Nov.) of 740, envoys from Samarkand presented a precious censer, white jade rings, carnelian, and rock crystal (*Ts'e-fu yüan-kuei* p.5029).

In the 12th month (Dec./Jan., 744) of the Chinese year 743, a chief from Samarkand presented objects (*Ts'e-fu yüan-kuei* p.5030).

In the 7th month (Aug./Sep.) of 744, envoys from Samarkand presented horses and valuables. Hsüan-tsung conferred on the king

[15] Both states adjoined Samarkand.

the title of King Who Respects Civilization, and on his mother that of Commandery Consort (*Chiu T'ang shu* 198:14b; *Ts'e-fu yüan-kuei* p.5030).

In the 1st month (Feb./Mar.) of 750, a chief sent by the king of Samarkand presented ten horses and regional objects (*Ts'e-fu yüan-kuei* p.5030).

In the 9th month (Sep./Oct.) of 751, envoys from Samarkand offered gifts (*Ts'e-fu yüan-kuei* p.5030).

In the 12th month (Jan./Feb., 753) of the Chinese year 752, envoys from Samarkand offered presents (*Chiu T'ang shu* 198:14b; *Ts'e-fu yüan-kuei* p.5030).

In 754, envoys from Samarkand offered gifts (*Chiu T'ang shu* 198: 14b; *Ts'e-fu yüan-kuei* p.5031).

On July 10, 758, the Chief Clerk of Samarkand was received at the T'ang court (*Chiu T'ang shu* 10:9a; *Ts'e-fu yüan-kuei* p.5031).

In the autumn of 772, envoys from Samarkand offered gifts (*Ts'e-fu yüan-kuei* p.5031).

KABŪDHĀN

This state, which was called Ts'ao in Chinese, was situated northeast of Samarkand, between it and the Syr-Darya. As will be seen, there are references to Eastern, and Western Kabūdhān.[16]

On Aug.29, 614, envoys from Kabūdhān to the Sui court offered regional objectst. On Feb.4, 615, the New Year's Day, Emperor Yang gave a great banquet for these and other envoys (*Sui shu* 4:9a, 9b; *Wen-hsien t'ung-k'ao* 338:48a).

In the 7th month (July/Aug.) of 624, envoys from Kabūdhān to the T'ang court offered gifts (*Ts'e-fu yüan-kuei* p.5023).[17]

In the 1st month (Feb./Mar.) of 642, envoys from Kabūdhān presented regional objects (*Ts'e-fu yüan-kuei* p.5024).

In the 10th month (Nov./Dec.) of 652, envoys from Kabūdhān offered gifts (*Ts'e-fu yüan-kuei* p.5025).

---

[16] *Wen-hsien t'ung-k'ao* 338:48a also mentions a Central Kabūdhān, but no missions from it are recorded.

[17] According to *Wen-hsien t'ung-k'ao* 338:48a, Eastern Kabūdhān sent envoys together with Samarkand between 618 and 626. Western Kabūdhān sent envoys between 605 and 626 (*T'ang hui-yao* 98:16a; *Wen-hsien t'ung-k'ao* 338:48a).

In the 11th month (Nov./Dec.) of 653, envoys from the king of Kabūdhān offered gifts (*Ts'e-fu yüan-kuei* p.5025).

In the 9th month (Sep./Oct.) of 659, Emperor Kao-tsung gave the unrealistic order to establish Chinese commanderies and prefectures out of Kashgar, Tashkent, Kabūdhān, Kish, Māimargh, Bukhara, Tokharia, Yi-ta, etc. (*Tzu-chih t'ung-chien* p.6317).

In 731, the king of Samarkand requested recognition of one of his sons as king of Kabūdhān. Emperor Hsüan-tsung complied (*Chiu T'ang shu* 198:14a-14b; *Wen-hsien t'ung-k'ao* 338:47b). This would mean that at that time Kabūdhān or part of it was a dependency of Samarkand.

In the 3rd month (Apr./May) of 742, envoys from the king of Kabūdhān[18] presented horses and regional objects (*Ts'e-fu yüan-kuei* p.5029; *Wen-hsien t'ung-k'ao* 338:48a).

In the 7th month (Aug./Sep.) of 744, envoys from Western Kabūdhān presented horses and valuables (*Ts'e-fu yüan-kuei* p.5030).

Some time in 744, Hsüan-tsung conferred on the king of Kabūdhān the title of King Who Cherishes Virtue(*T'ang hui-yao* 98:15b; *Wen-hsien t'ung-k'ao* 338:48a).

In 745, Hsüan-tsung received a letter from the king of Kabūdhān (*T'ang hui-yao* 98:15b).

In 752, envoys from the king of Kabūdhān proposed to the T'ang a joint attack on the black-robed Arabs.[19] This was one year after the Chinese defeat by the Arabs at the Talas River. Hsüan-tsung gave the envoys a banquet but did not respond (*T'ang hui-yao* 98:15b).

HO

Ho was situated Northwest of Samarkand.

On Feb.4, 615, the New Year's Day, Emperor Yang of Sui gave a great banqet for envoys from Ho and other states (*Sui shu* 4:9b; 83:14a; *Wen-hsien t'ung-k'ao* 338:48a).

In the 5th month (June/July) of 627, envoys from Ho to the T'ang court offered gifts (*Ts'e-fu yüan-kuei* p.5024).

In 641, envoys from Ho were received at the T'ang court (*Wen-hsien t'ung-k'ao* 338:48a).

---

[18] By *Wen-hsien t'ung-k'ao* referred to as Western Kabūdhān.

[19] The term "black-robed Arabs" refers to the Abbasid Caliphate.

In 658,[20] Emperor Kao-tsung created the imaginary Kuei-shuang Area Command and appointed the king of Ho as its Military Governor (*Wen-hsien t'ung-k'ao* 338:48a).

KISH

Kish, in Chinese Shih,[21] was situated directly south of Samarkand.

Between 605 and 617, envoys from Kish to the Sui court offered regional objects (*Sui shu* 83:13b; *T'ung-tien* 193:18a; *Ts'e-fu yüan-kuei* p.5023; *Wen-hsien t'ung-k'ao* 338:48a).

In the 1st month (Feb./Mar.) of 642, Kish offered gifts to the T'ang court (*Ts'e-fu yüan-kuei* p.5024; *Wen-hsien t'ung-k'ao* 338:48a).

In 658, Emperor Kao-tsung created the imaginary Ch'ü-sha Area Command and appointed the king of Kish as its Military Governor[22] (*T'ang hui-yao* 99:21b; *Wen-hsien t'ung-k'ao* 338:48a).

In the 9th month (Sep./Oct.) of 659, Kao-tsung gave the unrealistic order to establish Chinese commanderies and prefectures out of Kashgar, Tashkent, Kabūdhān, Kish, Māimargh, Bukhara, Tokharia, Yi-ta, etc. (*Tzu-chih t'ung-chien* p.6317).

In the 7th month (July/Aug.) of 727, the king of Kish presented barbarian (hu) twirling girls and a leopard (*Ts'e-fu yüan-kuei* p.5028; *Wen-hsien t'ung-k'ao* 338:48a).

In 739, Emperor Hsüan-tsung recognized the king of Kish (*T'ang hui-yao* 99:22a).

In 741, Kish offered gifts (*T'ang hui-yao* 99:22a).

Between 742 and 756,[23] Hsüan-tsung changed the Chinese name of Kish from Shih to Lai-wei (*Wen-hsien t'ung-k'ao* 338:48a).

In the 7th month (Aug./Sep.) of 744, envoys from Kish presented horses and valuables (*T'ung-tien* 193:18a; *Ts'e-fu yüan-kuei* p.5030).

In the intercalary month (Nov./Dec.) of 746, envoys from Kish were received at the T'ang court (*Ts'e-fu yüan-kuei* p.5030).

---

[20] *Wen-hsien t'ung-k'ao* gives the date of 650-656. But is has been seen that this text makes the same mistake about Samarkand. Emperor Kao-tsung established other Area Commands in 658, so that this date should also apply to Ho.

[21] In transliteration, Tashkent and Kish have the same name. This *shih*, however, is written with the character for clerk, historian or history.

[22] I emend Inspector to Military Governor.

[23] This must have been before the battle at the Talas River in 751.

MĀIMARGH

Māimargh, in Chinese Mi, was situated west of Kish, i.e. southwest of Samarkand.

Between 605 and 617, Māimargh offered gifts to the Sui court (*Sui shu* 83:13a).

In the 9th month (Sep./Oct.) of 659, Emperor Kao-tsung of T'ang gave the unrealistic order to establish Chinese commanderies and prefectures out of Kashgar, Tashkent, Kabūdhān, Kish, Māimargh, Bukhara, Tokharia, Yi-ta, etc. (*Tzu-chih t'ung-chien* p.6317).

In the 2nd month of 718, envoys from Māimargh were received at the T'ang court. In the 4th month, (May/June), envoys from the king of Māimargh presented dance mats and white copper[24] (*Ts'e-fu yüan-kuei* p.5027)

In the 11th month (Dec./Jan., 728) of the Chinese year 727, envoys from the king of Māimargh presented a lion (*Ts'e-fu yüan-kuei* p.5028).

In the 1st month (Feb./Mar.) of 729, envoys from Māimargh presented three barbarian (hu) twirling girls, one lion, and one leopard (*Ts'e-fu yüan-kuei* p.5028).

In the 4th month (May/June) of 730, envoys from Māimargh offered gifts (*Ts'e-fu yüan-kuei* p.5028).

In 731, the king of Samarkand requested recognition of one of his sons as king of Māimargh. Emperor Hsüan-tsung complied (*Chiu T'ang shu* 198:14a-14b; *Wen-hsien t'ung-k'ao* 338:47b). This would mean that at that time Māimargh or part of it was a dependency of Samarkand.

In the 7th month (Aug./Sep.) of 744, envoys from Māimargh presented horses and valuables (*Ts'e-fu yüan-kuei* p.5030).

In the intercalary month (Nov./Dec.) of 746, envoys from Māimargh were received at the T'ang court (*Ts'e-fu yüan-kuei* p.5030)

In the 4th month (Apr./May) of 754, envoys from Māimargh were received at the T'ang court (*Ts'e-fu yüan-kuei* p.5031).

In the 12th month (Dec./Jan., 773) of the Chinese year 772, envoys from Māimargh offered gifts (*Ts'e-fu yüan-kuei* p.5031).

---

[24] By Schafer, *Golden Peaches*, p.256, translated as brass.

BUKHARA

The regular Chinese name for Bukhara during Sui and T'ang was An. *T'ung-tien* and *Wen-hsien t'ung-k'ao* continued to use the earlier version of An-hsi.

The above-mentioned Attendant of the Director of the Retainers Tu Hsing-man, who had been dispatched by Emperor Yang of Sui, travelled as far as Bukhara (*Sui shu* 83:9a).

In 609, envoys from Bukhara to the Sui court offered gifts (*Sui shu* 83:9a; *T'ung-tien* 192:17a; *Wen-hsien t'ung-k'ao* 337:46b

On Feb.4, 615, the New Year's Day, Emperor Yang gave a great banquet for envoys from Bukhara and other states (*Sui shu* 4:9b)

In the 11th month (Dec./Jan., 639) of the Chinese year 638, envoys from Bukhara to the T'ang court offered regional objects (*Ts'e-fu yüan-kuei* p.5024).

In 639, envoys from Bukhara offered gifts (*Chiu T'ang shu* 3:6b).

In the 2nd month (Mar./Apr.) of 649, the king of Bukhara presented regional objects (*Ts'e-fu yüan-kuei* p.5025).

In the 4th month (Apr./May) of 654, envoys from the king of Bukhara offered gifts (*Ts'e-fu yüan-kuei* p.5025).

In the 9th month (Sep./Oct.) of 659, Emperor Kao-tsung gave the unrealistic order to establish Chinese commanderies and prefectures out of Kashgar, Tashkent, Kabūdhān, Kish, Māimargh, Bukhara, Tokharia, Yi-ta, etc. (*Tzu-chih t'ung-chien* p.6317).

In the 4th (May/June) and 6th month (June/July) of 697, envoys from Bukhara offered gifts (*Ts'e-fu yüan-kuei* p.5026).

In the 3rd month (Apr./May) of 717, envoys from Bukhara offered regional objects (*Ts'e-fu yüan-kuei* p.5027).

In the 2nd (Feb./Mar.) month of 719, the kings of Samarkand and Bukhara informed the T'ang court that they had been under attack by the Arabs. In the 3rd month (Mar./Apr.), envoys from Bukhara presented regional objects (*Ts'e-fu yüan-kuei* p.5027; *Tzu-chih t'ung-chien* p.6735).

In the 2nd month (Mar./Apr.) of 726, envoys from Bukhara presented one male and one female leopard. In the 5th month (June/July), a younger brother of the king of Bukhara offered horses and a leopard (*Ts'e-fu yüan-kuei* p.5028).

In the 5th month (May/June) of 727, Bukhara presented horses (*Ts'e-fu yüan-kuei* p.5028).

In the 10th month (Oct./Nov.) of 740, envoys from Bukhara

presented a valuable bed and cups made from ostrich eggs (*Ts'e-fu yüan-kuei* p.5029).

In the 3rd month (Apr./May) of 744, a chief sent by the king of Bukhara offered regional objects (*Ts'e-fu yüan-kuei* p.5030).

In the 7th month (August) of 745, envoys from the king of Bukhara offered gifts (*Ts'e-fu yüan-kuei* p.5030).

In the 1st month (Feb./Mar.) of 750, envoys from the king of Bukhara presented 100 horses (*Ts'e-fu yüan-kuei* p.5030).

In the 9th month (Sep./Oct.) of 751, envoys from Bukhara offered gifts (*Ts'e-fu yüan-kuei* p.5030).

In the 8th month (Sep./Oct.) of 753, envoys from Bukhara offered gifts (*Ts'e-fu yüan-kuei* p.5031).

In the 3rd month (Apr./May) of 759, an envoy from Bukhara was received at the T'ang court (*Ts'e-fu yüan-kuei* p.5031).

WU-NA-HO

Wu-na-ho[25] was situated on the left bank of the Amu Darya, south of Bukhara.

On Feb.4, 615, the New Year's Day, Emperor Yang of Sui gave a great banquet for envoys from Wu-na-ho and other states (*Sui shu* 4: 9b; *Wen-hsien t'ung-k'ao* 338:47b).

MU

Mu was situated on the left bank of the Amu Darya between Wu-na-ho and the Aral Lake.

On Feb.4, 615, the New Year's Day, Emperor Yang of Sui gave a great banquet for envoys from Mu and other states (*Sui shu* 4:9b; *Wen-hsien t'ung-k'ao* 338:48a).

TOKHARIA

Tokharia, in Chinese T'u-huo-lo, was situated on the left bank of the middle course of the Amu-Darya, centred on the modern city of Balkh.

---

[25] By *Wen-hsien t'ung-k'ao* called Wu-na-o, i.e. with radical 162 added.

On Feb.4, 615, the New Year's Day, Emperor Yang of Sui gave a great banquet for envoys from Tokharia and other states (*Sui shu* 4: 9b; 83:12b; *Wen-hsien t'ung-k'ao* 339:55b).

In the 5th month (June/July) of 635, envoys from Tokharia to the T'ang court offered regional objects (*Ts'e-fu yüan-kuei* p.5024).

In 639, envoys from Tokharia offered gifts (*Chiu T'ang shu* 3:6b).

On Feb.2, 645, the New Year's Day, envoys from a high Tokharian official congratulated at the T'ang court and offered regional objects (*Ts'e-fu yüan-kuei* p.5024).

In 647, envoys from Tokharia offered gifts (*Chiu T'ang shu* 3:11a).

On Jan.30, 648, the New Year's Day, envoys from Tokharia to the T'ang court offered gifts (*Ts'e-fu yüan-kuei* p.5025).

In the 5th month (June/July) of 650, envoys from Tokharia presented a black ostrich. The texts describe it as follows: it was 7 feet high, had feet resembling those of a camel, could run 300 Chinese miles (*li*) a day, ate bronze and iron, and was commonly called a camel bird. Emperor Kao-tsung sent it to be kept at the tomb of his father, T'ai-tsung (*Chiu T'ang shu* 4:2b; *T'ung-tien* 193:22a; *Wen-hsien t'ung-k'ao* 339:55b).

In 652, the king of Tokharia announced his enthronment to the T'ang court. Emperor Kao-tsung reponded with an envoy of his own (*T'ang hui-yao* 99:16a).

In the 4th month (Apr./May) of 654, envoys from Tokharia, led by a son of the king, offered gifts (*T'ang hui-yao* 99:16a; *Ts'e-fu yüan-kuei* p.5025).

On Jan.20, 657, the New Year's Day, Tokharia presented a lion (*Ts'e-fu yüan-kuei* p.5025).

On July 21, 661, Emperor Kao-tsung established out of Tokharia, Ya-ta, Kapiśa, Persia, and other states eight imaginary Area Commands, divided into 76 commanderies, 110 prefectures, and 126 army headquarters, all theoretically under the An-hsi protectorate in Kucha. The king of Tokharia was appointed Military Governor of the Yüeh-chih Area Command[26] (*T'ang hui-yao* 99:16b; *Tzu-chih t'ung-chien* pp.6324-6325).

In 665, a younger brother of the king of Tokharia presented carne-

[26] Earlier steps toward the establishment of this illusionary Area Command seem to have been taken in 652 (*T'ang hui-yao* 99:16a).

lian and two candlewood utensils which were more than 3 feet high (*T'ang hui-yao* 99:16b).

In the 5th month (June/July) of 671, envoys from Tokharia offered regional objects (*Ts'e-fu yüan-kuei* p.5026).

In the 5th month (May/June) of 681, envoys from Tokharia presented horses and regional objects. In the 12th month (Dec./Jan., 682) of the same Chinese year 681, envoys presented a golden garment. Emperor Kao-tsung rejected it (*Chiu T'ang shu* 5:10b; *Ts'e-fu yüan-kuei* p.5026).

Between 713 and 756, Tokharia frequently presented horses, mules, 200 varieties of drugs, jade, and glass (*Wen-hsien t'ung-k'ao* 339:55b).

In the 4th month (Apr./May) of 719, envoys from a high official in Tokharia offered gifts. In the 6th month (June/July), envoys from the king of Tokharia brought a letter and presented an astronomer/astrologer. There was nothing this man did not know (*Ts'e-fu yüan-kuei* p.5027).

In the 6th month (July/Aug.) of 720, Tokharia presented fine horses, big mules, and foreign drugs (*T'ang hui-yao* 99:16b; *Ts'e-fu yüan-kuei* p.5027).

In the 7th month (July/Aug.) of 724, envoys from Tokharia presented 300 kinds of drugs (*Ts'e-fu yüan-kuei* p.5028).

In the 11th month (Nov./Dec.) of 726, envoys from Tokharia were received at the T'ang court (*Ts'e-fu yüan-kuei* p.5028).

In the 7th month (July/Aug.) of 729, envoys from Tokharia presented a variety of drugs (*Ts'e-fu yüan-kuei* p.5028).

In the 5th month (May/June) of 730, a missions from Tokharia, including a Buddhist priest, presented red pears, green pears, baroos camphor, gold essence, and *chih-han* (citragandha) and other drugs (*T'ang hui-yao* 99:16b; *Ts'e-fu yüan-kuei* p.5028).

In the 9th month (Sep./*Ts'e-fu yüan-kuei* p.5Oct.) of 735, envoys from Tokharia offered regional objects (*Ts'e-fu yüan-kuei* p.5029).

In the 1st month (Jan./Feb.) of 738, a chief from Tokharia offered regional objects (*Ts'e-fu yüan-kuei* p.5029).

In the 7th month (Aug./Sep.) of 744, envoys from Tokharia presented horses and valuables (030).

In the 3rd month (Apr./May) of 745, envoys from Tokharia offered regional objects (*Ts'e-fu yüan-kuei* p.5030).

In the 4th month (Apr./May) of 749, envoys from Tokharia presented horses (*Ts'e-fu yüan-kuei* p.5030).

On Dec.18, 749, envoys from a high official of Tokharia informed the T'ang court that the king of Chieh-shih had joined the Tibetans and proposed that he be attacked (*Tzu-chih t'ung-chien* pp.6897-6898).[27]

In the 8th month (Sep./Oct.) of 753, envoys from a high official of Tokharia offered gifts (*Ts'e-fu yüan-kuei* p.5031).

In the 4th month (Apr./May) of 754, envoys from Tokharia were received at the T'ang court (*Ts'e-fu yüan-kuei* p.5031).

On July 10, 758, a high official of Tokharia offered gifts (*Chiu T'ang shu* 10:9a; *Ts'e-fu yüan-kuei* p.5031).

On Aug.9, 758, Envoys from Tokharia offered aid against the "bandits" (*Chiu T'ang shu* 10:9a). An Lu-shan had died im 757, but the rebellion was not suppressed until 763. According to *T'ang hui-yao* 99: 17a, nine western states (including the Arabs) actually sent troops.

PO-LAN

Po-lan was situated southwest of Balkh.

In 619, envoys from Po-lan were received at the T'ang court (*Wen-hsien t'ung-k'ao* 334:28a).

In the 11th month (November) of 631, envoys from Po-lan were received at the T'ang court (*Ts'e-fu yüan-kuei* p.5024).

YA-TA

Ya-ta was probably situated somewhere near Tokharia.

Between 605 and 617, envoys from Ya-ta to the Sui court offered regional objects (*Wen-hsien t'ung-k'ao* 338:49a).

On July 21, 661, Emperor Kao-tsung of T'ang established out of Tokharia, Ya-ta, Kapiśa, Persia, and other states eight imaginary Area Commands, divided into 76 commanderies, 110 prefectures, and 126

---

[27] Chieh-shih was situated north of Gilgit on the trade route from Kashgar to India and therefore was able to block it. In the 2nd month (Mar./Apr.) of 750, the Military Commissioner of the An-hsi Protectorate, Kao Hsien-chih, defeated and captured the king of Chieh-shih. On Apr.22, Emperor Hsüan-tsung recognized the king's elder brother as his successor. Kao Hsien-chih subsequently overran Tahskent. In the 1st month (Feb./Mar.) of 751, Kao Hsien-chih presented the captured king, the king of Tashkent, a Turkish qaghan, and Tibetan chiefs to the T'ang court (*Tzu-chih t'ung-chien* pp.6898, 6904).

army headquarters, all theoretically under the An-hsi protectorate in Kucha (*Tzu-chih t'ung-chien* pp.6324-6325).

YI-TA

Yi-ta was situated south of Tokharia.

Between 605 and 617, envoys from Yi-ta to the Sui court offered regional objects (*Sui shu* 83:13b; *Wen-hsien t'ung-k'ao* 338:49a).

In the 6th month (July) of 748, envoys from Yi-ta to the T'ang court offered gifts (*Ts'e-fu yüan-kuei* p.5030).

In the 9th month (Sep./Oct.) of 659, Emperor Kao-tsung gave the unrealistic order to establish Chinese commanderies and prefectures out of Kashgar, Tashkent, Kabūdhān, Kish, Māimargh, Bukhara, Tokharia, Yi-ta, etc. (*Tzu-chih t'ung-chien* p.6317).

KHUTTAL

Khuttal, in Chinese Ku-to, was situated north of the upper Amu-Darya.

On May 4, 720, Emperor Hsüan-tsung of T'ang sent envoys to recognize the king of Khuttal (*Tzu-chih t'ung-chien* p.6740).

In the 1st month (Feb./Mar.) of 729, a son of the king of Khuttal presented two horses (*Ts'e-fu yüan-kuei* p.5028; *Wen-hsien t'ung-k'ao* 335:35a).

In the 2nd month (Feb./Mar.) of 733, envoys from the king of Khuttal presented horses and female musicians. In the 8th month (Sep./Oct.) , a chief from Khuttal offered gifts (*Ts'e-fu yüan-kuei* pp.5028, 5029; *Wen-hsien t'ung-k'ao* 335:35a).

In the 3rd month (April) of 740, a chief from Khuttal was received at the T'ang court (*Ts'e-fu yüan-kuei* p.5029).

In the 1st month (Feb./Mar.) of 750, a chief sent by the king of Khuttal presented 43 humans and 30 barbarian (hu) horses (*Ts'e-fu yüan-kuei* p.5030).

CHIEH

Chieh, which was known to the Chinese since Sui times (*Wen-hsien t'ung-k'ao* 339:55b), was probably situated somewhere in West Turkestan.

In 619, envoys from Chieh to the T'ang court offered a valuable belt, a golden chain, a crystal cup, and 490 pieces of glass (*T'ung-tien* 193:22a; *Wen-hsien t'ung-k'ao* 339:55b).

SHIH-NI

Shih-ni was probably situated somewhere in West Turkestan.

In 646, envoys from Shih-ni were received at the T'ang court (*Wen-hsien t'ung-k'ao* 337:45b).

In 724, envoys from the king of Shih-ni presented horses and gold essence. That year, Emperor Hsüan-tsung appointed the king as General-in-chief of the Guards of the Golden Mace (*Ts'e-fu yüan-kuei* p.5028; *Wen-hsien t'ung-k'ao* 337:45b).

In the 3rd month (Apr./May) of 725, envoys from Shih-ni presented horses (*Ts'e-fu yüan-kuei* p.5028).

In the 10th month (Nov./Dec.) of 727, envoys from Shih-ni arrived at the T'ang court to congratulate on the New Year's Day of Feb.15, 728 (*Ts'e-fu yüan-kuei* p.5028).

In 747, the king of Shih-ni took part in Kao Hsien-chih's famous attack on Gilgit and fell in battle. Hsüan-tsung appointed his son and successor as Military Governor of an imaginary Area Command and as General-in-chief of the Martial Guards of the Left (*Wen-hsien t'ung-k'ao* 337:45b).

In contrast to East Turkestan, West Turkestan was never a true Chinese protectorate. The troops of the An-hsi protectorate in Kucha maintained a tenuous Chinese presence in West Turkestan, which waxed and wained in the course of time. It ended with Kao Hsien-chih's victory over the Tibetans in Kashmir in 747 and his defeat by the Arabs at the Talas River near Tashkent in 751. All attempts by the Chinese in 658, 661, and 747 to establish area commands in Ferghana, Tashkent, Samarkand, Ho, Kish, Tokharia, Ya-ta, Shih-ni, Kapiśa, and Persia were symbolic and futile. Since in each case, the king of the state was made Military Governor, the kings gained titles and the Chinese nothing. This is even more true about Emperor Kao-tsung's pathetic and unenforcable orders in 659 and 661 to establish commanderies and prefectures in Kashgar, Tashkent, Kabūdhān, Kish, Māimargh, Bukhara, Tokharia, Ya-ta, Yi-ta, Kapiśa, and Persia according to the Chinese model.

Emperor T'ai-tsung had rejected an alliance with Samarkand in 631, preferring to concentrate his energy on East Turkestan. This enabled the Western Turks to increase their influence in West Turkestan, so that Tashkent, Samarkand, Ho, Kish, Mu, Tokharia and other states fell under their sway from 639 (*Tzu-chih t'ung-chien* p.6151). However, the Western Turks were soon challenged by the Arabs. After the Arabs had won the battle of Nehavend in 641, the Sassanid Kingdom of Persia ceased to exist, and the Arabs soon appeared in West Turkestan. Between 650 and 656, Samarkand complained to the T'ang court that it was attacked and taxed by the Arabs (*T'ang-hui-yao* 99:18a). The policies of Emperor Kao-tsung and the Empress Wu had no lasting effects, and the Western Turks managed to maintain their loose control over the states of West Turkestan until the arrival of the great Arab warrior Qutayba ibn Muslim in 705. By the time he died in 715, he had added West Turkestan to the caliphate. Thereafter, the Western Turkish Turgesh tribe contested the presence of the Arabs. It defeated them in 724, but was defeated itself in 737. The Arab conquest was completed with their victory over the Chinese in 751 in the battle at the Talas River near Tashkent.

During this crucial period, the states of West Turkestan struggled to survive. In 719, Samarkand and Bukhara informed the T'ang court that they were under attack by the Arabs. Tashkent sought aid from China in 741. When this was not forthcoming, it surrendered to the Arabs (*Wen-hsien t'ung-k'ao* 339:55a). As late as 752, one year after the battle at the Talas River, Kabhūdān proposed to Emperor Hsüan-tsung a joint attack on the Arabs.

The remarkable thing is that in spite of the Western Turks, and in spite of the Arabs from 705, missions from West Turkestan managed to make it to China. Even after the Arab victory in 751, they only ceased gradually, from Ferghana after 762, from Tashkent after 777, from Samarkand after 772, from Māimargh after 772, from Bukhara after 759, and from Tokharia after 758. This does not mean that thereafter envoys from West Turkestan no longer arrived in China, only that henceforth they were labelled as those of their conquerors, the Arabs.

The T'ang married a Chinese princess to the king of Ferghana, it recognized the kings of at least Ferghana, Tashkent, Samarkand, Kabūdhān, Kish, Māimargh, and Khuttal, and it conferred honourary titles on many rulers. None of this had any lasting effect. No missions of condolence are recorded, no posthumous titles were conferred. There was no mourning at the T'ang court for deceased kings. There is no mention of hostages. West Turkestan was foreign country, and its kings were not politically close to China.

According to *Wen-hsien t'ung-k'ao* 338:47b, Ferghana offered annual gifts from 658. No mission is recorded until 738. According to *Wen-hsien t'ung-k'ao* 339:54b, Tashkent from 618 to 649 frequently offered regional objects. Three missions are recorded. According to *T'ang hui-yao* 99:15a, Tashkent repeatedly sent envoys from 742 until not later than 756. Nine missions are recorded. According to *Chiu T'ang shu* 198:14a, Samarkand annually offered gifts after 635. Ten missions are recorded until 648. According to *T'ang hui-yao* 98:15b, Kabūdhān offered gifts without interruption from 637 to 741. Four missions are recorded. According to *Wen-hsien t'ung-k'ao* 338:47b, Māimargh incessantly offered gifts from 605 to 617. One mission is recorded. It can be seen that the statistics for West Turkestan are similar to those for East Turkestan. The caravan traffic to China must have been so intense that the historians noted only the most important missions.

The preferred time for missions from West Turkestan to arrive in Ch'ang-an was the 1st month. Otherwise, they came fairly evenly during the other months.

This is the distribution by 20-year periods of the 169 recorded missions from West Turkestan to Sui and T'ang:

587-606:	0
607-626:	19
627-646:	23
647-666:	20
667-686:	6
687-706:	2
707-726:	22
727-746:	41
747-766:	32
767-786:	4

These 169 missions outstrip by far the 78 recorded ones for East Turkestan during the same period (587-786). Relations were opened in the reign of Emperor Yang (605-618). Missions were frequent during the reigns of Emperors T'ai-tsung (627-649) and Kao-tsung (650-683). During the Tibetan occupation of the Tarim Basin from 670 to 692, there is the same falling off which has been noticed for East Turkestan. The peak was reached in the reign of Emperor Hsüan-tsung (712-756).

The kings of West Turkestan had few matters of substance to discuss with the T'ang. Some warned against the Tibetans and Arabs. One announced his enthronement. But their obvious purpose in sending missions was, as usual, trade.

The specified goods brought by the missions from West Turkestan fall into the following categories:

Humans

718: one pygmy and barbarian (hu) twirling girls from Samarkand.
719: one astronomer/astrologer from Tokharia.
724: one pygmy from Samarkand.
727: barbarian (hu) twirling girls from Tashkent, Samarkand, and Kish.
729: 3 barbarian (hu) twirling girls from Māimargh.
733: female musicians from Khuttal.
750: 43 humans from Khuttal.

Animals and Animal Products

Felines

635: one lion from Samarkand.
657: one lion from Tokharia.
718: one leopard from Samarkand.
726: one leopard from Samarkand, one male, one female leopard, and one additional leopard from Bukhara.
727: one leopard from Kish, one lion from Māimargh.
751: one leopard from Ferghana.

Horses

624: fine horses from Samarkand.
626: fine horses from Samarkand.
628: fine horses from Samarkand.
681: horses from Tokharia.
720: horses from Tokharia.
724: 2 horses from Samarkand, horses from Shih-ni.
725: horses from Shih-ni.
726: horses from Bukhara.
729: 2 horses from Khuttal.

733: horses from Khuttal.
742: horses from Tashkent and Kabūdhān.
744: horses from Tashkent, Samarkand, Kabūdhān, Kish, Māimargh and Tokharia.
746: 15 horses from Tashkent.
749: horses from Tokharia.
750: 10 horses from Samarkand, 100 horses from Bukhara, and 30 barbarian (hu) horses from Khuttal.
751: 82 horses from Ferghana.
754: barbarian (hu) horses from Ferghana.

Mules

720: big mules from Tokharia.

Dogs

718: dogs from Samarkand.
724: 2 dogs from Samarkand.
751: one 'heavenly" dog from Ferghana.

Birds

650: one black ostrich from Tokharia.
718: ostrich eggs from Samarkand.

Aromatics

Aromatic and medical drugs

720: foreign drugs from Tokharia.
724: 300 kinds of drugs from Tokharia, gold essence from Shih-ni.
729: a variety of drugs from Tokharia.
730: aromatic drugs, gold essence, and *chih-han* (citragandha) drugs from Tokharia.

Camphor

730: baroos camphor from Tokharia.

Trees, Plants, Fruits, and Wine

637: gold and silver peach tree seedlings from Samarkand.
647: golden peaches from Samarkand.
727: grape wine from Tashkent.
730: red and green pears from Tokharia.

Minerals, Ores, and Metals

619: 490 pieces of glass from Chieh.
713-756: glass and jade from Tokharia.
718: white copper from Māimargh
740: rock crystal from Samarkand.

Manufactured Objects

Of metal

619: one golden chain from Chieh.
718: chain armour from Samarkand.
740: one precious censer from Samarkand.

Of crystal

619: one crystal cup from Chieh.
718: one rock crystal bowl from Samarkand.

Of precious stone

718: one carnelian pitcher from Samarkand.
740: white jade rings from Samarkand.

Other

619: one valuable belt from Chieh.
665: 2 candlewood utensils, more than 3 feet high, from Tokharia.
681: one golden garment from Tokharia (rejected).
718: dance mats from Māimargh.
740: one valuable bed and cups of ostrich eggs from Bukhara.

Textiles

Cottons

718: *yüeh-no* cloth from Samarkand.

Other

717: textiles from Samarkand.

Pigments

717: indigo from Samarkand.

Jewels

665: carnelian from Tokharia.
740: carnelian from Samarkand.

In contrast to the oasis states of East Turkestan, which locally produced relatively little, much of the merchandise from West Turkestan was native. Leopards and perhaps lions existed in the wild but could also have been bred. Horses and mules were raised on the pastures. Dogs must have been common. Ostriches in those days were found in a much more widespread area than now and may still have existed in West Turkestan. Seedlings came from local orchards. Much of the minerals, manufactured goods, textiles, and jewels was no doubt locally produced. The indigo plant may have been locally grown. Only much of the drugs and carnelian would have come from abroad and then have been passed along to China.

Nothing at all is recorded about how the Chinese paid for these goods.

KASHMIR AND AFGHANISTAN

KASHMIR

Kashmir (map 9) in Chinese was Ko-shih-mi.

In 720, envoys from Kashmir to the T''ang court offered barbarian (hu) drugs. Emperor Hsüan-tsung recognized its king and at a later date his brother and successor. At an unknown time, the latter also sent envoys, whom the Chinese questioned about the customs of their country and gave banquet (*Wen-hsien t'ung-k'ao* 335:34b).

HSI-LI

Hsi-li was probably situated somewhere in or near Kashmir.

In the intercalary 3rd month (Apr./May) of 646, envoys from Hsi-li to the T'ang court offered gifts (*T'ung-tien* 190:9b; *Ts'e-fu yüan-kuei* p.5024; *Wen-hsien t'ung-k'ao* 335:34b).

CHANG-CH'IU-PA

Chang-ch'iu-pa was situated southwest of Hsi-li and bordered in the south on India (*Ts'e-fu yüan-kuei* p.5024; *Wen-hsien t'ung-k'ao* 335:34b). That should place it somewhere in or near Kashmir.

In in the intercalary 3rd month (Apr./May) of 646, the king of Chang-ch'iu-pa attached envoys to the mission sent to the T'ang court by Hsi-li and offered gifts (*Hsin T'ang shu* 221A:13a; *Ts'e-fu yüan-kuei* p.5024; *Wen-hsien t'ung-k'ao* 335:34b; 338:51b).

GILGIT

The Chinese name of this state was Po-lü. It was situated north of Kashmir, between the Indus and Hindu Kush and was divided into a Greater and Lesser Gilgit (*Wen-hsien t'ung-k'ao* 335:34b).

In the 12th month (Dec./Jan., 687) of the Chinese year 686, envoys from Gilgit to the T'ang court offered gifts (*Ts'e-fu yüan-kuei* p.5026).

In the 10th month (Oct./Nov.) of 697, envoys from Gilgit offered gifts (*Ts'e-fu yüan-kuei* p.5026).

In the intercalary 12th month (Jan./Feb., 717) of the Chinese year 716, chiefs from Gilgit offered gifts (*Ts'e-fu yüan-kuei* p.5027).

In 720, Emperor Hsüan-tsung recognized the king of Gilgit (*Chiu T'ang shu* 198:13b; *Wen-hsien t'ung-k'ao* 335:34b) and aided him against the Tibetans in 722.

In the 2nd month (March) of 724, a chief from Gilgit was received at the T'ang court and was presented with 50 bolts of silk (*Ts'e-fu yüan-kuei* p.5027).

In the intercalary month (March) of 733, a chief from Gilgit was received at the T'ang court (*Wen-hsien t'ung-k'ao* 335:34b).

In 734,[28] a number of small principalities including Gilgit became dependencies of Tibet. A Tibetan princess was married to the king of Lesser Gilgit. Thereafter, connections between Gilgit and China were disrupted (*Chiu T'ang shu* 104:1a; 196A:10a-10b; 198:13b; *Tzu-chih t'ung-chien* p.6827 *Wen-hsien t'ung-k'ao* 335:34b).[29]

Tibet, in control of Gilgit, blocked the important trade route from Kashgar to Kashmir and India. Hsüan-tsung, who previously had protested against the conquest, therefore ordered in 747 the Military Commissioner of the An-hsi Protectorate, Kao Hsien-chih, to attack the Tibetans. Kao Hsien-chih marched his troops that year from Kucha through the Pamirs and Hindu Kush to Gilgit, a famous campaign in military history, defeated the Tibetans, and captured the king of Lesser Gilgit and his Tibetan Princess. They were presumably brought to Ch'ang-an. Hsüan-tsung treated the king well, appointed him General of the Martial Guards of the Right, and presented him with a purple robe and a belt of real gold (*Chiu T'ang-shu* 104:2a; *Wen-hsien t'ung-k'ao* 335:34b). But Kao Hsien-chih's victory in Gilghit of 747 and his subsequent one over Chieh-shih in 750 soon lost their significance with his defeat by the Arabs at the Talas River in 751.

---

[28] The date is according to *Chiu T'ang shu* 198:13b. The same text 196A:10a-10b has 736, and *Tzu-chih t'ung-chien* p.6827 has 737. The Tibetan conquest may have taken several years.

[29] In the 7th month (August) of 745, a Buddhist priest from Lesser Gilgit offered gifts to the T'ang court (*Ts'e-fu yüan-kuei* p.5030), but that was probably a private venture.

KAPIŚA

Kapiśa, in Chinese Chi-pin, was situated in Afghanistan and centred on what now is Kabul.

Between 605 and 617, envoys from Kapiśa to the Sui court offered regional objects (*Sui shu* 83:16a; *Ts'e-fu yüan-kuei* p.5023, *Wen-hsien t'ung-k'ao* 337:45a).

In 619, envoys from Kapiśa to the T'ang court offered valuable belts, golden chains, rock crystal cups, glass, and date seedlings (*Wen-hsien t'ung-k'ao* 337:45a).

In 637, envoys from Kapiśa presented fine horses. Emperor T'ai-tsung paid them with silken fabrics. He sent envoys of his own with rich gifts to the king (*Ts'e-fu yüan-kuei* p.5024; *Wen-hsien t'ung-k'ao* 337: 45a).

In the 5th month (May/June) of 640, envoys from Kapiśa offered regional objects (*Ts'e-fu yüan-kuei* p.5024).

In 642, envoys from Kapiśa presented a mongoose which could eat snakes (*Chiu T'ang shu* 198:13b; *Ts'e-fu yüan-kuei* p.5024; *Wen-hsien t'ung-k'ao* 337:45a).

In the 5th month (May/June) of 648, envoys from Kapiśa brought gifts, including saffron whose scent could be smelled from far away (*T'ang hui-yao* 99:20b; *Ts'e-fu yüan-kuei* p.5025).

In the 12th month (Jan./Feb., 652) of the Chinese year 651, envoys from Kapiśa presented a mongoose. Its snout was pointed and its tail red, and it could eat snakes. When its urine was smeared on boils, they were immediately cured (*T'ang hui-yao* 99:20b; *Ts'e-fu yüan-kuei* p.5025).

In the 11th month (Nov./Dec.) of 653, envoys of the king of Kapiśa offered gifts (*Ts'e-fu yüan-kuei* p.5025).

In the 4th month (Apr./May) of 654, envoys from Kapiśa offered gifts (*Ts'e-fu yüan-kuei* p.5025).

On July 21, 661, Emperor Kao-tsung established out of Tokharia, Ya-ta, Kapiśa, Persia, and other states eight imaginary Area Commands, divided into 76 commanderies, 110 prefectures, and 126 army headquarters, all theoretically under the An-hsi Protectorate in Kucha. The Kapiśa Area Command was called Hsiu-hsien *(Chiu T'ang shu* 198: 13b; *Tzu-chih t'ung-chien* pp.6324-6325; *Wen-hsien t'ung-k'ao* 337:45a).

In the 3rd month (Apr./May) of 670, Kapiśa presented regional objects (*Ts'e-fu yüan-kuei* p.5026).

In the 5th month (June/July) of 671, envoys from Kapiśa offered regional objects (*Ts'e-fu yüan-kuei* p.5026).

In the 9th month (Oct./Nov.) of 692, envoys from Kapiśa offered gifts (*Ts'e-fu yüan-kuei* p.5026).

Between 705 and 707, Emperor Chung-tsung confirmed the new king of Kapiśa as Military Governor of the imaginary Hsiu-hsien Area Command (*Wen-hsien t'ung-k'ao* 337:45a).

In the 10th month (Oct./Nov.) of 710, envoys from Kapiśa offered regional objects (*Ts'e-fu yüan-kuei* p.5026).

In the 2nd month (Feb./Mar.) of 719, envoys from Kapiśa presented a text on astronomy/astrology, and foreign drugs, and other objects. Emperor Hsüan-tsung conferred a title on the king. In the 9th month (Oct./Nov.) of the same year, Kapiśa presented fine horses (*Chiu T'ang shu* 198:13b; *Ts'e-fu yüan-kuei* p.5027).[30]

In 739, the king of Kapiśa informed Hsüan-tsung that he had abdicated because of old age and had been succeeded by his son. The emperor sent envoys to recognize the new king (*Chiu T'ang shu* 198:13b; *Wen-hsien t'ung-k'ao* 337:45a).

In 745, a new king of Kapiśa was by Emperor Hsüan-tsung appointed General of the Resolute Guards of the Left[31] and recognized as king (*Chiu T'ang shu* 198:13b; *Wen-hsien t'ung-k'ao* 337:45a).

In the 3rd month (Apr./May) of 745, envoys from Kapiśa presented Persian brocades and dance mats (*Ts'e-fu yüan-kuei* p.5030).

In the intercalary month (Nov./Dec.) of 746, envoys from Kapiśa offered gifts (*Ts'e-fu yüan-kuei* p.5030).

In the 6th month (July) of 748, envoys from Kapiśa offered gifts (*Ts'e-fu yüan-kuei* p.5030).

In 758, envoys from Kapiśa offered gifts (*Chiu T'ang shu* 198:13b; *Ts'e-fu yüan-kuei* p.5031; *Wen-hsien t'ung-k'ao* 337:45a).

HSIEH-YI

The Empress Wu changed the name of this state from Ho-ta-lo-chih to Hsieh-yi. It seems to have been situated southwest of Kapiśa.

In the 10th month (Oct./Nov.) of 710, envoys from Hsieh-yi to the

---

30 Both entries for 719 are by *Ts'e-fu yüan-kuei* p.5027 dated 720.

31 *T'ang hui-yao* 99:21a says "of the Right".

T'ang court offered regional objects (*Ts'e-fu yüan-kuei* p.5026; *Wen-hsien t'ung-k'ao* 337:45b).

In the 9th month (Oct./Nov.) of 720, envoys from Hsieh-yi were received at the T'ang court. Emperor Hsüan-tsung recognized the king (*Wen-hsien t'ung-k'ao* 337:45b).

In the 12th month (Jan., 721) of the Chinese year 720, envoys from Hsieh-yi offered gifts (*Ts'e-fu yüan-kuei* p.5027).

In the 7th month (Aug./Sep.) of 744, envoys from Hsieh-yi presented horses and valuables (*Ts'e-fu yüan-kuei* p.5030).

In the 3rd month (Apr./May) of 745, envoys from Hsieh-yi offered regional objects (*Ts'e-fu yüan-kuei* p.5030).

In the 3rd month (Apr./May) of 753, envoys from Hsie-yi offered regional objects (*Ts'e-fu yüan-kuei* p.5030).

The states in Kashmir and Afghanistan, like those in West Turkestan, faced threats to their independence but not from China. They had no tributary obligations to that country. *Wen-hsien t'ung-k'ao* 337: 45a claims that when T'ai-tsung's envoys arrived in Kapiśa in 637, the king saluted twice and accepted the imperial mandate, but that, as has been seen in other cases, is simply a quote from the self-serving report of the envoys. The king of Kapiśa had no need to humble himself, and would not have done so. According to *Chiu T'ang shu* 198: 13b and *Wen-hsien t'ung-k'ao* 337:45a, the king of Kapiśa "begged" in a "memorial" of 739 that because of his old age he should be succeeded by his son. Emperor Hsüan-tsung "allowed it". The succession was an internal matter, and all the king did was to inform the T'ang court. The Chinese historians later rephrased the account in sinocentric and dynastic terminology.

The T'ang recognized some and perhaps all of the kings and conferred courtesy titles on at least some of them. It did not condole at the death of kings, did not confer posthumous titles, and did not declare official mourning. The military intervention of 747 was directed against the Tibetans, and the king of Gilgit was a more or less innocent bystander. For the states of Kashmir and Afghanistan, the only purpose of their missions to China was trade. No missions are recorded beyond 753. They may have ceased because of Arab and Tibetan hostility.

According to *Wen-hsien t'ung-k'ao* 335:35a, missions from Kashmir arrived constantly after 720. None is recorded. According to *Wen-hsien t'ung-k'ao* 338:51b, missions from Chang-ch'iu-pa were uninerrupted from 648. None is recorded. According to *Wen-hsien t'ung-k'ao* 335:

34b, envoys from Gilgit arrived three times between 696 and 741. Four missions are recorded. The statistics are therefore partially incomplete. To the extent that any conclusions can be drawn from them, the majority of the missions arrived in Ch'ang-an during the winters and springs.

This is the distribution by 20-year periods of the 34 recorded missions from Kashmir and Afghanistan to T'ang:

607-626:	2
627-646:	5
647-666:	4
667-686:	3
687-706:	2
707-726:	10
727-746:	5
747-766:	3

The greatest numbers fall into the reign of Emperor Hsüan-tsung (712-756), followed by those of T'ai-tsung (627-649) and Kao-tsung (650-683).

The recorded goods were horses, mongooses, drugs, date seedlings, glass, valuable belts, golden chains, rock crystal cups, dance mats, Persian brocade, and a text on astronomy/astrology. This is a mixture of local and imported products.

The only Chinese payment recorded is silk.

THE MIDDLE EAST

PERSIA

For the Six Dynasties, three missions are recorded from Persia (Po-ssu) to Liang from 530 to 535, nine to Northern Wei from 437 to 522, and two to Western Wei from 553 to 555.[1]

Emperor Yang of Sui (r.605-618) took steps to open communications with Persia, and sent a Commandant of Cavalry Fleet as Clouds to that country. On the return of this envoy, the king of Persia, Chosroes II, attached his own envoys to him to present regional objects to the Sui court (*Sui shu* 83:15a-15b; *T'ung-tien* 193:21a; *Ts'e-fu yüan kuei* p.5023; *Wen-hsien t'ung-k'ao* 339:53b).

In 638, envoys from king Yazdgard III of Persia to the T'ang court presented a live ferret. It was 8-9 inches long and could enter hollows and catch mice (*Chiu T'ang shu* 198:15b; *Wen-h sien t'ung'kao* 339:53b). This was after the Arabs had invaded Persia in 633, and the Persians had lost the battle of Khadisiya in 637.

In the 1st month (Feb./Mar.) of 647,[2] after its defeat at Nehavend in 641, Persia offered regional objects and asked for help against the Arabs. None was given. Yazdgard III fled and was assassinated in Merv in 651 (*Chiu T'ang shu* 3:11a; 198:15b; *Ts'e-fu yüan kuei* p.5024; *Wen-hsien t'ung-k'ao* 339:53b).

The Sassanid Kingdom of Persia had come to an end and the Arabs were in possession, yet missions from Persia to the T'ang court are recorded fairly regularly until 771, and then once again in 824. Schafer[3] refers to these missions as coming from the ghost nation of Persia. It has to be assumed that they were sent by holdouts against the Arabs. One of these was Fīrūz, a son of Yazdgard III, until he fled to Ch'ang-an in 675. Thereafter, various tribes continued to resist the Arabs (*Chiu T'ang shu* 198:15b), such as those in Khurāsān in northeastern Persia. In fact, a dynasty of Muslim Persians was

---

[1] See my *Six Dynasties*, vol.II, p.104.

[2] *Ts'e-fu yüan kuei* dates the reception of this mission Jan.30, 648, the New Year's Day.

[3] *Golden Peaches*, p.244.

founded there by Tahir in 820, which only nominally recognized the caliphate. The missions consequently were from various pretenders who used the term of Persia in only a self-deluding sense.

In 661, Fīrūz informed the T'ang court that he was under attack by the Arabs and requested troops for his succor. Emperor Kao-tsung's response was preposterous. On July 21, 661, he established out of Tokharia, Ya-ta, Kapiśa, Persia, and other states eight Area Commands, divided into 76 commanderies, 110 prefectures, and 126 army headquarters, all theoretically under the An-hsi Protectorate in Kucha. Persia became the Chi-ling Area Command with Fīrūz as its Military Governor. The emperor even sent a Chinese official to organize these new imaginary territories (*Chiu T'ang shu* 198:15b; *Tzu-chih t'ung-chien* pp.6324-6325; *Wen-hsien t'ung-k'ao* 339:53b).

In the 10th month (Oct./Nov.) of 667, Persia offered regional objects (*Ts'e-fu yüan-kuei* p.5026).

In the 5th month (June/July) of 671, envoys from Persia offered regional objects (*Ts'e-fu yüan-kuei* p.5026).

On Jan.16, 675, the king of Persia, Fīrūz, having been defeated by the Arabs, arrived as a refugee at the T'ang court. Emperor Kao-tsung treated him well and appointed him General of the Martial Guards of the Left[4] (*Chiu T'ang shu* 198:15b; *Tzu-chih t'ung-chien* p.6374; *Wen-hsien t'ung-k'ao* 339:53b). In 677, Fīrūz was permitted to build his own Zoroastrian temple in Ch'ang-an, and died soon thereafter.

In 678,[5] Kao-tsung ordered a Gentleman-in-Attendance of the Ministry of Personnel to lead troops, escort Fīrūz's son Ni-nieh-shih back to Persia, and reinstall him as king of that country.[6] But in Central Asia the Chinese expeditionary force was diverted to another purpose, and Ni-nieh-shih continued alone. He was unable to enter Persia and instead spent decades in Tokharia (*Chiu T'ang shu* 198:15b; *Tzu-chih t'ing-chien* pp.6391-6392; *Wen-hsien t'ung-k'ao* 339:53b).

In the 5th month (June/July) of 682, envoys from Persia offered regional objects (*Ts'e-fu yüan-kuei* p.5026).

In the 7th month (Aug./Sep.) of 706, envoys from Persia offered gifts (*Ts'e-fu yüan-kuei* p.5026).

---

[4] *T'ang hui-yao* 100:4a says "of the Right".

[5] By *Tzu-chih t'ung-chien* and *Wen-hsien t'ung-k'ao* dated 679.

[6] *Chiu T'ang shu* claims that it was Fīrūz who was escorted back.

In the 3rd month (Mar./Apr.) of 708, envoys from Persia were received at the court (*Ts'e-fu yüan-kuei* p.5026).

Some time in 708, Ni-nieh-shih returned to Ch'ang-an. Emperor Chung-tsung appointed him General of the Awesome Guards of the Left. Later, he died of an illness. His son remained in Ch'ang-an (*Chiu T'ang shu* 198:15b).

In the 1st (Jan./Feb.), 2nd (Feb./Mar.), and 7th month (July./Aug.) of 719, envoys from Persia offered regional objects (*Ts'e-fu yüan-kuei* p.5027).

In the 10th month (Nov.Dec.) of 722, envoys from Persia presented a lion (*Chiu T'ang shu* 8:11b; *Ts'e-fu yüan-kuei* p.5027).

On Jan.23, 730, the New Year's Day, a son of a Persian king congratulated at the T'ang court and presented five kinds of aromatics (*Ts'e-fu yüan-kuei* p.5028).[7]

In the 9th month (Sep./Oct.) of 732, a chief and a Priest of Great Virtue,[8] sent by the king of Persia, offered gifts (*Ts'e-fu yüan-kuei* p.5028).

In the 1st month (Feb./Mar.) of 739, a royal son of Persia was received at the T'ang court (*Ts'e-fu yüan-kuei* p.5029).

In the 3rd month (Apr./May) of 745, envoys from Persia offered regional objects (*Ts'e-fu yüan-kuei* p.5030).

In the 7th month (July/Aug.) of 746, Persia presented through an intermediary one rhinoceros and one elephant (*Ts'e-fu yüan-kuei* p.5030).

In the 4th month (May/June) of 747, envoys from Persia presented a carnelian couch. In the 5th month (June/July), envoys from the king of Persia presented four leopards (*Ts'e-fu yüan-kuei* p.5030). (*Ts'e-fu yüan-kuei* p.5030).

In the 4th month (May/June) of 750, envoys presented dance mats and real pearls without holes (*Chiu T'ang shu* 198:15b; *Ts'e-fu yüan-kuei* p.5030).

In the 9th month (Sep./Oct.) of 751, envoys from Persia offered gifts (*Ts'e-fu yüan-kuei* p.5030).

---

[7] *Ts'e-fu yüan-kuei* has two entries, both for the 1st month. The first says that a royal son of Persia was received at the T'ang court and presented five kinds of aromatics. The second says that envoys from the king of Persia congratulated on the New Year's Day. I take these to refer to the same occasion.

[8] Perhaps a Zoroastrian priest.

In the 8th month (Aug./Sep.) of 759, Persia presented regional objects (*Ts'e-fu yüan-kuei* p.5031).

In the 5th (May/June) and 9th month (Sep./Oct.) of 762, Persia offered gifts (*Ts'e-fu yüan-kuei* p.5031).

In the 9th month (Oct./Nov.) of 771, envoys from Persia presented real pearls and amber (*Chiu T'ang shu* 198:15b; *Ts'e-fu yüan-kuei* p.5031).

On Sep.27, 824, an envoy from Persia offered gharu wood (*Tzu-chih t'ung-chien* p.7839).

After the 640's, the various Persian pretenders did not have the resources to send missions to China by ship. Consequently, they travelled by land. Even if ships had been available, the rhinoceros, elephant, and perhaps leopards could hardly have been transported over such a large distance by sea. It is even possible that at least the leopards were purchased en route in West Turkestan.

The prefered time for the arrival of Persian missions in Ch'ang-an was the fall, followed by the spring.

While the threat from the Arabs must have been a subject discussed by the Persian envoys, the chief purpose of the missions, at least on the Chinese side, must have been the exchange of goods.

THE ARABS

The Chinese name for the Arabs was Ta-shih, which transliterates the Persian Tāzīk. It is a frustrating and ambiguous term. Usually it refers to the real Arabs. But it can in some contexts mean Muslims outside the caliphate.[9] When the sources say "the Arab State", this normally although not always means the caliphate. But the envoys described as Arabs could have come from Baghdad, the conquered parts of Persia, from West Turkestan, conquered by 715 and reconquered in 751, and even from East Turkestan.

The first mission from the Arab State was received at the T'ang

[9] Wittfogel, *Liao*, pp.51, and 357, note 54, concludes that in the *Liao shih* the term Ta-shih probably refers to the caliphate in Baghdad in 924 and to the Muslim Qarā-khanid dynasty in East Turkestan in 1020 and 1021. This could, of course, be a lack of exactitude restricted to the *Liao shih*.

court on Aug.25, 651 (*Chiu T'ang shu* 4:3a; 198:17a; *Ts'e-fu yüan-kuei* p.5025).

In the 6th month (July/Aug.) of 655, envoys from the Arab State offered gifts (*Chiu T'ang shu* 4:5b).

In the 5th month (May-June) of 681, envoys from the Arab State, attached to a mission from Tokharia, presented horses and regional objects (*Ts'e-fu yüan-kuei* p.5026). This mission obviously came by land.

In the 5th month (June/July) of 682, envoys from the Arab State offered regional objects (*Ts'e-fu yüan-kuei* p.5026).

In the 3rd month (Apr./May) of 693, Arabs proposed to present a lion. A Chinese official advised the Empress Wu that lions are meat eaters. The lion would therefore be a great burden, since meat was difficult to get. Her Majesty had stopped the rearing of falcons and dogs, as well as fishing and hunting [for the imperial table]. What was the point of being frugal for oneself and yet making ample provisions for an animal? The empress thereupon rejected the lion (*Tzu-chih t'ung-chien* p.6505).

In the 3rd month (Mar./Apr.) of 703, envoys from the Arab State presented fine horses (*Ts'e-fu yüan-kuei* p.5026).

In 711, the Arab State offered regional objects (*Chiu T'ang shu* 198: 17a).

In 713 or soon thereafter, envoys from the Arab State were received at the T'ang court and presented horses, a precious ornamented belt, and other objects. The envoys refused to do obeisance, stating that in their country not even the king (caliph) was saluted, only the Spirit of Heaven (Allah). The Chinese high officials upbraided them sharply, whereupon they supposedly complied (*Chiu T'ang shu* 198:17a-17b; *Wen-hsien t'ung-k'ao* 339:56a).

In the 7th month (July/Aug.) of 716, envoys from the caliph Suleiman offered a letter, a robe embroidered with gold, and a precious jade-adorned pitcher for sprinkling water (*Ts'e-fu yüan-kuei* p.5027).

In the 6th month (June/July) of 719, envoys from the Arab State offered gifts (*Ts'e-fu yüan-kuei* p.5027).

In the 3rd month (Mar./Apr.) of 724, Arab envoys presented horses and baroos camphor (*Ts'e-fu yüan-kuei* p.5028).

In 725, an envoy from the Arab State named Su-li-man (Suleiman), leading a mission of 13 men, offered regional objects. He was presented with a purple robe and silver belt and appointed to the

Courageous Garrison (*T'ang hui-yao* 100:12b; *Ts'e-fu yüan-kuei* p.5028; *Wen-hsien t'ung-k'ao* 339:56a).[10]

In the 12th month (Jan./Feb., 734) of the Chinese year 733, a chief sent by the king (caliph) of the Arab State was received at the T'ang court (*Ts'e-fu yüan-kuei* p.5029).

In the 7th month (Aug./Sep.) of 744, envoys from the Arab State presented horses and valuables (*Ts'e-fu yüan-kuei* p.5030).

In the 5th month (June/July) of 745, Arab envoys offered gifts (*Ts'e-fu yüan-kuei* p.5030).

In the 5th month (June/July) of 747, envoys from the king (caliph) of the Arab State presented six leopards (*Ts'e-fu yüan-kuei* p.5030).

In the 12th month (Jan./Feb., 753) of the Chinese year 752, Arab envoys were received at the T'ang court (*Ts'e-fu yüan-kuei* p.5030).

In the 3rd (Apr./May) and 4th month (May/June) of 753, envoys of the black-robed Arabs [from the Abbasid caliphate] offered regional objects. In the 12th month (Dec./Jan., 754) of the same Chinese year, they presented 30 horses (*Ts'e-fu yüan-kuei* p.5030, 5031).

In the 4th month (Apr./May) of 754, envoys from the black-robed Arabs were received at the T'ang court (*Ts'e-fu yüan-kuei* p.5031).

In the 7th month (Aug./Sep.) of 755, 25 envoys from the black-robed Arabs were received at the T'ang court (*Ts'e-fu yüan-kuei* p.5031).

In c.756, Arab envoys offered gifts (*Hsin T'ang shu* 221B:12a).

On June 11, 758, six envoys of the black-robed Arabs entered the palace for an audience. 80 Uighur envoys entered at the same time, and at the Audience Gate both delegations wrangled for precedence. The Chinese receptionists separated them and made them enter simultaneously through the Eastern and Western Gates (*Chiu T'ang shu* 10:9a; 195:4a; *Ts'e-fu yüan-kuei* p.5031; *Wen-hsien t'ung-k'ao* 347:28b).

On June 26, 762, black-robed Arabs offered gifts (*Ts'e-fu yüan-kuei* p.5031).

In the 12th month (Dec./Jan., 763) of the Chinese year 762, envoys from the black-robed Arabs offered gifts (*Chiu T'ang shu* 11:15b; *Ts'e-fu yüan-kuei* p.5031).

In the autumn of 772, Arab envoys offered gifts (*Chiu T'ang shu* 11:20b).

---

[10] *Ts'e-fu yüan-kuei* records the reception of this mission for both the 1st (Feb./Mar.) and 3rd (Apr./May) month. According to *Wen-hsien t'ung-k'ao*, Suleiman arrived in 726.

In the 12th month (Dec./Jan., 773) of the Chinese year 772, Arab envoys offered gifts (*Ts'e-fu yüan-kuei* p.5031).

In the 7th month (Aug./Sep.) of 774, envoys from the black-robed Arabs were received at the T'ang court (*Ts'e-fu yüan-kuei* p.5032).

In the 1st month (Feb./Mar.) of 791, envoys from the black-robed Arabs offered gifts (*Chiu T'ang shu* 13:5b; *Ts'e-fu yüan-kuei* p.5032).

In the 9th month (Oct./Nov.) of 798, three envoys from the black-robed Arabs were received at the T'ang court, and all were appointed Generals of the Gentlemen-of-the-Household (*T'ang hui-yao* 100:13b; *Wen-hsien t'ung-k'ao* 339:56b). These appointments show that they were not lower-echelon envoys. At that time both the Arabs and the Chinese were at war with the Tibetans. It is possible that the mission came from the caliph Harūn al-Rashīd, proposing an alliance. If so, nothing came of it. This was the last recorded mission from the Arabs in T'ang times.

On Oct.28, 924, the Arab State offered gifts to the Liao court (*Liao shih* 2:4b).

When in 966, a Buddhist priest travelled west, Emperor T'ai-tsu of Sung entrusted to him a letter summoning the king (caliph) to his court (*Wen-hsien t'ung-k'ao* 339:56b).

On Jan.7, 969, envoys from the Arab State offered regional objects (*Sung shih* 2:7a; 490:17a; *Hsü Tzu-chih t'ung-chien ch'ang-pien* p.82; *Wen-hsien t'ung-k'ao* 339:56b).

In the 7th month (July/Aug.) of 971, the Arabs offered regional objects. On Aug.7, their chief envoy was appointed General Who Cherishes Civilization and presented with five-coloured damask with golden flowers (*Sung shih* 490:17a; *Hsü Tzu-chih t'ung-chien ch'ang-pien* p.103; *Wen-hsien t'ung-k'ao* 339:56b).

In the 3rd month (Apr./May) of 973, Arab envoys offered regional objects (*Sung shih* 490:17a; *Hsü Tzu-chih t'ung-chien ch'ang-pien* p.114; *Wen-hsien t'ung-k'ao* 339:56b).

On Jan.13, 974, an envoy from the king (caliph) of the Arab State offered regional objects (*Sung shih* 3:6b; 490:17a; *Wen-hsien t'ung-k'ao* 339:56b).[11]

On May 7, 975,[12] envoys from the Arab State offered presents (*Sung shih* 3:7b).

---

[11] The personal name of the king is by *Sung shih* 490:17a given as K'o-lo-fo (caliph).

[12] Correcting *chi-hai* to *yi-hai*.

On May 31, 976, the envoy P'u-hsi-mi from the king (caliph) of the Arab State offered regional objects (*Sung shih* 3:11a; 490:17a-17b; *Wen-hsien t'ung-k'ao* 339:56b).[13]

On Apr.21, 977, envoys from the Arab State offered regional objects. They were presented with garments, [porcelain] vessels, and silk (*Sung shih* 4:3b; 490:17b; *Wen-hsien t'ung-k'ao* 339:56b).

In 979, the Arabs offered gifts (*Sung shih* 490:17b; *Wen-hsien t'ung-k'ao* 339:56b).

In 984, an Arab envoy offered flowered brocade, *yüeh-no* cloth, aromatics, white baroos camphor, white granulated sugar, rose water, and opaque glass vessels (*Sung shih* 490:17b; *Wen-hsien t'ung-k'ao* 339: 56b).[14]

In 993, the Arab envoy Li-ya-wu[15] arrived on the China coast at the same time as the Arab shipmaster P'u-hsi-mi.[16] Because the latter was old and ill, he was unable to proceed to the palace in the capital. He therefore added his regional objects to the presents brought by Li-ya-wu, together with a written inventory. It listed 50 elephant tusks, 1,800 catties of frankincense, 700 catties of fine steel, one item of cotton with red threads, four items of variegated flowered brocades, two items of *yüeh-no* cloth, one opaque glass pitcher, one lump of limonite, and 100 bottles of rose water. Emperor T'ai-tsung presented P'u-hsi-mi with a letter, a brocade robe, silver vessels, and silk (*Sung shih* 490: 17b-18b; *Wen-hsien t'ung-k'ao* 339:56b).[17]

In the 4th month (May/June) of 994, envoys from the Arab State offered gifts (*Sung shih* 5:18b).

In 995, an Arab shipmaster sent an agent[18] with a letter to the Sung court and presented 100 ounces of baroos camphor, castoreum,

---

[13] *Sung shih* 3:11a, gives K'o-lo-fo (caliph) as the personal name.

[14] *Wen-hsien t'ung-k'ao* dates this mission 985.

[15] If he was the same Li-ya-wu who is mentioned in 1008, he was a shipmaster.

[16] Hirth and Rockhill, *Chao Ju-kua*, p.123, note 18, equate P'u-hsi-mi with Abu-Hamid.

[17] According to Chao Ju-kua, Li-ya-wu received as much gold as the presents were worth. See Hirth and Rockhill, *Chao Ju-kua*, p.118.

[18] According to *Wen-hsien t'ung-k'ao*, his name was P'u-hsi-mi. This name also occurs as that of the envoy of 976 and of the shipmaster of 993. While it is barely possibe, although hardly probable, that the entries for 976 and 993 concern the same person, this cannot be the case in 995. The P'u-hsi mi of 993 was too old and infirm to travel to the court and therefore cannot have acted for another shipmaster in 995.

dragon salt, drugs, white granulated sugar, dates, schisandra chinensis seeds, peaches, 20 bottles of rose water, frankincense, foreign brocade, mats, and *yüeh-no* cloth. The agent received a brocade robe, textiles, and gold and silver pitchers, the shipmaster real gold, equivalent to the value of the goods he had presented (*Sung shih* 490:18b-19a; *Wen-hsien t'ung-k'ao* 339:56b).

On Apr.7, 997, the Arab State offered gifts (*Sung shih* 5:25b; *Wen-hsien t'ung-k'ao* 339:56b).[19]

In the intercalary month (Apr./May) of 999, envoys from the Arab State congratulated on the enthronement of Emperor Chen-tsung (on May 8, 997) and presented 4 elephant tusks, 200 catties of aromatics, dates, white pebble sweets, grapes, opaque glass, and 40 bottles of rose water (*Sung hui-yao kao,* chüan 20,522).

On Aug.13, 999, envoys from the Arab State offered gifts (*Sung shih* 6:6b, 8b; 490:19a; *Wen-hsien t'ung-k'ao* 339:56b).

In the 3rd month (Apr./May) of 1000, an agent of the shipmaster T'o-p'o-li,[20] offered gifts. T'o-p'o-li was paid 2,700 ounces of silver, water sprinkling vessels, and gilded silver horse trappings (*Sung shih* 490: 19a; *Sung hui-yao kao,* chüan 20,522; *Wen-hsien t'ung-k'ao* 339:56b).

In the 6th month (July Aug.) of 1003, envoys from the king (caliph) of the Arab State offered a red parrot and regional objects.[21] On Chen-tsung's birthday,[22] they were given a great banquet and presented with garments (*Sung shih* 7:2b; 490:19b; *Sung hui-yao kao,* chüan 20, 522; *Wen-hsien t'ung-k'ao* 339:56b).

In 1004, envoys from the Arab State offered gifts. In the autumn, another envoy arrived at the Sung court (*Sung shih* 7:7b; 490:19b; *Wen-hsien t'ung-k'ao* 339:56b).

On Feb.12, 1005, the New Years Day, Arab envoys were invited to a banquet, given for them, for a royal son from Chiao-chih, and for envoys from Champa (*Sung hui-yao kao* 10,122:7b).

In 1007, envoys from the Arab State offered gifts. They arrived together with envoys from Champa, i.e. they had travelled by sea

---

[19] Chao Ju-kua reports this mission for 986, having mistaken *chih-tao* 3rd year (997) for *yung-hsing* 3rd year (986). See Hirth and Rocklhill, *Chao Ju-kua*, p.118.

[20] By *Wen-hsien t'ung-k'ao* called T'o-lo-li.

[21] According to Chao Ju-kua, these included pearls. See Hirth and Rockhill, *Chau* Ju-kua, p.118.

[22] It fell on Dec.27.

(*Sung shih* 7:15b; 490:19b; *Wen-hsien t'ung-k'ao* 339:56b).[23]

When Chen-tsung performed the *feng* and *shan* sacrifices at Mount T'ai on Nov.24 and 25, 1008, one Arab shipmaster attended it and at that occasion presented regional objects, while the shipmaster Li-ya-wu[24] sent the envoy Ma-wu (Mohammed) to present a jade tablet. Both shipmasters were given [porcelain] vessels, silk, robes, and belts. Simultaneously, the ruler (caliph) of their state was presented with a couch with silver ropes, water pitchers, mechanisms, banners, and horse trappings (*Sung shih* 7:15b, 20b; 490:19b-20a; *Wen hsien t'ung-k'ao* 339:56b). The Chinese presents to the caliph at this occasion prove that the Sung court regarded the shipmasters as at least quasi envoys. We do not know, of course, whether the Chinese gifts ever reached the caliph.

After Chen-tsung had sacrificed to Sovereign Earth at Fen-yin in Shan-hsi on Mar.24, 1011, an Arab envoy with the Chinese title of General Who Has Attached Himself to Virtue presented on Mar.25 aromatics, elephant tusks, amber, limonite, textiles, *yüeh-no* cloth, wine vessels of white opaque glass, rose water, and dates. He received caps, belts, and garments (*Sung shih* 8:1b; 490:20a).

An edict of Aug.8, 1014, mentions the presence of Arab envoys in K'ai-feng (*Sung hui-yao kao* 10122:11b).

In the 11th month (December) of 1016, envoys from the Arab State were received in audience by Chen-tsung (*Sung hui-yao kao,* chüan 20,522).

On June 6, 1019, envoys from the Arab State offered gifts (*Sung shih* 8:19b; 490:20a).

On Nov.12, 1020, envoys from the king of the Arab State[25] to the Liao court presented an elephant and regional objects, and requested the marriage of his son to a Liao princess (*Liao shih* 16:5a).

In the 3rd month (Apr./May) of 1021, envoys from the king of the Arab State to the Liao court again requested a marriage. The daughter

[23] According to Chao Ju-kua, the envoys were treated with great courtesy and allowed to visit Buddhist and Taoist temples and imperial gardens and parks. See Hirth and Rockhill, *Chao Ju-kua*, p.118.

[24] Perhaps the same Li-ya-wu who arrived on the China coast on 993.

[25] It has been seen that according to Wittfogel, this and the next embassy to the Liao may have come from the Muslim Qarā-khanid dynasty in East Turkestan. A marriage between a son of a caliph and a Liao princess is not, of course, within the realm of possibility.

of a Liao court noble was enfeoffed as a princess and married to him (*Liao shih* 16:5b).

In the 11th month (Dec./Jan., 1024) of the Chinese year 1023, envoys from the Arab State offered gifts to the Sung court (*Sung shih* 490: 20a; *Sung hui-yao kao,* chüan 20,522; *Wen-hsien t'ung-k'ao* 339:56b).

In the 10th month (Oct./Nov.) of 1055, an envoy from the the Arab State offered gifts (*Sung shih* 12:10a; *Sung hui-yao kao,* chüan 20,522).

In the 4th month (May/June) of 1056, envoys from the the Arab State offered regional objects (*Sung shih* 12:11b; *Sung hui-yao kao,* chüan 20,522).

In the 1st month (Feb./Mar.) of 1060, an envoy from the Arab State offered regional objects. He was appointed a Guard of the Staircase (*Sung shih* 12:17a).

On Jan.27, 1071, envoys from the Arab State offered gifts. They were presented with [porcelain] vessels, garments, drink, and food, each in accordance with his rank (*Sung hui-yao kao,* chüan 20,522).

On July 9, 1072, envoys from the Arab State took their leave and were presented with a white horse and trappings (*Sung hui-yao kao,* chüan 20,522).

On Oct.9. 1073, the Arabs offered presents (*Sung shih* 15:9b; 490: 20b).

On Jan.15, 1074, envoys from the Arab State offered frankincense etc. They were paid 2,900 strings of 1000 cash and 2000 ounces of silver (*Sung hui-yao kao,* chüan 20,522).

On May 9, 1084, the Arab State offered regional objects (*Sung shih* 16:12a).

In 1085, the Arab State offered gifts (*Sung shih* 17:4b).

On Dec.10, 1088, envoys from the Arab State offered gifts (*Sung shih* 17:11b).

On May 22, 1089, envoys from the Arab State offered gifts. The chief envoy was appointed a General of the Gentlemen Who Maintain Obedience (*Sung shih* 17:3b; *Sung hui-yao kao* chüan 20,522).

On Dec.30, 1089, the Arab State offered regional objects (*Sung hui-yao kao,* chüan 20,522).

In 1096, the Arabs offered gifts (*Sung shih* 18:7a).

On Mar.15, 1099, the Arabs offered gifts (*Sung shih* 18:13a).

On Aug.8, 1116, the Arab State offered gifts (*Sung shih* 21:7b; *Sung hui-yao kao,* chüan 20,522).

On Mar.28, 1129, envoys from the Arab State offered precious jade, pearls, and other valuables (*Sung shih* 490:21a; *Sung hui-yao kao,* chüan 20,522).

On Dec.17, 1131, the Maritime Trade Commission of the [Eastern] Kuang-nan Circuit [in Canton] reported to the court that the envoy P'u-ya-li had arrived from the Arab State by ship to offer 35 large, veined rhinoceros horns and 209 large elephant tusks. The tusks weighed more than 57 catties [each]. One catty of ivory was evaluated at 2 strings of 1000 cash. He was paid 600 ingots of silver, gold and silver vessels, and textiles. On July 28, 1134, the Judicial Commission of the Eastern Kuang-nan Circuit reported to the court that bandits had invaded P'u-ya-li's ship, had wounded him and killed four foreigners, and had robbed all the gold and silver (*Sung shih* 490:21b; *Sung hui-yao kao,* chüan 20,522; *Wen-hsien t'ung-k'ao* 339:57a).

On Sep.21, 1136, the Maritime Trade Commission of Fu-chien reported to the court that P'u-lo-hsin[26] from the Arab State had brought frankincese by ship and had handed it over to the Maritime Trade Commission of Ch'üan-chou. The estimated value was 300,000 strings of 1000 cash (*Sung hui-yao kao,* chüan 20,522; *Wen-hsien t'ung-k'ao* 339:57a).

In 1168, the Arabs offered regional objects (*Wen-hsien t'ung-k'ao* 339:57a).

Between 1205 and 1207, Arab envoys offered gifts (*Wen-hsien t'ung-k'ao* 339:57a).

The routes taken by the Arab missions to China are a problem. The regularity of the summer and winter monsoons was known to the Arabs not later than the 1st century A.D. , and by T'ang times they were capable to sail directly to China without changing shipa at the various ports of call.The biggest trading town on the China coast during T'ang was Canton,[27] during Sung Ch'üan-chou in Fu-chien. Envoys from Baghdad, unless they sailed on their own ships, could therefore take passage with the merchants. During Sung, Arab shipmasters are

---

[26] He must have been an envoy, since the arrival of a commercial ship would have been handled routinely by the authorities and would not have been reported to the court.

[27] On Oct.30, 758, the T'ang court was informed by local authorities that the Arabs and Persians had attacked Canton, had looted the granaries and arsenals, had burned houses, and had then departed by sea (*Chiu T'ang shu* 10:9b; 198:15b; *Tzu-chih t'ung-chien* p.7062).

When Huang Ch'ao sacked Canton in 879, Muslims were among those killed.

recorded to have brought gifts from the caliphs to the imperial court. They may have doubled as envoys or posed as such.

The other way taken by the missions was by land via Central Asia. Neither route was without risks. Ships could be wrecked and goods lost. An undated entry states that Arabs, when calling at Champa en route to China, at times had their goods confiscated (*Wen-hsien t'ung-k'ao* 339:57a). This could have happened to merchants and envoys alike. Caravans travelling through Central Asia encountered robbers. In both cases, the Arabs complained to the Chinese authorities. The Sung court advised them in 1023 that the sea route to Canton was to be preferred (*Wen-hsien t'ung-k'ao* 338:56b).

Unfortunately, the sources hardly ever specify how the missions had arrived in China. Only when a shipmaster is mentioned can we be absolutely sure, and these cases are only 7 out of 77. One has to rely on circumstantial evidence, where possible, to gain a better understanding of the situation. Horses would not have been brought from Arabia by a long sea voyage. It can be assumed, therefore, that when horses were offered by the envoys, these came by land from West Turkestan. This may also be true for the lion and leopards. But small luxury articles could be carried by land as well as sea.

The time element should help us to get a step further. The Arab ships left the Middle East with the beginning of the summer monsoon and reached China in 130 to 140 days. They returned with the beginning of the winter monsoon during the same or in subsequent years. This means that they departed from the Middle East about the middle of April and reached China in about the middle of August. Adding the necessary land travel, they would have arrived in the capital in early September or about the 8th month in the Chinese calendar. The ships could arrive a month later but not beyond that time because of the beginning of the adverse winter monsoon in middle October. In addition, the envoys might not have proceeded directly from the Chinese port of call to the capital. The agent of the shipmaster T'o-p'o-li was not received at the Sung court until the 3rd month of 1000, some seven months after his presumed landing. That narrows the time limit during which Arab missions must have arrived by land to the 4th, 5th, 6th, and 7th months.

Using this extremely rough calculation, only about 5 of the 30 Arab missions during T'ang could theoretically have come by sea.[28] During

[28] For three of the missions, the month of reception is not known.

Sung, only about 10 of the 47 missions could theoretically have come by land.[29] While these statistics are anything but exact, it is quite certain that the majority of the Arab missions during T'ang came by land and during Sung by sea.[30] It is also clear that the relations were much closer during Sung than T'ang.

Although the caliphate was a powerful state and had inflicted a serious defeat on China in 751, the T'ang and Sung upheld the fiction that it was a tributary. In 966, T'ai-tsu even had the arrogance to summon the caliph to his court. China and the caliphate were of course equals, but separated by a vast distance. The Chinese emperors conferred titles on Arab envoys but not on the caliphs. They did not bother to recognize the caliphs. They did not declare official mourning at the death of a caliph, they conferred no posthumous titles on the caliphs, and they sent no envoys to condole. The only common political interest of the Chinese and Arabs was to restrain the Tibetans, but they never cooperated against them. This makes it inescapable that the chief purpose of the Arab missions was trade.

FU-LIN

Fu-lin is generally accepted to be Syria. It does not mean Byzantium, and the term king does not stand for the Byzantine emperor. *T'ang hui-yao* 99:12a-12b states that Persia and Fu-lin were taken by the Arabs between 661 and 663.[31] Consequently, Fu-lin became an Arab possession and was no longer a Byzantine province. Hirth and Rockhill conclude that the term "king of Fu-lin" means the Nestorian Patriarch of Antioch.[32]

In 643, envoys from the king of Fu-lin to the T'ang court presented glass, red and green transparent glass, malachite, gold essence etc. T'ai-tsung reponded with a letter stamped with the imperial seal and thin silk (*Chiu T'ang shu* 198:16b; *Ts'e-fu yüan-kuei* p.5024).

---

[29] For nine of these missions, the month of reception is not known.

[30] The significant fact should also be noted that no animals were presented during Sung.

[31] The text is a few years off. The important town of Antioch in Syria was overrun by the Arabs in 633, and Persia was taken in the 640's.

[32] *Chau Ju-kua*, pp.105 note 2, 280. O.Franke, *Geschichte*, vol.III, p.361, maintains that Fu-lin is Byzantium.

In 667,[33] envoys from Fu-lin presented theriaca[34] (*Chiu T'ang shu* 198:16b).

In 701, envoys from Fu-lin were received at the T'ang court (*Chiu T'ang shu* 198:16b).

In 711, envoys from Fu-lin presented regional objects (*Ts'e-fu yüan-kuei* p.5026).

In the 1st month (Jan./Feb.) of 719,[35] the ruler of Fu-lin presented through a great Tokharian chief two lions and two goat antelopes. Later that year, a Priest of Great Virtue from Fu-lin offered gifts (*Chiu T'ang shu* 198:16b; *Ts'e-fu yüan-kuei* p.5027)

In the 5th month (June/July) of 742, a Priest of Great Virtue sent by the king of Fu-lin was received at the T'ang court (*Chiu T'ang shu* 198:16b; *Ts'e-fu yüan-kuei* p.5029).

In the 4th month (May/June) of 1081,[36] chiefs sent by the king of Fu-lin to the Sung court presented horse trappings, swords, and real pearls. They stated that their country was extremely cold[37] (*Wen-hsien t'ung-k'ao* 339:57a).

On Mar.3, 1091, envoys from Fu-lin offered gifts. On May 10, Emperor Che-tsung presented the king with 200 bolts of silk, silver pitchers, garments, and a golden belt (*Sung shih* 17:5a; 490:24a; *Sung hui-yao kao*, chüan 10,364; *Wen-hsien t'ung-k'ao* 339:57a).

On Feb.1, 1092, envoys from the Fu-lin State offered gifts (*Hsü Tzu-chih t'ung-chien ch'ang-pien* p.4387).

The question arises as to how the envoys from Fu-lin traveled to China. Luxury articles were not bulky and could be carried long distances by land or sea. In 719, Fu-lin made use of a Tokharian intermediary to present lions and antelopes. It means that this mission was organized in West Turkestan on behalf of Fu-lin and proceeded from there. Using the criteria suggested for the Arabs, the missions of 742 (5th month) and 1081 (4th month) should also have travelled by land. For the rest, no certainty is possible.

---

[33] By *T'ang hui-yao* 99:23b dated 666.

[34] According to Schafer, *Golden Peaches*, p.184, a truly universal antidote.

[35] By *T'ang hui-yao* 99:23b dated 1st month ((Jan./Feb.) of 722. According to the same entry, the Priest of Great Virtue arrived in the 4th month (Apr./May) of that year.

[36] *Sung hui-yao kao*, chüan 10,364, dates the reception of the mission Nov.9.

[37] Suffering from cold is a subjective matter. For the local people of Syria, their winters could feel cold.

Since Fu-lin and China had nothing in common, the link between them, at least from the Chinese point of view, was trade. Fu-lin may have had an additional aim, since the Priests of Great Virtue of 719 and 742 could have been Nestorian missionaries.[38]

According to *Chiu T'ang shu* 198:15b, Persia sent ten missions to the T'ang court from 722 to 747. Eight are recorded. According to *Sung shih* 490:20b and *Wen-hsien t'ung-k'ao* 339:56b, four Arab missions offered regional objects from 1054 to 1063. Three missions are recorded. The statistics are therefore reasonably reliable.

This is the distribution by 20-year periods of the 77 recorded missions from the Arabs to T'ang and Sung, the 27 missions from the Persians to T'ang, and the 9 missions from Fu-lin to T'ang and Sung, 113 in all from the Middle East:

Period	Missions
607- 626:	1
627- 646:	2
647- 666:	4
667- 686:	6
687- 706:	4
707- 726:	13
727- 746:	9
747- 766:	17
767- 786:	4
787- 806:	2
807- 826:	1
827- 846:	0
847- 866:	0
867- 886:	0
887- 906:	0
907- 926:	0
927- 946:	0
947- 966:	0
967- 986:	9
987-1006:	11
1007-1026:	7
1027-1046:	0

[38] Priest of Great Virtue is a flexible term, since, as has been seen, it might have refered to a Zoroastrian priest in 732. See p. 355, note 8.

1047-1066:	3
1067-1086:	7
1087-1106:	7
1107-1126:	1
1127-1146:	3
1147-1166:	0
1167-1186:	1
1187-1206:	1

The high point of foreign relations was the reign of Emperor Hsüan-tsung (r.712-756). After the rebellion of An Lu-shan in 755, with its reaction somewhat delayed because of the distance, the missions dropp off and then cease. They revive with the Sung, but with the Southern Sung (1126-1276) come to a virtual halt. Of the 49 missions to China during all of Sung only 5 arrived in Southern Sung. Yet, the Arabs could reach China by sea as easily as before. The collapse of foreign relations is still another proof for the xenophobia of Southern Sung.

The specified goods brought by the Persians, the Arabs, and Fu-lin fall into the following categories:

Animals and Animal Products

Elephants

746: one elephant from Persia.

Elephant tusks

993: 50 elephant tusks from the Arabs.
999: 4 elephant tusks from the Arabs.
1011: elephant tusks from the Arabs.
1131: 209 large elephant tusks from the Arabs.

Rhinoceroses

746: one rhinoceros from Persia.

Rhinoceros horns

1131: 35 large veined rhinoceros horns from the Arabs.

Felines

693: one lion from the Arabs (rejected).
719: 2 lions from Fu-lin.
722: one lion from Persia.
747: 4 leopards from Persia, 6 leopards from the Arabs.

Horses

681: horses from the Arabs.
703: fine horses from the Arabs.
c.713: horses from the Arabs.
724: horses from the Arabs.
744: horses from the Arabs.
753: 30 horses from the Arabs.

Other

638: one ferret from Persia.
719: 2 goat antelopes from Fu-lin.

Aromatics

Aromatic and medical drugs

643: gold essence from Fu-lin.
667: theriaca from Fu-lin.
730: five kinds of aromatics from Persia.
984: aromatics from the Arabs.
995: drugs and schisandra chinensis seeds from the Arabs.
999: 200 catties of aromatics from the Arabs.
1011: aromatics from the Arabs.

Frankincense

993: 1,800 catties of frankincense from the Arabs.
995: frankincense from the Arabs.

Rose water

984: rose water from the Arabs.
993: 100 bottles of rose water from the Arabs.
995: 20 bottles of rose water from the Arabs.

999: 40 bottles of rose water from the Arabs.
1011: rose water from the Arabs.

Fragrant woods

824: gharu wood from Persia.

Camphor

724: baroos camphor from the Arabs.
984: white baroos camphor from the Arabs.
995: 100 ounces of baroos camphor from the Arabs.

Cosmetics

995: castoreum from the Arabs.

Spices

995: dragon salt from the Arabs.

Trees and Fruits

995: dates and peaches from the Arabs.
999: dates and grapes from the Arabs.
1011: dates from the Arabs.

Minerals, Ores, and Metals

643: malachite from Fu-lin.
993: 700 catties of fine steel from the Arabs.
993: one lump of limonite from the Arabs.
1011: limonite from the Arabs.
1129: precious jade from the Arabs.

Manufactured Objects

Of metal

1081: swords from Fu-lin.

Of glass

643: glass and red and green transparent glass from Fu-lin.
984: opaque glass vessels from the Arabs.
993: one opaque glass pitcher from the Arabs.
999: opaque glass from the Arabs.
1011: wine vessels of white opaque glass from the Arabs.

Of precious stone

716: a precious jade-adorned pitcher for sprinkling water from the Arabs.
1008: a jade tablet from the Arabs.

Of leather

1081: horse trappings from Fu-lin.

Other

750: dance mats from Persia.
c.713: a precious ornamented belt from the Arabs.
995: mats from the Arabs.

Textiles

Cottons

984: *yüeh-no* cloth from the Arabs.
993: cotton with red threads and white *yüeh-no* cloth from the Arabs.
995: *yüeh-no* cloth from the Arabs.
1011: *yüeh-no* cloth from the Arabs.

Silks

984: flowered brocade from the Arabs.
993: variegated flowered brocades in five colours from the Arabs.
995: foreign brocades from the Arabs.

Other

1011: textiles from the Arabs.

Garments

716: one robe embroidered with gold from the Arabs.
1091: garments from Fu-lin.

Jewels

750: real pearls without holes from Persia.
771: real pearls and amber from Persia.
1011: amber from the Arabs.
1081: real pearls from Fu-lin.
1129: pearls from the Arabs.

Sweets

984: white granulated sugar from the Arabs.
995: white granulated sugar from the Arabs.
999: white pebble sweets from the Arabs.

As usual, some of the goods were native products, others not. The elephant and rhinoceros presented by the Persians did not come from Persia. The elephant tusks and rhinoceros horns of the Arabs did not come from Arabia. They were either from Africa or bought by the envoys in India or Southeast Asia. The lions and goat antelopes offered by Fu-lin came from West Turkestan. There are no leopards in Arabia. Although amber is an Arab word, this fossil resin is not found in Arabia. These and other cases show that the trade conducted by the missions was part of an exchange of goods involving the entire old world.

The Chinese paid with copper cash, gold, silver, gold and silver vessels, porcelain vessels, silk, damask, garments, caps, belts, banners, and horse trappings.

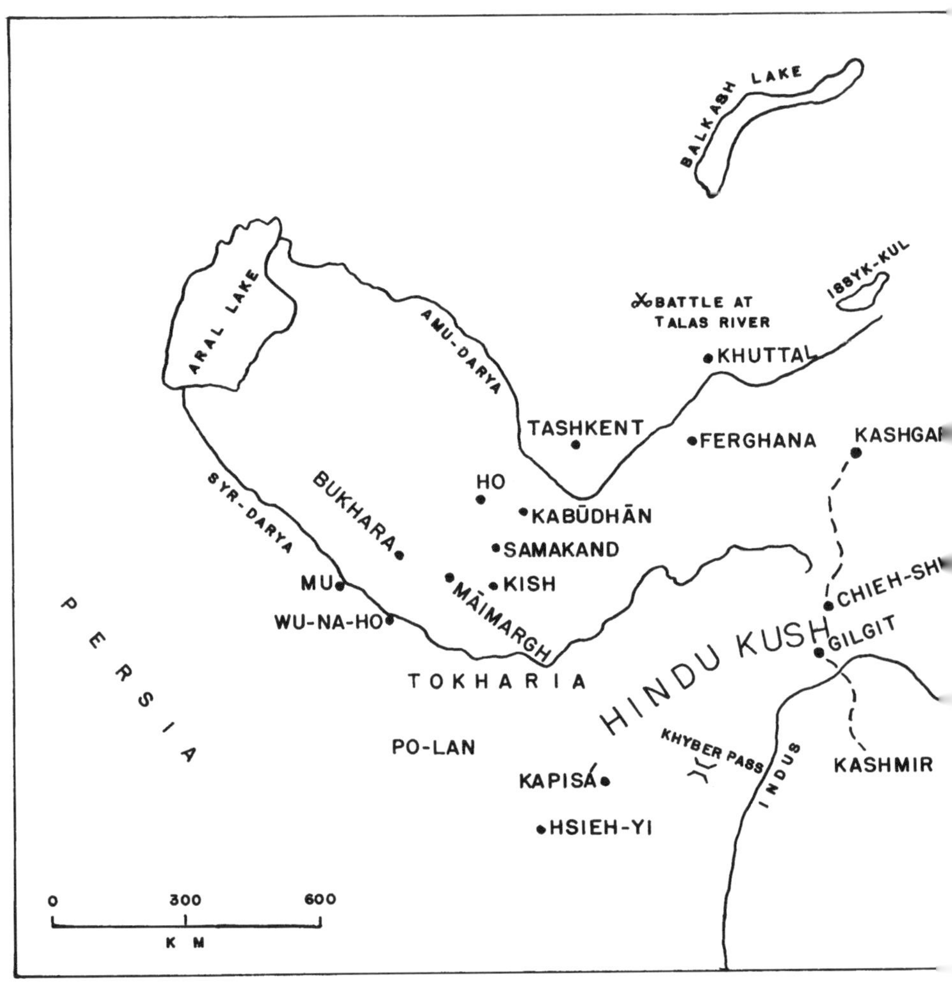

Map 9. West Asia.

THE TURKIC TRIBES

THE EASTERN TURKS

The Turks are the people who gave their name to their entire language family. The Chinese called them T'u-chüeh. Until 552, they had been a subject tribe of the Juan-juan, but that year they crushed their masters, and their chief T'u-men (Bumin) assumed the title of qaghan. His successors soon expanded the Turkish empire until it streched from the border of Manchuria to that of Persia. In the early 580's, it divided into two qaghanates, that of the Eastern Turks, also called the Northern, in what now is Inner and Outer Mongolia, and that of the Western Turks. Both were hostile to each other and also riven internally by factions and, at times, competing qaghans. These tensions were fomented and exploited by the Chinese.[1]

When the Sha-po-lüeh Qaghan of the Eastern Turks died in 587, he was briefly succeeded by a brother and then by a son who became the Hsieh-chia-shih-to-na-tu-lan Qaghan or Tu-lan for short. The latter sent envoys to the Sui court and was presented with 3000 items of objects (*Sui shu* 84:8b, 9b).

The stepmother of the new qaghan was Chinese. In 579, the last ruler of Northern Chou, Emperor Ching, had agreed to a marriage alliance with the Eastern Turks and had enfeoffed a lady of his imperial house as Princess of Ch'ien-chin. She was a granddaughter of Yü-wen T'ai, father of the first emperor of Northern Chou. In 580, she was escorted to the Turks, where she became the qatun of the Sha-po-lüeh Qaghan. After the overthrow of the Northern Chou

[1] The Chinese sources distinguish as a rule between the Eastern and Western Turks. Thus *Sui shu* 84:1a-14b, *Pei shih* 99:1a-16a, *Chiu T'ang shu* 194A, *Hsin T'ang shu* 215A and 215B:1a-3a, *T'ung-tien* 197:39a-198:44a, and *Wen-hsien t'ung-k'ao* 343:6b-344:11a are devoted to the Eastern Turks, and *Sui shu* 84:14b-18a, *Pei shih* 99:16a-19b, *Chiu T'ang shu* 194B, *Hsin T'ang shu* 215B:3a-10a, *T'ung-tien* 199:44a-46a, and *Wen-hsien t'ung-k'ao* 344:11b-13b to the Western Turks. However, one entry in the imperial annals of *Sui shu* and a number of entries in *Ts'e-fu yüan-kuei* and *Tzu-chih t'ung-chien* do not specify whether the Turks are eastern or western. Where internal evidence does not settle the matter, I have below marked the doubtful cases by an asterisc, i.e *Turks or *Turkish.

dynasty by the Sui in 581, she was bestowed the imperial surname of Yang and was entered into the imperial register. Her title was changed to Princess of Ta-yi, and in 589 or soon thereafter she was presented with valuable door screens which formed part of the loot taken from the defeated Ch'en dynasty in south China. However, the princess resented the fall of Northern Chou, and the Chinese believed that she was enciting the Eastern Turks against them. Emperor Wen therefore first demoted her to "Evermore Mean Princess", then made her a commoner, and slandered her to her husband (*Chou shu* 50:8a; *Sui shu* 84:8a, 8b, 9b, 10a).

On May 5, 591, a maternal uncle of Tu-lan presented a jade staff from Khotan. Emperor Wen appointed this envoy as Pillar of State and enfeoffed him as a duke (*Sui shu* 2:7a; 84:9b).

On Jan.9, 593, envoys sent by Eastern Turkish chiefs presented 10,000 horses, 20,000 sheep, 500 camels, and 500 heads of cattle. A subsequent mission negotiated with the Chinese the establishment of border markets (*Sui shu* 2:8a; 84:9b).

At this time, the Chinese had begun to deal with a lesser Eastern Turkish qaghan, who was a son of Sha-po-lüeh and consequently a half-brother of Tu-lan. This was the T'u-li Qaghan. He sent envoys to the Sui court and requested to marry a Chinese princess. At the advice of his central-Asian expert P'ei Chü, Emperor Wen agreed in 593, on the condition that the hostile Chinese qatun be killed. She was subsequently assassinated, the details being unknown (*Sui shu* 84: 10a; *T'ung-tien* 197:39a; *Wen-hsien t'ung-k'ao* 343:6b).

On Sep.10, 597, Emperor Wen approved the marriage of the Princess of An-yi to T'u-li. He gave T'u-li preferential treatment and sent envoys to him (*Sui shu* 84:10b; *T'ung-tien* 197:39a; *Wen-hsien t'ung-k'ao* 343:6b).

On Dec.28, 597, a Turkish mission was received at the Sui court. It had been sent by T'u-li to escort his bride to his camp (*Sui shu* 2: 12b, *Pei-shih* 11:24b; 99:13a).

The Chinese policy of driving a wedge between T'u-li and Tu-lan was successful, the former becoming friendly to Sui and the latter halting his missions to the court and turning hostile. Open warfare between the two broke out in 598 (*Sui shu* 84:10b).

In 599, T'u-li was defeated by Tu-lan and fled with five horsemen and a Sui envoy. In the 6th month (June/July), Emperor Wen gave him the new title of Yi-li-chen-tou-ch'i-min Qaghan or Ch'i-min for short.[2] Ch'i-min thanked in a letter which in the Chinese sources is called a "memorial". In this and further documents, he supposedly referred to himself as "subject". Since his Chinese wife, the Princess of An-yi was no longer alive, Emperor Wen married another lady of the imperial house to him, the Princess of Yi-ch'eng. Many Eastern Turkish tribes attached themselves to him (*Sui shu* 84:11a-11b; *T'ung-tien* 197:39a; *Wen-hsien t'ung-k'ao* 343:6b).

Tu-lan continued his attacks on T'u-li, and the latter temporarily withdrew with his followers to grazing grounds in the Ordos Region (map 10). Four Chinese armies were sent out against Tu-lan, and in the course of this campaign he was killed by his own men (*Sui shu* 84: 11a, 11b; *Pei-shih* 11:25b).

The qaghan of the Western Turks, Ta-t'ou (Tardu), a paternal uncle of Sha-po-lüeh, had allied himself with Tu-lan against T'u-li (Ch'i-min). After Tu-lan's death, he attempted to make himself Great Qaghan of all the Turks, adopting the title of Pu-chia Qaghan. This embroiled him in a largely unsuccessful war against both the Chinese and Ch'i-min. On Jan.21, 600, envoys of Ch'i-min to the Sui court expressed his thanks for support and presented regional objects (*Sui shu* 2:13b-14a; 84:6a, 11b; *Pei-shih* 11:25b).

From 601, Ch'i-min was was gradually recognized as qaghan by Eastern Turkish tribes. But Ta-t'ou kept up the pressure and captured a great number of people and domestic animals. Chinese troops pursued and routed his forces and returned the captured people and animals to Ch'i-min. After further fighting, Ta-t'ou was in 603 defeated by the T'ieh-le, fled to the T'u-yü-hun, and disappeared from history. Thereafter Ch'i-min was unchallenged as the Eastern Turkish ruler (*Sui shu* 84:12a).

A son of Ch'i-min was received at the Sui court on June 9, 607, and a nephew on June 18 (*Sui shu* 3:9b).

On June 23, 607, envoys of Ch'i-min proposed a meeting of the two rulers on Chinese soil, which was rejected by Emperor Yang.[4] But the emperor soon had a change of heart. On July 10, he arrived in Yü-lin commandery in what now is Sui-yüan, and there on July 19 met Ch'i-min and his qatun, the Princess of Yi-ch'eng. Ch'i-min

---

[2] *Wen-hsien t'ung-k'ao* avoids Li Shih-min's tabooed given name and calls him Ch'i-jen.

[4] He had succeeded his father Wen on Aug.13, 604.

presented 3000 horses, and Emperor Yang responded with 12,000 pieces of silk.[5] The emperor decreed that when Ch'i-min greeted him he did not have to mention his name and that his position in court should be in front of that of the feudal lords. On Aug.2, Ch'i-min "presented a memorial" in which he asked "permission" for the Turks to adopt Chinese clothing. Yang ordered a court discussion, in which the high dignitaries proposed that this be approved. The emperor rejected the advice and informed Ch'i-min that barbarians and Chinese had different customs and that a change of clothing was unnecessary. All the Turks had to do was to be good-hearted, filial, and obedient. A banquet was given for Ch'i-min and thousands of his tribe, and 2000 items of gifts were distributed among them, to each in accordance with his rank. Among the gifts to Ch'i-min were chariots, horses, fifes, and banners, and one golden jar each for him and the qatun. On Sep.2, the day of Yang's departure, the imperial chariot passed through the Turkish camp. Ch'i-min awaited it. The emperor entered his tent. Ch'i-min "knelt", raised a goblet, and wished him long life. This was followed by a banquet given by the qaghan, and gifts were exchanged. Meanwhile, the empress called on the qatun in her tent. On Sep.9, Ch'i-min returned by "imperial orders" to his homeland (*Sui shu* 3:9b, 10b, 11a; 84:12a-14a; *Pei shih* 99:14b-16a; *Wen-hsien t'ung-k'ao* 343:6b).

This account raises a number of questions, as does the one of 599. It is obviously adapted to put the Chinese side in the best possible light. The instruction on protocol was for Chinese consumption and would hardly have been communicated to the qaghan. He would not have addressed the emperor in the manner of a Chinese official, and he could not have been treated as an inferior to the Chinese high nobility. The emperor therefore decreed what was self-evident. Ch'i-min would naturally not have "presented a memorial". The request to adopt Chinese clothing is sheer nonsense. If the Turks had wished to do so, no one could have prevented them, and they needed no "permission". Ch'i-min would under no circumstances have "knelt" before the emperor. He was on good terms with the Chinese and had reason to be grateful to them. But he was the qaghan of the Eastern Turks, with no challenger in sight. Had there been a rival, he could conceivably have humbled himself, but that was not the case. Ch'i-min

[5] *Pei shih* says 13,000 pieces.

merely toasted the emperor in whatever the Turkish manner was, and this was wilfully interpreted by the Chinese as an act of homage. It goes without saying that Ch'i-min was not "ordered" to return to his homeland. Everything indicates that the meeting in Yü-lin was between equals. Ch'i-min and his qatun called on Emperor Yang, and then Yang called on Ch'i-min, and his the empress on the qatun. The rest is sino-centric window-dressing. The independence of Ch'i-min is also proved by the fact that envoys from Koguryŏ were in his entourage (*Sui shu* 84:15a; *Pei shih* 99:15b).

Ch'i-min died in 609 and was succeeded by his son, the Shih-pi Qaghan. Emperor Yang suspended the court for three days and recognized Shih-pi (*Sui shu* 84:14a-14b; *Wen-hsien t'ung-k'ao* 343:7a). According to custom, Shih-pi married the Princess of Yi-ch'eng, widowed qatun of his father.[6] (*Sui shu* 84:14a-14b; *Wen-hsien t'ung-k'ao* 343:7a).

On Feb.4, 615, the New Year's Day, Emperor Yang gave a great banquet for foreign envoys, including *Turks (*Sui shu* 4:9b). Later that year, Shih-pi and the princess were received in the Eastern Capital (Lo-yang) (*Sui shu* 84:14b).

But relations between Shih-pi and the Sui deteriorated because of Chinese meddling, and in the 8th month (Aug./Sep.) of 615 he invaded China and surrounded Emperor Yang in northern Shan-hsi. The emperor was barely saved from capture. Thereafter missions of the Eastern Turks no longer arrived. In 616, Shih-pi again raided Shan-hsi. During the troubles at the end of Sui, many Chinese found refuge among the Eastern Turks, and the state became strong and prosperous (*Sui shu* 84:14b; *Tzu-chih t'ung-chien* p.5792; *Wen-hsien t'ung-k'ao* 343:7a).

In the civil war at the end of Sui and during early T'ang, various pretenders such as Wang Shih-ch'ung, Liu Wu-chou, Liang Shih-tu, Li Kuei, and Kao K'ai-tao sought help from Shih-pi and declared themselves his subjects in exchange for titles and aid (*Sui shu* 84:14b). Among these, Li Yüan, the future Emperor Kao-tsu and founder of the T'ang dynasty, was the most successful. In 617, he sent an envoy to Shih-pi with a request for help. Shih-pi responded with 1000 horses and 2000 horsemen. Before and after Kao-tsu had ascended the throne on June 18, 618, "the gifts [to Shih-pi] were too many to

[6] He did not, of course, "memorialize" and ask Emperor Yang's permission, as claimed by *Sui shu* 84:14b and *Pei shih* 99:16a.

be recorded". That means, of course, that Shi-pi's support had to be bought. At the same time, the Eastern Turks who came to Ch'ang-an were oberbearing in their manners (*Chiu T'ang shu* 194A:1a; *Tzu-chih t'ung-chien* p.5792; *Wen-hsien t'ung-k'ao* 343:7a).

On June 25, 618, an envoy from Shih-pi to the T'ang court offered gifts. He was given a banquet in the Hall of the Grand Ultimate (*Chiu T'ang shi* 194A:1b; *Ts'e-fu yüan-kuei* p.5023; *Tzu-chih t'ung-chien* p.5792; *Wen-hsien t'ung-k'ao* 343:7a).

In the 9th month of 618, Kao-tsu sent a nephew and the Grand Master of Ceremonies to present singing girls to Shih-pi (*Tzu-chih t'ung-chien* p.5814).

On Oct.14, 618, an envoy from Shih-pi was received at the T'ang court. On Oct.30, the envoy was given a banquet and, as a special honour, summoned to the presence of the emperor (*Ts'e-fu yüan-kuei* p.5023; *Tzu-chih t'ung-chien* p.5814, 5816).

In the 2nd month (Feb./Mar.) of 619, Shih-pi raided the Ning-hsia Oasis, but in the 4th month (May/June), his envoys to the court offered gifts. He died about this time (*Chiu T'ang shu* 194A:1b; *Ts'e-fu yüan-kuei* p.5023; *Tzu-chih t'ung-chien* p.58547; *Wen-hsien t'ung-k'ao* 343:7a).

At the time of Shih-pi's death, a Chinese general was conveying silk to the Turks. Just before entering their territory, he learned about the death and halted. The Turks were enraged and became threatening. But the local Chinese Area Commander-in-chief was quickwitted enough to send on the silk and to call it now a contribution toward the funeral expenses (*Tzu-chih t'ung-chien* pp.5847-5848). Whether the silk originally had been sent as a Chinese tribute to the Eastern Turks or as payment for goods received, the Turks clearly regarded it as their property.

Since Shih-pi's son Shih-po-pi was considered too young, the Turks enthroned a younger brother of the late ruler. This was the Ch'u-lo Qaghan.[7] On July 28, 619, his envoys announced Shih-pi's death to the T'ang court. Kao-tsu proclaimed official mourning and suspended the court for three days. The officials were ordered to go to the guest lodge and condole with the Turkish envoys. A Member of the Suite of the Clerk of the Capital was sent to Ch'u-lo to condole and present 30,000 items as a contribution toward the funeral expenses. Ch'u-lo

[7] He is not to be confused with the Ch'u-lo Qaghan (d.619) of the Western Turks.

in turn married the Princess of Yi-ch'eng (*Chiu T'ang shu* 194A:1b; *T'ung-tien* 197:39b; *Tzu-chih t'ung-chien* p.5847, 5858; *Wen-hsien t'ung-k'ao* 343:7a).

In the 2nd month (Mar./Apr.) of 620, Ch'u-lo took the hostile step of setting up Yang Cheng-tao as king of Sui, with his residence in what now is Sui-yüan. Cheng-tao was a grandson of Emperor Yang of Sui. All the Chinese under Ch'u-lo's rule were assigned to him, and he appointed officials in accordance with the Sui official system (*Sui shu* 59:7b; *Tzu-chih t'ung-chien* p.5878). Ch'u-lo obviously intended to keep his options open by supporting rivals to the new T'ang house. He was surely also influenced by his wife, the Sui Princess of Yi-ch'eng, who could have had no love for the T'ang.

In the 6th month (July/Aug.) of 620, Ch'u-lo still played both sides by sending a younger brother with 2000 horsemen to support the T'ang (*Tzu-chih t'ung-chien* p.5884; *Wen-hsien t'ung-k'ao* 343:7a). But in the same month, he also entered Ping commandery in central Shan-hsi uninvited. He remained for three days, during which time the Turks looted and kidnapped many women without restraint. Emperor Kao-tsu sent the Grand Master of Ceremonies, Cheng Yüan-shou, to warn Ch'u-lo, which had no result (*Tzu-chih t'ung-chien* p.5912; *Wen-hsien t'ung-k'ao* 343:7a).

Ch'u-lo died suddenly, on the verge of a war with China. At that time, Cheng Yüan-shou was still among the Turks, who suspected him of having poisoned their qaghan. He was therefore detained and not allowed to return to Ch'ang-an (*Tzu-chih t'ung-chien* p.5912).

On Dec.25, 620, Turkish envoys announced Ch'u-lo's death to the T'ang court. Kao-tsu suspended the court for three days and ordered the officials to go to the guest lodge and condole with the Turkish envoys.The Princess of Yi-ch'eng was involved in arranging the succession. Because Ch'u-lo's son was deformed, he was dismissed, and Ch'u-lo's younger brother was enthroned. This was the Hsieh-li Qaghan (Illig), the third son of Ch'i-min. He in turn married the Princess of Yi-ch'eng and thereby became her fourth Turkish husband. Kao-tsu sent the Superintendent of the Imperial Household to present Hsieh-li with gold and silk (*Chiu T'ang shu* 194A:2a; *T'ung-tien* 197:39b; *Tzu-chih t'ung-chien* pp.5896, 5907; *Wen-hsien t'ung-k'ao* 343:7a).

Relations between the Hsieh-li qaghan and T'ang did not start well, and then became worse. In the 1st month (Jan./Feb.) of 621, envoys from Hsieh-li to the T'ang court offered gifts (*Ts'e-fu yüan-kuei* p.5023), but in the 3rd month (Mar./Apr.) the Turks raided Shan-hsi (*Tzu-chih-t'ung-chien* p.5907).

In the 4th month (Apr./May) of 621, Emperor Kao-tsu sent Li Kuei, a member of the imperial house, to present Hsieh-li with gold and silk. But this envoy was tactless and refused to salute the qaghan. He was detained by Hsieh-li, as well as the General-in-chief of the Resolute Guards of the Left, Chang-sun Shun-te. Kao-tsu retaliated by detaining Hsieh-li's envoys (*Tzu-chih t'ung-chien* p.5912).

During the same 4th month, Hsieh-li personally led an unsuccessful raid into Sui-yüan and Shan-hsi. He then proposed peace and presented several tens of catties of fish glue (*Chiu T'ang shu* 194A:2a; *Wen-hsien t'ung-k'ao* 343:7a).

In the 11th month (Dec./Jan., 622) of the Chinese year 621, Hsieh-li, cooperating with a Chinese pretender, raided border areas (*Tzu-chih t'ung-chien* p.5941).

In the 3rd month (Apr./May) of 622, Kao-tsu sent envoys with a conciliatory message. Hsieh-li thereupon released Cheng Yüan-shou, Li Kuei and Chang-sun Shun-te. He followed this up by a mission which was received at the T'ang court on May 4 and proposed better relations. Kao-tsu now set free the Turkish envoys whom he had detained. This did not prevent Hsieh-li, in cooperation with a Chinese pretender and a Chinse collaborator, from raiding Shan-hsi for more than a month (*Ts'e-fu yüan-kuei* p.5023; *Tzu-chih t'ung-chien* p.5948; *Wen-hsien t'ung-k'ao* 343:7a).

In the 8th month (Sep./Oct.) of 622, Kao-tsu sent Cheng Yüan-shou on another mission to Hsieh-li. According to his report, he told the qaghan that the customs of the Chinese and Turks were not the same. Even if the Turks took T'ang territory, they could not live in it. When they looted, the profit went to the people and the state. What did the qaghan gain from it? But if the armies were demobilized and good relations were established, the qaghan could sit and receive gold and silk and all went into his own treasury. In other words, Cheng Yüan-shou proposed the regular payment of Chinese tribute to the Turks (*Tzu-chih t'ung-chien* p.5955).[8]

In the 10th month (Oct./Nov.) of 623, Hsieh-li, again allied with a Chinese pretender, laid siege to Ma-yi in northern Shan-hsi. He also sent envoys to the T'ang court, proposing a marriage. Kao-tsu

---

[8] According to the same entry, Cheng Yüan-shou went as an envoy to the Turks on five occasions and several times risked his life.

responded that he was willing to discuss it if the Turks and their allies raised the siege of Ma-yi. Ssu-ma Kuang blames the Princess of Yi-ch'eng for Hsieh-li's refusal and the subsequent fall of the town. On Nov.22, 623, the Turks offered to evacuate Ma-yi in exchange for peace (*Tzu-chih t'ung-chien* pp.5973-5974).

In early 624, Hsieh-li again raided border territories, but in the 6th month (June/July) his envoys to the T'ang court offered gifts (*Ts'e-fu yüan-kuei* p.5023; *Tzu-chih t'ung-chien* pp.5974, 5983).

Subsequently, Hsieh-li with a large Turkish army forced his way deep into China and on Sept. 29,[9] 624, reached a point just west of Ch'ang-an. His second in command was the Shih-po-pi, son of the Shih pi Qaghan, who had not been allowed to succeed his father's in 619 because of his youth. Instead, he had been given the lesser title of T'u-li Qaghan.[10] He cannot but have resented that he had been deprived of his inheritance, and there were tensions between him and Hsieh-li. The Chinese knew about these and exploited them. Bypassing Hsieh-li, Li Shih-min, the middle son of Kao-tsu, sent an envoy to T'u-li to open negotiations He did not lecture T'u-li about "profit and harm", as claimed by the Chinese sources, but unquestionably offered peace with Chinese concessions. At this point Hsieh-li and T'u-li disagreed, the former wishing to continue the war and the latter willing to strike a bargain. Hsieh-li was persuaded to send T'u-li and A-shih-na Ssu-mo as envoys to Li Shih-min.[11] His conditions for peace were a marriage alliance and payments of gold and silk. A covenant was concluded between the Turks and Chinese, wherafter Hsieh-li withdrew. On Oct.17, Kao-tsu sent the Supervisor of the Left as envoy to the Turks (*Chiu T'ang shu* 194A:2b; *Tzu-chih t'ung-chien* pp.5992-5993; *Wen-hsien t'ung-k'ao* 343:7b).

The Chinese had temporarily extricated themselves from a dangerous situation, but at a cost. War broke out again before the end of October, 624 (*Tzu-chih t'ung-chien* p.5993).

In the 1st month (Jan./Feb.) of 625, envoys from Hsieh-li to

---

[9] Correcting *yi-mao* to *chi-mao*.

[10] He is not to be confused with the earlier T'u-li Qaghan who later was called the Ch'i-min Qaghan and died in 609. While still a teenager, the Sui had given Shih-po-pi the Princess of Huai-nan in marriage (*Chiu T'ang shu* 194A:5b; *T'ung-tien* 197:40b; *Wen-hsien t'ung-k'ao* 343:8a).

[11] I leave the question open as to how central Li Shih-min was to the events here discussed. A-shih-na Ssu-mo was a first paternal cousin of Hsieh-li's father, A-shih-na being the ruling clan of the Turks.

the T'ang court offered gifts. They also requested joint markets, to which the Chinese agreed (*Ts'e-fu yüan-kuei* p.5023; *Tzu-chih t'ung-chien* p.5994).

In the 7th month (Aug./Sep.) of 625, the Turks raided border areas. On Oct.2, Hsieh-li's envoys proposed peace. In the 9th month (Oct./Nov.) of the same year and in the 1st month (Feb./Mar.) of 626, they attacked again (*Chiu T'ang shu* 194A:2b; *Ts'e-fu yüan-kuei* p.5023; *Tzu-chih t'ung-chien* pp.5994, 5996, 5997, 5998, 5999; *Wen-hsien t'ung-k'ao* 343:7b).

In the late summer of 626, Hsieh-li and T'u-li invaded China once more. On Aug.27, Hsieh-li made a peace overture, but it was not at an opportune moment. Ch'ang-an was then in a period of transition. Li Shih-min had killed his two brothers on July 2 and was laying the ground for the abdication of his father, Kao-tsu. On Sep.3, Shih-min ascended the throne and in history is known as Emperor T'ai-tsung. Hsieh-li had meanwhile advanced further. On Sep.23, he once more reached the environs of Ch'ang-an and halted on the northern shore of the Wei River. It does not seem to have been his intention to make an assault on the city but rather to extract more tribute. For that purpose, he sent on that day (Sep.23) an envoy to intimidate the T'ang court. In the ensuing discussion, it was pointed out to the Turkish envoy that the qaghan had violated the covenant by which the T'ang already had paid uncountable amounts of gold and silk. Over the protests of Chinese officials against this breach of protocol, T'ai-tsung then placed the envoy under arrest in the Chancellery (*Chiu T'ang shu* 194A:2b; *Ts'e-fu yüan-kuei* p.5023; *Tzu-chih t'ung-chien* pp.6017, 6019; *Wen-hsien t'ung-k'ao* 343:7b).

On Sept.23 or 24, 626, T'ai-tsung with a suite of six men rode to the Wei River. There, on the southern shore, he negotiated with Hsieh-li on the northern shore by shouting across the river. T'ai-tsung supposedly blamed Hsieh-li for having violated the covenant, whereupon the Turks descended from their horses and saluted. On Sep.25, T'ai-tsung met Hsieh-li at the bridge across the Wei, a white horse was slaughtered, and a new covenant was concluded. Thereafter the Turks withdrew (*Tzu-chih t'ung-chien* pp.6019-6020; *Wen-hsien t'ung-k'ao* 343:7b). This account has to be summarily dismissed. Hsieh-li would not have accepted a moral lecture from Shih-min, and he would not have withdrawn empty-handed. What he wanted and surely got was more of the imperial treasury. The Chinese were meanwhile stalling for time. Ch'ang-an was poorly defended, and the emperor did not know Hsieh-li's ultimate plans. A Chinese army was approaching, and when this arrived, soon after T'ai-tsung's negotiations with Hsieh-li, the Chinese had become less vulnerable. It must be assumed, nevertheless, that the Turks got what they wanted and that the Chinese were the losers.

Having achieved his purpose, Hsieh-li was now eager to improve relations. In the 9th month (Sep./Oct.), he presented 3000 horses and 10,000 sheep. These were rejected by T'ai-tsung, who requested the return of the Chinese who had been kidnapped or detained by the Turks (*Chiu T'ang shu* 194A:4a; *T'ung-tien* 197:40a; *Ts'e-fu yüan-kuei* p.5023; *Tzu-chih t'ung-chien* p.6021; *Wen-hsien t'ung-k'ao* 343:7b).

In the 11th month (Nov./Dec.) of 626, envoys from Hsieh-li again offered gifts (*Chiu T'ang shu* 2:8a; *Ts'e-fu yüan-kuei* p.5023).

The winter of 627 to 628 was hard for the Turks. There was much snow, horses, cattle, and sheep died, the people suffered from famine, and there was disaffection among the tribes. T'ai-tsung was advised by some officials that he should take advantage of this opportunity and attack the Turks, but he refused (*Chiu T'ang shu* 194A:4b; *Tzu-chih t'ung-chien* p.6046; *Wen-hsien t'ung-k'ao* 343:7b).

In the spring of 628, T'u-li, who had been arrested briefly by Hsieh-li for not making a stand against the rebellious tribes, opened negotiations with the Chinese. Hsieh-li responded by attacking him. On May 19, envoys from T'u-li requested help from the T'ang court, but T'ai-tsung did not to act. T'u-li fled to China[12] (*Tzu-chih t'ung-chien* pp.6049-6050).

At this time, the Khitan chief Mo-hui offered the T'ang an alliance against the Eastern Turks. Hsieh-li requested through envoys that T'ai-tsung reject this, in exchange for which he would withdraw his backing of Liang Shih-tu.[13] T'ai-tsung refused the bargain (*Tzu-chih t'ung-chien* p.6050).

---

[12] On Apr.28, 630, T'ai-tsung appointed him General-in-chief of the Guards of the Right, enfeoffed him as king of Pei-p'ing commandery, and subsequently made him a Military Governor. He died in 631, aged 29. T'ai-tsung ordered state mourning for him and had a stele set up in his memory (*Chiu T'ang shu* 194A:6a; *T'ung-tien* 197:40b; *Tzu-chih t'ung-chien* p.6073; *Wen-hsien t'ung-k'ao* 343:8a). A younger brother of T'u-li was appointed General of the Gentlemen-of-the-Household. In 639, he attempted to escape back to the Turkish territory but was pursued and killed in the 4th month (May/June) (*T'ang hui-yao* 94:4b-5a).

[13] Liang Shih-tu was a Chinese holdout against the T'ang dynasty in the Ning-hsia Oasis. He was there besieged by Chinese forces and soon killed by a relative (*Tzu-chih t'ung-chien* p.6050).

In the 9th month (October) of 628, Turks raided Chinese border territory, but in the 11th month (Secember), Hsieh-li's envoys offered several 10,000 heads of horses and cattle (*Ts'e-fu yüan-kuei* p.5023; *Tzu-chih t'ung-chien* p.6057).

T'ai-tsung was now planning an attack on Hsieh-li and allied himself for that purpose with the Hsüeh-yen-t'o. This was a Turkish T'ieh-le tribe in northern Zungharia. Some Eastern Turkish tribes offered their support against Hsieh-li (*Chiu T'ang shu* 194A:4b; *Tzu-chih t'ung-chien* p.6061; *Wen-hsien t'ung-k'ao* 343:7b).

In the 8th month (Aug.Sep.) of 629, Hsieh-li requested through envoys a marriage with a Chinese princess. In the 11th month (Nov./ Dec.), he again invaded Chinese borderlands but suffered a crushing defeat on Mar.27, 630. He fled with a much reduced force (*Chiu T'ang shu* 194A:5a; *T'ung-tien* 197:40b; *Tzu-chih t'ung-chien* pp.6066, 6072; *Wen-hsien t'ung-k'ao* 343:8a).

In early 630, Hsieh-li proposed to personally call on the emperor and recognize his overlordship. T'ai-tsung sent the Superintendent of the Imperial Household, T'ang Chien, and others as his envoys to Hsieh-li. He also ordered the general Li Ching to meet and welcome Hsieh-li. The arrival of T'ang Chien reassured Hsieh-li. But Li Ching, whether acting on his own or by orders of T'ai-tsung, suddenly attacked him on Mar.27. T'ang Chien was barely able to save himself by escaping to the Chinese army. Li Ching killed many Turks and captured a great many. Among them were the Princess of Yi-ch'eng, her son Tieh-lo-shih, the Empress Dowager Hsiao, widow of Emperor Yang of Sui, who had found a refuge among the Eastern Turks, and Hsieh-li's protegé Yang Cheng-tao. The Sui empress and Yang Cheng-tao, were escorted to Ch'ang-an and treated well, Cheng-tao being made a a Supernumerary Cavalier Gentleman-in-Attendance. Many chiefs surrendered. Hsieh-li fled but was captured (*Sui shu* 59:9b; 67:3b; *Chiu T'ang shu* 194A:5a; *T'ung-tien* 197:40b; *Tzu-chih t'ung-chien* pp.6072, 6073; *Wen-hsien t'ung-k'ao* 343:8a).

On Apr.6, 630, T'ai-tsung issued an amnesty to celebrate the victory over the Eastern Turks (*Tzu-chih t'ung-chien* p.6073).

At this time, Hsieh-li was brought to Ch'ang-an. T'ai-tsung treated him leniently and reunited him with his family (*Chiu T'ang shu* 194A: 5a; *T'ung-tien* 197:40b; *Tzu-chih t'ung-chien* p.6074; *Wen-hsien t'ung-k'ao* 343:8a).

On May 20, 630, T'ai-tsung received Hsieh-li in audience and inflicted a gratuitous moral lecture on him. He then supplied him with lodgings in the ministry of the Grand Coachman and ample provisions of food (*Tzu-chih t'ung-chien* pp.6074-6075).

The *Tzu-chih t'ung-chien* (p.6073) claims that "all the barbarians" begged T'ai-tsung to adopt the title of Heavenly Qaghan and that he replied:"I am the Son of Heaven of the Great T'ang. Why should I lower myself to conduct the affairs of a qaghan?" Nevertheless, he did then allow the northwestern rulers and chiefs to call him Heavenly Qaghan. It is quite inconceivable that the defeated but proud Eastern Turks made such a proposal. T'ai-tsung, no doubt, wished to adopt the title and arranged to have it offered to him by sycophants.

In the 10th month (Nov./Dec.) of 632, T'ai-tsung appointed Hsieh-li Inspector of Kuo. This commandery, situated directly east of Ch'ang-an, had many deer, which gave an opportunity for hunting. Hsieh-li declined and was appointed General-in-chief of the Guards of the Left (*Tzu-chih t'ung-chien* p.6099).

In the 12th month (Jan./Feb., 634) of the Chinese year 633, T'ai-tsung gave a feast in Ch'ang-an in the old Eternal Palace (Wei-yang kung) of Han times, during which he requested Hsieh-li to dance (*Tzu-chih t'ung-chien* pp.6103-6104).

On Feb.13, 634, Hsieh-li died. T'ai-tsung ordered that he be buried according to the fashion of the Turks. He was therefore cremated. T'ai-tsung bestowed on him the posthumous title of King Who Has Attached Himself to Righteousness (*Chiu T'ang shu* 194A:5b; *T'ung-tien* 197:40b; *Tzu-chih t'ung-chien* p.6105; *Wen-hsien t'ung-k'ao* 343:8a).

In 639, A-shih-na Ssu-mo became the Yi-mi-ni-shu-ssu-li-pi Qaghan or Ssu-li-pi for short. He was conferred the imperial surname of Li by T'ai-tsung, and presented with drums and banners. This is the same Ssu-mo who was a first paternal cousin of Hsieh-li's father and who together with T'u-li had been a Turkish negotiator in 624. On Sep.22 of that year, Emperor Kao-tsu had given him the title of king of Ho-shun commandery. He had remained loyal to Hsieh-li and had been captured with him. On Apr.20, 630, Tai-tsung had appointed him General-in-chief of the Martial Guards of the Right. Subsequently he had made him a Military Governor and changed his title to king of Huai-hua commandery (*Chiu T'ang shu* 194A:7b; *T'ang hui-yao* 94:5a;[14] *Tzu-chih t'ung-chien* pp.5993, 6073; *Wen-hsien t'ung-k'ao* 343:8b).

[14] Note that the dates of *T'ang hui-yao* 94 are often at variance with the other sources.

Ssu-li-pi did not control much more than the area of present Sui-yüan. On Feb.28, 641, he requested that, when the Turks were raided by the Hsüeh-yen-t'o, he could seek refuge inside the border fortifications. This was approved (*Tzu-chih t'ung-chien* p.6165). In 643, T'ai-tsung agreed to that Ssu-li-pi and his followers could move to the Ning-hsia Oasis and northwestern Shensi (*Wen-hsien t'ung-k'ao* 343:8b-9a). This followed logically from T'ai-tsung's decision to settle large numbers of Eastern Turks in northern Chinese frontier areas.

In 645, Ssu-li-pi participated with Turkish horsemen in T'ai-tsung's attack on Koguryŏ. He was wounded by an arrow and died in 646 in Ch'ang-an. T'ai-tsung conferred on him the posthumous title of Master of Writing of the Ministry of Arms and Military Governor and ordered that a stele be set up in his memory (*Wen-hsien t'ung-k'ao* 343:9a).

The Eastern Turkish tribes north of the Gobi had not recognized Ssu-li-pi and had not submitted to China. After the defeat of Hsieh-li, they elected an A-shih-na clansman as qaghan. This man called himself the Yi-chu-chü-pi Qaghan or Chü-pi for short. He was not strong enough to withstand the Hsüeh-yen-t'o and had to accept a tributary status. Since he had a great following, the Hsüeh-yen-t'o wished to kill him. He succeeded in evading them. A son of his went as envoy to the T'ang court and was received in audience by T'ai-tsung in the 11th month (December) of 647.[15] Chü-pi offered to call on the emperor in person, whereupon T'ai-tsung sent a general to escort him. But Chü-pi never arrived, to the anger of the emperor. Ssu-ma Kuang records bitterly that Chü-pi was good at making promises but never had any intention to come (*Chiu T'ang shu* 194A:9a; *Ts'e-fu yüan-kuei* p.5024; *Tzu-chih t'ung-chien* p.6250; *Wen-hsien t'ung-k'ao* 343:9a).

In the 10th month (Oct./Nov.) of 648, Chü-pi's son-in-law Chü-lo-po arrived as his envoy at to the T'ang court. He was detained there (*Tzu-chih t'ung-chien* p.6262). In 649, the Chinese attacked Chü-pi, while the Uighurs and other tribes turned against him; he fled, was captured in 650, and brought to Ch'ang-an. Emperor Kao-tsung, who had ascended the throne on July 10, 649, scolded him but then appointed him General of the Martial Guards of the Left (*Chiu T'ang shu* 194A:9a; *T'ung-tien* 198:41b-42a; *Tzu-chih t'ung-chien* pp.6265-6266, 6271; *Wen-hsien t'ung-k'ao* 343:9a).

---

[15] Another son had at an unspecified time been sent to the T'ang court and had been appointed General of the Garrison Guards of the Left (*Chiu T'ang shu* 194A:9a; *Wen-hsien t'ung-k'ao* 343:9a).

For more than three decades thereafter, the Eastern Turks were a negligible force. In 682, there was an attempt to set up A-shih-na Fu-nien, a son of a first paternal cousin of Hsieh-li, as qaghan in the Ning-hsia Oasis. But Chinese forces captured him, he was brought to Ch'ang-an, and there decapitated on the Eastern Market (*Wen-hsien t'ung-k'ao* 343:9a).

Nevertheless, the humiliation of the Eastern Turks was almost over, and from the end of 682 their empire was restored by the qaghan Ku-to-lu[16] (Qutlugh), a distant relative of Hsieh-li (*Chiu T'ang shu* 194A: 9a; *Wen-hsien t'ung-k'ao* 343:9a).

In 683, Ku-to-lu began to raid Chinese border areas and defeated a Chinese army. In 686, he looted again and defeated another Chinese army. This was followed by raids in 687 and 688 (*Chiu T'ang shu* 194A: 10a; *Wen-hsien t'ung-k'ao* 343:9a).

No missions from Ku-to-lu to the T'ang court are recorded. He died in the early 690's.[17] Since his son was still young, his younger brother Mo-ch'o (Qapaghan) was enthroned as qaghan (*Chiu T'ang shu* 194A: 10b; *Tzu-chih t'ung-chien* p.6493; *Wen-hsien t'ung-k'ao* 343:9b).

In 693, Mo-ch'o sent envoys to the T'ang court (*Chiu T'ang shu* 194A:10b).

In 694, Mo-ch'o raided Chinese border areas, but thereafter envoys of his proposed peace.[18] The Empress Wu was pleased, appointed him General-in-chief of the Guards of the Left, entitled him Duke Who Has Attached Himself to the State, and presented him with 5000 items of objects (*Chiu T'ang shu* 194A:10b; *Tzu-chih t'ung-chien* p.6503; *Wen-hsien t'ung-k'ao* 343:9b).

In 695,[19] envoys from Mo-ch'o proposed peace. The Empress Wu sent envoys to entitle Mo-ch'o as Qaghan Who Has Reformed and Does Good (*Tzu-chih t'ung-chien* p.6510; *Wen-hsien t'ung-k'ao* 343:9b).

When the great Khitan war broke out in the summer of 695 and the Chinese armies had been crushed in the Peking area, Mo-ch'o offered

---

16 *Tzu-chih t'ung-chien* renders his name as Ku-tu-lu. This was the Elteriš Qaghan of the Orkhon inscriptions.

17 According to *Chiu T'ang shu* and *Wen-hsien t'ung-k'ao*, he died during the *t'ien-shou* period (690-692). *Tzu-chih t'ung-chien* p.6493 records that his death became known at the T'ang court in the 1st month (Feb./Mar.) of 694. *T'ang hui-yao* 94:7b also gives that date.

18 According to *T'ang hui-yao* 94:7b and *Tzu-chih t'ung-chien* p.6503, the envoys were received in the 10th month (Nov./Dec.) of 695 and "begged to surrender".

19 By *Tzu-chih t'ung-chien* dated 9th month (October) of 696.

help through envoys who were received at the T'ang court on Nov.22, 696. He did not "beg" to attack the Khitan, and a decree did not "allow" it, but he aided the Chinese in a desparate situation in order to gain benefits of his own. Of the two Khitan leaders, Li Chin-chung had died and Sun Wan-jung continued the fight. Mo-ch'o invaded their territory, captured their wives and children, and withdrew, no doubt, with considerable loot. The Empress Wu expressed her thanks by sending envoys to appoint Mo-ch'o as Specially Advanced, Hsieh-tieh-li-shih Great Shan-yü, and Qaghan Who Has Established Merit and Recompensed the State (*Chiu T'ang shu* 194A10b, 11a; *Tung-tien* 198:42b; *Tzu-chih t'ung-chien* p.6510; *Wen-hsien t'ung-k'ao* 343:9b)

In the 1st month (Jan./Feb.) of 697, Mo-ch'o raided Chinese border areas (*Tzu-chih t'ung-chien* p.6512).

In 698, Mo-ch'o offered peace, proposed to be like a son to the Empress Wu, and offered a daughter in marriage to an imperial prince. He simultaneously returned kidnapped Chinese (*Chiu T'ang shu* 194A:11a; *T'ung-tien* 198:42b; *Tzu-chih t'ung-chien* p.6509; *Wen-hsien t'ung-k'ao* 343:9b).[20]

Mo-ch'o furthermore made himself the spokesman for the Turks who had been settled in northern China by T'ai-tsung and demanded on their behalf agricultural implements and seeds. This could lead to a claim that these Turks were Mo-ch'o's subjects and set a dangerous precedent. The Empress Wu initially rejected the request. But she was afraid that she might be attacked and in the end agreed to all demands. She accepted the peace offer, provided 40,000 bushels of seed and 3000 agricultural implements, and selected a menber of her own family, her grandnephew and king of Huai-yang, Wu Yen-hsiu, as husband of Mo-ch'o's daughter. The General-in-chief of the Guards of the Leopard Bow-cases and Acting Master of the Ministry of Rights, Yen Chih-wei, and the General of the Gentlemen of the Guards of the Left and Acting Master of Guests,[21] T'ien Kuei-tao, were ordered to escort Wu Yen-hsiu to Mo-ch'o's court, appoint Mo-ch'o General-in-chief of the Guards of the Left, and present him with gold and silk (*Chiu T'ang shu* 194A:11a; *T'ung-tien* 198:42b; *Tzu-chih t'ung-chien* p.6515; *Wen-hsien t'ung-k'ao* 343:9b).[22]

---

[20] *Tzu-chih t'ung-chien* dates the reception of Mo-ch'o's envoys 9th month (October) 696.

[21] A variant of Herald.

[22] *Tzu-chih t'ung-chien* dates the departure of this mission 3rd month (Mar./Apr.)

While this mission was travelling to the court of Mo-ch'o, it met a Turkish envoy moving in the opposite direction. Yen Chih-wei gave him a purple robe and a silver belt and then memorialized the Empress Wu that when caitiffs went as envoys to the Chinese capital they should be properly equipped. T'ien Kuei-tao, who was on bad terms with Yen Chih-wei, memorialized on his part that now that Chih-wei had given the envoy a robe and a belt, he had preempted the gifts which would have been bestowed on him by the imperial court. The envoys of lesser caitiffs were not worthy to be fully equipped. The Empress Dowager approved of Kuei-tao's attitude (*Tzu-chih t'ung-chien* p.6515).

On Sep.10, 698, the Chinese mission reached Mo-ch'o's court. The qaghan informed Yen Chih-wei that his daughter had been offered in marriage to a son of the Son of Heaven of the Li house, whereas the envoys had arrived with a son of the Wu house. What use did he have for a son of the Wu house? How was he a son of the Son of Heaven? A daughter of his ought to marry a son of the Son of Heaven. The Wu was a lesser clan. He would now raise troops attack China, and enthrone one of the two surviving sons of Kao-tsung (*Tzu-chih t'ung-chien* p.6515). Mo-ch'o then arrested Yen Chih-wei and T'ien Kuei-tao and intended to execute them. A high Turkish official advised the qaghan that envoys from a great state should not be killed. Mo-ch'o spared their lives but detained them, as well as Wu Yen-hsiu. Another Chinese arrested at this time was the Investigating Secretary P'ei Huai-ku. He had rejected a possition among the Turks which Mo-ch'o had offered to him and was about to be executed, when he managed to escape and return to Ch'ang-an. There he was received by the Empress Wu and made his report (*Tzu-chih t'ung-chien* pp.6530, 6531).

When Mo-ch'o conducted a raid into the northern part of the Great Plain, the Empress Wu changed his name from Mo-ch'o to Chan-ch'o (Decapitated Ch'o) (*T'ung-tien* 198:42b; *Wen-hsien t'ung-k'ao* 343:9b).

Yen Chih-wei and T'ien Kuei-tao were released before the end of the year and confronted each other in an audience before the Empress Wu. Kuei-tao accused his colleague of having licked the boots of Mo-ch'o whereas he himself had neither bowed to nor saluted the qaghan.

---

of 697. According to the same source (p.6510), Yen Chih-wei and T'ien Kuei-tao had previously also been the envoys who in 695 had invested Mo-ch'o as Qaghan Who Has Reformed and Makes Good, and it claims that Mo-ch'o at that occasion was made General-in-chief of the Guards of the Left. This section of the *Tzu-chih t'ung-chien*, however, is poorly edited, with many contradictory dates, so that I am inclined to think it in error.

He insisted that Mo-ch'o had broken the covenant, that peace and a marriage alliance with the Turks would be impossible, and that preparations should be made for war. Chih-wei argued for peace and a marriage (*Tzu-chih t'ung-chien* p.6516). In other words, Kuei-tao was the worst type of a stiff, sino-centric, and tactless diplomat, while Chih-wei was polite and realistic. However, the Empress Wu once more sided with T'ien Kuei-tao and in the 10th month (Nov./Dec.) of 698 had Yen Chih-wei executed (*Tzu-chih t'ung-chien* p.6537).

In 700, Mo-ch'o sent an envoy and proposed that his daughter be married to a son of the heir-apparent (i.e. of Chung-tsung) (*Chiu T'ang shu* 194A:12a; *T'ung-tien* 198:42b; *Tzu-chih t'ung-chien* p.6563; *Wen-hsien t'ung-k'ao* 343:10a).[23] Later that year, Mo-ch'o sent a high official to present 1000 horses and regional objects to express his pleasure with the intended marriage. The Empress Wu gave him a banquet in which the heir-apparent, the kings, and the court officials from rank 3 and up participated. He left the court with rich presents. Subsequently, Mo-ch'o released Wu Yen-hsiu (*Chiu T'ang shu* 194A:12a; *T'ung-tien* 198:42b; *Ts'e-fu yüan-kuei* p.5026; *Tzu-chih t'ung-chien* pp.6568, 6569; *Wen-hsien t'ung-k'ao* 343:10a).[24]

After Chung-tsung had ascended the throne on Feb.23, 705, Mo-ch'o invaded the Ning-hsia Oasis and defeated a Chinese army. Chung-tsung ordered the proposed marriage to be cancelled. In early 707, Mo-ch'o again raided the Ning-hsia oasis (*Chiu T'ang shu* 194A:12a; *T'ung-tien* 198:42b; *Tzu-chih t'ung-chien* p.6607; *Wen-hsien t'ung-k'ao* 343:10a).

On Jan.30, 711, Mo-ch'o's envoys proposed peace and a marriage alliance. Emperor Jui-tsung agreed (*Chiu T'ang shu* 7:13a; 194A:13a-13b; *Tzu-chih t'ung-chien* p.6661). According to *T'ang hui-yao* 94:8b, the emperor then sent an envoy of his own. Mo-ch'o supposedly "saluted twice" and called himself a "subject". This account is due to another fraudulent report by a self-serving envoy.

In the 3rd month (Mar./Apr.) of 711, Jui-tsung enfeoffed a lady of the imperial house as Princess of Chin-shan to be the bride of Mo-ch'o. A son of the latter was received at the T'ang court and appointed Supernumerary General-in-chief of the Resolute Guards of the Right

[23] *T'ung-tien* dates the arrival of this mission 703, *Tzu-chih t'ung-chien* 6th month (July/Aug.) of 703, and *Ts'e-fu yüan-kuei* 11th month (December) of 704.

[24] *T'ung-tien* dates the arrival of this mission 703 and *Tzu-chih t'ung-chien* the 11th month (Dec./Jan., 704) of the Chinese year 703.

(*Chiu T'ang shu* 194A:13b; *Tzu-chih t'ung-chien* p.6664).

In the 8th (Sep./Oct.) and 9th month (Oct./Nov.) of 711, Turkish envoys were received at the T'ang court (*Ts'e-fu yüan-kuei* p.5026).

On Mar.7, 712, the emperor gave a banquet for a Turkish envoy and introduced the Princess of Chin-shan to him. But Jui-tsung abdicated on Aug.21, 712, and the marriage never took place (*Chiu T'ang-shu* 194A:13b; *Tzu-chih t'ung-chien* p.6671).

In the 1st (February) and 2nd month (March) of 713, Turkish envoys offered gifts (*Tzu-chih t'ung-chien* p.5027).

In the summer of 713, a son of Mo-ch'o was received at the T'ang court and again requested a marriage. Emperor Hsüan-tsung enfeoffed a lady of the imperial clan as Princess of Nan-ho, but that marriage also failed to be concluded (*Tzu-chih t'ung-chien* p.6686).

In the 2nd month (Feb./Mar.) of 714, Hsüan-tsung received a Turkish envoy in audience (*Tzu-chih t'ung-chien* p.5027).

In the same 2nd month of 714, Mo-ch'o sent a son and a brother-in-law to attack the Chinese garrison in Pei-t'ing (Besbalïq) near Urumchi in Zungharia. They were defeated and the son was killed. The brother-in-law feared to return and deserted to the Chinese. He was appointed General-in-chief of the Guards of the Left, enfeoffed as king of Yen-pei commandery, and given a residence, ten slaves, ten horses, and 1000 items of objects. His wife was made the Princess of Chin-shan (*Chiu T'ang shu* 194A:13b; *T'ung-tien* 198:43a; *Tzu-chih t'ung-chien* p.6696).

On June 11, 714, envoys from Mo-ch'o once more requested a marriage. He assumed at this time the title of Sheng-t'ien-ku-to-lu Qaghan (*Tzu-chih t'ung-chien* p.6699).

On Nov.26, 714, envoys from Mo-ch'o requested a marriage for the last time. Hsüan-tsung agreed and set 715 as the date for the occasion (*Tzu-chih t'ung-chien* p.6706), but other events superceded.

In 716, Mo-ch'o attacked the Uighurs and fell in battle. The victors sent his head to the Chinese capital (*Chiu T'ang shu* 8:7b; *T'ung-tien* 198:43a; *Tzu-chih t'ung-chien* p.6719; *Wen-hsien t'ung-k'ao* 343:10a).

Mo-ch'o had in 699 enfeoffed his heir as Junior Qaghan. On his father's death, he became qaghan but was immediately overthrown and killed with all his brothers by his first paternal cousin Ch'üeh-t'e-le (Kul-tegin). This was a son of Ku-to-lu. He enthroned his elder brother as the P'i-chia Qaghan (Bilgä) (*Chiu T'ang shu* 194A:14a; *T'ung-tien* 198:43a; *Tzu-chih t'ung-chien* p.6719; *Wen-hsien t'ung-k'ao* 343:10a).

In the 7th month (Aug./Sep.) of 717, Turkish envoys presented horses (*Ts'e-fu yüan-kuei* p.5027).

On Feb.10, 718, envoys from P'i-chia to the T'ang court proposed peace and a marriage alliance, but Hsüan-tsung was slow to respond. When Turkish envoys repeated the offer on Mar.11, 721, the emperor replied in a letter that in the past China had bought horses from the Turks and paid with silk. This trade had ceased because of the untrustworthyness and belligerence of Mo-ch'o. Should the qaghan be sincere, the Turks and Chinese could have good fortune together. Otherwise he did not wish envoys to come and go. It depended on the Turks (*Tzu-chih t'ung-chien* pp.6731, 6744; *Wen-hsien t'ung-k'ao* 343:10a).

In the 7th month (July/Aug.) of 724, Turkish envoys again requested a marriage (*Tzu-chih t'ung-chien* p.6760).

In the 12th (Dec./Jan., 725) and intercalary 12th month (Jan./Feb., 725) of the Chinese year 724, Turkish envoys were received at the T'ang court (*Ts'e-fu yüan-kuei* p.5028).

In 725, Hsüan-tsung sent the Acting Herald, Yüan Chen, to discuss peace with the Turks. P'i-chia gave him a banquet. According to Yüan Chen's report, the qaghan complained that while the Tibetans and Khitan had been given Chinese princesses in marriage, the Turks had not. Yüan Chen answered:"Since the qaghan and the emperor are like a son and a father, how could there be a marriage?"[25] Chia-p'i observed that barbarians had been bestowed the imperial surname of Li and yet been able to marry princesses. With this in mind, why should it be impossible for him? Moreover, none of the princesses had been the daughter of an emperor. He, Yüan Chen, had then promised to use his influence for the qaghan (*Chiu T'ang shu* 194A:15b; *T'ung-tien* 198:43a; *Wen-hsien t'ung-k'ao* 343:10a).

P'i-chia responded with an mission, led by a high official, to offer presents. Hsüan-tsung gave a banquet and rich gifts. The envoys departed in the 12th month (Jan./Feb., 726) of the Chinese year 725 (*Chiu T'ang shu* 194A:15b; *T'ung-tien* 198:44a; *Tzu-chih t'ung-chien* p.6768; *Wen-hsien t'ung-k'ao* 343:10b-11a). Although no formal peace treaty was drawn up and no Chinese princess was granted, relations between the Chinese and Turks improved.

In the 1st month (Feb./Mar.) of 726, a high-ranking Turkish envoy was received at the T'ang court (*Ts'e-fu yüan-kuei* p.5028).

---

[25] I.e. such a marriage would be incest.

In the 2nd month (Mar./Apr.) of 726, a mission of more than 300 Turks offered congratulations (*Ts'e-fu yüan-kuei* p.5028).

In the 5th month (June/July) of 726, another high-ranking Turkish envoy was received at the T'ang court (*Ts'e-fu yüan-kuei* p.5028).

In the 11th month (Nov./Dec.) of 726, Turkish envoys presented 30 fine horses (*Chiu T'ang shu* 8:14b; 194A:16b; *Ts'e-fu yüan-kuei* p.5028).[26]

On Oct.6, 727, a high official of P'i-chia offered gifts to the T'ang court. He also acquainted Hsüan-tsung with a letter from the Tibetans to the qaghan, in which they offered an alliance against the Chinese. The emperor was impressed and agreed to a joint market with the Turks in the Ning-hsia Oasis. Hencefort, the Chinese annually bought war-horses there for several 100,000 bolts of silk (*Tzu-chih t'ung-chien* p.6779; *Wen-hsien t'ung-k'ao* 343:11a).

In the 2nd (Feb./Mar.) and 4th month (Apr./May) of 730, Turkish envoys offered regional objects (*Ts'e-fu yüan-kuei* p.5028).[27]

In the 10th month (Nov./Dec.) of 731, a Turkish mission of 24 men, led by a high official, was received at the T'ang court (*Ts'e-fu yüan-kuei* p.5028).

In the 3rd month (April) of 732, it became known at the T'ang court that the younger brother of P'i-chia, the great general Ch'üeh-t'e-le (Kul-tegin), had died. Hsüan-tsung sent the General of the Gilded Mace and a Gentleman-of-the-Palace of [the Bureau of] Criminal Administration to condole and sacrifice and to present a letter stamped with the imperial seal. The Chinese also set up a stele in memory of Ch'üeh-t'e-le for which the emperor personally had written the inscription, and they built a temple for him with depictions of his battles on the four stone walls (*Chiu T'ang shu* 194A:16b; *Tzu-chih t'ung-chien* p.6795).

On Aug.24, 732, a Turkish mission led by a noble was received at the T'ang court (*Ts'e-fu yüan-kuei* p.5028).

In the 3rd month (Mar./Apr.) of 733, a Turkish mission of 16 men was received at the T'ang court. In the 4th month (May/June) of the same year, a high Turkish official arrived, and in the 9th month (Oct./Nov.) a mission of 13 men led by still another high Turkish official was received (*Ts'e-fu yüan-kuei* pp.5028, 5029).

---

26 By *Chiu T'ang shu* 194A:16b dated 727.

27 One of these missions was involved in a contretemps with the Turgesh. See the section on the latter below.

In the 4th month (May/June) of 734, a high Turkish official arrived at the T'ang court (*Ts'e-fu yüan-kuei* p.5029).

In the 1st month (Jan./Feb.) of 735, a Turkish envoy was received at the T'ang court (*Ts'e-fu yüan-kuei* p.5029).

On Jan.21, 735, envoys announced the death of P'i-chia to the T'ang court. He had been poisoned by a minister but was able to execute the culprit, his family, and his supporters before he died. P'i-chia was succeeded by his son the Yi-jan Qaghan. Hsüan-tsung sent the Director of the Imperial Clan to condole and sacrifice and to recognize Yi-jan. A stele and a temple were set up in memory of P'i-chia, and a Member of the Suite for the Diaries of Activity and Repose in the Office of History was ordered to write the inscription for the stele (*Chiu T'ang shu* 194A:16b; *Tzu-chih t'ung-chien* p.6809; *Wen-hsien t'ung-k'ao* 343:11a).

In the 1st month (Jan./Feb.) of 735, a Turkish envoy was received at the T'ang court (*Ts'e-fu yüan-kuei* p.5029).

In the 2nd month (Mar./Apr.) of 737, Turkish envoys congratulated and offered regional objects (*Ts'e-fu yüan-kuei* p.5029).

Yi-jan's death year is not recorded. However, his younger brother, the Teng-li Qaghan (Tengri), was recognized by the T'ang in 740. Yi-jan must therefore have died in 739 or 740. Hsüan-tsung sent the General of the Gilded Mace to recognize Teng-li and to present a letter stamped with the imperial seal (*Chiu T'ang shu* 194A:16b, 17a).

In the 3rd month (Mar./Apr.) of 741, envoys from Teng-li offered regional objects. Soon thereafter, Teng-li was killed by a relative. Turkish envoys announced his death to the T'ang court on Sep.2, 741. The assassin enthroned a son of the P'i-chia Qaghan. The latter was killed in turn by the sub-chief (yabghu) Ku-to, who enthroned his younger brother. Ku-to then killed this brother and enthroned himself (*Chiu T'ang shu* 9:4a; *Ts'e-fu yüan-kuei* p.5029; *Tzu-chih t'ung-chien* p.6844; *Wen-hsien t'ung-k'ao* 343:11a).

In 742, Ku-to was defeated by an alliance of Basmil, Uighurs, and Qarluks, whereupon there ensued chaos. Members of the ruling house with their followers submitted to China, including a grandson of Mo-ch'o, a concubine of Yi-jan, and daughters of P'i-chia and Teng-li. On Oct.12, 742, Hsüan-tsung gave them a banquet (*Chiu T'ang shu* 194A:17a; *Tzu-chih t'ung-chien* pp.6838, 6855; *Wen-hsien t'ung-k'ao* 343:11a).

In 745, the last nominal ruler of the Eastern Turks, the Po-mei Qaghan, was killed by the Uighurs, who sent his head to Ch'ang-an, the Dowager Qatun of P'i-chia surrendered to the Chinese, and

Emperor Hsüan-tsung wrote a poem to commemorate the fall of the Eastern Turkish empire (*Chiu T'ang shu* 194A:17a; *Tzu-chih t'ung-chien* p.6863; *Wen-hsien t'ung-k'ao* 343:11a).

THE WESTERN TURKS

The qaghanate of the Western Turks came into existance in the early 580's, when the Turkish empire split into an eastern and western part. The western comprised at its height what now is Zungharia and East and West Turkestan. The founder Ta-t'ou (Tardu), the Pu-chia Qaghan, ruled with the aide of his grandson, the Ni-li Qaghan. When the latter died in about 588, he was succeeded by his son, the Ni-chüeh-ch'u-lo Qaghan or Ch'u-lo for short.[28] Ch'u-lo's mother was Chinese, the Lady Hsiang, who after Ni-li's death married his younger brother P'o-shih. Toward the end of the century, she and her second husband visited Ch'ang-an. They remained there, possibly under duress (*Sui shu* 84:15a). With the disappearance of the Pu-chia Qaghan in 603, Ch'u-lo became temporarily the sole ruler of the Western Turkish empire.

On Mar.27, 591, *Turkish envoys to the Sui court presented seven precious bowls (*Sui shu* 2:7a).

In 592, *Turkish envoys to the Sui court offered gifts (*Pei shih* 11: 21b).

Early in his reign (605-618), Emperor Yang of Sui sent the Internuncio Ts'ui Chün-su as envoy to Ch'u-lo. Chün-su's account of the meeting is as self-serving, fraudulent, and preposterous as so many others. He claims that Ch'u-lo squatted when he received the "edict" and was not willing to rise. Having been corrected by the Chinese envoy he "was terrified, rose, wept, saluted twice, knelt, and accepted the edict" (*Sui shu* 84:16a).

In 610, Yang sent an envoy to Ch'u-lo and "summoned" him to meet him in the northwest. Ch'u-lo refused, which angered the emperor (*Sui shu* 84:16b; *T'ung-tien* 199:44a; *Wen-hsien t'ung-k'ao* 344:11b).

Soon thereafter, an opportunity opened up for the Chinese to sow discord among the Western Turks. Envoys from Ch'u-lo's paternal uncle She-kuei requested a marriage with a Chinese princess. At P'ei

[28] He is not to be confused with the Eastern Turkish Ch'u-lo Qaghan (d.620).

Chü's advice, Emperor Yang responded that if She-kuei killed Ch'u-lo, he would recognize him as Great Qaghan and a marriage would be arranged. She-kuei thereupon attacked and defeated Ch'u-lo. The latter fled to Turfan. Emperor Yang now sent P'ei Chü together with Ch'u-lo's mother, the Lady Hsiang, to the Jade Gate Pass (Yü-men kuan) in westernmost Kan-su. From there she persuaded her son through an envoy to surrender to China (*Sui shu* 84:16b-17a; *Pei shih* 99:18a-18b; *Wen-hsien t'ung-k'ao* 344:11b). Since Ch'u-lo had no hope of regaining his throne without Chinese help and was in danger of his life as long as he stayed in Central Asia, this was a real surrender.

In the winter of 611, with two younger brothers[29] and Turkish horsemen, Ch'u-lo arrived in Ch'ang-an and lodged in the Ministry of the Herald. When he was received by Emperor Yang, he knelt, kowtowed, and referred to himself as a subject. At the New Year's Reception on Feb.7, 612, Ch'u-lo wished Emperor Yang long life, stating that "from Heaven down and from Earth up, there is only one sagious man" (*Sui shu* 84:17a-17b). It is difficult to see how this account could be falsified, since it is based on the notes of the court diarists. Emperor Yang obviously intended to use Ch'u-lo as a rival to She-kuei, just he had done in the reverse before. But is also possible that Ch'u-lo had the same thought in mind, wishing to use Emperor Yang for his own restitution, and therefore was not adverse to blatant flattery .

Ch'u-lo partcipated in the campaign against Koguryŏ in 612 and was by Emperor Yang conferred the title of Ho-sa-na Qaghan[30] and richly rewarded. In 614, the Princess of Hsin-yi was married to him, and he was presented with 1000 brocade robes and 10,000 bolts of textiles (*Sui shu* 84:17b-18a; *Pei shih* 99:19a; *Chiu T'ang shu* 194B:1a; *Wen-hsien t'ung-k'ao* 344:11b).

On Dec.24, 618, Ch'u-lo was by Emperor Kao-tsu of T'ang enfeoffed

---

[29] One of these was A-shih-na Ta-nai, who like his elder brother participated in the campaign against Koguryŏ in 612 and was appointed Imperial Household Grandee of the Golden Seal and Purple Ribbon. He resided with his Turkish followers in northern Shan-hsi. From 617, he supported the future Emperor Kao-tsu of T'ang against other pretenders and was rewarded with three Palace Ladies, 5000 items of objects, and 10,000 items of variegated textiles. He was also given the Chinese family name of Shih. In 629, he was appointed General-in-chief of the Martial Guards of the Right and Governor, and was enfeoffed as a duke. He died in 638 and was bestowed the posthumous title of General-in-chief Who Supports the State (*Chiu T'ang shu* 195B:1b; *T'ung-tien* 199:44b; *Wen-hsien t'ung-k'ao* 344:11b).

[30] *Tzu-chih t'ung-chien* gives the name throughout as Ho-sha-na.

as king of Kuei-yi commandery. In the 4th month (May/June) of 619, he offered big pearls to Kao-tsu which the emperor rejected with the remark that pearls are useless (*T'ung-tien* 199:44b; *Ts'e-fu yüan-kuei* p.5023; *Tzu-chih t'ung-chien* p.5829; *Wen-hsien t'ung-k'ao* 344:11b).

In the 8th month (Sep./Oct.) of 619, envoys of Eastern Turks requested that Ch'u-lo be killed. The court officials took the view that the state should not be risked for the life of one man. To avoid future trouble, Ch'u-lo should be killed. Li Shih-min, the future Emperor T'ai-tsung, argued that it was not right to kill a man who had attached himself to China. But Kao-tsu, then as always, was unable to stand up to the Eastern Turks. He summoned Ch'u-lo to the palace and drank wine with him. Ch'u-lo was then taken to the Secretariat of the Palace Writers, where he was handed over to the Eastern Turkish envoys and murdered. After T'ai-tsung had ascended the throne of Sep.3, 626, he had Ch'u-lo reburied according to proper ritual (*Sui shu* 84:18a; *Chiu T'ang shu* 194B:1b; *T'ang hui-yao* 94:9b; *T'ung-tien* 199: 44b; *Tzu-chih t'ung-chien* p.5865; *Wen-hsien t'ung-k'ao* 344:11b).

From 611, with Ch'u-lo out of the way, She-kuei was the unchallenged qaghan of the Western Turks. He died in 618 and was succeeded by a younger brother, the T'ung-yeh-hu Qaghan (Ton-yabghu Qaghan) (*T'ung-tien* 199:44b; *Wen-hsien t'ung-k'ao* 344:11b).

On July 28,[31] 619, envoys from T'ung-yeh-hu to the T'ang court offered gifts (*Chiu T'ang shu* 1:6a; *Ts'e-fu yüan-kuei* p.5023; *Tzu-chih t'ung-chien* p.5859).

In the 1st month (Feb./Mar.) of 620, envoys from T'ung-yeh-hu presented ostrich eggs.[32] In the 3rd month (Apr./May), his envoys again offered gifts. In the 4th month (May/June), his envoys requested a marriage. Kao-tsu agreed because he wished to form an alliance with the Western Turks against the Eastern Turks (*Chiu T'ang shu* 1: 6a; 194B:2a; *Ts'e-fu yüan-kuei* p.5023; *Tzu-chih t'ung-chien* p.5995; *Wen-hsien t'ung-k'ao* 344:11b).

In the 3rd month (Mar./Apr.) of 621, envoys from T'ung-ych-hu offered gifts. In the 4th month (May/June) of 622, they presented a lion skin, in the 8th month (Sep./Oct.) of that year fine horses, in the 4th month (May/June) of 623 gifts, in the 3rd month (April) of 626

[31] Correcting *yi-yu* to *chi-yu*.

[32] *Chiu T'ang shu* 1:6a says ostriches.

gifts, and in the 6th month (June/July) of the same year once more gifts (*Ts'e-fu yüan-kuei* p.5023).

In the 12th month (Dec./Jan., 624) of the Chinese year 623, *Turkish envoys offered gifts (*Ts'e-fu yüan-kuei* p.5023).

In 625, Emperor Kao-tsu had sent a representative to T'ung-yeh-hu, presumably to negotiate the details of the coming marriage. In the 1st month (Jan./Feb.) of 627, this man returned to the court together with Turkish envoys who presented genuine pearls, 10,000 nails, a precious belt of fine gold, and 5000 horses as bridal presents for the princess. They stated that the Hsieh-li Qaghan of the Eastern Turks was attacking the Western Turks and blocking the roads in order to prevent the marriage (*Chiu T'ang shu* 194B:2b; *T'ung-tien* 199:44a; *Ts'e-fu yüan-kuei* p.5023; *Tzu-chih t'ung-chien* p.6046; *Wen-hsien t'ung-k'ao* 344:11b).

In the 10th month (Nov./Dec.) of 627 and in the 4th month (May/June) of 628, the Western Turks offered regional objects (*Ts'e-fu yüan-kuei* p.5023).

In the 12th month (January 629) of the Chinese year 628, T'ung-yeh-hu was killed by a paternal uncle, who enthroned himself as the Mo-ho-to-hou-ch'ü-li-ssu-pi Qaghan or Mo-ho-to for short. He did not win general acceptance among the Western Turks, and the tribes in West Turkestan enthroned a son of T'ung-yeh-hu as a rival qaghan. This was the Yi-p'i-po-lo-ssu-yeh-hu Qaghan or Ssu-yeh-hu for short (*Chiu T'ang shu* 194B:2b; *Tzu-chih t'ung-chien* pp.6061, 6084; *Wen-hsien t'ung-k'ao* 344:11b-12a).

In 629, both qaghans sent envoys to the T'ang court, each requesting a marriage. T'ai-tsung rejected this for the time being, since the outcome of the civil war between the Western Turks was as yet unknown. He also advised both sides to avoid armed conflict, which was an empty demand (*Chiu T'ang shu* 194B:2b; *Tzu-chih t'ung-chien* p.6061; *Wen-hsien t'ung-k'ao* 344:12a).

In 630, Mo-ho-to was defeated by Ssu-yeh-hu. He fled to the Altai Mountains and was killed. Ssu-yeh-hu was recognized by the Western Turks as Great Qaghan (*Tzu-chih t'ung-chien* p.6084; *Wen-hsien t'ung-k'ao* 344:12a).

In the 4th month (May/June) of 631, T'ai-tsung sent envoys to ransom for gold and silk Chinese who had been lost among the *Turks since Sui times (*Tzu-chih t'ung-chien* p.6087).

In 632, Ssu-yeh-hu attacked the Hsüeh-yen-t'o. He was defeated by them, fled to Samarkand, and subsequently died. His successor, the Hsi-li-pi-to-lu Qaghan, sent envoys to the T'ang court. On May 4, 633,[33] Emperor T'ai-tsung sent the Junior Herald to recognize him and to present him with drums, banners, and 10,000 items of textiles (*Chiu T'ang shu* 194B:3a, 5b-6a; *T'ung-tien* 199:45a; *Tzu-chih t'ung-chien* p.6097; *Wen-hsien t'ung-k'ao* 344:12a)

In the 10th month (Nov./Dec.) of 633, envoys of Hsi-li-pi-to-lu offered gifts (*Ts'e-fu yüan-kuei* p.5024).

Hsi-li-pi-to-lu died in 634. The empire of the Western Turks was that year divided between two rival qaghans. The western federation controlled West Turkestan, the eastern chiefly Zungharia, the two being divided by Issyk-Kul and the Ili River (*Tzu-chih t'ung-chien* pp.6110, 6118, 6142; *Wen-hsien t'ung-k'ao* 344:12a). Both contested the Tarim Basin, as did also the Chinese and Tibetans.

In the following, the sources do not usually distinguish which of the federations sent missions to the T'ang court. In 1st month (Jan./Feb.) of 635, one of the qaghans presented 500 horses and requested a marriage. T'ai-tsung responded with a letter stamped with the imperial seal but did not approve (*Chiu T'ang shu* 194B:3a; *T'ung-tien* 199:45a; *Ts'e-fu yüan-kuei* p.5024; *Wen-hsien t'ung-k'ao* 322:12a).

In the 8th (Sep./Oct.) and 12th month (Jan./Feb., 636) of the Chinese year 635 and in the 8th month (Sep./Oct.) of 636, Western Turkish envoys offered gifts (*Ts'e-fu yüan-kuei* p.5024).

In the 8th month (Sep./Oct.) of 638, envoys from one of the qaghans offered regional objects. In the10th month (Nov./Dec.), Western Turkish envoys offered regional objects. In 639, one of the qaghans offered gifts, and T'ai-tsung responded with a letter stamped with the imperial seal (*Chiu T'ang shu* 3:6b; 194B:4a; *Ts'e-fu yüan-kuei* p.5024; *Wen-hsien t'ung-k'ao* 344:12a).

On Aug.26, 641, T'ai-tsung sent the General of the Left Who Commands the Army to recognize one of the qaghans and to present him with drums and banners. Envoys of his rival arrived at the T'ang court (*Chiu T'ang shu* 194B:4a; *T'ung-tien* 199:45b; *Tzu-chih t'ung-chien* pp.6168, 6169; *Wen-hsien t'ung-k'ao* 344:12a).

In the 9th month (October) of 642, at the request of Western Turkish envoys, Emperor T'ai-tsung threw his support to and recognized

[33] *Tzu-chih t'ung-chien* gives the date of 632, 3rd month, *ting-yu*. *Chiu T'ang shu* 194B:5b only gives the year 632. *T'ung-tien* and *Wen-hsien t'ung-k'ao* have 633. Since the 3rd month of 632 did not have the cyclical characters of *ting-yu*, 633, 3rd month, *ting-yu* = May 4 is correct.

still another claimant, the Yi-p'i-she-kuei Qaghan. The latter showed his appreciation by releasing T'ang envoys who previously had been detained (*Chiu T'ang shu* 194B:4b; *T'ung-tien* 199:45b; *Tzu-chih t'ung-chien* p.6179; *Wen-hsien t'ung-k'ao* 344:12b).

In 646,[34] envoys from Yi-p'i-she-kuei offered regional objects and requested a marriage. T'ai-tsung agreed on the condition that the qaghan relinquished all claims on Kucha, Kashgar, Khotan, Chu-chü-po and Ts'ung-ling[35] (*Tzu-chih t'ung-chien* p.6236; *Wen-hsien t'ung-k'ao* 344:12b). With that, the negotiations fell through.

In the 2nd month (Mar./Apr.) of 649, the Western Turks presented regional objects (*Ts'e-fu yüan-kuei* p.5025).

In 651, the Western Turkish empire was reunited by A-shih-na Ho-lu, who assumed the title of Sha-po-lo Qaghan. Evading Yi-p'i-she-kuei, he had in 648 withdrawn to China, was received at the court, given a banquet, appointed General of the Resolute Guards of the Left, given a Military Area command, and promoted to General-in-chief of the Resolute Guards of the Left. As of 651, he had become a threat to China and in the 11th month (Dec./Jan., 652) of that Chinese year took the offensive. (*Chiu T'ang shu* 194B:4b; *T'ung-tien* 199:45b; *Tzu-chih t'ung-chien* p.6257, 6274; *Wen-hsien t'ung-k'ao* 344:12b).

But Sha-po-lo was not without opposition among the Western Turks, and in 655 a rival requested military help from the T'ang. On Dec.11 of that year, Emperor Kao-tsung attempted to invest him as qaghan, but Sha-po-lo blocked the Chinese envoy and forced him to return (*Tzu-chih t'ung-chien* pp.6295-6296).

In 657, a Chinese army with Turkish and Uigur allies defeated Sha-po-lo, and the Western Turkish empire ceased to exist. Sha-po-lo fled to Tashkent but was handed over to the Chinese and brought to Ch'ang-an. Kao-tsung spared his life, and he died in the T'ang capital in 659 (*Wen-hsien t'ung-k'ao* 344:12b).

Emperor Kao-tsung set up two Chinese protectorates in an attempt to control the Western Turks, but these lasted for less than one decade.

Relations between China and the Eastern Turks on the one hand and the Western Turks on the other were very different. The Eastern Turks, except for the years 650-682, were powerful northern neigh-

---

[34] By *T'ang hui-yao* 94:10b dated 645.

[35] Ts'ung-ling was situated northwest of Chu-chü-po.

bours, and in the early period China found itself politically subservient and militarily on the defensive. It treated the qaghans with respect. In 597 and 599, two Chinese princesses were consecutively given in marriage to the same qaghan. In 609, 619, and 620, court was suspended for three days at the death of qaghans. At the last two occasions, officials were ordered to condole with the Turkish envoys at their guest lodge. In 619, and 735, Chinese envoys went to the Turkish court to condole at the death of qaghans. In 732, they condoled at the death of Ch'üeh-t'e-le (Kul-tegin). In 732 and 735, Chinese workmen set up memorial steles and built temples. The stele inscription of 732 was written by Emperor Hsüan-tsung himself. Three qaghans were recognized by the Sui and T'ang.

When Emperor Yang met with the Ch'i-min Qaghan in 607, it was a carefully orchestrated encounter of equals. When the Shih-pi Qaghan and his Chinese princess visited Lo-yang in 615, he did not come as a supplicant or feudatory. This is proved by the fact that later that year he almost captured Emperor Yang in northern Shan-hsi. When the Hsieh-li Qaghan in 630 proposed to call on Emperor T'ai-tsung in Ch'ang-an and recognize his overlordship, he was in dire straits. Nothing came of his proposal, and it might have been a ploy, seeking to gain time. The Hsieh-li and Chü-pi Qaghans did not surrender with their states in 630 and 650 respectively but were taken prisoners. It cannot even be said that T'ai-tsung pacified the Eastern Turks and that these were dominated by the T'ang from 650 to 682. The Hsieh-li Qaghan was captured less by Chinese efforts than because such subordinate tribes as the Hsüeh-yen-t'o and Uighurs had rebelled, that there had been a harsh winter, and that Hsieh-li and T'u-li had fallen out with each other. The northern tribes kept their independence but did not have the strength or unity to raid China. This is what gave China more than three decades of peace at its northern border. After the resurgence of the Eastern Turks from 682, the Mo-ch'o Qaghan in 698 and 700 offered a daughter to marry a son of the T'ang heir-apparent (Chung-tsung), which would have made him the father-in-law of the next emperor, and he did not hesitate to insult the Empress Wu when he rejected her grandnephew as a son-in-law. Looking at it in reverse, Emperor Kao-tsu of T'ang can with some justification be called a vassal of the Shih-pi Qaghan. He allowed the murder of the refugee Ch'u-lo Qaghan of the Western Turks when presssured by the Eastern Turks. When the Empress Wu gave a banquet for an envoy of Mo-ch'o, such prominent guests participated as the heir-apparent, kings, and court officials from rank 3 and up.

This combined evidence is not commensurate with an overlord-vassal relationship in which the Eastern Turkish qaghans were subservient to China. The only qaghan who with any justification can be called a vassal was Ssu-li-pi.

Not much is said in the sources about the kind of gifts exchanged, i.e. government trade, and this may have played a subordinate role. There was little need for the Eastern Turks to present horses, since these could be sold in ordinary commercial transactions at border markets. Many missions may therefore have been concerned with political matters important to both sides, as for instance the Chinese seeking peace and the Turks seeking princesses. However, when relations improved from 726 and fewer contentious matters needed to be discussed, the number of Turkish missions increased. This would indicate an emphasis on the exchange of goods.

Relations between China and the Western Turks were much less intense, numerically, politically, and militarily. The interest of the Western Turks lay in the far west, where they dealt with Persia and even Byzantium, and they were no threat to Chinese borderlands. Conflicts only arose when the Pu-chia Qaghan tried to unite all the Turks from 600 and after China from 640 expanded into the Tarim Basin. No Western Turkish qaghan was a Chinese vasal. When Ch'u-lo surrendered in 611, he was isolated and only acted for himself. He was given a Chinese princess in marriage in 614. Only one qaghan was recognized by the T'ang. No Chinese state mourning was held for any Western Turkish qaghan.[36]

Since the Western Turks had little of substance to discuss with the Chinese other than the usual request for a princess, and since they did not have official joint markets with the Chinese, a chief purpose of their missions must have been trade.

According to *Sui shu* 84:12a, the Ch'i-min Qaghan of the Eastern Turks annually offered gifts. Three missions are recorded for 607. According to *Chiu T'ang shu* 194A:1b, the Ch'u-lo Qaghan of the Eastern Turks incessantly sent envoys from 619. No missions are recorded. According to *Tzu-chih t'ung-chien* p.6168, the Sha-po-lo Qaghan of

[36] The T'ang did not confer posthumous titles on deceased reigning qaghans of either the Eastern or Western Turks.

the Western Turks frequently sent envoys from 641. No missions are recorded. The statistics are therefore not complete.

This is the distribution by 20-year periods of the 77 recorded missions from the Eastern Turks 589-745 and the 32 missions from the Western Turks 589-657:

	Eastern Turks	Western Turks
587-606:	7	2
607-626:	19	13
627-646:	5	15
647-666:	2	2
667-686:	0	
687-706:	7	
707-726:	22	
727-746:	15	

The Eastern Turks came most often at their times of strength, the Western also when they were weak (634-651). The missions arrived during all months of the year, with no preference for any special season.

The products brought by the Eastern Turks were:

591: one jade staff from Kucha.
592: 10,000 horses,
20,000 sheep,
500 camels,
500 cattle.
607: 3000 horses.
617: 1000 horses.
621: fish glue.
626: 3000 horses,
10,000 sheep.
628: several 10,000 heads of horses and cattle.
700: 1000 horses.
704: 1000 fine horses.
717: horses.

The products brought by the Western Turks were:

591: *seven precious bowls.

618: big pearls (rejected).[37]
620: ostrich eggs (or ostriches).
622: one lion skin.
fine horses.
627: genuine pearls,
10,000 nails,
one precious belt of fine gold,
5000 horses.
635: fine horses.

It can be seen that the Eastern Turks traded almost exclusively in livestock, while the Western Turks had access to goods brought on the Silk Routes.

The Chinese paid with gold, silk, brocade robes, chariots, horses, banners, fifes, drums, objects of precious metal, Palace Ladies, and singing girls.

THE SHA-T'O

The Sha-t'o were a Western Turkish tribe, whose original grazing grounds were east of Zungharia. After the collapse of the two Turkish empires, they became dependents of the Uighurs and then the Tibetans but replaced the Uighurs later as a major power in Central Asia. Many of them settled in the Chinese northwest. One of their chiefs was conferred the T'ang imperial surname of Li, and his son Li K'o-yung founded the Later T'ang dynasty (923-936).

In 633, Emperor T'ai-tsung of T'ang recognized the Li-pi-to-lu Qaghan of the Sha-t'o and presented him with drums and banners (*Wen-hsien t'ung-k'ao* 347:30b).

THE BASMIL

The Basmil, Pa-hsi-mi in Chinese, lived to the northwest of the Eastern Turks and were their enemies.

---

[37] These were presented by the Ch'u-lo Qaghan after his surrender, which means that he had brought some of his treasury with him.

In 649, Basmil envoys were received at the T'ang court (*Wen-hsien t'ung-k'ao* 347:27b).

In 715, the Basmil together with the Qarluqs presented horses (*T'ang hui-yao* 100:10a).

After the defeat of the Eastern Turks by the Basmils and others in 742, Emperor Hsüan-tsung recognized the chief of the Basmil as Hsieh-tieh-yi-shih Qaghan (*Tzu-chih t'ung-chien* p.6854; *Wen-hsien t'ung-k'ao* 343:11a).

THE QARLUQS

The Qarluqs (Ko-lo-lu) had their grazing grounds north of Zungharia before they migrated west. In 742, they belonged to the alliance which defeated the Eastern Turks. In 751, they contributed to the Chinese defeat by the Arabs at the Talas River.

In 657, Emperor Kao-tsung of T'ang created three nominal Area Commands and made Qarluq chiefs their Military Governors (*T'ang-hui-yao* 100:10a).

In 715, the Qarluqs together with the Basmil presented horses. In the winter of the same year, the Qarluqs were again received at the T'ang court (*T'ang hui-yao* 100:10a).

In the 11th month (Dec./Jan., 753) of the Chinese year 752, Qarluq envoys were received at the T'ang court (*Wen-hsien t'ung-k'ao* 348: 32b).

In the 4th month (May/June) of 753, a Qarluq mission arrived at the T'ang court, consisting of 130 men (*Ts'e-fu yüan-kuei* p.5030).

In the 12th month (Dec./Jan., 754) of the Chinese year 753, Qarluqs offered regional objects (*Ts'e-fu yüan-kuei* p.5031). Thereafter, because of the enmity of the Uighurs to the Qarluqs, missions no longer reached China (*T'ang hui-yao* 100:10a).

THE TURGESH

The Turgesh (T'u-ch'i-shih) lived in the area between lake Balkash and Issyk-Kul.

On Sep.10, 699, a son of the Turgesh chief Wu-chih-le had an audience with the Empress Wu of T'ang. She sent an Attending Secretary in response (*Tzu-chih t'ung-chien* p.6540).

When Wu-chih-le died, he was succeeded by his son Sha-ko. On

Dec.18, 708, Emperor Chung-tsung conferred on him the title of king of Chin-ho commandery and presented him with four Palace Ladies (*Wen-hsien t'ung-k'ao* 344:13a). A rival presented 700 ounces of gold to the T'ang in an attempt to conspire against Sha-ko. Chung-tsung sent a Palace Assistant Secretary on a secret mission, but he was captured by the troops of Sha-ko and decapitated. After a brief clash with the Chinese, Sha-ko then sent an envoy to present horses. While this man was in Ch'ang-an, he learned about Chinese plans for an attack on Sha-ko, returned hurriedly, and reported it. This led to a further raid against the Chinese. Sha-ko then sent letters to the T'ang court, whereupon Chung-tsung recognized him as Qaghan of the Fourteen Tribes (*Tzu-chih t'ung-chien* pp.6625, 6627-6626, 6629; *Wen-hsien t'ung-k'ao* 344:13a).

In the 7th month (Aug./Sep.) of 709, envoys from Sha-ko offered peace. On Sep.4, Chung-tsung conferred on him the title of Qaghan Who Respects Civilization and the given name of Shou-chung (Observing Loyalty). In the 10th month (Nov./Dec.) of 709 and in the 9th month (Oct./Nov.) of 712, envoys from Sha-ko were again received at the T'ang court (*Ts'e-fu yüan-kuei* pp.5026, 5027; *Tzu-chih t'ung-chien* p.6636).

When Sha-ko was killed, Su-lu became his successor. In 714 or 715, he sent envoys to the T'ang court. In 715, Emperor Hsüan-tsung appointed Su-lu General-in-chief of the Guards of the Feathered Forest of the Left and enfeoffed him as Duke Who Is Obedient to the State (*Chiu T'ang shu* 194B:7b; *T'ung-tien* 199:46b; *Tzu-chih t'ung-chien* p.6733; *Wen-hsien t'ung-k'ao* 344:13b).[38]

In the 6th month (July/Aug.) of 717, the Turgesh presented camels and horses. Hsüan-tsung sent a letter in response (*Ts'e-fu yüan-kuei* p.5027).

In 718, Hsüan-tsung sent a letter stamped with the imperial seal to Su-lu and conferred on him the title of Qaghan Who Is Loyal and Obedient (*Chiu T'ang shu* 194B:7b; *T'ung-tien* 199:46b; *Tzu-chih t'ung-chien* p.6737; *Wen-hsien t'ung-k'ao* 344:13b).[39]

In spite of the exchange of missions, Su-lu had successfully attacked Chinese outposts in the Tarim Basin and east of Issyk-Kul. Hsüan-

[38] *Tzu-chih t'ung-chien* dates the appointment June 20, 718 and refers to Su-lu as Protector-general of the Turgesh.

[39] *Tzu-chih t'ung-chien* dates the appointment Dec.13, 719.

tsung countered by diplomacy. On Jan.14, 723, he enfeoffed a Turkish lady of the A-shih-na clan as Princess of Chin-ho[40] and gave her to Su-lu as a wife. This princess sent a Turgesh officer with 1000 horses to the joint market in Kucha, which since 649 was the headquarters of the Chinese An-hsi Protectorate. The Military Governor resented a message of the princess and undiplomatically detained her envoy. Su-lu retaliated by invading the Tarim Basin (*Chiu T'ang shu* 194B:7b; *T'ung-tien* 199:46b; *Tzu-chih t'ung-chien* p.6754; *Wen-hsien t'ung-k'ao* 344: 13b). But he also moved into West Turkestan where he contested the presence of the Arabs and defeated them in 724.

In the 1st month (Feb./Mar.) of 726, an envoy of Su-lu presented horses, and in the 12th month (Dec./Jan., 727) of the same Chinese years other envoys offered regional objects (*T'ung-tien* 199:46b; *Ts'e-fu yüan-kuei* p.5028; *Tzu-chih t'ung-chien* p.6776; *Wen-hsien t'ung-k'ao* 344: 13b).

In 730, envoys from Su-lu arrived in Ch'ang-an, and Emperor Hsüan-tsung invited them to a banquet. At this time, Eastern Turkish envoys were also at the court and had been asked to the same banquet. The Turgesh were to occupy the seats of honour, which caused a confrontation. The Eastern Turks insisted that the state of the Turgesh was small and that it originally had been a dependency of the [Western] Turks. Its envoys should not be placed above them. The Turgesh argued that, since the banquet had been arranged for them, they would not occupy a lower place. The Chinese court officials solved this problem of protocol by seating the Eastern Turks in the east and the Turgesh in the west (*Chiu T'ang shu* 194B:8a; *T'ung-tien* 199:46b; *Tzu-chih t'ung-chien* p.6792; *Wen-hsien t'ung-k'ao* 344:13b).

The formidable Su-lu was not only engaged with the Chinese and the Arabs but also negotiated with the Tibetans. In addition to his "Chinese" princess, he married a Tibetan and an Eastern Turkish lady, so that he had three qatuns (*T'ung-tien* 199:46b; *Wen-hsien t'ung-k'ao* 344:13b). But his long string of victories was coming to an end. In 731 he failed to take Samarkand, and in 737 he was decisively defeated by the Arabs. In 738, he was killed and replaced by his son T'u-huo-hsien. The latter and the Princess of Chin-ho were captured by the Military Governor of the An-hsi Protectorate and brought to Ch'ang-an. Emperor Hsüan-tsung gave T'u-huo-hsien a banquet and

[40] *Tzu-chih t'ung-chien* mistakenly writes Chiao-ho.

on Apr.28, 740, appointed him General-in-chief of the Gilded Mace of the Left. Thereafter, having failed to enthrone a Chinese puppet, Hsüan-tsung recognized Su-lu's killer Mo-ho-ta-kan as qaghan. On Dec.25, 740, Mo-ho-ta-kan made peace with China (*T'ung-tien* 199: 46b; *Tzu-chih t'ung-chien* pp.6841, 6843; *Wen-hsien t'ung-k'ao* 344:13b).

At about this time, the Yellow and Black Tribes of the Turgesh sent envoys to offer peace (*Wen-hsien t'ung-k'ao* 344:13b).

In the 9th month (Sep./Oct.) of 743, envoys of the Black tribe of the Turgesh offered regional objects (*Ts'e-fu yüan-kuei* p.5029).

On July 25, 747, Turgesh envoys were received at the T'ang court (*Ts'e-fu yüan-kuei* p.5030).

In the 7th month (Aug./Sep.) of 749, a certain Yi-po was recognized by Hsüan-tsung as qaghan of the Ten Tribes of the Turgesh. In the 8th month (Sep./Oct.), envoys of the Ten Tribes were received at the court. In the 11th month (Dec.), Turgesh envoys arrived to congratulate on the New Year's Day of 750 and to present regional objects (*Ts'e-fu yüan-kuei* p.5030; *Tzu-chih t'ung-chien* p.6897).

On Oct.7, 753, Hsüan-tsung recognized the qaghan of the Black Tribe as qaghan of all the Turgesh (*Tzu-chih t'ung-chien* p.6919).

In the 4th month (Apr./May) of 754, envoys of the Black Tribe of the Turgesh arrived at the T'ang court (*Ts'e-fu yüan-kuei* p.5031).

In the 8th month (Aug./Sep.) of 759, envoys from the Ten Tribes and the Black Tribe of the Turgesh were received at the T'ang court (*Ts'e-fu yüan-kuei* p.5030; *Wen-hsien t'ung-k'ao* 344:13b).

The qaghans of the Turgesh were independent rulers. When Emperor Chung-tsung in 708 recognized Sha-ko as qaghan of the Fourteen Tribes, he therefore did not "pardon his crimes" (*Tzu-chih t'ung-chien* p.6629). It was only after the final defeat of the Turgesh in 744, that they ceased to be a real problem for the T'ang.

According to *T'ung-tien* 199:46b and *Wen-hsien t'ung-k'ao* 344:13b, Su-lu annually sent envoys to offer presents to the T'ang court. Envoys are only recorded for 714/15, 717, twice for 726, for 730, and 736. This means that only the most important missions are recorded.

The Turgesh dealt in livestock. They had access to the joint market in Kucha but also traded in animals with the court: camels and horses in 717, and horses in 726.

The Chinese no doubt paid chiefly with silk, but in 708 they also presented four Palace Ladies.

THE LIU-KUEI

The Liu-kuei, Ku-li-kan, and Po-ma mentioned below may have been tribes in central Siberia. Nothing is known about their linguistic affiliation, and I list them among the Turkic tribes simply as a matter of convenience.

On Mar.31, 640, Li-kuei envoys were received at the T'ang court. This was the first contact between them and China. Emperor T'ai-tsung appointed the envoy as Chief Commandant of Cavalry (*T'ung-tien* 200: 49b; *Tzu-chih t'ung-chien* p.6153; *Wen-hsien t'ung-k'ao* 347:27b).

THE KU-LI-KAN

In the 8th month (Sep./Oct.) of 647, Ku-li-kan envoys presented 100 horses to the T'ang court. Emperor T'ai-tsung selected the ten best, called them the Ten Thorough-breds, and gave a name to each. The envoys were given rich presents. Out of the Ku-li-kan territory, T'ai-tsung created the imaginary Yüan-ch'üeh commandery (*Ts'e-fu yüan-kuei* p.5025; *Wen-hsien t'ung-k'ao* 348:31b).

In the 7th month (July/Aug.) of 694, Ku-li-kan envoys offered gifts (*Ts'e-fu yüan-kuei* p.5026).

THE PO-MA

In the 11th month (Dec./Jan., 653) of the Chinese year 652,[41] Po-ma envoys to the T'ang court offered gifts and congratulated (*Chiu T'ang shu* 4:4a; *Ts'e-fu yüan-kuei* p.5025; *Wen-hsien t'ung-k'ao* 348:33a).

THE HSÜEH-YEN-T'O

The T'ieh-le were divided into a number of tribes, among whom, until the rise of the Uighurs, the Hsüeh-yen-t'o were the most important. They had been a subject people of the Juan-juan against whom they rose in 546, only to become subjects of the Turks in 552. Their old grazing grounds stretched from northern Zungharia to the upper

[41] By *T'ang hui-yao* 100:14a dated 11th month (Dec./Jan., 652) of the Chinese year 651.

reaches of the Orkhon River. But although the Eastern Turks did their best to control the T'ieh-le, these frequently rose against them and had no difficulty in sending envoys to and in some cases forming military alliances with China. Although the sources use the term T'ieh-le for all the tribes collectively, it primarily refers to the Hsüeh-yen-t'o.

In 607, the T'ieh-le envoys to the Sui court offered peace and regional objects. Emperor Yang sent a Gentleman-in-Attendance at the Yellow Gates to conclude an alliance with them against the T'u-yü-hun (*Sui shu* 83:4b; 84:19a; *Wen-hsien t'ung-k'ao* 334:26a; 344:14a).

In 609, the T'ieh-le participated in the Chinese war against the T'u-yü-hun (*Sui shu* 3:13b; 83:4b-5a; *Tzu-chih t'ung-chien* p.5841).

When in 628 the power of the Eastern Turkish Qaghan was declining, Yi-nan of the Hsüeh-yen-t'o was elected rival qaghan. His envoys offered gifts to the T'ang court. In the 12th month (Dec./Jan., 629) of that Chinese year, Emperor Tai-tsung of T'ang recognized him as Chen-chu-p'i-chia Qaghan or P'i-chia for short (*Ts'e-fu yüan-kuei* p.5023; *Tzu-chih t'ung-chien* p.6061).

On Aug.31, 629, a younger brother of P'i-chia was received at the T'ang court and offered gifts. T'ai-tsung presented him with a precious sword and a precious horse whip. He joked that it was the custom of the Hsüeh-yen-t'o to decapitate those who had committed great crimes and to whip those who had committed lesser crimes (*Chiu T'ang shu* 2:10a; 199B:1b; *T'ung-tien* 197:40b; *Ts'e-fu yüan-kuei* p.5023; *Tzu-chih t'ung-chien* p.6065; *Wen-hsien t'ung-k'ao* 343:7b).

In the 2nd (Mar./Apr.) and 9th month Oct./Nov.) of 630, Hsüeh-yen-t'o envoys offered regional objects (*Ts'e-fu yüan-kuei* p.5023).

In the 10th month (Oct./Nov.) of 631, Hsüeh-yen-t'o envoys offered gifts (*Ts'e-fu yüan-kuei* p.5024).

In the 1st (Jan./Feb.) and 11th month (Dec./Jan., 633) of the Chinese year 632, Hsüeh-yen-t'o envoys offered gifts (*Ts'e-fu yüan-kuei* p.5024).

In the 4th (Apr./May) and 9th month (Oct./Nov.) of 635, Hsüeh-yen-t'o envoys offered regional objects (*Ts'e-fu yüan-kuei* p.5024).

At this time, the Hsüeh-yen-t'o were attacked by A-shih-na Mi-she, a son of the Ch'u-lo Qaghan of the Western Turks. They defeated him, whereupon he fled to Turfan and then in the 1st month (Feb./Mar.) of 636 to China[42] (*T'ang-hui-yao* 94:4b; *Tzu-chih t'ung-chien* p.6117).

[42] He was appointed General-in-chief of the Left Inspecting the Gates, attended

In the 11th month (Nov./Dec.) of 637, a son of the Hsüeh-yen-t'o qaghan was received at the T'ang court (*Ts'e-fu yüan-kuei* p.5024).

By 638, P'i-chia had become the most powerful qaghan north of the Gobi and the T'ang court was becaming apprehensive.T'ai-tsung nevertheless recognized two of his sons on Oct.30 as Junior Qaghans and presented them drums and banners (*Chiu T'ang shu* 199B:2a; *Tzu-chih t'ung-chien* p.6140).

After Turfan and the Western Turks had attacked Karashahr in 638, the qaghan of the Hsüeh-yen-t'o, [P'i-chia], proposed in the 3rd month (Apr./May) of 639 a joint attack on Turfan. T'ai-tsung sent a Master of Writing of the Ministry of Common People and the General-in-chief Who Commands the Army of the Right to present silk to the Hsüeh-yen-t'o and discuss the campaign. In the 7th month (Aug.Sep.), he furthermore sent the Minister of Agriculture with a letter stamped with the imperial seal (*Chiu T'ang shu* 198:4b; *Tzu-chih t'ung-chien* pp.6146-6147, 6148; *Wen-hsien t'ung-k'ao* 343:8b).

In the 9th month (October) of 639, Hsüeh-yen-t'o offered gifts (*Ts'e-fu yüan-kuei* p.5024).

On July 17, 640, envoys from P'i-chia proposed a marriage (*Chiu T'ang shu* 3:6b).

In the 12th month (Jan./Feb., 642) of the Chinese year 641, a son of P'i-chia was defeated by a Chinese army (*T'ang hui-yao* 94:13a).

On Jan.18, 642, envoys from Yi-nan (P'i-chia) informed the T'ang court that he had been defeated by the Turks and intended to form a marriage alliance with them. The envoys remained in Ch'ang-an until Jan.25,[43] T'ai-tsung advised them to live in peace with the Eastern Turks and that the Gobi should be the dividing line between them (*Chiu T'ang shu* 199B:2b; *Tzu-chih t'ung-chien* pp.6171, 6172).

In 642, Yi-nan (P'i-chia) sent a paternal uncle as envoy to the T'ang court and requested a marriage. He offered 3000 horses, 38,000 sable furs, and baroos camphor (*Chiu T'ang shu* 199B:3a; *Tzu-chih t'ung-chien* p.6177).

T'ai-tsung's attacks on Koguryŏ from 644, was enfeoffed as an earl, and married to an imperial younger sister, the Senior princess of Nan-yang (according to Hu San-hsing's commentary to the *Tzu-chih t'ung-chien* the Senior Princess of Heng-yang). In 657, he was made a General-in-chief of the Martial Guards of the Left. Subsequently, Kao-tsung made him a nominal qaghan of one half of the no longer existing Western Turkish empire (*Chiu T'ang shu* 194B:6a; 195:2b; *T'ung-tien* 199:46a; *Tzu-chih t'ung-chien* p.6118; *Wen-hsien t'ung-k'ao* 344:13a).

[43] Correcting *ping-tzu* to *ping-wu*.

In the 10th month (Oct./Nov.) of 642, T'ai-tsung observed to his attendant officials that the increasing strength of the Hsüeh-yen-t'o north of the Gobi forced him to make one of two decisions, either to attack them or to make a marriage alliance. Fang Hsüan-ling (578-648) answered:"Make peace and an alliance by marriage". The emperor said:"Yes. We are the father and mother of the people. If we can profit from it, why should we be stingy about one woman?" He ordered a Gentleman-in-Attendance of the Ministry of Arms to inform the [P'i-chia Qaghan] of the Hsüeh-yen-t'o that he would give him the Princess of Hsin-hsing as a wife. According to Hu San-hsing's commentary, she was an imperial daughter (*Tzu-chih t'ung-chien* pp.6179-6180).

On Jan.26, 643, the New Year's Day, the Hsüeh-yen-t'o presented regional objects. (*Ts'e-fu yüan-kuei* p.5024).

On July 31, 643, a nephew of P'i-chia offered 50,000 horses, 10,000 cattle and camels, and 100,000 sheep toward the promised marriage (*Chiu T'ang shu* 3:8b; *Tzu-chih t'ung-chien* p.6199). On Aug.12,[44] the same envoy presented delicacies, and the emperor gave him a banquet and rich gifts (*Tzu-chih t'ung-chien* p.6199).

At this point, a T'ieh-le in T'ai-tsung's entourage advised that a marriage alliance with the Hsüeh-yen-t'o should be out of the question. The emperor said:"I have already allowed it. How can I be the Son of Heaven and eat my words?" The T'ieh-le suggested that P'i-chia should be invited personally to welcome his bride in Ch'ang-an or at least in the Ning-hsia Oasis. He would not dare to come, whereupon the marriage could be cancelled. T'ai-tsung accepted this. He informed P'i-chia that he would personally conduct the bride to the Ning-hsia Oasis and meet him there. But the qaghan's ministers feared that this would involve to great a risk. P'i-chia refused the offer, and the marriage plans were cancelled off (*Hsin t'ang shu* 110:4a; *Tzu-chih t'ung-chien* pp.6199-2000). In short, the marriage was aborted by the emperor's trickery.[45]

In the 11th month (Nov./Dec.) of 643, the Hsüeh-yen-t'o offered regional objects (*Ts'e-fu yüan-kuei* p.5024). In one of the three missions of

---

[44] Emending 6th month to 6th intercalary month and *keng-tzu* to *keng-wu*.

[45] This conflicts with O. Franke's uncritical admiration of T'ai-tsung:"Dieser Mann hat durch sein ganzes Leben hundertfach bewiesen, dass ihm Hinterlist und Ungerechtigkeit ebenso fern lagen wie Grausamkeit und Härte" (*Geschichte*, vol.2, p.367).

643, Yi-nan (P'i-chia) also offered military assistance against Koguryŏ (*Chiu T'ang shu* 199B:3a).

In the 1st month (Feb./Mar.) of 644, Hsüeh-yen-t'o envoys offered regional objects (*Ts'e-fu yüan-kuei* p.5024).

In the 11th month (Nov./Dec.) of 645, Hsüeh-yen-t'o envoys came to congratulate and offer regional objects (*Ts'e-fu yüan-kuei* p.5024).

During 645, the P'i-chia Qaghan died and his two sons were killed. There ensued chaos. In in the 6th month (July/Aug.) of 646, the Hsüeh-yen-t'o were defeated by the Chinese and Uighurs. They enthroned To-mo-chih, a nephew of P'i-chia, who withdrew to the area of Karakorum. He there surrendered to a Chinese expeditionary force, was brought to Ch'ang-an, and there appointed General-in-chief of the Guards of the Right (*Chiu T'ang shu* 3:10a; *Tzu-chih t'ung-chien* pp.6228, 6237, 6238).

However, the Hsüeh-yen-t'o were not yet a spent force. On Oct.29, 646, several tribes of the T'ieh-le offered gifts and complained about the Turks. In the 9th month (Oct./Nov.) of the same year, various tribes of the T'ieh-le sent envoys to the Ning-hsia Oasis and offered regional objects (*Chiu T'ang shu* 3:10a, 10b).

In the 12th month (Jan./Feb., 647) of the Chinese year 646, the T'ieh-le were invited to participate in the attack on Kucha by the Chinese, Turks, Tibetans, and T'u-yü-hun (*Tzu-chih t'ung-chien* p.6251).

On Feb.18, 647, envoys from various T'ieh-le tribes including the Uighurs[46] had an audience with T'ai-tsung (*T'ang hui-yao* 196:13b; *Tzu-chih t'ung-chien* p.6245).

In the 2nd month (Feb./Mar.) of 648, Emperor T'ai-tsung gave a banquet for a T'ieh-le envoy (*Tzu-chih t'ung-chien* p.6252).

In 650, T'ieh-le envoys offered gifts to the T'ang court. Emperor Kao-tsung sent the General of the Cloud Flags on a return visit. When he came back, T'ieh-le envoys were attached to him and presented ten fine horses. Thereafter, connections broke off (*Chiu T'ang shu* 199B: 5a).

It goes without saying that the P'i-chia Qaghan of the Hsüeh-yen-t'o was an independent ruler. For the *Tzu-chih t'ung-chien* p.6146 to claim that P'i-chia in 639 presented a "memorial" to the emperor in which he referred to himself as "I, your slave" is therefore absurd. He was recognized by the T'ang, but at his death there was no official mourn-

[46] See further under that heading.

ing or condolence, and he was not conferred any posthumous title.

One purpose of the Hsüeh-yen-t'o missions was to discuss war and peace. But since the tribe had no joint markets with the Chinese, trade, chiefly in horses, cattle, camels, sheep, and furs, must have been another important aim. The Chinese payments are not recorded.

THE PA-YEH-KU

The Pa-yeh-ku were a T'ieh-le tribe.

In 629, Pa-yeh-ku envoys were received at the T'ang court (*Wen-hsien t'ung-k'ao* 344:14b).

In 647, Emperor T'ai-tsung established an imaginary Area Command out of the Pa-yeh-ku territory and appointed their chief as General-in-chief of the Martial Guards of the Right and Military Governor (*T'ung-tien* 199:47b; *Wen-hsien t'ung-k'ao* 344:14b).

Missions arrived between 742 and 756 (*Wen-hsien t'ung-k'ao* 344:14b).

THE T'UNG-LO

The T'ung-lo were a T'ieh-le tribe.

In 629, T'ung-lo envoys were received at the T'ang court (*Wen-hsien t'ung-k'ao* 344:14b).

During the reign of T'ai-tsung (627-649), the chief of the T'ung-lo sent envoys, but thereafter nothing was heard from him (*Wen-hsien t'ung-k'ao* 344:14b).

In 742 or soon afterwards, some T'ung-lo were by Emperor Hsüan-tsung settled in the Ordos Region (*Wen-hsien t'ung-k'ao* 344:14b).

THE P'U-KU

The P'u-ku were a T'ieh-le tribe. *Tzu-chih t'ung-chien* p.6239 refers to them as a tribe of the Uighurs.

In 629, P'u-ku envoys were received at the T'ang court (*Wen-hsien t'ung-k'ao* 344:14b).

In the 8th month (Sep./Oct.) of 646, P'u-ku envoys offered gifts (*T'ung-tien* 199:47b; *Tzu-chih t'ung-chien* p.6239; *Wen-hsien t'ung-k'ao* 344:14b).

THE TU-PO

The Tu-po were a T'ieh-le tribe.

In 647, Tu-po envoys offered gifts to the T'ang court (*T'ung-tien* 199:47b; *Wen-hsien t'ung-k'ao* 344:14b).

THE HU-HSÜEH

The Hu-hsüeh were a T'ieh-le tribe. *Tzu-chih t'ung-chien* p.6239 refers to them as a tribe of the Uighurs.

In the 8th month (Sep./Oct.) of 646, Hu-hsüeh envoys were received at the T'ang court. Their territory was divided into imaginary commanderies and prefecture (*Wen-hsien t'ung-k'ao* 344:15a).

THE A-PA

The A-pa were a T'ieh-le tribe.

During early T'ang, A-pa envoys were received at the court (*Wen-hsien t'ung-k'ao* 344:15a).

THE UIGHURS

The Uighurs (Hui-ku), also known as the Nine Tribes, were a T'ieh-le tribe. They had first been a subject people of the Eastern Turks until 630, then of the Hsüeh-yen-t'o until 646. In 745, they destroyed the Eastern Turkish empire and founded their own which lasted until their defeat by the Kirghiz in 840. They became, at a price, allies of the T'ang.[47]

In 629, the Uighurs offered regional objects to the T'ang court. This was the first official contact between them and China (*Wen-hsien t'ung-k'ao* 347:27b).

In 630, Uighurs were received at the T'ang court (*Wen-hsien t'ung-k'ao* 347:28a).

In the 11th month (Dec./Jan., 639) of the Chinese year 638, Uighur envoys offered gifts (*Tzu-chih t'ung-chien* p.5024).

---

[47] The two chapters devoted to the Uighurs in *Chiu T'ang shu* and *Hsin T'ang shu* have been translated and annotated for the period 744 to 840 by Colin Mackerras, *The Uighur Empire.*

In the 6th month (July/Aug.) of 646, the Uighur chief T'u-mi-tu, allied with the Chinese, defeated the Hsüeh-yen-to and in the following years annexed their territory (*Chiu T'ang shu* 195:1a; *Tzu-chih t'ung-chien* p.6237).

In the 8th month (Sep./Oct.) of 646, Uighurs offered gifts. On Sep.26, Emperor T'ai-tsung gave a banquet, appointed the envoys to offices, and gave them letters stamped with the imperial seal to their chiefs. He also sent the General of the Gentlemen-of-the-Household Who Commands the Army of the Right as his envoy in response (*Chiu T'ang shu* 195:1b; *Tzu-chih t'ung-chien* p.6239).

On Jan.31, 647, Uighur envoys were received at the T'ang court, and on Feb.2, T'ai-tsung gave them a banquet (*Tzu-chih t'ung-chien* p.6242).

On Feb.18, 647, envoys from the Uighurs and other T'ieh-le tribes had an audience with T'ai-tsung and were presented with gold, silver, silken materials, and brocade robes. They proposed that a road be opened from the land of the Uighurs to China, called the Road of the Heavenly Qaghan, with 68 postal stations, each providing horses, wine, and meat for passing envoys. They promised annually to offer sable furs (*T'ang hui-yao* 196:13b; *Tzu-chih t'ung-chien* p.6245).[48]

In 648, T'u-mi-tu was murdered by his nephew Wu-ku who then informed T'ai-tsung. Wu-ku and his ally Chü-lo-po were both sons-in-law of the Eastern Turkish qaghan Chü-pi and clearly wished to bring about a raprochement between the Uighurs and the Eastern Turks. In the 10th month (Oct./Nov) of 648, Chü-lo-po at Chü-pi's behest went to the T'ang court, where he was detained. T'ai-tsung sent a Master of Writing of the Ministry of Arms to the Uighurs, confered on T'u-mi-tu the posthumous title of General-in -chief of the Guards of the Left, and contributed to the funeral expenses. T'u-mi-tu's son and successor P'o-jun, who previously had been made General-in-chief of the Guards of the Garrison of the Left, was appointed General-in-chief of the Resolute Guards of the Left (*Chiu T'ang shu* 195:2a, 3a; *Tzu-chih t'ung-chien* p.6263).

In 649, the Uighurs and other tribes allied with the Chinese defeated the Eastern Turkish qaghan Chü-pi, who fled and was captured in 650 (*Chiu T'ang shu* 194A:9a; *T'ung-tien* 198:41b-42a; *Tzu-chih t'ung-chien*

---

[48] According to *Tzu-chih t'ung-chien*, the Uighur chiefs referred to themselves as "subjects and people of the T'ang" which is a sino-centric misstatement.

pp.6265-6266, 6271; *Wen-hsien t'ung-k'ao* 343:9a).

In 651, the Western Turkish empire was reunified by the Sha-po-lo Qaghan. He attempted to subdue the Eastern Turks as well but was defeated that year by a combined Chinese-Uighur army. In 657, the Western Turkish empire came to an end through another joint Chinese-Uighur action (*Chiu T'ang shu* 195:2b; *Wen-hsien t'ung-k'ao* 344:12b).

In the 10th month (Oct./Nov.) of 661 it became known at the T'ang court that the Uighur chief P'o-jun had died and had been succeeded by his nephew Pi-su-tu. Subsequently Uighur chiefs were appointed Military Governors of imaginary Area Commands (*Chiu T'ang shu* 195: 3a; *Tzu-chih t'ung-chien* p.6326).

In 716, the Eastern Turkish qaghan Mo-ch'o attacked the Uighurs and fell in battle. The victors sent his head to the Chinese capital (*Chiu T'ang shu* 8:7b; *T'ung-tien* 198:43a; *Tzu-chih t'ung-chien* p.6719; *Wen-hsien t'ung-k'ao* 343:10a).

In 719, it became known at the T'ang court that the Uighur chief Fu-ti-fu had died. Emperor Hsüan-tsung conferred on him the posthumous title of Specially Advanced. His son was appointed a Military Governor (*T'ang hui-yao* 98:2a).

In 742, the Uighur sub-chief Ku-li p'ei-lo sent envoys to offer gifts. At about the same time, another sub-chief, Hsieh-li-t'u-fa, sent envoys to the T'ang court. He was recognized as King Who Upholds Righteousness (*Chiu T'ang shu* 195:3a; *Tzu-chih t'ung-chien* p.6856).

In 744, Ku-li p'ei-lo attacked and defeated the Basmil and then adopted the title of Ku-to-lu-p'i-chia-ch'üeh Qaghan. He sent envoys to the T'ang court and was recognized as Qaghan Who Cherishes Benevolence.[49] In 745, he attacked the Po-mei Qaghan of the Eastern Turks, killed him, and sent his head to Ch'ang-an. T'ai-tsung appointed him as Supernumerary General-in-chief of the Resolute Guards of the Left. Henceforth, the Uighurs possessed the old territory of the Eastern Turks, and the Uighur empire had begun. Its capital was Karabalghasun at the upper Orkhon River (*Chiu T'ang shu* 194A:17a; 195:3a; *Tzu-chih t'ung-chien* p.6863; *Wen-hsien t'ung-k'ao* 343:11a).

In the 9th month (Sep./Oct.) of 745, an envoy from the Nine Tribes was received at the T'ang court (*Ts'e-fu yüan-kuei* p.5030).

In 745, the Ku-to-lu-p'i-chia-ch'üeh Qaghan received from Emperor Hsüan-tsung the title of Specially Advanced (*T'ang hui-yao* 98:2b). He

[49] *Hsin T'ang shu* 217A:3a and *T'ang hui-yao* 98:2b date the recognition 746.

died that year and was succeeded by his son, the Ko-le Qaghan (*Tzu-chih t'ung-chien* p.6863).

In the 4th month (May/June) of 747, the Nine Tribes presented 150 horses to the T'ang court (*Ts'e-fu yüan-kuei* p. 5030).[50]

In the 12th month (Jan./Feb., 748) of the Chinese year 747, the Nine Tribes presented horses (*Ts'e-fu yüan-kuei* p.5030).

In the 10th month (Nov./Dec.) of 749, a mission of ten men from the Nine Tribes was received at the T'ang court (*Ts'e-fu yüan-kuei* p.5030).

In the 10th month (Oct./Nov.) of 751, a chief from the Nine Tribes was received at the T'ang court (*Ts'e-fu yüan-kuei* p.5030).

In the 8th month (Sep./Oct.) of 752, Uighurs envoys were received at the T'ang court (*Ts'e-fu yüan-kuei* p.5030).

The outbreak of the rebellion of An Lu-shan in 755 brought on a fundamental change in Uighur-Chinese relations. The Uighurs became China's overbearing and self-conscious saviors, while the T'ang henceforth had to take care not to offend these demanding and powerful allies.

When Su-tsung had ascended the throne on Aug.12, 756, followed by the abdication of his father Hsüan-tsung, Lo-yang and Ch'ang-an were in the hands of the rebels and the survival of the dynasty was in doubt. In this crisis, Uighur envoys offered help. Su-tsung immediately sent his second cousin Li Ch'eng-shen, a great-grandson of Kao-tsung, and a general as his representatives to the Uighurs. The Ko-le Qaghan married his adopted daughter, a younger sister of his qatun, to Ch'eng-shen and sent a chief to accompany them back to China. Su-tsung received them warmly and recognized the Uighur princess as P'i-chia Princess[51] (*Chiu T'ang shu* 195:3a-3b; *Hsin T'ang shu* 217A:3a).

As a result of the agreement reached, the qaghan personally led an army to fight with the Chinese against An Lu-shan. On Dec.4, 756, he met with Kuo Tzu-yi north of the Ordos bend of the Yellow River and forced the Chinese general to salute the Uighur banners before receiving him (*Hsin T'ang shu* 217A:3b).

---

[50] The text says the Nine Tribes of the Turks which I take to be an error for Uighurs.

[51] According to *Chiu T'ang shu* 10:4a, the recognition was in 757. *Chiu T'ang shu* 195:7a states that *p'i-chia* in Uighuric means "having complete wisdom". See also infra note 62.

In the 1st month (Jan./Feb.) of 757, Su-tsung received a Uighur envoy in audience (*Hsin T'ang shu* 217A:3b).

In the 2nd month (Feb./Mar.) of 757, a Uighur mission of 15 men arrived at the T'ang court (*Chiu T'ang shu* 195:3a).

On Oct.20, 757, Su-tsung entitled Li Ch'eng-shen's Uighur wife a royal consort. The qaghan made Ch'eng-shen a sub-chief. The qaghan's heir-apparent, who commanded an army of Uighur infantry and cavalry, was given a banquet by Su-tsung and showered with presents. Su-tsung also ordered his eldest son, Li Yü, the future Emperor Taitsung, to meet with the heir-apparent and to treat him like a brother (*Chiu T'ang shu* 195:3a; *Hsin T'ang shu* 217A:3b).

On Nov.14, 757, the Chinese-Uighur army retook Ch'ang-an and on Dec.1 Lo-yang.[52] The Uighurs, but also Chinese troops, looted Lo-yang for three days. In addition, Li Yü presented the Uighur heir-apparent with silken brocade mats and valuables (*Chiu T'ang shu* 195: 3b; *Hsin T'ang shu* 217:4a).

On Dec.8, 757, Su-tsung returned to Ch'ang-an, and on Dec.13 the Uighur heir-apparent arrived there from Lo-yang. The emperor ordered the officials to welcome him. He then gave a banquet and presented the Uighur prince and his chiefs with silken fabrics and vessels of gold and silver. On Dec.30, Su-tsung issued an edict, replete with abject flattery, in which he appointed the qaghan a nominal Minister of Works and entitled him King Who Is Loyal and Righteous. He ordered that the Uighurs henceforth annually were to receive 20,000 bolts of pongee (*Chiu T'ang shu* 195:3b-4a).

On June 11, 758, 80 Uighur envoys and six envoys of the black-robed Arabs from the Abbasid caliphate entered the palace for an audience at the same time. At the Audience Gate, both delegations wrangled for precedence. The Chinese receptionists separated them and made them enter simultaneously through the Eastern and Western Gates. On July 7,[53] the Uighur envoys were given a banquet (*Chiu T'ang shu* 10:9a; 195:4a; *Ts'e-fu yüan-kuei* p.5031; *Wen-hsien t'ung-k'ao* 347:28b).

The Ko-le Qaghan had previously requested a marriage, and Su-tsung had agreed. In the 6th month (July/Aug.) of 758, a delegation of the qaghan arrived to welcome his future wife and to present 500

---

[52] Lo-yang fell again to the rebels on June 7, 760, but was retaken with Uighur help on Nov.20, 762.

[53] Correcting 6th month to 5th month. See Mackerras, *Uighur Empire*, p.133 note 48.

horses, sable furs, white cotton fabrics etc. Su-tsung appointed the chief envoy a Commander Unequalled in Honour. On Aug.25, 758, the emperor's second daughter, the Princess of Ning-kuo, was selected to become the bride of the qaghan (*Chiu T'ang shu* 10:9a; 195:4a-4b; *T'ang hui-yao* 98:3b; *Tzu-chih t'ung-chien* p.7059; *Wen-hsien t'ung-k'ao* 347: 28b).

On Aug 31, 758, Su-tsung recognized the Ko-le Qaghan of the Uighurs as P'i-chia-ch'üeh Qaghan, Who Is Brave and Martial and Awes the Distance. He appointed his own first cousin, the king of Han-chung Li Yü,[54] as Specially Advanced, Acting Grand Master of Ceremonies, Acting Grandee Secretary, and envoy for the ritual of conveying the document (*Chiu T'ang shu* 195:4b; *Tzu-chih t'ung-chien* p.7059; *Wen -hsien t'ung-k'ao* 347:28b).

On Sep.1, the princess departed from Ch'ang-an, escorted by Li Yü. His deputy Li Sun was a second cousin[55] of the emperor, who for that purpose was appointed a Gentleman-of-the-Palace of the Ministry of Arms, Acting Palace Assistant Secretary, and Acting Grand Herald. The Commander Unequalled in Honour and Acting Supervisor of the Right[56] of the Masters of Writing, the duke of Chi, P'ei Mien, was to conduct the cortège to the border. The emperor travelled with his daughter a short distance and then returned (*Chiu T'ang shu*195:4a-4b; *Tzu-chih t'ung-chien* p.7059; *Wen-hsien t'ung-k'ao* 347:28b).

The account of the reception by the Uighurs is based on Li Yü's report, which contained the usual self-serving and sino-centric mis-statements. When the Chinese reached the camp of the qaghan, the qaghan sat on a couch dressed in a yellow-ochre robe and a barbarian hat, surrounded by guards. Yü stood outside the tent. The qaghan asked him how he was related to the emperor, which he answered. The qaghan then inquired who was standing in front of him. Yü said a palace eunuch. The qaghan noted that a palace eunuch is a slave. How could he stand in front of a gentleman? The eunuch thereupon stepped back. Yü remained standing and did not salute the qaghan. The latter said that this was a breach of protocol. Yü answered that because of the qaghan's merit, the Son of Heaven of the T'ang had

---

[54] Not to be confused with the Liu Yü who became Emperor Tai-tsung. The names are written with different characters in the Chinese.

[55] Not a nephew as stated by *Chiu T'ang shu*. See Mackerras, op.cit., p.134 note 53.

[56] *Tzu-shih t'ung-chien* says Left.

given him a daughter in marriage. She was a real daughter of a Son of Heaven and not, as in other cases, a lady of the imperial house who had been entitled princess. She was also talented, virtuous, and good-looking and had come over a vast distance to marry the qaghan. That made him a son-in-law of the emperor. How could he thus receive the edict squatting on a couch? The qaghan thereupon was ashamed, rose, saluted, and accepted the edict (*Chiu T'ang shu* 195:4b; *Hsin T'ang shu* 217A:4a; *Tzu-chih t'ung-chien* p.7059; *Wen-hsien t'ung-k'ao* 347:28b). It is not probable that Li Yü lectured the qaghan and that the latter meekly accepted it. On the contrary, the qaghan knew that he had the upper hand and surely demanded and received homage from Yü.

On the following day, the Princess of Ning-kuo, was made the qatun. The silken fabrics and gold and silver vessels which Li Yü had presented were by the qaghan distributed among his chiefs and officials. When Yü returned, the qaghan presented him with 500 horses, 100 sable furs, white cotton fabrics, etc. (*Chiu T'ang shu* 195: 4b-5a; *Hsin T'ang shu* 217A:4b; *Tzu-chih t'ung-chien* p.7059; *Wen-hsien t'ung-k'ao* 347:28b).

In the 8th month (Sep./Oct.) of 758, fresh Uighur forces arrived in China, commanded by the qaghan's third son, the prince (tegin) Ku-ch'o, and the chief minister Ti-te. Su-tsung gave them a banquet (*Chiu T'ang shu* 195:5a; *T'ang hui-yao* 98:3b-4a).

On Oct.21, 758, a great chief of the Uighurs was received at the T'ang court. He conveyed the thanks of the qaghan for the marriage with the princess and also informed that the Uighurs had defeated the Kirghiz. The envoys were given a banquet and received gifts in accordance with their ranks (*Chiu T'ang shu* 195:5a).

On Jan.29, 759,[57] three ladies sent by the qaghan thanked for the marriage with the Princess of Ning-kuo. They were given a banquet (*Chiu T'ang shu* 195:4a).

From 758 to 760, the Uighurs annually requested joint border markets. Uighur envoys also frequently arrived in Ch'ang-an to trade horses for silk. The usual contingent was several 10,000 horses and the agreed price 40 bolts of pongee for one horse. Many envoys were waiting in the Ministry of the Herald for payment. The Chinese complained that the horses were inferior, weak, and useless, and that

[57] Correcting *chia-wu* to *chia-tzu*. See also Mackerras, *Uighur empire*, p.135 note 64.

the barbarians were insatiable in their demands for silk (*Chiu T'ang shu* 195:8b-9a; *Hsin T'ang shu* 217A:7a).

On Apr.7, 759, Ku-ch'o, Ti-te, and their Uighurs, under the command of Kuo Tzu-yi, suffered a defeat against the rebels at Hsiang-chou in southern Ho-pei. Ku-ch'o and Ti-te with an entourage of 13 men travelled from there to Ch'ang-an, where they arrived on Apr.19. Su-tsung gave them a banquet and presented gifts, to each in accordance with his rank. On Apr.25, when Ku-ch'o took leave to return to his encampment, the emperor gave another banquet and again distributed gifts (*Chiu T'ang shu* 195:5a; *Tzu-chih t'ung-chien* p.7072; *Wen-hsien t'ung-k'ao* 347:28b).

On Apr.30, 759, Ku-ch'o, who recently had been made a Supernumerary General-in-chief of the Army of the Feathered Forest of the Left, was appointed Supernumerary Imperial Household Grandee of the Silver Seal and Green Ribbon and Grand Herald (*Chiu T'ang shu* 195:5a).

In the 4th month (May) of 759, it became known at the T'ang court that the Ko-le Qaghan had died. His eldest son having been killed because of a crime, he was succeeded by his youngest son. This was the Teng-li Qaghan (Tengri),[58] also known as the Mou-yü Qaghan. His father had previously requested a marriage on behalf of him, whereupon Su-tsung had arranged for a daughter of the famous Chinese general of Uighur descent, P'u-ku Huai-en, to be given to him as a wife. She now became his qatun (*Chiu T'ang shu* 195:5a; *Hsin T'ang shu* 217A:4b-5a; *Tzu-chih t'ung-chien* p.7076; *Wen-hsien t'ung-k'ao* 347:28b).

On July 10, 759, Su-tsung appointed the General of the Guards of the Gilded Mace of the Left as Acting Grand Herald and Acting Palace Assistant Secretary to go to the Uighurs to condole and sacrifice (*Chiu T'ang shu* 195:5a).

When the Ko-le Qaghan had died, the Uighurs had wished to bury the Princess of Ning-kuo with him, but she had succeeded in talking them out of it. However, she had slashed her face and wailed according to Uighur custom. Since she was childless, the Uighurs permitted her to return to China. She arrived in Ch'ang-an on Sep.18 and was by the orders of Su-tsung welcomed by the officials outside the Gate

[58] Not to be confused with the Eastern Turkish Teng-li Qaghan, who had died in 741. The *li* is written with different Chinese characters.

of the Bright Phoenix[59] (*Chiu T'ang shu* 195:5a-5b; *Tzu-chih t'ung-chien* pp.7076, 7080).

On Oct.15, 760, a Uighur mission from the Teng-li Qaghan, led by a high official and numbering 20 men, arrived at the T'ang court to inquire about the well-being of the Princess of Ning-kuo. On Nov.10, Emperor Su-tsung received these envoys in audience (*Chiu T'ang shu* 195:5b; *Hsin T'ang shu* 217A:5a; *Tse-fu yüan-kuei* p.5031).

On Nov.23, 760, ten Uighur envoys were received in audience and given presents, each in accordance with his rank (*Chiu T'ang shu* 195: 5b; *Ts'e-fu yüan-kuei* p.5031).[60]

On June 16, 761, the Uighurs offered gifts (*Ts'e-fu yüan-kuei* p.5031).

In the 4th month (Apr./May) of 762, a Uighur mission of 18 men was received at the court T'ang (*T'ang hui-yao* 98:4a).

After Tai-tsung had ascended the throne on May 17, 762, he sent a eunuch to the Teng-li Qaghan to request military help against the last rebel, Shih Ch'ao-yi. But the latter had anticipated this and had himself formed an alliance with the Uighurs. These were already on the move and had reached the Chinese border. The eunuch managed to get a message through to the T'ang court, warning it of the emergency. Tai-tsung hurriedly sent the Palace Inspector Yao Tzu-ang to greet and spy on the qaghan, who by now had reached central Shan-hsi. Tzu-ang reported what he thought were the numbers of Uighur able-bodied men, of old and young, of wives, and of war horses (*Chiu T'ang shu* 195:5b-6a).

The qatun had accompanied the qaghan and was anxious to meet her father P'u-ku Huai-en. This enabled Emperor Tai-tsung to arrange a meeting between her, her husband, and her father. P'u-ku Huai-en succeeded in persuading the qaghan to change sides and to cooperate with the loyalists against the rebels (*Chiu T'ang shu* 195:6a; *Hsin T'ang shu* 217A:5a).

A Chinese army rendezvoused with the Teng-li Qaghan and his Uighurs in southernmost Shan-hsi. It was commanded by the emperor's

---

[59] This was the southern gate into the compound of the Palace of Great Brightness, which jutted out from Ch'ang-an in the northeast. See the map in Mackerras, *Uighurs Empire*, p.33.

[60] *Chiu T'ang shu* gives the date of 11th month, *mou-ch'en*, which did not exist. *Ts'e-fu yüan-kuei* has 10th month without cyclical characters. The 10th month did have a *mou-ch'en* day = Nov.23.

eldest son Li Kua, the future Emperor Te-tsung, with Yao Tzu-ang as one of his subordinates. The qaghan invited Li Kua to dance in front of the tent, which the latter refused. The qaghan accused him of haughtiness. Tzu-ang offered the excuse that Li Kua was in mourning for his great-grandfather Hsüan-tsung and grandfather Su-tsung (who had died earlier that year on May 3 and May 16, 762, respectively) and that it therefore was not proper for him to dance. The Uighurs replied that there was a covenant of brotherhood between the Teng-li Qaghan and Emperor Tai-tsung, which made Li Kua a nephew of the qaghan. He should observe the protocol of a nephew toward his uncle. Tzu-ang replied that this protocol had been superceded by the mourning. Moreover, Li Kua, as the eldest son of the emperor, was the heir-apparent. How could the heir-apparent of China dance before the qaghan of a foreign country? The Uighurs gave Tzu-ang and three other Chinese 100 strokes of the rod each, two of whom died from it in the following night.[61] Li Kua was allowed to return to his camp (*Chiu T'ang shu* 195:6a-6b; *Hsin T'ang shu* 217A:5b).

The Uighurs proceeded to defeat Shih Ch'ao-yi and to put an end to the rebellion by January 763. But the cost to the civilian population through brutality and pillage had been high. The qaghan sent envoys to the court, congratulated on the victory, and presented Shih Ch'ao-yi's banners. Tai-tsung summoned the envoys to an audience and presented them with 200 pieces of silk (*Chiu T'ang shu* 195:6b-7a; *Hsin T'ang shu* 217A:5b).

On Feb.22, 763, 15 Uighurs invaded the Ministry of the Herald by night. The guards at the gate did not dare to stop them (*Tzu-chih t'ung-chien* pp.7140-7141). The Herald was the official in charge of the reception of foreign envoys so that the Uighurs had official standing. They were no doubt the envoys who had just been sent by the qaghan and who according to the sources behaved abusively toward the Chinese officials.

On Aug.24, 763, Emperor Tai-tsung recognized the qaghan as Teng-li-hsieh-to-teng-mi-shih-han-chü-lu, Who Is Brave and Righteous and Has Established Merit, p'i-chia Qaghan. The *Chiu T'ang shu* here provides a translation from the Uighuric. It renders *hsieh-to* as "the lawful usage of the Gods of the Soils and Grains, *teng-mi-shih* as "enfeoffed territory", *han-chü-lu as* "skilfull", and *p'i-chia* as "having

[61] Yao Tzu-ang survived.

complete wisdom".[62] The qatun was recognized as P'o-mo, Who Is Bright and Loving, Beautiful and Glorious, p'i-chia Qatun. *P'o-mo* is translated as "to obtain compassion". A Regular Cavalier Attendant and Concurrent Grandee Secretary was sent to the Uighurs to convey these recognitions and confer titles on a number of dignitaries (*Chiu T'ang shu* 195:7a).

In the 10th month (Oct./Nov.) of 765, a Uighur chief with 200 men was received in audience by Emperor Tai-tsung. He was presented with 100,000 bolts of silken fabrics (*Chiu T'ang shu* 11:9a; *Ts'e-fu yüan-kuei* p.5031; *Tzu-chih t'ung-chien* p.7184).

After P'u-ku Huai-en had risen against the T'ang in 764, he received Uighur auxiliaries from his son-in-law, the Teng-li Qaghan, but also had the support of Tibetans, T'u-yü-hun, Tang-hsiang, and others. After his death on Sep.27/28, 765,[63] the Uighurs and Tibetans fell out with each other,[64] and peace feelers were exchanged in the 10th month (Oct./Nov.) between the former and the Chinese general Kuo Tzu-yi. Tzu-yi, with diplomatic skill and personal courage[65] negotiated an agreement. The Uighurs stipulated that the brothers [and sisters] of the qatun were not to be killed. This was followed by a banquet with toasts, speeches, and a Chinese presentation of silk, whereupon the Uighur chiefs danced (*Chiu T'ang shu* 195:7b-8a; *Tzu-chih t'ung-chien* pp.7180 ff).

The following day, Kuo Tzu-yi had a Uighur mission of 6 men, led by a chief, escorted to the capital for an audience with the emperor. Thereafter, the Uighurs attacked and defeated the Tibetans, who previously had fought with them under P'u-ku Huai-en (*Chiu T'ang shu* 195:8a-8b).

On Nov.14, 765, Kuo Tzu-yi sent on another Uighur mission of 196 men,[66] who were received in audience. Emperor Tai-tsung gave them a banquet and presented 100,000 bolts of silken fabrics. To

---

[62] Mackerras, *Uighur Empire*, p.141 note 101, points out that F.W.K Müller in his "Uigurika II" (in *Abhandlungen der königlichen preussischen Akademie der Wissenschaften zu Berlin, philosophisch-historische Klasse III,* 1910) gives a different translation. He renders *hsieh-to teng-mi-shih* as "holding the empire" *han* as "heroic", chü-lu as "glorious", and *p'i-chia* as "wise".

[63] For the date see Mackerras, *Uighur Empire*, p.144 note 117.

[64] They were at that time standing just north of the Wei River, not far from Ch'ang-an.

[65] He had entered the camp of the Uighurs unarmed.

[66] *Tzu-chih t'ung-chien* says more than 200.

raise funds for this, he had to dock the salaries of the court officials for the intercalary 10th, 11th, and 12th month (*Chiu T'ang shu* 195: 8b; *Tzu-chih t'ung-chien* p.7184).

In the 4th month (May/June) of 766, a Uighur mission of 100 men led by a chief was received at the T'ang court (*Ts'e-fu yüan-kuei* p.5031).

In the 10th (Oct./Nov.), 11th (Nov./Dec.), and the 12th month (Dec./Jan., 768) of the Chinese year 767, Uighur envoys offered gifts to the T'ang court (*Ts'e-fu yüan-kuei* p.5031).

In the 7th month (Aug./Sep.) of 768, Uighur envoys offered gifts and informed that the qatun had died. Tai-tsung sent a Regular Cavalier Attendant of the Right to condole and sacrifice (*Hsin T'ang shu* 217A: 6b-7a; *Ts'e-fu yüan-kuei* p.5031; *Tzu-chih t'ung-chien* p.7201; *Wen-hsien t'ung-k'ao* 347:28b).

On July 2, 769, Tai-tsung enfeoffed a younger daughter of P'u-ku Huai-en, i.e. a sister of the late qatun, as Princess Who Is Venerated and Virtuous to become the second qatun of the Teng-li Qaghan. A Gentleman-in-Attendance of the Ministry of Arms was ordered to escort her to her future husband. The qaghan was presented with 20,000 bolts of silken fabrics. The court was so impoverished that it did not have the mules and camels needed for the cortège and had to requisition them from the high officials (*Hsin T'ang shu* 217A:7a; *Wen-hsien t'ung-k'ao* 347:28b).

In the 12th month (January, 770) of the Chinese year 769, Uighur envoys offered gifts (*Ts'e-fu yüan-kuei* p.5031).

In the 1st month (Jan./Feb.) of 771,[67] Uighurs came out of the Ministry of the Herald without permission and robbed people in the wards and in the market places. Officials who tried to stop them were beaten. They then on horseback attacked palace gates which, however, were closed. Emperor Tai-tsung sent a eunuch to quieten them, whereupon they stopped (*Chiu T'ang shu* 195:8b; *Tzu-chih t'ung-chien* p.7218). These Uighurs cannot have been private merchants, who would not have been lodged in the Ministry of the Herald. As pointed out before, the Herald was in charge of the reception of foreign envoys, so that the perpetrators in this and similar cases described below must have been official envoys and their attendants.

[67] *Tzu-chih t'ung-chien* gives the date of Mar.3, 772.

In the 10th month (Nov./Dec.) of 771, Uighur envoys were received at the T'ang court (*Ts'e-fu yüan-kuei* p.5031).

In the autumn of 772, Uighur envoys offered gifts (*Chiu T'ang shu* 11:20b).

On Aug. 17, 772, Uighurs came out of the Ministry of the Herald and set on people in the wards and on the market places. They persued the Prefect of Ch'ang-an and seized his horse. He was barely able to escape on another horse. The officials did not dare to interfere (*Chiu T'ang shu* 195:8b; *Tzu-chih t'ung-chien* p.7219).

In the 12th month (Dec./Jan., 773) of the Chinese year 772, Uighur envoys offered gifts (*Ts'e-fu yüan-kuei* p.5031).

In the 4th month (Apr./May) of 773, a Uighur envoy was received in audience (*Ts'e-fu yüan-kuei* pp.5031-5032).

In the 6th month (June/July) 773, a Uighur envoy was received in audience (*Ts'e-fu yüan-kuei* p.5032).

On Sep.20, 773, a Uighur envoy offered 10,000 horses in trade. After an estimate of the tax income, Tai-tsung ordered the purchase of 6000 horses (*Chiu T'ang shu* 195:9a; *Tzu-chih t'ung-chien* p.7221).

In the intercalary 11th month (Dec./Jan., 774) of the Chinese year 773, a Uighur mission of 140 men returned to its homeland with its profit loaded on more than 1000 carts (*Chiu T'ang shu* 195:8b; *Ts'e-fu yüan-kuei* p.5032).

In the 3rd month (Apr./May) of 774, a Uighur envoy was received at the T'ang court. In the 4th month (May/June), he returned to his homeland (*Ts'e-fu yüan-kuei* p.5032).

In the 7th month (June/July) of 774, Uighur envoys presented 49 horses (*Ts'e-fu yüan-kuei* p.5032).

In the 10th month (Nov./Dec.) of 774, Uighur envoys were received in audience (*Ts'e-fu yüan-kuei* p.5032).

On Oct.15, 774, Uighurs came out of the Ministry of the Herald and killed people in broad daylight. They were captured by the officials, but Tai-tsung released them and cancelled the inquiry (*Tzu-chih t'ung-chien* p.7228).

In 775, a Uighur killed a man on the street. The Governor of the Capital arrested him, but Tai-tsung set him free and stopped the inquiry (*Hsin T'ang shu* 217A:7a).

On Oct.16, 775, another Uighur stabbed a man in broad daylight in the Eastern Market so that his intestines were hanging out. He was arrested and imprisoned. When his chief heard about it, he hurried from the Ministry of the Herald to the prison, brought out the captive by force, and wounded the goalers. Tai-tsung ignored it (*Chiu T'ang shu* 195:9a; *Hsin T'ang shu* 217A:7a; *Tzu-chih t'ung-chien* p.7232).

In the 12th month (Dec./Jan., 776) of the Chinese year 775, the Uighurs raided Chinese border areas. In the 1st month (Feb./Mar.) of 778, they invaded Shan-hsi and after some fighting withdrew. Later that year, a returning Uighur mission was robbed by Chinese soldiers in southern Shan-hsi, and the Uighurs retaliated by looting the populace (*Chiu T'ang shu* 195:9a; *Tzu-chih t'ung-chien* p.7236, 7251).

Emperor Tai-tsung died on June 10, 779, and was succeeded by his eldest son Li Kua or Te-tsung. This man had been through the experience of 762, hated the Uighurs, and even went so far as to consider an alliance with the Tibetans against them (*Tzu-chih t'ung-chien* p.7483). He nevertheless sent a eunuch to the Teng-li Qaghan to announce the death of his father. The envoy was not received (*Chiu T'ang shu* 195:9a).

While the Chinese envoy was at the Uighur court, the qaghan, together with his relatives and many Sogdians, was killed by his chief minister Tun. Tun enthroned himself as Ho-ku-to-lu-p'i-chia Qaghan. He apparently received the Chinese envoy and sent a chief to follow him back to the T'ang court (*Chiu T'ang shu* 195:9a-9b). In the 6th month (June/July), Te-tsung appointed the Herald as Cavalier Attendant and sent him to the Uighurs to condole (*T'ang hui-yao* 98:5a).

On Aug.28, 779, Te-tsung ordered that the Uighurs in Ch'ang-an were not allowed to adopt Chinese garments but had to wear Uighur clothing.[68]

On July 28, 780, Te-tsung ordered the Governor of the Capital to go to the Uighur court and recognize Tun as Qaghan Who Is Martial and Righteous and Achieves Merit (*Chiu T'ang shu* 195:9b).

At this time, the Uighur chief T'u-tung (a paternal uncle of the new qaghan), Yi-mi-shih, and others were returning to their homeland with a caravan of camels. They had halted for three months just northeast of Shan-hsi, near the northeastern bend of the Yellow River, at great expense to the Chinese government. There, it was discovered that they were attempting to smuggle Chinese women out of the country in bags. The local Army Commissioner, Chang Kuang-sheng, proposed to Te-tsung to kill these Uighurs, and the emperor apparently agreed. Kuang-sheng then ordered one of his officers to be publicly

---

[68] For details see Mackerras, *Uighur Empire*, p.153 note 150.

rude to T'u-tung, who had him whipped. This gave Kuang-sheng a pretext to massacre the Uighurs. He confiscated several 1000 of their camels and horses and 100,000 bolts of silk and sent the women back to Ch'ang-an.

Te-tsung summoned Chang Kuang-sheng to the capital and promoted him to General of the Gilded Mace of the Right. He also sent a eunuch to accompany a returning Uighur envoy and inform the qaghan that in view of the circumstances he was braking off relations with the [Uighur] barbarians (*Hsin T'ang shu* 217A:7b; *Tzu-chih t'ung-chien* pp.7287-7288).

In 781, Te-tsung sent the envoy Yüan Hsiu to return the corpses of T'u-tung, Yi-mi-shih, and two others to their country. A messenger of the qaghan told Hsiu that he should be killed in retaliation for the murder of T'u-tung. Hsiu blamed the death on Chang Kuang-sheng, absolving Emperor Te-tsung. He was not allowed to see the qaghan and was detained for 50 days. When he was permitted to return, the qaghan attached a Uighur envoy to him with the message that the T'ang had welshed on 1,800,000 strings of cash owed for Uighur horses. They reached Ch'ang-an on Aug.11, 782 The emperor "restrained his feelings" and paid 100,000 bolts of silk and 100,000 ounces of gold and silver (*Hsin T'ang shu* 217A:7b-8a; *Tzu-chih t'ung-chien* pp.7330-7331).[69]

On Oct.2, 787,[70] a chief sent by the qaghan offered regional objects[71] and requested a marriage alliance. Te-tsung was at first adamantly opposed but finally gave in to the insistant entreaties of the Grand Councilor Li Pi (722-789). He selected his eighth daughter, the Princess of Hsien-an, and ordered her to give an audience to the Uighur envoy. When the latter returned to his country on Oct.28, he brought with him a promise of the marriage as well as a portrait of the future bride (*Chiu T'ang shu* 12:25a-25b; 196:9b; *Hsin T'ang shu* 217A:8a-9a, 10a; *T'ang hui-yao* 98:5a; *Tzu-chih t'ung-chien* pp.7505-7506; *Wen-hsien t'ung-k'ao* 347:29a).

In the 5th month (June/July) of 788, Uighur envoys were received at the T'ang court (*Ts'e-fu yüan-kuei* p.5032).

---

[69] On the dates, see Mackerras, *Uighur Empire*, p.154 note 155.

[70] *Tzu-chih t'ung-chien* p.7501 dates the arrival of this mission 9th month (Oct./Nov.). *Chiu T'ang shu* 12:15a-25b has Oct.28, but that, according to *Tzu-chih t'ung-chien* p.7505, was the date of its return.

[71] These must have included horses, since the emperor paid 50,000 bolts of pongee specifically for horses (*Tzu-chih t'ung-chien* p.7506).

The Uighur qaghan sent a large cortège to welcome the Princess of Hsien-an. It consisted of his younger sister, the Ku-to-lu-p'i-chia Princess, his sister-in-law, the Mi-shu-to-lu Princess, the wives and concubines of his great chiefs, 56 women in all, the chief minister, and others, more than 1000 persons, and 2000 horses for the dignitaries. The chief minister was robbed and killed en route by the Shih-wei. Te-tsung ordered to detain 700 persons in T'ai-yüan and to send on the rest. The cortège arrived in Ch'ang-an on Nov.16, 788, and Emperor Te-tsung watched it from the Gate of Protracted Joy. The qaghan referred to himself in a letter as the emperor's son-in-law and half a son and promised to assist him against the Tibetans. He presented 3000 horses as a betrothal present. The Uighurs were lodged in the Ministries of the Herald and of the Court Architect (*Chiu T'ang shu* 195:9b; *Hsin T'ang shu* 217A:9a; *T'ang hui-yao* 98:5b; *Tzu-chih t'ung-chien* p.7515; *Wen-hsien t'ung-k'ao* 347:29a).[72]

On Nov.21 788,, the Uighur dignitaries had an audience in the Hall of All-Embracing Government (*Chiu T'ang shu* 195:9b).

On Nov.23, 788, Te-tsung gave an audience to the Uighur princesses and dignitaries in the Hall of Unicorn Virtue, after he had asked Li Pi about the protocol. The princesses were received by three Chinese Senior Princesses and conducted by the Palace Director of Guests. They saluted the emperor, and questions and answers were translated by an interpreter. This was followed by a banquet at which the emperor's favoured companion, the Sagacious Concubine, also participated and at which gifts were exchanged (*Chiu T'ang shu* 195: 9b; *Hsin T'ang shu* 217A:9a-9b; *T'ang hui-yao* 98:5b).

On Nov.28, 788, the emperor issued a formal edict that his daughter marry the qaghan. He appointed a staff for her, corresponding to the establishment of a king. On Nov.30, the Palace Inspector Li Chan-jan, a great-great-grandson of Kao-tsu, was made envoy for the marriage ritual. On Dec.5, a Master of Writing of the Ministry of Punishments was appointed Acting Supervisor of the Right for escorting the Princess of Hsien-an and for recognizing the qaghan as Long-lived, Beloved by Heaven, p'i-chia Qaghan and the princess as Wise, Good, Upright, Long-lived, Filial, and Obedient Qatun (*Chiu T'ang shu* 195:9b; *Hsin T'ang shu* 217A:9b; *Tzu-chih t'ung-chien* p.7516).

[72] For the number of Uighurs admitted to Ch'ang-an, see Mackerras, *Uighur Empire*, p.158 note 172.

On Dec.23, 789, it became known at the T'ang court that the Ho-ku-to-lu-p'i-chia Qaghan had died. Te-tsung suspended the court for three days and ordered the civilian and military officials from rank 3 and up to go to the Ministry of the Herald and condole with the envoys who had announced the death (*Chiu T'ang shu* 195:9b; *Tzu-chih t'ung-chien* p.7520).

On Dec.31, 789, the emperor sent the Herald and Concurrent Grandee Secretary to recognize the late qaghan's son as Ai-teng-li-lo-ku-mo-mi-shih-chü-lu-p'i-chia, Who Is Loyal and Upright, Qaghan (*Chiu T'ang shu* 195:10a; *Tzu-chih t'ung-chien* p.7520; *Wen-hsien t'ung-k'ao* 347:29a).

In the 2nd month (Feb./Mar.) of 790, Uighur envoys were received at the T'ang court (*Tse-fu yüan-kuei* p.5032).

In the 4th month (May/June)[73] of 790, it became known at the T'ang court that the Ai-teng-li-lo-ku-mo-mi-shih-chü-lu-p'i-chia, Who Is Loyal and Upright, Qaghan had been poisoned and killed by his Junior Qatun, a granddaughter of P'u-ku Huai-en, that his younger brother had enthroned himself, that the usurper had been killed, and that the murdered qaghan's son A-ch'o had succeeded (*Chiu T'ang shu* 195:10a; *Hsin T'ang shu* 217A:10a; *Tzu-chih t'ung-chien* p.7521).

In the 6th month (July/Aug.) of 790, a Uighur envoy was paid 300,000 bolts of pongee for the horses he had presented (*Chiu T'ang shu* 195:9b-10a).

In the 10th month (Nov./Dec.) of 790, the Uighurs officially announced the death of the Ai-teng-li-lo-ku-mo-mi-shih-chü-lu-p'i-chia, Who Is Loyal and Upright, Qaghan. Te-tsung commenced mourning (*Chiu T'ang shu* 13:5a).[74]

In the 1st month (Feb./Mar.) of 791, envoys from a Uighur chief were received at the T'ang court (*Ts'e-fu yüan-kuei* p.5032).

On Mar.21, 791, Te-tsung sent the Junior Herald to recognize A-ch'o as Qaghan Who Upholds Sincerity (*Chiu T'ang shu* 195:10b; *Tzu-chih t'ung-chien* p.2523).[75]

In the 5th month (June/July) of 791,[76] Uighur envoys announced that the Junior Princess of Ning-kuo had died. When the real Princess of

[73] According to *Tzu-chih t'ung-chien* the 3rd month (Mar./Apr.).

[74] Mackerras, *Uighur Empire*, p.191, dates the beginning of the mourning Jan.13, 791.

[75] For the date, see ibid., p.166 note 211.

[76] *T'ang hui-yao* 98:6b says 4th month (May/June).

Ning-kuo had been married to the Ko-le Qaghan in 758, she had been accompanied by a lady who was her first cousin. That lady's father, the king of Jung was Emperor Hsüan-tsung's sixth son. The Uighurs called her the Junior Princess of Ning-kuo. She became a secondary wife of the Ko-le Qaghan and after his death and the departure of the Princess of Ning-kuo in 759 the qatun of the Teng-li Qaghan. Her two sons had been killed by the Ho-ku-to-lu-p'i-chia Qaghan. Te-tsung suspended court in her memory for three days (*Chiu T'ang shu* 195:10b-11a; *Ts'e-fu yüan-kuei* p.5032).

In the 8th month (Sep./Oct.) of 791, Uighur envoys presented Tibetan and Qarluq captives and their cattle to the T'ang court (*Chiu T'ang shu* 195:11a; *Tzu-chih t'ung-chien* p.7524).[77]

On Jan.6, 792, a Uighur envoy presented a high-ranking Tibetan captive. Te-tsung inspected him from the Gate of Protracted Joy (*Chiu T'ang shu* 195:11a; *Tzu-chih t'ung-chien* p.7525).

In the 4th (Apr./May) and 5th month (May-June) of 792, Uighur envoys offered gifts (*Ts'e-fu yüan-kuei* p.5032).

In the 7th month (July/Aug.) of 792, a Uighur envoy offered horses. This man was a Chinese who had lived among the Uighurs and had become a fosterson of the qaghan. The emperor appointed him an Acting Supervisor of the Right and favoured him with presents. He was paid 70,000 bolts of pongee for the horses he traded (*Chiu T'ang shu* 195:11a).

In the 9th month (Oct./Nov.) of 793, Uighur envoys offered gifts (*Chiu T'ang shu* 195:11a; *Ts'e-fu yüan-kuei* p.5032).

On Mar.21, 795, Uighur envoys announced that A-ch'o had died and that, since he had no sons, he had been succeeded by his minister Ku-to-lu. Te-tsung commenced mourning (*Chiu T'ang shu* 13:11a; *Ts'e-fu yüan-kuei* p.5032; *Tzu-chih t'ung-chien*, p.7568; *Wen-hsien t'ung-k'ao* 347:29b).[78]

On June 15, 795,[79] Te-tsung sent the Inspector of the Imperial Library to recognize Ku-to-lu as the Ai-t'eng-li-lo-yü-lu-mo-mi-shih-ho-hu-lu-p'i, Who Cherishes Trustworthiness, Qaghan.[80] Ku-to-lu did

[77] By *T'ang hui-yao* 98:7a and *Tzu-chih t'ung chien* p.7524 dated 9th month (October).

[78] The date is controversial. See Mackerras, *Uighur Empire*, pp.167-168 note 226 and p.191.

[79] On the date, see Mackerras, op.cit., p.168 note 226.

[80] *Chiu T'ang shu* 13:11b gives the title as T'eng-li-lo-yü-lu-mo-mi-shih-ho-liu-ku-to-lu-p'i-chia, Who Cherishes Trustworthiness, Qaghan.

not come from the Yao-lo-ko (Yaghlaqar) clan, which had ruled so far, but from the Hsieh-tieh clan. He seized all the sons and grandsons of the [Ho-ku-to-lu-p'i-chia] Qaghan and presented them to the T'ang court (*Chiu T'ang shu* 12:11b; *Hsin T'ang shu* 217A:10b; *Wen-hsien t'ung-k'ao* 347:29b).

In the 12th month (Jan./Feb., 797) of the Chinese year 796, the Uighurs offered gifts (*Chiu T'ang shu* 13:13b).[81]

In the 2nd (Feb./Mar.), and 10th month (Nov./Dec.) of 806 and once more during that year, Uighur envoys offered gifts (*T'ang hui-yao* 98:7b; *Ts'e-fu yüan-kuei* p.5032).

On Feb.8, 807, a Uighur mission offering gifts for the first time brought along Manichaean priests.[82] On Feb.22, the Uighurs requested to build Manichaean temples in Lo-yang and T'ai-yüan, which the court was forced to accept. Manichaeans had, however, become frequent visitors to Ch'ang-an much earlier, and traded there illegally with merchants on the Western Market (*Hsin T'ang shu* 217A:10b; *Tzu-chih t'ung-chien* p.7638).

In the 2nd month (Mar./Apr.) of 807, Uighur envoys offered gifts (*Chiu T'ang shu* 14:13a; *Ts'e-fu yüan-kuei* p.5032).

On March 26, 808, Uighur envoys announced the death of the Princess of Hsien-an. She had lived among the Uighurs for 21 years and had been the wife of four successive qaghans.[83] Emperor Hsien-tsung conferred on her the posthumous title of Grand Senior Princess of Yen. In the 3rd month (April), the Uighur envoys were received in audience and presented with white brocade garments and silver vessels, each in accordance with his rank (*Chiu T'ang shu* 14:13a; *Hsin T'ang shu* 217A:10b; *T'ang hui-yao* 98:8a).

---

[81] According to the Chinese sources, it became known in the 11th month (Nov./Dec.) of 805 that Ku-to-lu had died. Emperor Hsien-tsung, who had ascended the throne on Sep.5 of that year, sent the Junior Herald to condole and recognize the successor as T'eng-li-yeh-ho-chü-lu-p'i-chia Qaghan (*Hsin T'ang shu* 217A:10b; *Tzu-chih t'ung-chien* p.7623; *Wen-hsien t'ung-k'ao* 347:29b). Mackerras, *Uighur Empire*, pp.187-190, has argued convincingly that Ku-to-lu did not die until 808 and that the T'ang court simply rerecognized him in 805 under a new title.

[82] After the second reconquest of Lo-yang in 762, the Teng-li Qaghan had met Manichaean priests and had become impressed by their religion. When he returned to his homeland in 763, he brought with him four missionaries, whereafter Manichaeism spread among the Uighurs.

[83] The Ho-ku-to-lu-p'i-chia Qaghan, the Teng-li-lo-ku-mo-mi-shih, Loyal and Upright, Qaghan, the qaghan A-ch'o, and the Ai-t'eng-li-lo-yü-lu-mo-mi-shih-ho-lu-hu-p'i, Who Cherishes Trustworthiness, Qaghan.

In the 5th month (May/June) of 808, it became known at the T'ang court that the Uighur qaghan had died. Hsien-tsung commenced mourning. On June 22, he sent the Junior Director of the Imperial Clan to recognize the new ruler as the Ai-teng-li-lo-ku-mi-shih-ho-p'i-chia, Who Maintains Righteousness, Qaghan (*Chiu T'ang shu* 14:13b; *Hsin T'ang shu* 217A:10b; *T'ang hui-yao* 98:7b-8a; *Wen-hsien t'ung-k'ao* 347:29b).

In 809, Uighur envoys were received at the T'ang court (*Chiu T'ang shu* 195:11a; *Chiu Wu-tai shih* 138:3b).[84]

On June 24, 810, a Uighur envoy was received at the T'ang court (*Hsin T'ang shu* 217A:10b).

In 813, a Uighur envoy proposed a marriage alliance on behalf of the qaghan. When he was about to leave in the 4th month (May/June), he was given a banquet and presented with silver vessels and silken fabrics. Before his actual departure, the qaghan appeared with horsemen at the Chinese border north of the Ordos bend of the Yellow River (*Chiu T'ang shu* 195:11a; *Hsin T'ang shu* 217A:10b).

Hsien-tsung ordered the high officials to estimate the expense of the proposed marriage, and they calculated that it would cost 5,000,000 strings of cash. This was more than the emperor thought he could afford. He sent the Director of the Imperial Clan and an Erudit as his envoys to the Uighurs to announce his decision (*Chiu T'ang shu* 195:11a; *Tzu-chih t'ung-chien* p.7730).

In the 5th month (May/June) of 814, the Master of Writing of the Ministry of Rites, Li Chiang, noted in a memorial that the Uighurs would probably launch an attack in the autumn and that a marriage alliance would prevent it. Opposing those who claimed that the cost of sending a princess was too high, he argued that it could be done for 200,000 strings of cash. That was no more than the annual tax revenue from one large prefecture (hsien) in the southeast, cheap when compared to that of the upkeep of the border defences which required one third of the entire annual tax revenue. A marriage alliance between the Uighurs and the Chinese would also set the Tibetans and Uighurs against each other. The emperor rejected this advice (*Hsin T'ang shu* 217A:10b-11b).

---

[84] They supposedly requested their name to be written differently in Chinese. While the Chinese did, in fact, substitute one character in the Uighur name by another, the date of the change is very much in doubt. See Mackerras, *Uighur Empire*, pp.158-159 note 173.

In the 11th month (Dec./Jan., 815 of the Chinese year 814, a Uighur mission of 37 men was received at the T'ang court (*Tse-fu yüan-kuei* pp.5032-5033).

In the 1st month (Feb./Mar.) of 816, Uighur envoys offered gifts. They were presented with brocade and silver vessels, each in accordance with his rank. In the 2nd month (Mar./Apr.),[85] they presented nine camels and 80 horses. In the winter, they offered gifts (*Chiu T'ang shu* 15:11b; *T'ang hui-yao* 98:8a, 8b; *Tse-fu yüan-kuei* p.5033).

In the 1st month (Jan./Feb.) of 817, the Uighurs again proposed a marriage. On Feb.20, a banquet was given for eight departing Uighur Manichaeans, who were entrusted with the answer that a marriage was not possible (*Tzu-chih t'ung-chien* p.7730).[86]

In 818, the Uighurs offered gifts (*Chiu T'ang shu* 15:16a).

Shortly before Emperor Hsien-tsung's death on Feb.14, 820, a Uighur envoy not only requested but demanded a marriage. The emperor agreed. His son Mu-tsung, who ascended the throne on Feb.20, chose a younger sister, the Senior Princess of Yung-an, as the bride of the qaghan. She was Hsien-tsung's fifteenth daughter On Apr.17, the Uighur envoy returned to his homeland (*Tzu-chih t'ung-chien* p.7779).

On Apr.2, 821, it became known at the T'ang court that the Ai-teng-li-lo-ku-mi-shih-ho-p'i-chia, Who Maintains Righteousness, Qaghan had died. Mu-tsung suspended the court for three days and ordered all official from rank 3 and up to go to the Ministry of the Herald and condole (*Chiu T'ang shu* 16:8b; 195:11a-11b; *Tzu-chih t'ung-chien* p.7789).

On May 25, 821, Mu-tsung appointed the Inspector of the Ministry of the Privy Treasurer as Acting Regular Cavalier Attendant of the Left and Concurrent Grandee Secretary as envoy to the Uighurs to condole and sacrifice and to recognize the new ruler as Teng-lo-yü-lu-mo-mi-shih-chü-chu-p'i-chia, Who Venerates Virtue, Qaghan[87] (*Chiu*

---

[85] *T'ang hui-yao* 98:8a has 3rd month (April).

[86] The estimate that the marriage would cost 5,000,000 strings of cash and the mission of the Junior Director of the Imperial Clan of 813 are by *Tzu-chih t'ung-chien* recorded for 817.

The return of the Manichaeans is by *Chiu T'ang shu* 195:11a dated [813], 12th month, 2nd day. Mackerras, *Uighur Empire*, pp.173-174 note 252, shows convincingly that this should be emended to *yüan-ho* 12th year (817), 2nd month. Feb.20 was the first day of the 2nd month.

[87] Also called Teng-lo-ku-mo-mi-shih-ho-p'i-chia Qaghan (*Chiu T'ang shu* 195: 11b).

T'ang shu 16:10a; 195:11b; *Hsin T'ang shu* 217B:1a; *Tzu-chih t'ung-chien* p.7791). This qaghan replaced his predecessor as the bridegroom of the Chinese princess.

In the 5th month (June/July) of 821, an enormous Uighur cortège, the largest ever, arrived in China. It included high-ranking officials, 2000 chiefs, two princesses, Manichaeans, and others. They brought as betrothal gifts 20,000 horses and 1000 camels. Mu-tsung allowed 500 members of the mission to proceed to Ch'ang-an and detained the rest in T'ai-yüan. 573 actually entered Ch'ang-an on June 4, where they were lodged in the Ministry of the Herald (*Chiu T'ang shu* 195: 11b-12a; *Hsin T'ang shu* 217B:1a).

However, the princess whom the Uighurs had come to meet was not the same who had been first selected by Mu-tsung. The Senior Princess of Yung-an, who later became a Taoist nun, was replaced. On July 1, Mu-tsung ordered that the Princess of T'ai-ho, a younger sister of his and the seventeenth daughter of Hsien-tsung was to be the bride of the qaghan. A Member of the Suite of the Imperial Secretariat was sent to the Ministry of the Herald to inform the Uighurs. 50 of the envoys were presented with brocade and silver vessels, each in accordance with his rank. The Uighurs offered white cotton, white silk, sable fur robes, jade belts, 1000 horses, 50 camels, camel wool, etc. A staff corresponding to that of a king was appointed for the princess. The General-in-chief of the Guards of the Gilded Mace of the Left was made Acting Master of Writing of the Ministry of Households to escort the Princess. The Privy Treasurer was made envoy for the mariage ritual. The Superintendent of the Imperial Household was made Concurrent Palace Assistant Secretary and deputy envoy. An Erudit of the Ministry of the Grand Master of Ceremonies was made Palace Assistant Secretary to act as an assistant (*Chiu T'ang shu* 195: 11b; *Hsin T'ang shu* 83:15a; 217B:1a; *T'ang hui-yao* 98:8b-9a).

When the Tibetans learned about the planned marriage, they showed their displeasure by raiding the Chinese border. On July 16, 821, the Uighurs informed the T'ang court that they were taking military action against the Tibetans (*Chiu T'ang shu* 195:11b; *Tzu-chih t'ung-chien* p.7791-7792).

On Aug.22, 821, Mu-tsung conferred on his sister, the Princess of T'ai-ho, the title of Qhatun Who is Benevolent, Filial, Upright, Beautiful, Bright, Wise, Superior, and Long-lived (*Hsin T'ang shu* 217B:1a).

On Aug.28, 821, the princess started from Ch'ang-an. The emperor said farewell. All the escorting officials were arranged according to their ranks. The populace poured out to watch it. The cortège travelled slowly, since it was not until the 11th month (Nov./Dec.) of that year (821) that it was met at the border by 760 Uighurs with camels, horses, and chariots (*Chiu T'ang shu* 195:12a; *Tzu-chih t'ung-chien* p.7796).

The escort of the princess returned to Ch'ang-an Nov.18, 822, and reported on the marriage ceremony. The Chinese envoys selected an auspicious day. On that day, the qaghan sat on a tower facing east. A felt tent had been set up for the princess below the tower. A number of Uighur princesses instructed the Chinese princess about their customs. She then removed her Chinese clothing and put on Uighur garments. She came out of the tent, stood in front of the qaghan, and saluted him facing west. Reentering the tent, she changed to the apparel of a qatun, a crimson robe and mantle, and a golden decorated headdress, pointed in front and straight in the back. She came out again and saluted the qaghan as before. Nine ministers, one each from the nine tribes of the Uighurs, carried her in a sedan chair nine times clockwise around the tower. She then ascended the tower and sat with the qaghan facing east. When ministers and courtiers made their obeisances, they henceforth saluted both the qaghan and the qatun. She had her own headquarters, where she gave a banquet for the departing Chinese officials and wept. On the last day, the qaghan presented the envoys with ample gifts (*Chiu T'ang shu* 195:12b; *Hsin T'ang shu* 217B:1a-1b).

In the 2nd month (Feb./Mar.) of 822, the emperor paid 50,000 bolts of pongee as the price for Uighur horses (*Chiu T'ang shu* 195:12a).

In the 3rd month (Mar./Apr.) of 822, Uighur envoys offered gifts. The same month, the emperor paid another 70,000 bolts of pongee for Uighur horses. Also in the 3rd month, Uighur troops entered China and offered support in suppressing unrest. The court feared a repetition of their behaviour in 757, and the emperor sent a eunuch asking them to return. They refused to do so until they had been presented with still another 70,000 bolts of silken fabrics (*Chiu T'ang shu* 195:12a; *Hsin T'ang shu* 217B:1b; *Ts'e-fu yüan-kuei* p.5033).

In the 10th month (Oct./Nov.) of 822, a Uighur envoy offered gifts, including six "bed women" (*Ts'e-fu yüan-kuei* p.5033).

In the 12th month (Jan./Feb., 823) of the Chinese year 822, Uighur envoys offered gifts (*Ts'e-fu yüan-kuei* p.5033).

In the 12th month (Dec./Jan., 825) of the Chinese year 824, Uighur envoys offered gifts (*Ts'e-fu yüan-kuei* p.5033).

In 824, it had become known at the T'ang court that the Teng-lo-yü-lu-mo-mi-shih-chü-chu-p'i-chia, Who Venerates Virtue, Qaghan had died and had been succeeded by a younger brother. On Apr.9, Emperor Ching-tsung, who had ascended the throne on Feb.25 of that year, sent the Gentleman-of-the Palace of the Transit Authorization Bureau to condole, sacrifice, recognize the new ruler as the Ai-teng-li-lo-ku-mo-mi-shih-ho-p'i-chia, Who Displays Propriety, Qaghan (*Chiu T'ang shu* 195:12a; *Hsin T'ang shu* 217B:1b; *T'ang hui-yao* 98:9a-9b; *Tzu-chih t'ung-chien* p.7843).[88]

In the 7th (July/Aug.), 10th (Nov./Dec.), and 12th month (Jan./Feb., 826) of the Chinese year 825, Uighur envoys offered gifts (*Ts'e-fu yüan-kuei* p.5033).

After Emperor Wen-tsung had ascended the throne on Jan.9, 827, he paid the Uighurs 500,000 bolts of pongee for their horses. Later that year, he ordered a eunuch to go to the Ministry of the Herald and pay the Uighurs 200,000 bolts of pongee for their horses (*Chiu T'ang shu* 195:12b; *Hsin T'ang shu* 217B:1b).

In the 1st month (Feb./Mar.) of 829, a eunuch paid the Uighurs 230,000 bolts of silk for their horses (*Chiu T'ang shu* 195:12b).

In the 3rd month (Mar./Apr.) of 833, Uighur envoys arrived with camels and horses and announced that the Ai-teng-li-lo-ku-mo-mi-shih-ho-p'i-chia, Who Displays Propriety, Qaghan had been murdered by his subordinates and had been succeeded by a nephew. On Apr.27, Emperor Wen-tsung suspended the court for three days and ordered all civilian and military officials from rank 3 and up and the officials of the Imperial Chancellery from rank 4 and up to go to the Ministry of the Herald and condole with the envoys (*Chiu T'ang shu* 17:9b; 195:12b-13a; *Tzu-chih t'ung-chien* p.7879; *Wen-hsien t'ung-k'ao* 347:29b).[89]

On May 22, 833, Wen-tsung appointed the General of the Resolute Guard of the Left and Regent of the Imperial City as General of the Gilded Mace and Concurrent Grandee Secretary to go as envoy to the Uighur court, condole and sacrifice, and recognize the new ruler as Ai-teng-li-lo-ku-mo-mi-shih-ho-chü-lu-p'i-chia, Who Manifests Trustworthiness, Qaghan (*Chiu T'ang shu* 195:13a; *Tzu-chih t'ung-chien* p.7884).

In the 6th month (June/July), 835, Uighur envoys offered seven female mounted archers and two children of the Sha-to Turks as

[88] By *Chiu T'ang shu* dated 822, 5th month (May/June).

[89] On the dates and the relationship of the new ruler to the deceased see Mackerras, *Uighur Empire*, pp.181-182 note 291.

presents from the Princess of T'ai-ho (*Chiu T'ang shu* 195:13a).

In the 12th month (Jan./Feb., 837) of the Chinese year 836, Uighur envoys offered gifts (*Ts'e-fu yüan-kuei* p.5033).

In the 10th month (Nov./Dec.) of 837, Uighur envoys offered gifts (*Ts'e-fu yüan-kuei* p.5033).

In the intercalary month (Feb./Mar.) of 839, Uighur envoys offered gifts (*Ts'e-fu yüan-kuei* p.5033).

During 839, the Ai-teng-li-lo-ku-mo-mi-shih-ho-chü-lu-p'i-chia, Who Manifests Trustworthiness, Qaghan killed two of his enemies but was subsequently attacked, defeated, and committed suicide. The Uighurs enthroned a certain Ho-sa as qaghan.[90] This was followed by an epidemic and a heavy snowfall in which many sheep and horses died (*Chiu T'ang shu* 195:13a; *Tzu-chih t'ung-chien* p.7983; *Wen-hsien t'ung-k'ao* 347:29b).

In 840, envoys from Ho-sa announced the death of his predecessor to the T'ang court. The same year, a Kirghiz army crushed the Uighurs and killed Ho-sa. The Uighur empire had come to an end (*Chiu T'ang shu* 195:13a; *T'ang hui-yao* 98:10a; *Wen-hsien t'ung-k'ao* 347:29b).

After their defeat, the Uighurs abandoned their old grazing grounds north of the Gobi and scattered in different directions. Some moved to Turfan and spread from there through East Turkestan. A large contingent moved to the territory north of the Ordos Bend in Inner Mongolia.

The Uighurs in Inner Mongolia were an obvious new danger to the T'ang, and the Chinese fell back on their old policy of creating dissent. In the 8th month (Aug.Sep.) of 841, the Wu-chieh Qaghan informed the T'ang court through envoys of the victory of the Kirghiz, of the death of the former qaghan (Ho-sa), and of his own election as qaghan by the tribesmen. The princess of T'ai-ho sent envoys of her own to announce the same matter. After the defeat of the Uighurs, she had fallen into the hands of the Kirghiz, who had attempted to escort her back to China. But the cortège had been intercepted by the Uighurs, the entire escort was killed, and she had been brought to the Wu-chieh Qaghan to become his wife. Emperor Wu-tsung, who had ascended the throne on Feb.10, 840, sent the Herald and the General of the Gilded Mace of the Left to recognize him (*Chiu T'ang shu* 18A: 4a; 195:12b, 12a-13b; *T'ang hui-yao* 98:9b).

---

[90] On Ho-sa, see ibid, p.182 note 295.

In the 2nd month (Mar./Apr.) of 842, the Wu-chieh Qaghan sent envoys to the T'ang court and requested grain. Attempts to persuade him and his tribe to return north were fruitless (*Tzu-chih t'ung-chien* p.7958; 7963).

On June 2, 842, envoys of the Uighur prince (great tegin), Wu-mo-ssu, offered his "surrender" to, i.e. cooperation with, China. The T'ang court immediately proceeded to promote him as an ally. On June 26, Wu-tsung ordered the Herald to enfeoff Wu-mo-ssu as as king of Huai-hua commandery, and to present him with 5000 bushels of rice and 3000 bolts of pongee. His chiefs received gifts, each in accordance with his rank. On Aug.1, Wu-tsung created out of the Uighurs following Wu-mo-ssu the imaginary Army Which Attaches Itself to Righteousness and appointed him General-in-chief of the Gilded Mace of the Left.[91] On Sep.23, Wu-tsung bestowed on Wu-mo-ssu and his younger brothers the imperial surname of Li and the given names of Ssu-chung (Thinking of Loyalty), Ssu-chen (Thinking of Uprightness), Ssu-hui (Thinking of Goodness), Ssu-en (Thinking of Kindness), Ssu-yi (Thinking of Righteousness), and Ssu-li (Thinking of Propriety) (*Chiu T'ang shu* 195:13b; *Tzu-chih t'ung-chien* pp.7961-7962, 7963). Thereafter, this branch of the Uighurs disappears from the sources.

In the 11th month (Dec./Jan., 843) of the Chinese year 842, Wu-tsung sent envoys with a letter to the Princess of T'ai-ho and presented her with winter garments (*Tzu-chih t'ung-chien* p.7968).

The collapse of the Uighur empire had the further result that the Hsi in Jehol and the Khitan in Manchuria, who previously had been tax-paying dependents of the Uighurs, rose against their former masters in 842 and massacred their inspecting envoys (*Tzu-chih t'ung-chien* p.7967).

Also in 842, open warfare broke out between China and the Uighurs of the Wu-chieh Qaghan. On Feb.13, 843,[92] the Chinese inflicted a crushing defeat on the Uighurs at the Sha-hu (Kill the Barbarians) Mountain. The Wu-chieh Qaghan was wounded and fled, and the Princess of T'ai-ho was rescued by the Chinese troops. She reached Ch'ang-an on Apr.4,[93] and there received the new title of Senior

[91] *Tzu-chih t'ung-chien* p.7961 records this appointment also under the date of June 26.

[92] By *Tzu-chih t'ung-chien* p.7972 correctly dated 1st month, *keng-tzu*. *Chiu T'ang shu* 18A:7b has 2nd month, which did not have these cyclical characters.

[93] By *Chiu T'ang shu* 18A:8a correctly dated 3rd month, *keng-yin*. By *Tzu-chih t'ung-chien* p.7974 dated 2nd month, which did not have these cyclical characters.

Grand Princess of An-ting (*Chiu T'ang shu* 18A:7b; *Tzu-chih t'ung-chien* p.7972, 7974).

In 847, the Wu-chieh Qaghan surrendered (*Chiu T'ang shu* 195: 14a), and the northern Chinese border was again secure. His surviving Uighurs moved westward and founded the Kan chou Qhaghanate in the eastern part of the Kan-su Corridor.[94] In the following accounts, some of the qaghans cannot be identified by their qaghanates. It is probable, however, that most of the unspecified missions came from Kan chou. These were not resumed on a regular basis until the Five Dynasties.

In the 11th month (December) of 875, a Uighur envoy offered gifts. The Uighurs were paid 10,000 bolts of pongee (*Tzu-chih t'ung-chien* p.8181).

On June 4, 902, Uighur envoys offered gifts and military assistance against the rebels. Emperor Chao-tsung sent a Han-lin scholar to follow up the matter (*Tzu-chih t'ung-chien* p.8573). But this was moot, as the T'ang dynasty fell in 907.

In the 5th month (May/June) of 909, a Uighur envoy to the Later Liang court offered gifts. Emperor T'ai-tsu gave him presents (*Ts'e-fu yüan-kuei* p.5034).

In the 11th month (Nov./Dec.) of 911, a Uighur envoy to the Later Liang court offered gifts.[95] T'ai-tsu appointed him a Supernumerary General-in-chief of the Guards Inspecting the Gates of the Right. His fellow envoys received similar supernumerary military titles. All were presented with silken fabrics and purple robes. A Chinese envoy accompagnied them back to their territory (*Chiu Wu-tai shih* 138:4a; *Wu-tai hui-yao* 28:2b; *Ts'e-fu yüan-kuei* p.5034).[96]

In the 12th month (Dec./Jan., 912)[97] of the Chinese year 911, a Tibetan and a Uighur chief were received in audience at the Later Liang court. The two chiefs and their 122 attendants prostrated themselves and presented letters and regional objects. They received gold and silk (*Wu-tai hui-yao* 30:2a; *Ts'e-fu yüan-kuei* p. 5034).

---

[94] The territory had since Former Han times been the Chang-yeh commandery. The Northern Wei and later the T'ang changed its name to Kan chou (Kan commandery).

[95] *Hsin Wu-tai shih* 74:9b remarks that the court historians had not noted the name of the ruler.

[96] By *Ts'e-fu yüan-kuei* dated 11th month (Dec./Jan., 913) of the Chinese year 912.

[97] *Wu-tai hui-yao* has 11th month (Nov./Dec.).

On Apr.3, 918, Uighur envoys to the Khitan court presented coral trees (*Liao shih* 1:10a-10b; 70:1b).[98]

On May 24, 924, two envoys with a mission of 66 men to the Later T'ang court presented regional objects, jade, and nine fine horses. They had been sent by the Uighur ruler of Kan chou, who called himself Qaghan Who Is Authoritative and Knowledgeable. Emperor Chuang-tsung summoned the envoys to the palace. He then sent the Minister of Agriculture and the Junior Court Architect to recognize the ruler of Kan chou as Qaghan Who Is Brave and Righteous (*Chiu Wu-tai shih* 31:9a; 138:4a-4b; *Ts'e-fu yüan-kuei* p.5034; Wen-hsien t'ung-k'ao 347:30a).

In the 9th month (October) of 924, Uighur envoys to the Khitan court offered gifts (Liao shih 2:5a).

On Nov.30, 924, a Uighur envoy informed the Later T'ang court that the qaghan of Kan chou had died and had been succeeded by a younger brother. The latter presented jade lumps, racehorses etc. (*Chiu Wu-tai shih* 32:8b; 138:4b; *Ts'e-fu yüan-kuei* p.5034; *Wen-hsien t'ung-k'ao* 347:30a).

On Dec.21, 924, a Uighur envoy was received at the Later T'ang court (*Hsin Wu-tai shih* 5:8a).

On May 6, 925, the Wu-wu-chu Qaghan offered gifts to the Khitan court (*Liao shih* 2:5b).

On Mar.15, 926, envoys from Kan chou to the Later T'ang court annnounced that the qaghan had died and had been replaced by a new one, whose relation to the ruling house, if any, is unknown. The envoys offered fine horses (*Chiu Wu-tai shih* 34:2a; 138:4b; *Ts'e-fu yüan-kuei* p.5034; *Wen-hsien t'ung-k'ao* 347:30a).

On Jan.27, 928, Uighurs offered gifts to the Later T'ang court (*Hsin Wu-tai shih* 6:6a; *Ts'e-fu yüan-kuei* p.5034)

The new qaghan of Kan chou did not survive for long. He was succeeded and perhaps overthrown by another Qaghan Who Is Authoritative and Knowledgable. On Mar.16, 928,[99] a mission of 128 men[100] from him to the Later T'ang court offered gifts. Emperor Ming-tsung received the envoys in audience and gave them presents, to each in accordance with his rank. On May 22,[101] Ming-tsung ordered

[98] By 70:1b misdated 3rd month.

[99] By *Hsin Wu-tai shih* 74:10a and *Wen-hsien t'ung-k'ao* 347:30a dated 927.

[100] *Wu-tai hui-yao* says 20 men and *Ts'e-fu yüan-kuei* 18 men.

[101] By *Chiu Wu-tai shih* 39:6a dated 5th month, *yi-ssu*. 138:4b has 3rd month

his own envoys to recognize the ruler of Kan chou as Qaghan Who Favours Civilization (*Chiu Wu-tai shih* 39:6a; 138:4b; *Hsin Wu-tai shih* 6:6b; *Wu-tai hui-yao* 28:9a *Ts'e-fu yüan-kuei* p.5034; *Wen-hsien t'ung-k'ao* 347:30a).

In the 12th month (Jan./Feb., 929) of the Chinese year 928, Uighurs offered gifts to the Later T'ang court (*Ts'e-fu yüan-kuei* p.5034).

On Mar.5, 929, a mission of five men from the qaghan of Kan chou was received at the Later T'ang court. All were appointed Managers of Lances (*Chiu Wu-tai shih* 138:4b; *Hsin Wu-tai shih* 6:7b; *Wu-tai hui-yao* 28:9a).

In June 13, 930, Uighurs offered gifts to the Later T'ang court. On June 16, Uighurs again offered gifts (*Hsin Wu-tai shih* 6:8b; *Ts'e-fu yüan-kuei* p.5035).

On June 20, 930, the Uighur qaghan of Kan chou offered gifts to the Later T'ang court (*Chiu Wu-tai shih* 41: 7a-7b; *Ts'e-fu yüan-kuei* p.5035).

On Jan.19, 931, a Uighur mission of 30 men from the qaghan of Kan chou to the Later T'ang court offered 80 horses and one jade lump (*Chiu Wu-tai shih* 41:13a; 138:4b; *Hsin Wu-tai shih* 6:9b).

On Jan.26, 932, a Uighur envoy to the Later T'ang court offered gifts (*Hsin Wu-tai shih* 6:10a *Ts'e-fu yüan-kuei* p.5035).

On Mar.6, 932, envoys from the Qaghan Who Favours Civilization, i.e. the ruler of Kan chou, to the Later T'ang court offered gifts (*Hsin Wu-tai shih* 6:10b; *Ts'e-fu yüan-kuei* p.5035).

On Aug.14, 933, a Uighur mission of 30 men[102] to the Later T'ang court presented a white falcon. Ming-tsung summoned the envoys to an audience and rewarded them liberally. He released the falcon (*Chiu Wu-tai shih* 138:4b-5a; *Hsin Wu-tai shih* 6:11a; *Wu-tai hui-yao* 28: 9b; *Ts'e-fu yüan-kuei* p.5035).

In the 1st month (Jan./Feb.) of 934, envoys from the newly enthroned Uighur qaghan of Kan chou to the Later T'ang court offered horse trappings and other testamentary gifts of his late predecessor. He presented on his own two jade lumps, horse trappings, uncut gems, goral horns, valuable Persian textiles, and a jade belt (*Ts'e-fu yüan-kuei* p.5035).

On Aug.6, 935, a Uighur mission of 78 men[103] to the Later T'ang

(Mar./Apr.), but that month did not have the cyclical characteres in question.

[102] *Ts'e-fu yüan-kuei* says 31 men.

[103] *Wu-tai hui-yao* says 70 men.

court offered 360 horses, 20 jade lumps, white cotton fabrics, yak tails, wild horse leather, and wild camels (*Chiu Wu-tai shih* 138:5a; *Hsin Wu-tai shih* 7:5a; *Wu-tai hui-yao* 28:9b; *Ts'e-fu yüan-kuei* p.5035).

In the 8th month (September) of 935, envoys from the Uighur qaghan of Kan chou to the Later T'ang court offered regional objects. The envoys were given the titles of General of the Gentlemen, Guard of the Staircase, and Manager of Lances (*Chiu Wu-tai shih* 47:8a; 138: 5a; *Wu-tai hui-yao* 28:9b).

On May 18, 936, Emperor T'ai-tsung of the Khitan presented Uighur envoys with garments, each in accordance with his rank (*Liao shih* 3:8b).

On Oct.30, 937, Uighurs offered gifts to the Khitan court. On Nov.6, Uighur envoys congratulated on the birthday of the Khitan Empress Dowager (widow of T'ai-tsu). On Nov.8, T'ai-tsung ordered the chief envoy to report on Uighur customs (*Liao shih* 3:12a).

On Apr.17, 938, the Uighur qaghan of Kan chou offered to the Later Chin court wild horses, dromedaries, jade horse trappings, uncut gems, goral horns, white sable furs, white cotton fabrics from An-hsi, yak tails, wild camels etc. (*Hsin Wu-tai shih* 8:5a; *Ts'e-fu yüan-kuei* p.5035).

In the 10th month (Oct./Nov.) of 938,[104] a Uighur envoy to the Later Chin court presented 100 horses and 12 camels. He was appointed General-in-chief . His deputy was made a General (*Chiu Wu-tai shih* 138:5a; *Ts'e-fu yüan-kuei* p.5035).

On Mar.16, 939, envoys from the Uighur qaghan of Kan chou to the Later Chin court offered regional objects, a jade lion, 100 fine horses, horse trappings, cotton fabrics, white sable furs, yak tails, a horse-like animal, and rare commodities. Emperor Kao-tsu responded by sending an envoy on May 1 to recognize him as Qaghan Who Upholds Civilization (*Chiu Wu-tai shih* 78:3a, 3b; 138:5a; *Hsin Wu-tai shih* 8:7a; *Ts'e-fu yüan-kuei* p.5035).

On May 28, 939, a Uighur shan-yü (>qaghan) requested recognition from the Khitan court (*Liao shih* 4:3b).

On Feb.8, 940, a knife fight broke out among the members of a Uighur mission to the Khitan court. They were ordered to hand over the culprits for punishment (*Liao shih* 4:4a).

In the 1st month (Feb./Mar.) of 940, the Uighur envoys to the

[104] By *Hsin Wu-tai shih* 8:6b dated 9th month (Sep./Oct.).

Khitan court requested permission to watch the ceremony in which the envoys from various states were received in audience. This was allowed (*Liao shih* 4:4a).

On Feb.26, 940,[105] envoys from the Uighur qaghan of Kan chou thanked Kao-tsu of Later Chin for his recgnition of their ruler and offered 100 fine horses, 100 lumps of white jade, horse trappings etc. (*Chiu Wu-tai shih* 138:5a-5b; *Hsin Wu-tai shih* 8:7b; *Ts'e-fu yüan-kuei* p.5035).

At the Dragon Boat Festival of June 13, 940, T'ai-tsung of the Khitan gave a banquet for the officials and for the envoys from the various countries. He ordered the two envoys from the Uighurs and from Tun-huang (Sha chou) to perform their native dances so that all the envoys might see them (*Liao shih* 4:4b-5a).

In the 3rd month (April) of 941, Uighur envoys to the Khitan court were presented with banners, bows, swords, garments, and horses (*Liao shih* 4:6b).

On Nov.30, 942, Uighur envoys were received at the Later Chin court (*Hsin Wu-tai shih* 9:2b).

On Sep.11, 944, Uighur envoys to the Khitan court requested a marriage. T'ai-tsung rejected it (*Liao shih* 4:10b).

In the 2nd month (Mar./Apr.) of 945, a Uighur qaghan presented to the Later Chin court jade lumps, jade horse trappings, uncut gems, red salt, white cotton fabrics from An-hsi, castoreum, goral horns, yak tails, sable furs etc. (*Ts'e-fu yüan-kuei* p.5036).

On July 15, 945, Uighurs offered gifts to the Khitan court (*Liao shih* 4:12a; 70:5b).

On Feb.12, 946, Uighurs offered gifts to the Khitan court (*Liao shih* 4:12b).

On Mar.20, 946, Uighur envoys to the Later Chin court offered gifts (*Chiu Wu-tai shih* 84:7b; *Hsin Wu-tai shih* 9:7a).

On June 20, 948, a Uighur envoy to the Later Han court offered 120 horses, jade horse trappings, 73 jade lumps, 127 pieces of white cotton fabrics, 225 sable furs, 148 yak tails, goral horns, uncut gems, various drugs etc. In the 7th month (Aug./Sep.) the envoy was by Emperor Yin appointed as General-in-chief, and his two deputies and assistant as Generals (*Chiu Wu-tai shih* 101:6b; 138:5b; *Ts'e-fu yüan-kuei* p.5036).

---

[105] By *Ts'e-fu yüan-kuei* dated 5th month (June/July).

On July 17, 949, Uighur envoys to the Later Han court offered regional objects (*Chiu Wu-tai shih* 102:4b).

In the 2nd month (Mar./Apr.) of 951, a Uighur envoy to the Later Chou court offered 77 jade lumps, 350 pieces of white cotton fabrics, 28 blue and black sable furs, one jade belt, jade horse trappings, 424 yak tails, 20 large pieces of amber, 300 catties of red salt, and 390 catties of tree tears (resin). Drugs were presented but not included in the inventory (*Chiu Wu-tai shih* 111:3b; *Ts'e-fu yüan-kuei* p.5036).

Even though their empire had collapsed in 840, Uighur merchants had remained a fixture and financial force in the Chinese capitals. The Later Chin and Later Han dynasties had attempted to make their trade a government monopoly and to impose punishment on the people who dealt with them directly. Emperor T'ai-tsu of Later Chou (r.952-954) abolished this regulation and allowed the Uighurs to trade privately. As a result, the price of jade fell (*Chiu Wu-tai shih* 138:5b).

On Apr.15, 952, Uighur envoys to the Later Chou court offered three jade lumps, 20 coral trees, 50 catties of amber, sable furs, coarse woolen stuffs, white cotton fabrics, leather boots, etc. The jade was rejected (*Chiu Wu-tai shih* 112:4b-5a; *Wu-tai hui-yao* 28:10b; *Ts'e-fu yüan-kuei* p.5036).

On Nov.15, 952, Uighur envoys to the Liao court of the Khitan offered gifts (*Liao shih* 6:2a).

On Feb.21, 953, Uighur envoys to the Later Chou court offered 770 pieces of white cotton fabrics, one jade lump, and 70 corals (*Chiu Wu-tai shih* 112:13b; *Ts'e-fu yüan-kuei* p.5036).

On Feb.8., 954, Uighurs offered gifts to the Liao court (*Liao shih* 6:3a).

On Mar.12, 954, Uighurs offered valuable jade to the Later Chou court (*Ts'e-fu yüan-kuei* p.5036; *Hsin Wu-tai shih* 12:1b).

On June 27, 954, Uighurs offered regional objects to the Later Chou court (*Ts'e-fu yüan-kuei* p.5036; *Hsin Wu-tai shih* 12:2b).

On May 27, 955, Uighur envoys to the Later Chou court offered regional objects (*Chiu Wu-tai shih* 115:4b).

In the 2nd month (Mar./Apr.) of 956, Uighur envoys to the Later Chou court offered regional objects (*Ts'e-fu yüan-kuei* p.5036).

In the 4th month (Apr./May) of 958, Uighur envoys were received at the Later Chou court (*Hsin Wu-tai shih* 12:5a).

On Apr.14, 959, Uighur envoys from Kan chou to the Later Chou court offered jade, uncut gems, etc. All were rejected (*Chiu Wu-tai shih* 138:5b; *Hsin Wu-tai shih* 12:5b; *Ts'e-fu yüan-kuei* p.5036).

In late 961 or early 962, envoys from the Uighur qaghhan of Kan chou to the Sung court offered regional objects (*Sung shih* 1:11a; 490: 13a; *Wen-hsien t'ung-k'ao* 347:30a).

On May 19, 962, a mission of 42 Uighurs[106] to the Sung court offered regional objects (*Sung shih* 1:12a; *Sung hui yao kao*, ts'e 197:1b; *Wen-hsien t'ung-k'ao* 347:30a).

In the 1st month (Feb./Mar.) of 964, Uighur envoys to the Sung court offered 100 jade lumps, 40 catties of amber,[107] 61 yak tails, 110 sable furs, 535 jade pearls, 125 pieces of broken jade, 65 horses, 19 racehorses, etc. (*Sung shih* 1:17a; 490:13a; *Sung hui-yao kao* ts'e 197: 1b; *Wen-hsien t'ung-k'ao* 347:30b).

On May 8, 965, a Uighur mission of 47 men to the Sung court offered 100 jade lumps,[108] 229 catties of amber, two lumps of white stone, four bags of uncut gems, 40 red and white yak tails, 50 sable furs, 50 pieces of coarse woolen stuffs, 30 pieces of white cotton fabrics, jade horse trappings, 10 horses, and 70 racehorses (*Sung shih* 2:1b; 490: 13a; *Sung hui-yao kao* ts'e 197:1b-2a; *Wen-hsien t'ung-k'ao* 347:30b).

On Dec.5, 965, a Buddhist priest sent by the Uighur qaghan of Kan chou to the Sung court presented a tooth of the Buddha, opaque glass vessels, and amber cups (*Sung shih* 2:2b; *Sung hui-yao kao* ts'e 197: 2a).

On Jan.16., 966, envoys from the Uighur qaghan of Kan chou to the Sung court offered 40 catties of uncut gems, eight branches of coral, 1000 bolts of coarse woolen stuffs, jade belts, jade horse trappings etc., and, together with Khotan and others, 1000 horses, 500 camels,[109] 500 jade lumps, and 500 catties of amber (*Sung shih* 2:2b-3a; *Sung hui-yao kao* ts'e 197: 2a; *Wen-hsien t'ung-k'ao* 337:41b).

In the 11th month (Nov./Dec.) of 968, Uighurs from Kan chou to the Sung court offered camels and regional objects (*Sung hui-yao kao* ts'e 197:2a).

Some time in 968, a Uighur chief minister offered horses to the Sung court (*Sung hui-yao kao* ts'e 197:2a).

On Dec.29, 969, Uighur envoys to the Sung court offered gifts. They also traded in the Ning-hsia Oasis (*Hsü Tzu-chih t'ung-chien ch'ang-pien* p.91).

---

[106] *Sung shih* says 41 men.

[107] *Sung hui-yao kao* says 229 catties and *Wen-hsien t'ung-k'ao* 10 catties.

[108] *Sung hui-yao kao* says seven lumps.

[109] *Sung hui-yao kao* says 500 race horses.

On July 8, 971, Uighur envoys to the Liao court offered gifts (*Liao shih* 8:2b).

In the winter of 976, Emperor T'ai-tsung of Sung sent an envoy to Kan chou to present vessels and silk (*Sung hui-yao kao* ts'e 197:2a).

In 977, a Uighur envoy was received at the Sung court. T'ai-tsung ordered that a sister's son of the Uighur qaghan of Kan chou be paid vessels and silk for fine horses and beautiful jade (*Sung shih* 490:13a; *Wen-hsien t'ung-k'ao* 347:30b).

On July 19, 977, Uighur envoys to the Liao court offered gifts (*Liao shih* 9:1a).

On May 15, 980, four envoys from the Uighur qaghan of Kan chou to the Sung court offered camels, fine horses, corals, and amber (*Sung shih* 4:12b; 490:13b; *Wen-hsien t'ung-k'ao* 347:30b).

In 987, Uighur envoys to the Sung court offered *t'ou* stones (*Sung hui-yao kao* ts'e 197:2b; *Sung-shih* 490:13b).

In the 9th month (Oct./Nov.) of 988, Uighurs offered gifts to the Sung court. They received brocade robes and silver belts (*Sung hui-yao kao* ts'e 197:2b; *Wen-hsien t'ung-k'ao* 347:30b).

On Mar.12, 989, Uighurs offered gifts to the Liao court (*Liao, shih* 12:5a).

In the 9th month (Oct./Nov.) of 989, Uighurs offered gifts to the Sung court. They were presented with brocade robes and silver belts (*Sung shih* 490:13b).

On Feb.28, 990, Uighur envoys to the Liao court offered gifts (*Liao shih* 13:1a).

On Dec.31, 990, Uighurs offered gifts to the Liao court (*Liao shih* 13:2a).

On May 21, 991, Uighurs offered gifts to the Liao court (*Liao shih* 13:2b).

On Nov.29, 992, Uighurs offered gifts to the Liao court (*Liao shih* 13:3b).

On Apr.8, 993, Uighurs offered gifts to the Liao court (*Liao shih* 13:3b).[110]

On Apr.1, 994, Uighurs offered gifts to the Liao court (*Liao shih* 13:4b).

In the 6th month (July/Aug.) of 994, Uighur envoys to the Liao court offered gifts (*Liao shih* 70:9a).

---

[110] By 70:9a dated 1st month (Jan./Feb.).

In the 10th month (Oct./Nov.) of 995, the qaghan of Kan chou offered regional objects to the Sung court (*Sung hui-yao kao* ts'e 197: 2b).

On Nov.3. 995, Uighurs offered gifts to the Liao court (*Liao shih* 13:6b).

In 996, the Uighur qaghan of Kan chou offered gifts to the Sung court (*Wen-hsien t'ung-k'ao* 347:30b).

On Mar.11, 996, Mar.29,[111] in the 6th month (June/July), and on Aug.6, 996, Uighurs offered gifts to the Liao court (*Liao shih* 13:7a, 7b; 70:9b).

In the 4th month (Apr./May) of 998, a Buddhist priest and other envoys from the qaghan of Kan chou to the Sung court offered gifts (*Sung hui-yao kao* ts'e 197:2b).

In the 12th month (Dec./Jan., 999) of the Chinese year 998, the Uighur qaghan of Kan-chou offered gifts to the Sung court (*Sung shih* 6:6a).

In the 12th month (Jan./Feb., 1001) of the Liao year 1000, Uighurs offered gifts to the Liao court (*Liao shih* 14:2a).

On Feb.7, 1001, Uighurs offered a Buddhist priest and a famous physician to the Liao court (*Liao shih* 14:2b).

In the 4th month (Apr./May) of 1001, an envoy from the Uighur qaghan Lu-sheng to the Sung court offered jade horse trappings, fine horses, dromedaries and humpless camels, iron swords and armour, and precious vessels of opaque glass. The envoy was appointed General-in-chief of the Army of Divine Warlikeness of the Left, and the qaghan was presented with vessels and garments (*Sung shih* 6:13a; 490: 13b-14a; *Wen-hsien t'ung-k'ao* 347:30b).

In the 9th month (Sep./Oct.) of 1004, a mission of 29 men from the Uighur qaghan of Kan chou to the Sung court offered gifts (*Sung shih* 490:14a; *Sung hui-yao kao* ts'e 197:3a; *Wen-hsien t'ung-k'ao* 347:30b).

In the autumn of 1004, the Uighurs living in the Western Capital (Lo-yang) were forbidden by the Sung government to trade privately (*Sung hui-yao kao* ts'e 197:3a).

On May 30, 1005,[112] Uighurs offered gifts to the Liao court (*Liao shih* 14:6a).

---

[111] Correcting *yi-yu* to *chi-yu*.

[112] *Liao shih* 14:6a has 2nd month *ting-mao*, 70:11b 3rd month. The 2nd month did not have the cyclical characters in question, so that 3rd month = May 30 is correct.

In 1007, the Uighur qaghan of Kan chou sent the Manichaean Fa-hsien and another envoy to the Sung court to present ten horses. Fa-hsien was allowed to travel to the Wu-t'ai Mountain in northern Shan-hsi. The qaghan furthermore sent a Buddhist priest to present 15 horses. He wished to build a Buddhist temple in the Chinese capital, which was denied (*Sung shih* 490:14a; *Sung hui-yao kao* ts'e 197: 3b; *Wen-hsien t'ung-k'ao* 347:30b).

In the 4th month (May/June) of 1008, envoys from the Uighur qaghan of Kan chou to the Sung court offered gifts. Emperor Chen-tsung presented the qaghan with aromatics and golden belts and his mother, the Princess of Pao-wu, with golden vessels (*Sung shih* 490:14b; *Sung hui-yao kao* ts'e 197:4a; *Wen-hsien t'ung-k'ao* 347:30b).

In the 9th month (October) of 1008, the qaghan of Kan chou presented a letter to Chen-tsung (*Sung hui-yao kao* ts'e 197:4a).

In the 11th month (December) of 1008, envoys from the the Princesses of Pao-wu and Mo-ku[113] and from the chief minister [of Kan chou] to the Sung court offered gifts (*Sung hui-yao kao* ts'e 197:4a).

In the 12th month (Dec./Jan., 1009) of the Chinese year 1008, Chen-tsung recognized the qaghan of Kan chou as Qaghan King Who Is Loyal and Obedient and Maintains Virtue. The Princess of Pao-wu was entitled Princess of Pao-wu Who Is Worthy and Enlightened (*Sung hui-yao kao* ts'e 197:4a).

In the 2nd month (March) of 1009, Chen-tsung appointed the envoy of the qaghan of Kan chou as General Who Brings Repose to the Distance, and the envoy of the Princess of Pao-wu as General of the Gentlemen. Both were presented robes (*Sung hui-yao kao* ts'e 197:4b).

On Dec.14. 1010, a Buddhist priest of the Kan chou Uighurs offered gifts to the Sung court. On Dec.22, the Foreign Relations Office informed Chen-tsung that a Uighur mission of 20 men wished to attend [the sacrifices to Sovereign Earth] in Fen-yin. It was allowed. On Dec.26, one of the envoys was appointed Manager of Lances, and another General of the Gentlemen. On Dec.28, the envoys from the Uighur qaghan of Kan chou to the Sung court offered gifts. On Jan.11, 1011, one of the envoys was made a Palace Servitor and given a robe and silver belt. At about this time, letters from the Princesses of Pao-wu and Mo-ku arrrived at the Sung court (*Sung shih* 7:25b; 490: 14b-15a; *Sung hui-yao kao* ts'e 197:4b).

---

[113] These titles had been conferred by the Sung.

In the 1st month (Feb./Mar.) of 1011, another Uighur envoy from Kan chou also requested permission to the attend the Sacrifices to Sovereign Earth in Fen-yin, and this was allowed. He was given the title of General-in-chief of the Army of Divine Fierceness of the Left and an associate of his was made General of the Gentlemen. Both received caps and belts, vessels, and silk. Chen-tsung performed the sacrifices on Mar.24, 1011. On Mar.25, the envoys from Kan chou offered gifts to him [in Fen-yin]. When they had returned to K'ai-feng, Chen-tsung presented the qaghan of Kan chou with 500 garments, 500 ounces of silver vessels, brocade gowns, and golden belts. The Princess of Pao-wu received 400 garments and 300 ounces of silver vessels, and the chief minister 200 garments and 100 ounces of silver vessels. The envoys were given silver vessels and golden head ornaments (*Sung shih* 8:1b; *Sung hui-yao kao* ts'e 197:5a-5b).

In the 4th month (May/June) of 1011, a Uighur envoy presented a jade belt to Chen-tsung and congratulated on the sacrifices in Fen-yin (*Sung hui-yao kao* ts'e 197:5b).

In the 6th month (July/Aug.) of 1011, a Uighur envoy from Kan chou was by Chen-tsung presented with a brocade robe and silver belt. On his way back, he was robbed. The emperor replaced what had been taken from him (*Sung hui-yao kao* ts'e 197:5b).

On Sep.22, 1011,[114] envoys from the Uighur qaghan of Kan chou announced a victory to the Sung court. The envoys were appointed Managers of Lances and Guards of the Staircase (*Sung shih* 8:3b; 490: 15a; *Sung hui-yao kao* ts'e 197:5b).

On May 31, 1012, envoys from the Uighur qaghan of Kan chou and the Princess of Pao-wu to the Sung court offered camels and horses. On June 6, an envoy from Kan chou presented one jade lump and three horses, while another Uighur offered one horse (*Sung hui-yao kao* ts'e 197:5b).

In the 12th month (Jan./Feb.,1014) of the Chinese year 1013, the Uighur qaghan of Kan chou offered 20 broken-in horses to the Sung court (*Sung shih* 8:8a; 490:15; *Sung hui-yao kao* ts'e 197:6a).

In the 9th month (Oct./Nov.) of 1015, an Interpreter of the Foreign Relations Office returned from Kan chou with a letter from the qaghan in which he sought a marriage and informed the Sung court that the Princess of Pao-wu had died in the 2nd month (Mar./Apr.)

[114] By *Sung hui-yao kao* dated 11th month (Nov./Dec.).

of 1013 (*Sung shih* 490:15b; *Sung hui-yao kao* ts'e 197:6a).

In late 1015, the Uighur qaghan Ho-lo offered gifts to the Sung court (*Sung shih* 8:12b).

On July 11, 1016, Uighurs offered peacocks to the Liao court (*Liao shih* 15:10b).

In 1016, Uighurs from Kan chou informed the Sung court that their qaghan had died (*Sung shih* 490:16a).

In the 3rd month (April) of 1017, Chen-tsung recognized the new Uighur qaghan of Kan chou as Qaghan King Who Cherishes Repose and Favours Civilization and presented him garments, golden belts, vessels, silk and horse trappings (*Sung hui-yao kao* ts'e 197:8a).

In the 2nd month (Feb./Mar.) of 1018, envoys from the Uighur qaghan of Kan chou to the Sung court offered gifts. Chen-tsung gave them ample presents (*Sung shih* 490:16a; *Sung hui-yao kao* ts'e 197:8a; *Wen-hsien t'ung-k'ao* 347:30b).

On Apr.4, 1020, envoys from the Uighur qaghan of Kan chou to the Sung court offered regional objects (*Sung hui-yao kao* ts'e 197:8b).

On Dec.27, 1020, envoys from the Uighurs of Kan chou and from the qaghan and Lion King of Kucha offered big-tailed white sheep to the Sung court (*Sung shih* 8:20b; 490:16a; *Sung hui-yao kao* 1076:3a; ts'e 197:8b).

In the 5th month (May/June) of 1023, envoys from the Uighur qaghan of Kan chou to the Sung court offered regional objects (*Sung shih* 490:16a).

In the 6th month (June/July) of 1023, Emperor Jen-tsung of Sung recognized the qaghan of Kan chou as Qaghan Who Attaches Himself to Loyalty and Maintains Obedience (*Sung shih* 490:16a).

On June 10, 1024, a mission of 14 men from the Uighur qaghan of Kan chou to the Sung court offered three horses, yellow barbarian pongee, and fine white cotton fabrics. The chief minister separately presented two horses (*Sung shih* 490:16a; *Sung hui-yao kao* ts'e 197:8b; *Hsü Tzu-chih t'ung-chien ch'ang-pien* p.904).

In the 2nd month (March) of 1025, Uighurs offered 20 horses to the Sung court (*Sung hui-yao kao* ts'e 197:8b).

In the 4th month (May) of 1025, the qaghan, princess, and chief minister [of Kan chou] offered horses and frankincense to the Sung court. They received silver vessels, golden belts, and brocade gowns, each in accordance with his rank (*Sung shih* 490:16a; *Sung hui-yao kao* ts'e 197:9a).

In the 8th month (Sep./Oct.) of 1027, a mission of 14 men from the Uighur qaghan of Kan chou to the Sung court offered regional objects (*Sung shih* 490:16b).

In the 2nd month (Mar.) of 1028, Uighurs offered regional objects to the Sung court (*Sung shih* 490:16b). That year, Kan chou became a dependency of Hsia.

On Dec.6, 1041, Uighur envoys to the Liao court offered gifts (*Liao shih* 19:2a).

On July 29, 1043, Uighur envoys to the Liao court offered gifts (*Liao shih* 19:4b).

On June 28, 1066, Uighurs offered gifts to the Liao court (*Liao shih* 22:4a).

On August 29, 1068, envoys from the Uighur qaghan of Kan chou to the Sung court offered gifts. They wished to buy the *Mahāprājñāpāramitā* Sutra in Golden Characters. Emperor Shen-tsung presented it to them, but only in black characters (*Sung shih* 14:7a; 490:16b; *Sung hui-yao kao* ts'e 197:9a).

In the 12th month (Dec./Jan., 1072) of the Liao year 1071, Uighurs offered gifts to the Liao court (*Liao shih* 70:20b-21a).

On Nov.30, 1072, Uighurs offered gifts to the Liao court (*Liao shih* 23:1b).

In 1073, Uighurs were received at the Sung court (*Sung shih* 490: 16b).

In the 10th month (Nov./Dec.) of 1073, Uighurs offered gifts to the Liao court (*Liao shih* 70:21a).

In the 6th month (July/Aug.) of 1076, Uighurs offered gifts to the Liao court (*Liao shih* 70:21a).

On July 3, 1077, Uighurs offered gifts to the Liao court (*Liao shih* 23:5b).

On Dec.25, 1078, Uighur envoys to the Liao court offered gifts (*Liao shih* 23:6b).

On Dec.6, 1080, Uighur envoys to the Liao court offered gifts (*Liao shih* 24:2b).

On Mar. 7, 1089, Uighur envoys to the Liao court offered fine horses (*Liao shih* 25:3a).

In the 5th month (June/July) of 1089, Uighur envoys to the Liao court offered fine horses (*Liao shih* 70:22b).

On July 2, 1091, Uighur envoys to the Liao court offered regional objects (*Liao shih* 25:4a).

On July 19, 1091, Uighur envoys to the Liao court offered rare objects. These were not accepted, but the envoys received ample presents (*Liao shih* 25:4a).

On Jan.14, 1114, Uighur envoys to the Liao court offered gifts (*Liao shih* 27:7b).

On Mar.11, 1127, envoys from the Uighur qaghan Ho-li to the Chin court of the Jurchen offered gifts (*Chin shih* 3:9b).

On Nov.20, 1127, envoys from the Huo-la-san Qaghan of the Uighurs to the Chin court offered gifts (*Chin shih* 3:10b).

On Sep.10, 1131, Uighur envoys to the Chin court offered gifts (*Chin shih* 3:15b).

On Sep. 15, 1138, Uighur envoys to the Chin court offered gifts (*Chin shih* 4:3b).

On July 27, 1142, Uighur envoys to the Chin court offered gifts (*Chin shih* 4:8b).

On Mar.21, 1144, Uighur envoys to the Chin court congratulated (*Chin shih* 4:9b).

On Jan.27, 1153, the emperor of Chin did not personally hold court. He ordered the high officials to receive the envoys from the Uighurs and others and accept their gifts (*Chin shih* 5:9a).

On Nov.29, 1156, a Uighur envoy to the Chin court offered gifts (*Chin shih* 5:15a).

In the 3rd (Mar./Apr.) and 4th month (Apr./May) of 1172, Uighur envoys to the Chin court offered gifts (*Chin shih* 7:2a).

The relation of the Uighurs to the Chinese was unique. They had been their allies against the Eastern and Western Turks and then saved the T'ang dynasty from An Lu-shan's rebellion in 755. But they exacted a price for it. While the alliance lasted until the collapse of the Uighur empire in 840, the Uighurs were the stronger partner. The Uighur qaghans considered themselves rightly the equals of the Chinese emperors, if not more so, and this self-confidence was shared by the Uighurs in general. Their envoys rioted in Ch'ang-an in 763, 771, 772, 774, and twice in 775. Minor Chinese officials tried to face up to them but Emperor Tai-tsung did not. From 757, the T'ang paid an annual tribute to the Uighurs of 20,000 bolts of pongee. That was not a large amount, compared to what the Sung later had to pay the Liao and Chin states. More importantly, the Uighurs foisted their horses on the T'ang at the average price of 40 bolts of silk. This trade was on the government level, conducted by Uighur envoys. The Chinese had their own pastures for breeding horses in the northwest and had no great need to import them as well. Not only did the Chinese have to buy several tens of thousands of horses a year, but these according to the sources were of poor quality. That is not unlikely, since the Uighurs not only had the upper hand but also were smart businessmen. In 781, the T'ang court owed the Uighurs 1,800,000 strings of cash for their horses. In 765 it paid 100,000 bolts of silk, in 782 100,000 bolts, in 787 50,000 bolts, in 790 300,000 bolts, in 792 70,000 bolts, in 822 120,000 bolts, in 827 700,000 bolts, and in 829 230,000 bolts. That adds up to 1,670,000 bolts or about 41,750 horses. Even if this included silk owed for earlier years, the expense was a burden to the T'ang. In fact, Emperor Tai-tsung had to dock the salaries of the court officials for three month in 765 in order to come up with the required amount. The Chinese were not fond of the Uighurs, but they knew that, whatever the cost, they had to be appeased.

The sources record that the T'ang court was suspended for mourning after the deaths of qaghans in 789, 790, 795, 808, 821, and 833. In 791, the court was suspended for mourning after the death of the Junior Princess of Ning-kuo. In 789, 821, and 833, officials were ordered to condole with the Uighur envoys at the Ministry of the Grand Herald. Chinese envoys condoled in Karabalghasun after the deaths of five qaghans in 759, 779, 821,824, and 833. They recognized eleven qaghans in 744, 758, 763, 780 (repeated in 787), 789, 791, 795, 808, 821, 824, and 833, and six of the of Kan chou qaghans in 924, 928, 939, 1008, 1017, and 1023. They once condoled at the death of a qatun in 768. This list is almost certainly incomplete.

The T'ang is not recorded to have conferred posthumous titles on Uighur qaghans,[115] and that may be a historical fact. The qaghans might have considered it an affrontery. A posthumous title was granted to the Princess of Hsien-an, the wife of four qaghans, in 808, but she was Chinese.

It stands to reason that the Chinese routinely informed the Uighurs about the deaths of all emperors, as the Uighurs did in reverse for their qaghans. But the texts omit to mention these instances, except that Te-tsung announced the death of his father Tai-tsung in 779. This gives the false impression that the Uighurs had to follow a protocol which did not apply to the Chinese.

The most important evidence of the subservience of the Chinese to the Uighurs is dynastic marriages. The Chinese used this device to

[115] It did confer posthumous titles on early Uighur chiefs in 648 and 719.

establish better relations with foreign rulers. Usually, a lady descending from the imperial house[116] who was not a princess in her own right was given that title and then sent off as a bride. The husbands were mostly aware of the subterfuge but did not object. But in the case of the Uighurs, no less than three imperial daughters became qatuns. The Princess of Ning-kuo in 758 was the second daughter of Su-tsung, the Princess of Hsien-an in 788 the eighth daughter of Te-tsung, and the Princess of T'ai-ho in 821 the seventeenth daughter of Hsien-tsung. It is true that the Princess of Ning-kuo had been married at least once before[117] and no longer was in her first youth.[118] The marriage was still a coup for the Uighurs and a shame to the Chinese.[119] In 758 and 788, the Chinese gave in quickly. They tried to resist the third time until the Uighurs in 820 simply demanded an imperial daughter. The wedding of the Princess of Hsien-an in 788 must have rankled Te-tsung in particular, since he was the emperor who hated the Uighurs most.

Te-tsung's rancor stemmed from his meeting with the Teng-li Qaghan in 762, who at that occasion had invited him to dance. He had refused, supported by officials in his entourage. The qaghan had thereupon put four Chinese to the rod, two of whom had died from it during the following night. The Chinese historians naturally look on this episode with disapproval. What is overlooked is the fact that ceremonial or native dancing was part of festive occasions. In the early 590's, Mo-ho envoys danced at a banquet given by Emperor Wen of Sui. When T'ai-tsung gave a banquet in Ch'ang-an in 634, he requested the captured Hsieh-li Qaghan of the Eastern Turks to dance. At a banquet of Uighur chiefs and Kuo Tzu-yi in 765, the chiefs danced. At a banquet given by the Liao court in 940, two envoys from the Uighurs and from Tun-huang (Sha chou) were asked by T'ai-tsung to perform their native dances. In 1112, Emperor T'ien-tso of Liao invited Jurchen chiefs dance. The Teng-li Qaghan may therefore have requested what was normal and perhaps even a courtesy, and, if this is so, it was he who was insulted and took revenge.

---

[116] But also girls of other families, such as the two daughters of P'u-ku Huai-en.

[117] Cf. Mackerras, *Uighur Empire*, p.133 note 49.

[118] Since her father was born in 711, she must have been in her late twenties.

[119] The dynastic historians nevertheless maintain the fiction that the Chinese did the Uighurs a favour and that the princesses were "sent down" as wives.

The Uighur missions served a number of purposes, such as discussing military strategy, announcing a victory, presenting prisoners, arranging a marriage, welcoming a bride, or announcing a death or enthronement. But by far the most important reason was trade. In 773 alone, Uighur envoys returned to Karabalghasun with their profit laden on 1000 carts.

According to *Hsin T'ang shu* 217A:3a, the Ko-le Qaghan annually sent envoys to the T'ang court. Missions are recorded for 747 (2), 749, 751, 752, 757 (2), 758 (3), and 759. According to *T'ang hui-yao* 98:9b, the Uighurs frequently sent envoys to the T'ang court from 825 to 827. Three missions are recorded for 826. According to *Wen-hsien t'ung-k'ao* 347:30, the Uighurs of Kan chou frequently offered gifts to the Later Chin court from 936 to 942. Missions are recorded for 938 (2), 939, 940, and 942. According to *Sung shih* 490:16b, the Uighurs offered gifts to the Sung court from 1119 to 1125. No missions are recorded. The statistics are therefore fairly but not entirely complete.

The Uighurs preferred the winter and spring for their missions, with well over half of all recorded for these seasons. This was probably because it was easier to move horses during the colder part of the year than in the hot summer and autumn. Also, by the winter the foaling season was over.

This is the distribution by 20-year periods of the 182 missions from the Uighurs to the T'ang, Later Liang, Later T'ang, Later Chin, Later Han, Later Chou, and Sung, the 46 missions to the Khitan/Liao, and the 10 mission to the Chin, 238 in all:

627- 646:	4
647- 666:	4
667- 686:	0
687- 706:	0
707- 726:	1
727- 746:	4
747- 766:	20
767- 786:	17
787- 806:	19
807- 826:	20
827- 846:	9
847- 866:	0
867- 886:	1
887- 906:	1

907- 926:	7	Khitan	3		
927- 946:	19	Khitan	10		
947- 966:	17	Liao	2		
967- 986:	5	Liao	3		
987-1006:	9	Liao	17		
1007-1026:	21	Liao	1		
1027-1046:	2	Liao	1		
1047-1066:	0	Liao	1		
1067-1086:	2	Liao	3		
1087-1106:		Liao	4		
1107-1126:		Liao	1	Chin	1
1127-1146:				Chin	5
1147-1166:				Chin	2
1167-1186:				Chin	2

It can be seen that during the 7th and early 8th centuries, when the Uighurs were a subject people of the Eastern Turks, their chiefs were nevertheless able to send missions to the T'ang court, which the Chinese encouraged by conferring posthumous titles and contributing toward funeral expenses. During the time of the Central Asian empire of the Uighurs, 745-840, missions arrived in great numbers, even as many as three times a year. Then followed a lull until the missions, now chiefly from Kan chou, increased again during the Five Dynasties and Sung. This is all the more remarkable, as the Kan chou Uighurs became politically dependent first on Liao and then from 1028 on Hsia.

Starting with the 10th century, the Uighurs also sent envoys to the Liao court. After the fall of Liao in 1125, the Uighurs dealt with the Chin court and not at all with the Southern Sung. This brings out the fact that the Uighurs, good businessmen as they were, understood how to profit from trade wherever they wished to go, even when they were politically dominated by others.

The specified goods brought by Uighurs embassies to the Chinese courts fall into the following categories:

Humans and Human Products

822: 6 "bed women".
835: 7 female mounted archers, 2 children of the Sha-t'o Turks.
965: one tooth of the Buddha.

Animals and Animal Products

Horses

747: horses.
758: 500 horses.
765: horses.
774: 49 horses.
816: horses.
821: 20,000 horses.
833: horses.
924: 9 fine horses, race horces.
926: fine horses.
930: 80 horses.
935: 360 horses, wild horse leather.
938: wild horses, 100 horses.
939: 100 fine horses.
940: 100 fine horses.
948: 120 horses.
964: 65 horses, 19 race horses.
965: 10 horses, 70 race horses.
966: 1000 horses (with Khotan).
968: horses.
980: fine horses (with Sha chou).
1001: fine horses.
1007: 10 horses, 15 horses.
1012: horses, 3 horses, 1 horse.
1013: 20 broken-in horses.
1024: 3 horses, 2 horses.
1025: 20 horses, horses.

Camels

816: camels.
821: 1000 camels, camel wool.
833: camels.
935: wild camels.
938: dromedaries, wild camels, 12 camels.
966: 500 camels (with Khotan).
968: camels.
980: camels (with Sha chou).

1001: dromedaries, humpless camels.
1012: camels.

Sheep

1020: big-tailed white sheep.

Birds

933: one white falcon.

Furs

758: 100 sable furs.
938: white sable furs.
939: white sable furs.
945: sable furs.
948: 225 sable furs.
951: 29 blue and black sable furs.
964: 110 sable furs.
965: 50 sable furs.

Other

934: goral horns.
935: yak tails.
938: goral horns, yak tails.
939: yak tails, a horse-like animal.
945: goral horns, yak tails.
948: 148 yak tails, goral horns.
951: 424 yak tails.
964: 61 yak tails.
965: 40 red and white yak tails.

Aromatics

Aromatic and medical drugs

948: various drugs.
951: drugs.

Frankincense

1025: frankincense.

Resins

951: tree tears.

Cosmetics

945: castoreum.

Spices

945: red salt.
951: 300 catties of red salt.

Minerals

924: jade, jade lumps.
930: one jade lump.
934: 2 jade lumps.
935: 20 jade lumps.
940: 100 lumps of white jade.
945: jade lumps.
948: 73 jade lumps.
951: 77 jade lumps.
952: 3 jade lumps (rejected).
953: one jade lump.
954: jade.
959: jades.
964: 100 jade lumps, 125 pieces of broken jade.
965: 500 jade lumps (with Khotan), 100 jade lumps, 2 lumps of white stone.
966: 500 jade lumps.
987: *t'ou* stones.
1012: one jade lump.

Manufactured Objects

Of metal

965: valuable vessels.
1001: iron swords and armour.

Of glass

965: opaque glass vessels.
1001: precious vessels of opaque glass.

Of precious stone

938: jade horse trappings.
939: one jade lion.
945: jade horse trappings.
948: jade horse trappings.
951: one jade belt, jade horse trappings.
964: 535 jade pearls.
965: jade horse trappings.
966: jade belts, jade horse trappings.
1001: jade horse trappings.
1011: one jade belt.

Of leather

934: horse trappings.
939: horse trappings.
940: horse trappings.
952: leather boots.

Other

965: amber cups.

Textiles

Cottons

758: white cotton fabrics.
935: white cotton fabrics.
938: white cotton fabrics from An-hsi.

939: cotton fabrics.
945: white cotton fabrics from An-hsi.
948: 127 pieces of white cotton fabrics.
951: 350 pieces of white cotton fabrics.
952: white cotton fabrics.
953: 770 pieces of white cotton fabrics.
965: 30 pieces of white cotton fabrics.
1024: fine white cotton fabrics.

Wool

952: coarse woolen stuffs.
965: 50 pieces of coarse woolen stuffs.
966: 1000 bolts of coarse woolen stuffs.

Silks

1024: yellow barbarian pongee.

Other

934: valuable Persian textiles.

Jewels

918: coral trees.
934: uncut gems.
938: uncut gems.
945: uncut gems,
948: uncut gems.
951: 20 large pieces of amber.
952: 20 coral trees, 50 catties of amber.
953: 70 corals.
959: uncut gems.
964: 40 catties of amber.
965: 229 catties of amber, 2 lumps of white stone, 4 bags of uncut gems.
966: 500 catties of amber (with Khotan), 40 catties of uncut gems, 8 branches of corals.
980: corals, amber (with Sha chou).

Like the Eastern Turks, the chief export of the Uighurs was livestock, in their case horses and camels. The country produced little else. It is also clear that the number of horses is vastly underrecorded. Only seven presentations of horses are mentioned until the collapse of the Uighur empire, although these were forced on the Chinese regularly. It has been seen that in 765, 782, 787, 790, 792, 822, 827, and 829 alone, the T'ang court paid for about 41,750 horses. In contrast, the Uighur missions, chiefly from Kan chou during the Five Dynasties and Sung brought a great variety of goods, including amber, corals, frankincense, and castoreum from far away. The reason is, of course, that Kan chou was situated on the Silk Route and, through the passing caravans, traded with distant lands.

The Chinese paid for these goods with gold, silver, copper cash, silk, brocade robes, garments, caps, gold and silver belts, golden vessels, silver vessels, [porcelain] vessels, and, although not mentioned, undoubtedly also tea.

SHA CHOU

The Tun-huang Oasis at the western end of the Kan-su Corridor owed its wealth to the fact that, travelling east, it was the place where the two Silk Routes met. It was inhabited by a people of mixed Chinese, Tibetan, and Turkic descent. The area had been the Chinese commandery of Tun-huang since Former Han times. The T'ang changed its name to Sha chou (Sha commandery), but the old name continued at times to be used. In the middle of the 8th century, the territory fell under Tibetan domination. In the middle of the 9th century, the Chinese warlord Chang Yi-ch'ao expelled the Tibetans and set up his own principality. It included Kua chou (Kua commandery) immediately northeast of Tun-huang.

In 851, Chang Yi-ch'ao sent a mission to the T'ang court and then visited it himself. The court regarded this as a submission and appointed him a Military Commissioner of the non-existant Army Which Attaches Itself to Righteousness. But in practice, Chang Yi-ch'ao and his successors were independent. (*Wen-hsien t'ung-k'ao* 335:35a).

In the early 10th century, the Chang family died out, and the people elected the Chief Clerk Ts'ao Yi-chin as their ruler. Like the Changs, he was Chinese (*Wen-hsien t'ung-k'ao* 335:35a).

On Mar.14, 926, envoys from Ts'ao Yi-chin of Sha chou to the Later T'ang court offered gifts (*Hsin Wu-tai shih* 5:9a).

In the 12th month (Dec./Jan., 931) of the Chinese year 930, envoys from Ts'ao Yi-chin of Sha chou were received at the Later T'ang court (*Hsin Wu-tai shih* 6:9b).

In the 1st month (Feb./Mar.) of 932, Sha chou presented 75 horses and 36 jade lumps to the Later T'ang court (*Ts'e-fu yüan-kuei* p.5035).

In the 1st month (Jan./Feb.) of 934, envoys from Sha chou were received at the Later T'ang court (*Hsin Wu-tai shih*7:2a).

In the 10th month (Nov./Dec.) of 934, Sha chou offered regional objects to the Later T'ang court (*Ts'e-fu yüan-kuei* p.5035).

In the 7th month (August) of 935, Sha chou offered three horses to the Later T'ang court (*Ts'e-fu yüan-kuei* p.5035).

In the 11th month (Dec./Jan., 940) of the Chinese year 939, Tun-huang (Sha chou) offered gifts to the Liao court (*Liao shih* 70:4b).

At the Dragon Boat Festival of June 13, 940, Emperor T'ai-tsung of the Khitan gave a banquet for the officials and the envoys from the various countries. He ordered the two envoys from the Uighurs and from Tun-huang (Sha chou) to perform their native dances so that all the envoys might see them (*Liao shih* 4:4b-5a).

On Feb.4, 943, envoys from Ts'ao Yüan-chung, son of Yi-chin, were received at the Later Chin court (*Hsin Wu-tai shih* 9:2b).

In 955, Ts'ao Yüan-chung offered gifts to the Later Chou court. He was appointed Military Commissioner, Acting Grand Commandant, and Manager of Affairs of the Palace Writers (*Wen-hsien t'ung-k'ao* 335: 35a).

In 962, the Sung appointed Ts'ao Yüan-chung Prefect of the Palace Writers. His son Yen-lu was made a Defense Commissioner (*Wen-hsien t'ung-k'ao* 335:35a).

In the 11th month (Nov./Dec) of 968, envoys from Sha-chou to the Sung court offered camels and regional objects (*Sung hui-yao kao*, ts'e 197:2a).

In the winter of 977, a Sung envoy to Sha chou presented vessels and silk (*Sung hui-yao kao*, ts'e 197:2a).

On May 15, 980, four envoys sent by Sha chou and the Uighur qaghan of Kan chou to the Sung court offered camels, fine horses, corals, and amber (*Sung shih* 4:12b; 490:13b; *Wen-hsien t'ung-k'ao* 347: 30b).

During the same year of 980, it became known at the Sung court that Ts'ao Yüan-chung had died. His son Yen-lu sent envoys with gifts. Emperor T'ai-tsung conferred on Yüan-chung the posthumous title of king of Tun-huang commandery. Yen-lu was appointed Military Commissioner and his younger brothers Yen-sheng and Yen-jui as Inspector and as Chief Inspector of the Headquarters respectively (*Wen-hsien t'ung-k'ao* 335:35a).

In 999, Sha chou offered gifts (*Sung shih* 6:8b).

In 1001, the Sung recognized Yen-lu as king (*Wen-hsien t'ung-k'ao* 335:35a).

In 1002, Ts'ao Yen-lu and his brother Yen-jui were killed by their nephew Tsung-shou who then took control of Sha chou. He sent envoys to the Sung court to offer gifts. Emperor Chen-tsung appointed him Military Commissioner and his son Hsien-shun Commander-in-chief of the Headquarter. Tsung-shou's younger brother Tsung-yün was made Acting Supervisor of the Left of the Masters of Writing and Administrator, (*Sung shih* 6:16a; *Wen-hsien t'ung-k'ao* 335:35a).

In 1004, Sha chou offered gifts to the Sung court (*Sung shih* 7:7b).

In the 8th month (Aug./Sep.) of 1006,[120] envoys from the king of Sha chou, Ts'ao [Tsung-]shou to the Liao court offered Arabian horses and beautiful jade, for which they received garments, silver vessels, and other objects (*Liao shih* 14:7a).

In 1006, Emperor Sheng-tsung of Liao recognized Ts'ao [Tsung-]shou as king of Sha chou.[121]

In 1007, Sha chou offered gifts to the Sung court (*Sung shih* 9:15b).

Ts'ao Tsung-shou died in about 1014. The Sung appointed his son and successor Ts'ao Hsien-shun as Military Commissioner and his younger brother Hsien-hui as Acting Master of Writing of the Ministry of Punishments. Hsien-shun requested from the Sung court the *Tripitaka in Golden Chacters*, brick tea, and drugs. All were provided (*Wen-hsien t'ung-k'ao* 335:35a-35b).

On May 22, 1014, envoys from the Sha chou Uighur Ts'ao [Hsien-]shun to the Liao court offered gifts (*Liao shih* 15:7b; 70:14a). It is important to note the the terminology of *Liao shih*, showing that by this time Sha chou and its ruling house had been uighurized.

On July 27, 1020, Sheng-tsung of Liao sent envoys to offer garments and other objects to the king of Sha chou Uighurs, Ts'ao [Hsien-]shun (*Liao shih* 16:4b; 70:15a).

---

[120] By *Liao shih* 70:12a dated 6th month (June/July).

[121] This is mentioned in a tomb inscription. See Wittfogel, *Liao*, p.226 note 4.

On Oct.16, 1020, envoys of the Sha chou Uighurs to the Liao court offered gifts (*Liao shih* 16:4b; 70:15a).

In 1023, envoys from Ts'ao Hsien-shun to the Sung court offered frankincense, uncut gems, and jade lumps (*Sung shih* 9:4b; *Wen-hsien t'ung-k'ao* 335:35b).

On Feb.5, 1031, Sha chou offered gifts to the Sung court (*Sung shih* 9:14a; *Hsü Tzu-chih t'ung-chien ch'ang-pien* p.979).

From 1034 to1054, Sha chou seven times offered regional objects to the Sung court (*Wen-hsien t'ung-k'ao* 335:35b).

In 1037, Sha chou offered gifts to the Sung court (*Sung shih* 9:4b).

In 1050, Sha chou offered gifts to the Sung court (*Sung shih* 12: 2a).

On Nov.1, 1052, Sha-chou envoys to the Sung court offered regional objects (*Hsü Tzu-chih t'ung-chien ch'ang-pien* p.1596).

The rulers of Sha chou traded at first exlusively with the Five Dynasties and Sung, but from the beginning of the 11th century also with Liao. They managed to keep their independence until the middle of that century when they lost it to Hsia. Their recorded merchandise was horses, camels, jade, uncut gems, corals, amber, and frankincense, i.e. not only local products but also goods (corals, amber, frankincense) obtained from far away through the caravans on the Silk Routes. They were paid with tea, drugs, [porcelain] vessels,silk and printed books such as the *Tripitaka*.

THE KIRGHIZ

The Kirghiz (Chieh-ku or Hsia-chia-ssu) lived originally in central Siberia at the upper course of the Yenisei River. After they had destroyed the Uighur empire, they took over the Orkhon region but soon after 900 were pushed back by the Khitan.

In 647, the chief of the Kirghiz came personally to the T'ang court (*T'ung-tien* 200:50a).

In 648, envoys of the Kirghiz to the T'ang court offered regional objects. Emperor T'ai-tsung created out of their territory the imaginary Chien-k'un Area Command and appointed the Kirghiz chief as General-in-chief of the Garrison Guards (*Wen-hsien t'ung-k'ao* 348:32a).

From 650 to 683, the Kirghiz were twice received at the T'ang court (*Wen-hsien t'ung-k'ao* 348:32a).

Between 707 and 710, the Kirghiz offered regional objects (*Wen-hsien t'ung-k'ao* 348:32a).

From 712 to756, the Kirghiz four times offered gifts (*Wen-hsien t'ung-k'ao* 348:32a).

Between 758 and 760, the Kirghiz were crushed by the Uighurs and became their subject tribe. Henceforth, they were unable to send missions to the T'ang (*Wen-hsien t'ung-k'ao* 348:32b).

In 840, the Kirghiz destroyed the Uighur empire and temporarily replaced them as the masters of the steppe (*Wen-hsien t'ung-k'ao* 348: 32b).

On Mar.16, 843, a Kirghiz mission of seven men to the T'ang court presented two fine horses. Emperor Wu-tsung ordered the Grand Coachman to entertain and reward the envoys (*Chiu T'ang shu* 18A: 8a; *T'ang hui-yao* 100:6b; *Tzu-chih t'ung-chien* p.7973).

In the 6th month (July) of 843, an envoy of the Kirghiz qaghan was received at the T'ang court. Wu-tsung sent an envoy of his own to recognize him and invite him to attack the remnants of the Uighurs (*Tzu-chih t'ung-chien* p.7985; *Wen-hsien t'ung-k'ao* 348:32b).

In the 8th month (Aug./Sep.) of 843, a Kirghiz envoy informed the T'ang court that his tribe was moving into the former Uighur territory[122] (*Chiu T'ang shu* 18A:9a; *Ts'e-fu yüan-kuei* p.5033; *Tzu-chih t'ung-chien* p.7999).

In 844, Wu-tsung sent the Grand Coachman and Concurrent Palace Assistant Secretary as his envoy to the Kirghiz (*T'ang hui-yao* 100:6b).

In 846, Wu-tsung intended to recognize the new qaghan of the Kirghiz but died on Apr.22, 846, before the envoy had departed. His successor Emperor Hsüan-tsung (r.847-859) was advised that it was not worthwhile to deal with a rustic and distant little country. After a court discussion, the matter was dropped. But in the following year, 847, Hsüan-tsung had a change of heart and in the 6th month (July/ Aug.) sent the Herald and Concurrent Palace Assistant Secretary to recognize the Kirghiz ruler as Qaghan Who Is Brave, Martial, Sincere, and Bright (*T'ang hui-yao* 100:7b; *Tzu-chih t'ung-chien* p.8030).

From 860 to 874, the Kirghiz were three times received at the T'ang court (*Wen-hsien t'ung-k'ao* 348:32b).

In the 8th month (Sep./Oct.) of 863, a Kirghiz envoy requested that his tribe henceforth send annual missions to the court, i.e. establish

[122] They certainly did not ask permission to do so as claimed by *Tzu-chih t'ung-chien*.

closer trade connections. This was rejected by the T'ang court (*Tzu-chih t'ung-chien* p.8107).

In the 12th month (Jan./Feb., 867) of the Chinese year 866, a Kirghiz envoy offered gifts and begged for the T'ang calendar (*Tzu-chih t'ung-chien* p.8117). This obviously was not a sign of surrender as traditionally interpreted by the Chinese.

The T'ang Office of History had no record of later missions (*Wen-hsien t'ung-k'ao* 348:32b).

In the 1st month (Jan./Feb.) of 931, Kirghiz were received at the Khitan court (*Liao shih* 70:3b).

In the 10th month (Oct./Nov.) of 953, Kirghiz offered gifts to the Liao court of the Khitan (*Liao shih* 70:6a).

In the 12th month (Dec./Jan., 977) of the Liao year 976, Kirghiz envoys to the Liao court offered gifts (*Liao shih* 70:6b).

THE TANG-HSIANG

The Tang-hsiang, like the Tibetans, were Tanguts. Their original habitat was to the southeast of Ch'ing-hai or Kokonor. They were not united but splintered into tribal groups under chiefs, hostile to each other and the Tibetans.

In 596, sons and younger brothers of Tang-hsiang chiefs were received at the Sui court (*Pei shih* 96:22a).

On May 17, 609, Tang-hsiang offered regional objects to Emperor Yang of Sui while he was in the northwest (*Sui shu* 3:13a; *Pei-shih* 12: 13a).

In the 11th month (Dec./Jan., 620) of the Chinese year 619, Tang-hsiang envoys to the T'ang court offered gifts (*Ts'e-fu yüan-kuei* p.5032).

In the 12th month (Dec./Jan., 627) of the Chinese year 626, Tang-hsiang envoys to the T'ang court offered gifts (*Chiu T'ang shu* 2:8a; *Ts'e-fu yüan-kuei* p.5023).

From 627 or soon thereafter, the Tang-hsiang of the Snowy Mountain frequently offered gifts to the T'ang court (*T'ang hui-yao* 98:19a).

In the 11th month (Nov./Dec.) of 631, Tang-hsiang were received at the T'ang court (*Ts'e-fu yüan-kuei* p.5023).[1]

In the 12th month (Jan./Feb., 633) of the Chinese year 632,[2] Tang-hsiang offered gifts to the T'ang court (*Ts'e-fu yüan-kuei* p.5024).

In 635, the Tibetans defeated the Tang-hsiang (*Tzu-chih t'ung-chien* p.6139). Due to this and subsequent attacks, the Tang-hsiang were dislodged from their homeland and gradually migrated into Chinese territories. They settled in an area extending from Kan-su to Sui-yüan, were mistreated by the Chinese officials, and retaliated by raiding and looting. When at the end of T'ang the government became more and more weakened, the Tang-hsiang began a slow territorial expansion. During the Five Dynasties, they became independent.

---

[1] According to *T'ang hui-yao* 98:19a, a Tang-hsiang chief called himself King Wo Esteems Goodness and offered gifts to the T'ang court. This may be the same mission.

[2] This is the second entry for 632 in *Ts'e-fu yüan-kuei* preceded by "11th month". I emend it to 12th month.

In the 2nd month (Mar./Apr.) of 918, Tang-hsiang envoys to the Khitan court offered gifts (*Liao shih* 1:10a-10b).

On Apr.17, 924, envoys from a Tang-hsiang chief to the Later T'ang court offered fine horses (*Hsin Wu-tai shih* 5:7a; *Ts'e-fu yüan-kuei* p.5034).

In the 11th month (Nov./Dec.) of 924, Tang-hsiang presented a white ass to the Later T'ang court (*Ts'e-fu yüan-kuei* p.5034).

In the 12th month (Dec./Jan., 925) of the Chinese year 924, Tang-hsiang offered fine horses to the Later T'ang court. The wife of the chief presented racehorses (*Ts'e-fu yüan-kuei* p.5034).

In the 2nd month (Feb./Mar.) of 925, Tang-hsiang offered regional objects to the Later T'ang court (*Ts'e-fu yüan-kuei* p.5034).

On Oct.20, 927, Tang-hsiang and others offered 40 horses to the Later T'ang court (*Hsin Wu-tai shih* 6:6a; *Ts'e-fu yüan-kuei* p.5034; *Wen-hsien t'ung-k'ao* 334:27b).

In the 11th month (Dec./Jan., 929) of the Chinese year 928, Tang-hsiang offered gifts to the Later T'ang court (*Ts'e-fu yüan-kuei* p.5034).

In the 8th month (Sep./Oct.) of 929, Tang-hsiang offered regional objects to the Later T'ang court. In the 9th month (Oct./Nov.), they presented horses. In the 10th month (Nov./Dec.), a Tang-hsiang chief offered horses (*Chiu Wu-tai shih* 40:7a; *Ts'e-fu yüan-kuei* p.5034).

In the 1st month (Jan./Feb.) of 930, a Tang-hsiang chief offered gifts to the Later T'ang court. He was appointed a Manager of Lances. In the 12th month (Dec./Jan., 931) of the same Chinese year 930, Emperor Ming-tsung of Later T'ang appointed one Tang-hsiang chief as Acting Master of Writing and Supervisor of the Right, and another as Acting Master of Writing in the Ministry of Works (*Wu-tai hui-yao* 29:11a-11b; *Wen-hsien t'ung-k'ao* 334:27b).

On Jan. 30, 931, Tang-hsiang in the Kan-su Corridor offered racehorses to the Later T'ang court (*Hsin Wu-tai shih* 6:9b; *Ts'e-fu yüan-kuei* p.5035).

In the 11th month (Dec./Jan., 932) of the Chinese year 931, Tang-hsiang offered gifts to the Later T'ang court (*Ts'e-fu yüan-kuei* p.5035).

In the 12th month (Jan./Feb., 932) of the Chinese year 931, a Tang-hsiang chief presented banners and horses he had taken from the Khitan to the Later T'ang court (*Ts'e-fu yüan-kuei* p.5035).

In the 4th month (Apr./May) of 933, Tang-hsiang offered gifts to the Khitan court (*Liao shih* 70:3b).

In the 1st month (Jan./Feb.) of 934, Tang-hsiang offered a deer to the Khitan court (*Liao shih* 70:4a).

In the 3rd month (Apr./May) of 935, Tang-hsiang offered gifts to the Khitan court (*Liao shih* 70:4a).

On Dec.15, 953, a Tang-hsiang envoy was received at the Later Chou court (*Hsin Wu-tai shih* 11:6b).

In the 10th month (Nov./Dec.) of 959, a Tang-hsiang chief offered 40 horses to the Later Chou court. Emperor Shih-tsung inspected the horses at the Hall of Restoration. The Military Affairs Commissioner memorialized that when the T'u[-yü-]hun and Tang-hsiang offered horses, the price they wanted was always paid. But at the time when the horses were inspected, the envoys were also presented with silken fabrics. When this expenditure was added to the price, the cost was doubled. He proposed that the custom be stopped. The emperor rejected this, since the state was in need of horses.[3] Henceforth, the horses and sheep of the barbarian tribes kept coming without interruption (*Wu-tai hui-yao* 29:11a).

In 961, a member of of a great Tang-hsiang lineage was received at the Sung court (*Sung shih* 491:12b; *Wen-hsien t'ung-k'ao* 334:27b).

In 968, Emperor T'ai-tsu of Sung appointed one chief of the Tang-hsiang as Acting Grand Guardian and General Who Has Attached himself to Virtue, and another as Acting Minister of the Multitude and General Who Cherishes Civilization (*Sung shih* 491:12b-13a; *Wen-hsien t'ung-k'ao* 334:27b).

In 977, T'ai-tsung of Sung presented a Tang-hsiang chief with gold and silk and made a covenant with him (*Sung shih* 491:13a).

In 981, Tang-hsiang offered horses to the Sung court (*Sung shih* 491: 13a; *Wen-hsien t'ung-k'ao* 334:27b).

In 982, the younger brother of a great Tang-hsiang chief, whose tribal area was just north of the Ordos bend of the Yellow River, offered horses to the Sung court (*Sung shih* 491:13a-15a; *Wen-hsien t'ung-k'ao* 334:27b).

In the 11th month (Dec./Jan., 987) of the Liao year 986, Tang-hsiang offered gifts to the Liao court of the Khitan (*Liao shih* 70: 8a).[4]

In the 6th month (July/Aug.) of 988, a Tang-hsiang envoy was received at the Liao court (*Liao shih* 70:8a).

---

[3] The Five Dynasties had no pastures at all.

[4] Correcting Hsiang-hsiang to Tang-hsiang.

In the 3rd month (Mar./Apr.) of 993, Tang-hsiang offered gifts to the Sung court and were presented with brocade robes, silver belts, vessels, and silk. In the 12 month (Jan./Feb., 994) of the same Chinese year 993, the chief of the Western Tribe of the Tsang-ts'ai offered gifts to the Sung court (*Sung shih* 491:15b; 16a).

In 994, T'ai-tsung of Sung appointed three Tang-hsiang chiefs as Generals Who Cherish Civilization, and three others as Generals of the Gentlemen Who Have Attached Themselves to Virtue (*Sung shih* 491:16a).

During the same year of 994, the great chief of the Yai-lo tribe and the chief of the Eastern Tribe of the Tsang-ts'ai each sent sons and younger brothers to offer gifts to the Sung court. Later that year, a Tang-hsiang chief was by T'ai-tsung appointed Acting General Who Cherishes Civilization (*Sung shih* 491:16a).

In the 9th month (Oct./Nov.) of 994, Tang-hsiang offered gifts to the Liao court (*Liao shih* 70:9a).

In the 4th month (May) of 995, the great chief of the Le-lang tribe was by T'ai-tsung appointed General-in-chief Who Attaches Himself to Virtue. Another chief was appointed as General of the Gentlemen Who find Peace in Civilization, and an assistant chief as General of the Gentlemen Who Observe Obedience. Later that year, a Tang-hsiang chief was presented with 50 bolts of silk and 50 catties of tea (*Sung shih* 491:16b, 17a).

In the 3rd month (Mar./Apr.) of 996, T'ai-tsung appointed a great chief of the Tang-hsiang as General-in-chief Who Keeps the Distance in Peace (*Sung shih* 491:17a).

In the 6th month (June/July) of 996, a mission of 193 men led by the Assistant Chief of the Le-lang tribe offered seven horses to the Sung court. The envoys were received in audience and presented with brocade robes and silver belts (*Sung shih* 491:17a; 18a).

In the 2nd month (Mar./Apr.) of 997, five Tang-hsiang envoys offered horses to the Sung court (*Sung shih* 491:17b-18a).

In the 3rd month (Apr./May) of 997, Tang-hsiang offered gifts to the Liao court. In the 7th month (Aug./Sep.), Tang-hsiang chiefs offered horses (*Liao shih* 70:9b).

In the 3rd month (April) of 998, envoys of the Shu-ts'ang tribe were received at the Sung court. Emperor Chen-tsung presented them with vessels and silk. Later that year, other Tang-hsiang offered gifts and were richly rewarded (*Sung shih* 491:18a).

In the 11th month (Dec./Jan., 1000) of the Chinese year 999, the great chiefs of the eight tribes of the Tsang-ts'ai presented fine horses to the Sung court (*Sung shih* 491:18b).

In the 7th month (July/Aug.) of 1001, Chen-tsung appointed one chief as General of the Gentlemen Who Observe Obedience, and another as General of the Gentlemen Who Find Peace in Civilization. During the same year, the chief of the Pi-ning tribe offered fine horses to the Sung court. An edict ordered that he be paid generously (*Sung shih* 491:18b).

In 1002, a son of the chief of the Mieh-pu tribe offered gifts to the Sung court. Chen-tsung conferred the titles of General Who Cherishes Civilization and of General Who Has Attached Himself to Virtue on prominent members of the tribe. Others were appointed General-in-chief to Keep the Distance in Peace and General Who Cherishes Civilization. Chen-tsung also presented gold and silk. In the 12th month (Jan./Feb., 1003) of the same Chinese year 1002, envoys of the Mieh-pu tribe offered gifts. The emperor questioned and rewarded them (*Sung shih* 491:19a-19b).

In the 2nd month (Mar./Apr.) of 1003, Chen-tsung presented tea to a Tang-hsiang chief. In the 3rd month (Apr./May), he gave brocade robes and silver belts to one Tang-hsiang mission and robes and belts to another. In the 7th month (August), he appointed the son of the chief of the Pu-li-yeh tribe[5] as General Who Cherishes Peace (*Sung shih* 491:20a; 20b, 21a).

In the 6th month (July) of 1003, Tang-hsiang were received at the Liao court (*Liao shih* 70:11a).

In the 1st month (Jan./Feb.) of 1004, Chen-tsung presented a Tang-hsiang chief with tea (*Sung shih* 491:21b).

In the 8th month (Aug./Sep.) of 1004, Tang-hsiang offered gifts to the Liao court (*Liao shih* 70:11b).

In 1005, Chen-tsung gave gifts to the new chief of the [Pu-]yeh-li tribe (*Sung shih* 491:22a).

In the 3rd (Apr./May) and 7th month (Aug./Sep.) of 1005, Tang-hsiang offered gifts to the Liao court (*Liao shih* 70:11b).

In 1006, Chen-tsung presented Tang-hsiang with brocade robes and silver belts (*Sung shih* 491:22a-22b).

On 1009, the great chief of the Wu-ni tribe offered gifts to the Sung court (*Sung shih* 491:23a).

---

[5] This may be an error for Pu-yeh-li. See infra.

In 1011, sons of the chiefs of the Western and Central tribes of the Tsang-ts'ai were received at the Sung court (*Sung shih* 491:23a).

In 1016, Chen-tsung presented a Tang-hsiang chief with brocade robes and silver belts (*Sung shih* 491:24a).

In 1021, Chen-tsung presented a Tang-hsiang chief with vessels and silk (*Sung shih* 491:24b).

In the 10th month (Nov./Dec.) of 1021, a Tang-hsiang chief offered gifts to the Liao court (*Liao shih* 70:15a).

According to *Wen-hsien t'ung-k'ao* 334:28a, the Tang-hsiang continued to send missions to the Sung court until about 1021.

The missions of the Tang-hsiang tribes to the Chinese courts were entirely for trade, the chief commodity being horses. The Tang-hsiang also warred with China when they did not fight each other. The Sung government tried to appease the chiefs by paying them good prices for their horses, and by offering gold, silk, brocade robes, silver belts, [porcelain] vessels, and tea, and by conferring titles. It also made some of them Inspectors of the territories they held already (*T'ang hui-yao* 98:18b). This was the old self-serving method of extending China on an imaginary map by creating fictitious administrative units. The relations of the Tang-hsiang to the Khitan/Liao were very much the same, alternating between trade missions and warfare. Official contacts between the Tang-hsiang and the Sung and Liao came to an end in 1021 when the former were under attack and soon absorbed by the Hsia State.

HSIA

When the Tang-hsiang in the latter half of the 7th century migrated into T'ang territories, the most powerful group, under chiefs of the T'o-pa clan[1], settled south of the Ordos steppe within the bend of the Yellow River. This was the nucleus of the future Hsia State.[2] Emperor T'ai-tsung of T'ang conferred on the chief T'o-pa Ch'ih-tz'u the imperial surname of Li. At the end of T'ang, another chief, T'o-pa Ssu-kung, supported the T'ang against the rebel Huang Ch'ao from 880 to 883. In recognition, he also was granted the imperial surname of Li and appointed Military Commissioner of the imaginary Army Which Fixes Difficulties. While he and his successors sported Chinese titles, they were, in fact, independent rulers.[3]

When Ssu-kung died, he was succeeded as Military Commissioner of the Army Which Fixes Difficulties by his younger brother Li Ssu-chien. Ssu-chien was succeeded by Ssu-kung's grandson Li Yi-ch'ang. Yi-ch'ang was soon killed and succeeded by his uncle Li Jen-fu. Jen-fu was given various Chinese titles and in 924 by the Later T'ang recognized as king of Shuo-fang. In 933, it became known at the Later T'ang court that Jen-fu had died. He was succeeded by his son Li Yi-ch'ao. In 935, it became known at the Later T'ang court that Yi-ch'ao had also died. His brother Li Yi-yin succeeded as Military Commissioner of the Army Which Fixes Difficulties.The Later Chou appointed him Prefect of the Masters of Writing, Grand Guardian, and Grand Tutor, and recognized him as king of Hsi-p'ing. After T'ai-tsu had founded the Sung dynasty in 960, he appointed Yi-yin as Grand Commandant. The Sung court henceforth refered to Yi-yin as Yi-hsing to avoid the tabooed given name of T'ai-tsu's father (*Chiu Wu-tai shih* 31:9a-9b; *Sung shih* 485:2a-2b; *Chin shih* 134:1a).

In 960 or soon thereafter, Li Yi-yin offered 300 horses to the Sung court. T'ai-tsu was greatly pleased with this support, personally made a jade belt, and sent an envoy to present it (*Sung shih* 485:2b-3a).

---

[1] Not to be confused with the T'o-pa ruling house of Northern Wei.

[2] In the sources, the state is more often referred to as Hsia than Hsi Hsia. Although Hsi Hsia is the common term in the West, I prefer to call it Hsia.

[3] For the internal history and foreign wars of the Hsia State see Ruth Dunnel, *The Cambridge History of China*, vol.6, pp.154-214.

In 967, it became known at the Sung court that Yi-yin had died. T'ai-tsu suspended the court for three days, conferred on him the posthumous titles of Grand Master and king of Hsia, appointed his son Kuang-jui as Grand Guardian, and recognized him as Military Commissioner of the Army Which Fixes Difficulties (*Sung shih* 485:3a). King of Hsia became henceforth the title of the Tangut rulers.

In 976, Kuang-jui defeated a Northern Han army and presented 1000 cattle and sheep he had captured to the Sung court. T'ai-tsu appointed him Acting Grand Commandant (*Sung shih* 485:3a).

After T'ai-tsung had ascended the Sung throne on Nov.15, 976, the sources refer to Kuang-jui as K'o-jui to avoid the tabooed given name of the new emperor (*Sung shih* 485:3a).

In 978, it became known at the Sung court that Li Kuang-jui had died. T'ai-tsung suspended the court for two days and conferred on Kuang-jui the posthumous title of Palace Attendant. Kuang-jui was succeeded by his son Chi-yün. T'ai-tsung appointed him Acting Minister over the Masses and recognized him as Military Commissioner of the Army Which Fixes Difficulties (*Sung shih* 485:3a).

When T'ai-tsung attacked the Northern Han in 979, Chi-yün supported him with troops (*Sung shih* 485:3a).

In 980, it became known at the Sung court that Li Chi-yün had died. He was succeeded by his brother Chi-p'eng. But Chi-p'eng met with opposition and was forced to seek Chinese support. In 982, he travelled to the court in K'ai-feng and there under duress ceded some territory to the Sung. T'ai-tsung presented him with 1000 ounces of silver, 1000 bolts of silk, and 1,000,000 cash, and his grandmother with one jade vessel and three golden vessels. He appointed Chi-p'eng Military Commissioner of the Army Which Displays Virtue and conferred offices on his brothers. The emperor then gave a banquet, bestowed on Chi-p'eng the imperial surname of Chao and the given name of Pao-chung (Maintaining Loyalty),[4] presented him with a painting by his own hand, appointed him Inspector of Hsia, recognized him as Military Commissioner of the Army Which Fixes Difficulties, and further presented him with 1000 ounces of golden vessels, 10,000 ounces of silver vessels, cash, and silk. When Chi-p'eng departed, T'ai-tsung gave another banquet and presented garments, jade belts, silver horse trappings, 3000 bolts of silken fabrics, 3000 ounces of silver vessels, 500 brocade robes, silver belts, and 500 horses (*Sung shih* 485:3a-4b).

---

[4] The Chinese sources henceforth refer to Chi-p'eng as Chao Pao-chung.

T'ai-tsung's attempt to buy the support of the Tanguts through Chi-p'eng failed. One party among them resented Chi-p'eng's concessions to the Sung and supported a rival. This was his third cousin Li Chi-ch'ien. Born in 963, he was in 982 only 20 years old, Chinese reckoning. A Chinese attack on Chi-ch'ien in 983 was a minor success, but he retaliated and defeated Chinese forces in 983 and 985. The Sung meanwhile courted Chi-p'eng by appointing him in 985 as Specially Advanced and Manager of the Affairs in the Secretariat-Chancellery (*Sung shih* 485:4a-6a).

Chi-ch'ien countered by allying himself with the Liao State, whose Emperor Sheng-tsung showed his support by appointing him in 986 as Specially Advanced and Acting Grand Master, and by recognizing him as the military commander of Hsia. In the 10th month (Nov./Dec.) of that year, envoys from Chi-ch'ien to the Liao court offered gifts. In the 12th month (Jan., 987) of the Liao year 986, his envoys requested a marriage. Sheng-tsung agreed. He recognized Chi-ch'ien as king of Hsia and presented him with 3000 horses (*Sung shih* 485:6a; *Liao shih* 11:9a-9b; 115:6b).

In 987, Chi-ch'ien inflicted a major defeat on a Sung army (*Sung shih* 485:6a).

On Apr.15, 988, envoys from Chi-ch'ien to the Liao court offered gifts (*Liao shih* 12:2a; 115:6b).

On Feb.18, 989, Chi-p'eng requested Sheng-tsung to mediate between himself and Chi-ch'ien. This was rejected (*Liao shih* 12:14a).

In the 2nd month (Mar./Apr.) of 989, envoys from Chi-ch'ien to the Liao court offered gifts (*Liao shih* 12:5a-5b; 115:6b).

On Apr.25, 989, Sheng-tsung enfeoffed a daughter of the Military Commissioner Yeh-lü Hsiang as Princess of Yi-ch'eng to be the bride of Chi-ch'ien (*Liao shih* 12:5b; 115:6b).

In about 990, the tensions between Chi-p'eng and Chi-ch'ien broke out into open warfare. Chi-ch'ien was wounded and withdrew. T'ai-tsung of Sung expressed his pleasure by presenting Chi-p'eng with 100 catties of tea and 10 *shih* of wine. Chi-p'eng on his part presented a white falcon which, however, was rejected (*Sung shih* 485:4b, 6a-6b).

In the 1st month (Jan./Feb.) of 990, envoys from Chi-ch'ien to the Liao court thanked for the recognition. On Mar.30, his envoys offered gifts. On Oct.11, his envoys presented Sung prisoners. In the 10th month (Oct./Nov.), his envoys announced that he had defeated a Sung army. On Dec.21, his envoys informed that he had conquered

Sung territories. On Feb.22, 991, his envoys announced another victory over Sung (*Liao shih* 13:1b, 2a, 2a; 115:6b).

On Dec.28, 990, Sheng-tsung of Liao once more recognized Li Chi-ch'ien as king of Hsia. On June 11, 991, an envoy from Chi-ch'ien thanked for the recognition. On Sep.3, his envoys informed the Liao court that he had recovered territory from the Sung. On Nov.15, his envoys acquainted Sheng-tsung with correspondence he had received from the Sung court (*Liao shih* (*Liao shih* 13:2a, 3a; 115:6b).

At the very end of 991, Chi-p'eng reversed his previous Sung-friendly policy and sought a rapprochement with Liao. Sheng-tsung appointed him Commander Unequalled in Honour, Acting Grand Master, and Concurrent Palace Attendant and recognized him as king of Hsi-p'ing (*Liao shih* 115:6b). Chi-ch'ien responded by also changing sides and making an approach to the Sung. T'ai-tsung granted him the given name of Pao-chi (Maintaining Auspiciousness). His son and future successor Te-ming was given a nominal office (*Sung shih* 485: 6b). This did not pass unnoticed in Liao, and Sheng-tsung sent the Commissioner of Bandit Suppression, Han Te-wei, to reprove Chi-ch'ien. When Te-wei arrived in Hsia, Chi-ch'ien refused to see him, under the pretext of illness. Te-wei then looted the countryside, took prisoners, returned to Liao, and handed in his report in the 2nd month (Mar.) of 992 (*Liao shih* 13:3a-3b; 115:7a).

In spite of the chilled relations, Chi-ch'ien did not burn his bridges to Liao, and on Apr.1, 992, envoys offered his explanations to Sheng-tsung. The emperor responded with a letter. On Nov.9, envoys from Chi-ch'ien offered gifts to the Liao court (*Liao shih* 13:3b; 115:7a).

In the 1st month (Feb./Mar.) of 994, Chi-p'eng informed the Sung court prematurely that he had patched up his quarrel with Chi-ch'ien and presented 50 horses. However, the latter made a surprise attack on him by night and captured his light baggage. Chi-p'eng fled and was brought by the Chinese to K'ai-feng. He remained there until his death, which made Chi-ch'ien the unchallenged king of Hsia. T'ai-tsung presented Chi-p'eng with caps, belts, vessels, and silk, and his mother with gold and silver vessels. Chi-ch'ien, on his part, played the Liao and Sung against each other. On Sep.3, he presented horses to the Sung court. Subsequently, a younger brother of his offered horses and camels. In the 11th month (Oct./Nov.), T'ai-tsung sent a eunuch to present Chi-ch'ien with vessels, silk, garments, tea, and drugs. But during the same year, Chi-ch'ien also offered gifts to the Liao court (*Sung shih* 5:19b; 485:4b-5a, 6b; *Liao shih* 115:7a).

On Mar.1, 995, envoys from Chi-ch'ien to the Sung court offered fine horses and camels (*Sung shih* 5:22a; 485:7a). On Apr.9, his envoys also offered gifts to the Liao court (*Liao shih* 13:6a; 70:9a). On July 11, 995, T'ai-tsung of Sung sent envoys to negotiate with Chi-ch'ien and to appoint him a Military Commissioner. Chi-ch'ien rejected it (*Sung shih* 5:22b; 485:7a).

On Aug.30, 995, envoys from Hsia to the Liao court offered horses (*Liao shih* 13:6b).

In the 9th month (Sep./Oct.) of 995, Chi-ch'ien looted Chinese border areas, and on Jan.2, 996, his envoys informed the Liao court that he had defeated Sung forces (*Liao shih* 13:7a; 115:7a).

On Feb.16, 996, envoys from Hsia to the Liao court offered gifts. Soon thereafter, Chi-ch'ien raided the Ning-hsia Oasis and captured provisions (*Liao shih* 13:7a; 115:7a; *Sung shih* 5:24a; 485:7b).

On Mar.22, 997, envoys from Hsia to the Liao court offered gifts. On Apr.14, envoys announced a victory over Sung forces. On Apr.24,[5] Sheng-tsung of Liao recognized the king of Hsia, Chi-ch'ien, as also king of Hsi-p'ing. On July 26, envoys from Chi-ch'ien thanked for the recognition. He then attacked the Ning-hsia Oasis. In the 9th month (Oct./Nov.), the Sung sent five armies by different routes against Hsia. They were defeated (*Sung shih* 485:7b-8a; *Liao shih* 13: 8a, 8b; 115:7a).

On Jan.22 and in the 2nd month (March) of 998, envoys from Hsia to the Liao court offered gifts (*Liao shih* 13:9a; 70:10a).

In 998 or soon thereafter, Chen-tsung of Sung appointed Chi-ch'ien as Inspector of Hsia, conferred on him the title of Meritorious Subject, and presented him with brocade robes and silver belts. He entitled his mother a Consort Dowager and made his son and successor Te-ming a Major in the Army Which Fixes Difficulties. Chi-ch'ien sent his younger brother Chi-yüan to express his thanks. Chen-tsung appointed Chi-yüan a Defense Commissioner (*Sung shih* 485:8a-8b).

On Mar.11, 998, envoys from Hsia to the Liao court offered gifts (*Liao shih* 14:1a; 115:76a).

On Nov.29, 1000, Shen-tsung of Liao appointed Te-ming[6] as Military Commissioner of the Shuo-fang Army (*Liao shih* 14:2a; 115:7a).

On Mar.30, 1001, an envoy from Hsia to the Liao court offered

[5] Correcting *yi-mao* to *chi-mao*.

[6] *Liao shih* at times writes his name Te-chao to avoid a taboo.

gifts. On July 11, Hsia informed the Liao court that it had conquered Sung territory. Sheng-tsung congratulated. In the 9th month (Sep/ Oct.), Chi-ch'ien made further conquests (*Sung shih* 485:8b; *Liao shih* 14:2b; 115:7a).

On Mar.24, 1002, envoys from Hsia to the Liao court offered horses and camels. In the 3rd month (Apr./May), Chi-ch'ien took Ling chou at the Ning-hsia Oasis, and in the 6th month (July/Aug.) his envoy announced this victory to the Liao court (*Liao shih* 14:3b; 115:7a).

In the spring of 1003, the Sung ceded territory to Hsia (*Sung shih* 485:8b).

On June 30, 1003, envoys from Te-ming to the Liao court announced that his father Li Chi-ch'ien had died. On July 22, Sheng-tsung confered on Chi-ch'ien the posthumous title of Prefect of the Masters of Writing and sent the Commissioner of the Palace Audience Gate of the West to condole. On Oct.10,[7] envoys of Te-ming thanked for the condolence and the posthumous title (*Liao shih* 14:4a, 5b; 115:7a).[8] In 1012, Te-ming conferred on his father the posthumous temple name of Wu-tsung. Li Yüan-hao (r.1032-1048) changed it to T'ai-tsu (*Sung shih* 485:9a, 11b). During his reign, Chi-ch'ien had enlarged the Hsia State to comprise the entire Ordos Region and the Ning-hsia Oasis.

Li Chi-p'eng died in K'ai-feng during 1004 and was by Chen-tsung given the posthumous title of Military Commissioner of the Army Which Awes the Border. Te-ming was presented with 10,000 ounces of silver, 10,000 bolts of pongee, 50,000 strings of cash, and 5000 ounces of tea (*Sung shih* 485:9b).

---

[7] *Liao shih* 115:7a has 8th month, but that month did not have the cyclical characters of *chi-hai*.

[8] The Liao account has to be reconciled with that of *Sung shih*. *Liao shih* 14:4a states unequivocably that "The king of Hsi-p'ing, Li Chi-ch'ien having died, his son Te-chao (=Te-ming) sent envoys on June 30, 1003, to come and announce it". The date refers to the reception of the envoys at the Liao court. According to *Liao shih* 115:7a, "[Li] Chi-ch'ien having died in 1003, his son Te-chao sent envoys to come and announce it". *Sung shih* 485:9a states that "on Jan.26, 1004, [it was learned that] Li Chi-ch'ien had died, aged 42". Jan.26 was the 2nd day of the 1st month of 1004, so that Chi-ch'ien must have died in the previous lunar year. All texts agree therefore that Li Chi-ch'ien died in 1003. The problem is his age. Since he was born in 963, he would by Chinese reckoning have been 41 in 1003. Why then does *Sung shih* give his age as 42, and why was the Sung informed so late of his death? I suggest that Hsia, being politically closer to Liao than to Sung, announced Chi-ch'ien's death to the Liao court first and to the Sung court seven month later in 1004. The Sung counted Chi-ch'ien's years of life from 963 to the time of the death announcement in 1004, which gives an age of 42.

On Apr.3, 1004, envoys from Te-ming to the Liao court presented Chi-ch'ien's testamentary gifts. On July 21, Sheng-tsung recognized Te-ming as king of Hsia and Hsi-p'ing. On Dec.13, envoys from Te-ming thanked for the recognition (*Liao shih* 14:4b-5a, 5b; 115:7b).

In early 1005,[9] envoys from Hsia to the Liao court announced a conquest of Sung territory (*Liao shih* 14:6a; 115:7b). During the same year, Hsia also offered gifts to the Sung court (*Sung shih* 7:10a).

In 1006, Te-ming sent a communication to Chen-tsung of Sung. The emperor entitled him a Specially Advanced and Meritorious Subject, appointed him Military Governor of Hsia, Acting Inspector of Hsia, Supreme Pillar of State, and Military Commissioner of the Army Which Fixes Difficulties, and recognized him as king of Hsi-p'ing. He presented him with garments, golden belts, silver horse trappings, 10,000 ounces of silver, 10,000 bolts of pongeee, 30,000 strings of cash, and 20,000 catties of tea. He also demanded that Te-ming send sons and younger brothers as hostages to the Sung court. Te-ming offered 725 horses and 300 camels but refused to provide hostages (*Sung shih* 485:9b-10a).

In 1007, Te-ming offered 500 horses and 300 camels to the Sung court and received garments, golden belts, vessels, and silk (*Sung shih* 7:15b, 485:10a).

Te-ming's mother having died,[10] Chen-tsung of Sung sent envoys to condole and sacrifice in the 5th month (May/June) of 1007. Sheng-tsung of Liao did the same on Aug.23 (*Sung shih* 485:10a; *Liao shih* 14:7b, 115:7b). When the lady had been buried, Te-ming requested Chen-tsung to let him worship and make offerings at the ten Buddhist Temples on the Wu-t'ai Mountain in northern Shan-hsi. The emperor agreed and sent an Audience Usher to escort Te-ming and make arrangements for the sacrifices. When Te-ming reached the mountain, he presented 500 horses (*Sung shih* 485:10a-10b).

In 1008, Chen-tsung appointed Te-ming a Meritorious Subject Who Observes Correctness. Te-ming sent envoys to thank. He was then appointed Concurrent Prefect of the Palace Writers (*Sung shih* 485:10b).

On Dec.30, 1009, Sheng-tsung sent envoys to Hsia to announce that his mother, the Empress Dowager, had died on the previous day (*Liao shih* 14:8a; 115:7b).

---

[9] The text says 2nd month, *ting-ssu*, which date did not exist.

[10] Missions announcing her death are not recorded.

In 1010, Hsia suffered from a famine. Te-ming requested 1,000,000 bushels of grain from the Sung, which was provided (*Sung shih* 485: 10b-11a).

On Oct.19, 1010, Sheng-tsung sent envoys to recognize Te-ming as king of the Great Hsia State (*Liao shih*15:1b; 115:7b; *Sung shih* 485: 10b).

When Chen-tsung performed the sacrifices to Sovereign Earth at Fen-yin on Mar.24, 1011, he appointed Te-ming Prefect of the Palace Writers. Hsia offered gifts to the Sung court (*Sung shih* 8:4a; 486:11a).

In 1012, Chen-tsung appointed Te-ming Acting Grand Guardian (*Sung shih* 485:11a).

On Apr.28, 1012, envoys from Hsia State to the Liao court offered fine horses. On Oct.22, Sheng-tsung conferred ranks on the Hsia envoys, to each in accordance with his standing (*Liao shih* 15:4a, 4b, 5a; 115:7b).

In the 7th month (Aug./Sep.) of 1013, Sheng-tsung invited Te-ming to attack rebellious Tang-hsiang. On Sep.10, Sheng-tsung sent the Commissioner of the Office of Presentations to present Te-ming and his widowed stepmother, the Princess of Yi-ch'eng, with chariots and horses (*Liao shih* 15:6b; 115:7b).

In the 2nd month (Mar./Apr.) of 1014, Hsia offered regional objects to the Sung court. Chen-tsung entitled Te-ming a Meritorious Subject Who Proclaims Virtue (*Sung shih* 8:10b; 485:11a).

In 1016, Te-ming sent a communication to Chen-tsung, in which, the claim of the dynastic historians notwithstanding, he most certainly did not refer to himself as a "subject" (*Sung shih* 484:11a-11b).

In the 1st month (February) of 1017, Chen-tsung appointed Te-ming as Acting Grand Tutor (*Sung shih* 485:11b).

In the winter of 1019, Chen-tsung entitled Te-ming a Meritorious Subject Who Venerates Benevolence (*Sung shih* 485:11b).

In 1021, Chen-tsung sent the Supreme General of the Guards of the Gilded Mace to present to Te-ming a golden seal as Prefect of the Masters of Writing and his recognition, carved on jade, as king of the Great Hsia State (*Sung shih* 485:12a).

In the 11th month (Dec./Jan.) of 1021, Hsia envoys to the Liao court offered gifts (*Liao shih* 16:6a; 115:7b).

In early 1022, Chen-tsung entitled Te-ming a Meritorious Subject Who Enlarges Sincerity. He sent a eunuch to present him with litchis, garments, belts, silver boxes with golden flowers, and gongs, in all

1000 ounces, 1000 bolts of silken fabrics, and silver horse trappings washed in gold. He also sent an Audience Usher to present winter garments (*Sung shih* 485:12a).

After Jen-tsung had ascended the Sung throne on Mar.23, 1022, he confirmed Te-ming as Prefect of the Masters of Writing (*Sung shih* 485:12a).

On Oct.24, 1022, Sheng-tsung of Liao sent a Secretariat Clerk to congratulate Te-ming on his birthday (*Liao shih* 16:7a).

In 1023, Hsia defeated Sung forces (*Sung shih* 485:12a).

On Nov.19, 1026, Liao envoys to Hsia inquired why Hsia had fought a battle with Sung in the 5th month (May/June) of that year (*Liao shih* 17:3a).

In 1028, Te-ming's son Yüan-hao conquered the Uighur qaghanate of Kan chou in the Kan-su Corridor (*Sung shih* 485:12b).

On June 30, 1031, Liao sent envoys to Hsia to announce the death of Emperor Sheng-tsung on June 25. On Oct.4, Hsia envoys condoled at the Liao court. On Nov.10, Hsia envoys to the Liao court contributed silk toward the funeral expenses (*Liao shih* 18:1b, 2a-2b; 115:7b).

Sheng-tsung's successor Hsing-tsung agreed to a marriage for Te-wen's son and successor Yüan-hao. He selected the Princess of Hsing-p'ing as Yüan-hao's bride, recognized him as duke of the Hsia State, and appointed him a Chief Commandant of Attendant Cavalry (*Liao shih* 18:3a; 115:7b; *Chin shih* 134:1a).

In the 10th month (Oct./Nov.) of 1031, the Sung court was informed that Li Te-ming had died, aged 51. Jen-tsung granted him the posthumous titles of Grand Master, Prefect of the Masters of Writing and Concurrent Prefect of the Palace Writers. He sent a Supernumerary Gentleman of the Revenue Section of the Masters of Writing to sacrifice, and contributed 700 bolts of pongee and 300 bolts of cotton toward the funeral expenses (*Sung shih* 485:12b).

Te-ming was succeeded by his son Yüan-hao, who conferred on his father the temple name of T'ai-tsung. Jen-tsung sent a Gentleman-of-the-Palace of the Ministry of Works to appoint Yüan-hao[11] as Specially Advanced, Acting Grand Master and Concurrent Palace Attendant, and Military Commissioner of the Army Which Fixes Difficulties in charge of the territory he held already, and to recognize him as king of Hsi-p'ing (*Sung shih* 485:12b-13b).

[11] *Sung shih* hencefort refers to Yüan-hao as Li Nang-hsiao.

On Dec.23, 1032, envoys from Hsia to the Liao court congratulated [on the enthronement of Hsing-tsung] (*Liao shih* 18:3b; 115:7b).

In the 11th month (Dec./Jan., 1033) of the Liao year 1032, Hsing-tsung recognized the duke of Hsia, Yüan-hao, as king of the Hsia State (*Liao shih* 18:3b; 115:7b).[12]

On Feb.20, 1033, Hsia envoys to the Liao court offered gifts (*Liao shih* 18:4a; 115:7b).

In 1034, Yüan-hao raided Sung border areas and defeated Sung forces. The same year, his mother died. He sent envoys to the Sung court to announce the death. Jen-tsung sent an Audience Usher to sacrifice and an Imperial Diarist to condole and inquire about the well-being of Yüan-hao (*Sung shih* 485:14a).

In 1035, Jen-tsung appointed Yüan-hao as Concurrent Prefect of the Palace Writers (*Sung shih* 485:15b).

On Apr.21, 1038, Hsia envoys to the Liao court offered gifts (*Liao shih* 18:8a; 70:16b; 115:7b).

At some time during 1038, Yüan-hao informed the Sung court that he wished to send envoys to the Wu-t'ai Mountain in order to make offerings to the Buddha (*Sung shih* 485:15b)

Meanwhile, Hsing-tsung of Liao had ordered an inquiry into the death of the Princess of Hsing-p'ing. She had not been on good terms with her husband Yüan-hao, and her death had apparently raised questions. Hsing-tsung on May 9, 1038, sent the Recepient of Edicts of the Northern Establishment to question Yüan-hao, but he found no evidence of wrongdoing (*Liao shih* 18:8a; 115:7b-8a).

On Dec.10, 1038, Yüan-hao proclaimed himself emperor of the Great Hsia State, which title was also adopted by his successors. He was 30 years old. In the following year, he sent a communication to Jen-tsung of Sung, informing him of this step.[13] War broke out immediately, and Jen-tsung stripped Yüan-hao of his Chinese titles (*Sung shih* 485:15b, 17a-17b; *Chin shih* 134:1a).

---

[12] The passage could be read: "The king of the Hsia State, Li Te-ming, died in the 11th month of 1032. [Hsing-tsung] recognized his son, the duke of the Hsia State Yüan-hao, as king of the Hsia State". However, according to *Sung shih* 485: 12b, Te-wen had died in 1031. The passage should therefore be read: "The king of the Hsia State, Li Te-ming, having died, [Hsing-tsung] in the 11th month of 1032 recognized his son, the Duke of the Hsia State Yüan-hao, as king of the Hsia State". Li Te-ming's relations to Liao had been cooler than those to Sung, which might explain the delay in the recognition.

[13] He would not have referred to himself a "subject" as claimed by *Sung shih*.

On Aug.30, 1040, envoys from Jen-tsung to the Liao court announced that Sung was at war with Hsia (*Liao shih* 18:8b; 115:8a).

On Oct.17, 1041, Hsia presented Sung prisoners of war to the Liao court (*Liao shih* 19:1b; 70:17a; 115:8a).

Liao had been at peace with Sung since 1004 and was eager to see the war ended. On Jan.29, 1042, Hsing-tsung sent envoys to the Sung court, asking why it was at war with Hsia (*Liao shih* 115:8a).

On Feb.14, 1043, Hsing-tsung sent an Associate Administrator and the Recepient of Edicts in the Bureau of Military Affairs to request Hsia to make peace with Sung (*Liao shih* 19:3b; 115:8a).

On Mar.24, 1043, Hsia congratulated Hsing-tsung on his honourable appelation (*Liao shih* 19:4a; 115:8a).[14]

On Mar.29, 1043, the Liao envoys who had been sent to Hsia returned to the court and reported that Yüan-hao had halted his armies. Hsing-tsung immediately sent envoys to inform the Sung court (*Liao shih* 19:4a; 115:8a).

On May 14, 1043, Hsia envoys to the Liao court offered horses and camels (*Liao shih* 19:4a; 70:17b; 115:8a).

The Sung court was quick to take advantage of the detente. On May 17, 1043, Jen-tsung sent an Administrative Assistant of the Army Which Protects Peace to again recognize Yüan-hao as ruler of Hsia. He was to be presented annually with 10,000 bolts of pongee and 30,000 catties of tea (*Sung shih* 11:5a).

On Sep.1, 1043, Hsia envoys to the Liao court requested Hsing-tsung to attack Sung. This was rejected (*Liao shih* 19:4b; 115:8a).

On Nov.22, 1043, Hsing-tsung sent the Commissioner of the Yen-ch'ang Palace to Hsia with the request that it rescind its attack on the Tang-hsiang (*Liao shih* 19:5a; 115:8a).

In the 4th month (May) of 1044, Hsing-tsung levied troops against five rebellious Tang-hsiang tribes which had joined the Hsia State. In the 6th month (June/July) he sent envoys to inform the Sung court about the coming attack (*Liao shih* 115:8a).

On Aug.16, 1044, Hsia envoys were received at the Liao court. On Aug.31, the authorities found these envoys to be deceitful, since they had not answered questions in accordance with the facts (*Liao shih* 19:6a; 70:17b; 115:8a).

---

[14] On Jan.1, 1043, Hsing-tsung had accepted from his officials the appelation of Emperor Who Is Astute, Refined, Sagacious, Martial, Brave, Strategic, Divine, Meritorious, Shrewd, Wise, Benevolent, and Filial (*Liao shih* 19:3a).

On Sep.28, 1044, another Hsia mission was received at the Liao court. The authorities once more concluded that the envoys were untruthful (*Liao shih* 19:6a; 70:17b).

In the 6th month (June/July) of 1044, Hsing-tsung sent the Commisioner of the Yen-ch'ang Palace as envoy to the Sung court to again announce that he intented to attack Hsia (*Liao shih* 19:5b-6a).

When Hsing-tsung took personal command against Hsia, a Sung envoy presented parting gifts on Oct.3, 1044 (*Liao shih* 19:6a).

On Oct.25, 1044, peace was concluded between Sung and Hsia. An oath letter[15] from Jen-tsung was handed to Yüan-hao in which Sung promised annually to pay 255,000 units of silver, silk, and tea (*Sung shih* 11:8a-8b; 485:19b-20a). In other words, peace was bought by the Sung. Even though the Chinese dynastic historian bravely states that the units were annual "bestowals", the appropriate word is "tribute".

On Nov.1, 1044, envoys from Yüan-hao to the Liao court announced his willingness to back down, and on Nov.3, he promised that the rebellious Tang-hsiang tribes would be abandoned to Liao. On Nov. 15, his envoys offered regional objects. However, the envoys were detained and the war continued. On Nov.16, Yüan-hao offered peace which was rejected. In the previous fighting, Hsing-tsung's brother-in-law had been captured by the Hsia forces. On Nov.21, Yüan-hao proposed an exchange of prisoners. The detained Hsia envoys were thereupon released. On Nov.28, Hsing-tsung left the army. Subsequently, the Liao forces withdrew for lack of provisions (*Sung shih* 485:20b-21a; *Liao shih* 19:6a-6b; 115:8a-8b).

On Dec.29, 1044, Jen-tsung of Sung appointed a Supernumerary Gentleman of the Bureau of Sacrifices of the Masters of Writing and an Audience Usher as envoys for presenting Yüan-hao with a belt of real gold, silver horse trappings, 20,000 ounces of silver, 20,000 bolts of pongee, 30,000 catties of tea, a lacquered bamboo tablet, and a silver seal washed in gold, 2.1 inches square, with the inscription "Ruler of the Hsia State" (*Sung shih* 11:8b; 485:20a-20b).

In the 12th month (Dec./Jan., 1045) of the Liao year 1044, Hsing-tsung's brother-in-law returned to Liao, and Hsia envoys offered gifts (*Liao shih* 155:8b).

On Feb.8, 1045, Liao envoys informed the Sung court that the war against Hsia had been concluded (*Sung shih* 11:9a).

[15] An oath letter took the place of a signed treaty.

On Feb.16, 1045, Hsia envoys to the Liao court offered falcons (*Liao shih* 19:7a).

On Feb.24, 1045, envoys from Yüan-hao arrived at the Sung court to congratulate on the New Year's Day for the first time during his reign (*Sung shih* 11:9a-9b).[16]

On Apr.12, 1045, Sung envoys to the Liao court congratulated on the conclusion of the war against Hsia (*Liao shih* 19:7a).

On Apr.24, 1045, envoys from Yüan-hao arrived at the Sung court to congratulate the birthday of Jen-tsung (*Sung shih* 11:10a).[17]

In the intercalary 5th month (June/July) of 1045, Hsia envoys to the Liao court offered gifts (*Liao shih* 19:7a).

On July 8, 1045, envoys from Yüan-hao to the Sung court thanked for his recognition (*Sung shih* 11:10a).

In the 6th month (July/Aug.) of 1045, Hsia envoys were received at the Liao court (*Liao shih* 70:18a).

In the 2nd month (Mar./Apr.) of 1048, Hsia informed the Sung and Liao courts that Li Yüan-hao had died (possibly assassinated). Yüan-hao was 46 years old. During his reign, the Hsia State had been expanded to the western end of the Kan-su Corridor and adjoining parts of Mongolia in the north. His temple name was Ching-tsung. Jen-tsung of Sung sent a Supernumerary Gentleman of the Bureau of Sacrifices of the Masters of Writing to be the envoy for sacrifing and an Inpector of a subcommandery to be envoy for condoling. He presented 1000 bolts of pongee, 500 pieces of cotton, 100 sheep, 100 bushels of flour, 100 bushels of rice, and 100 bottles of wine. At the funeral, he presented another 1,500 bolts of pongee. Hsing-tsung of Liao sent the Commissioner of the Yung-hsing Palace, the Grand Guardian of the Protective Guards of the Right, and the Junior Inspector of the Court Architect to condole. Yüan-hao was succeeded by his son Liang-tso, who had been born on Mar.5, 1047, and hence was a child (*Sung shih* 11:14a; 485:21b-22a; *Liao shih* 20:2a; 115:8b).

On Apr.23, 1048, Hsia envoys to the Liao court presented Yüan-hao's testamentary gifts (*Liao shih* 20:2a; 115:8b).

---

[16] The New Year's Day of 1045 fell on Jan.21. It is not clear whether the envoys congratulated belatedly or whether they stayed until the next New Year on Feb.9, 1046.

[17] As mentioned before, imperial birthdays were celebrated on a specified day of the Chinese lunar calendar. This made them movable feasts when translated to the solar calendar. Jen-tsung was born on the 14th day of the 4th month (*Sung shih* 9:1a), which in 1045 fell on May 3.

On May 16, 1048, Jen-tsung of Sung sent a Supernumerary Gentleman of the Ministry of Punishments and the Assistant Commissioner of the Imperial Larder to recognize Liang-tso as ruler of Hsia (*Sung shih* 11:14b; 485:22a).

On Oct.11, 1048, Hsia envoys to the Sung court thanked for the condolence and sacrifice. On Jan.23, 1049, they thanked for the recognition (*Hsü Tzu-chih t'ung-chien ch'ang-pien* pp.1516, 1520).

On Feb.9, 1049, the Liao court discussed whether to resume the war against Hsia. The envoys who had arrived from that state for the New Year's congratulations on Feb.5 were detained (*Liao shih* 20:3a; 115:8b).

On Feb.10, 1049, Hsing-tsung of Liao sent envoys to inform the Sung court that he was attacking Hsia. These envoys were received at the Sung court on May 1 (*Sung shih* 11:14b; *Liao shih* 20:3a; 115:8b).

On July 10, 1049, a Sung envoy presented parting gifts to Hsing-tsung (*Liao shih* 20:3b).

On July 22, 1049, Hsia envoys to the Liao court offered gifts. They were detained (*Liao shih* 20:3b; 115:8b).

In the 8th month (September) of 1049, a Liao army, other than the one commanded by the emperor, was defeated by Hsia *(Liao shih* 115:8b).

At some time in 1049, Hsia envoys informed the Sung court that Liang-tso's mother had died. Jen-tsung sent a Gentleman-of-the-Palace of the Ministry of Punishments and the Assistant Commissioner of [the Office of] Crafts to condole. Hsia envoys presented testamentary horses and camels (*Sung shih* 485:22a).

On Feb.7, 1050, Hsing-tsung of Liao sent envoys to reproach Hsia (*Liao shih* 20:4a).

On Apr.7. 1050, Liao envoys informed the Sung court that the armies had withdrawn from Hsia (*Sung shih*: 12:1a).

On July 10, 1050, Sung envoys to the Liao court congratulated on the war against Hsia (*Liao shih* 20:4b).

On Nov.4, 1050, envoys from Liang-tso's [step]mother[18] to the Liao court proposed that the two states return to the prewar status quo. Hsing-tsung replied that if Hsia sent a trusted official it would be considered. In the 12th month (Jan./Feb., 1051) of the Liao year

[18] It has been seen that Liang-tso's mother had died in the preceding year. This must have been his stepmother, the Empress Dowager.

1050, Hsia envoys arrived at the Liao court in accordance with Hsing-tsung's wish (*Liao shih* 20:5a, 5b; 115:9a).

On Mar.17, 1051, Hsing-tsung sent the Inspector-in-chief of the Northern Administration to Hsia to inquire about an uprising of the Tang-hsiang. This envoy returned on June 14 and reported that Liang-tso's [step]mother was willing to attack the Tang-hsiang, that she was willing to raze fortifications, and that she wished to offer horses and camels. On June 30, Hsia envoys repeated the offer to raze fortifications (*Liao shih* 20:5b; 115:9a).

On Nov.9, 1052, Hsia envoys to the Liao court proposed a cessation of hostilities. Hsing-tsung responded with an envoy of his own (*Liao shih* 20:7a; 115:9a-9b).

On Apr.14, in the 7th month (July/Aug.), and on Nov.9, 1053, Hsia envoys to the Liao court offered peace (*Liao shih* 20:7b; 115:9b).

On Mar.5, 1054, Hsia envoys to the Liao court offered regional objects (*Liao shih* 20:8a; 70:19b; 115:9b).

On June 14, 1054, Hsia proposed to offer horses and camels to Liao. Hsing-tsung decided to accept them annually (*Liao shih* 20:8a; 70:19b; 115:9b).

On July 7, 1054, Hsia envoys to the Liao court offered gifts (*Liao shih* 20:8a).

On Aug.13, 1054, Hsia envoys to the Liao court proposed a marriage (*Liao shih* 20:8a; 115:9b).

On Oct.18, 1054, Liao envoys to the Sung court announced that peace had been concluded between Hsia and Liao (*Sung shih* 12:8a).

On Nov.28, 1054, Hsia envoys to the Liao court offered an oath letter [confirming the peace] (*Liao shih* 20:8b; 115:9b).

On Mar.26, 1055, Hsia envoys to the Liao court congratulated (*Liao shih* 20:9a).

On May 11, Jen-tsung of Sung presented the *Tripitaka* to Hsia (*Hsü Tzu-chih t'ung-chien ch'ang-pien* p.1654).

On Sep.1, 1055, Emperor Tao-tsung of Liao sent envoys to Hsia to announce the death of his father Hsing-tsung on Aug.28. Hsia sent envoys to congratulate Tao-tsung on his enthronement. On Oct.20, Tao-tsung sent envoys to Hsia to present the testamentary gifts of the late emperor (*Liao shih* 21:1b, 2a; 115:9b).

On Jan.24, 1056, envoys from Liang-tso to the Sung court announced that his [step]mother had died. On Jan.25, Jen-tsung suspended the court for mourning (*Hsü Tzu-chih t'ung-chien ch'ang-pien* p.1704).

On Apr.23, 1057, envoys from Liang-tso to the Sung court presented his [step]mother's testamentary gifts (*Hsü Tzu-chih t'ung-chien ch'ang-pien* p.1704).

On July 17, 1057, Hsia envoys to the Sung court thanked for the condolence and sacrifice (*Sung shih* 12:12b).

On Jan.27, 1058, Tao-tsung of Liao sent envoys to Hsia to announce the death of the Grand Empress Dowager on Jan.24. She was his grandmother, widow of Sheng-tsung. The Grand Empress Dowager was buried on May 28, in the presence of envoys from Hsia (*Liao shih* 21:5a-5b).

On Jan.3, 1062, Liang-tso requested Chinese gowns and caps from the Sung court, announcing that he would wear them in the following year[19] and follow the Chinese etiquette when receiving envoys. The Sung agreed (*Sung shih* 485:23a; *Hsü Tzu-chih t'ung-chien ch'ang-pien* p.1807).

On May 23, 1062, Liang-tso presented 50 horses to the Sung court and requested the *T'ang shih*, the *Ts'e-fu yüan-kuei*, the *Sung cheng-chih ch'ao ho-yi*, the *Nine Confucian Classics*, and other works. He stated that he wished to establish a library. The horses were rejected, but the Confucian classics were provided (*Sung shih* 12:19b; 485:23a-23b; *Hsü Tzu-chih t'ung-chien ch'ang-pien* p.1812).

In the 1st month (Feb./Mar.) of 1063, Tao-tsung of Liao prohibited the sale of copper to Hsia (*Liao shih* 115:9b).

After Jen-tsung had died on Apr.30,1063, and Emperor Ying-tsung had ascended the throne on May 1, 1063, Hsia envoys to the Sung court on Aug.13 condoled and congratulated on the enthronement. The envoys were received in audience. One of them proceeded without permission to the Gate of Obedience to Heaven and moreover carried his fish tally in a fashion not approved by the Chinese. When detained, he went on a hunger strike. In the end, he was allowed to enter and was provided with food. Liang-tso was requested to punish him (*Sung shih* 485:23b; *Hsü Tzu-chih t'ung-chien ch'ang-pien* p.1841, 1874).

In the autumn of 1063, Hsia violated the Chinese border (*Sung shih* 485:23b).

In 1064 or soon thereafter, Hsia unsuccessfully tried to restore border markets with Sung (*Sung shih* 485:23b).

On Feb.8, 1065, the New Year's Day, Hsia envoys congratulated

---

[19] 1062, according to the Chinese calendar.

at the Sung court. On Feb.14, they presented a communication in which they put the blame for the border troubles on Sung (*Hsü Tzu-chih t'ung-chien ch'ang-pien* p.1884).

On June 28, 1065, Hsia envoys to the Liao court offered gifts (*Liao shih* 22:3b; 115:9b).

On Jan.17, 1066, Hsia envoys arrived at the Sung court for the New Year congratulations of Jan.29 (*Hsü Tzu-chih t'ung-chien ch'ang-pien* p.1914).

In 1066, Hsia attacked a Chinese town. In the 3rd month (Mar./Apr.), its envoys expressed regret over the incident and offered regional objects. They were presented with 500 bolts of pongee and 500 ounces of silver (*Sung shih* 13:7b; 485:24a).

In the 1st month (Jan./Feb.) of 1067, Ying-tsung of Sung sent a palace official to present Liang-tso with winter garments, silver, and pongee (*Sung shih* 14:2a; 485:24a).

After Shen-tsung had ascended the Sung throne on Jan.25, 1067, he sent the Assistant Commissioner of the Imperial Larder to announce the death of his father Ying-tsung in Hsia and at the same time to present Ying-tsung's testamentary gifts (*Sung shih* 485:24a).

On Apr.22, 1067, envoys from Liang-tso to the Sung court requested a normalization of relations. In the 8th month (Sep./Oct.) joint markets were restored. But in the winter, there was another border skirmish, instigated by the Chinese. Liang-tso responded by enticing Chinese officers to a meeting and killing them (*Sung shih* 14:3a, 4b; 485:24a-24b).

On Dec.21, 1067, Hsia envoys to the Liao court offered Uighur Buddhist priests and the *Chin-fo fan-chüeh* Sutra and proposed a border adjustment (*Liao shih* 22:5a; 115:9b).

In the 12th month (Jan./Feb., 1068) of the Chinese year 1067, Li Liang-tso of Hsia died at the age of 21. His temple name was Yi-tsung. He was succeeded by his 7-year-old son Ping-ch'ang. His mother, now the Empress Dowager, took over the government (*Sung shih* 485:25b; 486:1a; *Liao shih* 22:5a; 115:9b).

On Mar.15, 1068, Hsia envoys to the Liao court announced the death of Liang-tso. On Apr.8, Tao-tsung sent envoys to Hsia to condole and sacrifice (*Liao shih* 22:5b; 115:9b).

On Apr.12, 1068, a Hsia envoy to the Sung court announced the death of Liang-tso. Shen-tsung inquired about the killing of the Chinese officers. The envoy replied that the culprits had already been punished (*Sung shih* 14:6a; 486:1a).

On Apr.27, 1068, Hsia envoys thanked the Liao court for the condolence and presented Liang-tso's testamentary gifts (*Liao shih* 22:5b; 115:9b).

On Nov.26, 1068, Tao-tsung recognized Ping-ch'ang as king of Hsia (*Liao shih* 22:6a; 115:9b).

On Jan.8, 1069, Hsia envoys to the Liao court offered gifts (*Liao shih* 22:6a; 70:20a; 115:9b).

In the 2nd month (Feb./.Mar.) of 1069, Shen-tsung sent the Horse Pasturage Supervisor of Ho-nan and others to recognize Ping-ch'ang as ruler of Hsia (*Sung shih* 486:1b).

In the 3rd month (Mar./Apr.) of 1069, Hsia forces destroyed a Chinese fort. Sung protests were rejected (*Sung shih* 486:1b-2a).

On July 24, 1069, Hsia envoys to the Liao court thanked for the recognition (*Liao shih* 22:6a; 115:9b).

On Sep.2, 1069, Hsia envoys informed the Sung court that their state had relinquished Chinese garments and etiquette and resumed its old customs (*Sung shih* 14:9b; 486:2a).

In the 10th month (Oct./Nov.) of 1069, Hsia envoys to the Sung court thanked for the recognition (*Sung shih* 486:2a).

On Dec.31, 1069, Hsia envoys to the Liao court requested a seal and cord for Ping-ch'ang as king of Hsia (*Liao shih* 22:6b; 115:9b).

In the 5th month (June/July) of 1070, Hsia forces defeated Chinese troops. On Sep.28, they attacked a Chinese town and withdrew after nine days (*Sung shih* 15:2b; 486:2a, 2b).

In the 2nd month (Mar./Apr.) of 1071, Hsia forces attacked a Chinese stockade. On Oct.14, Hsia envoys offered gifts to the Sung court. They proposed an exchange of territory which was rejected (*Sung shih* 15:6b; 486:3a-3b).

In the intercalary month (Aug./Sep.) of 1072, Chinese armies were sent against Hsia (*Sung shih* 486:3b).

In the 12th month (Jan./Feb., 1073) of the Chinese year 1072, Hsia envoys to the Sung court presented horses and sought the *Tripitaka*. The *Tripitaka* was provided, and the horses were rejected (*Sung shih* 486:3b).

On Jan.23, 1074, Hsia envoys to the Liao court offered gifts (*Liao shih* 23:2b; 115:9b).

In the 3rd month (Mar./Apr.) of 1075, Shen-tsung of Sung remarked to his officials that when Yüan-hao had "usurped" the title of emperor, he had sent envoys with a "memorial" in which he had called himself a "subject" (*Sung shih* 486:4a). As previously remarked, it is out of the question that the Hsia emperor humbly referred to himself as a subject. His communication was no doubt recast at the Sung court in suitable terms, and these were by Shen-tsung accepted as accurate.

On Apr.13, 1076, Tao-tsung of Liao sent envoys to Hsia to announce the death of his mother, the Empress Dowager, on the preceding day and to deliver her testamentary gifts. On July 7, Hsia envoys to the Liao court condoled and sacrificed (*Liao shih* 23:4a; 115:9b-10a).

In the 6th month (July) of 1079, Hsia forces raided Chinese territory and on Aug.29 looted a Chinese town (*Sung shih* 15:23b; 486:4a-4b).

On Oct.30, 1079, Hsia envoys to the Liao court offered gifts (*Liao shih* 24:1b; 115:10a).

In 1081, Ping-ch'ang was supposedly persuaded by a Chinese favourite to cede territory in the southern Ordos Region to the Sung. When his mother, who controlled the government, learned about this, she had the Chinese executed and her son temporarily imprisoned. The Sung court considered this a rare opportunity to attack Hsia but its armies were repeatedly defeated (*Sung shih* 486:4b-5b).

On Mar.19, Hsia envoys presented a captured Sung officer to the Liao court. On July 4, other Hsia envoys offered gifts (*Liao shih* 24: 3b-4a).

In the 1st month (Jan./Feb.) of 1082, Liao informed the Sung court that the ruler of Hsia, Ping-ch'ang, had been imprisoned and abused by the faction of his mother (*Sung shih* 486:6a).

Fighting continued in 1082, centred on the area of present Lanchou in Kan-su (*Sung shih* 486:8b).

On July 18, 1083, Hsia envoys to the Sung court offered gifts (*Sung shih* 486:8b-9a; *Hsü Tzu-chih t'ung-chien ch'ang-pien* p.3126).

The war continued throughout 1084, even though Hsia envoys to the Sung court offered gifts on Dec.8 of that year (*Sung shih* 16:12b; 486:9b).

Shen-tsung died on Apr.1, 1085, whereafter Sung envoys presented his testamentary gifts to Hsia. In the 7th month (July/Aug.), Hsia envoys condoled at the Sung court, even though fighting still went on (*Sung shih* 486:9b).

On Oct.24, 1085, Hsia envoys to the Sung court offered 100 horses (*Sung shih* 17:3b; *Hsü Tzu-chih t'ung-chien ch'ang-pien* p.3316).

On Oct.28, 1085, envoys from Ping-ch'ang, to the Sung court announced that his mother had died (*Liao shih* 24:6b; 115:10a).

Sung sent a Gentleman-of-the Palace of the Ministry of Punishments as envoy for sacrificing and an Audience Usher as envoy for condoling. On Dec.25, 1085, envoys from Ping-ch'ang to the Sung court presented horses and a white camel as his mother's testamentary gifts (*Sung shih* 17:4a-4b; 486:9b).

On Mar.9, 1086, Hsia envoys to the Sung court offered gifts. On June 17, envoys congratulated on the enhronement of Emperor Che-tsung on Apr.1[20] (*Sung shih* 17:5a, 6a).

On Aug.19, 1086, Hsia requested Sung to cede territory, which at the advice of Ssu-ma Kuang was rejected (*Sung shih* 486:10a-10b; *Hsü Tzu-chih t'ung-chien ch'ang-pien* p.3603).

On Aug.21, 1086, it became known at the Sung court that Li Ping-ch'ang had died, aged 36. His temple name was Hui-tsung. He was succeed by his eldest son, the 3 year-old Ch'ien-shun (*Sung shih* 17:6b; 486:10b).

On Aug.26, 1086, Hsia envoys arrived at the Sung court to congratulate on the birthday of Che-tsung's grandmother, the Grand Empress Dowager (*Sung shih* 17:6b).[21]

On Nov.16, 1086, eight Hsia envoys to the Sung court officially announced the death of Ping-ch'ang. The Chinese government requested a return of the territory and people seized by Hsia since 1081 (*Sung shih* 17:7a; 486:10b; *Hsü Tzu-chih t'ung-chien ch'ang-pien* p.3667).

On Nov.24, 1086, Sung sent a Supernumerary Gentleman of the Treasury Bureau as envoy for sacrificing and the Commissioner of the Imperial Larder as envoy for condoling to Hsia (*Sung shih* 17:7a; 486:10b).

In the 10th month (Nov./Dec.) of 1086, Hsia envoys arrived at the Sung court to present 30 horses and 20 camels on the birthday of Che-tsung[22] (*Sung shih* 486:10b).

On Jan.16, 1087, Hsia envoys arrived at the Sung court for the New Year congratulations of Feb.6 (*Hsü Tzu-chih t'ung-chien ch'ang-pien* p.3716).

---

[20] He was born on Jan.4, 1076, and hence a child.

[21] It is not explicitly stated in the sources that the K'un-ch'eng Festival was the birthday of the Grand Empress Dowager. But since Che-tsung's birthday was the Hsing-lung chieh, there is no other possibility. Che-tsung did not have an empress until 1092. In 1086, the birthday of the Grand Empress Dowager fell on Aug.27.

This embassy must have set out before the death of Ping-ch'ang, since it did not announce it.

[22] It fell on Jan.14, 1087. According to *Hsü Tzu-chih t'ung-chien ch'ang-pien* p.3706, the gifts were offered on Jan.16.

On Jan.22, 1087, Hsia envoys presented Ping-ch'ang's testamentary gifts to the Liao court (*Liao shih* 24:8a; 115:10a).

On Feb.17, 1087, Sung sent the Probationary Supervisor of the Recepients of Edicts in the Bureau of Military Affairs and the Assistant Commissioner for Fostering Propriety to recognize Ch'ien-shun as ruler of Hsia and king of Hsi-p'ing (*Sung shih* 17:7b; 486:10b-11a).

In the 2nd month (Mar./Apr.) of 1087, Hsia envoys presented camels and horses to Che-tsung's grandmother, the Grand Empress Dowager, and thanked for the [condolence] and sacrifices.[23] On Apr.21, the envoys were received in audience (*Sung shih* 17:7b; 486:11a; *Hsü Tzu-chih t'ung-chien ch'ang-pien* p.3747)

In the 7th month (August), Hsia forces attacked Sung fortifications and then withdrew (*Sung shih* 486:11a).

On Sep.13, 1087, the Three Departments and the Bureau of Military Affairs reported to Che-tsung that the Hsia State had not congratulated on the birthday of his grandmother, the Grand Empress Dowager[24] (*Hsü Tzu-chih t'ung-chien ch'ang-pien* p.3822).

In the 3rd month (Mar./Apr.) of 1088, Hsia attacked a Sung stockade (*Sung shih* 486:11a).

On Aug.1, 1088, Tao-tsung of Liao sent envoys to recognize Ch'ien-shun as king of Hsia (*Liao shih* 25:2b; 115:10a).

On Feb.25, 1089, Sung and Hsia made peace (*Sung shih* 17:12a).

On Mar.28, 1089, Hsia envoys to the Sung court thanked for the recognition of their ruler (*Sung shih* 17:12a; 486:11a).[25]

In the summer of 1089, Hsia envoys to the Sung court offered gifts (*Sung shih* 17:12b). Subsequently, Hsia envoys thanked the Liao court for the recognition of Ch'ien-shun (*Liao shih* 25:3a; 115:10a).[26]

In the 6th month (July/Aug.) of 1089, the Hsia State returned some of the Chinese it had seized and received in exchange four stockades. Yet the border remained fluid. In the same 6th month, Sung sent the Commissioner for Fostering Propriety to present ritual objects and winter garments on the birthday of Ch'ien-shun (*Sung shih* 486: 11a-11b).

---

[23] By 486:11a dated 3rd month (Apr./May).

[24] It fell on Aug.16.

[25] By 17:12a dated 1st month, *yi-mao*, by 486:11a and *Hsü Tzu-chih t'ung-chien ch'ang-pien* p.3984 2nd month. The 1st month had no day with the cyclical characters *yi-mao*, so that 2nd month is correct.

[26] In both cases, the cyclical characters given did not occur in these months.

On July 18, 1089, Hsia envoys to the Sung court offered gifts (*Hsü Tzu-chih t'ung-chien ch'ang-pien* p.4045).

On Aug.20, 1089, Hsia envoys arrived at the Sung court to congratulate on the birthday [of the Grand Empress Dowager].[27] On Jan.8, 1090, Hsia envoys arrived to congratulate on the birthday of Che-tsung[28] (*Sung shih* 486:11b; *Hsü Tzu-chih t'ung-chien ch'ang-pien* pp.4053, 4099).

In the 6th month (July) of 1090, Hsia envoys to the Sung court found fault with the drawing of the border. On Aug.21, other envoys also discussed the drawing of the border (*Sung shih* 17:14b, 486:11b).

On Aug.10, 1090, Hsia envoys arrived at the Sung court to congratulate on the birthday [of the Grand Empress Dowager][29] (*Hsü Tzu-chih t'ung-chien ch'ang-pien* p.4188).

In the winter of 1090, Hsia attacked Sung. But on Dec.28, 1090, Hsia envoys also arrived at the Sung court for the New Year congratulations of Jan.23, 1091 (*Sung shih* 486:11b; *Hsü Tzu-chih t'ung-chien ch'ang-pien* p.4256).

On July 30, 1091, Hsia envoys arrived at the Sung court to congratulate on the birthday [of the Grand Empress Dowager].[30] This year, full-scale war between Sung and Hsia broke out again (*Sung shih* 486:11b).

On July 10, 1092, Hsia envoys sought help from the Liao court (*Liao shih* 25:4b; 115:10a).

In 1093, the war abated, and in the 4th month (Apr./May) Hsia envoys to the Sung court proposed a border adjustment. The Chinese replied with complaints of their own, and nothing came of the matter. Later that year, Hsia envoys sought a relaxation of enmity (*Sung shih* 17:19a). (*Sung shih* 486:12a).

On Feb.11, 1094, Hsia envoys to the Sung court offered gifts (*Sung shih* 18:1a).

In the 2nd month (Feb./Mar.) of 1094, Hsia presented horses to contribute toward the expenses of constructing the grave mound of Che-tsung's grandmother, the Grand Empress Dowager.[31] Hsia also sent envoys to discuss once more an exchange of territories, which the Sung rejected (*Sung shih* 486:12).

---

[27] It fell on Aug.24.
[28] It fell on Jan.10.
[29] It fell on Aug.14.
[30] It fell on Aug.3.
[31] She had died on Sep.26, 1093 (*Sung shih* 17:20a).

On Dec.11, 1095, Hsia envoys to the Liao court presented a Buddhist sutra written on palm leaves (*Liao shih* 26:2a).

In 1096, the war between Sung and Hsia started again. In the 6th month (July/Aug.) of 1097, Hsia envoys to the Liao court announced that Sung was fortifying strategic places. Tao-tsung sent envoys to the Sung court, requesting it to make peace with Hsia (*Liao shih* 26:3a; 155:10a).

On July 2, 1098, Hsia envoys to the Liao court asked for help against Sung. Tao-tsung sent two envoys to act as mediators between Hsia and Sung. On Nov.26, these remonstrated with the Sung court and urged it to make peace with Hsia. Later that year, Hsia once more sought rescue from Liao (*Liao shih* 26:3b, 4a; 115:10a).

In the 1st month (Jan./Feb.) of 1099, another Liao envoy arrived at the Sung court to mediate between Hsia and Sung (*Sung shih* 486: 13a).

On Mar.5, 1099, Hsia envoys to the Sung court announced the death of the National Mother. She was the formidable grandmother of the young ruler Ch'ien-shun. The envoys also requested peace. This was rejected, and the envoys were not received (*Sung shih* 18: 13a; 486:13b).[32]

On Apr.6, 1099, Liao envoys were received at the Sung court and requested that the war against Hsia be halted. On June 11, they returned to their court with the message that Sung was demobilizing its troops (*Sung shih* 18:13a; *Liao shih* 26:4a; *Wen-hsien t'ung-k'ao* 346: 24b).

On Sep.17, 1099, Hsia envoys offered peace to the Sung (*Sung shih* 18:14b). Soon thereafter, the war ended. On Dec.31, Hsia envoys to the Liao court thanked for its mediation. In the 12th month (Jan./Feb., 1100) of the Chinese year 1099, Hsia envoys presented an oath letter to the Sung court, in which, in spite of the claim of the dynastic historians, Ch'ien-shun would not have referred to himself as a "subject". As a matter of fact, the Chinese agreed to resume their tribute to Hsia (*Sung shih* 486:14a-14b; *Liao shih* 26:4b; 115:10a).

On Jan.15,1100, Hsia envoys arrived at the Sung court (*Hsü Tzu-chih t'ung-chien ch'ang-pien* p.4849), probably for the New Year's congratulations of Feb.12.

---

[32] 486:13b dates the reception of the envoys 9th month, but that month did not have the cyclical characters *chia-shen*. If 9th month were read as 9th intercalary month, the date would be Oct.31.

On Feb.23, 1100, Che-tsung of Sung died and was succeeded by his younger brother Hui-tsung. In the 9th month (Oct./Nov.), Hsia envoys condoled and sacrificed and congratulated on Hui-tsung's enthronement. On Nov.5, they arrived with gifts to congratulate on his birthday[33] (*Sung shih* 19:4a; 486:14b).

On Dec.28, 1100, envoys from Ch'ien-shun to the Liao court requested a marriage (*Liao shih* 26:5b; 115:10a).

Ch'ien-shun's great-grandfather Yüan-hao, the first emperor of Hsia, had taken steps toward establishing a bureaucracy partially modelled on the Sung system. In 1101, Ch'ien-shun for the first time established an Academy with 300 government-supported students (*Sung shih* 486:14b).

After Tao-tsung of Liao had died on Feb.12, 1101, and had been succeeded by his grandson T'ien-tso, the latter sent envoys on Mar.5 to announce the death in Hsia. On May 5, Hsia envoys condoled at the Liao court. On Jan., 1102, Hsia envoys congratulated T'ien-tso on his enthronement (*Liao shih* 27:1b, 2a; 115:10a).

On July 9, 1102, envoys from Ch'ien-shun to the Liao court requested a marriage (*Liao shih* 27:2b; 115:10b).

When fighting was resumed between Sung and Hsia, envoys from Ch'ien-shun sought rescue from Liao on July 15, 1102 (*Liao shih* 27:2b; 115:10b).

On July 19, 1103, envoys from Ch'ien-shun to the Liao court again requested a marriage (*Liao shih* 27:3a; 115:10b).

On Nov.15, 1103, Hsia envoys to the Liao court sought help against Sung (*Liao shih* 27:3a).

On July 6, 1104, two Hsia envoys to the Liao court again sought help against Sung (*Liao shih* 27:3b; 115:10b).

On Jan.23, 1105, Hsia envoys requested the Liao court to attack Sung (*Liao shih* 27:4a; 115:10b).

On Feb.14, 1105, T'ien-tso of Liao sent an Auxiliary Academician of the Bureau of Military Affairs to remonstrate with the Sung court and ask it to cease its attacks on Hsia (*Liao shih* 27:4a)

On Mar.21, 1105, T'ien-tso enfeoffed a lady of his house as Princess of Ch'eng-an and married her to Ch'ien-shun (*Sung shih* 486:14b-15a; *Liao shih* 27:4a; 115:10b).

---

[33] It fell on Nov.13.

On May 19, 1105, envoys from T'ien-tso to the Sung court demanded that it return territory to Hsia and withdraw its troops (*Sung shih* 20:2a).

On July 21, 1105, Hsia envoys to the Liao court thanked [for the marriage] and offered gifts (*Liao shih* 27:4a).

On Jan.12, 1106, Hsia envoys to the Liao court sought rescue from Sung attacks. On Jan.16, Hui-tsung of Sung sent an envoy to Hsia to discuss peace (*Liao shih* 27:4b).

On Feb.13, 1106, T'ien-tso sent the Commissioner of Military Affairs of the Northern Administration and the Commissioner of Military Affairs of the Southern Administration to the Sung court to remonstrate with it and demand the return of territory it had seized from Hsia (*Liao shih* 27:4b; 115:10b; *Wen-hsien t'ung-k'ao* 346:24b).

On July 23, 1106, Hsia envoys to the Liao court thanked [for the mediation] (*Liao shih* 27:4b; 115:10b).

On Nov.14, 1106, Hsia envoys to the Liao court announced that their state had made peace with Sung (*Liao shih* 27:4b).

In 1107, Hsia offered gifts to the Sung court in order to restore the old relationship (*Sung shih* 20:6b; 486:15a).

On Aug.2, 1108, envoys from Ch'ien-shun announced to the Liao court that the Princess of Ch'eng-an had given birth to a son (*Liao shih* 27:5b; 115:10b).

On Apr.15, 1109, Hsia envoys to the Liao court complained that Sung had not returned territory. During the same year, Hsia envoys offered gifts to the Sung court (*Sung shih* 20:6b; *Liao shih* 27:5b; 115:10b).

On Feb.18, 1110, Hsia offered gifts to the Sung court (*Sung shih* 20:10a).

On July 4, 1110, Hsia envoys offered gifts to the Liao court (*Liao shih* 27:6a; 115:10b).

On July 21, 1113, Hsia envoys offered gifts to the Liao court (*Liao shih* 27:7b; 115:10b).

In 1115, war between Sung and Hsia began anew. The Sung armies attacked victoriously by two routes in the spring but were utterly defeated in the fall. In the winter, Hsia cavalry raided Chinese territory and then withdrew (*Sung shih* 486:15b, 16a).

In spite of the war, Hsia offered gifts to the Sung court on Sep.11, 1115 (*Sung shih* 20:10a). Fighting continued until 1119 (*Sung shih* 20:10a; 486:16a-17a).

In the 10th month (Nov./Dec.) of 1119, Hsia envoys congratulated on the birthday of Hui-tsung of Sung[34] (*Sung shih* 486:17a).

In 1120, Hsia offered gifts to the Sung court (*Sung shih* 22:4b).

In the 6th month (July/Aug.) of 1122, Hsia forces arrived in Liao to assist the Khitan in their final struggle against the Jurchen. They were defeated. On Aug.18, a Hsia envoy inquired about the well-being of the Liao emperor.[35] Ch'ien-shun invited him to come to his state. T'ien-tso temporarily took advantage of this offer (*Liao shih* 29:4b; 115:10b; *Chin shih* 134:1b).

On May 19, 1123, envoys from Hsia to T'ien-tso requested that he recognize Ch'ien-shun as emperor of the Hsia State. He did so in the 6th month (June/July) (*Liao shih* 29:6b; 115:10b).

In the intercalary month (Apr./May) of 1124, Emperor T'ai-tsung of Chin sent a communication to Hsia (*Chin shih* 134:1b).

In the 9th month (Oct./Nov.) of 1124, Hsia envoys to the Sung court offered gifts (*Sung shih* 22:11a).

On Nov.8, 1124, Hsia envoys to the Chin court acknowledged the communication from T'ai-tsung. The *Chin shih* claims that Ch'ien-shun in his reply called himself a "subject", which is as implausible as all other cases previously examined (*Chin shih* 3:5a; 134:1b).

On Nov.22, 1124, Hsia envoys arrived at the Chin court to congratulate on the birthday of T'ai-tsung (*Chin shih* 3:5a).[36]

On Feb.5, 1125, the New Year's Day, Hsia envoys congratulated at the Chin court. On Feb.27, envoys congratulated T'ai-tsung on his enthronement. On Nov.11, envoys congratulated on the birthday of T'ai-tsung (*Chin shih* 3:5b, 6b).

After Ch'in-tsung had ascended the Sung throne on Jan.19, 1126, Hsia envoys congratulated on the New Year's Day of Jan.25 (*Sung shih* 486:17a).

On Nov.1, 1126, Hsia envoys to the Chin court congratulated on the birthday of T'ai-tsung (*Chin shih* 3:9a).

On Feb.13, 1127, the New Year's Day, Hsia envoys congratulated at the Chin court. In the 3rd month (Apr./May), Hsia envoys requested peace with Chin. They were arrested. On Nov.20, Hsia envoys to the Chin court congratulated on the birthday of T'ai-tsung (*Sung shih* 486:17b; *Chin shih* 3:9b, 10b).

---

[34] It fell on Nov.14.

[35] By *Liao shih* 70:31a dated 8th month, but that month did not have a *hsin-wei* day.

[36] It fell on Nov.23.

In the 1st month (Feb./Mar.) of 1128, Emperor Kao-tsung of Southern Sung sent a Supernumerary Gentleman of the Bureau of Reception and an Attendant Gentleman to Hsia with a communication for Ch'ien-shun (*Sung shih* 486:17b).

On Nov.9, 1128, Hsia envoys to the Chin court congratulated on the birthday of T'ai-tsung (*Chin shih* 3:12a).

On Jan.12, 1129, the New Year's Day, Hsia envoys congratulated at the Chin court (*Chin shih* 3:12a).

On Aug.5, 1129, Kao-tsung of Southern Sung sent a Supernumerary Gentleman of the Bureau of Reception as envoy to Hsia (*Sung shih* 25:17b; 486:18b).

On Nov.28, 1129, Hsia envoys to the Chin court congratulated on the birthday of T'ai-tsung (*Chin shih* 3:13a).

On Feb.10, 1130, the New Year's Day, Hsia envoys congratulated at the Chin court (*Chin shih* 3:13a).

In the 1st month (Feb./Mar.) of 1130, Kao-tsung of Southern Sung sent envoys to Hsia (*Sung shih* 26:2a, 486:18b-19a).

On Nov.17, 1130, Hsia envoys to the Chin court congratulated on the birthday of T'ai-tsung (*Chin shih* 3:14b).

On Jan.31, 1131, the New Year's Day, Hsia envoys congratulated at the Chin court (*Chin shih* 3:15a).

In the 8th month (Aug./Sep.) of 1131, an edict of Kao-tsung of Southern Sung stated that Hsia was basically an enemy state (*Sung shih* 486:19a).

On Nov.6, 1131, Hsia envoys to the Chin court congratulated on the birthday of T'ai-tsung (*Chin shih* 3:15b).

On Jan.20, 1132, the New Year's Day, Hsia envoys congratulated at the Chin court. On Nov.24, envoys congratulated on the birthday of T'ai-tsung (*Chin shih* 3:15b, 16a).

On Feb.7. 1133, the New Year's Day, Hsia envoys congratulated at the Chin court. On Nov.13, envoys congratulated on the birthday of T'ai-tsung (*Chin shih* 3:16b, 17a).

On Jan.27, 1134, the New Year's Day, Hsia cnvoys congratulated at the Chin court (*Chin shih* 3:17a).

On July 27, 1134, Kao-tsung of Southern Sung ordered the military commander Wu Chieh (1093-1139) to send a confidential envoy to the Hsia State (*Sung shih* 27:19b).[37]

---

[37] In the 11th month (Nov.Dec.) of 1131, Wu Chieh had sent an envoy with

On Nov.2, 1134, Hsia envoys to the Chin court congratulated on the birthday of T'ai-tsung (*Chin shih* 3:17a).

On Feb.13, 1135, Emperor Hsi-tsung of Chin sent envoys to inform Hsia that T'ai-tsung had died on Feb.9 (*Chin shih* 4:1b).

On Jan.29, 1136, the Chin court for the first time established a protocol for the envoys from Hsia and Koryŏ (*Chin shih* 4:2a).

On Feb.4, 1136, the New Year's Day, Hsia envoys congratulated at the Chin court. On Feb.20, they congratulated on the birthday of Hsi-tsung (*Chin shih* 4:2b).[38]

On Jan.23, 1137, the New Year's Day, Hsia envoys congratulated at the Chin court. On Feb.8, they congratulated on the birthday of Hsi-tsung (*Chin shih* 4:3a).

On Feb.12, 1138, the New Year's Day, Hsia envoys congratulated at the Chin court. On Feb.28, they congratulated on the birthday of Hsi-tsung (*Chin shih* 4:3b).

On Feb.1, 1139, the New Year's Day, Hsia envoys congratulated at the Chin court. On Feb.17, they congratulated on the birthday of Hsi-tsung (*Chin shih* 4:4b).

On June 30, 1139, Li Ch'ien-shun of Hsia died, aged 57. His temple name was Ch'ung-tsung. He was succeeded by his eldest son Jen-hsiao, aged 16 (*Sung shih* 29:6b; 486:20a).[39]

On Nov.19, 1139, Hsia envoys to the Chin court announced the death of Ch'ien-shun (*Chin shih* 4:5b).

On Jan.22, 1140,the New Year's Day, Hsia envoys congratulated at the Chin court. On Feb.7, they congratulated on the birthday of Hsi-tsung (*Chin shih* 4:5b, 6a).

In the 3rd month (Mar./Apr.) of 1140, Emperor Kao-tsung of Southern Sung sent an envoy to Hsia, inviting them to offer gifts. The Hsia government did not respond (*Sung shih* 29:9b; 486:20a-20b).

On May 23, 1140, Hsi-tsung recognized Jen-hsiao as king of Hsia (*Chin shih* 4:6a).

In the 9th month (Oct./Nov.) of 1140, Hsia envoys to the Chin court thanked for the contribution to the funeral expenses for Ch'ien-shun (*Chin shih* 4:6b).

---

a letter to Hsia. In the 12th month (Dec./Jan., 1135) of the Chinese year 1134, he memorialized Emperor Kao-tsung that the Hsia State frequently sent letters (*Sung shih* 26:21b-22a; 486:19a).

[38] Here and below, the congratulations were offered by separate delegations.

[39] 486:20a has July 1. Note that June 30 or July 1 is the date of the actual death.

On Nov.8, 1140, Hsia envoys to the Chin court thanked Hsi-tsung for the recognition (*Chin shih* 4:6b).

On Feb.9, 1141, the New Year's Day, Hsia envoys congratulated at the Chin court. On Feb.25, they congratulated on the birthday of Hsi-tsung (*Chin shih* 4:6b, 7a).

On Jan.27, 1142, Hsia envoys arrived at the Chin court. They congratulated on the New Year's Day of Jan.29. On Feb.14, they congratulated on the birthday of Hsi-tsung (*Chin shih* 4:8a).

On Jan.18, 1143, the New Year's Day, Hsia envoys congratulated at the Chin court. On Feb.3, the protocol for the Emperor's Birthday was made the same as for the New Year's Day (*Chin shih* 4:9a).

On Feb.6, 1144, the New Year's Day, Hsia envoys congratulated at the Chin court. On Feb.22, they congratulated on the birthday of Hsi-tsung (*Chin shih* 4:9b).

On Jan.25, 1145, the New Year's Day, Hsia envoys congratulated at the Chin court. On Feb.10, they congratulated on the birthday of Hsi-tsung (*Chin shih* 4:10b).

On Feb.13, 1146, the New Year's Day, Hsia envoys congratulated at the Chin court. On Mar.1, they congratulated on the birthday of Hsi-tsung. On Mar.4, Chin ceded border territory to Hsia (*Chin shih* 4:10b, 11a).

At some time during 1146, Hsia conferred on Confucius the title of Wen-hsüan Emperor (The Emperor Whose Literary Accomplishments Are Comprehensive) (*Sung shih* 486:20b).

On Feb.2, 1147, the New Year's Day, Hsia envoys congratulated at the Chin court. On Feb.18, the envoys congratulated on the birthday of Hsi-tsung (*Chin shih* 4:11b).

On Jan.23, 1148, the New Year's Day, Hsia envoys congratulated at the Chin court. On Feb.8, they congratulated on the birthday of Hsi-tsung (*Chin shih* 4:12a).

On Mar.15, Hsi-tsung appointed an envoy for taking gifts to Hsia (4:12a).

On Feb.10, 1149, the New Year's Day, Hsia envoys congratulated at the Chin court. On Feb.26, they congratulated on the birthday of Hsi-tsung (*Chin shih* 4:13a, 13b).

On Jan.9, 1150, Hsi-tsung was murdered by conspirators led by his first cousin Ti-ku-nai. The latter ascended the Chin throne. But since he in turn was overthrown eleven years later and subsequently assassinated, he never received a temple name. He is known in history as the Dismissed Emperor or by the posthumous title he received in

1162 as king of Hai-ling. In the 1st month (February) of 1150, he sent the Commander-in-chief of the Imperial Body Guards and others to inform Hsia. On Aug.18, a high-ranking Hsia envoy to the Chin court congratulated the Dismissed Emperor on his enthronement (*Chin shih* 5:2b`-4a, 5a; 134:4a).

On Jan.20, 1151, the New Year's Day, Hsia envoys congratulated at the Chin court. On Feb.4, they congratulated on the birthday of the Dismissed Emperor (*Chin shih* 5:6a).

In the 9th month (Oct./Nov.) of 1151, the Dismissed Emperor of Chin appointed an envoy to congratulate the Hsia ruler on his birthday (*Chin shih* 5:7b).

On Feb.8, 1152, the New Year's Day, Hsia envoys congratulated at the Chin court. On Feb.23, they congratulated on the birthday of the Dismissed Emperor (*Chin shih* 5:7b, 8a).

In the 9th month (Sep./Oct.) of 1152, the Dismissed Emperor appointed a Gentleman-of-the-Palace of the Ministry of Personnel as envoy to congratulate the Hsia ruler on his birthday (*Chin shih* 5:8b).

On the New Year's Day of Jan.27, 1153, the Dismissed Emperor did not hold court. He ordered his high officials to accept the New Year gifts of the Hsia envoys and others (*Chin shih* 5:9a).

On Feb.11, 1153, Hsia envoys to the Chin court congratulated on the birthday of the Dismissed Emperor (*Chin shih* 5:9a).

On Sep.20, 1153, the Dismissed Emperor appointed an Attendant of the Han-lin Academy as envoy to congratulate the Hsia ruler on his birthday (*Chin shih* 5:10a).

On the New Year's Day of Feb.14, 1154, the Dismissed Emperor was unwell. The Hsia envoys and others took up lodgings in Yen-ching (*Chin shih* 5:11a).[40]

On Feb.4, 1155, the New Year's Day, Hsia envoys congratulated at the Chin court. On Feb.19, they congratulated on the birthday of the Dismissed Emperor (*Chin shih* 5:12a).

On Jan.24, 1156, the New Year's Day, Hsia envoys congratulated at the Chin court. On Feb.8, they congratulated on the birthday of the Dismissed Emperor (*Chin shih* 5:14a).

On Feb.12, 1157, the New Year's Day, Hsia envoys congratulated at the Chin court. On Feb.27, they congratulated on the birthday of the Dismissed Emperor (*Chin shih* 5:15a, 15b).

[40] The Dismissed Emperor had moved his capital to Yen-ching (Peking) on Feb.25, 1153 (*Chin shih* 5:9a).

In the 3rd month (Apr./May) of 1157, the Dismissed Emperor of Chin appointed an Auxiliary General of the Guards as envoy to take gifts to Hsia. On Oct.7, he appointed another Auxiliary General of the Guards as envoy to congratulate the Hsia ruler on his birthday (*Chin shih* 5:15b, 16a).

On Feb.1, 1158, the New Year's Day, Hsia envoys congratulated at the Chin court. On Feb.16, they congratulated on the birthday of the Dismissed Emperor (*Chin shih* 5:16a).

On Oct.7, 1158, the Dismissed Emperor appointed an Auxiliary General of the Guards as envoy to congratulate the Hsia ruler on his birthday (*Chin shih* 5:16b).

On Jan.21, 1159, the New Year's Day, Hsia envoys congratulated at the Chin court. On Feb.5, they congratulated on the birthday of the Dismissed Emperor (*Chin shih* 5:17a, 17b).

In the 9th month (Oct./Nov.) of 1159, the Dismissed Emperor appointed an Auxiliary General of the Guards as envoy to congratulate the Hsia ruler on his birthday (*Chin shih* 5:18a).

On Feb.9, 1160, the New Year's Day, Hsia envoys congratulated at the Chin court. On Feb.24, they congratulated on the birthday of the Dismissed Emperor (*Chin shih* 5:18b).

On Jan.28, 1161, the New Year's Day, Hsia envoys congratulated at the Chin court. On Feb.12, they congratulated on the birthday of the Dismissed Emperor (*Chin shih* 5:19b, 20a).

In the 8th month (Aug./Sep.) of 1161, the Dismissed Emperor appointed an envoy to congratulate the Hsia ruler on his birthday (*Chin shih* 5:22a).

While the Dismissed Emperor was absent on a campaign against Southern Sung, his first cousin Wu-lu was enthroned as emperor of Chin on Oct.27, 1161. This was Emperor Shih-tsung. On Dec.15, the Dismissed Emperor, at the age of 40, was murdered in his camp by his officers (*Chin shih* 5:24a; 6:2b-3a). In the 4th month (May/June) of 1162, Hsia envoys to the Chin court congratulated Shih-tsung on his enthronement. They also offered regional objects and congratulated (belatedly) on the emperor's birthday.[41] On May 30, the Hsia envoys were given a banquet. On June 1, they departed (*Chin shih* 6:7a, 7b).

In the 8th month (Sep/Oct.) of 1162, Hsia envoys to the Chin court again congratulated (*Chin shih* 6:9a).

[41] In 1162, it fell on Apr.16.

In the 9th month (Oct./Nov.) of 1162, Shih-tsung appointed a Supernumerary Gentleman of the Left Office of the Masters of Writing as envoy to congratulate the Hsia ruler on his birthday (*Chin shih* 6:9b).

On Feb.5, 1163, the New Year's Day, Hsia envoys congratulated at the Chin court. On Apr.4, they arrived to congratulate on the birthday of Shih-tsung[42] (*Chin shih* 6:10a, 10b).

In the 6th month (July/Aug.) of 1163, Shih-tsung appointed an Auxiliary General of the Guards as envoy to take gifts to Hsia (*Chin shih* 6:11b).

On Jan.26, 1164, the New Year's Day, Hsia envoys congratulated at the Chin court. On Mar.25, they congratulated on the birthday of Shih-tsung (*Chin shih* 6:13a, 13b).[43]

On Sep.10, 1164[44] Shih-tsung appointed an Auxiliary General of the Guards as envoy to congratulate the Hsia ruler on his birthday (*Chin shih* 6:14b).

On Feb.13, 1165, the New Year's Day, Hsia envoys congratulated at the Chin court. On Apr.13,[45] they congratulated on the birthday of Shih-tsung. On Sep.23, they congratulated again (*Chin shih* 6:15a, 15b, 16a).

On Oct.10, 1165, Shih-tsung appointed an Auxiliary General of the Guards as envoy to congratulate the Hsia ruler on his birthday (*Chin shih* 6:16a).

On Feb.3, 1166, the New Year's Day, Hsia envoys congratulated at the Chin court. On Apr.6,[46] they congratulated on the birthday of Shih-tsung (*Chin shih* 6:16b).

On May 26, 1166, Shih-tsung appointed an Auxiliary General of the Guards as envoy to take gifts to Hsia. On Oct.6, he appointed a Han-lin academician as envoy to congratulate the Hsia ruler on his birthday (*Chin shih* 6:17a).

On Jan.23, 1167, the New Year's Day, Hsia envoys congratulated at the Chin court. On Mar.23, they congratulated on the birthday of Shih-tsung (*Chin shih* 6:18a).

On Oct.25, 1167, Shih-tsung of Chin appointed an Auxiliary

---

[42] It fell on Apr.6.

[43] *Chin shih* 134:4b gives the wrong date of Mar.23.

[44] Correcting *chi-hai* to *yi-hai*.

[45] The text gives the cyclical characters *mou-shen* which did not occur in the 3rd month. But since it is known that Shih-tsung's birthday was celebrated on the 1st day of the 3rd month (*Chin shih* 6:13a), the date can be corrected to Apr.13.

[46] Corrected date.

General of the Guards as envoy to congratulate the Hsia ruler on his birthday (*Chin shih* 6:18b).

On Feb.11, 1168, the New Year's Day, Hsia envoys congratulated at the Chin court. On Apr.10, they congratulated on the birthday of Shih-tsung (*Chin shih* 6:19b, 20b; 134:5a).

In the 7th month (Aug./Sep.) of 1168, Hsia envoys were received at the Southern Sung court (*Sung shih* 34:6a).

On Oct.13, Shih-tsung appointed the Commissioner of the Office of Presentations as envoy to congratulate the Hsia ruler on his birthday (*Chin shih* 6:21a-21b).

On Jan.30, 1169, the New Year's Day, Hsia envoys congratulated at the Chin court. On Mar. 30, they congratulated on the birthday of Shih-tsung (*Chin shih* 6:22a, 22b).

On May 28, 1169, Shih-tsung appointed an Auxiliary General of the Guards as envoy to take gifts to Hsia. On Sep.23, he appointed an Auxiliary General of the Guards as envoy to congratulate the Hsia ruler on his birthday (*Chin shih* 6:23a, 23b).

On Jan 19, 1170, the New Year's Day, Hsia envoys congratulated at the Chin court. On Mar.20, they congratulated on the birthday of Shih-tsung (*Chin shih* 5:24b).

On Oct.24, 1170, Shih-tsung appointed a Gentleman-of-the-Palace of the Ministry of Households as envoy to congratulate the Hsia ruler on his birthday (*Chin shih* 6:25b).

On Dec.26, 1170, Hsia envoys thanked the Chin court for support in the matter of Jen Te-ching's execution (*Chin shih* 6:26a).[47]

On Feb.7, 1171, the New Year's Day, Hsia envoys congratulated at the Chin court. On Apr.7, they congratulated on the birthday of Shih-tsung (*Chin shih* 6:26a, 26b).

On Sep.28, 1171, Shih-tsung appointed an envoy to congratulate the Hsia ruler on his birthday (*Chin shih* 6:27b).

On Jan.27, 1172, the New Year's Day, Hsia envoys congratulated at the Chin court. On Mar.26, they congratulated on the birthday of Shih-tsung (*Chin shih* 7:1a, 1b).

In the 4th month (Apr./May) of 1172, Shih-tsung appointed an Auxiliary General of the Guards as envoy to take gifts to Hsia. On Oct.4, he appointed the General of the Guards of the Right as envoy to congratulate the Hsia ruler on his birthday (*Chin shih* 7:2a, 2b).

---

[47] Jen Te-ching had been Li Jen-hsiao's treacherous chief minister.

At some time during 1172, Shih-tsung closed two border markets (*Chin shih* 134:6a).

On Jan.16, 1173, the New Year's Day, Hsia envoys congratulated at the Chin court. On Apr.14, they congratulated on the birthday of Shih-tsung (*Chin shih* 7:4a).

On Oct.9, 1173, Shih-tsung appointed an Auxiliary General of the Guards as envoy to congratulate the Hsia ruler on his birthday (*Chin shih* 7:5b).

On Feb.4, 1174, the New Year's Day, Hsia envoys congratulated at the Chin court. On Apr.4, they congratulated on the birthday of Shih-tsung (*Chin shih* 7:6a).

On Oct.8, 1174, Shih-tsung appointed an Auxiliary General of the Guards as envoy to congratulate the Hsia ruler on his birthday (*Chin shih* 7:7a).

On Jan.25, 1175, the New Year's Day, Hsia envoys congratulated at the Chin court. On Mar.24, 1175, they congratulated on the birthday of Shih-tsung.[48]

On Oct.27, 1175,[49] Shih-tsung appointed a Gentleman of Tallies and Seals as envoy to congratulate the Hsia ruler on his birthday (*Chin shih* 7:8a).

On Feb.13, 1176, the New Year's Day, Hsia envoys congratulated at the Chin court (*Chin shih* 7:8b).

The birthday of Shih-tsung in 1176 fell on Apr.11. But because of a solar eclipse that day, the celebration was postponed until Apr.12, when the Hsia envoys congratulated (*Chin shih* 7:9a).

On Oct.15, 1176, Shih-tsung appointed an Auxiliary General of the Guards as envoy to congratulate the Hsia ruler on his birthday (*Chin shih* 7:10a).

On Feb.1, 1177, the New Year's Day, Hsia envoys congratulated at the Chin court. On Apr.1, they congratulated on the birthday of Shih-tsung (*Chin shih* 7:10b, 11b).

In the 9th month (Sep./Oct.) of 1177, Shih-tsung appointed a Gentleman-of-the-Palace of the Ministry of Arms as envoy to congratulate the Hsia ruler on his birthday (*Chin shih* 7:13a).

On Jan.21, 1178, the New Year's Day, Hsia envoys congratulated

---

[48] Note that the text has a lacuna through the 6th month, but the dates for the New Year and birthday receptions can be reconstructed.

[49] Correcting 9th month to 9th intercalary month.

at the Chin court. On Mar.21, they congratulated on the birthday of Shih-tsung (*Chin shih* 7:14b-15a).

On Oct.23, 1178, Shih-tsung appointed an envoy to congratulate the Hsia ruler on his birthday (*Chin shih* 7:15b).

On Feb.9, 1179, the New Year's Day, Hsia envoys congratulated at the Chin court. On Apr.9, they congratulated on the birthday of Shih-tsung (*Chin shih* 7:17a).

On Oct.15, 1179, Shih-tsung appointed the Leader of the Guards of the Left of the Heir-apparent as envoy to congratulate the Hsia ruler on his birthday (*Chin shih* 7:18a).

On Jan.29, 1180, the New Year's Day, Hsia envoys congratulated at the Chin court. On Mar.28, they congratulated on the birthday of Shih-tsung (*Chin shih* 7:18b).

In the 9th month (Sep./Oct.) of 1180, Shih-tsung appointed the Junior Inspector of the Privy Treasurer as envoy to congratulate the Hsia ruler on his birthday (*Chin shih* 7:19a).

On Jan.17, 1181, the New Year's Day, Hsia envoys congratulated at the Chin court. Subsequently, a border market between Chin and Hsia was reopened (*Chin shih* 8:1a).

On Mar.17, 1181, Hsia envoys to the Chin court congratulated on the birthday of Shih-tsung (*Chin shih* 8:1b-2a).

On June 6, 1181, Shih-tsung appointed a Chief Clerk as envoy to take gifts to Hsia (*Chin shih* 8:3a).

In the 8th month (Sep./Oct.) of 1181, Shih-tsung appointed a Gentleman-of-the-Palace of the Ministry of Personnel as envoy to congratulate the Hsia ruler on his birthday (*Chin shih* 8:3a).

On Feb.5, 1182, the New Year's Day, Hsia envoys congratulated at the Chin court.[50]

On Apr. 5, 1182, Hsia envoys to the Chin court congratulated on the birthday of Shih-tsung (*Chin shih* 8:3b).

In the 9th month (October) of 1182, Shih-tsung appointed the Commissioner of the Service Supervising the Imperial Hand-drawn Carriage as envoy to congratulate the Hsia ruler on his birthday (*Chin shih* 8:4a).

On Jan.26, 1183, the New Year's Day, Hsia envoys congratulated at the Chin court. On Mar.26, they congratulated on the birthday of Shih-tsung (*Chin shih* 8:4b).

---

[50] The text has no entries for the 1st and 2nd months. A Hsia mission to the Chin court for the New Year congratulations of 1182 must, however, be assumed.

On Sep.25, 1183, Shih-tsung appointed an Auxiliary General of the Guards as envoy to congratulate the Hsia ruler on his birthday (*Chin shih* 8:6a).

On Feb.14, 1184, the New Year's Day, Hsia envoys congratulated at the Chin court. (*Chin shih* 8:7a).

In the 2nd month (Mar./Apr.) of 1184, Shih-tsung appointed the Commissioner of the Service of Imperial Utensils as envoy to take gifts to Hsia (*Chin shih* 8:7b).

On Apr.13, 1184, Hsia envoys to the Chin court congratulated on the birthday of Shih-tsung (*Chin shih* 8:7b).

In the 5th month (June/july) of 1184, Shih-tsung appointed an Attending Secretary as envoy to congratulate the Hsia ruler on his birthday (*Chin shih* 8:9a).

On Dec.13, 1184, Shih-tsung ordered that as long as he resided in the Supreme Capital, Hsia and Koryŏ did not have to send envoys to the birthday celebration because the distance was great and the cold severe (*Chin shih* 8:9a).

On Dec.20, 1185, Hsia envoys to the Chin court inquired about the well-being of Shih-tsung (*Chin shih* 8:11a).

On Jan.23, 1186, the New Year's Day, Hsia envoys congratulated at the Chin court. On Mar.23, they congratulated on the birthday of Shih-tsung (*Chin shih* 8:12a).

On Sep.29, 1186, Shih-tsung appointed an Auxiliary General of the Guards as envoy to congratulate the Hsia ruler on his birthday (*Chin shih* 8:15a).

On Feb.10, 1187, the New Year's Day, Hsia envoys congratulated at the Chin court. On Apr.11, they congratulated on the birthday of Shih-tsung (*Chin shih* 8:17b, 18b).

In the 8th month (Sep./Oct.) of 1187, Shih-tsung appointed the Prefect of the Office of Armaments as envoy to congratulate the Hsia ruler on his birthday (*Chin shih* 8:19b).

On Jan.30, 1188, the New Year's Day, Hsia envoys congratulated at the Chin court. On Mar.30, they congratulated on the birthday of Shih-tsung (*Chin shih* 8:20b, 21a).

On Sep.23, 1188, Shih-tsung appointed the Commissioner of the Imperial Falcon Cage as envoy to congratulate the Hsia ruler on his birthday (*Chin shih* 8:22a).

On the New Year's Day of Jan.19, 1189, Shih-tsung was ill with a great sweat and could not hold court. The Hsia envoys who had come to congratulate were sent home. On Jan.20, Shih-tsung died, aged 67, and was succeeded by Chang-tsung. On Jan.31, the new emperor sent the Grand Judge and others to announce Shih-tsung's death in Hsia (*Chin shih* 8:24a; 9:2b).

On Apr.10, 1189, Hsia envoys condoled at the Chin court. On Apr.26, they sacrificed. In the 5th month (May/June), they congratulated Chang-tsung on his enthronement (*Chin shih* 9:3a).

In the 6th month (July/Aug.) of 1189, the high officials of Chin sent envoys to Hsia to announce that Chang-tsung's birthday would be celebrated on the 1st day of the 9th month. On Oct.10, Hsia envoys arrived at the Chin court to congratulate on the birthday of Chang-tsung. Oct.12 was the imperial birthday, but because of the mourning for Shih-tsung the court was suspended (*Chin shih* 9:4b, 5a).

On Oct.22, 1189, Chang-tsung appointed the Commandant of the Guards of the Lung-ch'ing Palace as envoy to congratulate the Hsia ruler on his birthday (*Chin shih* 9:5b).

On Feb.5. 1190, Hsia envoys arrived at the Chin court to congratulate on the New Year's Day. Feb.7 was the New Year's Day, but because of the mourning for Shih-tsung the court was suspended (*Chin shih* 9:7a).

On June 7, 1190, Chang-tsung appointed the Commissioner of the Falcon Cage as envoy to take gifts to Hsia (*Chin shih* 9:8b).

On Sep.28, 1190, Hsia envoys arrived at the Chin court to congratulate on the birthday of Chang-tsung. Oct.1 was the imperial birthday, but because of the mourning for Shih-tsung the court was suspended (*Chin shih* 9:9b).

On Oct.8, 1190, Chang-tsung appointed the Assistant Commander-in-chief of the Army of the Martial Guards as envoy to congratulate the Hsia ruler on his birthday (*Chin shih* 9:9b).

On Jan.24, 1191, Hsia envoys arrived at the Chin court to congratulate on the New Year's Day. Jan 27 was the New Year's Day, but because of the mourning for Shih-tsung the court was suspended (*Chin shih* 9:10b).

On Feb.7, 1191, Chang-tsung's mother, the Empress Dowager of Chin, died. On Feb.12, he sent the Assistant Commander-in-chief and others to announce the death in Hsia. On Apr.4 and Apr.14, Hsia envoys condoled and sacrificed at the Chin court (*Chin shih* 9: 11a, 11b).

On Sep.19, 1191, Hsia envoys arrived at the Chin court to congratulate on the birthday of Chang-tsung. Sep.21 was the birthday, but because of the mourning for the Empress Dowager the court was suspended (*Chin shih* 9:12b).

In the 9th month (Sep./Oct.) of 1191, Chang-tsung appointed the Commissioner of the Palace Audience Gate of the West as envoy to congratulate the Hsia ruler on his birthday (*Chin shih* 9:12b).

On Dec.1, 1191, there was a border incident in which Hsia herdsmen killed a Chin official. It had no repercussions (*Chin shih* 9:13a).

On Jan.15, 1192, Hsia envoys arrived at the Chin court to congratulate on the New Year's Day. Jan.17 was the New Year's Day, but because of the mourning for the Empress Dowager the court was suspended (*Chin shih* 9:13b).

On Oct.5, 1192, Hsia envoys arrived at the Chin court to congratulate on birthday of Chang-tsung. Oct.8 was the imperial birthday but because of the mourning for the Empress Dowager, the court was suspended (*Chin shih* 9:17a).

On Oct.12, 1192, Chang-tsung appointed the Prefect of the Office of the National Altars as envoy to congratulate the Hsia ruler on his birthday (*Chin shih* 9:17b).

On Feb.2, 1193, Hsia envoys arrived at the Chin court to congratulate on the New Year's Day. Feb.4 was the New Year's Day, but because of the mourning for the Empress Dowager the court was suspended (*Chin shih* 10:1a).

In the 5th month (June) of 1193, Chang-tsung appointed the Commissioner of Livery Service as envoy to take gifts to Hsia (*Chin shih* 10:3a).

On Sep.27, 1193, Hsia envoys to the Chin court congratulated on the birthday of Chang-tsung (*Chin shih* 10:4a).

On Oct.16, 1193, Li Jen-hsiao of Hsia died, aged 70. His temple name was Jen-tsung. He was succeeded by his eldest son, Shun-yu, aged 17 (*Sung shih* 486:21b-22a).

On Dec.11. 1193, envoys of Shun-yu to the Chin court announced the death of his father. Chang-tsung appointed the Commissioner of the Palace Gate of the West as envoy to Hsia to condole, sacrifice, and inquire (*Chin shih* 10:4b).

On Jan.24, 1194, the New Year's Day, Hsia envoys congratulated at the Chin court (*Chin shih* 10:5a).

In the 1st month (Jan./Feb.) of 1194, Chang-tsung appointed the Libationer of the National Academy as envoy to recognize Shun-yu as king of Hsia (*Chin shih* 10:5a).

On Sep.16, 1194, Hsia envoys to the Chin court congratulated on the birthday of Chang-tsung (*Chin shih* 10:6b).

On Nov.15, 1194, Chang-tsung appointed the Commissioner of the Office of Presentations as envoy to congratulate the Hsia ruler on his birthday (*Chin shih* 10:8a).

On Feb.12, 1195, the New Year's Day, Hsia envoys congratulated at the Chin court. On Oct.5, they congratulated on the birthday of Chang-tsung (*Chin shih* 10:8b, 10b).

In the 9th month (Oct./Nov.) of 1195, Chang-tsung appointed a Gentleman-of-the-Palace of the Left Office of the Masters of Writing as envoy to congratulate the Hsia ruler on his birthday (*Chin shih* 10: 10b).

On Feb.1, 1196, the New Year's Day, Hsia envoys congratulated at the Chin court (*Chin shih* 10:11b).

On June 11, 1196, Chang-tsung appointed the Assistant Commissioner of the Medical Service as envoy to take gifts to Hsia (*Chin shih* 10:12a).

On Aug.3, 1196, Hsia envoys to the Chin court were received in audience and given communications (*Chin shih* 10:13a).

On Sep.24, 1196, Hsia envoys to the Chin court congratulated on the birthday of Chang-tsung (*Chin shih* 10:13a).

On Oct.22, 1196, Chang-tsung Chin appointed the Inspector of the National Academy as envoy to congratulate the Hsia ruler on his birthday (*Chin shih* 10:13b).

On Jan.20, 1197, the New Year's Day, Hsia envoys congratulated at the Chin court. On Oct.13, they congratulated on the birthday of Chang-tsung. The envoys departed on Oct.22 (*Chin shih* 10:14a, 16a; 134:7a).

On Dec.7, 1197, Chang-tsung appointed a Supernumerary Gentleman of the Ministry of Rites as envoy to congratulate the Hsia ruler on his birthday (*Chin shih* 10:16b).

On the New Year's Day of Feb.8, 1198, there was a solar eclipse. The Hsia envoys congratulated on Feb.10 (*Chin shih* 11:1a).

On June 17, 1198, Chang-tsung appointed the Commissioner of the Visitors' Bureau as envoy to congratulate the Hsia ruler on his birthday (*Chin shih* 11:2a)

On Oct.3, 1198, Hsia envoys to the Chin court congratulated on the birthday of Chang-tsung (*Chin shih* 11:2a).

On Jan.28, 1199, the New Year's Day, Hsia envoys congratulated at the Chin court (*Chin shih* 11:3a).

On June 6, 1199, Chang-tsung appointed a Gentleman-of-the-Palace of the Ministry of Arms as envoy to congratulate the Hsia ruler on his birthday. He appointed an Auxiliary General of the Guards as envoy to take gifts to Hsia (*Chin shih* 11:4b).

On Sep.22, 1199, Hsia envoys to the Chin court congratulated on the birthday of Chang-tsung (*Chin shih* 11:5a-5b).

On Jan.18, 1200, the New Year's Day, Hsia envoys congratulated at the Chin court (*Chin shih* 11:6a).

In the 10th month (Nov./Dec.) of 1200, Chang-tsung appointed an Auxiliary General of the Guards as envoy to congratulate the Hsia ruler on his birthday (*Chin shih* 11:8a).

On Feb.5, 1201, the New Year's Day, Hsia envoys congratulated at the Chin court. On Apr.9, they congratulated again. At this occasion or soon thereafter, they sought medicines for Shun-yu's sick mother. The Chin court provided these in the 8th month (Aug./Sep.) (*Chin shih* 11:8b, 9a; 134:7a).

On Sep.29, 1201, Hsia envoys to the Chin court congratulated on the birthday of Chang-tsung (*Chin shih* 11:10a).

On Nov.24, 1201, Chang-tsung appointed a Supernumerary Gentleman of the Ministry of Punishments as envoy to congratulate the Hsia ruler on his birthday (*Chin shih* 11:10b).

On Jan.16, 1202, the New Year's Day, Hsia envoys congratulated at the Chin court. On Sep.18, they congratulated on the birthday of Chang-tsung (*Chin shih*11:11a, 12a).

On Sep.30, 1202, Chang-tsung appointed an Auxiliary General of the Guards as envoy to congratulate the Hsia ruler on his birthday (*Chin shih* 11:12a).

On Feb.14, 1203, the New Year's Day, Hsia envoys congratulated at the Chin court. On Sep.7, they congratulated on the birthday of Chang-tsung (*Chin shih* 11:12b, 14a).

On Dec.2, 1203, Chang-tsung appointed an envoy to congratulate the Hsia ruler on his birthday (*Chin shih* 11:14b).

On Feb.3, 1204, the New Year's Day, Hsia envoys congratulated at the Chin court. On Sep.25, they congratulated on the birthday of Chang-tsung (*Chin shih* 12:1a, 3b).

On Jan.22, 1205, the New Year's Day, Hsia envoys congratulated at the Chin court. On Oct.14, they congratulated on the birthday of Chang-tsung (*Chin shih* 12:4a, 5b).

On Feb.10, 1206, Hsia envoys to the Chin court congratulated on the New Year's Day (*Chin shih* 12:6b).

On Mar.1, 1206, Li Shun-yu of Hsia was overthrown by his first cousin An-ch'üan and died soon thereafter, aged 30. His temple name was Huan-tsung. An-ch'üan enthroned himself. He forced Shun-yu's mother to send envoys to the Chin court, stating that she had found her son incompetent and with the support of the high officials had enthroned An-ch'üan. On Oct.26, Chang-tsung sent a Gentleman-of-the-Palace of the Left Office of the Masters of Writing to recognize An-ch'üan as king of the Hsia State (*Sung shih* 486:22a; *Chin shih* 12: 11a, 11b; 134:7a).

On Jan.30, 1207, the New Year's Day, Hsia envoys congratulated at the Chin court. On Sep.24, they congratulated on the birthday of Chang-tsung (*Chin shih* 12:13b, 15b).

On Dec.25, Chang-tsung appointed a Gentleman of Tallies and Seals as envoy to congratulate the Hsia ruler on his birthday (*Chin shih* 12:16b).

On Jan.19, 1208, the New Year's Day, Hsia envoys congratulated at the Chin court (*Chin shih* 12:16b).

On July 9, 1208, the celebration of the birthday of Emperor Chang-tsung was moved from the 1st day of the 9th month to the 15th day of the 10th month. On Nov.24, Hsia envoys congratulated according to the new schedule (*Chin shih* 12:18a, 18b).

In the 8th month (Aug./Sep.) of 1210, Hsia forces raided Chin territory (*Chin shih* 13:3b).

On Jan.17, 1211, the New Year's Day, Hsia envoys congratulated at the Chin court (*Chin shih* 13:4a).

On Sep.18, 1211, Li An-ch'üan of Hsia died, aged 42. His temple name was Hsiang-tsung. He was succeeded by his relative Tsun-hsü (*Sung shih* 486:22a-22b).

On Feb.5, 1212,the New Year's Day, Hsia envoys congratulated at the Chin court (*Chin shih* 13:5b).

In the 3rd month (Apr./May) of 1212, Emperor Ning-tsung of Southern Sung sent envoys to recognize Tsun-hsü as king of Hsia. During the same month, the Chin emperor[51] also sent envoys to recognize him as king (*Sung shih* 486:22b; *Chin shih* 13:5b).

On Dec.15, 1213, Hsia forces raided Chin (*Chin shih* 14:2b). That

[51] Emperor Chang-tsung had died on Dec.29, 1208, and had been succeeded by his brother. The latter was overthrown on Sep.10, 1213, and subsequently murdered. He therefore received no temple name and is in history known as the king of Wei-shao.

state had been under Mongol attack since 1211, and Tsun-hsü sought to turn this to Hsia's advantage.

In the 7th month (Aug./Sep.) of 1214, a Hsia agent reached Ssu-ch'uan in Southern Sung with a letter, proposing a joint attack on Chin. He received no response (*Sung shih* 39:11a).

On Sep.20, 1214, Hsia forces invaded Chin territory (*Chin shih* 14: 5a).

On Nov.1, 1221, another Hsia agent reached Ssu-ch'uan in Southern Sung, proposing a joint military action against Chin (*Sung shih* 40: 10b).

In 1223, Tsun-hsü abdicated in favour of his son Te-wang and assumed the title of Supreme Emperor (*Sung shih* 486:23a).

The attempts by Hsia to exploit the weakness of the Chin State having failed, envoys from Te-wang arrived at the Chin court on Dec.7, 1224, in order to make peace (*Chin shih* 17:3a).

In the 9th month (Oct./Nov.) of 1225, peace was concluded between Hsia and Chin. Emperor Ai-tsung[52] of Chin sent a mission in response, led by a Master of Writing of the Ministry of Rites, the Grand Judge, and an Attending Secretary (*Chin shih* 17:4a).

On Jan.30, 1226, the New Year's Day, Hsia envoys congratulated at the Chin court (*Chin shih* 17:4b).

In the spring of 1226, it became known at the Southern Sung court that the abdicated emperor of Hsia, Li Tsun-hsü, had died, aged 64. His temple name was Shen-tsung (*Sung shih* 486:23a).

In the 7th month (July/Aug.) of 1226, the Southern Sung court learned that Li Te-wang of Hsia had died as well, aged 46. His temple name was Hsien-tsung. He was succeeded by his relative Hsien (*Sung shih* 486:23a).

On Nov.6, 1226, Hsia envoys to the Chin court announced the death of Te-wang (*Chin shih* 17:5a).

On Dec.13, 1226, Hsia envoys arrived at the Chin court for the New Year congratulations of Jan.19, 1227. Two days later, on Dec.15, a goodwill mission from Hsia was also received at the Chin court. Soon thereafter, Ai-tsung of Chin sent a Palace Grandee to Hsia to condole and sacrifice (*Chin shih* 17:5b).

Hsia had been under Mongol pressure for a long time. In 1209, the

---

[52] The king of Wei-shao had on Sep.22, 1213 been succeeded by Emperor Hsüan-tsung. Hsüan-tsung died on Jan.19, 1223 and was succeeded by the last Chin emperor, Ai-tsung, on Jan.20.

Mongols had invaded Hsia, which had led to its nominal submission in 1210. In early 1226, the Mongols attacked again and in 1227 laid siege to the Hsia capital. In the the 6th month (July/Aug.) of 1227, Li Hsien surrendered to the Mongols and was killed. The remarkable Hsia State had ceased to exist (*Sung shih* 486:23a).

Relations between the Tanguts and China were at first relatively cordial. The Tangut chiefs supported the T'ang and were rewarded with the imperial surname of Li. Sung suspended the court after the deaths of Yi-yin and Kuang-jui. All rulers from Ssu-kung to Yüan-hao were during their lifetimes appointed to nominal Chinese offices. But these relations soured because of Chinese meddling. The Sung attempted to gain influence in Hsia through Chi-p'eng and thereby provoked a backlash led by Chi-ch'ien. Wars began and occupied almost a third of the time left until Hsia was destroyed by the Mongols. The peace treaty of Oct.25, 1044, in which Sung agreed to pay an annual tribute of 255,000 units in silver, silk, and tea, brought only temporary relief to China.

With the partial exception of Chi-p'eng, the Tangut chiefs were independant rulers, one of whom rejected a Sung request in 1006 to render hostages. They called themselves kings of Hsia from not later than 967. The Sung and Liao made no issue of this until Yüan-hao proclaimed himself emperor in 1038. This created a dilemma. While Sung and Liao reluctantly were forced to accept the imperial claims of each other, neither was prepared to do so from Hsia. The *Sung shih* persistantly uses the term "king of Hsia" or more often "ruler of Hsia", which probably reflects contemporary practice. The *Liao shih* always says "king of Hsia". Only when the Liao empire was in full dissolution did T'ien-tso recognize Ch'ien-shun as emperor in 1123. The Chin resumed the term "king".

During its time of existance, Hsia developed a remarkable culture, influenced but not dominated by Chinese civilization. In spite of lip service to Confucianism and the posthumous title granted to Confucius in 1146, it was a Buddhist state. Its missions to Sung, Liao, and Chin are richly documented in *Sung shih*, *Liao shih*, and *Chin shih*. But since the Hsia has no dynastic history of its own, there is no way of verifying or complementing that information.

The Sung recognized all Hsia rulers except Chi-ch'ien. That makes sense, since Emperor T'ai-tsung had given his support to Chi-p'eng. Recognitions ceased with the Southern Sung. The Liao is recorded to have recognized all contemporary Hsia rulers except Liang-tso, the

Chin all but three of the seven contemporary rulers.

China is not recorded to have announced the death of a single member of its imperial houses to Hsia. The Liao is recorded to have announced to Hsia the deaths of Emperor Sheng-tsung's mother, Sheng-tsung, Hsing-tsung, Tao-tsung's grandmother and mother, and Tao-tsung. That means every Liao emperor from 983 except, of course, the last. The Chin is recorded to have announced to Hsia the deaths of T'ai-tsung, Hsi-tsung, Shih-tsung, and Chang-tsung's mother. There is no mention of the Dismissed Emperor, nor of Chang-tsung and his successors.[53] Hsia is recorded to have announced the deaths of Yüan-hao's mother, Liang-tso's stepmother, Liang-tso, and Ch'ien-shun's grandmother to Sung, of Ping-ch'ang's mother to Liao, and of Ch'ien-shun and Te-wang to Chin.

It is recorded that Hsia condoled the Sung on the death of Jen-tsung, Shen-tsung, Che-tsung, and Che-tsung's grandmother. Chen-tsung and Ying-tsung are not mentioned. Hui-tsung, and Ch'in-tsung do not apply, since they died in Jurchen captivity. Hsia condoled Liao on the deaths of Sheng-tsung (contributing to the funeral expenses) and T'ao-tsung's mother. It condoled the Chin on the deaths of Shih-tsung and Chang-tsung's mother.

The Sung is recorded to have condoled Hsia on the deaths of Te-ming's mother, Te-ming (contributing to the funeral expenses), Yüan-hao's mother, Yüan-hao (contributing to the funeral expenses), Liang-tso's mother, Ping-ch'ang's mother, and Ping-ch'ang. Condolences ceased with the Southern Sung.

The Liao is recorded to have condoled Hsia on the deaths of Chi-ch'ien, Te-ming's mother, Yüan-hao, and Liang-tso.

The Chin is recorded to have condoled Hsia on the deaths of Ch'ien-shun and Jen-hsiao.

It became fashionable during this time to present testamentary gifts of deceased rulers, of Empresses Dowager, and of Grand Empresses Dowager to foreign courts. Hsia is recorded to have presented such gifts to Sung after the deaths of Liang-tso's stepmother and Ping-ch'ang's mother, to Liao after the deaths of Chi-ch'ien, Yüan-hao, Liang-tso's mother, Liang-tso, and Ping-ch'ang. Sung offered testamentary gifts of Ying-tsung and Shen-tsung to Hsia. Liao offered testamentary gifts

[53] The first emperor, T'ai-tsu, died before diplomatic relations were established between Hsia and Chin.

of Hsing-tsung and Tao-tsung's mother to Hsia. There is no mention of testamentary gifts to or from Chin.

The Sung, with the possible exception of Chi-yün, routinely conferred posthumous titles to the Hsia rulers from Yi-yin to Te-ming. But it granted no life or posthumous titles after Yüan-hao had proclaimed himself emperor in 1038. Liao and Chin did not confer posthumous titles to any of the Hsia rulers.

Hsia is recorded to have congratulated Sung after the enthronements of Ying-tsung, Che-tsung, and Hui-tsung, Liao after the enthronements of Hsing-tsung, Tao-tsung, and T'ien-tso, and Chin after the enthronements of T'ai-tsung, the Dismissed Emperor, Shih-tsung, and Chang-tsung. No congratulations from Sung to Hsia are recorded.

New Year congratulations from Hsia to Sung are recorded for 1045, 1065, 1066, 1087, 1090, 1091, and 1100.[54] New Year congratulations from Hsia to Liao are recorded only for 1049. On the other hand, New Year congratulations from Hsia to Chin became routine, and the only ones not recorded from 1125 to 1227 are for 1128, 1135, 1150, 1162, 1165, 1185, 1209, and 1213-1226. No congratulations from Sung to Hsia are recorded.

Finally, Hsia is recorded to have congratulated in Sung on the birthdays of Jen-tsung in 1045, of Che-tsung's grandmother, the Grand Empress Dowager, in 1086, 1089, 1090, and 1091, of Che-tsung in 1086 and 1089, and of Hui-tsung in 1100. Hsia did not congratulate on the imperial birthdays of Liao. But birthday congratulations to the Chin emperors again became routine. Hsia is recorded to have congratulated T'ai-tsung every year from 1124 to 1134, Hsi-tsung every year from 1136 to 1149, except 1143, the Dismissed Emperor every year from 1151 to 1161 except 1154, Shih-tsung every year from 1162 to 1188 except 1185, and Chang-tsung every year from 1189 to 1208 except 1200.[55]

Sung is recorded to have congratulated the Hsia ruler Ch'ien-shun on his birthday in 1089.The Liao is recorded to have congratulated Te-ming on his birthday once. The Chin is recorded to have con-

---

[54] There is also the general statement that Te-ming's envoys annually congratulated in Sung on the New Year Days (*Sung shih* 485:12a).

[55] In 1176, the birthday of Shih-tsung fell on Apr.11. Because of a solar eclipse that day, it was celebrated on Apr.12. Similarly, the New Year Day of 1198 fell on Feb.8. Because of a solar eclipse that day, it was celebrated on Feb.10. As remarked before, this was because of a superstition no longer supported by astronomical knowledge.

gratulated Jen-hsiao 36 times from 1151 to 1192, and Shun-yu every year from 1194 to 1203.

It is clear from this survey that the entries in *Sung shih*, *Liao shih*, and *Chin shih* cannot be complete. They are rich enough, however, to reveal an increasing sophistication in foreign relations, which became a routine by Chin times.

This is the distribution by 20-year periods of the 88 recorded missions from Hsia to Sung, the 109 missions to Liao, and the 187 missions to Chin:

Missions from Hsia

	To Sung	To Liao	To Chin
947- 966	1		
967- 986	1	2	
987-1006	8	31	
1007-1026	5	2	
1027-1046	6	18	
1047-1066	16	18	
1067-1086	18	11	
1087-1106	23	21	
1107-1126	7	6	7
1127-1146	0		40
1147-1166	0		40
1167-1186	1		41
1187-1206	0		47
1207-1226	2		12

It can be seen that Hsia at first cultivated closer ties with Liao than with Sung. Conflicts between the two states were few, tensions in 991 and 1043-1044, war from 1049 to 1051. Three Hsia rulers married Liao princesses, Chi-ch'ien in 989, Yüan-hao in 1031, and Ch'ien-shun in 1105, whereas there were never any marriage relations between the Hsia, Sung, and Chin houses. Liao desired stability and status quo and hence mediated between Hsia and Sung in 1042, 1043, 1098, 1099, 1105, and 1106. But when Hsia grew stronger and Liao weaker, the relations of Hsia to Sung improved. They came to an end after the fall of Northern Sung in 1127. Emperor Kao-tsung attempted to open diplomatic and commercial intercourse with Hsia from 1128 to

1140 but met with no success. He expressed his frustrations in 1131 by referring to Hsia as basically an enemy state. A single mission from Hsia was received at the Southern Sung court in 1168. Only in 1214 and 1221 did Hsia agents make their way to Ssu-ch'uan to propose a joint action against Chin. When Chin had replaced Liao as Hsia's powerful neighbour, the two states settled down to peaceful coexistance from 1225. The great increase in missions was due to the fact that diplomatic protocol by that time routinely required congratulations on the New Year Days and the birthdays of the emperors.

The missions from Hsia to its neighbours, then, were concerned with the niceties of diplomatic protocol, war and peace, the delineation of the border, marriage negotiations and the like. But most if not all missions also engaged in government trade and the private commerce of the envoys. That is easily documented.

In 1007, Hsia requested that its envoys to Sung should be allowed to trade in K'ai-feng. The court agreed to this (*Sung shih* 485:10a).

On Jan.10, 1034, Emperor Hsing-tsung of Liao prohibited the Hsia envoys to trade privately in gold and iron while en route to and from his court (*Liao shih* 18:4b; 115:7b).

On Oct.13, 1197, Hsia envoys to Chin congratulated on the birthday of Chang-tsung. When they departed on Oct.23, the court agreed to restore two border markets (*Chin shih* 10:16a; 134:7a). This means that a mission, which ostensibly was concerned only with ritual, also had negotiated on trade.

In 1157, 1163, 1166, 1169, 1172, 1181, 1184, 1190, 1193, 1196, and 1199, Chin sent missions to Hsia exclusively for government trade.

Above all, as already remarked in the section devoted to Koryŏ, Hsia envoys arrived in Chin in 1189, 1190, 1191, 1192, and 1193 for imperial birthday and New Year celebrations, even though they knew fully well that the court was suspended for state mourning. Apart from the conceivable dictates of protocol, the magnet which drew these missions was trade. On Jan.30, 1191, Emperor Chang-tsung instructed the high officials that the Hsia envoys could remain in their lodge and trade for one day in spite of the mourning. The Masters of Writing stated that according to precedent envoys were permitted to stay and trade for three days. The emperor accepted this (*Chin shih* 9:10b). In fact, it is documented that envoys stayed for longer than three days. For instance, for the New Year celebration on Jan.19, 1227, the Hsia envoys arrived at the Chin court as early as Dec.13, 1226 (*Chin shih* 17:5b).

Hsia exported horses, camels, cattle, falcons, carpets, herbs, salt, pearls, jade etc.,[56] but on the government level the sources for Sung chiefly record the offer of horses and camels, if they itemize the merchandise at all. Since Sung had a chronic shortage of horses, these may well have been the most coveted commodity. This is what the Sung is stated to have received:

960 or soon thereafter: 300 horses.
976: 1000 cattle and sheep.
990 or soon thereafter: one white falcon. Rejected.
994: horses and camels.
995: fine horses.
1002: horses and camels.
1006: 725 horses, 300 camels.
1007: 500 horses, 300 camels.
1049: horses and camels.
1062: 50 horses. Rejected.
1072: horses. Rejected.
1085: horses, one white camel.
1086: horses and camels.
1087: horses and camels.
1094: horses.

The Chinese paid with silver, cash, silk, gold, silver and [porcelain] vessels, silver boxes, gongs, brocade robes, garments, winter garments, caps, gold, silver and jade belts, silver horse trappings, litchis, tea, wine, drugs, and books.

[56] See *Cambridge History of China*, vol.6, p.196. Emperor Shih-tsung of Chin complained to his officials in 1172:"The Hsia State exchanges pearls and jade against our silk. That is not profitable" (*Chin-shih* 134:6a). The pearls had of course been obtained by Hsia through the caravan trade on the Silk Routes.

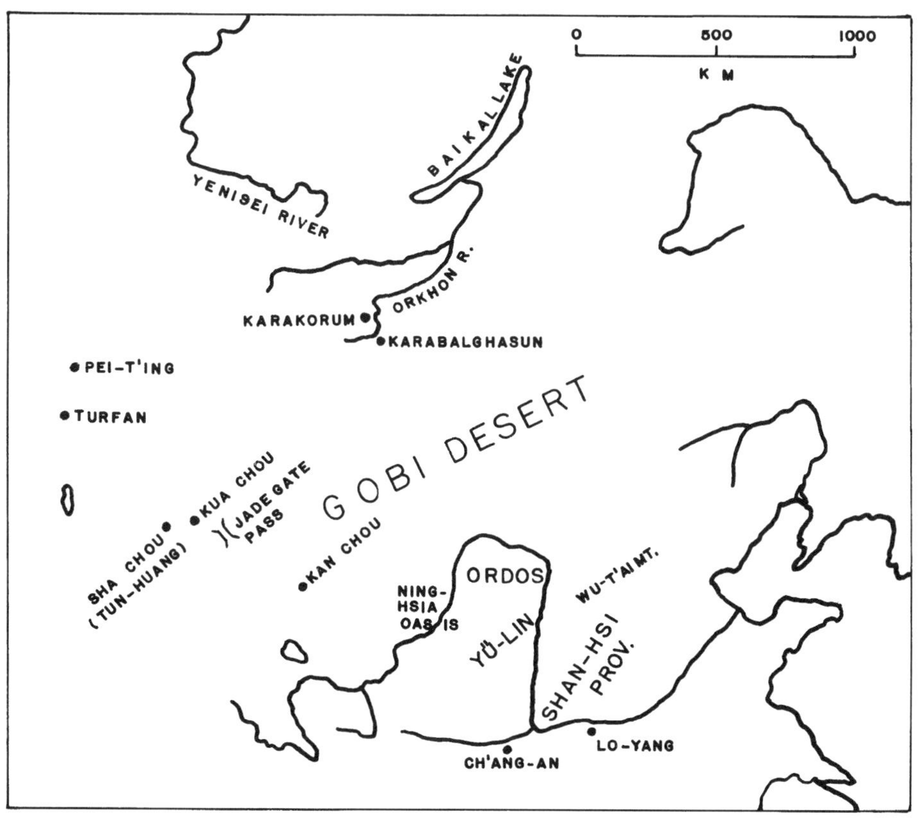

Map 10. Place names connected with the Turkic and Tangut tribes.

LIAO

The Khitan, in Chinese Ch'i-tan, may have belonged to the Mongol language family. When they appeared in history, they consisted of eight loosely federated tribes who lived in central Manchuria around the Sungari and Liao Rivers. This placed them west of Koguryŏ, later of Po-hai, and northeast of the Hsi. They had no common border with Sui or T'ang and therefore had to ally themselves with some of the Hsi tribes when they entered into hostilities with China. It was the Khitan who were destined to found the Liao dynasty in 947 (map 11).

On Dec.24, 590, Khitan envoys to the Sui court offered gifts (*Sui shu* 2:6b).

In the 1st month (February) of 591, Khitan envoys offered gifts (*Ts'e-fu yüan-kuei* p.5023).

On Feb.11, 593, Khitan envoys offered regional objects (*Sui shu* 2:8b).

In the 1st month (Jan./Feb.) of 600, Khitan envoys offered regional objects (*Sui shu* 2:13b-14a).

In 611, Khitan envoys offered regional objects (*Wen-hsien t'ung-k'ao* 345:16a).

On Feb.4, 615, Emperor Yang of Sui gave a great banquet for foreign envoys, including Khitan (*Sui shu* 4:9b).

In 619, Khitan looted Chinese border areas (*Chiu T'ang shu* 199B:5a; *Wen-hsien t'ung-k'ao* 345:16a).

In the 2nd month (Feb./Mar.) of 619, Khitan envoys to the T'ang court offered fine horses and luxuriant sable furs (*T'ang hui-yao* 96:1a).

The Khitan chief Sun Ao-ts'ao had by Emperor Yang of Sui been given the title of Imperial Household Grandee of the Golden Seal and Purple Ribbon. In 621, he sent envoys to the T'ang court and was appointed a General of the Cloud Flags (*Chiu T'ang shu* 199B:5b; *Wen-hsien t'ung-k'ao* 345:16a).

In 623, envoys from the Khitan chief To-lo offered fine horses and luxuriant sable furs (*Chiu T'ang shu* 199B:5a; *Wen-hsien t'ung-k'ao* 345:16a).

In the 6th month (July) of 623, envoys from Sun Ao-ts'ao offered gifts (*Ts'e-fu yüan-kuei* p.5023).

In the 2nd month (Feb./Mar.) of 624, Khitan envoys offered gifts (*Ts'e-fu yüan-kuei* p.5023).

In 628, the Khitan chief Mo-hui turned against the Hsieh-li Qaghan of the Eastern Turks and offered an alliance to the T'ang. Hsieh-li's envoys requested in vain that Emperor T'ai-tsung reject this offer (*Chiu T'ang shu* 199B:5a; *Tzu-chih t'ung-chien* p.6050; *Wen-hsien t'ung-k'ao* 345:16a).

On Feb.7, 629, a Khitan chief was received at the T'ang court (*Chiu T'ang shu* 2:10a; *Ts'e-fu yüan-kuei* p.5023).

In the 11th month (Nov./Dec.) of 629, a Khitan chief was received at the T'ang court (*Ts'e-fu yüan-kuei* p.5023).

In the 6th month (June/July) of 632, a Khitan chief was received at the T'ang court (*Ts'e-fu yüan-kuei* p.5024).

In the intercalary month (Sep./Oct.) of 632, Khitan were received at the T'ang court (*Ts'e-fu yüan-kuei* p.5024).

In the 1st month (Feb./Mar.) of 633, a Khitan chief was received at the T'ang court (*Ts'e-fu yüan-kuei* p.5024).

On Feb.16, 645, T'ai-tsung issued orders for his war against Koguryŏ, in which Silla, Paekche, the Hsi, and the Khitan were expected to attack by several routes (*Tzu-chih t'ung-chien* p.6215).

In the 1st month (Feb./Mar.) of 645, Khitan envoys congratulated, presumably on the New Year's Day of Feb.2, and offered regional objects (*Ts'e-fu yüan-kuei* p.5024).

En route to his war against Koguryŏ, T'ai-tsung met in 645 with Khitan chiefs and elders and gave them presents, to each in accordance with his rank. He appointed the chief K'u-ko a General of the Martial Guards of the Left (*Chiu T'ang shu* 199B:5b).

In 648, T'ai-tsung created the imaginary Sung-mo Area Command and made K'u-ko its Military Governor. He bestowed on him the imperial surname of Li and made him baron of Wu-chi. Subsequently, K'u-ko was appointed General-in-chief Inspecting the Gates of the Left (*Chiu T'ang shu* 199B:5b; *Wen-hsien t'ung-k'ao* 345:16a).[1]

In 685 or soon thereafter, the Empress Wu appointed Sun Wan-jung, a great-grandson of Sun Ao-ts'ao, as General of the Jade Bell Guards of the Right and Inspector of Kuei-ch'eng commandery and enfeoffed

[1] The Empress Wu (r.684-705) appointed K'u-ko's great-grandson Hu-mo-li a General of the Guards of the Left, Concurrent Acting Inspector of T'an-han commandery, and enfeoffed him as king of Kuei-shun commandery (*Chiu T'ang shu* 199B:5b).

him as duke of Yung-lo prefecture (*Chiu T'ang shu* 199B:5b).

In 696, the Empress Wu appointed the Khitan chief Li Chin-chung as General-in-chief of the Martial, Guards of the Right and Military Governor of the imaginary Sung-mo Area Command. But tensions between the Khitan and Chinese led to war that year, and commanded by Li Chin-chung and his brother-in-law, the above-mentioned Sun Wan-jung, the Khitan forces victoriously reached the area of present Peking. The Empress Wu changed Li's name from Chin-chung (Utterly Loyal) to Chin-mieh (Utterly Destroyed), and Sun's from Wan-jung (Ten-thousand Splendours) to Wan-chan (Ten-thousand Decapitations). Li Chin-chung assumed the title of Qaghan Who Has No Superior. He died at the end of 696 and was succeeded by Sun Wan-jung. The Eastern Turkish qaghan Mo-ch'o took advantage of the absence of so many Khitan forces, attacked the Khitan homeland, captured the wives and children of Chin-chung and Wan-jung, and then withdrew. The war ended in 697. For the next decades, the Khitan fell under the dominance of the Eastern Turks (*Chiu T'ang shu* 199B:5b; *T'ang hui-yao* 96:1b; *Tzu-chih t'ung-chien* pp.6509, 6510).

In 715, Li Chin-chung's first paternal cousin Li Shih-huo sought better relations with China. Emperor Hsüan-tsung reestablished the imaginary Sung-mo Area Command and made Shih-huo the Military Governor. He also appointed him General-in-chief of the Guards of the Gilded Mace of the Left in charge of the non-existant Army Which Gives Repose to the Imperial Domain, and recognized him as king of Sung-mo. These arrangements were confirmed in a letter written in vermilion ink (*Chiu T'ang shu* 199B:6a-6b; *T'ang hui-yao* 96:1b; *Wen-hsien t'ung-k'ao* 345:16a).

On Dec.10, 717, Shih-huo was received at the T'ang court. Hsüan-tsung enfeoffed a niece, the Lady Yang, as Princess of Yung-lo and married her to him (*Chiu T'ang shu* 8:8b; *Tzu-chih t'ung-chien* p.6730; *Wen-hsien t'ung-k'ao* 345:16a).[2]

In the 2nd month (Mar./Apr.) of 718, Khitan envoys were received at the T'ang court court (*Ts'e-fu yüan-kuei* p.5027).

In the 5th month (June/July) of 718, it became known at the T'ang court that Li Shih-huo had died. Hsüan-tsung ordered state mourning and conferred on him the posthumous title of Specially Advanced. Shih-huo was succeeded by his younger brother[3] Sha-ku, who was

[2] *Wen-hsien t'ung-k'ao* gives the date of 716.

[3] According to *Chiu T'ang shu* 199B:6b by his first paternal cousin.

recognized as king of Sung-mo by envoys from Hsüan-tsung (*Chiu T'ang shu* 8:8b; 199B:6b; *T'ang hui-yao* 96:2a; *Tzu-chih t'ung-chien* p.6733; *Wen-hsien t'ung-k'ao* 345:16a).

On Jan.26, 719, the New Year's Day, Khitan envoys congratulated at the T'ang court. In the 4th month (Apr./May), Sha-ku presented 10 horses (*Ts'e-fu yüan-kuei* p.5027).

In the 11th month (Dec./Jan., 721) of the Chinese year 720, Khitan envoys to the T'ang court announced that Li Sha-ku had been killed by his minister K'o-t'u-yü and been replaced by his first paternal cousin Yü-yü. Hsüan-tsung accepted the fait accompli and recognized Yü-yü as Military Governor of the imaginary Sung-mo Area Command (*Chiu T'ang shu* 199b:6b; *Tzu-chih t'ung-chien* p.6743; *Wen-hsien t'ung-k'ao* 345:16a).

On Nov.29, 721, a Khitan envoy was received at the T'ang court and appointed an [officer of the] Assault-resisting Garrison (*Ts'e-fu yüan-kuei* p.5027).

On May 16, 722, Yü-yü was received at the T'ang court and requested a marriage. Hsüan-tsung enfeoffed the Lady Mu-jung, a daughter of the Princess of Yü-yao, as Princess of Yen commandery and married her to him, recognized him as king of Sung-mo, appointed him Supernumerary General-in-chief of the Guards of the Gilded Mace of the Left and Concurrent Commissioner of the non-existant Army Which Gives Repose to the Imperial Domain, and presented him with 1000 objects. Yü-yü then returned. Subsequently, K'o-t'u-yü was also received at the court and appointed General of the Feathered Forest of the Left (*Chiu T'ang shu* 8:10b; 199B:6b; *T'ang hui-yao* 96:2a-2b; *Tzu-chih t'ung-chien* p.6750; *Wen-hsien t'ung-k'ao* 345:16a).

In 723, Li Yü-yü died and was succeeeded by his younger brother T'u-yü. He in turn married the Princess of Yen commandery (*Chiu T'ang shu* 199B:6b; *Tzu-chih t'ung-chien* p.6762; *Wen-hsien t'ung-k'ao* 345:16b).

In the 2nd month (March) of 724, a Khitan envoy offered regional objects. In the 3rd month (Mar./Apr.) of the same year, Khitan envoys were again received at the T'ang court. In the 5th month (May/June), envoys from T'u-yü arrived at the court. In the 12th month (Dec./Jan., 725) of the Chinese year 724, Khitan envoys offered horses, and other Khitan envoys presented regional objects (*Ts'e-fu yüan-kuei* p.5028).

In the 1st month (Feb./Mar.) of 725, Khitan envoys were received at the T'ang court (*Ts'e-fu yüan-kuei* p.5028). That year, T'u-yü and his Chinese princess fled from K'o-t'u-yü to China. Hsüan-tsung enfeoffed him as king of Liao-yang, whereafter the refugees remained in Ch'ang-an. K'o-t'u-yü enthroned Li Chin-chung's younger brother Shao-ku, who was then recognized by Hsüan-tsung[4]. In the winter of 725, Hsüan-tsung made a tour of inspection to the northeast and met with Shao-ku (*Chiu T'ang shu* 199B:6b-7a; *Tzu-chih t'ung-chien* p.6769; *Wen-hsien t'ung-k'ao* 345:16b).

In the 1st month (Feb./Mar.) of 726,[5] K'o-t'u-yü personally offered regional objects. But he was insulted by a Gentleman-in-Attendance of the Masters of Writing and departed angrily (*Chiu T'ang shu* 199B: 7a; *Tzu-chih t'ung-chien* p.6789; *Ts'e-fu yüan-kuei* p.5028).

In 726, Shao-ku personally paid a visit to the T'ang court. Hsüan-tsung appointed him on Feb.10, 726,[6] as General of the Feathered Forest, Supernumerary General-in-chief, and Grand Commissioner of the non-existant Army Which Gives Repose to the Imperial Domain, and enfeoffed him as king of Kuang-hua commandery. He also enfeoffed the Lady Ch'en, a daughter of one of his sisters, as Princess of Tung-hua and on Apr.10[7] married her to him. She returned with him to the Khitan homeland (*Chiu T'ang shu* 8:14a; 199B:7a; *Tzu-chih t'ung-chien* p.6770).

In the 4th month (May/June) of 726, the Khitan chief Li-nao and others, six men in all, were received at the T'ang court. In the 7th month (August), the chief Su Ku-to came to the court (*Ts'e-fu yüan-kuei* p.5028).

On June 15, 730, it became known at the T'ang court that K'o-t'u-yü had killed Li Shao-ku, had replaced him with a certain Ch'ü-lieh, and had allied himself with the Eastern Turks. Shao-ku's widow, the Princess of Tung-hua, fled to China. Later in June, unidentified Khitan envoys presented 12 horses. In the 11th month (Dec./Jan., 731) of the same Chinese year 730, other Khitan envoys offered gifts (*Chiu T'ang shu* 8:17a, 199B:7a; *Ts'e-fu yüan-kuei* p.5028; *Tzu-chih t'ung-chien* p.6789; *Wen-hsien t'ung-k'ao* 345:16b).

In 732, a Chinese army defeated K'o-t'u-yü. In 733, he was murdered by his subordinate Li Kuo-che who then proclaimed himself king. In 735, Hsüan-tsung appointed him Acting Chief Commandant,

---

[4] Hsüan-tsung "allowed it", as *Wen-hsien t'ung-k'ao* would have it.

[5] *Ts'e-fu yüan-kuei* dates the visit 725, but according to the sequence of events given in *Chiu T'ang shu* it must have taken place in 726.

[6] The date is according to *Tzu-chih t'ung-chien*. *Chiu T'ang shu* gives the cyclical characters of *kuei-hai* which did not occur in the 1st month.

[7] Correcting *jen-tzu* to *jen-wu*.

enfeoffed him as king of Pei-p'ing commandery, and presented him with brocade garments, ten kinds of silver vessels, and 3,000 bolts of pongee. That winter, a surviving supporter of K'o-t'u-yü, Huang-li, killed Li Kuo-che and all his sons except La-ch'ien, who managed to escape. Hsüan-tsung appointed La-ch'ien General of the Resolute Guards of the Left. Huang-li informed the T'ang court that the murder had been justified by Kuo-che's harshness. Hsüan-tsung recognized Huang-li as Military Governor of the imaginary Sung-mo Area Command but objected in a letter to the killing[8] (*Chiu T'ang shu* 199B:7a, 7b; *Tzu-chih t'ung-chien* p.6813).

After several years of military conflicts, a Khitan chief with a mission of 80 men was received at T'ang the court in the 1st month (Jan./Feb.) of 743 (*Ts'e-fu yüan kuei* p.5029).

In 745, the Khitan chief Li Huai-chich[9] made peace with China. Hsüan-tsung recognized him as Military Governor of the imaginary Sung-mo Area Command and entitled him King Who Venerates Obedience. On Apr.20, he enfeoffed the Lady Tu-ku, an orphaned daughter of one of his daughters, as Princess of Ching-lo and married her to him. But as soon as the 9th month (October) of that year, Li Huai-chieh and a Hsi king, acting in unison, murdered their Chinese wives and turned against the T'ang. They were defeated by An Lu-shan (*Chiu T'ang shu* 9:7a; *Tzu-chih t'ung-chien* pp.6864, 6868; *Wen-hsien t'ung-k'o* 345:16b).

On Apr.26, 746, Hsüan-tsung entitled the Khitan chief Chieh-lo as King Who Respects Benevolence (*Tzu-chih t'ung-chien* p.6871).

In the 6th month (July/Aug.) of 750, Khitan envoys were received at the T'ang court (*Ts'e-fu yüan-kuei* p.5030).

In 751, the Khitan defeated An Lu-shan (*Chiu T'ang shu* 199B:7b). Thereafter, relations between the Khitan and T'ang settled down to peaceful routine.

In the 8th month (Aug./Sep.) of 762, Khitan offered gifts (*Ts'e-fu yüan-kuei* p.5031).

In the 8th month (Aug./Sep.) of 767 and in the 12th month (Dec./Jan., 768) of the same Chinese year, Khitan envoys offered gifts (*Ts'e-fu yüan-kuei* p.5031).

In the 12th month (January 770) of the Chinese year 769, Khitan envoys offered gifts (*Ts'e-fu yüan-kuei* p.5031).

---

[8] He did not, of course "pardon the crime" as claimed by *Tzu-chih t'ung-chien.*

[9] By *Wen-hsien t'ung-k'ao* called Li Huai-hsiu.

In the 11th month (Dec./Jan., 772) of the Chinese year 771, Khitan envoys offered gifts (*Ts'e-fu yüan-kuei* p.5031).

In the 12th month (Dec./Jan., 773) of the Chinese year 772, Khitan envoys offered gifts (*Ts'e-fu yüan-kuei* p.5031).

In the 12th month (Jan./Feb., 774) of the Chinese year 773, Khitan envoys offered gifts (*Ts'e-fu yüan-kuei* p.5032).

In the 12th month (Jan./Feb., 775) of the Chinese year 774, Khitan envoys were received at the T'ang court (*Ts'e-fu yüan-kuei* p.5032).

In the 1st month (Feb./Mar.) of 775 and in the 12th month (Dec./Jan., 776) of the same Chinese year, Khitan envoys offered gifts (*Ts'e-fu yüan-kuei* p.5032).

In the 4th (May/June), 6th (July/Aug.), 8th (Sep./Oct.), and 12th month (January 778) of the Chinese year 777, Khitan envoys offered regional objects (*Ts'e-fu yüan-kuei* p.5032).

In the 9th month (Oct./Nov.) of 785, Khitan envoys were received at the T'ang court (*Chiu T'ang shu* 12:21a).

788 was the only year during this period when the Khitan looted Chinese border areas (*Chiu T'ang shu* 199B:7b).

In the 9th month (October) of 791, Khitan envoys were received at the T'ang court (*Ts'e-fu yüan-kuei* p.5032).

In 793 and 794, Khitan envoys were received at the T'ang court (*Chiu T'ang shu* 199B:7b; *Ts'e-fu yüan-kuei* p.5032).

In the 10th month (Nov./Dec.) of 795, the Khitan chief Je-su with a mission of 25 men was received at the T'ang court (*Chiu T'ang shu* 199B:7b; *Ts'e-fu yüan-kuei* p.5032).

In 801, Khitan were received in audience by Emperor Te-tsung (*Ts'e-fu yüan-kuei* p.5032).

In the 12th month (Jan./Geb., 807) of the Chinese year 806, Khitan envoys offered gifts (*Ts'e-fu yüan-kuei* p.5032).

In the 2nd month (Mar./Apr.) of 807, Khitan offered gifts (*Ts'e-fu yüan-kuei* p.5032).

In the 11th month (December) of 810, Khitan envoys offered gifts (*Ts'e-fu yüan-kuei* p.5032).

In the 11th month (Nov./Dec.) of 813, a Khitan chief offered gifts (*T'ang hui-yao* 96:3b).

In the 11th month (Dec./Jan., 816) of the Chinese year 815, a Khitan mission of 29 men offered gifts (*Chiu T'ang shu* 15:19b; *T'ang hui-yao* 96:3b).

In 816, Khitan envoys offered gifts (*Chiu T'ang shu* 15:11b).

In the 11th month (Dec./Jan., 818) of the Chinese year 817,[10] a Khitan chief offered gifts (*Chiu T'ang shu* 15:16a; *T'ang hui-yao* 96:3b; *Ts'e-fu yüan-kuei* p.5033).

In the 12th month (Jan./Feb., 823) of the Chinese year 822, Khitan envoys offered gifts (*Ts'e-fu yüan-kuei* p.5033).

On Jan.1, 825, Khitan envoys offered gifts (*Chiu T'ang shu* 17A:4b; *Ts'e-fu yüan-kuei* p.5033).

In the 12th month (Jan./Feb., 826) of the Chinese year 825, Khitan envoys offered gifts (*Ts'e-fu yüan-kuei* p.5033).

In the 12th month (Dec./Jan., 830) of the Chinese year 829, Khitan envoys offered gifts (*Ts'e-fu yüan-kuei* p.5033).

In the 12th month (Dec./Jan., 831) of the Chinese year 830, Khitan envoys offered gifts (*Ts'e-fu yüan-kuei* p.5033).

In the 11th month (Dec./Jan., 832) of the Chinese year 831, Khitan envoys offered gifts (*Ts'e-fu yüan-kuei* p.5033).

In the 11th month (Nov./Dec.) of 835,[11] a Khitan chief with a mission of 29 men[12] was received at the T'ang court (*T'ang hui-yao* 96: 3b-4a; *Ts'e-fu yüan-kuei* p.5033).

In the 11th month (Dec./Jan., 837) of the Chinese year 836, a Khitan chief with a mission of 31 men was received at the T'ang court. In the 12th month (Jan./Feb., 837) of the same Chinese year, Khitan envoys offered gifts (*Ts'e-fu yüan-kuei* p.5033).

In the 11th month (December) of 837, Khitan envoys offered gifts (*Ts'e-fu yüan-kuei* p.5033).

In the 12th month (Jan./Feb., 840) of the Chinese year 839, a Khitan chief with a mission of 30 men offered gifts (*T'ang hui-yao* 96:4a; *Ts'e-fu yüan-kuei* p.5033).

During the height of the Uighur empire, the Khitan and Hsi had fallen under its domination, and Uighur inspectors had collected taxes annually. In the 9th month (Oct./Nov.) of 842, the Hsi and Khitan killed hundreds of these inspectors. The Uighurs attacked and defeated the Khitan chief Ch'ü-jung, who thereafter allied himself with the Chinese. Emperor Wu-tsung appointed him General of the Cloud Flags and Acting General of the Martial Guards of the Right (*Chiu T'ang shu* 199B:7b-8a; *Tzu-chih t'ung-chien* p.7967; *Wen-hsien t'ung-k'ao* 345:16b).

---

[10] *Ts'e-fu yüan-kuei* has 12th month (Jan./Feb, 818).

[11] *Ts'e-fu yüan kuei* has 12th month (Jan./Feb., 836) of the Chinese year 835.

[12] *Ts'e-fu yüan-kuei* says 19 men.

On Feb.16, 846, Khitan envoys were received at the T'ang court (*Chiu T'ang shu* 18A:16b; *Ts'e-fu yüan-kuei* p.5033).

In about 874, the Khitan king Jih-hsi-erh-chih-lei[13] offered regional objects (*Ts'e-fu yüan-kuei* p.5033).

In 906, the two most powerful men in T'ang were the Chinese Chu Wen and the Sha-to Turk Li K'o-yung. Both were overshadowed by the Khitan A-pao-chi.[14] He belonged to the Yi-la tribe which adopted Yeh-lü as its surname. This became the lineage of the Khitan emperors.[15] It was due to A-pao-chi that the loose Khitan tribal federation was gradually transformed into a united expansionist empire which by the time of his death in 926 comprised all of Manchuria and Mongolia.

On Feb.27, 907, A-pao-chi, or to refer to him by his temple name T'ai-tsu,[16] proclaimed himself emperor of the Khitan (*Liao shih* 1: 2b).[17]

After Chu Wen had founded the Later Liang dynasty in 907,[18] he sent envoys to the Khitan to inform T'ai-tsu (*Liao shih* 1:2b-3a).

In the 4th (May/June) and 5th month (June/July) of 907, a Khitan chief was received at the Later Liang court and presented fine horses and regional objects. The Later Liang sent the Grand Treasurer and others as envoys in response (*Ts'e-fu yüan-kuei* p.5033; *Tzu-chih t'ung-chien* p.8676).

On Apr.3, 908, envoys from T'ai-tsu to the Later Liang court offered fine horses and regional objects. In the 5th month (June) of the same year, his envoys presented 10 fine horses, horse trappings with golden flowers, caps and garments of sable fur, brocade, one male, and one young girl. His wife presented one fine horse, caps embroidered with golden flowers, and aromatics. The Later Liang sent the Minister of Agriculture and a lesser official as envoys in response (*Chiu Wu-tai*

[13] *Wen-hsien t'ung-k'ao* 345:16b gives his name as Hsi-erh-chih.

[14] For various renderings of his name see *Cambride History of China*, vol.6, p.60 note 14.

[15] For the history of Liao see, Karl A. Wittfogel and Fêng Chia-shêng, *History of Chinese Society, Liao (907-1125)*, and Denis Twichett and Klaus-Peter Titze, *Cambridge History of China*, vol.6, pp.43-153.

[16] Not to be confused with Chu Wen, founder of Later Liang, whose temple name also was T'ai-tsu.

[17] For questions about A-pao-chi's chronology see *Cambridge History of China*, vol.6, p.60.

[18] According to *Chiu Wu-tai shih* 3:3a, he proclaimed himself emperor on June 5, 907. According to *Hsin Wu-tai shih* 1:2a, he ascended the throne in June and proclaimed an amnesty on June 5.

shih 4:1b; *Hsin Wu-tai shih* 72:3b; *Wu-tai hui-yao* 29:2a; *Ts'e-fu yüan-kuei* p.5033).

On Feb.23, 909, a goodwill mission from Later Liang was received at the Khitan court (*Liao shih* 1:3a).

On Sep.27, 909, 50 Khitan envoys to the Later Liang court presented gilded iron and silver armour, horse trappings ornamented with rock crystal, jade, and 100 horses. T'ai-tsu's mother and wife also sent presents. The envoys were received in audience and received gold and silk in accordance with their ranks (*Hsin Wu-tai shih* 2:4b; *Wu-tai hui-yao* 29:2a; *Ts'e-fu yüan-kuei* p.5034).

On May 19, 911, envoys from T'ai-tsu to the Later Liang court offered gifts. On Nov.25, other Khitan envoys were received at the court (*Liao shih* 1:4a; *Ts'e-fu yüan-kuei* p.5034).

On July 19, 912, the founder of Later Liang was murdered by his son Chu Yu-kuei who then enthroned himself.[19] In the 10th month (Nov./Dec.), Khitan envoys [condoled,] sacrificed, and offered gifts (*Chiu Wu-tai shih* 8:1b; *Liao shih* 1:4b; *Ts'e-fu yüan-kuei* p.5034).

Later Liang and its successors of the Five Dynasties were not the only Chinese states which had dealings with the Khitan. On Nov.30, 915, envoys from the ruler of Wu-yüeh, whose domain chiefly comprised what now is Che-chiang, offered gifts to the Khitan court (*Liao shih* 1:5a).

In spite of military clashes between Later Liang and the Khitan from 916 to 922, diplomatic channels were kept open.

On May 24, 916, an envoy from the Later Liang congratulated at the Khitan court (*Liao shih* 1:9a).

On July 9, 916, an envoy from the ruler of Wu-yüeh to the Khitan court offered gifts. The envoy stayed with the Khitan for several month and was in the 11th month (Nov./Dec.) of that year bestowed the given name of Shu-lü (*Liao shih* 1:9a).

In the 2nd month (Feb./Mar.) of 917, envoys from the ruler of Wu, whose state was situated between Wu-yüeh and Later Liang and comprised the territory of present Chiang-hsi, southern An-hui, and northern Chiang-su, presented to the Khitan fierce-burning oil (naphta). They explained that if a city was attacked with this oil, it would burn the towers and turrets, and if the enemy poured water on

---

[19] He was in the 2nd month (Mar./Apr.) of the following year killed by his younger brother Yu-chen who became the Last Emperor of Later Liang (*Chiu Wu-tai shih* 8:2b-3a).

it, it would burn all the more. T'ai-tsu was greatly pleased (*Tzu-chih t'ung-chien* p.8814).

On May 6, 917, the Last Emperor of Later Liang sent the General-in-chief of the Personal Guard as envoy to the Khitan (*Hsin Wu-tai shih* 3:3b).

In the 2nd month (Mar./Apr.) of 918, Later Liang envoys on a goodwill mission to the Khitan court offered gifts. In the same month, envoys from Wu-yüeh also offered gifts (*Liao shih* 1:10a, 10b).

On May 25, 920, an envoy from the ruler of Wu-yüeh to the Khitan court offered rhinoceros horns and corals. He was appointed to a nominal Khitan office and sent back (*Liao shih* 2:1b).

On Oct.16, 920, the Last Emperor of Later Liang appointed a member of the Office of Palace Service as envoy to lead a goodwill mission to the Khitan court (*Hsin Wu-tai shih* 3:4a-4b)

On Apr.23, 923, another goodwill mission from Later Liang was received at the Khitan court.[20] In the same month, envoys from the ruler of Wu-yüeh offered gifts (*Liao shih* 2:3b).

In the 5th month (May/June) of 925, an envoy from T'ai-tsu to the Later T'ang court offered regional objects (*Ts'e-fu yüan-kuei* p.5034).

On Oct.27, 925, the Later T'ang belatedly informed the Khitan court that it had replaced the Later Liang. T'ai-tsu immediately sent envoys with gifts on a goodwill mission (*Liao shih* 2:5b).

On Mar.7, 926, envoys from T'ai-tsu offered gifts to the Later T'ang court. They were treated extremely well, and envoys with presents were sent in in response (*Chiu Wu-tai shih* 34:14b; *Wen-hsien t'ung-k'ao* 345:17a).

In the 1st month (Feb./Mar.) of 926, 37 envoys from T'ai-tsu to the Later T'ang court offered 30 horses (*Wu-tai hui-yao* 29:2b).

In the 2nd month (Mar./Apr.) of 926, envoys from T'ai-tsu informed the Later T'ang court that he had conquered the Po-hai State (*Liao shih* 2:6b). He changed its name to Tung-tan and made his eldest son and heir-apparent T'u-yü its king (*Liao shih* 2:6b).

In the 7th month (Aug./Sep.) of 926, Emperor Ming-tsung of Later T'ang sent a Palace Servitor to the Khitan court to announce the death of his adoptive father Chuang-tsung on May.15. T'ai-tsu received him, dressed in a brocade robe with a great belt. According to

[20] This embassy must have set out before the Later Liang was overthrown by the Later T'ang on Apr.13.

the envoy's subsequent report, the Khitan emperor went through the act of weeping. He then demanded territorial concessions. When the envoy refused to collaborate, he was imprisoned and almost executed (*Hsin Wu-tai shih* 72:6a-6b; *Tzu-chih t'ung-chien* p.8989).

On Aug.16, 926, envoys from a Khitan chief to the Later T'ang court offered two horses, garments, a golden bracelet ornamented with real pearls, golden hair pins etc. (*Chiu Wu-tai shih* 36:7b; *Ts'e-fu yüan-kuei* p.5034).

On Sep.6, 926, the Khitan emperor T'ai-tsu died, aged 55. On Nov.25, envoys to the Later T'ang court announced the death, whereupon Ming-tsung suspended the court for three days. Meanwhile, the Khitan went through a succession struggle in which the heir-apparent T'u-yü was bypassed and T'ai-tsu's second son Te-kuang entroned on Dec.16. This was emperor T'ai-tsung (*Chiu Wu-tai shih* 137:2a, 6b; *Hsin Wu-tai shih* 6:5a; *Liao shih* 2:7a-7b; *Tzu-chih t'ung-chien* p.8991; *Wen-hsien t'ung-k'ao* 345:17a).

In the 9th month (Sep./Oct.) of 927, 30 Khitan on a goodwill mission were received at the Later T'ang court and offered gifts (*Chiu Wu-tai shih* 38:1b; 137:7a; *Ts'e-fu yüan-kuei* p.5034).

On Oct.22, 927, envoys from T'ai-tsung to the Later T'ang court presented fine horses and requested a stele for the tomb of his father. Ming-tsung agreed to it and in the 12th month (Dec./Jan., 928)[21] sent rich presents, including silken fabrics, silver vessels with golden flowers, and wine vessels, as well as a necklace, an embroidered coverlet, and brocade for T'ai-tsung's mother (*Chiu Wu-tai shih* 38:12b, 14b; 137:2a; *Hsin Wu-tai shih* 6:6a; *Hsin Wu-tai shih* 72:8b-9a; *Wu-tai hui-yao* 29:3b).

In the 1st month (Jan./Feb.) of 928, 50 Khitan envoys to the Later T'ang court offered gifts. Ming-tsung responded with envoys of his own who conveyed presents to the wife of T'ai-tsung (*Chiu Wu-tai shih* 39:2a; *Ts'e-fu yüan-kuei* p.5034).

In the 5th month (May/June) of 928, the Khitan supported a rebellion in Later T'ang, but their forces were defeated and their commander captured and executed. When the Khitan later sought the return of his bones, Ming-tsung had the envoy executed as well (*Chiu Wu-tai shih* 39:6b-7a; *Wen-hsien t'ung-k'ao* 345:17a).

In the intercalary month (Sep./Oct.) of 928, a Khitan envoy to

---

[21] *Wu-tai hui-yao* has 11th month (Nov./Dec.).

the Later T'ang court offered gifts (*Ts'e-fu yüan-kuei* p.5034; *Tzu-chih t'ung-chien* p.9023).

On Nov. 3, 928, T'ai-tsung sent envoys to the Later T'ang court (*Liao shih* 3:2b).

In the 10th month (Nov./Dec.) of 928, Later T'ang envoys were received at the Khitan court and presented a jade flute (*Liao shih* 3: 3a).

In the 12th month (Jan./Feb., 929) of the Chinese year 928, a goodwill mission from the Later T'ang was received at the Khitan court (*Liao shih* 3:3a).

On May 25, 929, Khitan envoys to the Later T'ang court offered gifts (*Hsin Wu-tai shih* 6:7b; *Ts'e-fu yüan-kuei* p.5034).

The king of Tung-tan, T'u-yü, threatened by his brother T'ai-tsung, fled by sea with an entourage of more than 40 men to the Later T'ang, arriving at the court on Dec.19, 930. The Secretariat-Chancellery memorialized in the 12 month (Dec./Jan., 931) of the same Chinese year 930 that T'u-yü should be granted a Chinese name. Ming-tsung named him Tung-tan Mu-hua and and conferred on him a number of honory titles. In the 9th month (October) of 932, T'u-yü's Chinese name was changed to Li Tsan-hua (*Hsin Wu-tai shih* 6:9b; 72:9a; *Wu-tai hui-yao* 29:4b-5a; *Wen-hsien t'ung-k'ao* 345:17a).

On May 11, 931, a goodwill mission from the Later T'ang was received at the Khitan court (*Liao shih* 3:5a).

On Sep.18, 931, a Khitan envoy to the Later T'ang court offered gifts (*Hsin Wu-tai shih* 6:10a; *Ts'e-fu yüan-kuei* p.5035).

On Dec.13, 931, a goodwill mission from the Later T'ang was received at the Khitan court (*Liao shih* 3:5b).

On Feb.25, 932, a goodwill mission from the Later T'ang was received at the Khitan court (*Liao shih* 3:5b).

On Feb.26, 932, Khitan envoys to the Later T'ang court offered gifts (*Chiu Wu-tai-shih* 43:1a; *Ts'e-fu yüan-kuei* p.5035).

On Feb.29, 932, T'ai-tsung sent envoys to the Later T'ang court (*Liao shih* 3:5b).

In the 2nd month (Mar./Apr.) of 932, the Khitan presented 3 horses and drugs to the Later T'ang court (*Ts'e-fu yüan-kuei* p.5035).

On Mar.14. 932, a Khitan envoy returned to his court from a mission to Wu-yüeh. Envoys from the ruler of Wu-yüeh accompanying him presented precious vessels. T'ai-tsung responded with still another mission to Wu-yüeh (*Liao shih* 3:5b).

On Apr.10, 932, a Khitan mission of 116 men led by a Military

Governor offered the Later T'ang court 100 horses and regional objects (*Chiu Wu-tai shih* 43:3b; *Ts'e-fu yüan-kuei* p.5035).

In the 3rd month (Apr./May) of 932, a Khitan envoy presented 30 horses to the Later T'ang court (*Ts'e-fu yüan-kuei* p.5035).

On May 30, 932, a goodwill mission from the Later T'ang was received at the Khitan court (*Liao shih* 3:5b).

In the 4th month (May/June) of 932, Khitan envoys arrived at the Later T'ang court (*Chiu Wu-tai shih* 43:4b-5a).

In the 7th month (Aug./Sep.) of 932, a Khitan envoy to the Later T'ang court offered 30 horses (*Wu-tai hui-yao* 29:5b).

On Sep.15, 932, Later T'ang envoys to the Khitan court presented a flute of red ivory (*Liao shih* 3:6a).

In the 9th month (October) of 932, a Khitan envoy to the Later T'ang court presented 40 horses (*Ts'e-fu yüan-kuei* p.5035).

On Nov.7, 932 a goodwill mission from Later T'ang was received at the Khitan court (*Liao shih* 3:6a).

On Mar.7, 933, an envoy to the Later T'ang returned to the Khitan court (*Liao shih* 3:6b).

On Apr.17, 933, Later T'ang envoys to the Khitan court requested a cessation of their war against the Tang-hsiang (*Liao shih* 3:6b).

On June 6, 933, Khitan envoys to the Later T'ang court offered gifts (*Chiu Wu-tai shih* 44:4b; *Ts'e-fu yüan-kuei* p.5035).

On Oct.29, 933, a goodwill mission from Later T'ang was received at the Khitan court (*Liao shih* 3:7a).

On Nov.6, 933, T'ai-tsung sent an envoy to the Later T'ang court (*Liao shih* 3:7a).

On Dec.18, 933, the Khitan Grand Empress Dowager (mother of T'ai-tsu) died.[22] T'ai-tsung sent envoys to announce her death to the Later T'ang court (*Liao shih* 3:7a).

On Jan.21, 934, a Khitan mission led by a Military Governor offered the Later T'ang court 400 horses, 10 racehorses, and 2000 sheep (*Chiu Wu-tai shih* 45:2b; *Ts'e-fu yüan-kuei* p.5035). They probably had not been aware, when they left their homeland, that Emperor Ming-tsung was already dead.

On Mar.5, 934, envoys from Emperor Min of Later T'ang officially informed the Khitan court that his father Ming-tsung had died on

[22] *Liao shih* 71:2a dates her death 936.

Dec.15, 933. That very day, T'ai-tsung sent a mission to condole and sacrifice (*Liao shih* 3:7a).

On July 16, 934, envoys from Min[23] of Later T'ang to the Khitan court thanked for the condolence and sacrifice (*Liao shih* 3:7b).

In the 8th month (Sep./Oct.) of 934, a Khitan envoy to the Later T'ang court offered gifts (*Ts'e-fu yüan-kuei* p.5035).

On Aug.21, 936, Khitan envoys were received at the Later T'ang court (*Chiu Wu-tai shih* 48:7b).

On Nov.28, 936, Shih Ching-t'ang proclaimed himself emperor of Later Chin. This was Emperor Kao-tsu. He was recognized by T'ai-tsung of the Khitan. Subsequently, Kao-tsu met with T'ai-tsung, who had arrived with horsemen to support him. In the negotitions, Kao-tsu agreed to pay the Khitan an annual tribute of 130,000 bolts of pongee and to cede territory to them. When they were about to part, T'ai-tsung gave a banquet, at which both emperors became intoxicated. They held hands, and Kao-tsu promised to treat T'ai-tsung as a son would his father (*Chiu Wu-tai shih* 76:13a; *Hsin Wu-tai shih* 8:3b; 75:9b; *Wu-tai hui-yao* 29:5b, 6a; *Liao shih* 3:10b). He thereby accepted a status below that of the Khitan ruler.

When the forces of Kao-tsu entered Lo-yang, the Last Emperor of Later T'ang immolated himself on a tower. Kao-tsu sent a Grand Councilor to the Khitan court to thank for the support (*Chiu Wu-tai shih* 48:7b; 138:8a).

On Mar.28, 937, a Khitan goodwill mission was received at the Later Chin court (*Hsin Wu-tai shih* 8:4b; *Wu-tai hui-yao* 29:6a).

On Apr.3, 937, Kao-tsu returned two Khitan, who previously had been seized by the Later T'ang, to their country (*Liao shih* 3:11b).

On Apr.20, 937, Later Chin envoys to the Khitan court offered gifts (*Liao shih* 3:11b).

On Apr.20, T'ai-tsung sent the Court Architect as envoy to the Later Chin court (*Liao shih* 3:11b).

On May 12, 937, Later Chin envoys to the Khitan court were received in audience by T'ai-tsung (*Liao shih* 3:11b).

On July 12, 937, a goodwill mission from the Khitan was received at the Later Chin court and presented 200 horses, racehorses, sable

---

[23] This mission must have set out before the Last Emperor overthrew Min on May 19 and proclaimed himself emperor on May 21.

furs, wooden bowls, and ginseng (*Chiu Wu-tai shih* 76:13a; *Ts'e-fu yüan-kuei* p.5035).

On July 13, 937, a Master of Writing of the Ministry of Households and other Later Chin envoys to the Khitan court proposed the return to their state of three territories occupied by the Khitan in exchange for honorific titles and an annual tribute raised to 300,000 bolts of silk. T'ai-tsung rejected the offer (*Liao shih* 3:11b).

On Aug.22, 937, Later Chin envoys informed the Khitan court of a rebellion (*Liao shih* 3:11b).

On Aug.28, 937, T'ai-tsung sent an envoy to the Later Chin court (*Liao shih* 3:11b).

On Sep.10, 937, Later Chin envoys to the Khitan court begged to offer honorific titles. This was rejected (*Liao Shih* 3:12a).

On Sep.17, 937, envoys from the rulers of both Later Chin and Southern T'ang[24] to the Khitan court offered gifts (*Liao shih* 3:12a).

On Sep.27, 937, Later Chin envoys informed the Khitan court that Kao-tsu had moved his capital to Pien (K'ai-feng) and that a rebellion had been suppressed (*Liao shih* 3:12a).

On Oct.17, 937, T'ai-tsung sent an envoy to the Later Chin and Southern T'ang courts (*Liao shih* 3:12a).

On Nov.6, 937, Later Chin envoys congratulated on the birthday of the Khitan Empress Dowager (widow of T'ai-tsu) (*Liao shih* 3:12a).

On Dec.15, 937, Khitan envoys to the Later Chin court requested physicians. On Jan.14, 938, these physicians arrived at the Khitan court (*Liao shih* 3:12a).

On Feb.2, 938, the New Year's Day, envoys from the Later Chin and other countries congratulated at the Khitan court (*Liao shih* 4:1a).

On Feb.22, 938, T'ai-tsung sent envoys to the Later Chin court (*Liao shih* 4:1a).

On June 8, 938, Later Chin envoys to the Khitan court again proposed that T'ai-tsung accept honorific titles from their ruler. This time, it was approved (*Liao shih* 4:1b).

On July 15, 938, Southern T'ang envoys offered gifts to the Khitan court (*Liao shih* 4:1b).

On Aug.16, 938, T'ai-tsung sent envoys to offer horses to the Later Chin court (*Liao shih* 4:1b).

On Aug.20, T'ai-tsung sent one envoy to the Later Chin court and

[24] Southern T'ang had replaced the Wu State and occupied the same territory.

another to the Southern T'ang court (*Liao shih* 4:1b).

On Aug.21, 938, T'ai-tsung sent the Minister of the Right of the Department of State Affairs as envoy to the Later Chin court (*Liao shih* 4:1b).

On Aug.31, 938, Emperor Kao-tsu sent two envoys to present the honorific titles to the Khitan Empress Dowager and Emperor T'ai-tsung. They arrived at the Khitan court in the 9th month (Sep./Oct.) (*Chiu Wu-tai shih* 77:4b; 137:8a; *Liao shih* 4:1b-2a; *Wen-hsien t'ung-k'ao* 345:17b).

On Oct.12, 938, Khitan envoys arrived in Lo-yang to escort the Princess of Hsing-p'ing to their country. She was a daughter of Emperor Ming-tsung of Later T'ang and had been married into the prominent Chao family. Chao Te-kou had been the king of Pei-p'ing and a Military Commissioner. His son Yen-shou had become the husband of the princess and had had with her the son Tsan. Both Te-kou and Yen-shou had been captured by the Khitan, but the princess and her son had remained in China. Emperor Kao-tsu of Later Chin now allowed the family to be reunited (*Chiu Wu-tai shih* 77:6a; *Sung shih* 254:11b-12a).

On Oct.26, 938, T'ai-tsung sent a Court Attendant and others as envoys to the Later Chin court (*Liao shih* 4:2a).

On Oct.30. 938, the Khitan Prefect of the Palace Writers, who had been sent as envoy to the Later Chin, was welcomed outside the capital and conducted to the palace. He there presented to Emperor Kao-tsu the honorific title of Emperor Who Is Bravely Martial and Shiningly Righteous. On Nov.23, envoys from Kao-tsu to T'ai-tsung thanked for the title (*Chiu Wu-tai shih* 77:8a, 137:8a; *Hsin Wu-tai shih* 8:6b; *Liao shih* 4:2a; *Wen-hsien t'ung-k'ao* 345:17b).

In the 11th month (Nov./Dec.) of 938, the Later Chin envoys who had arrived at the Khitan court in order to present the honorific titles were given a banquet. On Nov.27, they were given an audience (*Liao shih* 4:2a).

On Dec.3, 938, the Later Chin envoys presented to the Khitan Empress Dowager the honorific title of Empress Dowager Who Is Extensively Benevolent, Luminously Illustrious, Respectfully Grand, and Responsive to Heaven . On Dec.17, they presented to T'ai-tsung the honorific title of Emperor Who Is Astutely Refined, Divinely Martial, Takes Heaven as His Model, Is Initiator of Fortune, Brightly Virtuous, Displayer of Sincerity, Reacher of Truth, Broadly Reverent, Luminously Filial, and Heir of Sagacity (*Liao shih* 4:2a).

Soon thereafter and not later than Dec.24, the Later Chin ceded to the Khitan 16 commanderies (chou) at its northern border (*Liao shih* 4:2b).

On Jan.18, 939, the Later Chin envoys who had brought the honorific titles were by T'ai-tsung appointed to such nominal offices as Acting Grand Tutor, Acting Grand Guardian etc. On Jan.27, they were given a banquet and gifts in accordance with their ranks (*Liao shih* 4:2b-3a, 3b).

On Jan.25, 939, T'ai-tsung sent envoys to the Southern T'ang court to announce that he had accepted honorific titles from the Later Chin (*Liao shih* 4:3a).

On Jan.28, 939, a General-in-chief of the Guards of the Gilded Mace and a Gentleman-of-the-Palace of the Bureau of Evaluations, who had been sent as envoys by the Later Chin to the Khitan court, offered precious gifts. T'ai-tsung ordered them to be distributed among his officials (*Liao shih* 4:3a).

On Feb.5, 939, Later Chin envoys thanked the Khitan court for suspending the cash and silk payments in return for four border commanderies (*Liao shih* 4:3a).

In early May, 939, Southern T'ang envoys to the Khitan court offered gifts. On May 27, T'ai-tsung distributed these gifts among his officials (*Liao shih* 4:3b).

On July 27, 939, Later Chin envoys to the Khitan court presented a belt of rhinoceros hide (*Liao shih* 4:3b).

On Sep.2, 939, T'ai-tsung sent an envoy to the Later Chin court to offer fine horses (*Liao shih* 4:3b).

On Oct.12, 939, Later Chin envoys to the Khitan court announced that the annual tribute in gold and silk for 938 and 939 had been delivered to Yen-ching (Peking) (*Liao shih* 4:3a).

On Oct.26, 939,[25] two Khitan envoys on a goodwill mission were received at the Later Chin court. They presented cattle, horses, 14 horses with white forelegs, and dogs (*Chiu Wu-tai shih* 78:3b; *Hsin Wu-tai shih* 8:7b; *Liao shih* 4:4a; *Ts'e-fu yüan-kuei* p.5035).

In the 11th month (Dec./Jan., 940) of the Chinese year 939, a Khitan envoy was received at the Later Chin court. He then proceeded to Wu-yüeh (*Tzu-chih t'ung-chien* p.9208).

On Feb.2, 940,[26] a Khitan envoy was received at the Later Chin court (*Hsin Wu-tai shih* 8:7b).

---

[25] *Hsin Wu-tai shih* gives the date of Oct.23.

[26] Correcting *mou-tzu* to *mou-wu*.

On Mar.3, 940, envoys from the ruler of Wu-yüeh to the Khitan court offered gifts (*Liao shih* 4:4a).

On Mar.7, 940, T'ai-tsung sent an envoy to the Later Chin court to congratulate on the birthday of Kao-tsu[27] (*Liao shih* 4:4a).

On Apr.12, 940, T'ai-tsung sent envoys to the Later Chin court to announce that he was visiting his Southern Capital (*Liao shih* 4:4b).

On May 9, 940, envoys from Later Chin and Southern T'ang to the Khitan court were received in audience by T'ai-tsung (*Liao shih* 4:4b).

On May 16, 940, T'ai-tsung sent envoys to the Later Chin court (*Liao shih* 4:4b).

On May 20, 940, the Commissioner of Palace Attendants and other Later Chin envoys to the Khitan court inquired about the well-being of T'ai-tsung (*Liao shih* 4:4b).

On May 26, 940, T'ai-tsung gave a banquet for the envoys from Later Chin and other countries (*Liao shih* 4:4b).

On May 30, 940, Later Chin envoys to the Khitan court presented tea and drugs (*Liao shih* 4:4b).

On June 6, 940, Later Chin envoys arrived at the Khitan court to congratulate on the Dragon Boat Festival of June 13. T'ai-tsung distributed the presents among his officials (*Liao shih* 4:4b).

On June 8, 940, Southern T'ang envoys to the Khitan court presented a white tortoise (*Liao shih* 4:4b).

On the Dragon Boat Festival of June 13, 940, T'ai-tsung gave a banquet for his officials and the envoys from the various countries. He ordered the two envoys from the Uighurs and from Tun-huang (Sha chou) to perform their native dances so that all the envoys might see them (*Liao shih* 4:4b-5a).

On June 23, 940, the Later Chin envoys offered bows and arrows to the Khitan court (*Liao shih* 4:5a).

On June 27, 940, T'ai-tsung sent one of his sons and an Acting Minister over the Masses as envoys to the Later Chin court (*Liao shih* 4:5a).

On July 13, 940,[28] Later Chin envoys to the Khitan court were received in audience (*Liao shih* 4:5a).

On Sep.2, 940, Later Chin envoys to the Khitan court announced

---

[27] It fell on Apr.8.

[28] Correcting 5th month to 6th.

[Kao-tsu's] intention to perform the Southern Suburban Sacrifice (*Liao shih* 4:5b).

On Sep.13, 940, T'ai-tsung sent envoys to the Southern T'ang court (*Liao shih* 4:5b).

In the 8th month (Sep./Oct.) of 940, Southern T'ang envoys to the Khitan court requested blue felt tents. These were provided (*Liao shih* 4:5b).

On Oct.17, 940, envoys from the ruler of Wu-yüeh to the Khitan court offered gifts (*Liao shih* 4:6a).

On Oct.27, 940, Later Chin envoys to the Khitan court offered fine horses (*Liao shih* 4:6a).[29]

On Nov.11, 940, T'ai-tsung sent one envoy to the Wu-yüeh court and another to Southern T'ang court (*Liao shih* 4:6a).

On Nov.17, 940, a Khitan envoy on a goodwill mission was received at the Later Chin court. He presented 100 horses, jade horse trappings, fox furs, embroidered bow cases etc. (*Chiu Wu-tai shih* 79:6b; *Ts'e-fu yüan-kuei* p.5035).

On Nov.30, 940, Later Chin envoys to the Khitan court offered plain cloth and announced [Kao-tsu's] intention personally to sacrifice to the Southern Sacred Mountain (in Hu-nan) (*Liao shih* 4:6a).

On Dec.9, 940, a Southern T'ang envoy to the Khitan court offered a letter on secret affairs in a ball of wax (*Liao shih* 4:6a).[30]

On Jan.5, 941, T'ai-tsung sent envoys to the Later Chin court (*Liao shih* 4:6a).

On Feb.14, 941, envoys from Southern T'ang to the Khitan court offered gifts (*Liao shih* 4:6a).

On Mar.14, 941, Later Chin envoys to the Khitan court offered aromatics and drugs (*Liao shih* 4:6b).

On Mar.29, 941, a Later Chin envoy to the Khitan court offered gifts (*Liao shih* 4:6b).

On Apr.12, 941, Later Chin envoys to the Khitan court presented 200 ounces of real gold (*Liao shih* 4:6b).

On May 28, 941,[31] Later Chin envoys to the Khitan court offered cherries (*Liao shih* 4:6b).

---

[29] If the two last entries are correctly dated, they are listed in the wrong sequence by *Liao shih*.

[30] Letters on intelligence were protected in this fashion from unauthorized readers.

[31] *Liao shih* gives the cyclical characters of *chi-mao*, but these did not occur in the 4th month. *Hsin Wu-tai shih* has *chi-wei* = May 28.

In the 6th month (June/July) of 941, a Later Chin envoy to the Khitan court unsuccessfully complained about rising tensions (*Liao shih* 4:6b).

In the 7th month (July/Aug.) of 941, Southern T'ang envoys to the Khitan court presented a letter in a ball of wax (*Liao shih* 4:6b).

On Aug.9, 941, Later Chin envoys to the Khitan court presented an inkstone of crystal (*Liao shih* 4:7a).

On Aug.30, 941, Southern T'ang envoys to the Khitan court presented a letter in a ball of wax (*Liao shih* 4:7a).

On Sep.6, 941, Later Chin envoys to the Khitan court presented a bow decorated with rhinoceros horn, and bamboo arrows (*Liao shih* 4:7a).

In the 8th month (Aug./Sep.) of 941, envoys from the ruler of Wu-yüeh to the Khitan court presented a letter in a ball of wax (*Liao shih* 4:7a).

On Sep.20, 941, Kao-tsu sent the Superintendent of the Imperial Household as envoy to the Khitan court (*Hsin Wu-tai shih* 8:8b).

On Oct.11, 941, Kao-tsu sent the Military Commissioner of the Army Which Keeps the State in Peace as envoy to the Khitan court (*Hsin Wu-tai shih* 8:8b).

On Nov.8, 941, envoys of the ruler of Wu-yüeh to the Khitan court offered gifts (*Liao shih* 4:7a).

On Dec.1, 941, Later Chin envoys to the Khitan court announced that their forces were attacking the Chinese strongman An Ch'ung-jung. He was much opposed to the Khitan, had abused their envoys, and even executed some of those passing through his territory (*Hsin Wu-tai shih* 51:13a; *Liao shih* 4:7a).

On Dec.23, 941, Later Chin envoys to the Khitan court announced that one of their Military Commissioners had rebelled (*Liao shih* 4:7a).

On Dec.25, 941, Southern T'ang envoys to the Khitan court presented a letter in a ball of wax (*Liao shih* 4:7b).

On Dec.31, 941, Khitan envoys were received at the Later Chin court (*Hsin Wu-tai shih* 8:9a).

In the 1st month (Jan./Feb.) of 942, T'ai-tsung sent the Commissioner of the Visitors Bureau to the Later Chin court to congratulate on the birthday of Kao-tsu[32] (*Liao shih* 4:7b-8a).

---

[32] It fell on Mar.17.

On Jan.2, 942, a Later Chin envoy to the Khitan court offered gifts (*Liao shih* 4:7b).

On Jan.12, 942, the Later Chin informed the Khitan court that An Ch'ung-jung had been killed. A Later Chin envoy who had previously been detained by the Khitan to protest An Ch'ung-jung's hostility was now released. On Jan.15, envoys to the Khitan court announced that the Later Chin was demobilizing its troops (*Chiu Wu-tai shih* 98: 4b; *Liao shih* 4:7b).

On Feb.3. 942, a Khitan envoy was received at the Later Chin court (*Hsin Wu-tai shih* 8:9a).

On Feb.6, 942, T'ai-tsung sent envoys to Later Chin (*Liao shih* 4: 7b).

On Feb.27, 942, T'ai-tsung sent a goodwill mission of 31 men to the Later Chin court to offer horses and regional objects (*Chiu Wu-tai shih* 80:7b; *Liao shih* 4:8a; *Ts'e-fu yüan-kuei* p.5035).

On Mar.25, 942,[33] the Later Chin sent a former Defense Commissioner of a local unit and the Tea Libationer of the Han-lin Academy as envoys to the Khitan court to inquire about the wellbeing of T'ai-tsung (*Chiu Wu-tai shih* 80:8a; *Liao shih* 4:8a).

In the 4th month (May/June) of 942, Khitan envoys to the Later Chin court complained that Kao-tsu had established relations with the T'u-yü-hun (*Tzu-chih t'ung-chien* p.9236).

On June 9, 942, Later Chin envoys to the Khitan court offered horse trappings for the ceremony of Shooting at Willows[34] (*Liao shih* 4:8a).

On July 16, 942, envoys from Shih Ch'ung-kuei, the nephew and heir of Kao-tsu of Later Chin, offered gifts to the Khitan court (*Liao shih* 4:8a-8b).

On July 28, 942, Emperor Kao-tsu died and was succeeded by Shih Ch'ung-kuei. This was Emperor Shao.[35] On July 31, envoys from Shao informed the Khitan court of the death. T'ai-tsung suspended the court for seven days. On Aug.2, T'ai-tsung sent envoys to condole and sacrifice (*Liao shih* 4:8b).

In the 6th month (July/Aug.) of 942, a Khitan envoy was received at the Later Chin court (*Hsin Wu-tai shih* 9:1b).

---

[33] The date is questionable, since according to *Liao shih* this mission was received on Mar.20.

[34] According to Wittfogel, *Liao*, p.216, this may have been a ritual symbolizing birth after death.

[35] By *Wen-hsien t'ung-k'ao* called the Last Emperor.

On Aug.11, 942, Shao sent two envoys, the General-in-chief of the Guards of the Gilded Mace of the Right and the Supervisor of the Lodges of the Four Quarters [for envoys], to the Khitan court. They were there received on Aug.22. T'ai-tsung was furious because Shao had not first petitioned to succeed Kao-tsu but had enthroned himself, and because he had referred to himself as a "grandson" but not a "subject"[36] (*Chiu Wu-tai shih* 81:2b; 137:8b; *Hsin Wu-tai shih* 9: 2a; *Liao shih* 4:8b; *Wen-hsien t'ung-k'ao* 345:17b).

On Sep.5, 942, T'ai-tsung sent the Commissioner of the Visitors Bureau to the Later Chin court to protest. This man was a Chinese. Shao had him briefly arrested but then released. The high officials who advised caution were overruled by Shao. The court spokesman was Ching Yen-kuang, leader of the anti-Khitan party. He agreed that Kao-tsu had been helped to the throne by T'ai-tsung, i.e. the Khitan, but insisted that the present ruler had succeeded by the code of the Later Chin. This meant that the term "grandson" was appropriate but "subject" not. The envoy considered that Yen-kuang lacked humility and on his return reported this to T'ai-tsung. The latter became even more incensed, planned an attack on Later Chin, but changed his mind (*Chiu Wu-tai shih* 137:8b; *Hsin Wu-tai shih* 9:2a; *Liao shih* 4: 8b; *Wen-hsien t'ung-k'ao* 345:17b).

On Sep.8, 942, Later Chin envoys to the Khitan court announced the death of the imperial grandmother (*Liao shih* 4:8b).

On Sep.25, 942, Khitan envoys to the Later Chin court offered 20 horses and pongee (*Chiu Wu-tai-shih* 81:5a; *Hsin Wu-tai shih* 9:2a).

On Oct.4, 942,[37] T'ai-tsung sent the Military Commissioner of the Army of the Great City with a mission of 26 men to attend the burial of Kao-tsu on Dec.20 and to contribute two horses, 1000 sheep, and 1000 pieces of pongee toward the funeral expenses (*Chiu Wu-tai shih* 81:5a; *Wu-tai hui-yao* 29:6b; *Liao shih* 4:9a).

On Oct.23, 942, T'ai-tsung sent envoys to the Later Chin court to congratulate Shao on his enthronement. These were received at the Later Chin court on Nov.19, 942 (*Hsin Wu-tai shih* 9:2b; *Liao shih* 4:9a).

---

[36] Since Kao-tsu in 936 had agreed to be like a son to T'ai-tsung, Shao, being one generation lower, was logically like a grandson.

[37] Both text give the same date, even though *Liao shih* normally records the departure and *Chiu Wu-tai shih* the arrival. In the present context, it probably refers to the departure.

Toward the end of December, 942, another Khitan envoy was received at the Later Chin court (*Hsin Wu-tai shih* 9:2b).

On Dec.29, 942, Shao sent an official of the Cattle and Sheep Office as envoy to the Khitan court (*Hsin Wu-tai shih* 9:2b).

On Jan.22, 943, envoys from Shao thanked at the Khitan court (*Liao shih* 4:9a).

In the 1st month (Feb./Mar.) of 943, a Khitan envoy was received at the Later Chin court (*Hsin Wu-tai shih* 9:3a).

On Mar.15, 943, Later Chin envoys to the Khitan court offered Kao-tsu's testamentary gifts (*Liao shih* 4:9a).

On Mar.21, 943, Later Chin envoys to the Khitan court announced that Shao would reside in Pien (K'ai-feng) (*Liao shih* 4:9a).

On Apr.8, 943, envoys from the ruler of Wu-yüeh to the Khitan court offered gifts (*Liao shih* 4:9a).

On Apr.17, 943, envoys from Southern T'ang to the Khitan court offered a letter in a ball of wax (*Liao shih* 4:9a).

On Apr.30, 943, the Later Chin sent an envoy to the Khitan court (*Chiu Wu-tai shih* 81:10b).

On May 6, 943, Later Chin envoys to the Khitan court announced that Shao had arrived in Pien (*Liao shih* 4:9a).

On May 29, 943, Shao sent an envoy to the Khitan court (*Hsin Wu-tai shih* 9:3a).

On June 27, 943, T'ai-tsung sent envoys to the Later Chin court to congratulate on the birthday of Shao[38] (*Liao shih* 4:9a).

In the 6th month (July/Aug.) of 943, Later Chin envoys to the Khitan court offered gold (*Liao shih* 4:9b).

In the 7th month (July/Aug.) of 943, a Khitan envoy was received at the Later Chin court (*Hsin Wu-tai shih* 9:3b).

On Sep.3, 943, Later Chin envoys to the Khitan court again offered gold (*Liao shih* 4:9b).

In the 8th month (September) of 943, Shao's eldest son was received at the Khitan court (*Liao shih* 4:9b).

On Nov.21 of 943, a Khitan envoy was received at the Later Chin court (*Hsin Wu-tai shih* 9:3b).

On Dec.4, 943, Shao sent an envoy to the Khitan court (*Hsin Wu-tai shih* 9:3b).

---

[38] It fell on July 31.

On Dec.20, 943, a Khitan envoy was received at the Later Chin court (*Hsin Wu-tai shih* 9:3b).

On Jan. 7, 944, Shao sent a Serving Within the Palace and a former local Inspector as envoys to the Khitan. But after prolonged Chinese provocation, the war had begun, and when the envoys approached the border they were unable to proceed. They stayed in a public lodge for several months and then returned (*Chiu Wu-tai shih* 82:4a; *Hsin Wu-tai shih* 9:4a).

On Feb.4, 944, Shao sent an envoy to the Khitan court. He was unable to proceed and returned (*Hsin Wu-tai shih* 9:4a).

On Feb.22, 944, Shao sent an interpreter with a letter to the Khitan, seeking a restoration of the former good relations. This envoy was received on Feb.24, which means that he must have waited on T'ai-tsung in the field. T'ai-tsung replied that it was up to the Later Chin (*Chiu Wu-tai shih* 82:6a; *Liao shih* 4:9b; *Tzu-chih t'ung-chien* p.9262).

On Aug.12, 944, a Later Chin envoy to the Khitan court proposed peace. He was detained (*Liao shih* 4:10b).

When on Nov.11, 944, envoys from foreign countries to the Khitan court congratulated on the birthday of T'ai-tsung,[39] Later Chin envoys were conspicuously absent (*Liao shih* 4:11a).

In the 7th month (Aug./Sept.) of 944, a Later Chin envoy to the Khitan court begged for peace (*Liao shih* 4:11a).

In the 10th month (Oct./Nov.) of 946, the Later Chin army surrendered to the Khitan. In the 12th month (Dec./Jan., 947) of the same Chinese year, the Khitan entered the Later Chin capital Pien. Shao and his family were placed under arrest (*Chiu Wu-tai shih* 99:3b; *Liao shih* 4:13b; *Wen-hsien t'ung-k'ao* 345:18a).

On Jan.25, 947, T'ai-tsung entered Pien, held court in the Hall of Reverence for the Supreme, and received the homage of the Later Chin officials. On Jan.29, he demoted Emperor Shao to Grandee of Imperial Entertainments and Acting Grand Commandant, and enfeoffed him as Marquis Who Has Turned His Back on Righteousness. On Feb.10, the former emperor, his mother, his wife, a younger brother, and two sons were escorted to Jehol. He was allowed an entourage of 50 Palace Ladies, 3 eunuchs, 50 East and West File Officials,[40] 1 physician, 4 grooms, 7 cooks, 3 tea libationers, 3 members of the

[39] The date of his birth is not known.
[40] These were of low rank.

Imperial Regalia Office, and 10 able-bodied soldiers. Shao never saw China again (*Chiu Wu-tai shih* 99:4a; *Liao shih* 4:14a, 14b).

On Feb.24, 947, T'ai-tsung named his state the Great Liao (*Liao shih* 4:15a).[41]

On Mar.10, 947, the Military Commissioner Liu Chih-yüan proclaimed himself emperor in T'ai-yüan, founding the Later Han Dynasty. This was Emperor Kao-tsu[42] (*Chiu Wu-tai shih* 99:4b; *Liao shih* 4:15a).

On Apr.10, 947, T'ai-tsung emptied the imperial palace in Pien of personnel and paraphernalia and sent them to his Supreme Capital north of the Shira Muren. On Apr.24, he departed from Pien himself, abandoning north China to the Later Han. While still in Ho-pei, he died on May 15, aged 46. On May 16, his nephew, the eldest son of T'u-yü, ascended the throne. This was Emperor Shih-tsung. He sent envoys to announce T'ai-tsung's death to the Later Han (*Liao shih* 4: 15a, 16a; *Wen-hsien t'ung-k'ao* 345:18b).

On Mar.10, 948, Emperor Kao-tsu of Later Han also died, aged 54. On Mar.14, he was succeeded by his second son. This was Emperor Yin (*Chiu Wu-tai shih* 100:10a; 101:10b; *Liao shih* 5:2a).

On May 12, 948, envoys from the Southern T'ang to the Liao court congratulated on the ascension of Shih-tsung. They also presented a letter in a ball of wax which recommended a joint attack on the Later Han (*Liao shih* 5:2a).

Om Mar.21, 950, Southern T'ang envoys to the Liao court congratulated Shih-tsung on a successful raid against Later Han (*Liao shih* 5:2b).

On Dec.28, 950, Emperor Yin of Later Han was murdered. On Feb.13, 951, the general Kuo Wei ascended the throne and founded the Later Chou Dynasty. This was Emperor T'ai-tsu.[43] However, his aspirations were rejected by Liu Ch'ung, a brother of Kao-tsu of Later Han, who proclaimed himself emperor in T'ai-yüan. This was Emperor Shih-tsu. His state comprised the northern part of Shan-hsi and is known as Northern or Eastern Han (*Chiu Wu-tai shih* 103:8b, 13b; *Liao shih* 5:3a).

---

[41] The date is in doubt. On this and the name of the dynasty see *Cambridge History of China*, vol.6, p.60 note 14.

[42] Not to be confused with Kao-tsu of Later Chin.

[43] Not to be confused with T'ai-tsu (A-pao-chi) of the Khitan and T'ai-tsu of Later Liang.

On Mar.25, 951, T'ai-tsu sent the General of the Personal Guard of the Left as envoy to the Liao court to announce his ascension.[44] Shih-tsung responded with envoys, who presented a team of four fine hoses and congratulated (*Chiu Wu-tai shih* 111:2b; *Wu-tai hui-yao* 29: 9a; *Tzu-chih t'ung-chien* p.9456).

On Apr.4, 951, T'ai-tsu sent an Assistant of the Left of the Masters of Writing as envoy to the Liao court (*Chiu Wu-tai shih* 111:3b; *Liao shih* 5:3a; *Tzu-chih t'ung-chien* p.9457).

On June 3, 951, T'ai-tsu dispatched the same envoy to the Liao court. Shih-tsung sent the General of the Gilded Mace of the Left and the General of Divine Fierceness of the Right in response to the Later Chou court and presented jade horse trappings, washed with gold and lined with silver, bows and arrows, sable furs etc., and 40 horses (*Chiu Wu-tai shih* 111:6b-7a; *Wu-tai hui-yao* 29:9a).

On June 15, 951, T'ai-tsu sent the General of the Gilded Mace of the Left as envoy to the Liao court. He was detained, because Liao had allied itself with Northern Han (*Tzu-chih t'ung-chien* p.9460).

On July 7, 951, a Member of the Suite of the Interpreters, who had been sent as envoy by Shih-tsu of Northern Han, was received at the Liao court. In his communication, Shih-tsu called himself a nephew of the Liao emperor and requested recognition. Shih-tsung immediately sent a high-ranking envoy to recognize him as the Divinely Martial Emperor of the Great Han (*Liao shih* 5:3a; *Tzu-chih t'ung-chien* p.9457).

In the 6th month (July/Aug.) of 951, Southern T'ang envoys to the Liao court proposed a joint action against Later Chou (*Liao shih* 5:3a).

On Sep.16, 951, Liao returned the corpse of Chao Ying (*Hsin Wu-tai shih* 11:5b).[45]

On Oct.7, 951, Emperor Shih-tsung of Liao was murdered, aged 34. On Oct.11, he was succeeded by T'ai-tsung's eldest son. This was Mu-tsung. He sent an envoy to Northern Han to announce the death of his predecessor (*Liao shih* 6:1a).

In the 11th month (December) of 951, envoys from Northern Han,

---

[44] This was in the 2nd month. *Wu-tai hui-yao* dates the mission 1st month (Feb./Mar.).

[45] He was one of the Later Chin officials whom the Liao emperor T'ai-tsung had transferred to his Supreme Capital in 947. When he died, he expressed the wish to be buried in China.

Later Chou, and Southern T'ang condoled at the Liao court (*Liao shih* 6:1a).

In the 12th month (January 952) of the Chinese year 951, Northern Han envoys to the Liao court presented bows, arrows, and horse trappings (*Liao shih* 6:1a).

On Jan.30, 952, Southern T'ang envoys to the Liao court presented a letter in a ball of wax and offered 10,000 sets of rhinoceros hide armour (*Liao shih* 6:1b).

On Apr.4, 952, Southern T'ang envoys to the Liao court presented a letter in a ball of wax (*Liao shih* 6:1b).

On Apr.8 and June 23, 952, Southern T'ang envoys to the Liao court offered gifts (*Liao shih* 6:1b).

On July 2, 952, Northern Han envoys to the Liao court announced that their state was invaded by the Later Chou. Emperor Mu-tsung sent the Minister of the Right of the Department of State Affairs to lead troops in support of Northern Han (*Liao shih* 6:1b).

On Oct.22, 952, Northern Han envoys to the Liao court offered grape wine (*Liao shih* 6:2a).

On Jan.18, 953,[46] Northern Han envoys to the Liao court thanked for the aid in repelling the Later Chou army (*Liao shih* 6:2a).

On Apr.16, 953, Southern T'ang envoys to the Liao court offered gifts (*Liao shih* 6:2b).

On May 3, 953, Northern Han envoys to the Liao court offered garments and polo horses (*Liao shih* 6:2b).

On July 7, 953, Northern Han envoys to the Liao court announced that a stone stele which had been set up by Later Chin in commemoration of the Liao Emperor T'ai-tsung had been destroyed by the Later Chou. They proposed to carve a new one. Liao agreed to it (*Liao shih* 6:2b).

On Sep.22, 953, Northern Han envoys to the Liao court thanked for military support (*Liao shih* 6:2b).

On Nov.2, 953, Northern Han envoys to the Liao court offered drugs (*Liao shih* 6:2b).

On Mar.18, 954, Northern Han envoys to the Liao court offered tea and drugs (*Liao shih* 6:3a).

On Aug.14, 954, Northern Han envoys to the Liao court requested the return of people who had been seized by the Liao army (*Liao shih* 6:3a).

---

[46] Correcting *jen-tzu* to *jen-wu*.

On Oct.24, 954, Northern Han envoys to the Liao court announced that their state had been invaded by the Later Chou (*Liao shih* 6:3a).

On Jan.26, 955, Northern Han envoys to the Liao court offered gifts (*Liao shih* 6:3b).

On Mar.17, 955, Northern Han envoys to the Liao court proposed that their ruler present an honorific title to Mu-tsung. This was rejected (*Liao shih* 6:3b).

On May 5, 955, Northern Han envoys to the Liao court sought help against a Later Chou invasion (*Liao shih* 6:3b).

On Oct.3, 955, Northern Han envoys to the Liao court announced that their ruler (Shih-tsu) was ill (*Liao shih* 6:3b).

On Nov.30, 955, Southern T'ang envoys to the Liao court offered gifts (*Liao shih* 6:3b).

On Jan.6, 956, Northern Han envoys from Liu Ch'eng-chün to the Liao court announced that his father (Shih-tsu) had died and that he had succeeded him. This was Emperor Jui-tsung. He requested recognition. Mu-tsung sent envoys to condole and sacrifice and to recognize him (*Liao shih* 6:3b).

On Feb.2 and July 13, 956, Northern Han envoys were received at the Liao court to discuss military matters (*Liao shih* 6:3b).

On Mar.7, 957, Southern T'ang envoys to the Liao court presented a letter in a ball of wax (*Liao shih* 6:4a).

On June 5, 957, Northern Han envoys to the Liao court offered gifts (*Liao shih* 6:4a).

On June 30, 957, a goodwill mission from the Later Chou was received at the Liao court. At about the same time, Southern T'ang envoys offered gifts (*Liao shih* 6:4a).

On Sep.1, 957, a goodwill mission from the Later Chou was received at the Liao court (*Liao shih* 6:4a).

On Dec.27, 958, Northern Han envoys to the Liao court announced that their country had again been invaded by the Later Chou (*Liao shih* 6:4b).

In the 1st month (Jan./Feb.) of 960, Chao K'uang-yin overthrew the Later Chou and enthroned himself (*Sung shih* 1:1b; *Liao shih* 6:5a). This was Emperor T'ai-tsu, founder of the Sung dynasty.

In the 6th month (June/July) of 960,[47] Northern Han envoys to the Liao court announced that there country was being invaded by Sung.

---

[47] *Liao shih* gives the cyclical characters of *keng-shen*, but these did not occur in the 6th month.

Mu-tsung sent five regiments to its rescue. On July 27, 960, Northern Han envoys announced Sung victories (*Liao shih* 6:5a).

On Mar.5, 963, Northern Han envoys to the Liao court discussed military matters (*Liao shih* 6:6a).

On July 24, 963, and in the 10th month (Oct./Nov.) of the same year, Northern Han envoys to the Liao court announced a Sung raid (*Liao shih* 6:6a).

On Feb.24, 964, Northern Han envoys to the Liao court announced a Sung invasion. Emperor Mu-tsung sent troops to the rescue. On Apr.10, Northern Han envoys reported a victory. On May 25, they thanked for the support (*Liao shih* 7:1a).

On Aug.23, 966, Northern Han envoys to the Liao court presented golden vessels and armour (*Liao shih* 7:3a).

On Dec.4, 966, envoys from the Northern Han ruler to the Liao court announced the death of his mother. Mu-tsung sent envoys to condole and contribute to the funeral expenses (*Liao shih* 7:3a).

On Aug.16, 968, Northern Han envoys to the Liao court announced that Emperor Jui-tsung had died and that his son Liu Chi-en[48] had succeeded him. Mu-tsung sent envoys to condole and sacrifice (*Liao shih* 7:4b).

On Feb.25, 969,[49] envoys from [Chi-en's brother] Chi-yüan to the Liao court announced that he had ascended the Northern Han throne and asked to be recognized. This was Emperor Ying-wu. On Mar.4, Mu-tsung sent an envoy to recognize him (*Liao shih* 7:5a).

On Mar.7, 969, Northern Han envoys to the Liao court presented a white single-horned deer (*Liao shih* 7:5a-5b).

On Mar.12, 969, Emperor Mu-tsung of Liao was murdered by night, aged 39. He was succeeded by Shih-tsung's second son. This was Emperor Ching-tsung (*Liao shih* 7:5b; 8:1b).

In the 2nd month (Feb./Mar.) of 971, Northern Han envoys were received at the Liao court (*Liao shih* 70:6b).

On July 7, 971, Northern Han envoys to the Liao court inquired

---

[48] Correcting Chi-yüan to Chi-en. He was murdered the same year and received no posthumous title.

[49] None of the cyclical characters given by *Liao shih* 7:5a-5b for the 3rd month of 969 occurred in that month. That is because 3rd month is an error for 2nd. This is proved by the entries for Mu-tsung's death. *Liao shih* 7:5b has the date of 3rd month, *chi-ssu*, which is impossible, whereas 8:1a correctly has 2nd month, *chi-ssu* = Mar.12.

about the well-being of the new emperor. They also announced that their state was under attack by Sung (*Liao shih* 8:2b; 70:6b).

On Nov.11, 971, Northern Han envoys to the Liao court offered gifts (*Liao shih* 8:3a).

On Feb.19, 972, Northern Han envoys to the Liao court congratulated on the birth of an imperial son (*Liao shih* 8:3a).

In the 1st month (Feb./Mar.) of 973, Northern Han envoys to the Liao court offered gifts (*Liao shih* 8:3b).

On July 16, 973, Northern Han envoys were received at the Liao court to confer on a joint policy against Sung (*Liao shih* 8:3b).

In the 3rd month (Mar./Apr.) of 974, Sung envoys to the Liao court requested peace. Ching-tsung sent a Palace Attendant to Sung to discuss it (*Liao shih* 8:4a).

On Feb.14, 975, the New Year's Day, Sung envoys congratulated at the Liao court (*Liao shih* 8:4b).

On Apr.4, 975, a Military Commissioner from Northern Han was received at the Liao court and offered regional objects (*Liao shih* 8: 4b).

On May 10, 975, 28 Liao envoys to the Sung court presented a letter with a peace proposal. On May 12, T'ai-tsu received them in audience and presented garments, golden belts, black gauze caps, silver horse trappings etc. The envoys were given garments, [porcelain] vessels, and silk, in accordance with their ranks. They were invited to watch archery practice by horsemen. On May 13, they were given a banquet (*Sung shih* 3:7b; *Sung hui-yao kao* 5257:2a; *Wen-hsien t'ung-k'ao* 346:20a).

On Aug.19, 975, T'ai-tsu sent the Audience Commissioner and an Assistant of the Grand Master of Ceremonies as envoys to the Liao court (*Sung shih* 3:8a; *Wen-hsien t'ung-k'ao* 346:20a).

On Sep.30, 975, the General-in-chief of the Guards of the Left, sent by Liao as an envoy to the Sung court, presented garments, jade belts, and fine horses. T'ai-tsu gave him ample presents and invited him to a hunt in which the emperor himself participated (*Sung shih* 3: 8b; *Wen-hsien t'ung-k'ao* 346:20a).

On Dec.23, 975, T'ai-tsu sent a Gentleman of the Construction Office and two Palace Eunuchs as envoys to the Liao court to congratulate on the New Year's Day of Feb.3, 976 (*Sung shih* 3:9b).

On Feb.8, 976, a goodwill mission from Sung was received at the Liao court (*Liao shih* 8:4b).

In the 2nd month (Feb.Mar.) of 976, T'ai-tsu watched archery on horseback by Chinese cavalry and Liao envoys in the Northern Park (*Sung hui-yao kao* 5257:3b).

In the 2nd month (Mar./Apr.) of 976, a Liao envoy arrived at the Sung court to congratulate on T'ai-tsu's birthday[50]. He presented garments, jade belts, fine horses, and white falcons (*Sung shih* 3:9b).

On June 18, 976, T'ai-tsu sent an Assistant Audience Commissioner and others to Liao to congratulate Ching-tsung on his birthday. These congratulations were offered on Aug.4 (*Sung shih* 3:11a; *Liao shih* 8:5a).

On Sep.5 and 11, 976, Northern Han envoys were received at the Liao court. On Oct.14 and 20, other envoys reported a Sung invasion. Ching-tsung sent troops in support. On Nov.2, Northern Han envoys thanked the Liao for having forced the Sung army to withdraw (*Liao shih* 8:5a-5b).

On Nov.14, 976, Emperor T'ai-tsu died, aged 50, and was succeeded by his younger brother. This was Emperor T'ai-tsung. On Nov.26,[51] T'ai-tsung sent a Gentleman of the Editorial Service and an Adjunct to announce the news to the Liao court. This mission was received on Dec.7. On Dec.22, Ching-tsung sent a Court Attendant and others as envoys to Sung to condole. On Jan.2, 977, he sent another envoy to congratulate T'ai-tsung on his ascension.[52] On Jan.18, Liao envoys arrived at the Sung court to contribute 30 horses, three trained horses, horse trappings of real gold, garments, and two golden belts toward the funeral expenses of T'ai-tsu (*Sung shih* 3:12a; 4:2b; *Liao shih* 8:5b; *Wen-hsien t'ung-k'ao* 346:20a).

On Jan.22, 977, the New Year's Day, Liao envoys congratulated at the Sung court. They offered garments, golden belts, weapons adorned with gold and silver, 100 horses, and jade horse trappings. The 82 envoys and attendants were given garments, belts, [porcelain] vessels, and silk, each in accordance with his rank (*Sung hui-yao kao* 5257:4a).

Meanwhile, on Jan.7, 977, Northern Han envoys to the Liao court had reported an attack by Sung. They also requested grain (*Liao shih* 8:5b).

On Mar.1, 977, Sung envoys to the Liao court presented T'ai-tsu's testamentary gifts (*Liao shih* 9:1a).

---

[50] The date of his birth is not known.

[51] Correcting *chi-ch'ou* to *yi-ch'ou*.

[52] This mission was received at the Sung court on Mar.16, 977 (*Sung shih* 4:3a).

In the 2nd month (Feb./Mar.) of 977, Sung and Liao agreed on common border markets (*Sung shih* 4:3b).

On Apr.19, 977, Ching-tsung ordered 200,000 bushels of grain to be sent to Northern Han (*Liao shih* 9:1a).

On Apr.21, 977, the Junior Herald and other Liao envoys, who had received their orders on Jan.18, arrived at the Sung court to attend the funeral of T'ai-tsu. He was buried on May 15 (*Sung shih* 4:3b; *Hsü Tzu-chih t'ung-chien ch'ang-pien* p.153; *Wen-hsien t'ung-k'ao* 346:20a).[53]

On May 30, 977, Northern Han envoys to the Liao court thanked for the grain and also discussed policy matters concerning Sung (*Liao shih* 9:1a).

In the 5th month (May/June) of 977, T'ai-tsung sent a Member of the Suite of the Imperial Diarists on a goodwill mission to Liao. He was received at the Liao court on July 23 (*Sung shih* 4:3b; *Liao shih* 9: 1a-1b; *Wen-hsien t'ung-k'ao* 346:20a).

On July 31, 977, Northern Han envoys to the Liao court announced a Sung raid. On Aug.4, Liao sent envoys with war horses to aid the Northern Han (*Liao shih* 9:1b).

In the 8th month (Sep./Oct.) of 977, Northern Han envoys to the Liao court offered grape wine (*Liao shih* 9:1b).

On Nov.17, 977, Liao envoys arrived at the Sung court to congratulate on the birthday of T'ai-tsung[54] On Nov.25, T'ai-tsung watched a riding and archery contest between these envoys and the Chinese guards. Afterwards, he gave a banquet (*Sung shih* 4:4b; *Wen-hsien t'ung-k'ao* 346:20a).

On Dec.11, 977, and Jan.10, 978, Northern Han envoys to the Liao court conferred on a common policy against Sung (*Liao shih* 9:1b).

On Jan.19, 978,[55] T'ai-tsung sent envoys to Liao to congratulate on the New Year's Day of Feb.10 (*Sung shih* 4:5a).

On Feb.10, 978, the New Year's Day, the Grand Coachman and a deputy congratulated as Liao envoys at the Sung court and presented fine horses and regional objects (*Sung hui-yao kao* 5257:4a-4b).

On June 17, 978, Sung sent envoys to Liao (*Sung shih* 4:6b).

On Nov.4, 978, the Grand Coachman and other Liao envoys arrived at the Sung court to congratulate on the birthday of T'ai-tsung.[56] They

---

[53] *Hsü Tzu-chih t'ung-chien ch'ang-pien* has May 14.

[54] It fell on Nov.30.

[55] Correcting *chia-wu* to *chia-tzu*.

[56] It fell on Nov.20.

presented garments, golden belts, bows and arrows, 100 horses, four trained horses, and golden horse trappings. On Nov.5, the envoys were given a banquet (*Sung shih* 4:8a; *Sung hui-yao kao* 5257:4b; *Hsü Tzu-chih t'ung-chien ch'ang-pien* p.166).

On Dec.8, 978, T'ai-tsung sent envoys to the Liao court to congratulate on the New Year's Day of Jan.31, 979 (*Hsü Tzu-chih t'ung-chien ch'ang-pien* p.166).

On Jan.28, 979, Liao envoys arrived at the Sung court to congratulate on the New Year's Day of Jan.31. They presented fine horses and regional objects. T'ai-tsung summoned them to the Jade Ford Park to watch archery practice (*Sung shih* 4:8a; *Sung hui-yao kao* 5257:4b).

On Feb.4, 979, Ching-tsung sent an envoy to the Sung court to inquire why T'ai-tsung was attacking the Northern Han. This envoy returned on Feb.15 with the answer that there could be no peace unless the Liao refused aid to the Northern Han (*Liao shih* 9:2a).

In the 2nd month (March) of 979, a Liao envoy to the Sung court inquired about T'ai-tsung's well-being. He was presented with golden belts and silver horse trappings (*Sung hui-yao kao* 5257:5a; *Wen-hsien t'ung-k'ao* 346:20a).

Also in the 2nd month of 979, Northern Han envoys to the Liao court asked for military help. On Apr.6, envoys thanked for the aid. On Apr.9, envoys reported on the Sung invasion. On Apr.17, a Sung army decisively defeated Liao forces in Shan-hsi. On May 1, Northern Han envoys to the Liao court discussed the conduct of the war. On May 29, the Sung army won a victory over Northern Han. On June 3, Emperor Ying-wu surrendered to Sung, and the Northern Han State ceased to exist (*Sung shih* 4:10a; *Liao shih* 9:2a, 2b). But the war between Sung and Liao continued until 1005, largely in favour of Liao.

On Oct.13, 982, Emperor Ching-tsung of Liao died, aged 35. On Oct.14, he was succeeded by his 12-year old son. This was Emperor Sheng-tsung. His mother, the Empress Dowager, took over the government (*Liao shih* 9:5a; 10:1a).

In the 12th month (Dec./Jan.983), of the Chinese year 982, Sung envoys to the Liao court presented a belt adorned with rhinoceros horn. They also proposed peace, which the Liao rejected (*Liao shih* 10:1b).

On Sep.13 and Oct.19, 994, Sung envoys to the Liao court proposed peace. This was rejected (*Liao shih* 13:5a-5b).

Emperor T'ai-tsung of Sung died on May 8, 997, aged 59, and was succeed by his third son. This was Emperor Chen-tsung (*Sung shih* 5:25b; 6:1b).

On Dec.10, 1004, while the war was in progress, Liao envoys to the Sung court proposed that relations be improved (*Sung hui-yao kao* 5257:28b).

In the 11th month (Dec./Jan., 1005) of the Liao year 1004, after invading Liao forces had reached the Yellow River, the Sung responded with a peace feeler of its own. It used a certain Wang Chi-chung as a middleman, a former Sung official who had been captured by the Khitan in 1003, had entered their civil service, had become Commissioner of the Department of Revenue, and was much respected by Emperor Sheng-tsung and the Empress Dowager. Chen-tsung sent a man to present a bow and arrow to Chi-chung and secretely ask for peace. Chi-chung referred this request to the Liao court and was ordered to negotiate peace with Chinese envoys (*Liao shih* 14:5b).

On Jan.10, 1005, the Sung Assistant Commissioner for Fostering Propriety, Ts'ao Li-yung, was received at the Liao court for further peace negotiations. Sheng-tsung sent the Flying Dragon Commissioner on a goodwill mission in response. On Jan.16, Ts'ao Li-yung returned to the Liao court, offering annual payments but refusing to cede territory. Sheng-tsung sent the General-in-chief of the Palace Guards to respond with a letter (*Liao shih* 14:5b-6a).

On Jan.21, 1005, a Sung envoy was received at the Liao court whereupon the peace treaty was concluded. This was the peace of Shan-yüan.[57] The Chinese emperor agreed to consider the Liao Empress Dowager as his aunt and undertook to pay annually 100,000 ounces of silver and 200,000 bolts of silk. The border between the two states would be clearly delineated. Neither state would accept fugitive criminals. No new border fortifications were to be built, nor canals constructed near the border. Both states were to live in peace. Sheng-tsung sent the Commissioner for Audience Ceremonies on a goodwill mission to the Sung court to confirm the agreement. On Dec.2, 1005, the annual gifts (i.e. tribute) of Sung arrived in Liao for the first time (*Liao shih* 14:5b-6a, 6b).

On June 10, 1005, Sung envoys arrived at the Liao court to congratulate on the birthday of the Empress Dowager[58] (*Liao shih* 14: 6b).

---

[57] It was concluded in the Chinese/Liao year of 1004 and is usually dated that way.

[58] The date of her birth is not known.

On June 28, 1005, Sung envoys were received at the Liao court (*Liao shih* 14:6b).

On Nov.3, 1005, Sheng-tsung sent the Grand Commandant and the Grand Tutor to the Sung court to congratulate on the birthday of Chen-tsung.[59] On Dec.5, 1005, the Supreme General of the Guards of the Golden Mace of the Left arrived at the Sung court as an envoy from the Liao Empress Dowager, and also to congratulate on the birthday of Chen-tsung. He offered a letter, seven garments, 200 horses, horse trappings of gold and jade, brocade, deer tongues etc., while Sheng-tsung's envoys presented five garments, 200 horses, horse trappings, brocade, bows and arrows, falcons etc. Chen-tsung received the envoys in audience and made them rich gifts (*Sung hui-yao kao* 5257:35a-35b; *Liao shih* 14:6b; *Wen-hsien t'ung-k'ao* 346:21b).

On Dec.7, 1005, Sheng-tsung sent the Grand Guardian and an Executive Assistant, and the Empress Dowager sent the Grand Master and a Member of the Retinue of the Department of Administration as envoys to the Sung court to congratulate on the New Year's Day of Feb.1, 1006. One of the envoys fell ill and was unable to participate in the ceremony. Chen-tsung sent a physician to treat him (*Sung hui-yao kao* 5257:38a; *Liao shih* 14:6b-7a; *Wen-hsien t'ung-k'ao* 346:21b).

On Dec.25, 1005, Sung envoys arrived at the Liao court to congratulate on the New Year's Day of Feb.1, 1006 (*Liao shih* 14:7a; *Wen-hsien t'ung-k'ao* 346:21b).

On Jan.24, 1006, Sung envoys arrived at the Liao court to congratulate on the birthday of Sheng-tsung[60] (*Liao shih* 14:7a).

On Feb.11, 1006, Chen-tsung ordered officials to announce at the grave mounds of T'ai-tsu and T'ai-tsung that good relations had been establised with Liao (*Hsü Tzu-chih t'ung-chien ch'ang-pien* p.536).

At the end of the Chinese year 1006,[61] Liao envoys arrived at the Sung court to congratulate on the birthday of Chen-tsung.[62] The chefs were ordered to prepare Khitan food for them. From their lodgings, the envoys heard drums and asked whether Sung was preparing for war. They were told that the sound was made by actors. The emperor interfered and decided that it was best to tell the truth, namely that

[59] It fell on Jan.4, 1006.

[60] It fell on Apr.12, 1006.

[61] The text has 11th month, *hsin-mao*, but these cyclical characters did not occur in that month.

[62] It fell on Dec.24.

the art of war was a constant concern of the Sung State. It would also show the envoys that the Sung had no secrets from them (*Hsü Tzu-chih t'ung-chien ch'ang-pien* p.586). This may have been an attempt to impress the envoys with Sung's martial spirit.

On Jan.17, 1007, the Supreme General of the Awesome Guards of the Right, a Military Commissioner, the Junior Director of the Imperial House, and the General of the Guards of the Gilded Mace arrived as Liao envoys at the Sung court to congratulate on the New Year's Day of Jan.22 (*Hsü Tzu-chih t'ung-chien ch'ang-pien* p.558).

In the 4th month (Apr./May) of 1007, Liao envoys were received at the Sung court. Later that year, Sung envoys on their return from the Liao court reported all they had observed (*Sung hui-yao kao* 5257: 38a-38b).

In the 2nd month (Mar./Apr.) of 1008, a Sung envoy on his return from the Liao court reported all he had observed (*Sung hui-yao kao* 5257:39b).

In the 6th month (July/Aug.) of 1008, Chen-tsung sent a Supernumerary Gentleman of the Criminal Administration as envoy to the Liao court to announce that in the 10th month (November) he would sacrifice at Mount T'ai[63] (*Sung hui-yao kao* 5257:39b).

On Feb.5, 1008,[64] Liao envoys arrived at the Sung court to congratulate on the New Year's Day of Feb.10 (*Hsü Tzu-chih t'ung-chien ch'ang-pien* p.588).

On Dec.25, 1008, the Supreme General of the Martial Guards of the Left and other Liao envoys arrived at the Sung court to congratulate on the birthday of Chen-tsung.[65] They were given a banquet (*Sung hui-yao kao* 5257:40a).[66]

On Jan.24, 1009, Liao envoys arrived at the Sung court to congratulate on the New Year's Day of Jan.29 (*Sung shih* 7:20b).

In the 9th month (Sep./Oct.) of 1009, Chen-tsung appointed a Gentleman-in-Attendance of the Ministry of Works as envoy to the Liao court (*Sung shih* 7:22b).

In the 10th month (Oct./Nov.) of 1009, Liao envoys to the Sung

[63] That sacrifice was performed on Nov.24 (*Sung shih* 7:18b).

[64] Correcting the Chinese year of 1006 to 1007 (= 1008 Western calendar).

[65] It fell on Dec.31.

[66] One Liao mission, whose arrival at the Sung court is not recorded, returned on Jan.7, 1009. Another returned on Mar.24, 1009 (*Sung hui-yao kao* 5257:40a; *Hsü Tzu-chih t'ung-chien ch'ang-pien* p.614).

court announced that their state would attack Koryŏ (*Wen-hsien t'ung-k'ao* 346:22a).

On Dec.12, 1009, Liao envoys arrived at the Sung court to congratulate on the birthday of Chen-tsung[67] (*Hsü Tzu-chih t'ung-chien ch'ang-pien* p.638).

On Dec.29, 1009, the Empress Dowager of Liao, mother of Sheng-tsung, died, aged 57. On Dec.30, Sheng-tsung sent envoys to the Sung court to announce her death. Chen-tsung suspended the court for seven days. On Jan.16, 1010, Sheng-tsung cancelled his birthday celebrations[68] and on the New Year Day of Jan.18 he suspended the court (*Liao shih* 14:7b; 15:1a; *Hsü Tzu-chih t'ung-chien ch'ang-pien* pp.638-639).

On Feb.22, 1010, Sung envoys condoled and sacrificed at the Liao court and contributed 10,000 bolts of silk toward the funeral expenses. Subsequently, Sheng-tsung sent the Supreme General of the Dragon Tiger Guards of the Left to the Sung court with a testamentary letter of the Empress Dowager and jade bracelets, amber necklaces, vessels of carnelian, jugs of rhinoceros horn and jade, and fine horses etc. as testamentary gifts. Thereafter, he dispatched a Military Commissioner and the Supreme General of the Metropolitan Guard of the Left to thank for the condolence and sacrifice. Chen-tsung sent two generals to the Liao court to present garments, belts with veined rhinoceros horn, bows and arrows, and fine horses to thank for the testamentary gifts (*Sung hui-yao kao* 5257:42a-42b; *Liao shih* 15:1a; *Hsü Tzu-chih t'ung-chien ch'ang-pien* p.639; *Wen-hsien t'ung-k'ao* 346:21b).

On May 31, 1010, the Empress Dowager of Liao was buried in the presence of Sung envoys. Chen-tsung suspended the Sung court on that day and prohibited border towns from playing music for three days (*Liao shih* 15:1b; *Hsü Tzu-chih t'ung-chien ch'ang-pien* p.647).

On Oct.1, 1010, Sheng-tsung sent envoys to the Sung court to announce that he had personally taken command of an army against Koryŏ. This mission was received at the Sung court on Dec.14 (*Sung hui-yao kao* 5257:42b; *Liao shih* 15:1b).

On Dec.18, 1010, Liao envoys arrived at the Sung court to congratulate on the birthday of Chen-tsung[69] (*Sung hui-yao kao* 5257:43a).

On Feb.1, 1011, Liao envoys arrived at the Sung court to con-

---

[67] It fell on Dec.20.

[68] They would have fallen on Apr.17.

[69] It fell on Jan.8, 1011.

gratulate on the New Year's Day of Feb.6 (*Hsü Tzu-chih t'ung-chien ch'ang-pien* p.659).

On May 17, 1011, a Liao envoy to the Sung court gave an account of the war against Koryŏ (*Sung hui-yao kao* 5257:44a).

On Jan.21, 1012, Liao envoys arrived at the Sung court to congratulate on the New Year's day of Jan.26 (*Hsü Tzu-chih t'ung-chien ch'ang-pien* p.676).

On Jan.26, 1012, the New Year's Day, Sung envoys congratulated at the Liao court (*Liao shih* 15:3b).

In the 7th month (July/Aug.) of 1012, Sheng-tsung sent two envoys to the Sung court to congratulate on the birthday of Chen-tsung[70] and the Assistant Commissioner for National Credentials and another envoy to congratulate on the New Year's Day of Feb.13, 1013. The latter mission arrived at the Sung court on Feb.8 (*Liao shih* 15:4a; *Hsü Tzu-chih t'ung-chien ch'ang-pien* p.700).

In 1013, a Sung envoy, on returning from Liao, reported on the conditions in that state. Another returning envoy reported on the customs of the Khitan (*Sung hui-yao kao* 5257:44b, 46a-46b).

In the 10th month (Nov./Dec.) of 1013, Sheng-tsung sent envoys to the Sung court to congratulate on the birthday of Chen-tsung[71] (*Liao shih* 15:7a).

On Dec.20, 1014, Liao envoys arrived at the Sung court to congratulate on the birthday of Chen-tsung[72] (*Hsü Tzu-chih t'ung-chien ch'ang-pien* p.735).

On Feb.5, 1016, Liao envoys arrived at the Sung court to congratulate on the New Year's Day of Feb.11 (*Hsü Tzu-chih t'ung-chien ch'ang-pien* p.756).

On Dec.27, 1016, Liao envoys arrived at the Sung court to congratulate on the birthday of Chen-tsung[73] (*Hsü Tzu-chih t'ung-chien ch'ang-pien* p.783).

On Jan.25, 1017, Liao envoys arrived at the Sung court to congratulate on the New Year's Day of Jan.31 (*Hsü Tzu-chih t'ung-chien ch'ang-pien* p.784).

On Jan.27, 1017, two envoys from Chen-tsung arrived at the Liao

---

[70] It fell on Jan.16, 1013.
[71] It fell on Jan.5, 1014.
[72] It fell on Dec.26.
[73] It fell on Jan.2, 1017.

court to congratulate on the birthday of Sheng-tsung[74] (*Liao shih* 15: 10b).

On Oct.4, 1017, Sheng-tsung sent the [Chief Commandant of] Attendant Cavalry, a Military Commissioner, two Drafters, and others to the Sung court to congratulate on the birthday of Chen-tsung[75] and on the New Year's Day of Jan.20, 1018. The birthday mission arrived at the Sung court on Dec.18, 1017, and the New Year's mission on Jan.14, 1018 (*Sung shih* 8:17a; *Liao shih* 15:11b; *Hsü Tzu-chih t'ung-chien ch'ang-pien* p.806).

On Jan.13, 1018, four envoys from Chen-tsung arrived at the Liao court, two to congratulate on the birthday of Sheng-tsung,[76] and two to congratulate on the New Year's Day of Jan.20 (*Liao shih* 15:12a).

On Oct.12, 1018,[77] Sheng-tsung sent four envoys to the Sung court, two to congratulate on the birthday of Chen-tsung[78] and two to congratulate on the New Year's Day of Feb.8, 1019. The birthday mission arrived on Jan.6, 1019, and the New Year's mission on Feb.2 (*Liao shih* 16:1b; *Hsü Tzu-chih t'ung-chien ch'ang-pien* pp.820, 821).

On Jan.17, 1019, two envoys from Chen-tsung arrived at the Liao court to congratulate on the birthday of Sheng-tsung[79] (*Liao shih* 16: 2b).

On Feb.8, 1019, the New Year's Day, Sung envoys congratulated at the Liao court (*Liao shih* 16:3b).

In the 7th month (August) of 1019, Sheng-tsung sent two envoys to the Sung court to congratulate on the birthday of Chen-tsung.[80] (*Liao shih* 167:3b).

In the 9th month (October) of 1019, Sung envoys arrived at the Liao court to congratulate on the birthday of Sheng-tsung[81] (*Liao shih* 16:4a).

On Nov.4, 1019, Sheng-tsung sent two envoys to the Sung court to congratulate on the New Year's Day of Jan.28, 1020. They arrived on Jan.23 (*Liao shih* 16:4a; *Hsü Tzu-chih t'ung-chien ch'ang-pien* p.837).

---

74 It fell on Mar.31.
75 It fell on Jan.23, 1018.
76 It fell on Mar.20.
77 Correcting 8th month to 9th.
78 It fell on Jan.10, 1019.
79 It fell on Apr.8.
80 It fell on Dec.30.
81 It fell on Mar.27, 1020.

[On Jan.28], 1020, [the New Year's Day,] two Sung envoys congratulated at the Liao court (*Liao shih* 16:4b).

In the 7th month (July/Aug.) of 1020, Sheng-tsung sent two envoys to the Sung court to congratulate on the birthday of Chen-tsung[82] and on the New Year's Day of Feb.15, 1021. The birthday mission arrived in the 11th month (Nov./Dec.) and the New Year's mission in the intercalary month (Jan./Feb., 1021) of the Chinese year 1020 (*Liao shih* 16:4b; *Hsü Tzu-chih t'ung-chien ch'ang-pien* pp.837, 860).

In the 9th month (Sep./Oct.) of 1020, Chen-tsung sent two envoys to the Liao court to congratulate on the birthday of Sheng-tsung[83] (*Liao shih* 16:5a).[84]

On Feb.15, 1021, the New Year's Day, two Sung envoys congratulated at the Liao court (*Liao shih* 16:5b).

On Nov.17, 1021, two Sung envoys arrived at the Liao court to congratulate on the birthday of Sheng-tsung[85] and another two envoys to congratulate on the New Year's Day of Feb.4, 1022. Sheng-tsung immediately sent two envoys on a goodwill mission in response (*Liao shih* 16:6a).

In the 11th month (Dec./Jan., 1022) of the Liao year 1021, a Sung goodwill mission arrived at the Liao court (*Liao shih* 16:6b).

On Jan.1, 1022, Liao envoys arrived at the Sung court to congratulate on the birthday of Chen-tsung[86] (*Hsü Tzu-chih t'ung-chien ch'ang-pien* p.868).

On Feb.4, 1022, the New Year's Day, Liao envoys congratulated at the Sung court (*Hsü Tzu-chih t'ung-chien ch'ang-pien* p.869).[87]

On Mar.23, 1022, Emperor Chen-tsung died, aged 55, and was succeeded by his sixth son. This was Emperor Jen-tsung. He had not yet reached majority, and until 1027 the Empress Dowager, widow of Chen-tsung but not Jen-tsung's mother, conducted the government. She

[82] It fell on Dec.18.

[83] It fell on Apr.15, 1021.

[84] These envoys or those who returned from the New Year congratulations reported on the customs of the Khitan (*Sung hui-yao kao* 5257:47b).

[85] It fell on Apr.4, 1022.

[86] It fell on Jan.7.

[87] The text dates the arrival of the mission 12th month, *mou-tzu*, of the Chinese year 1021, but these cyclical characters did not occur in that month. Although *wu* often is miswritten *tzu*, *mou-wu* is in this case not a reasonable emendation. It would give the date of Jan.22, 1022, which does not fit into the chronological pattern discussed below. The date of arrival must therefore be questionable.

sent envoys to the Liao court to announce the death of her husband (*Sung shih* 9:1b; *Wen-hsien t'ung-k'ao* 346:22b).

On Mar.31, 1022, Sung sent envoys with Chen-tsung's testamentary gifts to Liao. This mission was received at the Liao court on June 28[88] (*Sung shih* 9:1b; *Wen-hsien t'ung-k'ao* 346:22b).

On Apr.11, 1022, Sheng-tsung sent the Inspector-general to the Sung court to sacrifice and the Assistant Commissioner for Libations to condole with the Empress Dowager. This mission was received at the Sung court on July 20. It also presented a letter from the Liao Empress to the Sung Empress Dowager and offered such things as pearls and inferior jade (*Sung shih* 9:2a; *Wen-hsien t'ung-k'ao* 346:22b; *Liao-shih* 16:6b).

On Apr.12, 1022, Sheng-tsung sent the Bearer of the Gilded Mace and a member of the Office of Presentations to condole with the new ruler of Sung (*Liao shih* 16:6b).

On May 16, 1022, Sung sent envoys to the Liao court to announce the ascension of Jen-tsung (*Sung shih* 9:2a).

In the 6th month (July), of 1022, Sung sent envoys to the Liao court to present drinking and eating vessels of tortoise shell adorned with gold, elephant tusks, carnelian cups, tea vessels and drinking cups [of porcelain], five robes, objects of rhinoceros horn, golden belts, musical instruments of tortoise shell adorned with gold, horse trapping of carnelian adorned with gold, jade horse whips, and 3000 bolts of brocade as Chen-tsung's testamentary gifts (*Sung hui-yao kao* 5257:50a-50b).

On Sep.3, 1022, Sung sent envoys to congratulate Sheng-tsung and his empress on their birthdays[89] and on the New Year's Day of Jan.25, 1023. "The custom of congratulating the Liao empresses on their birthdays began from this". The birthday mission arrived on Jan.13, 1023 (*Sung shih* 9:2b; *Liao shih* 16:7b; *Hsü Tzu-chih t'ung-chien ch'ang-pien* p.882).

On Sep.30, 1022, the Sung court ordered that the Liao emperors should henceforth be annually presented with garments and golden belts (*Hsü Tzu-chih t'ung-chien ch'ang-pien* p.882).

On Oct.24, 1022, Sheng-tsung sent two Masters of Writing to con-

---

[88] Correcting 6th month to 5th.

[89] Sheng-tsung's birthday fell on Mar.24, 1023. The birthdate of his empress is not known.

gratulate the Sung ruler on his ascension. This mission was received at the Sung court on Nov.2 (*Sung shih* 9:2b; *Liao shih* 16:7a; *Wen-hsien t'ung-k'ao* 346:22b-23a).

On Nov.2, 1022,[90] Sheng-tsung sent two envoys to the Sung court to congratulate on the birthday of the Empress Dowager[91] and two other envoys to congratulate on the New Year's Day of Jan. 25, 1023. The New Year mission arrived on Jan.21, 1023, and the birthday mission on Jan.29, 1023 (*Sung shih* 9:3a; *Liao shih* 16:7a).

On Dec.16, 1022, Sung envoys to the Liao court thanked [for the congratulations on Jen-tsung's ascension] (*Liao shih* 16:7b).

On May 6, 1023, the birthday of Jen-tsung, the Chinese officials and Liao envoys wished long life in the Hall for Venerating Virtue (*Sung shih* 9:3b).

On Oct.18, 1023, Sheng-tsung sent two envoys to the Sung court to congratulate on the New Year's Day of Feb.13, 1024, and another two envoys to congratulate on the birthday of Jen-tsung[92] (*Liao shih* 16:8a).

On Dec.10, 1023, two Sung envoys arrived at the Liao court to congratulate on the birthday of Sheng-tsung's empress and two other envoys to congratulate on the birthday of Sheng-tsung[93] (*Liao shih* 16: 8a).

On Feb.7, 1024, Liao envoys arrived at the Sung court to congratulate on the New Year's Day of Feb.13 (*Hsü Tzu-chih t'ung-chien ch'ang-pien* p.900).

On Feb.13, 1024, the New Year's Day, four Sung envoys congratulated at the Liao court (*Liao shih* 16:8b).

In the 3rd month (Apr./May) of 1024, Liao envoys to the Sung court presented a letter and were received in audience (*Sung hui-yao kao* 5257:50b).

In the 7th month (Aug./Sep.) of 1024, Sung sent envoys to the Liao court to discuss territorial matters (*Sung hui-yao kao* 5257:52b).

In the 8th month (Sep./Oct.) of 1024, Liao envoys arrived at the Sung court with an oath letter (*Sung hui-yao kao* 5257:52b).

On Oct.23, 1024, Sung sent two envoys to Liao to congratulate

---

[90] Correcting 9th month to 10th.
[91] It fell on Feb.1, 1023.
[92] It fell on May 24, 1024.
[93] It fell on Apr.11, 1024.

on the birthday of Sheng-tsung.[94] They arrived at the Liao court in the 10th month (Nov./.Dec.). During the same month, Liao envoys were received at the Sung court (*Sung hui-yao kao* 5257:53b-54a; *Liao shih* 16:9a-9b; *Hsü Tzu-chih t'ung-chien ch'ang-pien* p.909).

In the 12th month (January, 1025) of the Liao year 1024, Sheng-tsung of Liao sent two envoys to Sung to congratulate on the New Year's Day of Feb.1, 1025. They arrived at the Sung court on Jan.27, 1025 (*Liao shih* 16:9b; *Hsü Tzu-chih t'ung-chien ch'ang-pien* p.910).

On Feb.5, 1025, Liao envoys arrived at the Sung court to congratulate on the birthday of the Empress Dowager. On Feb.8, the actual birthday, the Chinese officials and Liao envoys wished long life in the Hall for Venerating Government. The Empress Dowager sat behind a screen. The Liao envoys complained that Sung envoys to the Liao court met an Empress Dowager face to face. They were told that when a Chinese Empress Dowager conducted the government, she always sat behind a screen and was not seen by even the Sung officials (*Sung shih* 9:5b; *Hsü Tzu-chih t'ung-chien ch'ang-pien* p.911).

On May 10, 1025, Liao envoys arrived at the Sung court to congratulate on the birthday of Jen-tsung[95] (*Hsü Tzu-chih t'ung-chien ch'ang-pien* p.913).

On Nov.15, 1025, two envoys from the Sung Empress Dowager arrived at the Liao court to congratulate on the birthday of Sheng-tsung's empress (*Liao shih* 17:1b).

On Jan.12, 1026, Sheng-tsung sent two envoys to the Sung court to congratulate Jen-tsung on the New Year's Day of Jan.22. On Jan.16, other envoys arrived to congratulate the Empress Dowager on the New Year's Day. "The custom to congratulate a Sung Empress Dowager on the New Year's Day began from this" (*Liao shih* 17:2a; *Hsü Tzu-chih t'ung-chien ch'ang-pien* p.920).

On Jan.18, 1026, two Sung envoys arrived a the Liao court to congratulate on the birthday of Sheng-tsung[96] (*Liao shih* 17:2a).

On Jan.22, 1026, the New Year's Day, four Sung envoys congratulated at the Liao court (*Liao shih* 17:2a).

On Jan.26, 1026, Liao envoys arrived at the Sung court to congratulate on the birthday of the Empress Dowager.[97] They had received

---

[94] It fell on Apr.1, 1025.
[95] It fell on May 13.
[96] It fell on Mar.22.
[97] It fell on Jan.29.

their orders on Aug.15, 1025 (*Liao shih* 17:1b; *Hsü Tzu-chih t'ung-chien ch'ang-pien* p.921).

On Apr.30, 1026, Liao envoys arrived at the Sung court to congratulate on the birthday of Jen-tsung[98] (*Hsü Tzu-chih t'ung-chien ch'ang-pien* p.923).

On Nov.28, 1026,[99] two Sung envoys arrived at the Liao court to congratulate on the birthday of Sheng-tsung's empress (*Liao shih* 17: 3b).

On Feb.3, 1027, Liao envoys arrived at the Sung court to congratulate the Empress Dowager on the New Year's Day of Feb.9 (*Hsü Tzu-chih t'ung-chien ch'ang-pien* p.933).

On Feb.4, 1027, Liao, envoys arrived at the Sung court to congratulate [Jen-tsung] on the New Year's Day of Feb.9 (*Hsü Tzu-chih t'ung-chien ch'ang-pien* p.933).

On Feb.9, 1027, the New Year's Day, Liao envoys to the Sung court congratulated the Empress Dowager who sat behind a screen. They saluted twice. On the same day, four Sung envoys congratulated at the Liao court (*Liao shih* 17:4a; *Hsü Tzu-chih t'ung-chien ch'ang-pien* p.933).

On Feb.13, 1027,[100] Liao envoys arrived at the Sung court to congratulate on the birthday of the Empress Dowager[101] (*Hsü Tzu-chih t'ung-chien ch'ang-pien* p.934).

On May 19, 1027, Liao envoys arrived at the Sung court to congratulate on the birthday of Jen-tsung.[102] The chief envoy complained that he was not received at the throne but placed with envoys from lesser states at a distance. He was told that the protocol had been approved by Chen-tsung and could not be changed but that Liao and Sung in any event were equals. Jen-tsung ordered a court discussion. One Grand Councilor considered this a trivial matter not worth wrangling about. Another insisted that small concessions would lead to big ones. His view was approved by the emperor (*Liao shih* 17:3b; *Hsü Tzu-chih t'ung-chien ch'ang-pien* p.936).

In the 11th month (December) of 1027, two Sung envoys arrived at the Liao court to congratulate on the birthday of Sheng-tsung,[103]

---

[98] It fell on May 3.
[99] Correcting *yi-ch'ou* to *chi-ch'ou*.
[100] Correcting *ping-wu* to *ping-tzu*.
[101] It fell on Feb.16.
[102] It fell on May 22.
[103] It fell on Mar.29, 1028.

and another two envoys to congratulate on the birthday of his empress (*Liao shih* 17:4b).

On Jan.25, 1028, Liao envoys arrived at the Sung court to congratulate the Empress Dowager on the New Year's Day of Jan.30. They had received their orders on Dec.31, 1027. On Jan.27, 1028 other envoys arrived to congratulate Jen-tsung on the New Year's Day (*Liao shih* 17:4b; *Hsü Tzu-chih t'ung-chien* p.944).

On Feb.3, 1028, Liao envoys arrived at the Sung court to congratulate on the birthday of the Empress Dowager.[104] They had received their orders on Dec.31, 1017 (*Liao shih* 17:4b; *Hsü Tzu-chih t'ung-chien ch'ang-pien* p.945).

On May 8, 1028, Liao envoys arrived at the Sung court to congratulate on the birthday of Jen-tsung[105] (*Hsü Tzu-chih t'ung-chien ch'ang-pien* p.949).

In the 10th month (Oct./Nov.) of 1028, two Sung envoys arrived at the Liao court to congratulate on the birthday of Sheng-tsung's empress (*Liao shih* 17:5b).

On Jan.12, 1029, Liao envoys arrived at the Sung court to congratulate the Empress Dowager on the New Year's Day of Jan.18. On Jan.13, other envoys arrived to congratulate Jen-tsung on the New Year's Day (*Hsü Tzu-chih t'ung-chien ch'ang-pien* p.955).

On Jan.14, 1029, two Sung envoys arrived at the Liao court to congratulate on the birthday of Sheng-tsung[106] (*Liao shih* 17:6a).

On Jan.22, 1029, Liao envoys arrived at the Sung court to congratulate on the birthday of the Empress Dowager.[107] They had received their orders in the 6th month (July/Aug.) (*Liao shih* 17:5a; *Hsü Tzu-chih t'ung-chien ch'ang-pien* p.956).

On May 26, 1029, Liao envoys arrived at the Sung court to congratulate on the birthday of Jen-tsung[108] (*Hsü Tzu-chih t'ung-chien ch'ang-pien* p.963).

On Jan.29, 1030, two Sung envoys arrived at the Liao court to congratulate on the birthday of Sheng-tsung[109] (*Liao shih* 17:7b).

On Jan.31, 1030, Liao envoys arrived at the Sung court to congratu-

[104] It fell on Feb.6.
[105] It fell on May 11.
[106] It fell on Apr.17, 1029.
[107] It fell on Jan.25.
[108] It fell on May 29.
[109] It fell on Apr.6.

late the Empress Dowager on the New Year's Day of Feb.5. On Feb.1, other envoys arrived to congratulate Jen-tsung on the New Year's Day. On the same day, four Sung envoys congratulated at the Liao court (*Liao shih* 17:7b; *Hsü Tzu-chih t'ung-chien ch'ang-pien* p.971).

On Feb.10, 1030, Liao envoys arrived at the Sung court to congratulate on the birthday of the Empress Dowager[110] (*Hsü Tzu-chih t'ung-chien ch'ang-pien* p.971).

On May 15, 1030, Liao envoys arrived at the Sung court to congratulate on the birthday of Jen-tsung[111] (*Hsü Tzu-chih t'ung-chien ch'ang-pien* p.974).

On Jan.20, 1031, Liao envoys arrived at the Sung court to congratulate the Empress Dowager on the New Year's Day of Jan.26. On Jan.21, other envoys arrived to congratulate Jen-tsung on the New Year's Day (*Hsü Tzu-chih t'ung-chien ch'ang-pien* pp.978, 979).

On Jan.22, 1031, two Sung envoys arrived at the Liao court to congratulate on the birthday of Sheng-tsung[112] (*Liao shih* 17:8b).

On Jan.30, 1031, Liao envoys arrived at the Sung court to congratulate on the birthday of the Empress Dowager[113] (*Hsü Tzu-chih t'ung-chien ch'ang-pien* p.979).

On May 4, 1031, Liao envoys arrived at the Sung court to congratulate on the birthday of Jen-tsung[114] (*Hsü Tzu-chih t'ung-chien ch'ang-pien* p.981).

On June 25, 1031, Emperor Sheng-tsung of Liao died, aged 61. He was succeeded by his eldest son. This was Emperor Hsing-tsung (*Liao shih* 17:8b; 18:1a). He had not been born by the empress but was raised by her. On his ascension, he had not yet reached majority, being born in 1016. In a power struggle for the regency, his natural mother proclaimed herself Empress Dowager[115] and contrived the banishment and death of Sheng-tsung's legitimate empress (*Liao shih* 18:71:5a-5b).

On June 30, 1031, the Liao Empress Dowager sent envoys to Sung to announce Sheng-tsung's death. This mission was received at the Sung court on July 22. Jen-tsung and his empress faced north and

---

[110] It fell on Feb.12.
[111] It fell on May 18.
[112] It fell on Mar.26.
[113] It fell on Feb.2.
[114] It fell on May 8.
[115] She was also called the State Mother.

went through the act of weeping. He suspended the court for seven days and sent four envoys to the Liao court to condole, another two to sacrifice, two to congratulate Hsing-tsung on his enthronement, and two to congratulate his mother on becoming the Empress Dowager. This mission was received at the Liao court on Sep.25 (*Sung shih* 9: 13a-13b; *Liao shih* 18:1a-1b, 2a; *Wen-hsien t'ung-k'ao* 346:23a).

On Oct.18, 1031, the Liao court sent the Palace Assistant Secretary, the Minister of Agriculture, a general, and the Commissioner of the Lodges for the Four Quarters to thank the Sung for the condolence and sacrifice (*Sung shih* 9:13b; *Liao shih* 18:2b).

On Oct.29, 1031, Jen-tsung appointed an envoy to congratulate on the birthday of the new Liao emperor Hsing-tsung,[116] other envoys to congratulate the Empress Dowager on the New Year's Day of Feb.14, 1032, and still other envoys to congratulate Hsing-tsung on the New Year's Day (*Liao shih* 18:3a; *Hsü Tzu-chih t'ung-chien ch'ang-pien* p.986).

On Oct.30, 1031, the Liao Empress Dowager sent a Master of Writing of the Ministry of Works and the Minister of Imperial Entertainments to the Sung court to convey Sheng-tsung's testamentary gifts. The Supreme General of the Metropolitan Guard of the Right and the Inspector of the Privy Treasury were to express further thanks on behalf of the Empress Dowager, and the Supreme General of the Palace Gate Guards and the Commissioner of the Office of Presentations were to do the same on behalf of Hsing-tsung. The envoys with the testamentary gifts arrived at the Sung court on Nov.22, and the others on Jan.18, 1032 (*Sung shih* 9:13b; *Liao shih* 18:2b; *Hsü Tzu-chih t'ung-chien ch'ang-pien* pp.986, 988).

On Feb.7, 1032, Liao envoys arrived at the Sung court to congratulate the Empress Dowager on the New Year's Day of Feb.14. On Feb.8, other envoys arrived to congratulate Jen-tsung on the New Year's Day. They had received their orders on Nov.11, 1031 (*Liao shih* 18:2b; *Hsü Tzu-chih t'ung-chien ch'ang-pien* p.988).

On Feb.16, 1032, two Sung envoys arrived at the Liao court to congratulate on the birthday of the Empress Dowager[117] (*Liao shih* 18:3a).

---

[116] The birth date of Hsing-tsung is not recorded. However, on Apr.30, 1040, a general amnesty was proclaimed in Liao because of his birthday (*Liao shih* 18:9a-9b). If, as must be assumed, the amnesty was granted on his actual birthday, he was born on the 17th day of the 3rd month. In 1032, it fell on Apr.29.

[117] The date of her birth is not known.

On Feb.17, 1032, Liao envoys arrived at the Sung court to congratulate on the birthday of the Empress Dowager[118] (*Hsü Tzu-chih t'ung-chien ch'ang-pien* p.988).

On May 22, 1032, Liao envoys arrived at the Sung court to congratulate on the birthday of Jen-tsung[119] (*Hsü Tzu-chih t'ung-chien ch'ang-pien* p.990).

In the 7th month (Aug./Sep.) of 1032, the Liao court sent envoys to the Sung court to congratulate on the birthday of Jen-tsung in the following year[120] (*Liao shih* 18:3b).

On Dec.20, 1032, two Sung envoys arrived at the Sung court to congratulate on the birthday of Hsing-tsung (18:3b).[121]

On Jan.16, 1033, four Sung envoys arrived at the Liao court to congratulate on the New Year's Day of Feb.3 (*Liao shih* 18:3b).

On Jan.28, 1033, Liao envoys arrived at the Sung court to congratulate the Empress Dowager on the New Year's Day of Feb.3. On Jan.29, other envoys arrived to congratulate Jen-tsung on the New Year's Day (*Hsü Tzu-chih t'ung-chien ch'ang-pien* p.998).

On Feb.7, 1033, Liao envoys arrived at the Sung court to congratulate on the birthday of the Empress Dowager[122] (*Hsü Tzu-chih t'ung-chien ch'ang-pien* p.998).

On Apr.30, 1033, the Sung Empress Dowager, widow of Chen-tsung, died. On May 2, an envoy was sent to announce her death to the Liao Empress Dowager. On May 6, two other envoys were sent to offer her testamentary gifts. The Liao Empress Dowager immediately sent the Commissioner of the Palace of Increasing Sagacity, a Serving within the Palace and Drafter, the Commissioner for Sacrifices and Military Commissioner of the Army of Heavenly Virtue, the Grand Judge, the Military Commissioner of the Army West of the [Yellow] River, and the Commissioner of the Office of Presentations to condole and sacrifice. This mission was received at the Sung court on Aug.28 (*Sung shih* 10:4a; 242:9a; *Liao shih* 18:4a; *Hsü Tzu-chih t'ung-chien ch'ang-pien* pp.1001, 1009).

On Sep.2, 1033, Jen-tsung ordered that because the ritual gifts of Liao after the death of the Empress Dowager had been more ample

[118] It fell on Feb.21.
[119] It fell on May 25.
[120] It fell on May 15, 1033.
[121] It fell on Apr.18, 1033.
[122] It fell on Febr.10.

than usual, it should receive 300 ounces of gold over and above the value of these gifts (*Hsü Tzu-chih t'ung-chien ch'ang-pien* p.1009).

On Dec.16, 1033, four Sung envoys to the Liao court thanked for the condolence (*Liao shih* 18:4b).

On Dec.27, 1033, two Sung envoys arrived at the Liao court to congratulate on the birthday of Hsing-tsung[123] (*Liao shih* 18:4b).

In the 12th month (Dec./Jan., 1034) of the Chinese year 1033, envoys from the Liao Empress Dowager and of Hsing-tsung arrived at the Sung court to congratulate on the New Year's Day of Jan.23, 1034 (*Hsü Tzu-chih t'ung-chien ch'ang-pien* p.1019).

On Jan.15, 1034, six Sung envoys arrived at the Liao court to congratulate on the birthday of the Empress Dowager and on the New Year's Day of Jan.23. One of these envoys died on Jan.28. The Empress Dowager ordered the high officials to contribute to the funeral expenses and Court Attendants to escort the corpse back to Sung (*Liao shih* 18:4b).

On May 1, 1034, envoys from the Liao Empress Dowager and of Hsing-tsung arrived at the Sung court to congratulate on the birthday of Jen-tsung[124] (*Hsü Tzu-chih t'ung-chien ch'ang-pien* p.1026).

Subsequently, Hsing-tsung foiled an attempted coup by his mother, the Empress Dowager, and banished her from the court. On Aug.17, 1034, he took over the government himself and immediately sent three envoys to the Sung court to congratulate on the New Year's Day of Feb.11, 1035 (*Sung shih* 10:6a; *Liao shih* 18:4b, 5a).

In the 12th month (Jan./Feb.1035) of the Liao year 1034, two Sung envoys arrived at the Liao court to congratulate on the New Year's Day of Feb.11, 1036, and another two envoys to congratulate on the birthday of the Empress Dowager (*Liao shih* 18:5a). In spite of her banishment, the Empress Dowager and her faction remained powerful, and Hsing tsung did not prevent the congratulations.

On May 20. 1035, Liao envoys arrived at the Sung court to congratulate on the birthday of Jen-tsung[125] (*Hsü Tzu-chih t'ung-chien ch'ang-pien* p.1046).

On Jan.11, 1036, four Sung envoys arrived at the Liao court to congratulate on the birthday of the Empress Dowager and on the New Year's Day of Jan.31, 1036 (*Liao shih* 18:5b).

---

123 It fell on Apr.8, 1034.
124 It fell on May 4.
125 It fell on May 23.

On Jan.26, 1036, Liao envoys arrived at the Sung court to congratulate on the New Year's Day of Jan.31 (*Hsü Tzu-chih t'ung-chien ch'ang-pien* p.1062).

On May 9, 1036, Liao envoys arrived at the Sung court to congratulate on the birthday of Jen-tsung[126] (*Hsü Tzu-chih t'ung-chien ch'ang-pien* p.1067).

In the 10th month (Oct./Nov.) of 1036, two Sung envoys arrived at the Liao court to congratulate on the birthday of the Empress Dowager. During the same month, Hsing-tsung sent envoys to Sung to congratulate on the New Year's Day of Jan.19, 1037. These arrived at the Sung court on Jan.14, 1037 (*Liao shih* 18:6a; *Hsü Tzu-chih t'ung-chien ch'ang-pien* p.1078).

On Apr.28, 1037, Liao envoys arrived at the Sung court to congratulate on the birthday of Jen-tsung[127] (*Hsü Tzu-chih t'ung-chien ch'ang-pien* p.1082-1083).

In the 12th month (Jan./Feb., 1038) of the Liao year 1037, Hsing-tsung sent four envoys to the Sung court to congratulate on the New Year's Day of Feb.7, 1038 (*Liao shih* 18:7b).[128]

On Feb.7, 1038, the New Year's Day, four Sung envoys congratulated at the Liao court. They also congratulated on the birthday of the Empress Dowager (*Liao shih* 18:7b).

On May 17, 1038, Liao envoys arrived at the Sung court to congratulate on the birthday of Jen-tsung[129] (*Hsü Tzu-chih t'ung-chien ch'ang-pien* p.1100).

On Nov.19, 1038, Hsing-tsung sent envoys to the Sung court to congratulate on the New Year's Day of Jan.27, 1039. These arrived on Jan.22, 1039 (*Liao shih* 18:8a; *Hsü Tzu-chih t'ung-chien ch'ang-pien* p.1106).

On Jan.18, 1039, two Sung envoys arrived at the Liao court to congratulate on the birthday of the Empress Dowager (*Liao shih* 18:8b).

On Jan.27, 1039, the New Year's Day, two Sung envoys congratulated at the Liao court (*Liao shih* 18:9a).

---

[126] It fell on May 12.

[127] It fell on May 1.

[128] *Hsü Tzu-chih t'ung-chien ch'ang-pien* p.1090 dates the arrival of this mission in 12th month, *kuei-wei*, of the Chinese year 1037 = Jan.23, 1038. That is an unlikely date, considering the chronological pattern to be discussed below. *Kuei-wei* is probably error for *Kuei-ssu* = Feb.2, 1038.

[129] It fell on May 20.

On May 6, 1039, Liao envoys arrived at the Sung court to congratulate on the birthday of Jen-tsung[130] (*Hsü Tzu-chih t'ung-chien ch'ang-pien* p.1112).

On Feb.10, 1040, Liao envoys arrived at the Sung court to congratulate on the New Year's Day of Feb.15 (*Hsü Tzu-chih t'ung-chien ch'ang-pien* p.1130).

On Feb.15, 1040, the New Year's Day, two Sung envoys congratulated at the Liao court (*Liao shih* 18:9a).

On the same New Year's Day of Feb.15, 1040, the reception at the Sung court was cancelled because of an eclipse of the sun. The Liao envoys were provided with drink and food at their lodge but not received (*Hsü Tzu-chih t'ung-chien ch'ang-pien* p.1135).

On May 24, 1040, envoys from the Liao Empress Dowager, who had been rehabilitated and been recalled in 1039, and envoys from Hsing-tsung arrived at the Sung court to congratulate on the birthday of Jen-tsung[131] (*Sung shih* 10:14b; *Hsü Tzu-chih t'ung-chien ch'ang-pien* p.1150).

On Aug.30, 1040, a Sung envoy to the Liao court announced that Sung was at war with Hsia (*Liao shih* 18:8b; 115:18a).

In the 11th month (Dec./Jan., 1041) of the Liao year 1040, two Sung envoys arrived at the Liao court to congratulate on the birthday of Hsing-tsung[132] (*Liao shih* 18:9b).

On Jan.13, 1041, Liao envoys arrived at the Sung court on a goodwill mission (*Hsü Tzu-chih t'ung-chien ch'ang-pien* p.1171).

On Jan.30, 1041, envoys from the Liao Empress Dowager and from Hsing-tsung arrived at the Sung court to congratulate on the New Year's Day of Feb.4 (*Hsü Tzu-chih t'ung-chien ch'ang-pien* p.1176).

On Feb.4, 1041, the New Year's Day, four Sung envoys congratulated at the Liao court (*Liao shih* 19:1a).

On Feb.17, 1041, two Sung envoys arrived at the Liao court to congratulate on the birthday of the Empress Dowager (*Liao shih* 19:1a).

On May 13, 1041, envoys from the Liao Empress Dowager and from Hsing-tsung arrived at the the Sung court to congratulate on the

[130] It fell on May 9.
[131] It fell on May 27.
[132] It fell on Apr.20, 1041.

birthday of Jen-tsung[133] (*Hsü Tzu-chih t'ung-chien ch'ang-pien* pp.1192-1193).

On Dec.26, 1041, two Sung envoys arrived at the Liao court to congratulate on the birthday of Hsing-tsung[134] (*Liao shih* 19:2a).

When Hsing-tsung learned that Sung, in violation of the treaty of Shan-yüan in 1005, was stengthening fortifications and improving waterways at the border, he made plans in the 12th month (Dec./Jan., 1942) of the Liao year of 1041 to seize ten contested prefectures (hsien)[135] (*Liao shih* 19:2a-2b).

On Jan.9, 1042, six Sung envoys arrived at the Liao court to congratulate on the birthday of the Empress Dowager and on the New Year's Day of Jan.25, 1042 (*Liao shih* 19:2b).

On Jan.16, 1042, a discussion was held at the Liao court on whether to go to war with Sung (*Liao shih* 19:2b).

On Jan.19, 1042, envoys from the Liao Empress Dowager and from Hsing-tsung arrived at the Sung court to congratulate on the New Year's Day of Jan.25 (*Hsü Tzu-chih t'ung-chien ch'ang-pien* p.1228).

On Jan.29, 1042, Hsing-tsung sent the Commissioner of Court Ceremony of the Southern Administative Division and a Han-lin Academician[136] as envoys to the Sung court to announce that he intended to retake the ten prefectures. They also were to inquire why Sung had attacked Hsia. These envoys were received at the Sung court on Apr.18 (*Sung shih* 11:3a; *Liao shih* 19:2b).

On May 3, 1042, envoys from the Liao Empress Dowager and from Hsing-tsung arrived at the Sung court to congratulate on the birthday of Jen-tsung.[137] They had received their orders on July 1, 1041 (*Liao shih* 19:1b; *Hsü Tzu-chih t'ung-chien ch'ang-pien* p.1239).

On June 23, 1042, two Sung envoys arrived at the Liao court on a goodwill mission. Hsing-tsung responded with a letter (*Liao shih* 19:2b).

On Sep.12, 1042, two Sung envoys arrived at the Liao court on a goodwill mission. They presented a letter from Jen-tsung and proposed,

---

[133] It fell on May 16.

[134] It fell on Apr.9, 1042.

[135] These had been first ceded by the Later Chin to the Khitan in 938 as part of the Sixteen Commanderies, were then occupied by the Later Chou in 959, and had thereafter been under Chinese rule.

[136] The Han-lin Academician was Liu Liu-fu, a Chinese in Liao service, who also had been sent on previous missions.

[137] It fell on May 6.

in at times vehement discussions, to increase the annual payments of silver and silk in return for keeping the ten prefectures. Hsing-tsung temporarily broke off the negotiations and replied with a letter (*Liao shih* 19:3a).

On Sep.18, 1042, Hsing-tsung sent two envoys including Liu Liu-fu to the Sung court to negotiate a covenant. They argued that since the Later Chin had ceded the ten prefectures, their occupation by the Later Chou was improper, and the rights and wrongs of the issue clear. Jen-tsung accepted the advice of Fu Pi, who had previously represented the Sung in the negotiations at the Liao court on June 23 and Sep.12, that annual payments to the Liao were better than war. He therefore agreed that the annual payments to Liao should be increased to 200,000 ounces of silver and 300,000 bolts of silk and, under protest, also agreed that these be called "tribute".[138] In exchange, Sung kept the ten prefectures. On Oct.11, 1042, three Liao envoys including Liu Liu-fu presented an oath letter to the Sung court. On Oct.29,[139] the Liao envoys informed Hsing-tsung. The emperor was pleased and gave a banquet to the officials in the Hall of Luminous Blessings (*Sung shih* 11:4a; *Liao shih* 19:3a; 96:1a-1b; *Wen-hsien t'ung-k'ao* 346:23a).

On Nov.16, 1042,[140] the Liao envoys returned to their court with an oath letter from the Sung State. On Dec.11, 1042, Liao envoys to the Sung court presented another oath letter from their state (*Sung shih* 11:4b; *Liao shih* 19:3a). That concluded the treaty.

On Feb.2, 1043, Sung envoys arrived at the Liao court to congratulate on the New Year's Day of Feb.13 and on the birthday of the Empress Dowager (*Liao shih* 19:3b).

On Feb.8, 1043, envoys from the Liao Empress Dowager and from Hsing-tsung arrived at the Sung court to congratulate on the New Year's Day of Feb.13 (*Hsü Tzu-chih t'ung-chien ch'ang-pien* p.1272).

On Feb.14, 1043, Hsing-tsung sent an Associate Administrator and the Recepient of Edicts of the Bureau of Military Affairs to Hsia to request it to make peace with Sung. They returned to their court on Mar.29 and informed that Hsia had halted its armies. Hsing-tsung

---

[138] As pointed out by Wittfogel, *Liao*, p.358 note 60, *Sung shih* 313:4b gives a different version. It claims that Liao accepted the term "payment".

[139] Correcting 9th month to 9th intercalary month.

[140] See previous note.

immediately sent envoys to convey this information to the Sung court (*Liao shih* 19:3b, 4a; 115:8a).

On May 22, 1043, envoys from the Liao Empress Dowager and from Hsing-tsung arrived at the Sung court to congratulate on the birthday of Jen-tsung[141] (*Hsü Tzu-chih t'ung-chien ch'ang-pien* p.1286).

On Sep.1, 1043, Hsia envoys requested Hsing-tsung of Liao to attack Sung. This was rejected (*Liao shih* 19:4b; 115:8a).

On Jan.28, 1044, envoys from the Liao Empress Dowager and from Hsing-tsung arrived at the Sung court to congratulate on the New Year's Day of Feb.2 (*Hsü Tzu-chih t'ung-chien ch'ang-pien* p.1343).

On May 3, 1044, it was learned at the Sung court that Liao was building two fortifications in northern Shan-hsi. When the Liao envoys who had congratulated on the birthday of Jen-tsung[142] returned home, they were requested to ask that these fortifications be abolished. Liao accepted it (*Hsü Tzu-chih t'ung-chien ch'ang-pien* p.1364).

In the 6th month (June/July) of 1044, Hsing-tsung sent the Commissioner of the Yen-ch'ang Palace to Sung court to announce that he was about to attack Hsia. This envoy was received at the court on Aug.19 (*Sung shih* 11:7b; *Liao shih* 19:5b-6a).

When Hsing-tsung had taken personal command of the army against Hsia, a Sung envoy presented parting gifts on Oct.3, 1044 (*Liao shih* 19:6a).

On Jan.16, 1045, envoys from the Liao Empress Dowager and from Hsing-tsung arrived at the Sung court to congratulate on the New Year's Day of Jan.21 (*Hsü Tzu-chih t'ung-chien ch'ang-pien* p.1424).

On Feb.8, 1045, Liao envoys to the Sung court announced that the war against Hsia had been concluded. On Feb.12, Jen-tsung sent a Drafter to congratulate on the end of the war. This envoy was received at the Liao court on Apr.12 (*Sung shih* 11:9a; *Liao shih* 19:7a).

On Apr.30, 1045, envoys from the Liao Empress Dowager and from Hsing-tsung arrived at the Sung court to congratulate on the birthday of Jen-tsung[143] (*Hsü Tzu-chih t'ung-chien ch'ang-pien* p.1439).

On Nov.14, 1045, Liao envoys to the Sung court presented a Nine Dragon Chariot and sheep and horses which their army had captured from Hsia (*Sung shih* 11:10a).

On Feb.4, 1046, envoys from the Liao Empress Dowager and from

---

[141] It fell on May 25.
[142] It fell on May 13.
[143] It fell on May 3.

Hsing-tsung arrived at the Sung court to congratulate on the New Year's Day of Feb.9 (*Hsü Tzu-chih t'ung-chien ch'ang-pien* p.1457).

On May 19, 1046, envoys from the Liao Empress Dowager and from Hsing-tsung arrived at the Sung court to congratulate on the birthday of Jen-tsung[144] (*Hsü Tzu-chih t'ung-chien ch'ang-pien* p.1461).

On Aug.21, 1046,[145] Jen-tsung appointed an envoy to congratulate the Liao Empress Dowager on her birthday, another to congratulate Hsing-tsung on his birthday,[146] another to congratulate the Empress Dowager on the New Year's Day of Jan.29, 1047, and another to congratulate Hsing-tsung on the New Year's Day (*Hsü Tzu-chih t'ung-chien ch'ang-pien* p.1467).

On Jan.24, 1047, envoys from the Liao Empress Dowager and from Hsing-tsung arrived at the Sung court to congratulate on the New Year's Day of Jan.29 (*Hsü Tzu-chih t'ung-chien ch'ang-pien* p.1473).

In the 4th month (Apr./May) of 1047, envoys from the Liao Empress Dowager and from Hsing-tsung arrived at the Sung court to congratulate on the birthday of Jen-tsung[147] (*Hsü Tzu-chih t'ung-chien ch'ang-pien* p.1478).

On Jan.13, 1048, envoys from the Liao Empress Dowager and from Hsing-tsung arrived at the Sung court to congratulate on the New Year's Day of Jan.18 (*Hsü Tzu-chih t'ung-chien ch'ang-pien* p.1487).

On May 26, 1048, envoys from the Liao Empress Dowager and from Hsing-tsung arrived at the Sung court to congratulate on the birthday of Jen-tsung[148] (*Hsü Tzu-chih t'ung-chien ch'ang-pien* p.1505).

On Jan.31, 1049, envoys from the Liao Empress Dowager and from Hsing-tsung arrived at the Sung court to congratulate on the New Year's Day of Feb.5 (*Hsü Tzu-chih t'ung-chien ch'ang-pien* p.1520).

On Feb.10, 1049, Hsing-tsung sent envoys to inform Sung that he was attacking Hsia. These were received at the Sung court on May.31 (*Sung shih* 11:14b; *Liao shih* 20:3a; 115:8b).

On May 15, 1049, envoys from the Liao Empress Dowager and from Hsing-tsung arrived at the Sung court to congratulate on the birthday of Jen-tsung[149] (*Hsü Tzu-chih t'ung-chien ch'ang-pien* p.1528).

---

144 It fell on May 22.
145 Emending *chi-wei* to *yi-wei*.
146 It fell on Apr.14, 1047.
147 It fell on May 11.
148 It fell on May 29.
149 It fell on May 18.

On Jan.21, 1050, envoys from the Liao Empress Dowager and from Hsing-tsung arrived at the Sung court to congratulate on the New Year's Day of Jan.26 (*Hsü Tzu-chih t'ung-chien ch'ang-pien* p.1540).

On Feb.6, 1050, Liao envoys arrived at the Sung court and announced that their state was attacking Hsia (*Hsü Tzu-chih t'ung-chien ch'ang-pien* p.1543).

On Apr.7, 1050, Liao envoys to the Sung court announced that their armies had withdrawn from Hsia. Jen-tsung sent a Han-lin Apprentice as his envoy in response (*Sung shih* 12:1a, 1b).

On May 4, 1050, envoys from the Liao Empress Dowager and from Hsing-tsung arrived at the Sung court to congratulate on the birthday of Jen-tsung[150] (*Hsü Tzu-chih t'ung-chien ch'ang-pien* p.1544).

On July 10, 1050, Sung envoys to the Liao court congratulated on the war against Hsia (*Liao shih* 20:5a).

On Feb.9, 1051, envoys from the Liao Empress Dowager and from Hsing-tsung arrived at the Sung court to congratulate on the New Year's Day of Feb.14 (*Hsü Tzu-chih t'ung-chien ch'ang-pien* p.1558).

On May 23, 1051, envoys from the Liao Empress Dowager and from Hsing-tsung arrived at the Sung court to congratulate on the birthday of Jen-tsung[151] (*Hsü Tzu-chih t'ung-chien ch'ang-pien* p.1564).

In the 6th month (July/Aug.) of 1051, Hsing-tsung sent envoys to the Sung court to present objects captured in the war with Hsia (*Liao shih* 20:5b-6a).

On Jan.30, 1052, envoys from the Liao Empress Dowager and from Hsing-tsung arrived at the Sung court to congratulate on the New Year's Day of Feb.4 (*Hsü Tzu-chih t'ung-chien ch'ang-pien* p.1577).

On May 12, 1052, envoys from the Liao Empress Dowager and from Hsing-tsung arrived at the Sung court to congratulate on the birthday of Jen-tsung[152] (*Hsü Tzu-chih t'ung-chien ch'ang-pien* p.1584).

On Jan.18, 1053, envoys from the Liao Empress Dowager and from Hsing-tsung arrived at the Sung court to congratulate on the New Year's Day of Jan.23 (*Hsü Tzu-chih t'ung-chien ch'ang-pien* p.1600).

On Jan.28, 1053, Hsing-tsung requested from Sung envoys a portrait of their emperor Jen-tsung, saying that he had for a long time wished to see one (*Liao shih* 20:8a).

On May 1, 1053, envoys from the Liao Empress Dowager and from

150 It fell on May 7.

151 It fell on May 26.

152 It fell on May 15.

Hsing-tsung arrived at the Sung court to congratulate on the birthday of Jen-tsung[153] (*Hsü Tzu-chih t'ung-chien ch'ang-pien* p.1606).

On Feb.6, 1054, envoys from the Liao Empress Dowager and from Hsing-tsung arrived at the Sung court to congratulate on the New Year's Day of Feb.11 (*Hsü Tzu-chih t'ung-chien ch'ang-pien* p.1620).

On May 20, 1054, envoys from the Liao Empress Dowager and from Hsing-tsung arrived at the Sung court to congratulate on the birthday of Jen-tsung[154] (*Hsü Tzu-chih t'ung-chien ch'ang-pien* p.1626).

On Oct.18, 1054, Liao envoys to the Sung court announced that Liao and Hsia had made peace (*Sung shih* 12:8a; *Wen-hsien t'ung-k'ao* 346:23b).

On Oct.24, 1054, Jen-tsung sent the State Finance Commissioner as envoy to the Liao court (*Sung shih* 12:8a).

On Jan.26, 1055, envoys from the Liao Empress Dowager and from Hsing-tsung arrived at the Sung court to congratulate on the New Year's Day of Jan.31 (*Hsü Tzu-chih t'ung-chien ch'ang-pien* p.1642).

On Feb.21, 1055, Sung envoys to the Liao court presented a tame elephant. On Mar.3, Hsing-tsung summoned the Chinese envoys to a reading of *fu* and *shih* poetry (*Liao shih* 20:9a).

On May 10, 1055, envoys from the Liao Empress Dowager and from Hsing-tsung arrived at the Sung court to congratulate on the birthday of Jen-tsung[155] They presented paintings with the likenesses of Hsing-tsung and his predecessors painted on silk and requested a portrait of Jen-tsung (*Sung shih* 12:9a; *Hsü Tzu-chih t'ung-chien ch'ang-pien* p.1654; *Wen-hsien t'ung-k'ao* 346:23b).

On Aug.28, 1055, Emperor Hsing-tsung died, aged 40. He was succeeded by his eldest son. This was Emperor Tao-tsung (*Liao shih* 20:9a; 21:1a).

On Sep.9, 1055, Jen-tsung appointed an envoy to congratulate on the birthday of the Liao Empress Dowager, another to congratulate on the birthday of the emperor,[156] another to congratulate the Empress Dowager on the New Year's Day of Jan.20, 1056, and another to congratulate the emperor on the New Year's Day. This roster was

[153] It fell on May 4.

[154] It fell on May 23.

[155] It fell on May 13.

[156] The congratulation must have been intended for Hsing-tsung, since news of his death did not reach the Sung court until Sep.26. His birthday would have fallen on Apr.4, 1056.

adjusted on Oct.22, presumably because of Hsing-tsung's death (*Hsü Tzu-chih t'ung-chien ch'ang-pien* p.1669).

On Sep.26, 1055, Liao envoys to the Sung court announced the death of Hsing-tsung. Jen-tsung ordered mourning and prohibited music. He sent envoys to condole and sacrifice, all in accordance with precedent (*Sung shih* 12:9b; *Wen-hsien t'ung-k'ao* 346:23b).

On Oct.9, 1055, Tao-tsung sent the Tribal Judge of the Left and a Han-lin Academician to present the testamentary gifts of his late father to the Sung court, and to thank for the condolence and sacrifice. This mission was received at the Sung court on Jan.6, 1056 (*Sung shih* 12: 10a; *Liao shih* 21:2a).

On Oct.11, 1055, Tao-tsung sent envoys to officially announce his enthronement (*Liao shih* 21:2a).

On Dec.1, 1055, Hsing-tsung was buried in the presence of Sung envoys (*Liao shih* 21:3a).

On Jan.2, 1056, the later famous Ou-yang Hsiu (1007-1072) congratulated as Sung envoy to the Liao court on the enthronement of Tao-tsung (*Liao shih* 21:3b).

On Jan.15, 1056, envoys from the Liao [Grand] Empress Dowager[157] and from Tao-tsung arrived at the Sung court to congratulate on the New Year's Day of Jan.20. When these envoys took leave on Jan.25, they were given a banquet (*Hsü Tzu-chih t'ung-chien ch'ang-pien* p.1676).

On Apr.8, 1056, Liao envoys to the Sung court, a Military Commissioner and a Grandee Remonstrant and Consultant of the Left, thanked for the congratulation, presented a portrait of Tao-tsung, and requested a portrait of Jen-tsung. This was agreed upon, but apparently no action was taken (*Sung shih* 12:10b; *Sung hui-yao kao* 5257:56a; *Wen-hsien t'ung-k'ao* 346:23b).

Jen-tsung's birthday celebration on May 30, 1056, was cancelled for that year (*Hsü Tzu-chih t'ung-chien ch'ang-pien* p.1682), presumably to observe the mourning for Hsing-tsung.

On Feb.2, 1057, envoys from the Liao [Grand] Empress Dowager and from Tao-tsung arrived at the Sung court to congratulate on the New Year's Day of Feb.7 (*Hsü Tzu-chih t'ung-chien ch'ang-pien* p.1704).

On Apr.25, 1057, a Liao envoy to the Sung court again requested a

---

[157] I.e. Tao-tsung's grandmother, Hsing-tsung's mother. She was the former Empress Dowager, who became Grand Empress Dowager after Hsing-tsung's death in 1055.

portrait of the emperor.[158] Jen-tsung sent an envoy in response (*Sung shih* 12:12a; *Hsü Tzu-chih t'ung-chien ch'ang-pien* p.1707).

On May 16, 1057, envoys from the Liao [Grand] Empress Dowager and from Tao-tsung arrived at the Sung court to congratulate on the birthday of Jen-tsung[159] (*Hsü Tzu-chih t'ung-chien ch'ang-pien* p.1708).

On Oct.27, 1057, Liao envoys to the Sung court once more sought a portrait of the emperor (*Sung shih* 12:13a).

On Nov.1, 1057, Jen-tsung sent an envoy to the Liao court (*Sung shih* 12:13a).

On Jan.22, 1058, envoys from the Liao [Grand] Empress Dowager and from Tao-tsung arrived at the Sung court to congratulate on the New Year's Day of Jan.27[160] (*Hsü Tzu-chih t'ung-chien ch'ang-pien* p.1718).

On Jan.24, 1058, the Liao [Grand] Empress Dowager died. On Jan.27, Tao-tsung sent envoys to announce her death to the Sung court. They were received on Feb.27. Jen-tsung suspended the court for seven days (*Sung shih* 12:13a; *Liao shih* 21:5a).

On Jan.28, 1058, Sung envoys to the Liao court presented a portrait of Jen-tsung (*Liao shih* 21:5a). These envoys had obviously left K'ai-feng before the death of the Grand Empress Dowager had become known.

On May 6, 1058, Liao envoys arrived at the Sung court to congratulate on the birthday of Jen-tsung[161] (*Hsü Tzu-chih t'ung-chien ch'ang-pien* p.1721).

On May 22, 1058, Sung envoys to the Liao court condoled and sacrificed (*Sung shih* 12:13a; *Liao shih* 21:5a).[162]

On June 18, 1058, Liao envoys to the Sung court presented the testamentary gifts of the Grand Empress Dowager (*Sung shih* 12:13b).

On Oct.11, 1058, Liao envoys to the Sung court thanked for the condolence (*Sung shih* 12:14a).

In the intercalary month (Jan./Feb., 1059) of the Chinese year 1058, a Liao envoy was received at the Sung court (*Sung shih* 12:14b).

On Feb.10, 1059, envoys from the Liao Empress Dowager[163] and

---

158 By *Hsü Tzu chih t'ung chien ch'ang-pien* expressed as the "divine countenance".

159 It fell on May 20.

160 Unbeknownst to Sung and the envoys, the Grand Empress Dowager was already dead on Jan.27.

161 It fell on May 9.

162 The date is according to *Liao shih*.

163 I.e. Hsing-tsung's widow and Tao-tsung's mother.

from Tao-tsung arrived at the Sung court to congratulate on the New Year's Day of Feb.15. They departed on Feb.29 (*Hsü Tzu-chih t'ung-chien ch'ang-pien* pp.1735, 1736).

On May 25, 1059, envoys from the Liao Empress Dowager and from Tao-tsung arrived at the Sung court to congratulate on the birthday of Jen-tsung[164] (*Hsü Tzu-chih t'ung-chien ch'ang-pien* p.1736).

On Jan.31, 1060, envoys from the Liao Empress Dowager and from Tao-tsung arrived at the Sung court to congratulate on the New Year's Day of Feb.5 (*Hsü Tzu-chih t'ung-chien ch'ang-pien* pp.1758-1759).

On May 13, 1060, envoys from the Liao Empress Dowager and from Tao-tsung arrived at the Sung court to congratulate on the birthday of Jen-tsung[165] (*Hsü Tzu-chih t'ung-chien ch'ang-pien* p.1764).

On Jan.19, 1061, envoys from the Liao Empress Dowager and from Tao-tsung arrived at the Sung court to congratulate on the New Year's Day of Jan.24 (*Hsü Tzu-chih t'ung-chien ch'ang-pien* p.1777).

On May 3, 1061, envoys from the Liao Empress Dowager and from Tao-tsung arrived at the Sung court to congratulate on the birthday of Jen-tsung[166] (*Hsü Tzu-chih t'ung-chien ch'ang-pien* p.1781).

On Feb.7, 1062, envoys from the Liao Empress Dowager and from Tao-tsung arrived at the Sung court to congratulate on the New Year's Day of Feb.12 (*Hsü Tzu-chih t'ung-chien ch'ang-pien* p.1808).

On Apr.30, 1063, Emperor Jen-tsung died, aged 54, and was succeeded by a great-grandson of T'ai-tsung. This was Emperor Ying-tsung. The Empress Dowager of Liao sent two and Tao-tsung six envoys to condole and sacrifice. They performed that task on Aug.14 (*Sung shih* 12:20b; 245:1a, 16a; *Sung hui-yao kao* 5257:57b; *Liao shih* 22: 1b; *Hsü Tzu-chih t'ung-chien ch'ang-pien* p.1841).

In the 4th month (May) of 1063, Liao envoys arrived at the Sung court to congratulate on the birthday of Jen-tsung[167] (*Sung hui-yao kao* 5257:57b). They must have set out before the news of Jen-tsung's death had reached the Liao court.

On Jan.20, 1066, Liao envoys arrived at the Sung court to congratulate on the birthday of Ying-tsung[168] (*Hsü Tzu-chih t'ung-chien ch'ang-pien* p.1914).

---

164 It fell on May 28.
165 It fell on May 16.
166 It fell on May 6.
167 It would have fallen on May 14.
168 It fell on Jan.31.

On Jan.29, 1066, the New Year's Day, Sung envoys congratulated at the Liao court. Soon thereafter, one of the envoys died. His corpse was sent back in accordance with ritual requirements (*Liao shih* 22: 54a).

On Apr.4, 1066, Sung envoys returned from the Liao court (*Hsü Tzu-chih t'ung-chien ch'ang-pien* p.1926).

On Jan.18,1067, the New Year's Day, Liao envoys congratulated at the Sung court. They were invited to a banquet, but since Ying-tsung was dying, he ordered officials to be the hosts (*Hsü Tzu-chih t'ung-chien ch'ang-pien* p.1939).

On Jan.25, 1067, Emperor Ying-tsung died, aged 36. He was succeeded by his eldest son. This was Emperor Shen-tsung. His envoys announced the death of Ying-tsung to the Liao court. On Mar.20, Tao-tsung sent the Grand Guardian of the Imperial Bodyguards of the Right and a Han-lin Academician to condole and sacrifice. On July 16, these envoys and envoys from the Liao Empress Dowager were received at the Sung court (*Sung shih* 13:7b; 14:1b; *Sung hui-yao kao* 5257:58b; *Liao shih* 22:4b; *Wen-hsien t'ung-k'ao* 346:24a).

On July 17, 1067, Sung envoys to the Liao court presented Ying-tsung's testamentary gifts (*Liao shih* 22:5a).

On Aug.7, 1067, a Sung envoy to the Liao court announced Shen-tsung's enthronement. Tao-tsung immediately sent a local administrator and a Member of the Suite of the Palace Writers to congratulate. They were received at the Sung court on Oct.29 (*Sung hui-yao kao* 5257:59a; *Liao shih* 22:5a).

In the 9th month (Oct./Nov.) of 1067, Sung envoys to the Liao court thanked [for the congratulations]. They also congratulated on the birthday of Tao-tsung[169] and on the New Year's Day of Feb.6, 1068 (Sung shih 14:4b).

On Sep.26, 1068, Sung envoys to the Liao court congratulated on the birthday of Tao-tsung and on the New Year's Day of Jan.26, 1069 (*Sung shih* 14:7b).

On Jan.21, 1069, Liao envoys arrived at the Sung court to congratulate on the New Year's Day of Jan.26 (*Sung shih* 14:8a).

On Apr.29, 1069, Liao envoys arrived at the Sung court to congratulate on the birthday of Shen-tsung[170] (*Sung shih* 14:8b).

---

[169] From Tao-tsung to the end of Liao the imperial birth dates are not known.
[170] It fell on May 3.

On Oct.1, 1069, Sung envoys to the Liao court congratulated on the birthday of Tao-tsung and on the New Year's Day of Feb.14, 1070 (*Sung shih* 14:10a).

On Feb.9, 1070, Liao envoys arrived at the Sung court to congratulate on the New Year's Day of Feb.14 (*Sung shih* 14:11a).

On May 17, 1070, Liao envoys arrived at the Sung court to congratulate on the birthday of Shen-tsung[171] (*Sung shih* 15:1b).

In the 8th month (Sep./Oct.) of 1070, Sung envoys to the Liao court congratulated on the birthday of Tao-tsung and on the New Year's Day of Feb.3, 1071 (*Sung shih* 15:2b).

On Jan.29, 1071, envoys from Tao-tsung and from the Empress Dowager arrived at the Sung court to congratulate on the New Year's Day of Feb.3 (*Sung shih* 15:4a; *Hsü Tzu-chih t'ung-chien ch'ang-pien* p.2034).

On May 8, 1071, envoys from Tao-tsung and from the Empress Dowager arrived at the Sung court court to congratulate on the birthday of Shen-tsung[172] (*Sung shih* 15:5b; *Hsü Tzu-chih t'ung-chien ch'ang-pien* p.2070).

On Sep.17, 1071, Sung envoys to the Liao court congratulated on the birthday of Tao-tsung and on the New Year's Day of Jan.23, 1072 (*Sung shih* 15:6a).

On Jan.18, 1072, envoys from Tao-tsung and from the Empress Dowager arrived at the Sung court to congratulate on the New Year's Day of Jan.23 (*Sung shih* 15:7a; *Hsü Tzu-chih t'ung-chien ch'ang-pien* p.2132).

On May 26, 1072, envoys from Tao-tsung and from the Empress Dowager arrived at the Sung court to congratulate on the birthday of Shen-tsung[173] (*Sung shih* 15:7b; *Hsü Tzu-chih t'ung-chien ch'ang-pien* p.2159).

On Oct.1, 1072, Sung envoys to the Liao court congratulated on the birthday of Tao-tsung and on the New Year's Day of Feb.10, 1073 (*Sung shih* 15:8a).

On Feb.4, 1073, envoys from Tao-tsung and from the Empress

---

[171] It fell on May 22. The Diplomacy Office had previously reported to Shen-tsung that when these envoys had reached a certain Postal Relay Station en route to K'ai-feng, one of the Khitan had during the night stabbed and killed four men of the mission and wounded twelve (*Hsü Tzu-chih t'ung-chien ch'ang-pien* pp.1947-1948).

[172] It fell on May 12.

[173] It fell on May.30.

Dowager arrived at the Sung court to congratulate on the New Year's Day of Feb.10 (*Sung shih* 15:8b; *Hsü Tzu-chih t'ung-chien ch'ang-pien* p.2264).

On May 15, 1073,[174] envoys from Tao-tsung and from the Empress Dowager arrived at the Sung court to congratulate on the birthday of Shen-tsung[175] (*Sung shih* 15:9b; *Hsü Tzu-chih t'ung-chien ch'ang-pien* p.2278).

On Sep.5, 1073,[176] Shen-tsung sent envoys to the Liao court to congratulate on the birthday of Tao-tsung (*Sung shih* 15:10a).

On Sep.16, 1073, Shen-tsung appointed an envoy to congratulate Tao-tsung on the New Year's Day of Jan.30, 1074, another to congratulate the Empress Dowager on her birthday, and another to congratulate her on the New Year's Day (*Hsü Tzu-chih t'ung-chien ch'ang-pien* p.2306).

On Jan.27, 1074, envoys from Tao-tsung and from the Empress Dowager arrived at the Sung court to congratulate on the New Year's Day of Jan.30 (*Sung shih* 15:10b; *Hsü Tzu-chih t'ung-chien ch'ang-pien* p.2334).

On Apr.17, 1074, two Liao envoys arrived at the Sung court to confer on border demarcation. They were received in audience. On Apr.23, the border discussion took place. On Apr.25, Sung sent a goodwill mission in response (*Sung shih* 15:11a; *Sung hui-yao kao* 5257:60a, 60b; *Wen-hsien t'ung-k'ao* 346:24b).

In May 4, 1074, envoys from Tao-tsung and from the Empress Dowager arrived at the Sung court to congratulate on the birthday of Shen-tsung[177] (*Sung shih* 15:11a; *Sung hui-yao kao* 5257:61a; *Hsü Tzu-chih t'ung-chien ch'ang-pien* p.2368).

In the 4th month (Apr./May) of 1074, the Assistant Commissioner of the Bureau of Military Affairs arrived as Liao envoy in Sung to discuss border demarcation. Shen-tsung sent the Junior Master of Ceremonies to meet with him in northern Shan-hsi, i.e. near the disputed border (*Sung shih* 15:22b; *Wen-hsien t'ung-k'ao* 346:24b).

In the 8th month (Aug./Sep.) of 1074, Shen-tsung sent envoys to the Liao court to congratulate on the birthday of Tao-tsung and on

---

[174] *Sung shih* has May 13, but considering the chronological pattern which will be discussed below May 15 is the more probable date.

[175] It fell on May 19.

[176] By *Hsü Tzu-chih t'ung-chien ch'ang-pien* p.2306 dated Sep.16.

[177] It fell on May 8.

the New Year's Day of Jan.20, 1075 (*Sung shih* 15:12a).

On Jan.15, 1075, envoys from Tao-tsung and from the Empress Dowager arrived at the Sung court to congratulate on the New Year's Day of Jan.20 (*Sung shih* 15:12b; *Hsü Tzu-chih t'ung-chien ch'ang-pien* pp.2426-2427).

In the 3rd month (Mar./Apr.) of 1075, a Liao envoy arrived at the Sung court with a proposal for border demarcation. Shen-tsung rejected this and made a counterproposal. This was in turn rejected by the envoy. After having been given a banquet, the envoy departed on Apr.22 with a letter from Shen-tsung (*Hsü Tzu-chih t'ung-chien ch'ang-pien* p.2453; *Wen-hsien t'ung-k'ao* 346:24b). The conflict wasa finally resolved in 1076.

On Apr.23, 1075, envoys from Tao-tsung and from the Empress Dowager arrived at the Sung court to congratulate on the birthday of Shen-tsung[178] (*Sung shih* 15:13b; *Hsü Tzu-chih t'ung-chien ch'ang-pien* p.2462).

On Sep.19, 1075, Shen-tsung sent envoys to the Liao court to congratulate on the birthday of Tao-tsung and on the New Year's Day of Feb.8, 1076 (*Sung shih* 15:14b).

On Feb.3, 1076, envoys from Tao-tsung and from the Empress Dowager arrived at the Sung court to congratulate on the New Year's Day of Feb.8 (*Sung shih* 15:15a; *Hsü Tzu-chih t'ung-chien ch'ang-pien* p.2560).

On Apr.11, 1076, the Empress Dowager, mother of Tao-tsung, died. On Apr.12, Tao-tsung sent the Palace Assistant Inspector-general to announce her death to the Sung court (*Liao shih* 23:4a).

On May 11, 1076, Liao envoys arrived at the Sung court to congratulate on the birthday of Shen-tsung. On May 15, which was the birthday, Shen-tsung cancelled the celebration to observe the mourning for the Liao Empress Dowager (*Sung shih* 15:16a).

On May 26, 1076, Shen-tsung sent envoys to condole at the Liao court (*Sung shih* 15:16a).

On June 3, 1076, Liao envoys to the Sung court instructed Shen-tsung that he should wear mourning garments for the Empress Dowager and suspend the court for seven days (*Sung shih* 15:16a).[179]

On Sep.6, 1076, Shen-tsung sent envoys to the Liao court to con-

---

[178] It fell on Apr.27.

[179] According to *Hsü Tzu-chih t'ung-chien ch'ang-pien* p.2588, he had apparently failed to do so because of the late arrival of the Liao envoys.

gratulate on the birthday of Tao-tsung and on the New Year's Day of Jan.27, 1077 (*Sung shih* 15:17a).

On Oct.26, 1076, Liao envoys to the Sung court were received in audience (*Hsü Tzu-chih t'ung-chien ch'ang-pien* p.2615).

On Jan.22, 1077, envoys from Tao-tsung arrived at the Sung court to congratulate on the New Year's Day of Jan.27 (*Sung shih* 15:18a; *Hsü Tzu-chih t'ung-chien ch'ang-pien* p.2639).

On Apr.30, 1077, envoys from Tao-tsung arrived at the Sung court to congratulate on the birthday of Shen-tsung[180] (*Sung shih* 15:18b; *Hsü Tzu-chih t'ung-chien ch'ang-pien* p.2656).

In the 8th month (Aug./Sep.) of 1077, Shen-tsung sent envoys to the Liao court to congratulate on the birthday of Tao-tsung and on the New Year's Day of Jan.17, 1078 (*Sung shih* 15:19a).

On Jan.11, 1078, envoys from Tao-tsung arrived at the Sung court to congratulate on the New Year's Day of Jan.17, 1078 (*Sung shih* 15: 19b-20a; *Hsü Tzu-chih t'ung-chien ch'ang-pien* p.2699).

On May 19, 1078, Liao envoys arrived at the Sung court to congratulate on the birthday of Shen-tsung[181] (*Sung shih* 15:20b).

On Sep.21, Shen-tsung sent envoys to the Liao court to congratulate on the birthday of Tao-tsung and on the New Year's Day of Feb.5, 1079 (*Sung shih* 15:21a).

On Jan.31, 1079, Liao envoys arrived at the Sung court to congratulate on the New Year's Day of Feb.5 (*Sung shih* 15:22a).

On May 9, 1079, Liao envoys arrived at the Sung court to congratulate on the birthday of Shen-tsung.[182] On May 17, they were given a banquet and departed (*Sung shih* 15:22b; *Hsü Tzu-chih t'ung-chien ch'ang-pien* p.2789).

In the 8th month (Aug./Sep.) of 1079, Shen-tsung sent envoys to the Liao court to congratulate on the birthday of Tao-tsung and on the New Year's Day of Jan.25, 1080 (*Sung shih* 15:23b).

On Jan.20, 1080, Liao envoys arrived at the Sung court to congratulate on the New Year's Day of Jan.25 (*Sung shih* 15:24a).

On Apr.28, 1080, Liao envoys arrived at the Sung court to congratulate on the birthday of Shen-tsung[183] (*Sung shih* 16:1b).

On Sep.9, 1080, Shen-tsung sent envoys to the Liao court to con-

---

[180] It fell on May 4.
[181] It fell on May 23.
[182] It fell on May 13.
[183] It fell on May 2.

gratulate on the birthday of Tao-tsung and on the New Year's Day of Feb.12, 1081 (*Sung shih* 16:1b).

On Feb.7, 1081, Liao envoys arrived at the Sung court to congratulate on the New Year's Day of Feb.12 (*Sung shih* 16:3a; *Hsü Tzu-chih t'ung-chien ch'ang-pien* p.2906).

On May 17, 1081, Liao envoys arrived at the Sung court to congratulate on the birthday of Shen-tsung[184] (*Sung shih* 16:3b).

On Jan.27, 1082, Liao envoys arrived at the Sung court to congratulate on the New Year's Day of Feb.1 (*Sung shih* 16:6a).

On May 6, 1082, Liao envoys arrived at the Sung court to congratulate on the birthday of Shen-tsung[185] (*Sung shih* 16:6b-7a).

On Sep.17, 1082, Shen-tsung sent envoys to the Liao court to congratulate on the birthday of Tao-tsung and on the New Year's Day of Jan.21, 1083 (*Sung shih* 16:8a).

On Jan.16, 1083, Liao envoys arrived at the Sung court to congratulate on the New Year's Day of Jan.21 (*Sung shih* 16:9a).

On Apr.25, 1083, Liao envoys arrived at the Sung court to congratulate on the birthday of Shen-tsung[186] (*Sung shih* 16:10a).

On Sep.26, 1083, Shen-tsung sent envoys to the Liao court to congratulate on the birthday of Tao-tsung and on the New Year's Day of Feb.9, 1084 (*Sung shih* 16:11a).

On May 13, 1084, Liao envoys arrived at the Sung court to congratulate on the birthday of Shen-tsung[187] (*Sung shih* 16:12a).

On Sep.16, 1084, Shen-tsung sent envoys to the Liao court to congratulate on the birthday of Tao-tsung and on the New Year's Day of Jan.29, 1085 (*Sung shih* 16:12b).

On Jan.24, 1085, Liao envoys arrived at the Sung court to congratulate on the New Year's Day of Jan.29 (*Sung shih* 16:13a).

Emperor Shen-tsung died on Apr.1, 1085, aged 38, and was succeeded by his sixth son. This was Emperor Che-tsung. On May 14th, he sent envoys to Liao to announce the death of his father and his own enthronement. These were received at the Liao court on May 18 (*Sung shih* 16:13b; 17:2b; *Liao shih* 24:6a).

In the 6th month (June/July) of 1085, Tao-tsung sent envoys to the Sung court to condole and sacrifice. They performed that task on

[184] It fell on May 21.
[185] It fell on May 10.
[186] It fell on Apr.29.
[187] It fell on May 17.

Aug.7 (*Liao shih* 24:6a; *Hsü Tzu-chih t'ung chien ch'ang-pien* p.3301).

On July 10, 1085, Sung envoys to the Liao court presented Shen-tsung's testamentary gifts (*Liao shih* 24:6a-6b).

On Aug.6, 1085, Tao-tsung sent envoys to Sung to congratulate on the enthronement of Che-tsung. These were received at the Sung court on Dec.8 (*Sung shih* 17:4a; *Liao shih* 24:6b).

On Sep.3, 1085, Sung envoys to the Liao court congratulated on the birthday of Tao-tsung and on the New Year's Day of Jan.18, 1086. On Oct.9, 1085, Sung sent other envoys to the Liao court (*Sung shih* 17:3b).

On Jan.2, 1086, a Sung envoy to the Liao court thanked for the condolence and sacrifice (*Liao shih* 24:6b).

On Jan.13, 1086, Liao envoys arrived at the Sung court to congratulate on the New Year's Day of Jan.18 (*Sung shih* 17:4b).

On Aug.27, 1086, the birthday of the Sung Grand Empress Dowager,[188] Liao envoys congratulated at the Sung court (*Hsü Tzu-chih t'ung-chien ch'ang-pien* p.3607).

On Jan.11, 1087, Liao envoys arrived at the Sung court to congratulate on the birthday of Che-tsung[189] (*Hsü Tzu-chih t'ung-chien ch'ang-pien* p.3705).

On Feb.1, 1087, Liao envoys arrived at the Sung court to congratulate on the New Year's Day of Feb.6 (*Hsü Tzu-chih t'ung-chien ch'ang-pien* p.3717).

On Aug.9, 1087, Liao envoys arrived at the Sung court to congratulate on the birthday of the Grand Empress Dowager.[190] They were given a banquet and departed on Aug.19 (*Sung shih* 17:8b; *Hsü Tzu-chih t'ung-chien ch'ang-pien* pp.3809, 3816).

On Dec.31, 1087, Liao envoys arrived at the Sung court to congratulate on the birthday of Che-tsung[191] (*Sung shih* 17:9b; *Hsü Tzu-chih t'ung-chien ch'ang-pien* p.3851).

On Jan.22, 1088, Liao envoys arrived at the Sung court to congratulate on the New Year's Day of Jan.27 (*Hsü Tzu-chih t'ung-chien ch'ang-pien* p.3855).

---

[188] The sources fail to identify the imperial birthday called the K'un-cheng Festival. But it was undoubtedly that of Che-tsung's grandmother, widow of Ying-tsung, since these congratulations ceased after her death in 1093.

[189] It fell on Jan.14.

[190] It fell on Aug.16.

[191] It fell on Jan.3, 1088. *Sung shih* wrongly says Jan.4.

On July 29, 1088, Liao envoys arrived at the Sung court to congratulate on the birthday of the Grand Empress Dowager[192] (*Hsü Tzu-chih t'ung-chien ch'ang-pien* p.3901).

On Dec.19, 1088, Liao envoys arrived at the Sung court to congratulate on the birthday of Che-tsung[193] (*Hsü Tzu-chih t'ung-chien ch'ang-pien* p.3948).

On Feb.8, 1089, Liao envoys arrived at the Sung court to congratulate on the New Year's Day of Feb.13 (*Hsü Tzu-chih t'ung-chien ch'ang-pien* p.3958).

On Feb.13, 1089, the New Year's Day, Che-tsung did not hold court. The Liao envoys congratulated at the Audience Gate (*Sung shih* 17:12a).

On Aug.17, 1089, Liao envoys arrived at the Sung court to congratulate on the birthday of the Grand Empress Dowager[194] (*Sung shih* 17:12b).

On Oct.30, 1089, Tao-tsung sent envoys to the Sung court to present dried venison (*Liao shih* 25:3b).

On Jan.7, 1090, Liao envoys arrived at the Sung court to congratulate on the birthday of Che-tsung[195] (*Sung shih* 17:13b).

On Jan.29, 1090, Liao envoys arrived at the Sung court to congratulate on the New Year's Day of Feb.3 (*Hsü Tzu-chih t'ung-chien ch'ang-pien* p.4103).

On Dec.27, 1090, Liao envoys arrived at the Sung court to congratulate on the birthday of Che-tsung[196] (*Hsü Tzu-chih t'ung-chien ch'ang-pien* p.4246).

On Jan.18, 1091, Liao envoys arrived at the Sung court to congratulate on the New Year's Day of Jan.23 (*Hsü Tzu-chih t'ung-chien ch'ang-pien* p.4256).

On Jan.23, 1091, the New Year's Day, Che-tsung did not hold court. The Liao envoys congratulated at the Audience Gate (*Sung shih* 17:15a).

On Mar.1, 1092, Che-tsung suspended the court for one day, because of the death of a Liao envoy (*Sung shih* 17:7a).

On July 27. 1091, Liao envoys arrived at the Sung court to con-

[192] It fell on Aug.5.
[193] It fell on Dec.22.
[194] It fell on Aug.24.
[195] It fell on Jan.10.
[196] It fell on Dec.30.

gratulate on the birthday of the Grand Empress Dowager[197] (*Hsü Tzu-chih t'ung-chien ch'ang-pien* p.4318).

On Jan.15, 1092, Liao envoys arrived at the Sung court to congratulate on the birthday of Che-tsung[198] (*Hsü Tzu-chih t'ung-chien ch'ang-pien* p.4385).

On Feb.5, 1092, Liao envoys arrived at the Sung court to congratulate on the New Year's Day of Feb.10 (*Hsü Tzu-chih t'ung-chien ch'ang-pien* p.4387).

On Aug.14, 1092, Liao envoys arrived at the Sung court to congratulate on the birthday of the Grand Empress Dowager[199] (*Hsü Tzu-chih t'ung-chien ch'ang-pien* p.4442).

On Nov.2, 1092, Tao-tsung sent envoys to the Sung court to present dried venison (*Liao shih* 15:4b).

On Jan.3, 1093, Liao envoys arrived at the Sung court to congratulate on the birthday of Che-tsung.[200] They were received in audience (*Hsü Tzu-chih t'ung-chien ch'ang-pien* p.4475).

On Jan.,25, 1093, Liao envoys arrived at the Sung court to congratulate on the New Year's Day of Jan.30 (*Hsü Tzu-chih t'ung-chien ch'ang-pien* p.4479).

On Sep.26, 1093, the Grand Empress Dowager of Sung, grandmother of Che-tsung, died.[201] On Sep.28, Che-tsung sent envoys to Liao to announce it. These envoys were received at the Liao court on Nov.11. Tao-tsung immediately responded with envoys to condole and sacrifice. The Liao envoys were received at the Sung court on Jan.3, 1094 (*Sung shih* 17:20a; 242:22a; *Liao shih* 25:6a).

On Jan.2, 1094, Sung envoys to the Liao court presented the testamentary gifts of Che-tsung's [grand]mother (*Liao shih* 25:6a).

On July 16, 1094, Sung envoys to the Liao court thanked for the condolence and sacrifice (*Liao shih* 25:7a).

On Oct.24, 1095, Tao-tsung ordered catapultiers and crossbow men to teach their skills to Chinese troops (*Liao shih* 26:1b).

---

197 It fell on Aug.3.

198 It fell on Jan.18.

199 It fell on Aug.21.

200 It fell on Jan.6.

201 According to *Liao shih*, Che-tsung announced the death of his mother, the Lady Ts'ao. That is an error. The Lady Ts'ao had been the second empress of Jen-tsung and had died in 1079 (*Sung shih* 15:24a; 242:16b). The Grand Empress Dowager who died in 1093 was the Lady Kao, widow of Ying-tsung and grandmother of Che-tsung.

On Jan.16, 1097, the New Year's Day, Che-tsung did not hold court. The Liao envoys congratulated at the Audience Gate (*Sung shih* 18:7a-7b).

On July 30, 1097, Tao-tsung sent envoys to the Sung court, advising it to make peace with Hsia (*Liao shih* 26:3a).

On Jan.9, 1098, Liao envoys arrived at the Sung court to congratulate on the birthday of Che-tsung[202] (*Hsü Tzu-chih t'ung-chien ch'ang-pien* p.4602).

On Jan.30, 1098, Liao envoys arrived at the Sung court to congratulate on the New Year's Day of Feb.4 (*Hsü Tzu-chih t'ung-chien ch'ang-pien* p.4606).

On Feb.25, 1098, Sung envoys to the Liao court presented brocade and silk (*Liao shih* 26:3b).

On Nov.22, 1098, Tao-tsung sent the Tribal Judge of the Right and an Auxiliary Academician of the Bureau of Military Affairs as envoys to the Sung court, urging it to make peace with Hsia (*Liao shih* 26:4a).

On Dec.29, 1098, Liao envoys arrived at the Sung court to congratulate on the birthday of Che-tsung[203] (*Hsü Tzu-chih t'ung-chien ch'ang-pien* p.4714).

On Jan.24, 1099, the New Year's Day, Che-tsung did not hold court because of a snowfall. The Liao envoys congratulated at the Audience Gate (*Sung shih* 18:12b).

On Apr.6, 1099, an Administrative Assistant of the Bureau of Military Affairs and other Liao envoys were received at the Sung court and given a banquet. They requested that the war against Hsia be halted and presented a jade belt. Che-tsung sent envoys in response. On May 11, the Liao envoys were given another banquet. On June 11, they returned to their court with the message that Sung was demobilizing its troops (*Sung shih* 18:13a; *Liao shih* 26:4a; *Hsü Tzu-chih t'ung-chien ch'ang-pien* pp.4742, 4757; *Wen-hsien t'ung-k'ao* 346:24b).

On Dec.13, 1099, two Sung envoys on a goodwill mission were received at the Liao court (*Liao shih* 26:4b).

On Jan.16, 1100, Liao envoys arrived at the Sung court to congratulate on the birthday of Che-tsung[204] (*Hsü Tzu-chih t'ung-chien ch'ang-pien* p.4850).

---

[202] It fell on Jan.12.

[203] It fell on Jan.1, 1099.

[204] It fell on Jan.19.

On Feb.7, 1100, Liao envoys arrived at the Sung court to congratulate on the New Year's Day of Feb.12. On Feb.16, these envoys were given a banquet. On Feb.17, they departed (*Hsü Tzu-chih t'ung-chien ch'ang-pien* p.4854).

On Feb.23, 1100, Emperor Che-tsung died, aged 25. He was succeeded by a younger brother, the eleventh son of Shen-tsung. This was Emperor Hui-tsung. He sent envoys to Liao to announce the death of his brother. These were received at the Liao court on Apr.5. That very day, Tao-tsung sent envoys to Sung to condole and sacrifice in accordance with precedent. His envoys were received at the Sung court on July 9 (*Sung shih* 18:15b; 19:1b, 3b; *Liao shih* 26:5a; *Wen-hsien t'ung-k'ao* 346:24b).

On Apr.10, 1100, Hui-tsung sent two envoys to Liao to present Che-tsung's testamentary gifts. These envoys were received at the Liao court on July 4 (*Sung shih* 19:2b; *Liao shih* 26:5a).

On Apr.14, 1100, Hui-tsung sent two envoys to the Liao court to announce his enthronement (*Sung shih* 19:2b).

On July 13, 1100, Tao-tsung sent envoys to Sung to congratulate Hui-tsung [on his enthronement]. These were received at the Sung court on Oct.7. In January, 1102, Sung envoys to the Liao court thanked for these congratulation (*Sung shih* 19:4a; *Liao shih* 26:5a, 5b).

On Sep.17, 1100, Hui-tsung sent an envoy to the Liao court to congratulate on the birthday of Tao-tsung, and another envoy to congratulate on the New Year's Day of Jan.31, 1101 (*Sung shih* 19:4a).

On Jan.27, 1101, Liao envoys arrived at the Sung court to congratulate on the New Year's Day of Jan.31.

On Feb.12, 1101, Emperor Tao-tsung died, aged 70. He was succeeded by a grandson. This was Emperor T'ien-tso. On Mar.5, he sent envoys to Sung to announce the death of Tao-tsung. These were received at the Sung court on Apr.4 (*Sung shih* 19:5a; *Liao shih* 27:1a, 1b).

In the 3rd month (April) of 1101, Hui-tsung sent envoys to Liao to condole and sacrifice in accordance with precedent. These were received at the Liao court on May 3 (*Sung shih* 19:5a; *Liao shih* 27:1b; *Wen-hsien t'ung-k'ao* 346:24b).

On Nov.2, 1101, Hui-tsung's birthday, Liao envoys congratulated at the Sung court (*Sung shih* 19:6a).

On Dec.28, 1101, Sung envoys to the Liao court congratulated on the enthronement of T'ien-tso. Subsequently, Liao envoys to the

Sung court presented Tao-tsung's testamentary gifts (*Sung shih* 19:5a, 6b; *Liao shih* 27:2a).

On Feb.14, 1105, an Auxiliary Academician of the Bureau of Military Affairs and other Liao envoys to the Sung court requested that Sung demobilize the troops attacking Hsia (*Liao shih* 27:4a).

On May 19, 1105, Liao envoys to Sung sought a return of territory to Hsia and the withdrawal of troops. These envoys departed from the Sung court on June 24 (*Sung shih* 20:2a; *Sung hui-yao kao* 5257:69b).

On July 29, 1105, two Sung envoys on a goodwill mission were received at the Liao court (*Liao shih* 27:4a).

On Feb.13, 1106, T'ien-tso sent the Commissioner of Military Affairs of the Northern Administration and the Commissioner of Military Affairs of the Southern Administration as envoys to the the Sung court. They were to urge Sung to return territory it had seized from Hsia and to discuss with it the delineation of the border (*Liao shih* 27:4b; 115:10b; *Wen-hsien t'ung-k'ao* 346:24b).

On Nov.14 1106, two Sung envoys to the Liao court announced that their state had made peace with Hsia (*Liao shih* 27:4b).

On Apr.15, 1109, Hsia envoys to the Liao court announced that Sung had not returned any territory (*Liao shih* 27:5b).

On July 26, 1115, Sung envoys arrived at the Liao court to present silver and silk for the support of the army (*Liao shih* 27:10b). This may have been a last half-hearted attempt to support the Khitan against the Jurchen. It would hardly have been a regular tribute payment, since such was delivered at the border.

On Mar.11, 1118, Hui-tsung sent the Grandee of Martial Loyalty by sea to the Jurchen to form an alliance with them against Liao (*Sung shih* 21:9a).

War broke out between the Khitan and Jurchen, and the strength of Liao was sapped by bad leadership, continuous defeats, and internal uprisings. In early 1125, T'ien-tso was captured and on Sep.3 brought before the Jurchen emperor T'ai-tsu (A-ku-ta). On Sep.6 he was demoted to king of Hai-pin. On Oct.22, Jurchen envoys to the Sung court announced T'ien-tso's capture. He died a natural death, aged 54[205] (*Sung shih* 22:12a; *Liao shih* 30:1b).

Chinese and Khitan/Liao diplomatic relations can be divided into three distinct historical periods. The first comprised the time from Sui

---

[205] Since he was born in 1075 (*Liao shih* 27:1a), he ought to have died in 1128.

through T'ang, i.e. 589 to 906, when Chinese superiority was never in doubt. The second can be dated 907 to 1005, i.e. the Five Dynasties and Sung until the treaty of Shan-yüan, when the Khitan/Liao State outgrew China in power. The third lasted from 1005 to about 1115, when relations settled down to diplomatic routine and the superiority of Liao was unchallenged. The final collapse of Liao came in 1125.

During the first period, 589 to 906, the Khitan posed no serious threat to China, even though they invaded it 696 to 697, fought minor engagements in the first half of the 740's, defeated An Lu-shan in 751, and looted border areas in 788. On the contrary, they were a potential asset to the T'ang as a counterweight to the Hsi. In a classical diplomatic endeavour, the Chinese attempted to form an alliance with a people behind a possible enemy. But this policy met with no great succcss. Thc Khitan were divided, some favouring China and others preferring an alliance with the Turks. 16 Khitan chiefs visited the T'ang court between 629 and 830.[206] Chinese official and noble titles were conferred on 15 chiefs from Sui until 842. One chief was granted the imperial surname of Li in 648. Emperor Hsüan-tsung recognized at least seven chiefs as kings in 715, 718, 722, 725, 735, 745, and 746. Above all, Hsüan-tsung sought to improve relations by marrying Chinese princesses to prominent Khitan. In 717, the Princess of Yung-lo was married to Li Shih-huo. When it became known in 718 that he had died, Hsüan-tsung suspended the court for mourning and conferred on him the posthumous title of Specially Advanced. In 722, the Princess of Yen commandery was married to Li Yü-yü. After Yü-yü's death in 723, she married his younger brother T'u-yü. But in 725, the couple was forced to flee to China. In 726, the Princess of Tung-hua was married to Li Shao-ku. After he had been killed, she fled to China in 730. In 745, the Princess of Ching-lo was married to Li Huai-chieh. He murdered her the same year. Hostility to China was obviously strong among the Khitan. Chinese attempts to turn their territory into an imaginary Area Command were mere wishful thinking. The Khitan never submitted to the T'ang, They preserved their independence from the Chinese, although not always from the Turks and Uighurs.

Little is known of the purpose of the Khitan missions to Sui and T'ang. In 628, they offered an alliance against the Turks. They con-

[206] One of these, K'o-t'u-yü, was received twice, in 722 and 726.

gratulated on the New Year's Day probably in 645 and certainly in 719.They informed about an internal upheaval in 733 and offered peace in 745. This paucity of information must be due to the fact that the overwhelming number of all other missions was for the sake of trade.

The second period begins in 907 with the partitioning of China into lesser states and the unification of the Khitan into a single state. A-pao-chi (T'ai-tsu) proclaimed himself emperor of the Khitan that year, and Chu Wen founded the Later Liang dynasty (907-923). From 916 to 922 the Khitan were at war with the Later Liang, in 928 with the Later T'ang (923-936), from 944 to 946 with the Later Chin (936-946), and from 952 with the Later Chou (951-960). Only the brief Later Han (947-950) was free of conflicts. The Five-Dynasties emperor who had the best relations with the Khitan was Kao-tsu of Later Chin (r.936-942), but he could not have founded his dynasty without their help, and throughout his reign he had to appease them. In 936, he agreed to treat T'ai-tsung of the Khitan like a father, which placed him one step below T'ai-tsung. He also agreed to pay an annual tribute of gold and 130,000 bolts of silk. No other of the Five Dynasties is recorded to have paid tribute. In 938, he had to cede the Sixteen Commanderies to the Khitan, which has rankled so bitterly with the Chinese historians ever since. But, as often has been pointed out, he was a pragmatic Turk and not concerned with Chinese sensibilities. When his successor, Emperor Shao under the influence of an anti-Khitan party attempted to take a more independant line and refused to call himself a subject, this provoked the invasion of the Khitan in 944 and his arrest, dethronement, and deportation in 946. From 952, Liao supported the Northern Han against the Later Chou, another classical example of an alliance across a common enemy. A close relationship was established, in which Shih-tsu of Northern Han called himself a nephew of the Liao emperor in 951. The war of Later Chou against Northern Han and Liao was carried on by the Sung from 960 until 1005. The Khitan extended the alliance they had with the Northern Han to the Chinese states southwest of the Five Dynasties, Wu (902-937), its successor the Southern T'ang (937-975), and Wu-yüeh (908-979). This threatened the Five Dynasties and early Sung with possible wars on two fronts and also povided the Khitan with valuable intelligence, forwarded in secret letters encased in wax.

But even when relations were at their best between one or another of the Chinese states and the Khitan, the former never offered princesses in marriage and the latter never sought them.

In spite of tensions, there were attempts to observe diplomatic protocol. Since, as will be seen, there seem to be many missed opportunities at ceremonial occasions, it is possible that the sources are incomplete. But it is equally possible and even more probable that a routine exchange of missions was still in the process of coming into existance.

The Southern T'ang congratulated in 948 on the entronement of Shih-tsung of Liao, but no similar acts by the Five Dynasties are recorded. On the other hand, the Khitan congratulated on the enthronement of Shao of Later Chin in 942, of T'ai-tsu of Later Chou in 951, and of T'ai-tsung of Sung in 977.

The Later Chin congratulated in 937 on the birthday of the Khitan Empress Dowager, widow of T'ai-tsu. The Khitan congratulated on the birthdays of of the Later Chin emperors Kao-tsu in 940 and 942 and of Shao in 943. This was the dynasty which at first was closest to them.

The Later T'ang announced to the Khitan the death of Chuang-tsung in 926 and of Ming-tsung in 934. At the former occasion, the Khitan emperor T'ai-tsu pretended to weep. In 942, the Later Chin announced the death of Kao-tsu to the Khitan. In the same year, the Later Chin announced the death of Shao's grandmother. The Northern Han informed the Khitan of the death of Shih-tsu in 956, of Jui-tsung's mother in 966, and of Jui-tsung in 968. In 976, Sung announced the death of T'ai-tsu to Liao. The Khitan announced the death of T'ai-tsu in 926, and of the Grand Empress Dowager, mother of T'ai-tsu, in 933, both to the Later T'ang. In 951, Liao informed the Northern Han of the death of Shih-tsung.

In 951, Later Chou, Northern Han, and Southern T'ang condoled on the death of the Khitan emperor Shih-tsung. In 912, the Khitan condoled on the death of the founder of Later Liang and in 934 on that of Ming-tsung. In 942, they contributed toward the funeral expenses of the grandmother of Shao of Later Chin. They condoled in 956 on the death of Shih-tsu, in 966 on that of Jui-tsung's mother, and in 968 on that of Jui-tsung, all of Northern Han. In 977, they condoled on the death of T'ai-tsung of Sung and contributed toward his funeral expenses in 976.

In 926, the Later T'ang suspended the court for three days after the death of the Khitan emperor T'ai-tsu. The Khitan suspended the court for seven days after the death of Kao-tsu of Later Chin.

The Later Chin offered Kao-tsu's testamentary gifts to the Khitan in 943. The Sung offered T'ai-tsu's testamentary gifts to the Liao in 977.

Neither the Chinese nor the Khitan granted posthumous titles to each other, but they did present honorific titles. Kao-tsu of Later Chin offered such titles to the Khitan Empress Dowager, widow of T'ai-tsu, and to T'ai-tsung twice in 937 and again in 938. On the last occasion T'ai-tsung accepted. Later Chin envoys conferred the titles on Dec.3 and 17, 938. In 939, T'ai-tsung informed the Southern T'ang of these titles, which shows that they were some source of pride to him. The whole account looks therefore like a diplomatic coup for the Later Chin. It was not. The Khitan and Later Chin did in actual fact exchange honorific titles, and T'ai-tsung conferred his on Kao-tsu earlier, on Oct.30, 938. He thereby emphasized the precedence of Liao.

Still other missions were undertaken to announce the founding of a new dynasty, the delivery of tribute, a conquest, a rebellion, the move to a new capital, to express thanks, to inquire about well-being, to ask for physicians, to discuss border markets, and to request peace. But it can be taken for granted that trade was not neglected on any of these occasions.

As was common in China, missions moved in both directions even in times of war.

The third period began in 1005 with the treaty of Shan-yüan. Sung bought itself peace with an annual payment to Liao of 100,000 ounces of silver and 200,000 bolts of silk, in 1042 raised to 200,000 ounces of silver and 300,000 bolts of silk. The Sung could easily afford the expense. But, whatever euphemisms the Chinese resorted to, this placed them in a tributary relationship to Liao. The Sung struggled unsuccessfully for equality, and the Liao maintained its supremacy. Chinese princesses were not offered and would not have been accepted. Honorific titles were not exchanged. Posthumous titles were not granted. When informed of Sheng-tsung's death in 1031, the Sung emperor Jen-tsung not only suspended the court for seven days but together with his empress faced north. According to Chinese ritual, an emperor faced south and a subject north. When in 1076 Shen-tsung of Sung was tardy in ordering mourning for the Liao Empress Dowager, the Liao instructed him curtly to suspend the court for seven days and wear mourning garments. In 1092, Che-tsung of Sung suspended the court for one day after the death of a mere Liao envoy. In contrast, the Liao rulers never mourned Sung emperors, their widows, or envoys.

Due to the treaty of Shan-yüan, Sung and Liao henceforth had few substancial issues to discuss. There were border tensions in 1042, 1044 and 1074-1076, which required an exchange of envoys. Liao acted as a peacemaker between Sung and Hsia. It announced to Sung the beginning, progress, and end of wars. Sung congratulated Liao on the outbreak and end of wars. It sent some missions for the purpose of goodwill and espionage. Liao asked for and presented imperial portraits. Both states occasionally exchanged news on imperial activities. All other missions, and these were the overwhelming majority, were for ceremonial purposes and are recorded until 1101. It must be stressed that even when a mission was concerned with ritual, other matters of mutual interest were not neglected. For instance, when Liao envoys congratulated on an imperial birthday in 1044, the Sung government negotiated with them the razing of Liao border fortifications. It is also clear that at these occasions trade was not neglected. When Jen-tsung considered that the ritual gifts offered by Liao after the death of the Sung Empress Dowager in 1033 had been more ample than usual, he ordered that the envoys should receive 300 ounces of gold over and above the value of the goods received. It follows that even ritual gifts were objects of commerce.

According to the sources, Sung announced the enthronment of all relevant emperors but Ying-tsung, and Liao for all but Sheng-tsung. Sung announced the death of all emperors but Jen-tsung, Liao for all. Sung and Liao condoled each other on the death of all emperors. Sung declared mourning for all Liao emperors but Tao-tsung. After the death of Sheng-tsung, Jen-tsung suspended the Sung court for seven days. After the death of Hsing-tsung, Jen-tsung suspended the Sung court and prohibited music. Sung sent testamentary gifts of all emperors but Jen-tsung, Liao of all. Sung and Liao announced the death of every Empress Dowager/Grand Empress Dowager, and both states condoled on the deaths of all and sent testamentary gifts of all. Sung suspended the court for seven days after the death of every Liao Empress Dowager/Grand Empress Dowager. On the day of burial of one Liao Empress Dowager (May 31, 1010) Chen-tsung not only suspended court but also prohibited border towns to play music for three days. As has been seen, there are four omissions, which concern Ying-tsung and Jen-tsung of Sung and Sheng-tsung and Tao-tsung of Liao. Whether this is due to negligence by the dynastic historians or to special circumstances is difficult to say.

All mutual congratulations on New Year's Days and birthdays ceased after 1101. That gives a time span of 97 years from 1005 to 1101. The following table shows the years for which the ceremonies are not recorded:

New Year congratulations of Sung to Liao	-51
New Year congratulations of Liao to Sung	-11
Sung congratulations on the birthdays of Liao emperors	-56
Liao congratulations on the birthdays of Sung emperors	-18

For the 55 years when Liao Empresses Dowager/Grand Empress Dowager were alive, no birthday congratulations by Sung are recorded for 35 years.

For the 38 years when Sung Empresses Dowager/Grand Empresses Dowager were alive, no birthday congratulations by Liao are recorded for 22 years.[207]

Clearly, as far as the sources reveal, Liao was more eager than Sung to send congratulatory missions. It is possible that the committee under T'o T'o, which compiled both the *Sung shih* and *Liao shih*, ignored relevant data, but it is also possible that the chronological gaps are real. The Liao court coveted luxury goods and their envoys profited economically. Greed can therefore not be excluded as a motive for the frequency of the Liao missions.

It was under these circumstances in the interest of the Sung government to limit the stay of the Liao missions. It is not known when these set out. When the sources state that an emperor sent a mission, this refers to the time when the envoys received their orders, not to their departure.[208] Fortunately, the sources frequently give the day of the arrival of a mission. If it was for New Year's Days, their dates are known, and if it was for imperial birthdays, the dates can usually be calculated. This makes it possible to determine how many days before an event a mission arrived.

For the New Year's Day reception of Sung emperors, the arrival

[207] In spite of the decisions of 1022 and 1026, congratulations to empresses on their birthdays and Empresses Dowagers on the New Year's Day were sporadic.

[208] In 16 cases, the sources record when the Sung envoys received their orders, and in 10 cases give the correponding information for Liao. This corpus is too small for meaningful statistics. The information for Southern Sung and Chin is much richer and will be discussed below.

dates of 81 Liao missions are known. 60 of these arrived 5 days earlier. The average interval was 5.2 days.[209]

For the birthday congratulations of Sung emperors, the arrival dates of 70 Liao missions are known. 39 of these arrived 3 days earlier. The average interval was 5.0 days.

For the birthday congratulations of Chen-tsung's widow (d.Mar.23, 1022), the arrival dates of 9 Liao missions are known. 7 of these arrived 3 days earlier. The average interval was 3.0 days.

For the birthday congratulations of Ying-tsung's widow (d.Jan.25, 1067), the arrival dates of 8 missions are known. All of these arrived 7 days earlier.

In only two cases are the dates known when Liao missions returned home. The Liao mission which arrived at the Sung court on Feb.7, 1100 for the New Year reception of Feb.12 was given a banquet on Feb.16. A banquet normally concluded the visit of envoys. Excluding the day of arrival, the mission would consequently have stayed for 9 days. The Liao mission which arrived at the Sung court on May 9, 1079, for the birthday celebration of Emperor Shen-tsung on May 13 departed on May 17. It had therefore stayed for 8 days.

The Sung obviously attempted to standardize the arrival and limit the stay of Liao missions. The Liao took a completely different attitude. For the New Year's Day receptions of Liao emperors, the arrival dates of 6 Sung missions are known.The average interval between arrival and event was 18.5 days. For the birthday congratulations of Liao emperors, the arrival dates of 13 Sung missions are known. The average interval between arrival and event was 81.4 days.

The New Year and birthday congratulations required only one day. The Sung envoys to the Liao court presented 4000 bolts of silk and 2000 ounces of silver objects at the former occasion, and 5000 bolts of silk and 5000 ounces of silver objects at the latter.[210] The Liao envoys to the Sung court no doubt made similar gifts, in each case with reciprocity. The remainder of the time had to be used by the envoys for other purposes. There can be no doubt that, apart from amusement,

---

[209] When Liao congratulated on a New Year's Day to both a Sung empress dowager and an emperor, it sometimes sent separate missions. When that was the case, the missions to the empress dowager had precedence and usually arrived in K'ai-feng one day earlier.

[210] See Wittfogel, *Liao*, p.358 note 60. These gifts must have become a rule from 1005 at the earliest.

this was trade. Even though the Sung attempted to prevent its envoys from engaging in private commerce, such a prohibition was difficult to enforce, and trade could always be disguised as an exchange of gifts. The Chinese needed little of what Liao had to offer and limited the stay of of the Khitan envoys. The Liao welcomed the Chinese envoys for much longer periods, perhaps because they had goods to offer which the Khitan desired.

It happened that envoys found at their arrivals that celebrations were cancelled. On Feb.14, 1040, the Sung New Year's reception was omitted because of an eclipse of the sun.[211] The Liao envoys were merely provided with food and drink in their lodge. Shen-tsungs's birthday celebration in Sung on May 15, 1076, was cancelled because of mourning for the Liao Empress Dowager. The Liao envoys were not received. On Jan.23, 1092, and Jan.16, 1097, Che-tsung held no receptions on the New Year's Days. The Liao envoys congratulated at the Audience Gate. On Jan.24, 1099, Che-tsung did not hold the New Year's reception because of a snowfall. The Liao envoys again congratulated at the Audience gate.

Envoys profited from their missions and probably eagerly sought such assignments. The Liao envoys are known to have received garments, caps, belts, shoes, silver, silver objects, and silk.[212] All envoys engaged in private trade. Entertainment was another benefit. Banquets were a matter of course. In 975, T'ai-tsu, founder of Sung, invited the Liao envoys to a hunt. In 976, he watched an archery contest on horseback between Liao envoys and Chinese. In 997, T'ai-tsung of Sung watched another archery contest on horseback between Liao envoys and Chinese guards. In 979, T'ai-tsung summoned Liao envoys to watch archery practice. In 1005, a sick Liao envoy was treated by a Chinese physician, sent by the Sung emperor himself. In 1006, Khitan food was prepared for the Liao envoys. In 1005, the Liao emperor summoned the Chinese envoys to a poetry reading.

On the other hand, envoys also faced danger and even death. In 926, a Later T'ang envoy to the Khitan court was imprisoned and almost executed. In 928, a Khitan envoy was executed by Ming-tsung of Later T'ang. In 937, the Later Chin released two Khitan envoys

---

[211] As remarked before, it was a persistant Chinese superstition, although discredited by their astronomers long since, that a solar eclipse was a baneful event.

[212] See Wittfogel, *Liao*, pp.358-359 note 60.

who had previously been detained by the Later T'ang. Khitan envoys passing through the territory of An Ch'ung-jung some time before 942 were executed by him. In 942, the Khitan released a Later Chin envoy who had been detained as a protest against the actions of An Ch'ung-jung. In 951, a Later Chou envoy was detained by Liao because Liao had allied itself with Northern Han. In 1006, a Liao envoy fell ill at the Sung court. In 1034, 1066, and 1092, Sung envoys died at the Liao court. In 1070, four members of a Liao mission en route to the Sung court were killed and twelve wounded when one of the Khitan ran amok with a knife.

The *Wen-hsien t'ung-k'ao,* as is its habit, gives at times totals of missions rather than individual listings. It claims (345:16a) that after 628, the Khitan chief Mo-hui constantly offered gifts to the T'ang court. Five Khitan missions are recorded until 633, which may be constant enough. It claims that from 713 to756 the Khitan offered gifts about 20 times. Twenty-three missions are recorded. It claims that from 756 to 763, the Khitan offered gifts twice. One mission is recorded. It claims that from 766 to 779, the Khitan came to the court thirteen times. Thirteen missions are recorded. It claims that from 785 to 805, the Khitan came to the court three times. Six missions are recorded. It caims that from 806 to 820, the Khitan came to the court seven times. Ten missions are recorded. It claims that from 827 to 840, the Khitan came to the court four times. Eight missions are recorded. It claims that from 860 to 874, the Khitan came to the court twice. One mission is recorded. It follows that the statistics are close to complete.

This is the distribution by 20-year periods of the 446 recorded Khitan/Liao missions to Sui, T'ang, Later Liang, Later T'ang, Later Chin, Later Chou, Wu-yüeh, and Southern T'ang:

587- 606	4
607- 626	7
627- 646	6
647- 666	0
667- 686	0
687- 706	0
707- 726	17
727- 746	4
747- 766	2
767- 786	12
787- 806	7

807- 826	9
827- 846	9
847- 866	0
867- 886	1
887- 906	0
907- 926	12
927- 946	77
947- 966	2
967- 986	15
987-1006	7
1007-1026	50
1027-1046	67
1047-1066	50
1067-1086	44
1087-1106	44

After the middle of the 7th century, relations between the Khitan and the T'ang cooled, culminating in the war of 696-697. They thereafter improved until after the middle of the 9th century, when they again lapsed. With the Five Dynasties, relations once more warmed, reaching the highest intensity with the Later T'ang (923-936) and especially the Later Chin (936-946). Even though the Later Chou and Sung were at war with the Khitan from 951 to 1005, missions kept coming. Relations became regular after 1005 and settled into diplomatic routine.

The specified goods brough by the Khitan/Liao missions fall into the following categories:

Humans

908: one male and one young girl.

Animals and Animal Products

Horses

619: fine horses.
623: fine horses.
719: 10 horses.
724: horses.

730: 12 horses.
907: fine horses.
908: fine horses.
909: 100 horses.
926: 32 horses.
927: fine horses.
932: 203 horses.
934: 400 horses, 10 racehorses.
937: 200 horses, racehorses.
938: horses.
939: fine horses, 14 horses with white forelegs.
940: horses.
942: horses.
951: team of 4 fine horses, 40 horses.
975: fine horses.
976: fine horses, 30 horses, 3 trained horses.
977: 100 horses.
978: fine horses, 100 horses, 4 trained horses.
979: fine horses.
1005: 400 horses.
1010: fine horses.
1045: horses.

Cattle

939: cattle.

Dogs

939: dogs.

Birds

976: white falcons.
1005: falcons.

Sheep

934: 2000 sheep.
942: 1000 sheep.
1045: sheep.

Furs

619: sable furs.
623: sable furs.
937: sable furs.
940: fox furs.
951: sable furs.

Meat

1005: deer tongues.
1089: dried venison
1092: dried venison.

Aromatics

Aromatic and medical drugs

908: aromatics.
932: drugs.

Herbs

937: ginseng.

Minerals

909: jade.
1022: inferior jade.

Manufactured Objects

Of metal

908: horse trappings with golden flowers.
909: gilded iron and silver armour.
926: golden bracelet ornamented with real pearls, golden hair pins.
976: horse trappings of real gold, 2 golden belts.
977: golden belts, weapons adorned with gold and silver.
978: golden belts, golden horse trappings.
1005: golden horse trappings.

Of crystal

909: horse trappings ornamented with rock crystal.

Of precious stone

940: jade horse trappings.
951: jade horsetrappings, washed with gold and lined with silver.
975: jade belts.
976: jade belts.
977: jade horse trappings.
1005: jade horse trappings.
1010: jade bracelets, vessels of carnelian, jugs of jade.
1099: jade belt.

Of amber

1010: amber necklaces.

Of fur

908: caps and garments of sable fur.

Of leather

1005: horse trappings.

Of wood

937: wooden bowls.

Other

940: bows and arrows, blue felt tents.
951: bows and arrows.
978: bows and arrows.
1005: bows and arrows.
1010: jugs of rhinoceros horn.
1045: Nine Dragon Chariot.
1055: portraits of Liao emperors on silk.
1056: portrait of Tao-tsung.

Textiles

Silks

908: brocade.
942: pongee.
1005: brocade.

Garments

908: caps embroidered with golden flowers.
975: garments.
976: garments.
977: garments.
978: garments.
1005: 12 garments.

Other

940: embroidered bow cases.

Jewels

1022: pearls.

The information for Sung is much poorer than for T'ang and the Five Dynasties. Horses, furs, and manufactured objects were the chief exports. Amber and pearls were not regional objects but passed along by the Khitan.

The Chinese paid for these goods with gold, silk, brocade, gold, silver and porcelain vessels, wine vessels, drinking and eating vessels of tortoise shell adorned with gold, teapots and cups of porcelain, elephant tusks, rhinoceros horns, corals, carnelian cups, necklaces, jade and ivory flutes, musical instruments of tortoise shell adorned with gold, inkstones, plain cloth, garments, black gauze caps, golden belts, belts of rhinoceros hide, belts adorned with rhinoceros horn, embroidered coverlets, naphta, tea, cherries, aromatics, drugs, a tame elephant, fine horses, horse trappings, silver horse trappings, horse trappings of carnelian adorned with gold, jade horse whips, a white single-horned deer, a white tortoise, armour, rhinoceros hide armour, bows decorated with rhinoceros horn, arrows, and a portrait of Jen-tsung. These were chiefly luxury goods. Some of them were of foreign origin, such as the elephant tusks, rhinoceros horns and hides, corals, and naphta. Tea did not grow in the Northern Han, and the shipment this state presented in 954 had therefore to have been imported. The tame elephant of 1055 had originally come from Chiao-chih/Annam or Champa. The Sung had a surfeit of these animals and was probably glad to pass on one of them to the Liao court.

CHIN

The Jurchen were a Tungusic-speaking people, ancestors of the Manchus, who originally lived as hunters and fishermen in the forests of eastern Manchuria. They spread from there to the lowlands around the Sungari River and took up agriculture and animal husbandry. The sedentary Jurchen became subjects of Po-hai, and after the destruction of that kingdom in 926 of the Khitan/Liao. The forest-dwelling Jurchen on the periphery of these states remained semi-independent. They managed to send missions to the Five Dynasties and Sung, mostly by sea.

The Chin dynasty of the Jurchen was founded by A-ku-ta of the Wan-yen clan in 1115. The *Liao shih* 27:6b records that in 1112 the last emperor of Liao, T'ien-tso, attended the spring hunting and fishing at the Sungari River. At a banquet for Jurchen chiefs, he requested them to dance. A-ku-ta refused and soon thereafter rebelled. Later historians have blamed T'ien-tso for his tactlessness. But it has been seen that ceremonial or native dancing was part of festive occasions. In the early 590's, Mo-ho envoys danced at a banquet given by Emperor Wen of Sui. When T'ai-tsung of T'ang gave a banquet in Ch'ang-an in 634, the captured Hsieh-li Qaghan of the Eastern Turks danced at his request. In 762, the Teng-li Qaghan of the Uighurs invited the Chinese heir-apparent and future Empeor Te-tsung to perform a ceremonial dance, which the prince refused to do. At a banquet of Uighur chiefs and Kuo Tzu-yi in 765, the chiefs danced. In 940, two envoys from the Uighurs and from Tun-huang (Sha chou) were asked by Emperor T'ai-tsung of the Khitan to perform their native dances. T'ien-tso therefore probably only requested what was normal, bonhomie under the influence of alcohol, and perhaps even a courtesy, and the episode could not have been a casus belli. It must also be remembered that the unification of the Jurchen was an effort begun by A-ku-ta's grandfather, continued by his elder brother, and only completed by him. The dance had nothing to do with his uprising.

On June 11, 925, Jurchen envoys to the Later T'ang court offered gifts (*Chiu Wu-tai shih* 32:14b).

On Jan.21, 926, Jurchen envoys to the Khitan court offered gifts (*Liao shih* 3:2a).

In the 12th month (Dec./Jan., 928) of the year 927, Jurchen envoys to the Khitan court offered gifts (*Liao shih* 70:3a).

In the 1st month (Jan./Feb.) of 928, a Jurchen envoy to the Khitan court offered gifts (*Liao shih* 3:2a).

In the 5th month (June/July) of 929, Jurchen offered gifts to the Khitan court (*Liao shih* 3:3b).

On Jan.15, 930, Jurchen offered gifts to the Khitan court (*Liao shih* 3:4a).

On June 4, 932, Jurchen offered gifts to the Khitan court (*Liao shih* 3:6a).

On Aug.6, 933, Jurchen offered gifts to the Khitan court (*Liao shih* 3:7a).

On Mar.9 and Apr.19, 934, Jurchen offered gifts to the Khitan court (*Liao shih* 3:7a).

On Mar.26 and May 8, 936, Jurchen offered gifts to the Khitan court (*Liao shih* 3:8b).

On Oct.20, 937, Jurchen offered gifts to the Khitan court (*Liao shih* 3:12a).

In the 3rd month (Apr./May) and on May 9, 938, Jurchen envoys to the Khitan court offered gifts. On May 22, they presented bows and arrows, and on Sep.15 they again offered gifts (*Liao shih* 4:1b; 70:4b).

On Mar.29, 939, Jurchen offered gifts to the Khitan court (*Liao shih* 4:3a).

On Mar.17, 940, Jurchen offered gifts to the Khitan court. On Mar.30, Jurchen of the Yalu River had an audience at the Khitan court. On Oct.29, Jurchen offered gifts to it (*Liao shih* 4:4a, 4b, 5b-6a).

On Dec.11, 941, Jurchen of the Yalu River offered gifts to the Khitan court (*Liao shih* 4:7a).

On Feb.19, in the 5th month (June/July), and on Aug.24, 946, Jurchen offered gifts to the Khitan court (*Liao shih* 4:12b; 70:5b).

In the 1st month (Jan./Feb.), and on Mar.15, 952, Jurchen offered gifts to the Liao court of the Khitan (*Liao shih* 6:1b; 70:6a).

On Nov.24, 955, Jurchen offered gifts to the Liao court (*Liao shih* 6:3b).

On Feb.25, 959, Jurchen envoys to the Later Chou court offered gifts (*Chiu Wu-tai shih* 119:1a; *Ts'e-fu yüan-kuei* p.5036).

On Jan.24, 961, Jurchen envoys to the Sung court offered gifts. On Oct.2, another mission offered fine horses. In the 12th month (Jan./Feb., 962) of the same Chinese year, envoys arrived by sea to offer regional objects (*Sung shih* 1:10b; *Sung hui-yao kao*, ts'e 196; *Hsü Tzu-chih t'ung-chien ch'ang-pien* p.20).

On Feb.28 and Apr.26, 962, Jurchen envoys to the Sung court offered regional objects (*Sung shih* 1:11a, 11b).

In the 8th month (Sep./Oct.) of 962, Jurchen presented a small boy with hair on his nose to the Liao court (*Liao shih* 70:6a).

On Feb.22, 963, Jurchen envoys to the Sung court offered gifts. On Sep.4, they offered fine horses, and on Oct.9 56 fine horses and falcons (*Sung shih* 1:13b, 15b, 16a; *Sung hui-yao kao*, ts'e 196; *Hsü Tzu-chih t'ung-chien ch'ang-pien* p.40).

In 964, Jurchen envoys to the Sung court offered horses and sable furs (*Sung hui-yao kao*, ts'e 196).

In the 9th month (Sep./Oct.) of 965, Jurchen envoys to the Sung court offered gifts (*Sung hui-yao kao*, ts'e 196).

In 967, Jurchen offered horses to the Sung court (*Sung hui-yao kao*, ts'e 196).

In 968, Jurchen offered horses to the Sung court (*Sung hui-yao kao*, ts'e 196).

On Oct.20, 970, Jurchen envoys to the Sung court offered regional objects (*Sung shih* 2:10b).

On July 26, 973, a Jurchen chief was received at the Liao court (*Liao shih* 8:3b).

In the 12th month (Dec./Jan., 974) of the Chinese year 973, Jurchen envoys to the Sung court offered gifts (*Hsü Tzu-chih t'ung-chien ch'ang-pien* p.120).

On Jan.26, 977, Jurchen envoys to the Liao court offered gifts. On June 18, 21 Jurchen requested that the Liao emperor confer honourary offices on them. These were granted, to each in accordance with his rank. On Nov.28, Jurchen envoys offered gifts (*Liao shih* 9:1a, 1b).

On May 24, 978, Jurchen envoys to the Liao court offered gifts (*Liao shih* 9:1b).

On Apr.11, 979, Jurchen envoys to the Liao court offered gifts (*Liao shih* 9:2b).

In the 11th month (December) of 981, Jurchen envoys to the Sung court offered gifts (*Sung shih* 4:15a).

In the 9th month (Oct./Nov.) of 985, a Jurchen chief offered gifts to the Liao court (*Liao shih* 70:8a).

In 987, a Jurchen envoy arrived by sea en route to the Sung court (*Sung hui-yao kao*, ts'e 196).

In the 8th month (Sep./Oct.) of 988, a Jurchen chief offered gifts to the Liao court (*Liao shih* 70:8a).

In 989, a Jurchen mission was received at the Sung court (*Sung shih* 491:3a)

On Mar.25, May 2, June 11, and July 7, 990, and in the 12th month (Dec./Jan., 991) of the same Liao year, Jurchen envoys to the Liao court offered gifts (*Liao shih* 13:1a, 1b, 2a).

In 991, a Jurchen chief and others complained to the Sung court that the Khitan tried to prevent their travelling to it with gifts (*Sung shih* 491:3a; *Wen-hsien t'ung-k'ao* 327:61b).

On Jan.21, 991, Jurchen envoys to the Liao court offered gifts. On Sep.22, the Jurchen presented deer-callers (*Liao shih* 13:2a, 3a).

On Aug.15, 994, Jurchen envoys to the Liao court offered gifts (*Liao shih* 13:5a).

On Jan.19, 995, Jurchen envoys informed the Liao court that the Sung had been offering them bribes to rebel against it. On Mar.4 and July 30, they offered gifts (*Liao shih* 13:5b, 6b).

On Mar.4, 997, Jurchen offered gifts to the Liao court (*Liao shih* 13:8a).

On Apr.4, 998, Jurchen envoys to the Liao court offered gifts (*Liao shih* 14:1a).

On Mar.11 and Mar. 27, 1002, Jurchen offered gifts to the Liao court (*Liao shih* 14:3b).

On May 9, 1003, Jurchen envoys to the Liao court offered gifts (*Liao shih* 14:4a).

On Feb.23, 1004, Jurchen envoys to the Liao court offered gifts. In the 9th month (Sep./Oct.), they presented ravens (*Liao shih* 14:4b).

On May 19 and Aug.28, 1005, Jurchen envoys to the Liao court offered gifts (*Liao shih* 14:6b).

On Nov.9, 1010, Jurchen proposed to the Liao court that they would join the attack on Koryŏ with 10,000 fine horses. This was accepted (*Liao shih* 15:2a).

On Feb.9, 1012, Jurchen chiefs offered gifts to the Liao court and requested ranks. Other chiefs were received on Feb.13 (*Liao shih* 15:3b).

On Nov.13, 1013, Emperor Sheng-tsung of Liao questioned Jurchen envoys as to the best way of attacking and defeating Koryŏ and accepted their advice (*Liao shih* 15:7a).

In 1014, Jurchen offered gifts to the Sung court (*Sung shih* 8:10b).

On Feb.12, 1014, Jurchen offered gifts to the Liao court (*Liao shih* 15:7b).

In the 3rd month (Mar./Apr.) and on May 10, 1015, Jurchen offered gifts to the Liao court (*Liao shih* 15:8b; 70:14b).

In 1017, a Jurchen chief was received at the Sung court (*Sung hui-yao kao*, ts'e 196).

On Dec.25, 1019, Eastern and Western Jurchen chiefs had an audience at the Sung court and offered gifts. The cloth they offered was rejected. They requested the Buddhist *Tripitaka*. This was provided, together with garments and silken fabrics (*Hsü Tzu-chih t'ung-chien ch'ang-pien* p.836).

On May 17, 1021, Sheng-tsung of Liao was informed that 30 Jurchen chiefs and their sons wished to call on him. He accepted. On Aug.11, he invited them to a hunt and presented them with autumn garments (*Liao shih* 16:5b-6a).

On Mar.4, 1032, Jurchen offered gifts to the Liao court (*Liao shih* 18:4a).

In the 1st month (Feb./Mar.) of 1033, Jurchen chiefs offered gifts to the Liao court (*Liao shih* 70:16b).

On Dec.20, 1047, Jurchen envoys to the Liao court offered gifts (*Liao shih* 20:1b).

In the 2nd month (Mar./Apr.) of 1071, Jurchen offered horses to the Liao court (*Liao shih* 70:20b).

On July 8, 1080, Jurchen envoys to the Liao court offered gifts (*Liao shih* 24:2a-2b).

On Mar.9, 1081, Jurchen offered fine horses to the Liao court (*Liao shih* 24:3a).

On May 15, 1084, Jurchen offered fine horses to the Liao court (*Liao shih* 24:5b).

On May 18, 1086, Jurchen offered fine horses to the Liao court (*Liao shih* 24:7a).

On May 3, 1087, Jurchen offered fine horses to the Liao court (*Liao shih* 25:1a).

On Apr.8, 1090, Jurchen envoys to the Liao court offered gifts (*Liao shih* 25:3b).

On May 16, 1095,[1] Jurchen envoys to the Liao court offered gifts. On Dec.23, they offered horses (*Liao shih* 26:1a, 2a).

---

[1] Correcting *chi-hai* to *yi-hai*.

On Jan.4, 1100, Jurchen envoys to the Liao court offered gifts (*Liao shih* 26:5b).

On Feb.9, 1103, envoys from Jurchen chiefs to the Liao court offered gifts (*Liao shih* 27:3a).

In the 3rd (Apr./May) and 11th month (August) of 1114, Jurchen envoys were received at the Liao court (*Liao shih* 70:27a).

On Jan.28, 1115, A-ku-ta proclaimed himself emperor and founded the Chin dynasty. He had been born on Aug.1, 1068. This was Emperor T'ai-tsu (*Chin shih* 2:1a, 8a). The Liao State was reeling but not yet defeated and tried to survive by a combination of military actions and a flurry of diplomatic initiatives.[2]

Meanwhile, the Sung court saw an opportunity for allying itself with the Jurchen and regaining the lost Sixteen Commanderies. In the 12th month (Dec./Jan., 1118) of the Sung year 1117, Emperor Hui-tsung sent a Defense Commissioner to the Chin court. He brought a letter which said: "The land where the sun rises has truly given birth to a sage. We have ventured to learn that you are attacking Liao and that you frequently have crushed your powerful enemy. After you have subjugated Liao, we wish the towns below (i.e. south) of the border, forming the Chinese territory which in the time of the Five Dynasties fell to the Khitan". On Mar.11, 1118, a Grandee of Martial Loyalty was sent by sea to the Chin court to offer an alliance against Liao (*Sung shih* 21:9a; *Chin shih* 2:12a).

On Feb.21, 1119, a goodwill mission from Chin reached the Sung port of Teng in northern Shan-tung but then returned (*Sung shih* 22: 1a).

In the 6th month (July/Aug.) of 1119, a Sung goodwill mission was received at the Chin court. T'ai-tsu responded with envoys of his own. In the 2nd month (March) of 1120, these returned and reported (*Chin shih* 2:14a).

On Mar.5, 1120, Hui-tsung sent envoys to the Chin court to discuss the territorial concessions which he expected. On May 14, T'ai-tsu took personal command of the troops attacking Liao and invited the

[2] Approaches by Liao to Chin are recorded for the 4th month (Apr./May) and June 24 of 1115, for Feb.22, May 21, and the 7th (July/Aug.), 8th (Aug./Sep.), 9th month (Sep./Oct.), and 12th month (Jan.Feb., 1119) of the Liao year 1118, for the 3rd month (Apr./May), July 25 and the 11th month (Dec./Jan., 1120) of the Liao year 1119, for the 4th month (May) of 1120, and for the 5th month (June/July) of 1122 (*Chin shih* 2:9a; 2:12a, 12b, 13a, 13b; 2:14a, 14b, 17b).

Chinese envoys to accompany him. These congratulated him on his victories (*Sung shih* 22:3a; *Chin shih* 2:14a-14b).

On Sep.28, 1120, a Chin mission was received at the Sung court. Hui-tsung responded with an envoy of his own who received his orders on Oct.12 (*Sung shih* 22:4a).

In the 12th month (Dec./Jan., 1121) of the Chinese year 1120, Sung envoys to the Chin court again requested territorial concessions (*Chin shih* 2:15b).

On May 30, 1121, Chin envoys were received at the Sung court (*Sung shih* 22:5a).

In the 3rd month (Apr./May) of 1122, Chin envoys to the Sung court proposed a joint attack on Liao. On Oct.5, other Chin envoys discussed the timing of this offensive (*Sung shih* 22:6b, 7a).

On Oct.20, 1122, Hui-tsung sent a goodwill mission to the Chin court (*Sung shih* 22:7a).

On Dec.23, 1122, Chin envoys were received at the Sung court (*Sung shih* 22:7b).

On Jan.2, 1123, Hui-tsung sent a goodwill mission to the Chin court (*Sung shih* 22:7b).

On Jan.5. 1123, Chin forces conquered Yen (Peking) (map 11). The Liao officials surrendered and were spared (*Chin shih* 2:19b).

On Jan.6, 1123, Chin envoys to the Sung court announced the victory (*Sung shih* 22:7b).

On Feb.1, 1123, Chin envoys to the Sung court discussed mutual obligations. On Feb.2, Sung sent a goodwill mission to the Chin court and again asked for territorial concessions in exchange for annual payments of silk. The envoys proposed that the border be delineated and that a protocol be drawn up for the exchange of congratulatory missions on the New Year's Days and imperial birthdays (*Sung shih* 22:8a; *Chin shih* 2:20b).

On Mar.30, 1123, Chin envoys were received at the Sung court (*Sung shih* 22:8b). On Apr.3, Hui-tsung sent a goodwill mission to the Chin court (*Sung shih* 22:8b).

In the 4th month (Apr./May) of 1123, a Sung army belatedly reached Yen (*Chin shih* 2:21a).

The intense negotiations between Sung and Chin led to a treaty, which was confirmed by oath letters from both sides. The Chin oath letter was received at the Sung court on May 7, 1123. Even though this treaty in its terminology was between equal partners, Sung was in a much weaker position as its armies had contributed next to nothing to the war. It had to agree to paying Chin the same annual tribute it previously had rendered Liao, i.e. 200,000 ounces of silver and 300,000 bolts of silk, and it did not receive the long-desired Sixteen Commanderies but only Yen and adjoing territories in return for a large indemnity (*Sung shih* 22:8b).

On Sep.19, 1123, Emperor T'ai-tsu of Chin died, aged 56. He was succeeded by a younger brother, born in 1075, who ascended the throne on Sep.37. This was Emperor T'ai-tsung. In the 12th month (Dec./Jan., 1124) of the Chin year 1123, T'ai tsung sent two envoys to the Sung court to announce T'ai-tsu's death (*Chin shih* 2:22b; 3: 1a-1b, 2a).

On Jan.14, 1124, Chin envoys arrived at the Sung court to congratulate on the New Year's Day of Jan.24, but because of the death of T'ai-tsu the Sung court was suspended (*Sung shih* 22:9b).

In the 3rd month (Mar./Apr.) of 1124, Chin requested grain from Sung. It was not provided (*Sung shih* 22:10a). By this time, relations between Sung and Chin had soured. There was no agreement as to how the treaty of 1123 should be implemented, and Chin had realized the feebleness of Sung.

In the 4th month (Apr./May) of 1124, Sung envoys condoled and sacrificed at the Chin court on the death of T'ai-tsu. They had received their orders on Feb.16, 1124 (*Sung shih* 22:9b; *Chin shih* 3:4a).

On Sep.10, 1124, T'ai-tsung sent envoys to the Sung court to congratulate on the birthday of Hui-tsung[3] (*Chin shih* 3:5a).

On Nov.4, 1124, Chin envoys to the Sung court presented T'ai-tsu's testamentary gifts (*Sung shih* 22:10b).

On Nov.22, 1124, Sung envoys to the Chin court congratulated on the birthday of T'ai-tsung (*Chin shih* 3:5a).

On Feb.5, 1125, the New Year's Day, two Chin envoys congratulated at the Sung court. They had received their orders on Jan.11 (*Chin shih* 3:5b).

In the 1st month (Feb./Mar.) of 1125, Sung envoys to the Chin court congratulated on the enthronement of T'ai-tsung. They had received their orders on Aug.24, 1124, and presented three horse trappings adorned with gold and silver, three horse whips of ivory and tortoise shell, eight gold and silver cups, three incense braziers shaped like lions, three garments, ten baskets of fruit, ten jugs of honey, and

[3] It fell on Nov.17.

three pounds of tea. On his return to the Sung court, the chief envoy reported on what he had noticed of Chin fortifications (*Sung shih* 22: 10a; *Chin shih* 3:5b).[4]

On July 22, 1125, T'ai-tsung sent envoys to Sung to announce that the last Liao emperor, T'ien-tso, had been captured. These envoys were received at the Sung court on Oct.22 (*Chin shih* 3:6a; *Sung shih* 22:12a).

In the 7th month (August) of 1125, T'ai-tsung sent envoys to the Sung court (*Chin shih* 3:6a).

On Nov.11, 1125, Sung envoys to the Chin court congratulated on the birthday of T'ai-tsung (*Chin shih* 3:6b).

On Dec.4, 1125, Hui-tsung sent envoys to the Chin court to congratulate (*Sung shih* 22:12b), presumably on the capture of T'ien-tso.

But war had broken out, the Chin forces had invaded northern China, and the Sung court in K'ai-feng was in a state of shock. Hui-tsung abdicated on Jan.18, 1126, and was succeeded by his eldest son. This was Emperor Ch'in-tsung, born in 1100 (*Sung shih* 22:13a; 23:2a).

On Jan.30, 1126, the Chin army crossed the Yellow River and on Jan.31 unsuccessfully attacked one of the city gates of K'ai-feng by night (*Sung shih* 23:3b)

On Feb.1, 1126 peace negotiations were begun, in which the Jurchen sent first one envoy and then another. After a second unsuccessful attack on K'ai-feng on Feb.2, negotiations were resumed, and in the end Sung promised to pay a huge indemnity in gold, silver, and silk, cede three territories in Ho-pei and Shan-hsi, and render an imperial prince as a hostage. The annual tribute was settled at 300,000 ounces of silver, 300,000 bolts of silk, and 1,000,000 strings of cash. The Chin army then withdrew on Feb.10 (*Sung shih* 23:3b). The Sung had been deeply humiliated, its weakness was all too apparent, and in a communication brought by a Sung envoy to the Jurchen camp, the Chin State was even referred to in characters larger than all others. On Feb.24, breaking the recent agreement, a Sung Chief Commandant made a feeble suprise attack on the Chin army, was defeated, and had to flee (*Sung shih* 23:3b, 4b). Peace held a little longer, and a new

[4] The gifts are enumerated in the private acount of the envoy Hsü K'ang-tsung. See H.Franke in Rossabi, ed., *China among Equals*, pp.130, 138.

outbreak of the war was briefly postponed by an intensive diplomatic exchange.

On Feb.27, 1126, Ch'in-tsung sent a Chief Commandant of Attendant Cavalry as envoy to the withdrawing Chin army. The Chin reponded with an envoy of its own. On Mar.2, another Sung envoy was dispatched to the Chin army. On Mar.3, still another two Sung envoys were sent with a letter to the Chin army. On May 10, two Chin envoys were received at the Sung court (*Sung shih* 23:4b, 5a, 8a; *Chin shih* 3:7b-8a).

But by this time fighting had broken out again, and the Chin forces had resumed their attack on K'ai-feng. On Oct.16, 1126, Ch'in-tsung sent a Serving within the Palace by sea to Chin in order to discuss peace, and on Oct.23 two Chin envoys were received at the Sung court. But it was too late (*Sung shih* 23:12b, 13a).

On Nov.21, 1126,[5] the Chin forces crossed the Yellow River. From Dec.3, 1126, to Jan.3, 1127, they attacked the gates of K'ai-feng. On Jan.9, K'ai-feng surrendered (*Sung shih* 23:15a, 15b, 16a, 16b).

On the New Year's Day of Feb.13, 1127, Ch'in-tsung of Sung sent two of his half-brothers to congratulate the Chin army, and Chin envoys entered K'ai-feng and congratulated (*Sung shih* 23:17b; 246:7b, 8a).

On Mar.20, 1127, the Chin demoted the abdicated Emperor Hui-tsung and current Emperor Ch'in-tsung to commoners. With the first departures on May 10, they and their immediate families and entourages were by stages transferred to the north, arriving in the Supreme Capital in Manchuria in the 7th month (July/Aug.) of 1128. Dressed in plain garments, they were there on Sep.21 presented in the temple of T'ai-tsu. Thereafter, they were received in audience by T'ai-tsung, who conferred on Hui-tsung the title of Duke of Stupified Virtue and on Ch'in-tsung that of Marquis of Aggravated Stupidity. They were then, again by stages, transferred to their final place of exile, Wu-kuo town at the Sungari River east of present Charbin (*Sung shih* 22:13a, 18b; 23:18b; 24:7b-8a,10b; *Chin shih* 3:9b, 10b, 11b, 12a).

Meanwhile, Chinese resistance to the Jurchen had stiffened and on June 12, 1127, Hui-tsung's ninth son, a half-brother of Ch'in-tsung had been enthroned as emperor. This was Kao-tsung, born in 1107 (*Sung shih* 24:1a; 5b; *Chin shih* 3:9b). His dynasty was henceforth known as the Southern Sung. The war continued and was to last until 1142,

---

[5] Correcting *ping-tzu* to *ping-wu*.

but this did not stop the diplomatic intercourse.

In the 3rd month (April) of 1128, Kao-tsung sent an envoy to the Chin court (*Sung shih* 25:3b).

In the 1st month (Jan./Feb.) of 1129, Chin envoys reached the headquarters of the Sung army. On Sep.6, Oct.25, and Dec.26, Sung envoys were sent to the Chin army (*Sung shih* 25:18a, 19a, 20b).

The Jurchen did not at first intend to govern the conquered north Chinese territories. Their first attempt to set up a Chinese puppet as emperor of Ch'u failed. They next installed a certain Liu Yü as emperor of Ch'i, probably in early 1130. This state was abolished on Jan.1, 1138, whereafter the north-Chinese conquests were incorporated into the Chin empire.[6]

On July 9, 1130, T'ai-tsung ordered that Hui-tsung's six daughters be married to members of the imperial Chin clan. On July 23, he bestowed two sets of seasonal garments on Hui-tsung and Ch'in-tsung (*Chin shih* 3:13b; 15b).

On Oct.15, 1132, the Southern Sung envoy Wang Lun, who had gained fame in the defense of K'ai-feng and had been on a mission to the Jurchen, returned to his court and reported in an audience. Kao-tsung sent new envoys to the Chin army (*Sung shih* 27:7a).

On June 17, 1133, Kao-tsung sent envoys to the Chin army (*Sung shih* 27:12b).

On June 25, 1133, Southern Sung offered peace to Chin (*Sung shih* 27:13a).

On Jan. 25, 1134, a Chin envoy was received at the Southern Sung court (*Sung shih* 27:16a).

---

[6] Ch'i envoys congratulated at the Chin court on the New Year's Days of Jan.31, 1131, Feb.7, 1133, Jan.27, 1134, Feb.4, 1136, and Jan.23, 1137. They congratulated on the birthdays of T'ai-tsung on Nov.17, 1130, Nov.6, 1131, Nov.24, 1132, Nov.13, 1133, and Nov.2, 1134. After T'ai-tsung had died on Feb.9, 1135, his son and sucessor Hsi-tsung sent envoys to inform the Ch'i State. He also instructed Liu Yü that in communications to the Chin court he was no longer allowed to refer to himself as "I" but had to call himself a "subject". On Apr.20, Ch'i envoys condoled at the Chin court. On May 29, they congratulated Hsi-tsung on his enthronement. They congratulated Hsi-tsung on his birthdays of Feb.20, 1136, and Feb.8, 1137. On Jan.29, 1136, Chin established a protocol for congratulations by Ch'i and other states. On Sep.25, 1136, Ch'i was ordered in all official correspondence to use the Chin reign titles.

On Jan.1, 1138, Hsi-tsung abolished the Ch'i State, and Liu Yü was demoted to king of Shu. On Jan.23, he thanked for his demotion. In the 2nd month (March) of 1142, his title was changed to king of Ts'ao. On Oct.18, 1146, he died in Manchuria (*Chin shih* 3:14b, 15a, 15b, 16a, 16b, 17a; 4:1b, 2a, 2b, 3a, 8b, 11a).

In the 1st month (Feb./Mar.) of 1134, Kao-tsung sent envoys to the Chin court (*Sung shih* 27:16b).

On Feb.9, 1135, Emperor T'ai-tsung of Chin died, aged 61. He was succeeded by a son, born in 1119, who ascended the throne on Feb.10. This was Emperor Hsi-tsung (*Chin shih* 3:17a; 4:1a-1b).

On June 4, 1135,[7] Hui-tsung died in Wu-kuo town, aged 54. Hsi-tsung sent envoys to sacrifice and contribute to the funeral expenses. In the 1st month (Jan./Feb.) of 1137, the Southern Sung court for the first time learned of Hui-tsung's death and of that of his empress, the Lady Cheng, aged 52 (*Sung shih* 243:11a; *Chin shih* 4:2a). The Chinese had the natural wish to bring the corpses home, the Jurchen the political interest in holding on to them. On Mar.1, 1137, Kao-tsung sent Wang Lun to Chin to negotiate the release of the coffins. Lun returned on Feb.7, 1138, and reported in an audience that Chin was willing to relinquish the coffins and also to make some territorial concessions. Three days later, on Febr.11, Wang Lun set out again for the coffins. He came back without them. On Aug.8, he was sent for the third time on the same errand. He returned on Nov.28 together with two Chin envoys, once more without success (*Sung shih* 22:13a; 28:4a, 14b, 19a; 29:2b, 3a; *Chin shih* 4:2a).

On Dec.19, 1138, Wang Lun had an audience with Kao-tsung. On Dec.20, he was ordered to return to the Chin court. His deputy excused himself on the grounds of illness (*Sung shih* 29:3a-3b).

On Dec.22, 1138, Kao-tsung ordered that Chin envoys be admitted (*Sung shih* 29:3b).

On Jan.25, 1139, Kao-tsung appointed envoys to go to the Chin court (*Sung shih* 29:4a).

On Jan.27, 1139, Kao-tsung again ordered that Chin envoys be admitted (*Sung shih* 29:4a).

On Apr.29, 1139, Southern Sung envoys at the Chin court thanked for the territorial concessions (*Chin shih* 4:4b).

On June 29, 1139, the Lady Hsing died in Wu-kuo, town. She had been the legitimate wife of the future Emperor Kao-tsung, and when he ascended the throne in 1127 he had made her empress in absentia (*Sung shih* 29:6b; 243:17b).

In the 6th month (June/July) of 1139, Wang Lun was again sent as envoy to the Chin court (*Sung shih* 29:7a).

---

[7] *Chin shih* dates his death June 6.

On Sep.17, 1139, Kao-tsung sent envoys to the Chin court to congratulate on the New Year's Day of Jan.22, 1140 (*Sung shih* 29: 7b-8a).

On Oct.19, 1139, the by now well-seasoned Southern Sung diplomat Wang Lun[8] requested the Chin court that Kao-tsung's still-living mother, the Lady Wei,[9] be released and escorted to the Southern Sung court, and that the corpse of Hui-tsung be returned. He was arrested. In the 10th month (Oct./Nov.), Wang Lun had an audience with Hsi-tsung who urged him to take service with the Chin. He refused but was allowed to send his deputy back to Southern Sung (*Sung shih* 29:8a; *Chin shih* 4:8b).

On Mar.25, 1141, Hsi-tsung changed the title of the late Emperor Hui-tsung posthumously from Duke of Stupified Virtue to king of T'ien-shui commandery and that of the still living Emperor Ch'in-tsung from Marquis of Aggravated Stupidity to Duke of T'ien-shui commandery (*Chin shih* 4:7a). This was a political move, signaling that an end of the long war between Chin and Southern Sung was in sight. In the latter state, whose capital from 1138 had been Lin-an, the peace party under Ch'in Kuei had come to power, and the famous general and war advocate Yüeh Fei was executed in 1141.

On Oct.2, 1141, Kao-tsung sent envoys to the Chin court to propose that the troops be halted and the Huai River be made the border. These envoys returned to the Southern Sung court on Nov.10, whereupon two further envoys were dispatched. On Dec.6, Chin envoys were received at the Southern Sung court, and on Dec.17, a covenant of peace was agreed on. This was, as usual, confirmed by oath letters. That of Kao-tsung was sent on Dec.20 by an envoy, who was received in audience by the Chin ruler Hsi-tsung on Jan.9, 1142. In this letter, Kao-tsung referred to himself by his first name, called himself a subject, and referred to Chin as the "Superior State". He agreed that with minor exceptions the Huai River should be the border, that Southern Sung from 1142 would pay an annual tribute of 250,000 ounces of silver and 250,000 bolts of silk delivered at the border in the last month of spring, that it would not place large garrisons at the border, that it would return fugitives from the north, and that it

---

[8] This was his sixth mission to Chin.

[9] She had been a concubine of Hui-tsung. After Kao-tsung in 1137 had learned of the death of Hui-tsung's empress, the Lady Cheng, he promoted his mother in absentia to Empress Dowager.

annually would congratulate the Chin emperor on his birthday and on the New Year's Day. (*Sung shih* 29:17b, 18a, 18b, 19a; *Chin shih* 4: 8a; 77:5a-6b).

On Apr.20, 1142, Hsi-tsung sent the Commissioner of Palace Attendants to recognize Kao-tsung as emperor and to inform him that his mother, the Lady Wei, and the corpses of his first empress, the Lady Hsing, of Hui-tsung, and of Hui-tsung's empress, the Lady Cheng, would be returned (*Chin shih* 4:8b).

On Apr.28, 1142, Kao-tsung sent envoys to meet the imperial coffins. On May 1, the cortège conveying the Empress Dowager[10] and the imperial coffins left Wu-kuo town with a Jurchen escort (*Sung shih* 30:1b).

On May 29, 1142, Kao-tsung sent envoys to congratulate Hsi-tsung on his birthday[11] (*Sung shih* 30:1b).

On Aug.23, 1142, Chin envoys were received at the Southern Sung court to discuss the border (*Sung shih* 30:1a).

On Sep.5, 1142, Kao-tsung sent envoys to the Chin court (*Sung shih* 30:2a).

On Sep.13, 1142, Kao-tsung's mother, the Empress Dowager, arrived in Lin-an and took up residence in the Palace of Compassionate Repose (*Sung shih* 30:2a).

On Sep.16, 1142, the coffins of Hui-tsung, his empress, the Lady Cheng, and Kao-tsung's empress, the Lady Hsing arrived in Lin-an. On Sep.20, Kao-tsung paid obeisance to them, dressed in coarse mourning garments (*Sung shih* 22:13a; 30:2a-2b).

In the 8th month (Aug./Sep.) of 1142, the border between Chin and Southern Sung was delineated (*Sung shih* 30:2b).

On Oct.7, 1142, Kao-tsung received nine Chin envoys in audience. It was probably this mission which brought an oath letter confirming the recent treaty. This was stored in the office of the Palace Domestic Service (*Sung shih* 30:2b).

In the 9th month (Sep./Oct.) of 1142, Kao-tsung sent another envoy to the Chin court (*Sung shih* 30:2b).

Diplomatic relations between Southern Sung and Chin now settled down to routine, just as they had done between Northern Sung and Liao after the peace of Shan-yüan in 1005.

---

[10] I.e. Kao-tsung's mother, the Lady Wei.
[11] It fell on Feb.3, 1143.

On the New Year's Day of 1143, Hsi-tsung did not hold a reception because of the death of his heir-apparent. The Southern Sung envoys, who had received their orders in the 9th month (Sep./Oct.) of 1142, congratulated in the emperor's absence in the Hall of the August Ultimate (*Sung shih* 30:2b; *Chin shih* 4:9a).

On Feb.3, 1143, the Chin court decided that the etiquette for the emperor's birthday should be the same as that for the New Year's Day (*Chin shih* 4:9a).

On Aug.7, 1143, Hsi-tsung released Hung Hao and two other Chinese. Hung Hao had been sent as a Southern Sung envoy in 1129 and had been detained by the Jurchen under harsh conditions, because he had refused to enter their service. On Sep.24, 1143, he was received in audience by Kao-tsung (*Sung shih* 30:4b, 5a).

On Feb.6, 1144, the New Year's Day, Southern Sung envoys congratulated at the Chin court. They had received their orders on Sep.25, 1143. On the same day, Chin envoys congratulated at the Southern Sung court. They had arrived on Jan.9. On Feb.10, Kao-tsung sent envoys to the Chin court to thank for the congratulations (*Sung shih* 30:5a; *Chin shih* 4:9b).

On Feb.12, 1144, Hsi-tsung appointed a Chinese envoy to his court as Fiscal Commissioner. When the envoy refused to serve, he was sentenced for "insurrection" and executed (*Chin shih* 4:9b).

On Feb.22, 1144, Southern Sung envoys to the Chin court congratulated on the birthday of Hsi-tsung and presented 10,000 ounces of real gold. They had received their orders on Sep.25, 1143 (*Sung shih* 30:5a; *Chin shih* 4:9b).

On June 21, 1144, Chin envoys arrived at the Southern Sung court to congratulate on the birthday of Kao-tsung[12] (*Sung shih* 30:6b).

On Aug.9, 1144, Chin executed the envoy Wang Lun who since 1139 had steadfastly refused to serve it (*Sung shih* 30:7a).

On Jan.25, 1145, the New Year's Day, Southern Sung envoys congratulated at the Chin court. They had received their orders on Sep.15, 1144. On the same day, Chin envoys congratulated at the Southern Sung court. They had arrived on Jan.21 (*Sung shih* 30:7a; *Chin shih* 4:10b).

On Feb.10, 1145, Southern Sung envoys to the Chin court congratulated on the birthday of Hsi-tsung. They had received their orders

---

[12] It fell on June 22.

on Sep.15, 1144 (*Sung shih* 30:7a; *Chin shih* 4:10b).

On June 11, 1145, Chin envoys arrived at the Southern Sung court to congratulate on the birthday of Kao-tsung[13] (*Sung shih* 30:8b).

On Feb.13, 1146, the New Year's Day, Southern Sung envoys congratulated at the Chin court. They had received their orders on Oct.6, 1145. On the same day, Chin envoys congratulated at the Southern Sung court. They had arrived on Feb.9 (*Sung shih* 30:9a, 10a; *Chin shih* 4:10b-11a).

On Mar.1, 1146, Southern Sung envoys to the Chin court congratulated on the birthday of Hsi-tsung. They had received their orders on Oct.6, 1145 (*Sung shih* 30:9a; *Chin shih* 4:10b-11a).

On June 29, 1146, Chin envoys arrived at the Southern Sung court to congratulate on the birthday of Kao-tsung[14] (*Sung shih* 30:10b).

On Oct.14, 1146, Kao-tsung sent envoys to the Chin court (*Sung shih* 30:10b).

On Feb.2, 1147, the New Year's Day, Southern Sung envoys congratulated at the Chin court. They had received their orders on Sep.22, 1146. On the same day, Chin envoys congratulated at the Southern Sung court. They had arrived on Jan.29 (*Sung shih* 30:10b, 11a; *Chin shih* 4:11b).

On Feb.18, 1147, Southern Sung envoys to the Chin court congratulated on the birthday of Hsi-tsung. They had received their orders on Sep.22, 1146 (*Sung shih* 30:1b; *Chin shih* 4:11b).

On June 18, 1147, Chin envoys arrived at the Southern Sung court to congratulate on the birthday of Kao-tsung[15] (*Sung shih* 30:11b).

On Jan.23, 1148, the New Year's Day, Southern Sung envoys congratulated at the Chin court. They had received their orders on Sep.13, 1147. On the same day, Chin envoys congratulated at the Southern Sung court. They had arrived on Jan.19 (*Sung shih* 30:12b; *Chin shih* 4:12a).

On Feb.8, 1148, Southern Sung envoys to the Chin court congratulated on the birthday of Hsi-tsung. They had received their orders on Sep.13, 1147 (*Sung shih* 30:12a; *Chin shih* 4:12a).

On June 7, 1148, Chin envoys arrived at the Southern Sung court to congratulate on the birthday of Kao-tsung[16] (*Sung shih* 30:13a).

---

[13] It fell on June 12.

[14] It fell on June 30.

[15] It fell on June 19.

[16] It fell onJune 8.

On Feb.10, 1149, the New Year's Day, Southern Sung envoys congratulated at the Chin court. They had received their orders on Oct.1, 1148. On the same day, Chin envoys congratulated at the Southern Sung court. They had arrived on Feb.6 (*Sung shih* 30:13b, 14a; *Chin shih* 4:13a).

On Feb.26, 1149, Southern Sung envoys to the Chin court congratulated on the birthday of Hsi-tsung. They had received their orders on Oct.1, 1148 (*Sung shih* 30:13b, *Chin shih* 4:13b).

On June 26, 1149, Chin envoys arrived at the Southern Sung court to congratulate on the birthday of Kao-tsung[17] (*Sung shih* 30: 14b-15a).

On Jan.9, 1150, the self-indulgent and paranoid Emperor Hsi-tsung of Chin was murdered, aged 31. The assassination had been planned by his second cousin Ti-ku-nai,[18] born in 1122, who then ascended the throne. This was the Dismissed Emperor, also known by his posthumous title as King of Hai-ling (*Chin shih* 4:15a; 5:2b, 3a).

On Jan.29, 1150, Chin envoys arrived at the Southern Sung court to congratulate on the New Year's Day of Jan.31. These must have been sent before Hsi-tsung's assassination (*Sung shih* 30:15b).

In the 1st month (February) of 1150, the Dismissed Emperor sent the Commander-in-chief of the Imperial Bodyguards to Southern Sung to announce his enthronement. The envoy was received at the Southern Sung court on Apr.2 (*Sung shih* 30:15b; *Chin shih* 5:35-4a).

On Apr.8, 1150, Southern Sung envoys to the Chin court congratulated on the enthronement of the Dismissed Emperor (*Sung shih* 30:16a; *Chin shih* 5:4a).

On June 15, 1150, Chin envoys arrived at the Southern Sung court to congratulate on the birthday of Kao-tsung[19] (*Sung shih* 30:16b).

On Jan.20, 1151, the New Year's Day, Southern Sung envoys congratulated at the Chin court. They had received their orders on Sep.10, 1150. On the same day, Chin envoys congratulated at the Southern Sung court. They had arrived on Jan.16 (*Sung shih* 30:16b, 17a; *Chin shih* 5:6a).

On Feb.4, 1151, Southern Sung envoys to the Chin court congratulated on the birthday of the Dismissed Emperor. They had received

[17] It fell on June 27.

[18] Ti-ku-nai's father was the eldest son of T'ai-tsu by a concubine (*Chin shih* 5: 1a; 59:8b; 69:1a; 76:12a-15a).

[19] It fell on June 16.

their orders on Sep.10, 1150 (*Sung shih* 30:16b; *Chin shih* 5:6a).

On Mar.10, 1151, Kao-tsung sent envoys to the Chin court to beg for the release of Emperor Ch'in-tsung (*Sung shih* 30:17a). They were not successful.

On July 4, 1151, a Han-lin Academician and other Chin envoys arrived at the Southern Sung court to congratulate on the birthday of Kao-tsung.[20] They had received their orders on Apr.7 (*Sung shih* 30:17b; *Chin shih* 5:6b).

In the 6th month (July/Aug.) of 1151, Southern Sung envoys to the Chin court requested a minor territorial adjustment. This was rejected (*Chin shih* 5:7b).

On Feb.8, 1152, the New Year's Day, Southern Sung envoys congratulated at the Chin court. They had received their orders on Sep.28, 1151. On the same day, Chin envoys congratulated at the Southern Sung court. They had arrived on Feb.4 (*Sung shih* 30:18a; *Chin shih* 5:7b).

On Feb.23, 1152, Southern Sung envoys to the Chin court congratulated on the birthday of the Dismissed Emperor. They had received their orders on Sep.28, 1151 (*Sung shih* 30:18a; *Chin shih* 5:8a).

On June 23, 1152, a Master of Writing of the Ministry of Punishments and other Chin envoys arrived at the Southern Sung court to congratulate on the birthday of Kao-tsung.[21] They had received their orders on Apr.7 (*Sung shih* 30:18b; *Chin shih* 5:8a).

On Jan.27, 1153, the New Year's Day, the Dismissed Emperor did not hold a reception. He ordered the high officials to receive the tribute and gifts of the Southern Sung envoys. On the same day, a Fiscal Commissioner-in-chief and other Chin envoys congratulated at the Southern Sung court. They had received their orders on Jan.7 and arrived on Jan.24 (*Sung shih* 30:9a; *Chin shih* 5:9a).

On Feb.11, 1153, Southern Sung envoys to the Chin court congratulated on the birthday of the Dismissed Emperor (*Chin shih* 5:9b).

On June 13, 1153, the Commissioner of the Palace Attendants of the Left and other Chin envoys to the Southern Sung court congratulated on the birthday of Kao-tsung. They had received their orders on Apr.27 (*Sung shih* 31:1b; *Chin shih* 5:9b).[22]

---

[20] It fell on July 5.

[21] It fell on June 24.

[22] Kao-tsung's birthday was the 20th day of the 5th month, which in 1153 fell

On Feb.14, 1154, the New Year's Day, the Dismissed Emperor was unwell and did not hold a reception. The Southern Sung envoys, who had received their orders on Oct.21, 1153, stayed in their lodge. On the same day, a Master of Writing of the Ministry of Households and other Chin envoys congratulated at the Southern Sung court. They had received their orders on Nov.28, 1153, and arrived on Feb.10, 1154 (*Sung shih* 31:2b; *Chin shih* 5:10b, 11a).

On Mar.1, 1154, Southern Sung envoys to the Chin court congratulated on the birthday of the Dismissed Emperor. They had received their orders on Oct.21, 1153 (*Sung shih* 31:2a; *Chin shih* 5:11a).

On July 1, 1154, Chin envoys arrived at the Southern Sung court to congratulate on the birthday of Kao-tsung[23] (*Sung shih* 31:3a).

On Feb.4, 1155, the New Year's Day, Sung envoys congratulated at the Chin court. They had received their orders on Nov.15, 1154. On the same day, Chin envoys congratulated at the Southern Sung court. They had received their orders on Jan.31 (*Sung shih* 31:4a, 4b; *Chin shih* 5:12a).

On Feb.19, 1155, Southern Sung envoys to the Chin court congratulated on the birthday of the Dismissed Emperor. They had received their orders on Nov.15, 1154 (*Sung shih* 31:4a; *Chin shih* 5:12a).

On Apr.5, 1155, a Gentleman-of-the-Palace of the Right Office returned to the Southern Sung court from a mission to Chin. He was sentenced to dismissal for having been disrespectful in his duty (*Sung shih* 31:5a).

On June 20, 1155, Chin envoys arrived at the Southern Sung court to congratulate on the birthday of Kao-tsung.[24] They had received their orders on Apr.26 (*Sung shih* 31:5a; *Chin shih* 5:12b).

On Jan.24, 1156, the New Year's Day, Sung envoys congratulated at the Chin court. They had received their orders on Nov.4, 1155. On the same day, Chin envoys congratulated at the Southern Sung court. They had arrived on Jan.20 (*Sung shih* 31:6a, 7b; *Chin shih* 5:14a).

On Feb.8, 1156, Southern Sung envoys to the Chin court congratulated on the birthday of the Dismissed Emperor (*Chin shih* 5:14a).

On May 10, 1156, Kao-tsung sent envoys to the Chin court to

on June 13. *Sung shih* dates the arrival of the Chin envoys June 16, which is, of course, impossible.

[23] It fell on July 2.

[24] It fell on June 21.

congratulate the Dismissed Emperor on his honoured title (*Sung shih* 31:8b-9a).

On June 8, 1156, Chin envoys arrived at the Southern Sung court to congratulate on the birthday of Kao-tsung[25] (*Sung shih* 31:9a).

On June 29, 1156, the last Northern Sung emperor Ch'in-tsung died in Manchurian captivity. The Southern Sung court learned about this only on June 14, 1161 (*Sung shih* 23:19a). (*Chin shih* 5:15a).

On Feb.12, 1157, the New Year's Day, Southern Sung envoys congratulated at the Chin court. They had received their orders on Nov.17, 1156.[26] On the same day, Chin envoys congratulated at the Southern Sung court. They had arrived on Feb.8 (*Sung shih* 31:10b, 11a; *Chin shih* 5:15a).

On Feb.27, 1157, Sung envoys to the Chin court congratulated on the birthday of the Dismissed Emperor. They had received their orders on Nov.17, 1156 (*Sung shih* 31:10b; *Chin shih* 5:15b).

On June 27, 1156, Chin envoys arrived at the Southern Sung court to congratulate on the birthday of Kao-tsung[27] (*Sung shih* 31:11b).

On Feb.1, 1158, the New Year's Day, Sung envoys congratulated at the Chin court. They had received their orders on Dec.6, 1157. On the same day, Chin envoys congratulated at the Southern Sung court. They had arrived on Jan.28 (*Sung shih* 31:12b; *Chin shih* 5:16a).

On Feb.16, 1158, Southern Sung envoys to the Chin court congratulated on the birthday of the Dismissed Emperor. They had received their orders on Dec.22, 1157 (*Sung shih* 31:12b; *Chin shih* 5:16a).

In the 5th month (May/June) of 1158, a Master of Writing of the Ministry of Arms and other Chin envoys to the Southern Sung court congratulated on the birthday of Kao-tsung.[28] They had received their orders on Apr.21 (*Sung shih* 31:13b; *Chin shih* 5:16b).

On Jan.21, 1159, the New Year's Day, Southern Sung envoys congratulated at the Chin court. They had received their orders on Oct.24, 1158. On the same day, Chin envoys congratulated at the Southern Sung court. They had arrived on Jan.17 (*Sung shih* 31:14b; *Chin shih* 5:17a).

On Feb.5, 1159, Sung envoys to the Chin court congratulated on the birthday of the Dismissed Emperor. They had received their orders

---

25 It fell on June 9.
26 Correcting 10th month to 10th intercalary month.
27 It fell on June 28.
28 It fell on June 18.

on Oct.24, 1158 (*Sung shih* 31:14b; *Chin shih* 5:17b).

On Apr.27, 1159, the Director of Studies of the Directorate of Education returned to the Southern Sung court from a mission to Chin and reported that the Dismissed Emperor would move his residence to K'ai-feng (*Sung shih* 31:15b).

In the 5th month (May/June) of 1159, the Inspector of the Imperial Library and other Chin envoys to the Southern Sung court congratulated on the birthday of Kao-tsung. They had received their orders in the 4th month (Apr./May) (*Sung shih* 31:16a; *Chin shih* 5:18a).

On June 18, 1159, Southern Sung sent envoys to the Chin court.[29] On their return, they reported in an audience on Oct.17 that the Chin State wanted friendship (*Sung shih* 31:16a, 17a). That was a falsehood by the Dismissed Emperor, who actually was planning a war against Southern Sung.

On Nov.1, 1159, the Southern Sung Empress Dowager, the Lady Wei, died. On Nov.4, Kao-tsung sent envoys to Chin to announce the death of his mother. These were received at the Chin court on Jan.15, 1160 (*Sung shih* 31:17a. 17b; *Chin shih* 5:18a).

On Feb.9, 1160, the New Year's Day, Southern Sung envoys congratulated at the Chin court. On the same day, Chin envoys congratulated at the Southern Sung court. They had arrived on Feb.5 (*Sung shih* 31:18a; *Chin shih* 5:18b).

On Feb.24, 1160, Southern Sung envoys to the Chin court congratulated on the birthday of the Dismissed Emperor (*Chin shih* 5:18b).

On Mar.12, 1160, Southern Sung envoys to the Chin court presented the testamentary gifts of the Empress Dowager. On Mar.15, 1160, Chin envoys to the Southern Sung court condoled and sacrificed. On Mar.18, Southern Sung envoys were sent to the Chin court to thank for the condolence (*Sung shih* 31:18a; *Chin shih* 5:18b).

On June 24, 1160, Chin envoys arrived at the Sung court to congratulate on the birthday of Kao-tsung[30] (*Sung shih* 31:19a).

A Southern Sung envoy, who had been sent to the Chin court on Dec.18, 1159, returned on Sep.8, 1160, and reported that Chin inevitably would break the covenant and that Southern Sung should prepare for war (*Sung shih* 31:17b, 19b).

---

[29] *Sung shih* 31:16a states that the envoys received their orders on the 1st day of the 6th month (June 18). This means that the cyclical characters *chia-ch'en* must be corrected to *chia-shen*.

[30] It fell on June 25.

On Jan.28, 1161, the New Year's Day, Southern Sung envoys congratulated at the Chin court. They had received their orders on Nov.2, 1160. On the same day, Chin envoys congratulated at the Southern Sung court. They had arrived on Jan.21 (*Sung shih* 31:20a; *Chin shih* 5:19b).

On Feb.12, 1161. Southern Sung envoys to the Chin court congratulated on the birthday of the Dismissed Emperor. They had received their orders on Nov.2, 1160 (*Chin shih* 5:20a).

On May 25, 1161, Kao-tsung sent envoys to the Chin court to congratulate on the Dismissed Emperor's intended move to K'ai-feng (*Sung shih* 32:2a).

On the same June 14, 1161, Chin envoys arrived at the Southern Sung court to congratulate on the birthday of Kao-tsung.[31] One of the envoys threatened the Southern Sung with war (*Sung shih* 32:2a-2b).

On July 4, 1161, Chin envoys to the Southern Sung court announced that the Dismissed Emperor was about to move to K'ai-feng (*Sung shih* 32:3a).

On Aug.14, 1161, Southern Sung envoys were arrested by the Dismissed Emperor (*Sung shih* 32:3b).

The war broke out on Oct.28, 1161, when the Chin troops, led by the Dismissed Emperor, crossed the Huai River and soon reached the Yangtze. But a strong Jurchen faction, opposed to him, his cruelties, and his policies, proclaimed on Oct.27 a new ruler in his absence. This was Emperor Shih-tsung, born in 1123 as a son of the eighth son of T'ai-tsu, and hence a second cousin of the Dismissed Emperor. On Dec.15, the Dismissed Emperor was murdered by his own officers. He was posthumously demoted first to king of Hai-ling and then to commoner (*Chin shih* 5:24a, 24b; 6:2b-3a, 4a).

On Jan.9, 1162, Shih-tsung sent the Marshal and Inspector of the Army of the Left to the Southern Sung court to inform about the recent events, and on Feb.7 other envoys announced his enthronment (*Sung shih* 32:11b; *Chin shih* 32:13b). The war continued however until 1165.

On July 28, 1162, Southern Sung envoys to the Chin court congratulated on Shih-tsung's enthronement (*Chin shih* 6:7b).

On July 24, 1162, Emperor Kao-tsung of Southern Sung abdicated. He died on Nov.9, 1187, aged 81. Kao-tsung was succeeded

[31] It fell on June 15.

by a seventh-generation descendant of T'ai-tsu, born in 1127. This was Emperor Hsiao-tsung. In the 7th month (Aug./Sep.), he sent envoys to the Chin court to announce his ascension (*Sung shih* 32: 15a; 33:1a, 5a

On Dec.15, 1163, Hsiao-tsung sent envoys to negotiate with the Chin court. On Sep.17, 1164, he sent Wei Ch'i for the same purpose. Wei Ch'i was detained at the Huai River because of the war and was not able to cross it until Jan.21, 1165. Meanwhile, another Southern Sung envoy had been sent on Jan.9, and Chin envoys had arrived at the Southern Sung court on Jan.10. On Feb.21, 1165, Wei Ch'i was finally received at the Chin court (*Sung shih* 33:12a; 15a, 15b, 17b; 35: 21a; 36:2a; *Chin shih* 6:15a-15b).

These negotiations led to a peace treaty in 1165 in which the border between the two states and the tribute rendered by Southern Sung remained the same as before, but in which the Chin made certain concessions. In communications, the Southern Sung emperor still had to refer to himself by his given name. However, his status was no longer that of a subject but that of a nephew, and instead of tribute Chin accepted the euphemism of payment.

On Mar.16, 1165, the Vice Inspector of the Left and other Southern Sung envoys were received at the Chin court (*Chin shih* 6:15b).

On Apr.13, 1165,[32] Southern Sung envoys to the Chin court congratulated on the birthday of Shih-tsung. The envoys had received their orders in the 12th month (Jan.Feb., 1165) of the Chinese year 1164 (*Sung shih* 33:18a; *Chin shih* 6:15b).

On June 2, 1165, Hsiao-tsung received Chin envoys in audience (*Sung shih* 33:19a).

On July 8, 1165, Hsiao-tsung sent envoys to Chin to congratulate Shih-tsung on his honoured title. These were received at the Chin court on Sep.23 (*Sung shih* 33:19b; *Chin shih* 6:16a).

On Nov.26, 1165, a Master of Writing of the Ministry of Personnel and other Chin envoys arrived at the Southern Sung court to congratulate on the birthday of Hsiao-tsung.[33] They had received their orders on Oct.7 (*Sung shih* 33:21a; *Chin shih* 6:16a).

---

[32] *Chin shih* has the cyclical characters of *mou-shen*, but these did not occur in the 3rd month. However, Shih-tsung's birthday in 1165 fell on Apr.13.

[33] It fell on Nov.27.

On Feb.3, 1166, the New Year's Day, Southern Sung envoys congratulated at the Chin court. They had received their orders on Nov.8, 1165. On the same day, Chin envoys congratulated at the Southern Sung court. They had arrived on Jan.30 (*Sung shih* 33:20b-21a, 21b; *Chin shih* 6:16b).

On Apr.2, 1166,[34] Southern Sung envoys to the Chin court congratulated on the birthday of Shih-tsung. They had received their orders on Jan.11 (*Sung shih* 33:21a-21b; *Chin shih* 6:16b).

On Nov.15, 1166, a Master of Writing of the Ministry of Households and other Chin envoys arrived at the Southern Sung court to congratulate on the birthday of Hsiao-tsung.[35] They had received their orders on Oct.2 (*Sung shih* 33:24a; *Chin shih* 6:17a).

On Jan.23, 1167, the New Year's Day, Southern Sung envoys congratulated at the Chin court. They had received their orders on Oct.30, 1166. On the same day, Chin envoys congratulated at the Southern Sung court. They had arrived on Jan.19 (*Sung shih* 33:24a, 25a; *Chin shih* 6:18a).

On Mar.23, 1167, Southern Sung envoys to the Chin court congratulated on the birthday of Shih-tsung. They had received their orders on Dec.29, 1166 (*Sung shih* 33:24b; *Chin shih* 6:18a).

On June 27, 1167, Chin envoys to the Southern Sung court sought the release of prisoners of war. This was agreed to (*Sung shih* 34:2a).

On Dec.4, 1167, the Commissioner for Encouraging Agriculture and other Chin envoys arrived at the Southern Sung court to congratulate on the birthday of Hsiao-tsung.[36] They had received their orders in the 9th month (Oct./Nov.) (*Sung shih* 34:3b; *Chin shih* 6:18b).

On Feb.11, 1168, the New Year's Day, Southern Sung envoys congratulated at the Chin court. They had received their orders on Nov.16, 1167. On the same day, Chin envoys congratulated at the Southern Sung court. They had arrived on Feb.7 (*Sung shih* 34:3b, 4a; *Chin shih* 6:19b).

On Apr.10, 1168, Southern Sung envoys to the Chin court congratulated on the birthday of Shih-tsung. They had received their orders on Jan.17 (*Sung shih* 34:4a; *Chin shih* 6:20b).

On Nov.22, 1168, the Commissioner of the Palace Attendants of

---

[34] *Chin shih* has the cyclical characters of *jen-yin*, which did not occur in the 3rd month. However, Shih-tsung's birthday in 1166 fell on Apr.2.

[35] It fell on Nov.16.

[36] It fell on Dec.5.

the Right and other Chin envoys to the Southern Sung court congratulated on the birthday of Hsiao-tsung. They had received their orders on Oct.7 (*Sung shih* 34:6b; *Chin shih* 6:21a).

On Jan.30, 1169, the New Year's Day, Southern Sung envoys congratulated at the Chin court. They had received their orders on Nov.5, 1168. On the same day, Chin envoys congratulated at the Southern Sung court. They had arrived on Jan.26 (*Sung shih* 34:16b; 34:7a; *Chin shih* 6:22a).

On Mar.30, 1169, Southern Sung envoys to the Chin court congratulated on the birthday of Shih-tsung. They had received their orders on Jan.8 (*Sung shih* 34:7a; *Chin shih* 6:22b).

On Nov.11, 1169, a Master of Writing of the Ministry of Punishments and other Chin envoys arrived at the Southern Sung court to congratulate on the birthday of Hsiao-tsung.[37] They had received their orders on Sep.23 (*Sung shih* 34:8b; *Chin shih* 6:23b).

On Jan.19, 1170, the New Year's Day, Southern Sung envoys congratulated at the Chin court. They had received their orders on Oct.24, 1169. On the same day, the Governor of the Capital and other Chin envoys congratulated at the Southern Sung court. They had received their orders on Nov.29, 1169 and arrived on Jan.15, 1170 (*Sung shih* 34:8b, 9a; *Chin shih* 6:24a, 24b).

On Mar.20, 1170, Southern Sung envoys to the Chin court congratulated on the birthday of Shih-tsung. They had received their orders on Dec.27, 1169 (*Sung shih* 34:9a; *Chin shih* 6:24b).

On June 24, 1170, Hsiao-tsung sent envoys to the Chin court to seek a territorial adjustment and a change in the protocol by which Southern Sung communications were received by the Chin. They returned in the 9th month (Oct./Nov.) and reported that Chin had agreed to release the coffin of Ch'in-tsung but that it would not change the protocol (*Sung shih* 34:11a, 12a).

On Nov.30, 1170, a Notary of the Ministry of Military Affairs and other Chin envoys arrived at the Southern Sung court to congratulate on the birthday of Hsiao-tsung.[38] They had received their orders on Oct.16 (*Sung shih* 34:12a; *Chin shih* 6:25b).

On Feb.7, 1171, the New Year's Day, Southern Sung envoys congratulated at the Chin court. They had received their orders on

[37] It fell on Nov.12.
[38] It fell on Dec.1.

Nov.24, 1170. On the same day, the Supervisor of the Household of the Heir-apparent and other Chin envoys congratulated at the Southern Sung court. They had received their orders in the 11th month (Dec./Jan., 1171) of the Chin year 1170 and arrived on Feb.3, 1171 (*Sung shih* 34:12a, 12b; *Chin shih* 6:26a).

On Apr.7, 1171, Southern Sung envoys to the Chin court congratulated on the birthday of Shih-tsung (*Chin shih* 6:26b).

On Nov.20, 1171, a Gentleman-in-Attendance of the Ministry of Punishments and other Chin envoys arrived at the Southern Sung court to congratulate on the birthday of Hsiao-tsung. On Nov.21, which was the birthday, the envoys were received in audience (*Sung shih* 34:14b; *Chin shih* 6:27b).

On Jan.27, 1172, the New Year's Day, Southern Sung envoys congratulated at the Chin court. They had received their orders on Nov.7, 1171. On the same day, Chin envoys congratulated at the Southern Sung court. They had arrived on Jan.23 (*Sung shih* 34:14b; *Chin shih* 7:1a).

On Mar.5, 1172, Hsiao-tsung sent envoys to the Chin court to congratulate Shih-tsung on his honoured title and once more to request a change in the protocol of receiving communications. They returned in the 7th month (July/Aug.) with the answer that Chin had rejected the request (*Sung shih* 34:15a, 16a).

On Mar.26, 1172, Southern Sung envoys to the Chin court congratulated on the birthday of Shih-tsung. They had received their orders on Jan.4 (*Sung shih* 34:154b; *Chin shih* 7:1b).

On May 23, 1172, a Southern Sung mission was received at the Chin court (*Chin shih* 7:2a).

On Nov.8, 1172, the Vice Inspector-general of the Right and other Chin envoys arrived at the Southern Sung court to congratulate on the birthday of Hsiao-tsung.[39] They had received their orders on Oct.4 (*Sung shih* 34:16a-16b; *Chin shih* 7:2b).

On Jan.16, 1173, the New Year's Day, Southern Sung envoys congratulated at the Chin court. They had received their orders on Oct.30, 1172. On the same day, Chin envoys congratulated at the Southern Sung court. They had arrived on Jan.12 (*Sung shih* 34:16a, 16b; *Chin shih* 7:4a).

---

[39] It fell on Nov.9.

On Apr.14, 1173, Southern Sung envoys to the Chin court congratulated on the birthday of Shih-tsung. They had received their orders on Jan.8 (*Sung shih* 34:16b; *Chin shih* 7:4a).

On Nov.27, 1173, the Vice Inspector-general of the Left and other Chin envoys arrived at the Southern Sung court to congratulate on the birthday of Hsiao-tsung.[40] They had received their orders on Oct.4. On Dec.4, they entered the palace and discussed the protocol for receiving communications (*Sung shih* 34:18a; *Chin shih* 7:5a).

On Feb.4, 1174, the New Year's Day, Southern Sung envoys congratulated at the Chin court. They had received their orders on Nov.11, 1173. On the same day, Chin envoys congratulated at the Southern Sung court. They had arrived on Jan.31. On his return, the chief Jurchen envoy was on Mar.9 sentenced for a crime he had committed during his mission. He was given a bastinado of more than 150 lashes, and the presents he had received were confiscated (*Sung shih* 34:18a-18b; *Chin shih* 7:5b, 6a).

On Mar.13, 1174, Shih-tsung appointed a Master of Writing of the Ministry of Punishments and other envoys to conduct discussions with Southern Sung. They were received at the Southern Sung court on Apr.29 (*Sung shih* 34:19a; *Chin shih* 7:6a).

On Apr.4, 1174, Southern Sung envoys to the Chin court congratulated on the birthday of Shih-tsung. They had received their orders in the 12th month (Jan./Feb., 1174) of the Chinese year 1173 (*Sung shih* 34:18b; *Chin shih* 7:6a).

On Oct.22, 1174, a Southern Sung goodwill mission was received at the Chin court (*Chin shih* 7:7a).

On Nov.17, 1174, a Master of Writing of the Ministry of Punishments and other Chin envoys arrived at the Southern Sung court to congratulate on the birthday of Hsiao-tsung.[41] They had received their orders on Oct.8 (*Sung shih* 34:20a; *Chin shih* 7:7a).

On Jan.25, 1175, the New Year's Day, Southern Sung envoys congratulated at the Chin court. They had received their orders on Nov.4, 1174. On the same day, a Palace Assistant Secretary and other Chin envoys congratulated at the Southern Sung court. They had received their orders on Dec.8, 1174 (*Sung shih* 34:20a, 20b; *Chin shih* 7:7b).[42]

---

[40] It fell on Nov.28.

[41] It fell on Nov.18.

[42] For 1175, *Chin shih* has a lacuna from the 1st month through the 6th, but the main events can be reconstructed from entries for 1174.

On Mar.24, 1175, Southern Sung envoys to the Chin court congratulated on the birthday of Shih-tsung. They had received their orders on Jan.3 (*Sung shih* 34:20a-20b).

On Sep.15, 1175, the Remonstrator of the Left and other Southern Sung envoys were sent to the Chin court for discussions (*Sung shih* 34: 21b).

On Dec.5, 1175, a Governor and other Chin envoys arrived at the Southern Sung court to congratulate on the birthday of Hsiao-tsung.[43] They had received their orders on Oct.27 (*Sung shih* 34:22a; *Chin shih* 7:8a).

On Feb.13, 1176, the New Year's Day, Southern Sung envoys congratulated at the Chin court. They had received their orders on Nov.22, 1175. On Feb.12,[44] the Commissioner of the Palace Attendants of the Right and other Chin envoys congratulated at the Southern Sung court. They had received their orders on Dec.25, 1175, and arrived on Feb.9, 1176 (*Sung shih* 34:22a, 22b; *Chin shih* 7:8b).

The birthday of Shih-tsung of Chin in 1176 fell on Apr.11. But because of an eclipse of the sun, the celebration was postponed until the following day. On Apr.12, the Sung envoys congratulated. They had received their orders in the 12th month (Jan./Feb., 1176) of the Chinese year 1175 (*Sung shih* 34:22b; *Chin shih* 7:9a).

On Nov.23, 1176, the Palace Inspector-general and other Chin envoys arrived at the Southern Sung court to congratulate on the birthday of Hsiao-tsung.[45] They had received their orders Oct.15, 1176 (*Sung shih* 34:24a; *Chin shih* 7:10a).

On Feb.1, 1177, the New Year's Day, Southern Sung envoys congratulated at the Chin court. They had received their orders on Nov.14, 1176. On the same day, the Associate Administrator of the Court of Palace Attendants and other Chin envoys congratulated at the Southern Sung court. They had received their orders on Dec.19, 1176, and arrived on Jan.28 (*Sung shih* 34:24a; *Chin shih* 7:10a, 10b).

On Apr,1, 1177, Southern Sung envoys to the Chin court congratulated on the birthday of Shih-tsung. They had received their orders on Dec.31, 1176 (*Sung shih* 34:24a; *Chin shih* 7:11b).

---

[43] It fell on Dec.6.

[44] The New Year's Day in Southern Sung in 1176 fell on Feb.12 and in Chin on Feb.13.

[45] It fell on Nov.24.

On Nov.13, 1177, the Vice Inspector-general of the Right and other Chin envoys arrived at the Southern Sung court to congratulate on the birthday of Hsiao-tsung[46] (*Sung shih* 34:25b; *Chin shih* 7:13a).

On Jan.21, 1178, the New Year's Day, Sung envoys congratulated at the Chin court. They had received their orders in the 10th month (Oct./Nov.) of 1177. On the same day, a Governor and other Chin envoys congratulated at the Southern Sung court. They had received their orders on Dec.12, 1177, and arrived on Jan.17, 1178 (*Sung shih* 34:25b, 26a; *Chin shih* 7:14a, 14b).

On Mar.21, 1178, Southern Sung envoys to the Chin court congratulated on the birthday of Shih-tsung. They had received their orders on Dec.19, 1177 (*Sung shih* 34:26a; *Chin shih* 7:15a).

On Dec.2, 1178, the Grand Judge and other Chin envoys arrived at the Southern Sung court to congratulate on the birthday of Hsiao-tsung.[47] They had received their orders on Oct.23 (*Sung shih* 35:2b; *Chin shih* 7:15b).

On Feb.9, 1179, the New Year's Day, Southern Sung envoys congratulated at the Chin court. They had received their orders on Nov.21, 1178. On the same day, Chin envoys congratulated at the Southern Sung court. They had arrived on Feb.5, 1179 (*Sung shih* 35: 2b, 3b; *Chin shih* 7:17a).

On Apr.9, 1179, Southern Sung envoys to the Chin court congratulated on the birthday of Shih-tsung. They had received their orders on Jan.11 (35:3a; *Chin shih* 7:17a).

On Nov.22, 1179, the Commissioner of the Palace Attendants of the Left and other Chin envoys arrived at the Southern Sung court to congratulate on the birthday of Hsiao-tsung.[48] They had received their orders on Oct.5 (*Sung shih* 35:5a; *Chin shih* 7:18a).

On Jan.29, 1180, the New Year's Day, Southern Sung envoys congratulated at the Chin court. They had received their orders on Nov.7, 1179. On the same day, Chin envoys congratulated at the Southern Sung court. They had arrived on Jan.25, 1180 (*Sung shih* 35:4b, 5a; *Chin shih* 7:18b).

On Mar.28, 1180, Southern Sung envoys to the Chin court congratulated on the birthday of Shih-tsung (*Sung shih* 35:5a; *Chin shih* 7: 18b).

---

[46] It fell on Nov.14.
[47] It fell on Dec.3.
[48] It fell on Nov.23.

On Nov.10, 1180, the Inspector of the Imperial Treasury and other Chin envoys arrived at the Southern Sung court to congratulate on the birthday of Hsiao-tsung.[49] They had received their orders in the 9th month (Sep./Oct.) (*Sung shih* 35:17b; *Chin shih* 7:19a).

On Jan.17, 1181, the New Year's Day, Souther Sung envoys congratulated at the Chin court. They had received their orders on Oct.29, 1180. On the same day, Chin envoys congratulated at the Southern Sung court. They had received their orders on Dec.5, 1180, and arrived on Jan.13, 1181 (*Sung shih* 35:7a, 8a; *Chin shih* 7:20a; 8:1a).

On Mar.17, 1181, Southern Sung envoys to the Chin court congratulated on the birthday of Shih-tsung. They had received their orders on Dec.13, 1180 (*Sung shih* 35:7b; *Chin shih* 8:1b-2a).

On Nov.29, 1181, Chin envoys arrived at the Southern Sung court to congratulate on the birthday of Hsiao-tsung[50] (*Sung shih* 35:10a).

On Feb.5, 1182, the New Year's Day, Southern Sung envoys congratulated at the Chin court. They had received their orders on Nov.14, 1181. On the same day, the Vice Inspector-general and other Chin envoys congratulated at the Southern Sung court. They had received their orders on Oct.1, 1181, and arrived on Feb.1, 1182 (*Sung shih* 35: 10a, 11a; *Chin shih* 8:3a).[51]

On Apr.5, 1182, Southern Sung envoys to the Chin court congratulated on the birthday of Shih-tsung. They had received their orders on Jan.1 (*Sung shih* 35:10b; *Chin shih* 8:3b).

On Nov.18, 1182, the General of the Guards of the Left and other Chin envoys arrived at the Southern Sung court to congratulate on the birthday of Hsiao-tsung.[52] They had received their orders in the 9th month (October) of 1181 (*Sung shih* 35:13a; *Chin shih* 8:4a).

On Jan.26, 1183, the New Year's Day, Southern Sung envoys congratulated at the Chin court. They had received their orders on Oct.29, 1182. On the same day, a Master of Writing of the Ministry of Personnel and other Chin envoys congratulated at the Southern Sung court. They had received their orders on Dec.6, 1182, and arrived on Jan.22, 1183 (*Sung shih* 35:13a; *Chin shih* 8:4a, 4b).

On Mar.26, 1183, Southern Sung envoys to the Chin court con-

---

[49] It fell on Nov.11.

[50] It fell on Nov.30.

[51] For 1182, *Chin shih* has a lacuna for the 1st and 2nd months, but the main events can be reconstructed from entries for 1181.

[52] It fell on Nov.19.

gratulated on the birthday of Shih-tsung. They had received their orders on Dec.16, 1182 (*Sung shih* 35:13a; *Chin shih* 8:4b).

On Nov.7, 1183, the Deputy Grand Director of the Imperial Clan and other Chin envoys arrived at the Southern Sung court to congratulate on the birthday of Hsiao-tsung.[53] They had received their orders on Sep.25, 1182 (*Sung shih* 35:14b; *Chin shih* 8:6a).

On Feb.14, 1184, the New Year's Day, Sung envoys congratulated at the Chin court. They had received their orders on Oct.11, 1183. On the same day, Chin envoys congratulated at the Southern Sung court. They had arrived on Feb.10 (*Sung shih* 35:14b, 15a; *Chin shih* 8:7a).

On Apr.13, 1184, Southern Sung envoys to the Chin court congratulated on the birthday of Shih-tsung. They had received their orders on Jan.11 (*Sung shih* 35:14b; *Chin shih* 8:7b).

On Nov.25, 1184, the Inspector of the Imperial Treasury and other Chin envoys arrived at the Southern Sung court to congratulate on the birthday of Hsiao-tsung.[54] They had received their orders on Sep.13 (*Sung shih* 35:16b; *Chin shih* 8:9a).

On June 11, 1184, Shih-tsung arrived in his Supreme Capital. On Dec.13, he ordered that because the weather there was cold and the distance to it great, the Southern Sung was not allowed to send envoys for the New Year's Day of Feb.2, 1185, and for his birthday on Apr.2. As a matter of fact, the Southern Sung had already appointed envoys, for the New Year's Day on Sep.10 and for the birthday on Nov.14. (*Sung shih* 35:16a, 16b; *Chin shih* 8:8a-8b). But since *Chin shih* does not record any congratulations by these envoys, they apparently never set out or turned back. On May 27, 1185, Shih-tsung left the Supreme Capital (*Chin shih* 8:10a).

On Jan.23, 1186, the New Year's Day, Southern Sung envoys congratulated at the Chin court. They had received their orders on Oct.6, 1185. On the same day, a Governor and other Chin envoys congratulated at the Southern Sung court. They had received their orders on Dec.8, 1185, and arrived on Jan.19, 1186 (*Sung shih* 35:17b, 18a; *Chin shih* 8:11a, 12a).

On Mar.23, 1186, Southern Sung envoys to the Chin court congratulated on the birthday of Shih-tsung. They had received their orders on Dec.6, 1185 (*Sung shih* 35:18a; *Chin shih* 8:12a).

53 It fell on Nov.8.
54 It fell on Nov.26.

On Dec.3, 1186, Chin envoys arrived at the Southern Sung court to congratulate on the birthday of Hsiao-tsung.[55] They had received their orders on Oct.1 (*Sung shih* 35:19b; *Chin shih* 8:15a).

On Feb.10, 1187, the New Year's Day, Sung envoys congratulated at the Chin court. They had received their orders in the 8th month (Sep./Oct.). On the same day, a Master of Writing of the Ministry of Punishments and other Chin envoys congratulated at the Southern Sung court. They had received their orders on Dec.20, 1186, and arrived on Feb.6, 1187 (*Sung shih* 35:19a-19b; *Chin shih* 8:16a, 17b).

On Apr.11, 1187, Southern Sung envoys to the Chin court congratulated on the birthday of Shih-tsung. They had received their orders on Dec.29, 1186 (*Sung shih* 35:19b; *Chin shih* 8:18b).

On Nov.23, 1187, a Governor and other Chin envoys to the Southern Sung court congratulated on the birthday of Hsiao-tsung. They had received their orders in the 8th month (Sep./Oct.) (*Sung shih* 35: 21b; *Chin shih* 8:19b).

On Jan.15, 1188, Southern Sung envoys to the Chin court announced the death of the abdicated Emperor Kao-tsung [on Nov.9, 1187]. They presented 2000 ounces of gold, 30,000 ounces of silver, and 2000 bolts of silk (*Chin shih* 8:20a).

On Jan.30, 1188, the New Year's Day, Southern Sung envoys congratulated at the Chin court. They had received their orders on Oct.11, 1187. On the same day, the Vice Inspector-general and other Chin envoys congratulated at the Southern Sung court. They had received their orders on Dec.14, 1187, and arrived on Jan.26, 1188 (*Sung shih* 35:21a, 22b; *Chin shih* 8:20a, 20b).

On Mar.20, 1188, the Commissioner of Palace Attendants and other Chin envoys to the Southern Sung court condoled and sacrificed on the death of Kao-tsung. They were received in audience by Hsiao-tsung. These envoys had been given their orders on Feb.5 (*Sung shih* 35:22b; *Chin shih* 8:20b).

On Mar.22, 1188, Southern Sung envoys arrived at the Chin court to present Kao-tsung's testamentary gifts. On Mar.26, they were received in audience. Shih-tsung rejected the gifts, among them 5 jade vessels, 20 glass vessels, and bows and arrows, saying:"These were all enjoyed objects of the late ruler of your state which it is proper to value and store in order not to forget the deceased. If [We] now

---

[55] It fell on Dec.4.

accept them, it would be immoral. When you return, inform your ruler and make him understand Our sentiment" (*Sung shih* 35:22b; *Chin shih* 8:20b, 21a).

On Mar.30, 1188, Southern Sung envoys to the Chin court congratulated on the birthday of Shih-tsung. They had received their orders on Dec.12, 1187 (*Sung shih* 35:22a; *Chin shih* 8:21a).

On June 9, 1188, Southern Sung envoys to the Chin court thanked for the condolence and sacrifice (*Chin shih* 8:21b).

On Nov.11, 1188, the Military Commissioner of the Peace and War Army and other Chin envoys arrived at the Southern Sung court to congratulate on the birthday of Hsiao-tsung.[56] They had received their orders on Sep.23 (*Sung shih* 35:24b; *Chin shih* 8:22a).

In the 11th month (Nov./Dec.) of 1188, Hsiao-tsung sent envoys to congratulate Shih-tsung on his birthday in 1189 (*Sung shih* 35:24b. These congratulations could not be delivered, since Shih-tsung died.[57]

On Jan,19, 1189, the New Year's Day, Shih-tsung was ill with a great sweat and could not attend court. The Southern Sung envoys, who had received their orders on Oct.8, 1188, and were at the Chin court for the congratulations, were sent home. On the same day, a Governor and other Chin envoys congratulated at the Southern Sung court. They had received their orders on Dec.2, 1188, and arrived on Jan.15, 1189 (*Sung shih* 35:24a, 24b; *Chin shih* 8:22b-23a; 24a).

On Jan.20, 1189, Emperor Shih-tsung of Chin died, aged 67. He was succeeded by a grandson, the eldest son by the legitimate wife of his own eldest son (d.1185). This was Emperor Chang-tsung (*Chin shih* 8:24a; 9:1a, 2a).

On Jan.31, 1189, Chang-tsung appointed the Grand Judge and others as envoys to announce the death of Shih-tsung to Southern Sung. These were received at the Southern Sung court on Mar.31. Southern Sung envoys condoled and sacrificed at the Chin court on Apr.26 (*Sung shih* 36:3a, 3b; *Chin shih* 9:2b, 3a).[58]

On Feb.18, 1189, Emperor Hsiao-tsung of Southern Sung abdicated. He died on June 28, 1194, aged 68. Hsiao-tsung was succeeded by his third son, Emperor Kuang-tsung, born in 1147. On Feb.28, he sent envoys to Chin to announce his enthronement. These were

---

[56] It fell on Nov.12.

[57] The birthday would have fallen on Mar.19, 1189.

[58] Correcting the entries in *Sung shih*, which there are reversed.

received at the Chin court on May 29 (*Sung shih* 35:25a, 25b; 36:2b, 3a; *Chin shih* 9:3a).

On Apr.15, 1189, Chin envoys to the Southern Sung court presented Shih-tsung's testamentary gifts (*Sung shih* 36:3b).

On May 5, 1189, Chin envoys to the Southern Sung court announced the enthronement of Chang-tsung (*Sung shih* 36:4a).

In the 5th month (May/June) of 1189, Chang-tsung sent the Commissioner for Bandit-suppression of the Northeastern Circuit and other envoys to the Sung court to congratulate on the enthronement of Kuang-tsung (*Chin shih* 9:3b).

On July 6, 1189, Southern Sung envoys to the Chin court congratulated on the enthronement of Chang-tsung (*Chin shih* 9:3b).[59]

In the 6th month (July/Aug.) of 1189, the high officials of Chin informed Southern Sung that the birthday of Chang-tsung would be celebrated on the 1st day of the 9th month (*Chin shih* 9:4b).

On Oct.10, 1189, Southern Sung envoys arrived at the Chin court to congratulate on the birthday of Chang-tsung. They had received their orders on Sep.2. The birthday fell on Oct.12, but because of the mourning for Shih-tsung the court was suspended, and the envoys were not received (*Sung shih* 36:5a; *Chin shih* 9:5a).

On Oct.17, 1189, a Master of Writing of the Ministry of Punishments and other Chin envoys to the Southern Sung court congratulated on the birthday of Kuang-tsung.[60] They had received their orders in the 6th month (July/Aug.) (*Sung shih* 36:5a; *Chin shih* 9:5a).

On Feb.5, 1190, Southern Sung envoys arrived at the Chin court to congratulate on the New Year's Day of Feb.7. They had received their orders in the 9th month (Oct./Nov.) of 1189. But because of the mourning for Shih-tsung the court was suspended and the envoys were not received. On the same New Year's Day, the Commissioner of the Court of Palace Attendants of the Right and other Chin envoys congratulated at the Southern Sung court. They had received their orders on Dec.14, 1189, and arrived on Feb.3, 1190 (*Sung shih* 36:5b; *Chin shih* 9:6a, 7a).

---

[59] *Sung shih* 36:3b records that Southern Sung sent an earlier congratulatory mission on Mar.24. If that is correct, this would have been sent before the Southern Sung got official news of Chang-tsung's enthronement, and so there would have been two missions for the same purpose.

[60] He was born on the 4th day of the 9th month (*Sung shih* 36:1a), but the birthday was celebrated on the 6th day.

On Sep.28, 1190, Sung envoys arrived at the Chin court to congratulate on the birthday of Chang-tsung. They had received their orders on July 8. The birthday was on Oct.1, but because of the mourning for Shih-tsung the court was suspended (*Sung shih* 36:6b; *Chin shih* 9:9b).

On Oct.6, 1190, a Master of Writing of the Ministry of Rites and other Chin envoys to the Southern Sung court congratulated on the birthday of Kuang-tsung (*Sung shih* 36:6b; *Chin shih* 9:9a).

On Jan.24, 1191, Southern Sung envoys arrived at the Chin court to congratulate on the New Year's Day of Jan.27. They had received their orders on Oct.19, 1190. But because of the mourning for Shih-tsung the court was suspended. On the same New Year's Day, a Notary of the Bureau of Military Affairs and other Chin envoys congratulated at the Southern Sung court. They had received their orders in the 11th month (November) of 1190, and arrived on Jan.23 (*Sung shih* 36: 6b, 7a; *Chin shih* 9:10a, 10b).

On Feb.7, 1191, the Empress Dowager of Chin, mother of Chang-tsung, died.[61] On Feb.12, Chang-tsung sent the Vice Inspector-general of the Left and other Chin envoys to the Sung court to announce her death. These were received on Mar.25. Kuang-tsung sent envoys to the Chin court to condole and sacrifice.[62] They were received on Apr.24 (*Sung shih* 36:7b; *Chin shih* 9:10b, 11b).

On Sep.19, 1191 Southern Sung envoys arrived at the Chin court to congratulate on the birthday of Chang-tsung. They had received their orders on June 26. The birthday fell on Sep.21, but because of the mourning for the Empress Dowager the court was suspended (*Sung shih* 36:8b; *Chin shih* 9:12b).

On Sep.26, 1191, the Deputy [Commissioner] of the Court of the Imperial Clan and other Chin envoys to the Southern Sung court congratulated on the birthday of Kuang-tsung. They had received their orders in the 7th month (July/Aug.) (*Sung shih* 36:9a; 9:12b).

On Jan.15, 1192, Southern Sung envoys arrived at the Chin court to congratulate on the New Year's Day of Jan.17. They had received their orders on Oct.7. 1191. On Jan.13, 1192, a royal Tutor and

---

[61] It has been seen that her husband, the eldest son of Shih-tsung, had preceded his father in death in 1185. Therefore, the lady had never been an empress. Chang-tsung had nevertheless entitled her Empress Dowager.

[62] According to *Sung shih* 36:7b, Kuang-tsung gave orders for this mission on Mar.21, but the official news from Chin only arrived four days later.

other Chin envoys arrived at the Southern Sung court for the same purpose. They had received their orders on Nov.30, 1191 Neither celebration took place, because both courts were suspended, the one in Sung because of an illness of Kuang-tsung and the one in Chin because of the mourning for the Empress Dowager (*Sung shih* 36:9a, 9b, 10a; *Chin shih* 9:13a, 13b).

On Oct.5, 1192, Southern Sung envoys arrived at the Chin court to congratulate on the birthday of Chang-tsung. They had received their orders on July 14. The birthday fell on Oct.8, but the celebration was cancelled because of the mourning for the Empress Dowager (*Sung shih* 36:11a; *Chin shih* 9:17a).

On Oct.13, 1192, the Palace Inspector-general and other Chin envoys to the Southern Sung court congratulated on the birthday of Kuang-tsung. They had received their orders on Aug.30 (*Sung shih* 36: 11b; *Chin shih* 9:16b).

On Feb.2, 1193, Southern Sung envoys arrived at the Chin court to congratulate on the New Year's Day of Feb.4. They had received their orders on Oct.26, 1192. But because of the mourning for the Empress Dowager the court was suspended. On Jan.31, 1193, the Vice Inspector-general of the Right and other Chin envoys arrived at the Southern Sung court for the New Year's Day of Feb.4. They had received their orders in the 11th month (Nov./Dec.) of 1192 (*Sung shih* 36:11b, 12b; *Chin shih* 9:16b, 18b; 10:1a).

On Sep.27. 1193, Chang-tsung of Chin for the first time celebrated his birthday, after the long mourning period for his grandfather and mother. He received the kings of the imperial house, the high officials, and the envoys of foreign states. The Southern Sung envoys had received their orders on July 4 (*Sung shih* 36:13b; *Chin shih* 10:4a).

On Oct.3, 1193,[63] the Palace Assistant Secretary and other Chin envoys to the Southern Sung court congratulated on the birthday of Kuang-tsung. They had received their orders in the 7th month (July/Aug.) (*Sung shih* 36:14a; *Chin shih* 10:3b).

On Jan.24, 1194, the New Year's Day, Southern Sung envoys congratulated at the Chin court. They had received their orders on Oct.15, 1193. On the same day, an Auxiliary Academician of the Han-lin Academy and other Chin envoys congratulated at the Southern Sung

[63] The birthday should have fallen on Oct.2 (6th day of 9th month) but was this year for an unknown reason celebrated one day later.

court. They had received their orders on Dec.10, 1193, and arrived on Jan.20, 1194 (*Sung shih* 36:14a; *Chin shih* 10:4b, 5a).

After the abdicated Emperor Hsiao-tsung of Southern Sung had died on June 28, 1194, Kuang-tsung sent envoys to Chin on June 30 to announce it. These were received at the Chin court on Sep.30 (*Sung shih* 36:17b; *Chin shih* 10:7a).).

On July 24, 1194, Emperor Kuang-tsung was overthrown in a coup and forced to abdicate. He died on Sep.17, 1200, aged 54. Kuang-tsung was succeeded by his second son, born in 1168. This was Emperor Ning-tsung (*Sung shih* 36:18a; 37:2b, 15a).

In the 7th month (July/Aug.) of 1194, Ning-tsung sent envoys to the Chin court to announce his father's abdication (*Sung shih* 37:3a).

On Sep.16, 1194, Southern Sung envoys to the Chin court congratulated on the birthday of Chang-tsung. They had received their orders in the 6th month (June/July) (*Sung shih* 36:17a; *Chin shih* 10:6b).

On Oct.6, 1194, Chang-tsung sent a local Administrator and other Chin envoys to Southern Sung to condole and sacrifice on the death of the abdicated Emperor Hsiao-tsung. These were received at the Southern Sung court on Nov.25. Ning-tsung responded with envoys to the Chin court who thanked for the condolence (*Sung shih* 37:5b; *Chin shih* 10:7a)

In the 10th month (Oct./Nov.) of 1194, Southern Sung envoys presented Hsiao-tsung's testamentary gift to the Chin court (*Chin shih* 10:7a).

On Nov.15, 1194, Southern Sung envoys to the Chin court announced the enthronement of Ning-tsung (*Chin shih* 10:7b).

On Jan.29, 1195, Chin envoys to the Southern Sung court congratulated on the enthronement of Ning-tsung (*Sung shih* 37:6a).

On Feb.12, 1195, the New Year's Day, Southern Sung envoys congratulated at the Chin court. They had received their orders on Nov.9, 1194. On the same day, the Commissioner of the Palace Attendants of the Right and other Chin envoys congratulated at the Southern Sung court. They had received their orders on Dec.27, 1194, and arrived on Feb.8, 1195 (*Sung shih* 37:5a, 6a-6b; *Chin shih* 10:8a, 8b).

On Apr.9. 1195, Southern Sung envoys to the Chin court thanked for the congratulations on Ning-tsung's enthronement (*Chin shih* 10: 8b).

On Oct.5, 1195, Southern Sung envoys to the Chin court congratulated on the birthday of Chang-tsung. They had received their order on July 14 (*Sung shih* 37:7b; *Chin shih* 10:19b).

On Nov.20, 1195, a Master of Writing of the Ministry of Personnel and other Chin envoys arrived at the Southern Sung court to congratulate on the birthday of Ning-tsung.[64] They had received their orders in the 8th month (Sep./Oct.) (*Sung shih* 37:8a; *Chin shih* 10:10b).

On Feb.1, 1196, the New Year's Day, Southern Sung envoys congratulated at the Chin court. They had received their orders on Oct.27. On the same day, a Master of Writing of the Bureau of Punishments and other Chin envoys congratulated at the Southern Sung court. They had received their orders on Dec.18, 1195, and arrived on Jan.28, 1196 (*Sung shih* 37:8a; *Chin shih* 10:11a, 11b).

On Sep.24, 1196, Southern Sung envoys to the Chin court congratulated on the birthday of Chang-tsung. They had received their orders on June 29 (*Sung shih* 37:9b; *Chin shih* 10:13a).

On Nov.8, 1196, a Master of Writing of the Ministry of Personnal and other Chin envoys arrived at the Southern Sung court to congratulate on the birthday of Ning-tsung.[65] They had received their orders in the 9th month (Sep./Oct.) (*Sung shih* 37:10a; *Chin shih* 10:13a).

On Jan.20, 1197, the New Year's Day, Southern Sung envoys congratulated at the Chin court. They had received their orders on Oct.14, 1196. On the same day, the Army Commander of a Circuit and other Chin envoys congratulated at the Southern Sung court. They had received their orders on Dec.10, 1196, and arrived on Jan.16, 1197 (*Sung shih* 37:10a; *Chin shih* 10:13b, 14a).

On Oct.13, 1197, Southern Sung envoys to the Chin court congratulated on the birthday of Chang-tsung.[66] They had received their orders on July 19 (*Sung shih* 37:10b; *Chin shih* 10:16a).

On Nov.27, 1197, Chin envoys arrived at the Southern Sung court to congratulate on the birthday of Ning-tsung[67] (*Sung shih* 37:11a).

In the middle of December, 1197, the Grand Empress Dowager of Southern Sung died. She had been the second empress of Kao-tsung. On Dec.18, Ning-tsung sent an envoy to the Chin court to announce her death (*Sung shih* 37:11b).

On Feb.8, 1198, the New Year's Day, there was an eclipse of the sun. The Chin court moved the celebration to Feb.10, on which day the Southern Sung envoys congratulated. They had received their

[64] It fell on Nov.22.
[65] It fell on Nov.10.
[66] It fell on Oct.13.
[67] It fell on Nov.29.

orders on Nov.2, 1197. Chin envoys had arrived at the Southern Sung court on Feb.4 to congratulate on the same occasion, but no reception is recorded. An eclipse of the sun was not needed for the suspension of the Southern Sung court, since this was required in any event by the death of the Grand Empress Dowager (*Sung shih* 37:11a; *Chin shih* 11:1a, 11b).

Because there had been no proper mourning after the death of his grandfather Hsiao-tsung in 1194, Ning-tsung sent envoys to the Chin court who there announced the death once more on Mar.6, 1198 (*Chin shih* 11:1a).

On May 5, 1198, the Commander-in-chief of the Martial Guards and other Chin envoys to the Southern Sung court condoled and sacrificed on the death of the Grand Empress Dowager. They had received their orders in the 2nd month (Mar./Apr.). In the 8th month (Sep./Oct.), Southern Sung envoys thanked for the condolence. (*Sung shih* 37:12a; *Chin shih* 11:1b).

On Oct.3, 1198, Southern Sung envoys to the Chin court congratulated on the birthday of Chang-tsung. They had received their orders on July 8 (*Sung shih* 37:12a; *Chin shih* 11:2a).

On Nov.24, 1198, a Fiscal Commissioner-in-chief and other Chin envoys to the Sung court congratulated on the birthday of Emperor Ning-tsung.[68] They had received their orders in the 9th month (October) (*Sung shih* 37:12b; *Chin shih* 11:2a).

On Jan.28, 1199, the New Year's Day, Southern Sung envoys congratulated at the Chin court. They had received their orders on Oct.27, 1198. On the same day, the Grand Master of Ceremonies and other Chin envoys congratulated at the Southern Sung court. They had received their orders on Dec.13, 1198, and arrived on Dec.31 (*Sung shih* 37:12b; *Chin shih* 11:2b, 3a).

On Sep.22, 1199, Southern Sung envoys to the Chin court congratulated on the birthday of Chang-tsung. They had received their orders on June 27 (*Sung shih* 37:13a; *Chin shih* 11:5a-5b).

On Nov.7, 1199, a local Administrator and other Chin envoys arrived at the Southern Sung court to congratulate on the birthday of Ning-tsung.[69] They had received their orders on Oct.21 (*Sung shih* 37:13b; *Chin shih* 11:5b).

---

[68] The birthday should have fallen on Nov.19 (19th day of 10th month) but was that year for an unknown reason celebrated on the 24th.

[69] It fell on Nov.9.

On Jan.18, 1200, the New Year's Day, Southern Sung envoys congratulated at the Chin court. They had received their orders on Oct.18, 1199. On the same day, a local Administrator and other Chin envoys congratulated at the Southern Sung court. They had received their orders in the 11th month (Nov./Dec.) of 1199, and arrived on Jan.14, 1200 (*Sung shih* 37:13b; *Chin shih* 11:5b, 6a).

On July 16, 1200, the Southern Sung Empress Dowager died. She had been Kuang-tsung's empress and was the mother of Ning-tsung. On July 20, Ning-tsung sent envoys to the Chin court to announce her death (*Sung shih* 37:14b).

After the abdicated Emperor Kuang-tsung had died on Sep.17, 1200, Ning-tsung on Sep.20 sent envoys to the Chin court to announce his death (*Sung shih* 37:15a).

On Oct.10, 1200, Southern Sung envoys to the Chin court congratulated on the birthday of Chang-tsung. They had received their orders on July 20 (*Sung shih* 37:14b; *Chin shih* 11:7b).

On Nov.11, 1200, Ning-tsung sent envoys with Kuang-tsung's testamentary gifts to the Chin court, where they were received on Feb.15, 1201 (*Sung shih* 37:15a-15b; *Chin shih* 11:8b).

On Dec.14, 1200, the Southern Sung empress died. Envoys to the Chin court announced her death on Dec.24 (*Sung shih* 37:15b; *Chin shih* 11:8b).

In the 11th month (Dec./Jan., 1201) of the Chin year 1200, Chang-tsung sent a Master of Writing of the Ministry of Works and other envoys to Southern Sung to condole and sacrifice [on the death of Kuang-tsung]. This mission was received at the Southern Sung court on Jan.23, 1201. In the 12th month (Jan./Feb., 1201), Chang-tsung sent the Army Commander of a Circuit and other envoys to condole and sacrifice [on the death of the empress]. This mission was received on Mar.1, 1201 (*Sung shih* 37:15b; 38:1a; *Chin shih* 11:8b).

During the 12th month (Jan./Feb., 1201) of the Chinese year 1200, Ning-tsung sent envoys to the Chin court to thank for the condolence [for Kuang-tsung] (*Sung shih* 37:15b-16a).

On Feb.5, 1201, the New Year's Day, Southern Sung envoys congratulated at the Southern Sung court. They had received their orders on Nov.13, 1200. On the same day, the Vice Palace Inspector of the Right and other Chin envoys congratulated at the Southern Sung court. They had received their orders in the 11th month (Dec./Jan., 1201) of the Chin year 1200, and arrived on Feb.1, 1201 (*Sung shih* 37:15b, 16a; *Chin shih* 11:8b).

On Mar.17, 1201, Ning-tsung sent envoys to Chin to thank for the condolence [for the empress]. This mission was received at the Chin court on Apr.19 (*Sung shih* 38:1a; *Chin shih* 11:9a).

On Sep.29, 1201, Southern Sung envoys to the Chin court congratulated on the birthday of Chang-tsung. They had received their orders on July 4 (*Sung shih* 38:2a; *Chin shih* 11:10a).

On Nov.14, 1201, the Commissioner of the Palace Attendants of the Right and other Chin envoys arrived at the Southern Sung court to congratulate on the birthday of Ning-tsung.[70] They had received their orders in the 9th month (Sep./Oct.) (*Sung shih* 38:3a; *Chin shih* 11:10a-10b).

On Jan.26, 1202, the New Year's Day, Southern Sung envoys congratulated at the Chin court. They had received their orders on Oct.22, 1201. On the same day, the General of the Guards of the Right of the Palace and other Chin envoys congratulated at the Sourthern Sung court. They had received their orders on Dec.10, 1201, and arrived on Jan.22, 1202 (*Sung shih* 38:2b, 3a; *Chin shih* 11:11a).

On Sep.18, 1202, Southern Sung envoys to the Chin court congratulated on the birthday of Chang-tsung. They had received their orders on June 24 (*Sung shih* 38:3b; *Chin shih* 11:12a).

On Nov.3, 1202, the Auxiliary Commander of the Saluting Guards and other Chin envoys arrived at the Southern Sung court to congratulate on the birthday of Ning-tsung.[71] They had received their orders on Sep.30, on which occasion Chang-tsung had instructed the chief envoy to admonish Ning-tsung, saying:"Our two states have been at peace for a long time. It is not proper that you wrangle for petty reasons and thereby destroy the great propriety" (*Sung shih* 38: 4a; *Chin shih* 11:12a).

On Feb.14, 1203, the New Year's Day, Southern Sung envoys congratulated at the Chin court. They had received their orders on Nov.10, 1202. On the same day, Chin envoys congratulated at the Southern Sung court. They had arrived on Feb.10 (*Sung shih* 38:3a, 4b; *Chin shih* 11:12b).

On Oct.7, 1203, Southern Sung envoys to the Chin court congratulated on the birthday of Chang-tsang. They had received their orders on July 15 (*Sung shih* 38:5b; *Chin shih* 11:14a).

---

[70] It fell on Nov.16.
[71] It fell on Nov.5.

On Nov.22, 1203, a Master of Writing of the Ministry of Punishments and other Chin envoys arrived at the Southern Sung court to congratulate on the birthday of Ning-tsung.[72] They had received their orders on Oct.13 (*Sung shih* 38:6b; *Chin shih* 11:14a).

In the 10th month (Nov./Dec.) of 1203, the Chief Steward returned to the Chin court from a mission to Southern Sung and reported that the Chinese were buying horses and drilling troops, and that they would start a war (*Chin shih* 11:14b).

On Feb.3, 1204, the New Year's Day, Sung envoys congratulated at the Chin court. They had received their orders in the 9th month (Oct./Nov.) of 1202. On the same day, a Notary of the Bureau of Military Affairs and other Chin envoys congratulated at the Southern Sung court. They had received their orders on Dec.11, 1203 (*Sung shih* 38:6a, 6b; *Chin shih* 11:14b; 12:1a).

On Feb.20, 1204, the Branch Department of State Affairs in Chin informed Chang-tsung that one of the Southern Sung envoys who had congratulated on the New Year's Day had died on his way home. The emperor ordered a Defense Commissioner to sacrifice to the deceased, to contribute 220 bolts of pongee and 220 bolts of cotton to the funeral expenses, and to escort the corpse back (*Chin shih* 12:1a).

On Sep.24, 1204, Southern Sung envoys to the Chin court congratulated on the birthday of Chang-tsung. They had received their orders on June 30 (*Sung shih* 38:7b; *Chin shih* 12:3b).

On Nov.6, 1204, a local Administrator and other Chin envoys arrived at the Southern Sung court to congratulate on the birthday of Ning-tsung.[73] They had received their orders on Sep.20 (*Sung shih* 38:8a; *Chin shih* 12:3b).

On Jan.22, 1205, the New Year's Day, Southern Sung envoys congratulated at the Chin court. They had received their orders on Oct.17, 1204. On the same day, a former Palace Vice Inspector-general and other Chin envoys congratulated at the Southern Sung court. They had received their orders on Dec.1, 1204, and arrived on Jan.18, 1205 (*Sung shih* 38:8a, 8b; *Chin shih* 12:3b, 5b).

On Oct.14, 1205, Southern Sung envoys to the Chin court congratulated on the birthday of Chang-tsung. They had received their orders on July 1 (*Sung shih* 38:9b; *Chin shih* 12:6a).

---

[72] Ot fell on Nov.24.

[73] It fell on Nov.12.

In Southern Sung, a war party led by Han T'o-chou had come to power, and tensions with the Jurchen had been steadily rising. Even though missions continued to be exchanged, the war began on Oct.28, 1205, with an unprovoked attack by Chinese troops (*Chin shih* 12:6a).

On Nov.29, 1205, an Army Commander and other Chin envoys arrived at the Southern Sung court to congratulate on the birthday of Ning-tsung.[74] They had received their orders in the 9th month (Oct./Nov.) (*Sung shih* 38:10b; *Chin shih* 12:6a).

On Feb.10, 1206, the New Year's Day, Southern Sung envoys congratulated at the Chin court. They had received their orders on Nov.6, 1205. On the same day, the Grand Master of Ceremonies and other Chin envoys congratulated at the Southern Sung court. They had received their orders on Dec.17, 1205 and arrived on Feb.5, 1206. A misunderstanding led to sharp protests by the Chin envoys, to which a Chinese official responded by proposing their execution. Ning-tsung took no action (*Sung shih* 38:10b, 11a; *Chin shih* 12:6a, 6b)

When the Southern Sung envoys to the Chin court took leave on Feb.14, 1206 Chang-tsung sent the Grandee Secretary to their lodge with a message to Ning-tsung. It reminded him that ever since the treaty of 1165 the Chin emperors had permitted the Southern Sung emperors to call themselves their nephews, and that Chin had kept peace, whereas its borders had been violated by the Southern Sung. "When you, gentlemen, return to you state, you must entirely inform your ruler about Our sentiment" (*Chin shih* 12:6b-7a).

This did not stop the fighting. On July 5, 1206, Ning-tsung formally declared war, and on July 11 announcements were made in Lin-an to Heaven and Earth, the imperial ancestors, and the Gods of the Soils and the Crops (*Sung shih* 38:12b).[75]

On the New Year's Day of Jan.30, 1207, there were no mutual congratulations. But when the Grand Empress Dowager, widow of Hsiao-tsung, died on June 13, the Southern Sung on July 15 sent envoys to the Chin court to announce it (*Sung shih* 38:17b). On the same day, another envoy was appointed to congratulate Chang-tsung on his birthday, but no Southern Sung representatives are mentioned

74 It fell on Dec.1.

75 Correcting 5th month to 6th.

among those congratuling on Sep.24 (*Sung shih* 38:17b; *Chin shih* 12: 15b).

It became soon apparent that the Chinese could not win the war. On Aug.29, 1207, they requested peace. On Oct.21, the Southern Sung sent a Gentleman-of-the-Palace of the Left Office who was received at the Chin court on Nov.25. He brought a letter which proposed that the Southern Sung emperor would refer to the Chin emperor as uncle and that the annual tribute would be raised. The Jurchen made it a condition that Han T'o-chou be handed over. Ning-tsung decided on a compromise. Han T'o-chou was dismissed and by Ning-tsung's secret orders killed. A letter informed the Chin court of these events on Dec.11 (*Sung shih* 38:18a; *Chin shih* 12:15b, 16a)

In the 12th month (Dec./Jan., 1208) of the Chinese year 1207, Ning-tsung sent a negotiator to the Chin court (*Sung shih* 38:19a).

On the New Year's Day of Jan.19, 1208, there were again no mutual congratulations (*Chin shih* 12:16b).

On Jan.30. 1208, the Southern Sung court was informed that the Jurchen insisted that the head of Han T'o-chou be delivered to them. Ning-tsung complied (*Sung shih* 39:1a).

In the 1st month (Jan./Feb.) of 1208, Ning-tsung sent an envoy to the Chin court, and on Feb.22, another envoy presented a letter (*Sung shih* 39:1a; *Chin shih* 12:7a).

On Apr.7, 1208, Chin agreed to a peace treaty in which the annual Southern Sung tribute was raised to 300,000 ounces of silver and 300,000 bolts of silk. On Aug.23, Chang-tsung sent an oath letter to the Southern Sung court, confirming the peace (*Chin shih* 12:17a, 18b).

On Nov.5, 1208, Ning-tsung received a Chin envoy in audience (*Sung shih* 39:2b).

On Nov.24, 1208, Sung envoys to the Chin court congratulated on the birthday of Chang-tsung according to the new schedule.[76] They had received their orders on July 22 (*Sung shih* 39:2a; *Chin shih* 12:18b).

On Nov.26, 1208, a Master of Writing of the Ministry of Households and other Chin envoys arrived at the Southern Sung court to congratulate on the birthday of Ning-tsung.[77] They had received their orders on Nov.8 (*Sung shih* 39:3a; *Chin shih* 12:18b).

---

[76] The celebration of Chang-tsung's birthday had on July 9, 1208 been shifted from the 1st day of the 9th month to the 15th day of the 10th (*Chin shih* 12:18b).

[77] It fell on Nov.28.

On Dec.29, 1208, Emperor Chang-tsung of Chin died, aged 41. He was succeeded by the 7th son of Shih-tsung, born by a concubine, who in 1197 had been enfeoffed as king of Wei-shao. Since he never received a posthumous title, he is called by the sources the King of Wei-shao (*Sung shih* 9:3a; *Chin shih* 12:19a; 13:1a-1b, 2a).

On Jan.20, 1209, Ning-tsung sent envoys to the Chin court to condole and sacrifice, and on Jan.31 other envoys to congratulate the new Chin ruler on his enthronement (*Sung shih* 39:3a). These actions were taken before the Southern Sung had been officially informed of the events. On Feb.12. 1209, Chin envoys announced the death of Chang-tsung, and as late as Mar.12 the enthronement of the successor (*Sung shih* 39:3b).

On Mar.3, 1209, Chin envoys to the Southern Sung court presented Chang-tsung's testamentary gifts (*Sung shih* 39:3b).

In the 8th month (September) of 1209, Southern Sung envoys to the Chin court congratulated on the birthday of the ruler.[78] They had received their orders on July 8 (*Sung shih* 39:4b; *Chin shih* 13:2b).

On Nov.15, 1209, Chin envoys arrived at the Southern Sung court to congratulate on the birthday of Ning-tsung[79] (*Sung shih* 39:5a).

On Jan.27, 1210, the New Year's Day, Southern Sung envoys congratulated at the Chin court. They had received their orders on Oct.4, 1209. On the same day, Chin envoys congratulated at the Southern Sung court. They had arrived on Jan.23 (*Sung shih* 39:5a; 5b).

In the 8th month (Aug./Sep.) of 1210, Southern Sung envoys to the Chin court congratulated on the birthday of the ruler. They had received their orders on June 29 (*Sung shih* 39:6b; *Chin shih* 13:3b).

On Nov.5, 1210, Chin envoys arrived at the Southern Sung court to congratulate on the birthday of Ning-tsung[80] (*Sung shih* 39:7a).

On Jan.17, 1211, the New Year's Day, Southern Sung envoys congratulated at the Chin court. They had received their orders on Oct.17, 1210. On the same day, Chin envoys congratulated at the Southern Sung court. They had arrived on Jan.13 (*Sung shih* 39:7a; *Chin shih* 13:4a).

On July 18, 1211, Ning-tsung sent an envoy to congratulate the Chin ruler on his birthday. But the Chin State was in turmoil, since in

[78] The exact date of the birthday is unknown.
[79] It fell on Nov.17.
[80] It fell on Nov.7.

the spring of 1211 the Mongols had begun their raids into its north-Chinese territories. The envoy was unable to proceed and returned (*Sung shih* 39:8a, 8b).

On Feb.5, 1212, the New Year's Day, Southern Sung envoys congratulated at the Chin court. They had received their orders on Nov.5, 1211. On the same day, Chin envoys congratulated at the Southern Sung court. They had arrived on Feb.1 (*Sung shih* 39:8a, 8b; *Chin shih* 13:5b).

In the 8th month (Aug./Sep.) of 1212, Southern Sung envoys to the Chin court congratulated on the birthday of the ruler. They had received their orders on July 8. Because of deep inroads by the Mongols at this time, the traditional banquet was omitted. (*Sung shih* 39:8b; *Chin shih* 13:6a). On Nov.10, 1212, Chin envoys arrived at the Southern Sung court to congratulate on the birthday of Ning-tsung[81] (*Sung shih* 39:9a).

On Jan.24, 1213, the New Year's Day, Southern Sung envoys congratulated at the Chin court. They had received their orders in the 9th month (Sep./Oct.) of 1212. On the same day, Chin envoys congratulated at the Southern Sung court. They had arrived on Jan.20 (*Sung shih* 39:9a).

On June 27, 1213, Ning-tsung ordered envoys to congratulate the Chin ruler on his birthday. But the Mongols blocked the roads, and the envoys had to return (*Sung shih* 39:9b).

On Sep.10, 1213, the Chin ruler (King of Wei-shao) was overthrown. On Sep.11, he was removed from the palace and subsequently assassinated. On Sep.22, Chang-tsung's older brother was enthroned. This was Emperor Hsüan-tsung, born in 1163 (*Sung shih* 39:10a; *Chin shih* 13:6b, 7a, 7b, 10a; 14:1b).

On Nov.15, 1213, Ning-tsung attempted to congratulate Hsüan-tsung on his enthronement, but the envoy was also unable to proceed because of the Mongols and had to return. Official announcement of the ascension of Hsüan-tsung did not reach the Southern Sung court until Dec.11 (*Sung shih* 39:10a).

On Nov.27, 1213, Ning-tsung sent envoys to the Chin court to congratulate on the New Year's Day of Feb.12, 1214. They could not proceed because of the Mongols. However, Chin envoys did reach

[81] It fell on Nov.13.

the Southern Sung court on Feb.8, 1214 for the celebration on the 12th (*Sung shih* 39:10a, 10b).

On Apr.26, 1214, Chin officials arrived in Southern Sung and attempted to collect the annual tribute for the past two years. They were not only unsuccessful, but after a memorial by a Member of the Suite of the Imperial Diarists to Ning-tsung, the Chinese on Sep.3 stopped the annual tribute altogether (*Sung shih* 39:10b, 11a).

On Aug.19, 1214, Chin envoys to the Southern Sung court announced that Hsüan-tsung was moving his residence to the Southern Capital (K'ai-feng) (*Sung shih* 39:11a).

In the 8th month (Sep./Oct.) of 1214, Chin officials again attempted unsuccessfully to collect the annual tribute in Southern Sung (*Sung shih* 39:11a).

On Feb.1, 1215, the New Year's Day, Southern Sung envoys congratulated at the Chin court. They had received their orders on Dec.3, 1214. On the same day, Chin envoys congratulated at the Southern Sung court. They had arrived on Jan.28 (*Sung shih* 39:11b; *Chin shih* 14:6a).

On Apr.13, 1215, Southern Sung envoys to the Chin court congratulated on the birthday of Hsüan-tsung. They had received their orders on Feb.19 (*Sung shih* 39:11b; *Chin shih* 14:8a).

On Nov.9, 1215, Chin envoys arrived at the Southern Sung court to congratulate on the birthday of Ning-tsung[82]

By the end of 1215, the Chin State was in dire straits. Manchuria and Shan-tung had been lost through local uprisings. The Mongols operated freely in northern China and on May 31, 1215, had received the surrender of the Central Capital (Peking). Chin and Hsia had been at war since 1214. All that was left of a once mighty empire was Honan, southern Shan-hsi, and Shensi, with K'ai-feng as the capital.

On Jan.21, 1216, the New Year's Day, Southern Sung envoys congratulated at the Chin court. They had received their orders on Nov.30, 1215. On the same day, Chin envoys congratulated at the Southern Sung court. They had arrived on Jan.17 (*Sung shih* 39:13a).

On Nov.17, 1216, the Commandant of the Palace Guards and other Chin envoys arrived at the Southern Sung court to congratulate on the birthday of Ning-tsung.[83] They had received their orders in the

[82] It fell on Nov.11.
[83] It fell on Nov.29.

9th month (Oct./Nov.) (*Sung shih* 39:13b; *Chin shih* 14:21b).

On Feb.8, 1217, the New Year's Day, Southern Sung envoys congratulated at the Chin court. On the same day, a Gentleman-in-Attendance of the Ministry of Works and other Chin envoys congratulated at the Southern Sung court. They had received their orders on Jan.4 and arrived on Feb.4 (*Sung shih* 39:14a; *Chin shih* 14:23b; 15:1a).

On Mar.1, 1217, Ning-tsung sent envoys to Chin, who congratulated on Hsüan-tsung's birthday of Apr.20 (*Sung shih* 40:1a; *Chin shih* 15:2a). The war with the Mongols continued, but their main interest was at this time directed toward western Asia. Chin used this respite for an attack on Southern Sung in 1217.

On Feb.2, 1223, the New Year's Day, Chin rescinded the exchange of congratulatory missions (*Chin shih* 16:15a).

On Jan.14, 1224, Emperor Hsüan-tsung of Chin died, aged 61. He was succeeded by his third son. This was Emperor Ai-tsung, born in 1198. Ai-tsung made peace with Southern Sung in 1224 and Hsia in 1225. He ratified the cessation of tribute payments by Southern Sung, and both sides agreed to discontinue all congratulatory missions.

On Sep.6, 1224, Ning-tsung of Southern Sung fell ill and could no longer attend to government. He died on Sep.17, aged 51, and was succeeded by a distant relative. This was Emperor Li-tsung, born in 1205 (*Sung shih* 40:13a; 41:2a).

After the death of Chinggis Qan on Aug.25, 1227, there followed a lull in the Mongol operations, but these were resumed with an attack on Chin in 1230. The siege of K'ai-feng began on Apr.8, 1232, and lasted until its surrender on May 29, 1233. Emperor Ai-tsung fled to Ts'ai-chou, situated just north of the upper course of the Huai River. He was there attacked by Mongol and Southern Sung troops but held out until early 1234. On Feb.8 of that year, he abdicated to a distant relative. This was Wan-yen Ch'eng-lin, sometimes called the Last Emperor. On Feb.9, Ts'ai-chou was taken. Ai-tsung hanged himself, and the Last Emperor fell against the invaders. Chin had perished (*Sung shih* 41:17a-17b; *Chin shih* 11b; *Yüan shih* 2:23a-23b; 4:4a; 3:4a).

The Southern Sung had foolishly cooperated with the Mongols in the last stage of the war against Chin. But its hope of regaining the lost northern Chinese territories came to naught. The Mongols had no intention of giving them up but on the contrary were soon to embark on the conquest of all of China. Their next step was to defeat Nanchao in 1254, whereafter the Southern Sung was outflanked. Raids into Chinese territory were followed by full-scale war. The death of Great

Qan Möngke on Aug.12, 1259, and a subsequent succession crisis, brought on a pause in hostilities. This was not used by the Southern Sung to its advantage, and Mongol envoys to its court in 1260 and 1261 were treated badly. After renewed border clashes, the war began again in 1268. From 1273, the famous general Bayan was in command of the Mongol troops. He crossed the Yangtze in 1275 and thereafter defeated the main Chinese forces. The Empress Dowager, on behalf of the child emperor Kung-tsung, sent an envoy to Bayan and proposed that the Southern Sung become a nephew country to the Great Qan and pay an annual tribute. The envoy returned on Mar.19, 1276, with a flat rejection. The Empress Dowager and the child emperor then surrendered, and on Mar.26 the Mongols entered the Palace.

Relations between the Chinese and Jurchen can be divided into two periods. The earlier should be dated 925 to 1142. The first recorded mission from the Jurchen to China was to the Later T'ang in 925, followed by another to the Later Chou in 959. From 961, the Jurchen traded with the Sung. But, for good reasons, the chief dealings of the Jurchen until their unification by A-ku-ta in 1115 were with their Khitan overlords. The various tribes had different aims. Some circumvented the Khitan prohibition of trading with China and complained to the Sung in 991 that the Khitan attempted to prevent the traffic. Others reported to the Liao court in 995 that the Sung tried to incite them against it. Some Jurchen sought titles from the Liao and offered aid against Koryŏ. This fragmention of the Jurchen made them valueless to China as a counterweight to the Liao. Their missions were consequently for trade. But when after 1115 the Liao State began to disintegrate, an alliance of the classical type across a common enemy became a Sung desideratum, with the recovery of the Sixteen Commanderies as the ultimate goal. This failed because of the weakness of Sung and the incompetence of its government. The Sung contribution toward the defeat of Liao was negligible and therefore the treaty with the Jurchen in 1123 was not to Sung's advantage. It meant in practice little more than that the tributary relationship of Sung to Liao had been transferred to Chin. Conflicting interests led to war in 1125, the fall of K'ai-feng in 1127, the detention of Hui-tsung and Ch'in-tsung with their families in Manchuria, and the end of Northern Sung.

Hui-tsung died in captivity in 1135, and his empress, the Lady Cheng, at about the same time. When this became known in Southern Sung in 1137, diplomatic efforts were concentrated on the return of their coffins. These efforts became even more urgent after the Lady Hsing, whom Kao-tsung had made empress in absentia, had also died in Manchuria in 1139. In addition, Kao-tsung sought the release from captivity of his mother, the Lady Wei.

With the peace treaty of 1142, the relations of Southern Sung and Chin entered their second phase which lasted until 1224. Even though there were brief wars from 1161 to 1165, and 1205 to 1208, this was a period of coexistance in which the Southern Sung until 1214 was the junior partner. It ended with the unilateral rescinding by Southern Sung of its tribute payments to Chin in 1214, a last war from 1217, the unilateral rescinding by Chin of all congratulatory missions in 1223, and the peace of 1224 in which the two revocations were recognized by both sides. The remaining years from 1224 to 1234 were occupied by Chin's last struggle against the Mongols and the cessation of all relations with Southern Sung.

In accordance with the treaty of 1142, a tight protocol was set up which governed the exchange of congratulatory missions between reigning rulers. Empresses Dowager/Grand Empresses Dowager no longer congratulated through messengers of their own, nor did they receive personal congratulations.

The exchange of congratulatory missions on the New Year's Days and birthdays of the emperors began to function routinely in 1144 and ceased after 1217. Its rescinding by Chin in 1223 therefore simply acknowledged what had already happened. From 1144 to 1217, there are only four unexplainable gaps gaps in these missions. There is no mention of a New Year congratulation in 1209 by Chin, birthday congratulations in 1200 and 1214 by Chin, and a birthday congratulation in 1216 by Southern Sung. Four possible omissions compared to 261 recorded missions give us remarkably accurate statistics.[84]

The statistics concerning the enthronements and deaths of emperors are equally reliable. From 1142 to 1223, the Southern Sung and Chin announced the enthronement of every emperor to each other. They congratulated each other on the enthronement of every emperor with one exception. Chin did not congratulate Ning-tsung in 1194. They announced the death of every emperor, including that of abdi-

[84] Note that the Chin court twice postponed congratulations because of solar eclipses, for the birthday celebration of 1176 and for the New Year reception of 1198. It shows that the Jurchen shared the outdated Chinese superstitious fear of these events.

cated emperors, to each other, with three exceptions. Chin did not announce the murder of Hsi-tsung in 1150, the murder of the Dismissed Emperor in 1161, and the overthrow and assassination of the King of Wei-shao in 1213. While condolences otherwise were a routine, the Southern Sung did not condole on these three occasions. It did not have to do so, since it had not been officially informed of the deaths. With the same three exceptions, Southern Sung and Chin presented the testamentary gifts of all emperors to each other. The only unexplained omission is therefore the congratulation on the enthronement of Ning-tsung in 1194.

This far, Southern Sung and Chin largely followed the protocol established in Liao times. There was, however, a sharp difference when it came to announcing the death of an Empress Dowager or Grand Empress Dowager. The protocol of Sung-Liao times had been based on reciprocity. That of Southern Sung and Chin was not. The Southern Sung announced the death of Grand Empresses Dowager in 1197 and 1207, and of an Empress Dowager in 1200.[85] The Chin made not a single corresponding announcement. This means that the traffic was distinctly one-sided. Southern Sung was deferential, Chin was not. Another change of protocol was the fact that Chin at no time held official mourning for Southern Sung. The latter, on the other hand, suspended the New Year celebration on Jan.14, 1124, because of T'ai-tsu's death on Sep.19, 1123. It therefore held official mourning for Chin on at least this occasion.

All missions discussed so far had chiefly, but not exclusively, ritual purposes. Others were concerned with border delineations and territorial concessions, espionage, peace negotiations, release of prisoners of war, thanks for condolences, goodwill, congratulations on the move of an imperial residence, dates when birthdays were to be celebrated, and the like.

The intense diplomatic traffic between Southern Sung and Chin did not disguise the fact that Southern Sung was the lesser partner. During all the years of their coexistance, the Southern Sung never offered honorific or posthumous titles to the Chin emperors, knowing, no doubt, that these would not be accepted. The titles confered by T'ai-tsung on Hui-tsung and Ch'in-tsung in 1128, Duke of Stupified

---

[85] I exclude titular empresses, who had not been legitimate empresses in their lifetimes.

Virtue and Marquis of of Aggravated Stupidity, were blatant insults. No Chin emperor requested a Chinese princess in marriage. On the contrary, T'ai-tsung of Chin ordered in 1130 that Hui-tsung's six captive daughters in Manchuria be married to members of the imperial Chin clan. Since Hui-tsung's consent was not asked and the marriages were performed on T'ai-tsung's dictum, these were a severe humiliation to the Chinese. When Hui-tsung died in 1135, Chin did not bother to inform the Southern Sung, and the death did not become known there until 1137. After the peace treaty of 1142, Chin released Kao-tsung's mother and the coffins of Hui-tsung, Hui-tsung's empress and Kao-tsung's empress, but Ch'in-tsung remained in captivity. Kao-tsung's request in 1151 for the release of Ch'in-tsung was refused. When Ch'in-tsung died in 1156, his death did not become known at the Southern Sung court until 1161. In 1170, Chin agreed to return the coffin of Ch'in-tsung, but there is no record that it ever arrived in Lin-an. Attempts by Southern Sung to change the protocol, which was irksome to it, in 1170 and 1172 were rejected.

The protocol dictated when missions were to arrive at the courts. *Chin shih* as a rule does not record the arrival days of Southern Sung missions for the New Year celebrations, except for the years 1190-1193. On three of these occasions they came two days before the event and on one three days. For the birthday celebrations of the Chin emperors, the arrival days of the Southern Sung missions are recorded for 1189-1192. They twice came two days before the event and twice three days. In contrast, *Sung shih* as rule does note the arrival times of the Chin missions. For the New Year celebrations, it gives this information for 63 years. The missions came once two days before the event, once three days, fifty-seven times four days, once five days, once seven days, and twice twenty-eight days. For the birthday celebrations of the Southern Sung emperors, the arrival days of the Chin missions are recorded 40 times. The missions came twenty-nine times one day before the event, nine times two days, once three days, and once five days. The preferred arrival time to the Southern Sung court for the New Year celebrations was obviously four days before the events and for the birthday celebrations one day before the events.

The missions in either direction could be large and comprise hundreds of persons. It took time to set them up, and the courts gave orders well in advance. *Sung shih* records the orders for 56 New Year missions and 50 birthday missions to the Chin court. *Chin shih* gives the corresponding information for 26 New Year missions and

24 birthday missions to the Southern Sung court. That makes it possible to calculate the days elapsed from the orders to the events. On the average, Southern Sung gave orders for the New Year missions 97 days before the events, Chin only 27 days. On the average, Southern Sung gave orders for the birthday missions 50 days before the events, Chin only 24 days. The discrepancy is hard to explain. Distance cannot apply, since this affected both sides. All missions brought gifts, and these had to be assembled. But the rule of reciprocity exludes the possibility that Southern Sung offered substantially more goods and therefore needed more time to bring them together. The same rule also prevented Southern Sung missions from being larger than their counterparts. The simple explanation may be that the Southern Sung was more bureaucratic and therefore more inefficient and slower in setting up its missions.

It is not known how long the missions stayed at the courts they visited. The Chin mission for Hsiao-tsung's birthday on Nov.28, 1173, was still in Lin-an on Dec.4. The Southern Sung mission for the New Year celebration at the Chin court on Feb.10, 1206, left four days later on Feb.14. No conclusions can be drawn from these two instances.

It will have been noted that Southern Sung, like Koryŏ and Hsia, sent missions to the Chin court in 1189, 1190, 1191, 1192, and 1193, even though it knew that these would not be received because of state mourning. As remarked before, the magnet must have been government and private trade. Trade could take place in spite of mourning and therefore was an opportunity not to be missed. It has also been seen that in 1191, Emperor Chang-tsung allowed the envoys from Hsia to remain and trade for three days. This was according to a precedent, which must have applied to all foreign missions.

While the great majority of missions exchanged by Southern Sung and Chin was for ritual purposes, there can be no question that the concominant exchange of gifts was a form of trade and that the envoys profited from the gifts they received and their own private enterprise. In 1174, the chief Chin envoy to the Southern Sung court for the New Year celebration was on his return sentenced for a crime to a bastinado of more than 150 lashes and had all his presents confiscated. To be a real punishment, these gifts had to have been considerable. Envoys faced hazards, whether dishonest or honest. Wang Lun was detained by the Jurchen in 1139 and executed in 1144. In 1144, another Southern Sung envoy was executed by Chin. In 1143, the Jurchen released a Southern Sung envoy whom they had detained under harsh conditions since 1129. In 1155, a Southern Sung envoy on his return from a mission was sentenced to dismissal for disrespect. In 1161, Southern Sung envoys were arrested by the Dismissed Emperor. In 1204, a Southern Sung envoy died on his way home from a New Year celebration in Chin. In 1206, a Southern Sung official proposed the execution of Chin envoys. The fact that men still were willing to serve as envoys was patriotism only in a very few instances, such as that of Wang Lun, and the lure of making profit in the majority of cases.

This is the distribution by 20-year period of the 71 recorded missions from the Jurchen to Liao and the 208 recorded missions from the Jurchen/Chin to the Later T'ang, Later Chou, Northern Sung, and Southern Sung:

Missions from the Jurchen/Chin

	To Sung	To Liao
907- 926	1	1
927- 946	0	23
947- 966	11	4
967- 986	5	7
987-1006	2	14
1007-1026	3	6
1027-1046	0	2
1047-1066	0	1
1067-1086	0	6
1097-1106	0	6
1107-1126	20	1
1127-1146	16	
1147-1166	40	
1167-1186	40	
1187-1206	47	
1207-1226	23	

Before 1115, relations between the Jurchen and Sung swung like a pendulum. When the Jurchen were politically close to the Liao, they were distant to Sung and vice versa. The last Jurchen mission to Liao was in 1114. After A-ku-ta had founded the Chin empire in 1115, relations between Chin and Southern Sung were lively and reached their peak between 1187 and 1206. With the disintegration of Chin, the missions fell off and ceased alltogether after 1217.

It is a peculiarity of *Sung shih* from 1115 and the entire *Chin shih* that they do not list the goods offered by Chin. That must be due to an editorial decision by T'o T'o. *Wen-hsien t'ung-k'ao* 346:25a mentions in general terms that the Jurchen traded in gold, pearls, and beeswax. The other sources record that the Jurchen offered horses in 961, 963, 964, 967, and 968, falcons in 963, and sable furs in 964. In 1019, they offered cloth which was rejected. The Sung responded with real gold, vessels of gold, silver, jade, and glass, incense braziers, silken fabrics, garments, horse trappings, horse whips, bows and arrows, fruit, honey, tea, and the Buddhist *Tripitaka.*

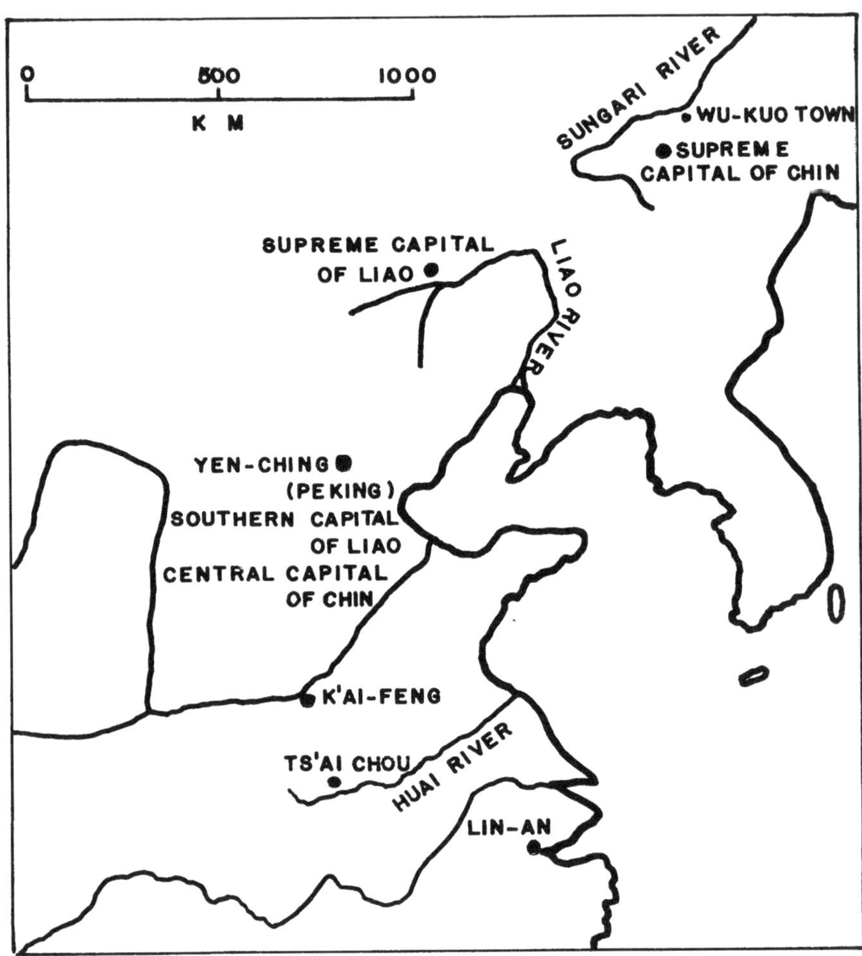

Map 11. Place names connected with the Khitan and Jurchen.

CONCLUSION

Emperor Yang of Sui (r.605 to 618) made efforts to establish relations with foreign countries, and his envoys reached as far as Ch'ih-t'u in South Asia, Bukhara in West Turkestan, and Persia. His intention must have been to announce the restoration of the Chinese empire, to invite homage, and to encourage trade.

When missions arrived from abroad, the Chinese considered this a recognition of, and submission to, the Son of Heaven, and proceeded to incorporate the foreign countries into their imginary world empire. They did this by two methods, by either establishing non-existant armies under the foreign rulers as Military Commissioners, or by establishing equally non-existant Area Commands under the foreign rulers as Military Governors.

These are the imaginary armies with the dates of their first creation:

The Army Which Protects the Border, of the Hsi, 722.
The Army Which Gives Repose to the Imperial Domain, of the Khitan, 715.
The Army Which Cherishes Virtue, in Southern India, 720.
The Army Which Brings Repose to the Sea, in Silla, 733.
The Army Which Attaches Itself to Righteousness, of the Uighurs, 840.
The Army Which Attaches Itself to Righteousness, in Sha chou, 851.
The Army Which Fixes Difficulties of the Tang-hsiang/Hsia, c.883.
The Army West of the [Yellow] River, in the Kan-su Corridor, 926-933.
The Army of Great Righeousness, in Koryŏ, 932.
The Army Which Quiets the Sea, in Chiao-chih/Annam, 973.
The Army of Great Obedience, in Koryŏ, 976.
The Army Which Displays Virtue, in Hsia, 980.
The Army Which Quiets the Sea, in Koryŏ, 988.
The Shuo-fang Army, in Hsia, 1000.
The Army Which Guarantees Obedience, in Tsong-kha, 1036.
The Army West of the [Yellow] River, in Tsong-kha, 1041.

The Army Which Cherishes the Distance, in Tsong-kha, 1100.
The Army Which Cherishes the Distance, in Champa, 1120.
The Army Which Cherishes the Distance, in She-p'o, 1129.

This pleasing but meaningless bookkeeping device allowed the same name to be used more than once. There was supposedly an Army Which Attaches Itself to Righteousness among the Uighurs in 840 and another in Sha chou in 851, an Army West of the [Yellow] River in the Kan-su Corridor in 926-933 and another in Tsong-kha in 1041, an Army Which Quiets the Sea in Chiao-chih/Annam in 973 and another in Koryŏ in 988, and an Army Which Cherishes the Distance in Tsong-kha in 1100, in Champa in 1120 and in She-p'o in 1129. Since the armies did not exist and only were a self-serving conceit of the Chinese, their names could be duplicated even simultaneously and scattered about at will.

These were the imaginary Area Commands:

Unnamed Area Command of the Pa-yeh-ku, 647.
The Jao-lo Area Command, of the Hsi, 648.
The Chien-k'un Area Command, of the Kirghiz, 648.
The Sung-mo Area Command, of the Khitan, 648.
Three unnamed Area Commands, of the Qarluqs, 657.
The Hsiu-hsün Area Command, in Ferghana, 658.
The Ta-wan Area Command, in Tashkent, 658.
The K'ang-chü Area Command, in Samarkand, 658.
The Kuei-shang Area Command, in Ho, 658.
The Ch'ü-sha Area Command, in Kish, 658.
The Yüeh-chih Area Command, in Tokharia, 661.
The Hsiu-hsien Area Command in Kapiśa, 661.
The Chi-ling Area Command, in Persia, 661.
Unamed Area Commands, of the Uighurs, 661.
The Chi-lin Area Command, in Silla, 663.
The P'i-sha Area Command, in Khotan, c.682.
The Hu-han Area Command, in Po-hai, 712.
The Black River Area Command of the Black River Mo-ho, 726.
The Kuei-yi Area Command, of the Hsi, 732.
Unnamed Area Command, in Shih-ni, 747.
Unnamed Area Command, of the Shih-wei, 792.
The Yün-nan Area Command, in Nan-chao, 1117.

In this fashion, the Chinese surrounded themselves with ficticious armies and Area Commands on all their borders except Tibet, and reached out as far as maritime South Asia and Persia. This may have had an ideological significance to them but served no purpose in practice.

In reality, none of the 121 foreign countries and tribes, which have accounts under their own headings in the sources and are discussed in this work, recognized the Son of Heaven.[86] None was subservient to China, and only Chiao-chih/Annam at times paid what amounted to tribute. On the contrary, China was the lesser partner in its relations to Hsia, Liao, and Chin and had to buy itself peace. A tributary system centred on China did not exist

The Chinese graded foreign states in accordance with their supposed importance, but the hierarchy cannot be reconstructed. All which is known is that the Sung authorities considered Chiao-chih/Annam, She-p'o, Pagan, Chu-lien, and the Arabs as equals, and that Koryŏ from 1105 outranked Hsia. Chiao-chih/Annam, Koryŏ, and Hsia seem to have occupied a special position, in that the Sung granted only their rulers the title of Meritorious Subject. The foreign states were status conscious, and quarrels arose among their envoys about prescedence.

The aim of the Chinese governments was to keep potentially dangerous neighbours off-balance by supporting internal rivals and forming alliances against them, or to create a milieu in which China and its neighbours could coexist peacefully. As part of the latter policy, all Chinese dynasties recognized foreign rulers and and gave them and their envoys nominal and usually appreciated titles. In special cases, they granted the imperial surname, which meant that the recepients were entered into the imperial family registers.

The T'ang conferred its imperial surname of Li on Tang-hsiang chiefs between 627 and 649 and in c.883, on the Yi-mi-ni-shu-ssu-li-pi Qaghan of the Eastern Turks in 639, on a Khitan chief in 648, on Hsi chiefs in 648 and 808, on a Black River Mo-ho chief in 728, probably on an Indian prince visiting Ch'ang-an in 741, on a Uighur prince who was a rival of the Wu-chieh Qaghan and his five younger

[86] East Turkestan during the times of T'ang occupation is, of course, a different matter.

brothers in 842, and on a Sha-t'o chief (father of Li K'o-yung) at the end of the dynasty.

The Later T'ang conferred its imperial surname of Li[87] on a Hsi chief in 923 and on a T'u-[yü-]hun chief between 923 and 926.

The Sung conferred its imperial surname of Chao on a Tang-hsiang chief friendly to Sung in 980 and on members of the Tsong-kha Tibetan royal house who surrendered at the end of the 10th century and in 1100.

With the exception of the Indian prince, all grants had political aims. That the imperial surnames were appreciated is shown by the fact that the king of Khotan, Li Sheng-t'ien, claimed in 938 to be a relation to the then defunct T'ang house.

In extreme cases, the T'ang emperors consented to the marriage of a Chinese princess with a foreign ruler. At times, they took the initiative but more often were reluctantly forced into it. Such marriages were usually coveted by foreign rulers other than the self-confident emperors of Liao and Chin. The marriages were unquestionably status symbols but did not turn the bridegrooms into Chinese vassals or pliant tools. They kept their independence, and it was the brides who had to adapt themselves to alien customs. This included further marriages to close relatives of late husbands, a practice abhorrent to the Chinese. These are the instances:

The Hsi

In 717, Hsüan-tsung enfeoffed a daughter's daughter of an unspecified T'ang emperor, the Lady Hsin, as Princess of Ku-an and married her to the Hsi king Li Ta-fu. After he had fallen in battle in 720, she married his younger brother and successor Lu-su. She was divorced due to a Chinese intrigue, whereupon Hsüan-tsung enfeoffed a daughter's daughter of Chung-tsung, the Lady Wei, as Princess of Tung-kuang, and married her to Lu-su in 726. Both fled to China from the Turks in 730.

In 745, Hsüan-tsung enfeoffed a daughter's daughter of Jui-tsung, the Lady Yang, as Princess of Yi-fang and married her to the Hsi king Li Yen-ch'ung. Within half a year, he murdered her and began a war with T'ang.

[87] Itself conferred by the T'ang on Li K'o-yung's father.

Tibet

In 635, the Tibetan king Srong-btsan-sgam-po requested a marriage which was rejected. After having attacked China, he repeated his request in 640. T'ai-tsung enfeoffed a lady of the T'ang imperial house as Princess of Wen-ch'eng and married her to the king in 641. She survived her husband by thirty years and died in about 680.

In 659, 663, 665, 675, and 679, the Tibetans unsuccessfull requested marriages. In 703, the Empress Wu agreed, but the Tibetan king fell in battle against the Nepalese before the marriage could take place. In 705, the Tibetans again requested a marriage. In 707, Chung-tsung enfeoffed a great-granddaughter of Kao-tsung, whom he had brought up himself, as Princess of Chin-ch'eng and married her in 710 to the Tibetan king Tsuk-tsen. She died fifteen years before her husband in about 740. In 797 and thereafter once more, the Tibetans unsuccessfully requested a marriage.

Nan-chao

Soon after 878 and in 882, Nan-chao requested a marriage. Hsi-tsung agreed and enfeoffed a lady of the T'ang imperial house as Princess of An-hua. But he was persuaded to cancel the marriage and in 883 had the bridal envoys from Nan-chao murdered.

The T'u-yü-hun

In 596, Emperor Wen of Sui married the Princess of Kuang-hua to the T'u-yü-hun king Shih-fu. He was killed almost immediately, whereupon the princess married his younger brother and successor Yün-fu.

In 634, Yün-fu requested a marriage on behalf of his son. T'ai-tsung agreed, but the marriage was cancelled because of border troubles.

In 640, T'ai-tsung enfeoffed a lady of the T'ang imperial house as Princess of Hung-hua (later promoted to Senior Princess) and married her to the T'u-yü-hun king No-ho-po. She visited Ch'ang-an in 652. Her husband died in 688.

Turfan

In 612, Emperor Yang of Sui enfeoffed a lady of the Yü-wen clan[88] as Princess of Hua-jung and married her to the king of Turfan, Ch'ü Po-ya. When he died in 619, she married his son and successor Ch'ü Wen-t'ai. He died in 640.

Ferghana

In 744, Hsüan-tsung enfeoffed a lady of the T'ang imperial house as Princess of Ho-yi and married her to the king of Ferghana.

The Eastern Turks

In 579, Emperor Ching of Northern Chou had enfeoffed a lady of the imperial house as Princess of Ch'ien-chin and in 580 had married her to the Sha-po-lüeh Qaghan of the Eastern Turks. She was a granddaughter of Yü-wen-t'ai (d.556).[89] In 581, Emperor Wen of Sui had granted her his own surname (Yang) and had changed her title to Princess of Ta-yi. She resented the fall of Northern Chou and agitated among the Turks against Sui. Emperor Wen therefore changed her title to "Evermore Mean Princess", then demoted her to commoner, and between 593 and 597 managed to have her murdered.

In 597, Emperor Wen agreed to marry a lady of the Sui imperial house, the Princess of An-yi, to the T'u-li Qaghan (from 599 called the Yi-li-chen-tou-ch'i-min Qaghan), a brother and rival of the Hsieh-chia-shih-to-na-tu-lan Qaghan of the Eastern Turks. She was escorted to the camp of her bridegroom in 597 and died no later than 599.

In 599, Emperor Wen married the Princess of Yi-ch'eng, another lady of the Sui imperial house, to the widowed Yi-li-chen-tou-ch'i-min Qaghan. When he died in 609, she married his son and successor, the Shih-pi Qaghan. He died in c.619, whereupon she married his younger brother and successor, the Ch'u-lo Qaghan. When he died in 620, she married his younger brother and successor, the Hsieh-li Qaghan. The T'ang resented her hostility, and in 629 she was killed by its forces.

---

[88] She may have been a member of the imperial clan of Northern Chou.

[89] Father of the first emperor of Northern Chou.

At some time during Sui, the Princess of Huai-nan was married to Shih-po-pi, son of the Shih-pi Qaghan.

In 711, Mo-ch'o, Qaghan of the Eastern Turks, requested a marriage. Jui-tsung agreed and enfeoffed a lady of the T'ang imperial house as Princess of Chin-shan to be his bride. But Jui-tsung abdicated on Aug.21, 712, and the marriage did not take place.

In 713, Mo-ch'o again requested a marriage. Hsüan-tsung enfeoffed a lady of the T'ang imperial house as Princess of Nan-ho to be his bride, but this marriage also fell through.

In 714, Mo-ch'o twice requested a marriage. Hsüan-tsung agreed, but Mo-ch'o was killed in battle against the Uighurs in 716.

In 718, 721, and 724, the P'i-chia Qaghan of the Eastern Turks unsuccessfully requested a marriage. In 725, he complained to a Chinese envoy and did not accept his sophistries.

The Western Turks

In 610, a Western Turkish contender requested a marriage. In spite of certain promises, it did not take place.

In 614, Emperor Yang married the Princess of Hsin-yi to the fugitive Ch'u-lo Qaghan of the Western Turks.

In 620, the T'ung-yeh-hu Qaghan of the Western Turks requested a marriage. Kao-tsu agreed, but nothing happened and Tung-yeh-hu was killed in 628.

In 629, 635, and 646, Western Turks unsuccessfully requested marriages.

In 635 or soon thereafter, A-shih-na Mi-she fled to the T'ang court. He was a son of the late Ch'u-lo Qaghan of the Western Turks. He received in marriage the Senior Princess of Nan-yang (or Heng-yang), the sister of an unspecified T'ang emperor.

The Hsüeh yen t'o

In 642, T'ai-tsung agreed to marry the Princess of Hsin-hsing, a lady of the T'ang imperial house to the Chen-chu-p'i-chia Qaghan of the Hsüeh-yen-t'o. This marriage was aborted by Chinese trickery.

The Uighurs

In 758, Su-tsung married his second daughter, the Princess of Ning-kuo, to the Ko-le Qaghan of the Uighurs. He died within a year. The princess escaped being buried with him and, being childless, was able to return to Ch'ang-an. Her first cousin, the Junior Princess of Ning-kuo, had become a secondary wife of the Ko-le Qaghan. After the qaghan's death, she married his son and successor, the Teng-li Qaghan. She died in c.791.

In 787, Te-tsung agreed that his eighth daughter, the Princess of Hsien-an, marry the Ho-ku-to-lu-p'i-chia Qaghan of the Uighurs and sent her portrait to the Uighur court. The marriage was performed in 789, but the qaghan died within the year. The princess married her husband's son and successor, the Ai-teng-li-lo-ku-mo-mi-shih-p'i-chia, Who Is Loyal and Upright, Qaghan. When he was killed in c.790, she married his son and successor A-ch'o. When he died in c.795, she married the Ai-t'eng-li-lo-yü-lu-mo-mi-shih-ho-hu-lu-p'i-chia, Who Cherishes Trustworthiness, Qaghan. He was no relation. She died in c.808.

In 813, the Uighurs requested a marriage. Hsien-tsung had the expenses estimated and found them too high.

In 817, the Uighurs unsuccessfully requested a marriage.

In 820, the Uighurs demanded a marriage. Hsien-tsung had to agree but died on Feb.14. His son and successor, Mu-tsung, selected the Senior Princess of Yung-an, who was his younger sister and the fifteenth daughter of Hsien-tsung. However, the bridegroom died, and his successor, the Teng-lo-yü-lu-mo-mi-shih-chü-chu-p'i-chia, Who Venerates Virture, Qaghan, took his place. Meanwhile, the Senior Princess of Yung-an had been replaced by the Princess of T'ai-ho, the seventeenth daughter of Hsien-tsung. The marriage was performed in 822. The qaghan died in 839. In 840 or 841, she was forced to marry the Wu-chieh Qaghan of the Uighurs. In 843, she was rescued by Chinese troops, brought to Ch'ang-an, and there retitled Senior grand Princess of An-ting.

The Khitan

In 717, Hsüan-tsung enfeoffed a daughter's daughter of Jui-tsung, the Lady Yang, as Princess of Yung-lo and married her to the Khitan chief Li Shih-huo. He died within the year.

In 722. Hsüan-tsung enfeoffed the Lady Mu-jung, daughter of the Princess of Yü-yao, as Princess of Yen commandery and married her to the Khitan chief Li Yü-yü. When he died in 723, she married his younger brother and successor T'u-yü. In 725, both fled to China.

In 726, Hsüan-tsung enfeoffed a daughter's daughter of Jui-tsung, the Lady Ch'en, as Princess of Tung-hua and married her to the Khitan chief Li Shao-ku. When he was killed in 730, she fled to China.

In 745, Hsüan-tsung enfeoffed an orphaned daughter's daughter of his, the Lady Tu-ku, as Princess of Ching-lo and married her to the Khitan chief Li Huai-chieh. He murdered her within half a year and began a war with T'ang.

Considering only those marriages which were with actual rulers, these were 20 in all. In spite of the short duration of the Sui as a national dynasty (589-618), four of these took place and one was recognized during it. The political focus was on the northeast and north, one marriage each with kings of Turfan and the T'u-yü-hun, and three with Eastern Turkish qaghans.

The T'ang emperor most willing to accept foreign marriages was Hsüan-tsung (8), followed by T'ai-tsung (2), Su-tsung (2), Chung-tsung (1), Te-tsung (1), and Mu-tsung (1), 15 in all. The political focus was on the northeast and north, three marriages with Hsi chiefs, four with the Khitan, four with Uighur qaghans, one with a king of the T'u-yü-hun, one with a king of Ferghana, and only two in the southwest with Tibetan kings. Marriages with Korean or South Asian rulers were never an issue.

The T'ang emperors were ambivalent about political marriages and reneged at least four times on given promises. But they could see possible advantages. As T'ai-tsung put it in 642: "If we profit from it, why should we be stingy about one woman?" Hsüan-tsung probably took the initiative in 745, when he simultaneously married princesses to a Hsi chief and a Khitan chief, and it may have been they who were under pressure to agree. Why would both otherwise have murdered their Chinese wives half a year later and turned against the T'ang? On the other hand, T'ai-tsung acted under duress when he agreed to a marriage with the king of Tibet in 641, and Su-tsung, Te-tsung, and Mu-tsung were forced to marry princesses to Uighur qaghans in 758, 789, and 822.

During Sui, the relationship of three princesses to the imperial house is unknown. Of the other two, one with certainty and one with probability belonged to the defunct imperial house of Northern Chou.

During T'ang, seven princesses with certainty and one with probablity[90] were daughter's daughters of emperors and one a great-granddaughter. Significantly, the three princesses who were married to Uighur qaghans were imperial daughters.[91] Theirs are the only documented cases of a such a magnitude and proof for the irresistible demands of the Uighurs. In three cases, the the exact relation of the princesses to the T'ang imperial house is unknown. It should be noted that with the exception of the three imperial daughters, none of the ladies was a princess in her own right. Each received the title only after she had been chosen for the marriage. The bridegrooms did not object.

It was a Central Asian custom that widows married brother-in-laws or stepsons. Since many of the husbands must have been considerably older than their Chinese wives, the princesses could expect several marriages in their future. Thus, during Sui, the Princess of Yi-ch'eng was married four times, and the Princesses of Kuang-hua and Hua-jung twice each. During T'ang, the Princess of Hsien-an was married four times, and the Junior Princess of Ning-kuo and the Princesses of Ku-an, T'ai-ho, and Yen Commandery twice each.

Twice, foreign princesses were unsuccessfully suggested as brides to the Chinese courts. In 591, the king of the T'u-yü-hun, Shih-fu, offered a daughter, presumably to be married to a Sui prince. Emperor Wen refused. In 698, The Eastern Turkish qaghan Mo-ch'o proposed that a daughter of his marry a T'ang prince. The Empress Wu agreed but substituted a member of her own family. This led to a haughty refusal by Mo-ch'o. In 700, Mo-ch'o repeated his offer and specified a son of the heir-apparent, i.e. of Chung-tsung, as the bridegroom. This was also agreed to, but after Chung-tsung had ascended the throne in 705 he cancelled the marriage. One marriage actually took place. In 756, the Ko-le Qaghan of the Uighurs married his adopted daughter, a younger sister of his qatun, to a second cousin of Su-tsung. The emperor received her warmly and recognized her as a princess.

After the fall of T'ang, all foreign marriages came to an end. Chinese princesses were no longer requested or offered. Instead, the orientation of Sung's northeastern, northern, and northwestern neighbours was

[90] The Princess of Yen commandery who married the Khitan chief Li Yü-yü in 722.

[91] In addition, the Junior Princess of Ning-kuo was an imperial daughter-daughter.

toward Liao. In 944, Uighur envoys to the Khitan court unsuccessfully requested a marriage. In 986, Li Chi-ch'ien of Hsia requested a marriage from Liao. Emperor Sheng-tsung approved and in 989 married the Princess of Yi-ch'eng to him. In 996, the Lion King (Arslan) of probably Turfan unsuccessfully requested a marriage from the Liao court. In 996, the king of Koryŏ, Wang Ch'ih (Sŏngjong), married a daughter's daughter of Emperor Ching-tsung of Liao. In 1031, the Liao Princess of Hsing-p'ing was married to the Hsia heir-apparent Li Yüan-hao. In 1054, 1100, 1102, and 1103, Hsia envoys to the Liao court unsuccessfully requested marriages. In 1105 the Liao Princess of Ch'eng-an was married to Li Ch'ien-shun of Hsia. That adds up to three Liao princesses married to Hsia rulers and one to a Koryŏ king.

It has been seen that the rulers of only eight foreign countries or tribes (the Hsi, the Khitan, the T'u-yü-hun, Turfan, Ferghana, the Eastern Turks, the Uighurs, and Tibet) entered into political marriages with Chinese imperial families.

In the same way, only certain foreign countries and tribes (Chiao-chih/Annam, Champa, Koguryŏ, Paekche, Silla, Koryŏ, the Hsi, Po-hai, Tibet, Nan-chao, the Eastern Turks, the Uighurs, Kan chou, Sha chou, the Arabs, Hsia, and the Khitan) had sporadic ritual relations (congratulations, death announcements, testamentary gifts, state mournings, condolences) with China, until these vastly increased and reached full maturity in the mutual exchange of missions by Sung, Liao, and Chin. It is clear that with few exceptions China had ritual relations only with countries and tribes close to it. South Asia (except for Vietnam) and the islands, Japan, East and West Turkestan, Kashmir, Afghanistan, and the Middle East (except for the Arabs) were not involved.

This is the total number of recorded datable missions from all foreign countries and tribes to Sui, T'ang, the Five Dynasties, Northern Sung, and Southern Sung, 2809 in all, arranged by 20-year periods:

578- 606:	45
607- 626:	142
627- 646:	239
647- 666:	116
667- 686:	45
686- 706:	55
707- 726:	198
727- 746:	168

747- 766:	129
767- 786:	116
787- 806:	75
807- 826:	107
827- 846:	75
847- 866:	7
867- 886:	11
887- 906:	2
907- 926:	59
917- 946:	162
947- 966:	67
967- 986:	92
987-1006:	85
1007-1026:	148
1027-1046:	100
1047-1066:	87
1067-1086:	119
1087-1106:	108
1107-1126:	48
1127-1146:	29
1147-1166:	34
1167-1186:	54
1187-1206:	54
1207-1226:	26
1227-1246:	2
1247-1266:	3
1267-1276:[92]	2

The highest point in international relations was during the reign of T'ai-tsung (627-649), followed by a reduction in the reigns of Kao-tsung (650-683) and the Empress Wu (684-704). Then followed another high under Hsüan-tsung (712-756). After the rebellion of An Lu-shan in 755, the figures gradually decreased and reached their nadir at the end of T'ang. During the Five Dynasties (907-960) and Northern Sung (960-1127), the figures were steadily high but during the Southern Sung (1127-1276) in the aggregate were the lowest for the entire period. The average number of missions per year during

[92] 10-year period.

T'ang was 4.8, during the Five Dynasties and Northern Sung 4.9, and during Southern Sung a lowly 1.4. As has been shown, the Southern Sung decrease was due to the persistant xenophobia of the time.

The purposes of the missions depended on the locations of their home countries and also on their attitudes to China. Some sought inspiration from Chinese civilization and statecraft, and from Buddhism, Confucianism, and Taoism, while at the same time trading with the Chinese courts. This was true in various degree for the Japanese, Koreans, Mo-ho, Tanguts, Khitan, and Jurchen, less so for the Vietnamese, and hardly at all for the Tibetans. The countries of South Asia, the islands, and the Middle East had their own civilizations, religions, and forms of government. The countries of East and West Turkestan, Kashmir, and Afghanistan were not interested in Chinese culture. Missions from these states consequently did not come to China to learn or negotiate. Their only purpose was commerce. China's immediate neighbours had political issues to discuss, particularly the Tibetans, Turks, Uighurs, Tanguts, Khitan, and Jurchen. Alliances were formed to keep others in check. The Khitan and Jurchen set up protocols for the exchange of missions on the New Year Days, imperial enthronements, birthdays, and deaths, which became more rigid in the course of time. But these missions for negotiations and ritual also conducted trade. This commerce was conducted on two levels, official exchange of goods by the governments and private trade by the envoys.

Proof for this trade is the frequent mention in the sources of Chinese payments, consisting chiefly of gold, silver, copper cash, and silk, and from Sung onward also porcelain and tea. Another proof is the fact that the foreign missions not only offered luxury articles and curiosities for the pleasure of the court but also goods of value for China as a whole. To these belonged naphta, various ores, fish glue, nails, yak tails, and vast herds of horses, camels, and sheep, to give only a few examples.[93]

---

[93] Small flocks of horses were actually brought to the capitals. In 647, T'ai-tsung of T'ang personally selected for his own use the ten best horses out of 100 offered by the Ku-li-kan and gave each a name. In 959, Shih-tsung of Later Chou personally inspected 40 horses offered by the Tang-hsiang. It stands to reason, however, that herds of thousands of horses, camels, and sheep were not trotted to the capitals but delivered to pastures near the border, and that the envoys then proceeded, perhaps with receipts. In a similar case, the Sung court accepted an elephant from Champa in 983, but ordered that it be kept in Canton. At times, foreigners first inquired whether an animal was acceptable. In 693, Arabs proposed to offer a lion, which was

The foreign countries traded not only in native products but also in goods they had received by sea from or via the Middle East or on the Silk Routes from the West. This included the Chinese government into a vast international network of commerce, which was only broken when Southern Sung withdrew into isolationism. It was not until the Mongols that this kind of trade was again revived.

---

rejected by the T'ang court. In 971, Khotan proposed to offer a dancing elephant, which was accepted by the Sung court.

WEIGHTS AND MEASURES

The values of Chinese weights and measures changed in the course of history. I give below those of T'ang times, following Wittfogel, *Liao*, p.609.

1 peck (*tou*) = 5.944 litres or 362.73 cubic inches
1 bushel (*hu* or *shih*) = 59.44 litres or 1.6869 U.S. bushels

1 inch (*ts'un*) = 3.11 centimetres or 1.2244 inches
1 foot (*ch'ih)* = 31.1 centimetres or 12.244 inches
1 mile (*li*) = 0.559 kilometres or 0.3478 miles

1 ounce (*liang*) = 37.3 grams or 1.315 ounces
1 catty (*chin*) = 0.5968 kilograms or 1.3129 pounds

1 bolt of silk = 0.5598 x 12.44 metres or 22 x 489.76 inches

QUOTED LITERATURE

Sources

Sui shu 隋書, 85 chüan. By Wei Cheng 魏徵 (580-643) and others. Facsimily reproduction of ta-te 大德 (1297-1307) edition by Po-na 百衲 edition, *Ssu-pu ts'ung-k'an* 四部叢刊, 1920-1922.

Pei shih 北史, 100 chüan. By Li Yen-shou 李延壽 (fl.629). Facsimily reproduction of ta-te (1297-1307) 大德 edition by Po-na edition, *Ssu-pu ts'ung-k'an*, 1920-1922.

Chiu T'ang shu 舊唐書, 200 chüan. By Liu Hsü 劉昫 (887-946) and others. Facsimily reproduction of undated Sung edition by Po-na edition, *Ssu-pu ts'ung-k'an*, 1920-1922.

Hsin T'ang shu 新唐書, 225 chüan. By Ou-yang Hsiu 歐陽修 (1007-1072) and others. Facsimily reproduction of two combined Sung editions by Po-na edition, *Ssu-pu ts'ung-k'an*, 1920-1922.

Chiu Wu-tai shih 舊五代史, 150 chüan. By Hsüeh Chü-cheng 薛居正 (912-981). Facsimily reproduction of undated edition by Po-na edition, *Ssu-pu ts'ung-k'an*, 1920-1922.

Wu-tai shih 五代史 (>*Hsin Wu-tai shih* 新五代史), 74 chüan. By Ou-yang Hsiu 歐陽修 (1007-1072). Facsimily reproduction of ch'ing-yüan 慶元 (1195-1200) edition by Po-na edition, *Ssu-pu ts'ung-k'an*, 1920-1922.

Sung shih 宋史, 496 chüan. By T'o T'o 脫脫 (1313-1355) and others. Facsimily reproduction of chih-cheng 至正 (1341-1368) edition by Po-na edition, *Ssu-pu ts'ung-k'an*, 1920-1922.

Liao shih 遼史, 114 chüan. By T'o T'o 脫脫 (1313-1355) and others. Facsimily reproduction of undated Yüan edition by Po-na edition, *Ssu-pu ts'ung-k'an*, 1920-1922.

Chin shih 金史, 135 chüan. By T'o T'o 脫脫 (1313-1355) and others. Facsimily reproduction of chih-cheng 至正(1341-1368) edition by Po-na edition, *Ssu-pu ts'ung-k'an*, 1920-1922.

Yüan shih 元史, 210 chüan. By Sung Lien 宋濂 (1310-1381) and others. Facsimily reproduction of hung-wu 洪武 (1368-1398) edition by Po-na edition, *Ssu-pu ts'ung-k'an*, 1920-1922.

T'ang hui-yao 唐會要, 100 chüan. By Wang P'u 王溥 (922-982), 1884.

Wu-tai hui-yao 五代會要, 30 chüan. By Wang P'u 王溥 (922-982), 1884.

Sung hui-yao 宋會要, 200 ts'e. Reconstituted by Hsü Sung 徐松 (1781-1848) from the *Yung-lo ta-tien* 永樂大典. Facsimily reproduction of 1809 edition by Pei-p'ing t'u-shu kuan 北平圖書館, 1936, entitled *Sung hui-yao kao* 宋會要稿.

T'ung-tien 通典, 200 chüan. By Tu Yu 杜佑 (735-812), Hung-pao shu-chü 鴻寶書局, Shanghai 1900.

Ts'e-fu yüan-kuei 冊府元龜, 100 chüan. Completed 1013 by Wang Ch'in-jo 王欽若, Yang Yi 楊億 and others, Taipei 1984.

Wen-hsien t'ung-k'ao 文獻通考, 348 chüan. By Ma Tuan-lin 馬端林 (fl.1273), *Kuo-hsüeh chi-pen ts'ung shu* 國學紀本叢書.

Tzu-chih t'ung-chien 資治通鑑, 294 chüan. By Ssu-ma Kuang 司馬光 (1019-1086), commentary by Hu San-hsing 胡三省 (1230-1287), Chung-hua shu-chü 中華書局, Hong Kong 1976.

Hsü Tzu-chih t'ung-chien ch'ang-pien 續資治通鑑長編, 520 chüan. By Li T'ao 李燾 (1115-1184), Shanghai 1986.

Analytical Literature

Bielenstein, Hans, *The Restoration of the Han Dynasty*, vol.III, *Bulletin of the Museum of Far Eastern Antiquities* vol.39, Stockholm 1967.

——, *The Six Dynasties*, vols.I-II, *Bulletin of the Museum of Far Eastern Antiquities*, nos.68-69, Stockholm 1996, 1997.

Dunnel, Ruth, "The Hsi Hsia", in Franke, Herbert, and Twichett, Denis, eds., *The Cambridge History of China*, vol.6, *Alien Regimes and Border States, 907-1368*, Cambridge 1994.

Franke, Herbert, "Sung Embassies. Some General Observations", in Rossabi, Morris, ed., *China among Equals*.

Franke, Herbert, and Twitchett, Denis, eds., *The Cambridge History of China*, vol.6, *Alien Regimes and Border States, 907-1368*, Cambridge 1994.

Franke, Otto, *Geschichte des chinesischen Reiches*, vols. II-III, Berlin and Leipzig 1936 and 1937.

Herrmann, Albert, *Atlas of China*, Cambridge 1935.

Hirth, Friedrich, and Rockhill, W.W., *Chau Ju-kua on the Chinese and Arab Trade in the Twelfth and Thirteenth Centuries*, Amsterdam 1966.

Legge, James, *A Record of Buddhism Kingdoms*, New York 1965.

Mackerras, Collin, *The Uighur Empire according to the T'ang Dynastic Histories*, Canberra 1972.

Marcus, Richard, *Korean Studies Guide*, Berkeley and Los Angeles 1954.

Needham, Joseph, *Science and Civilisation in China*, vols.4:1-2, Cambridge 1962, 1965.

Petech, Luciano, "Tibetan Relations with Sung China and with the Mongols", in Rossabi, Morris, ed., *China among Equals*.

Rogers, Michael, "Sung-Koryŏ Relations: some inhibiting Factors", in *Oriens*, vol.XI, Leiden 1958.

——, "Factionalism and Koryŏ Policy under the Northern Sung", *Journal of the American Oriental Society*, vol.79, 1959.

——, "National Consciousness in Medieval Korea: The Impact of Liao and Chin on Koryŏ", in Rossabi, Morris, ed., *China among Equals*.

Rossabi, Morris, ed., *China among Equals*, Berkeley, Los Angeles, London, 1983.

Sansom, George B., *Japan. A short cultural History*, New York 1931.

Tchang, Mathias, *Synchronismes chinois*, Shanghai 1905.

Tsunoda Ryasaku and Goodrich, L.Carrington, *Japan in the Chinese Dynastic Histories, Later Han through Ming Dynasties*, Pasadena 1951.

Twichett, Denis, and Tietze, Klaus-Peter, "The Liao", in Franke, Herbert, and Twitchett, Denis, eds., *The Cambridge History of China*, vol.6, *Alien Regimes and Border States, 907-1368*, Cambridge 1994.

——, ed., *The Cambridge History of China*, vol.3:1, *Sui and T'ang China, 589-906*, Cambridge 1997.

Schafer, Eward H., *The Golden Peaches of Samarkand*, Berkeley and Los Angeles 1963.

Wittfogel, Karl A., and Fêng Chia-shêng, *History of Chinese Society, Liao*, *Transactions of the American Philosophical Society, New Series*, vol.36, Philadelphia 1949.

Worthy, Edmund H., "Diplomatic Survival: Domestic and Foreign Relations of Wu Yüeh, 907-978", in Rossabi, Morris, ed., *China among Equals*.

INDEX

HANDBOOK OF ORIENTAL STUDIES

SECTION 4 : CHINA

2. Literature.
1. Debon, G. *Chinesische Dichtung.* Geschichte, Struktur, Theorie. 1989. ISBN 90 04 08700 1
4. Religions and Customs.
1. Eichhorn, W. *Die alte chinesische Religion und das Staatskultwesen* 1976. ISBN 90 04 04487 6
6. Law.
   Weggel, O. *Chinesische Rechtsgeschichte.* 1980. ISBN 90 04 06234 3
9. Wagner, D.B *Iron and Steel in Ancient China.* 1996. ISBN 90 04 09632 9
10. Zurndorfer, H.T. *China Bibliography.* A Research Guide to Reference Works about China Past and Present. 1995. ISBN 90 04 10278 7
11. Lust, J. *Chinese Popular Prints.* 1996. ISBN 90 04 10472 0
12. Rhie, M.M. *Early Buddhist Art of China and Central Asia,* 1. Later Han, Three Kingdoms and Western Chin in China and Bactria to Shan-shan in Central Asia. 1999. ISBN 90 04 11201 4
13. Lee, T.H.C. *Education in Traditional China.* A History. 2000. ISBN 90 0410363 5
14. Kohn, L. (ed.) *Daoism Handbook.* 2000. ISBN 90 04 11208 1
15/1. Standaert, N. (ed.) *Handbook of Christianity in China.* Volume One : 635 - 1800. In preparation. ISBN 90 04 11431 9
15/2. Tiedemann, R.G. (ed.) *Handbook of Christianity in China.* Volume Two : 1800 - present. In preparation. ISBN 90 04 11430 0
16. Loewe, M. *A Biographical Dictionary of the Qin, Former Han and Xin Periods (221 BC - AD 24).* 2000. ISBN 90 04 10364 3
17. Loewe, M. *The Men Who Governed Han China.* Companion to a Biographical Dictionary of the Qin, Former Han and Xin Periods. 2004. ISBN 90 04 13845 5
18. Bielenstein, H. *Diplomacy and Trade in the Chinese World, 589-1276.* 2005. ISBN 90 04 14416 1